Anti-Machiavel:
A Discourse upon the Means of Well Governing

Innocent Gentillet

Translated by Simon Patericke
Edited by Ryan Murtha

A DISCOVRSE

VPON THE MEANES

OF VVEL GOVERNING AND

MAINTAINING IN GOOD

PEACE, A KINGDOME, OR

OTHER PRINCIPALITIE.

Divided into three parts, namely, The Counsell, the Religion, and the Policie, which a Prince ought to hold and follow.

Againſt *Nicholas Machiavell* the Florentine.

Tranſlated into Engliſh by Simon Patericke.

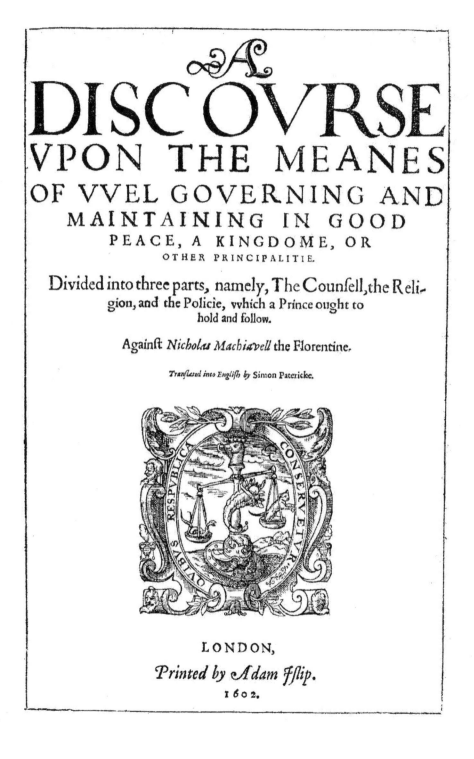

RESPVBLICA · CONSERVETVR · QVIBVS

LONDON,

Printed by Adam Iſlip.

1602.

For Donald

Contents

A Discourse Upon the Means of Well Governing

Part I: Counsel

Part II: Religion

Part III: Policy

Introduction

The life and works of Innocent Gentillet, like all France of his time, were shaped in large part by the religious conflict which escalated into a series of civil wars waged intermittently over the latter half of the sixteenth century. Though termed the Wars of Religion, historians agree that the division between Catholic and Protestant was not the sole contributing factor, and since the time of the wars many writers have argued that religion was not the primary cause. At its highest point, the Protestant (or Huguenot) population comprised around ten percent of France, drawn mostly from the nobility, merchant, and professional classes; of these, "Huguenots of state" were politically motivated, while "Huguenots of religion" were concerned with reform of the church.[1] The distinction was not always clear, and a contemporary observer remarked of both Protestant and Catholic institutions that "those which held and persuaded pressure of consciences, were commonly interested therein themselves for their own ends."[2] In the most tragic event of the wars, the St. Bartholomew's Day massacres,

> Atrocious deeds were done, in which religious passion was often the instrument, but policy was the motive . . . When the King of France undertook to kill all the Protestants, he was obliged to do it by his own agents. It was nowhere the spontaneous act of the population, and in many towns and in entire provinces the magistrates refused to obey. The motive of the Court was so far from mere fanaticism that the Queen [Catherine de Medici] immediately challenged Elizabeth to do the like to the English Catholics.[3]

The order for the killings had been given by twenty-two-year-old Charles IX, under the guidance of his mother, Catherine de Medici, and her Italian advisers. Catherine had had little influence while queen of Henry II; after his death in 1559, however, she wielded great power for thirty years while her three ineffectual sons nominally reigned. In the wake of Bartholomew, it was said that Catherine was governing by the

---

[1] See J.H.M. Salmon, *The French Wars of Religion: How Important Were Religious Factors?* Boston: D.C. Heath, 1967.

[2] Quoted in Francis Bacon, "Of Unity in Religion" (source unknown).

[3] Dalberg-Acton, John. *The History of Freedom and Other Essays*, pp. 43-4. London: MacMillian, 1907.

principles of Machiavelli, her bedside reading and her Bible. This was polemic, but not without foundation; Machiavelli viewed religion as a tool to be cynically manipulated for political ends; and he approved political violence, provided it is done expeditiously and all at once. Moreover, *The Prince* had been addressed to Catherine's father, Lorenzo de Medici, advising him that "on the other hand, it would be easier to conquer the kingdom of France, but there would be great difficulty in holding it . . . The contrary is the case in kingdoms governed like that of France, because it is easy to enter them by winning over some baron of the kingdom, there being always malcontents, and those desiring innovations. These can, for the reasons stated, open the way to you and facilitate victory..."[4] If this was not enough, Machiavelli implied in *The Prince* and the *Discourses on Livy* that French incompetence, barbarism, and greed made them wothy of such handling. In this context, it is unsurprising that French reaction to Machiavelli was particularly hostile; and that reaction found its ultimate expression in Gentillet's *Anti-Machiavel*.

~

Gentillet was born around 1532, the same year *The Prince* was published, in Vienne, a city in south-eastern France whose proximity to Geneva made it more strongly Protestant than most of the country.[5] After a period of military service, he studied law and theology, acquiring a solid grounding in classical humanism. Beginning in 1547 he appears on court lists for twenty-nine years, but was probably rarely in attendance. In 1562 Vienne was sacked by Protestants, and Gentillet was sent to Geneva and Bern to recruit ministers for the Protestant congregation. He is listed in Vienne as a bailiff's attorney in 1564 and as a deacon in 1566. In 1568 he refused to take an oath required by the Edict of Longjumeau, and was prosecuted for *lèse-majesté* in absentia. In 1572 he took a post in Toulouse, but fled to Geneva after the St. Bartholomew events. In 1574 he published his *Remonstrance au roy tres-christien Henri III*, outlining Protestant grievances; the following year he published the Duke of Alençon's *Protestation*, followed by his own response, *Brieve Remonstrance de la declaration de Mgr. le duc d' Alençon;*

---

[4] *The Prince*, ch. 4.
[5] Rathé, C. Edward. "Innocent Gentillet and the First 'Anti-Machiavel'." *Bibliothèque D'Humanisme Et Renaissance* 27, no. 1 (1965): 186-225.
D'Andrea, Antonio. "The Political and Ideological Context of Innocent Gentillet's Anti-Machiavel." *Renaissance Quarterly* 23, no. 4 (1970): 397-411.
D'Andrea, "The Last Years of Innocent Gentillet: `Princeps Adversariorum Machiavelli'." *Renaissance Quarterly* 20, no. 1 (1967): 12-16.

in 1576 he dedicated the *Anti-Machiavel* to the duke. After local Italians complained about *Anti-Machiavel*'s recriminations against their countrymen, Gentillet was summoned to the Geneva city council; he published an apology of sorts, but in early 1577 was assaulted in the street by an Italian, Francesco Lamberto; another Italian was arrested after being overheard threatening to kill Gentillet if he met him out of town. Later that year Gentillet returned to France and was named to the *Chambre mi partie* (a court with both Catholic and Protestant members) of the Parlement of Grenoble. In 1578 he published a translation from Latin, *La République des Suisses*. In 1581 he was nominated to the presidency of the Parlement of Grenoble. In 1584 he published *Apologie ou défense pour les chretiens de France de la religion reformée*; the following year the Treaty of Nemours again banned Protestantism, and Gentillet returned to Geneva. In 1586 he published *Le Bureau du concile de Trente*. He died in Geneva on 23 June, 1588.

These are the facts as we have them now, more or less; but in 1702 the *Dictionnaire historique et critique* complained, "I wonder we have so few particulars about the life of a person who distinguished himself both by his writings and employments . . . those who have given us an account of the authors of his province could not fill up six lines concerning him without committing several faults."[6] One of the editors of *Les bibliothèques françoises* questioned whether Gentillet had written the book at all: "For my part, I believe that all these Gentillets are masks, and that the author of *Anti-Machiavel* is not known."[7]

Further controversy was sparked by Edward Meyer's *Machiavelli and the Elizabethan Drama* (1897). Because *The Prince* was not printed in English translation until 1640, Meyer questioned the origins of what he thought an unfair hostility in Elizabethan "Machiavel" allusions (of which he counted almost four hundred). On finding a copy of *Anti-Machiavel* in the British Museum, Meyer felt he had discovered "the source of all Elizabethan misunderstanding," the vitriolic invective of Gentillet.[8] After T.S. Eliot remarked Shakespeare's "shameless lifting" from *Anti-Machiavel*,[9] it was dismissed as "never of any importance in

---

[6] *The Dictionary Historical and Critical of Peter Bayle: The Second Edition,* Volume III, pp. 156-7. London, 1736.

[7] *Les bibliothèques françoises de La Croix du Maine et de Du Verdier*, p. 220. Paris: Saillant & Nyon, 1772.

[8] Meyer, Edward. *Machiavelli and the Elizabethan Drama*. Weimar: E. Felber, 1897.

[9] G. Wilson Knight. *The Wheel of Fire*, p. xvi. London: Routledge, 2001.

England,"[10] which in turn has been refuted. Recent editors differed as to the book's significance; C. Edward Rathé, who in 1968 published a reissue of the French first edition, enthusiastically called for more attention; while Antonio D'Andrea and Pamela Stewart, who collated several early editions to produce an authoritative French text in 1974, declared the matter closed:

> It would be anachronistic indeed to imagine even for a moment that the *Discours* could still be read, quoted, and discussed, as in the past, in connection with the interpretation of Machiavelli's thought. Nor is it possible to expect of today's readers, even of scholars, the impassioned curiosity for erudite puzzles, that also contributed much for about two centuries to the success of a book, published anonymously by an author completely unknown beyond the restricted provincial horizon of the Dauphiné and the confines of Calvinist Geneva. These reasons for interest in the book have long since ceased to exist. From the nineteenth century on the only conceivable reason for studying the *Discours* has been the role they played in the origins and development of anti-Machiavellism.[11]

This has proven something of an overstatement, however, and Gentillet continues to draw attention outside the province of Machiavelli studies. More recently Sydney Anglo hinted that in attributing Elizabethan "Machiavel" tropes to Gentillet's influence, Meyer "may have got something like the right answer for the wrong reasons,"[12] though unfortunately he did not give any indication as to what the right reasons might be. Another writer has suggested that "there are many more allusions [to Gentillet] waiting to be discovered by scholars who know what to look for . . . It would be helpful if readers of texts from the last quarter of the sixteenth century were to keep alert for more signs of his influence, so that we can estimate that effect more precisely."[13] We will now note some of these allusions, a majority for the first time, hoping to shed some light on the "erudite puzzle" of Gentillet.

---

[10] Raab, Felix. *The English Face of Machiavelli*. London: Routeledge and Kegan Paul, 1965.

[11] D'Andrea, Antonio and Pamela Stewart, eds. *Discours contre Machiavel*, pp. xi-xii. Florence: Casalini Libri, 1974.

[12] Anglo, Sydney. *Machiavelli – The First Century: Studies in Enthusiasm, Hostility, and Irrelevance*, p. 284. Oxford: Oxford University Press, 2005.

[13] Bawcutt, N. W. "The "Myth of Gentillet" Reconsidered: An Aspect of Elizabethan Machiavellianism." *The Modern Language Review* 99, no. 4 (2004): 863-74.

~

In September of 1575 the Duke of Alençon, brother of Henry III and heir to the throne, leader of the moderate *politiques*, joined with Huguenot forces opposed to the Catholic crown. His *Protestation*, calling for reforms and an end to foreign influence at court, was published in Geneva by Gentillet, who then printed his own response. Months later Gentillet dedicated the *Anti-Machiavel* to the duke; *The Prince* had been dedicated to Alençon's grandfather, Lorenzo de Medici. In 1583 Alençon, formerly a suitor to Queen Elizabeth, disastrously tried to attack Antwerp under the color of amity; when Shakespeare called his ancestor in *1 Henry VI* "that notorious Machiavel," adding "take this compact of a truce/Although you break it when your pleasure serves," he was alluding to the more recent duke's maneuvers. According to Meyer, "That Shakespeare had Gentillet in mind is perfectly evident."[14] *Shakespeare's Answer to Machiavelli* notes "the only two times the world "Machiavel" is uttered in the history plays, it is spoken first by Richard York and second by his true son, Richard Gloucester."[15] York is himself Machiavellian, deriding "churchlike humours [that] fits not for a crown"; but Shakespeare tells us that the father, who "will hunt this deer to death," is surpassed in perfidy by the son (Richard III), who "must hunt this wolf to death." In *2 Henry VI* the latter, who "always has piety on his lips in public, though he never observes any piety in private," says "Priests pray for enemies, but princes kill." In *3 Henry VI* he says

> I can add colours to the chameleon,
> Change shapes with Proteus for advantages,
> And set the murderous Machiavel to school.

Anti-Machiavel states: "as soon as the prince shall clothe himself with Proteus' garments, and has no hold nor certitude of his word, nor in his actions, men may well say that his malady is incurable, and that in all vices he has taken the nature of the chameleon." This is unique to Simon Patericke's English translation; in the original French, followed by the Latin, "the nature of the chameleon" reads *le ply du camelot*, or the ply of a peddler. Patericke's *Anti-Machiavel* did not appear until

---

[14] Ibid., p. 58

[15] Hollingshead, Stephen. *Shakespeare's Answer to Machiavelli: The Role of the Christian Prince in the History Plays*. Diss., Marquette University, 1996. (Incidentally, Hollingshead is a descendant of Raphael Holinshed, whose *Chronicles* were Shakespeare's primary source for English history.)

that men are not fitly to be wrought otherwise but by fear, and therefore that he seek to have every man obnoxious, low, and in strait," which the Italians call *seminar spine*, to sow thorns: or that other principle, contained in the verse which Cicero citeth, *Cadant amici, dummodo inimici intercidant* [Let friends fall, provided our enemies perish with them], as the Triumvirs, which sold every one to other the lives of their friends for the deaths of their enemies: or that other protestation of L. Catilina, to set on fire and trouble states, to the end to fish in droumy waters, and to unwrap their fortunes . . .

Anti-Machiavel relates the story of "Catiline, who with his companions went about to destroy his country with fire and sword"; twice uses the phrase "fish in troubled waters," and devotes a chapter to the policy of keeping subjects poor. It also speaks of Cicero being traded to Antony: "Antony, to have his enemy Cicero (whom Octavian favored as his friend), was content to deliver in exchange Lucius Caesar, his own uncle on his mother's side; so that the one was exchanged for the other, and they both died." This brutal bargaining is depicted in Shakespeare's *Julius Caesar*:

Octavius. Prick him down, Antony.

Lepidus. Upon condition Publius shall not live,
Who is your sister's son, Mark Antony.

Antony. He shall not live; look, with a spot I damn him.

Two scenes later, we learn that Cicero is one of the victims:

Brutus. Therein our letters do not well agree;
Mine speak of seventy senators that died
By their prescription, Cicero being one.

Gentillet asked: "Is it not a strange thing to hear that a friend should be betrayed to death, to have the cruel pleasure of slaying an enemy? Yet by this course died a hundred and thirty senators, besides many other persons of quality."

In *The Advancement of Learning* Bacon wrote: "Achilles was brought up under Chiron the Centaur, who was part a man and part a beast: expounded ingeniously but corruptly by Machiavel, that it belongeth to the education and discipline of princes to know as well how to play the part of the lion in violence and the fox in guile. . ." Earlier Gentillet wondered, "should we call this beastliness or malice, what Machiavelli says of Chiron? Or has he read that Chiron was both a man and a beast?

Who has told him that he was delivered to Achilles to teach him that goodly knowledge to be both a man and a beast?" Shakespeare's *Timon of Athens* displays similar impatience with Machiavelli's advice:

> A beastly ambition, which the gods grant thee t'
> attain to! If thou wert the lion, the fox would
> beguile thee; if thou wert the lamb, the fox would
> eat three: if thou wert the fox, the lion would
> suspect thee . . . What beast couldst thou be, that
> were not subject to a beast? and what a beast art
> thou already, that seest not thy loss in
> transformation!

Another place in *The Advancement of Learning* reads "Machiavel noteth wisely, how Fabius Maximus would have been temporizing still, according to his old bias, when the nature of war was altered and required hot pursuit." Gentillet relates that "the Roman Senate sent against Hannibal Fabius Maximus, who was not so forward (and it may be not so hardy) as Flaminius or Sempronius were; but he was more wise and careful, as he showed himself." Bacon elaborates in *Apophthegms New and Old*:

> Fabius Maximus being resolved to draw the war in length, still waited upon Hannibal's progress, to curb him; and for that purpose, he encamped upon the high grounds. But Terentius his colleague fought with Hannibal, and was in great peril of overthrow. But then Fabius came down from the high grounds, and got the day. Whereupon Hannibal said, *That he did ever think, that that same cloud that hanged upon the hills, would at one time or other, give a tempest.*

This is a strong echo of *Anti-Machiavel*:

> On his arrival he did not set upon Hannibal, who desired no other thing, but began to coast him far off, seeking always advantageous places. And when Hannibal approached him, then would he show him a countenance fully determined to fight, yet always seeking places of advantage. But Hannibal, who was not so rash as to join with his enemy to his own disadvantage, made a show to recoil and fly, to draw him after him. Fabius followed him, but upon coasts and hills, seeking always not the shortest way, but that way which was most for his advantage. Hannibal saw him always upon some hill or coast near him, as it were a cloud over his head; so that after Hannibal had many times essayed to draw Fabius into a place fit for himself, and where he might give battle for his own good, and yet could not thereunto draw him, said: "I see well now that the Romans also have gotten a Hannibal; and

I fear that this cloud, which approaching us, still hovers upon those hills, will one of these mornings pour out some shower on our heads."

Francis Bacon is known for advocating inductive reasoning, or the Baconian method, a precursor of the scientific method. Anglo remarked that "Gentillet's appeals to historical exemplars are really no more rigid, and no further removed from true inductive reasoning, than is Machiavelli's use of Livy."[20] Bacon's *Novum Organum* strongly echoes Gentillet on the subject; Bacon wrote:

> There are and can be only two ways of searching into and discovering truth. The one flies from the senses and particulars to the most general axioms, and from these principles, the truth of which it takes for settled and immovable, proceeds to judgment and middle axioms. . . The other derives axioms from the senses and particulars, rising by a gradual and unbroken ascent, so that it arrives at the most general axioms last of all.

Anti-Machiavel reads:

> Aristotle and other philosophers teach us, and experience confirms, that there are two ways to come unto the knowledge of things. The one, when from the causes and maxims, men come to knowledge of the effects and consequences. The other, when contrary, by the effects and consequences we come to know the causes and maxims. . . The first of these ways is proper and peculiar unto the mathematicians, who teach the truth of their theorems and problems by their demonstrations drawn from maxims, which are common sentences allowed of themselves for true by the common sense and judgment of all men. The second way belongs to other sciences, as to natural philosophy, moral philosophy, physic, law, policy, and other sciences. . .

The Great Assizes holden in Parnassus (1645, attributed to George Wither) features a court of poets and scholars, with Francis Bacon as Chancellor, before whom are arraigned authors charged with "strange abuses, committed against [Apollo] and the Nine Muses":

> Hee was accus'd, that he had us'd his skill,
> Parnassus with strange heresies to fill,
> And that he labour'd had for to bring in,
> Th' exploded doctrines of the Florentine,
> And taught that to dissemble and to lie,

---

[20] Anglo, Sydney. "The Reception of Machiavelli in Tudor England: A Re-Assessment." *Il Politico* 31, no. 1 (1966): 127-38.

Were vitall parts of humane policie...

"Th' exploded doctrines of the Florentine" can only refer to *Anti-Machiavel*; the court of Parnassus also includes Shakespeare, Ben Jonson, and the scholar Isaac Casaubon, a friend of Bacon's who was born in Geneva to Huguenot refugee parents. Bacon wrote in a letter to Casaubon: "to write at leisure that which is to be read at leisure matters little; but to bring about the better ordering of man's life and business, with all its troubles and difficulties, by the help of sound and true contemplations — this is the thing I am at."[21] He comments on the edifying potential of the stage in *The Advancement of Learning*:

> Dramatic poesy, which has the theatre for its world, would be of excellent use if well directed. For the stage is capable of no small influence both of discipline and of corruption. Now of corruptions in this kind we have enough; but the discipline has in our times been plainly neglected. And though in modern states play-acting is esteemed but as a toy, except when it is too satirical and biting; yet among the ancients it was used as a means of educating men's minds to virtue.

A similar concern with the didactic effects of the theatre is expressed in the dedication of *Anti-Machiavel* (after the first edition):

> After Solon had seen Thespis' first edition and action of a tragedy, and meeting with him before the play, he asked if he was not ashamed to publish such feigned fables under so noble, yet a counterfeit personage. Thespis answered that it was no disgrace upon a stage, merrily and in sport, to say and do anything. Then Solon, striking hard upon the earth with his staff, replied thus: "Yea but shortly, we that now like and embrace this play, shall find it practiced in our contracts and common affairs." This man of deep understanding saw that public discipline and reformation of manners, attempted once in sport and jest, would soon quail; and corruption, at the beginning passing in play, would fall and end in earnest.

This dedication ("for kinred") is to Francis Hastings and Edward Bacon, half-brother of Francis Bacon. It is dated 1577, and first appeared in the Latin edition of that year (Geneva). It is anonymous, and critics have accepted it as the work of a different author, but the possibility of a literary fiction cannot be discounted; the vitriolic tone

---

[21] Spedding, James. *The Letters and the Life of Francis Bacon,* Vol. IV, p. 147. London: Longman, Green, Reader, and Dyer, 1868.

of Gentillet is also present in the dedication. Antonio D'Andrea attributes it to Lambert Daneau,[22] a Huguenot theologian who had been a tutor of Francis and Anthony Bacon; Daneau later dedicated his commentary on the minor prophets (1586) to Anthony.[23] D'Andrea also suggests the possible involvement of Theodore Beza, Calvin's successor in Geneva and a colleague of Daneau's, who approved the *Anti-Machiavel* for publication.[24] While in Geneva Anthony Bacon lodged with Beza, who later dedicated his *Meditations* (1582) to Lady Anne Bacon, mother of Francis and Anthony. The Bacon family's connections in Geneva went back to Lady Anne's father, Sir Anthony Cooke, who corresponded with Calvin and met Beza while living on the continent as a Protestant exile during the reign of Mary I.[25] Beza's *Meditations* dedication echoes the one in *Anti-Machiavel*; while the former speaks of "that right vertuous and right renowmed Lord, my Lord Nicholas Bacon your husband, & most worthy Keeper of the seale of England,"[26] the latter exhorts Edward Bacon to "imitate the wisdome, sanctimonie, and integritie of your father, the Right Honorable Lord Nicholas Bacon, Keeper of the broade Seale of England, a man right renowned. . ."

Machiavelli's influence on Bacon is now taken for granted; however, Bacon's family motto, *Mediocria firma* ("moderation is stable" or "the middle way is sure"), is flatly contradicted by Machiavelli, who complained that "men take certain middle ways that are very harmful, for they do not know how to be altogether wicked or altogether good." This is handled in *Anti-Machiavel* III.28. Machiavelli counseled a prince "to appear merciful, faithful, humane, religious, upright, and to be so, but with a mind so framed that should you require not to be so, you may be able and know how to change to the opposite." Bacon wrote

---

[22] D'Andrea, Antonio. "Machiavelli, Satan, and the Gospel." *Yearbook of Italian Studies* (1971): 156-77.

[23] Vickers, Brian. *Francis Bacon: The Major Works*, p. 562. Oxford: Oxford University Press, 1996.

[24] D'Andrea, Antonio. "Geneva 1576-78: The Italian Community and the Myth of Italy." In *Peter Martyr Vermigli and Italian Reform*, edited by Joseph McLelland, 60-3. Waterloo: Wilfrid Laurier University Press, 1980.

[25] McIntosh, Marjorie Keniston. "Sir Anthony Cooke: Tudor Humanist, Educator, and Religious Reformer." *Proceedings of the American Philosophical Society* 119, no. 3 (1975): 233-50.

[26] Beza, Theodore. *Christian Meditations upon Eight Psalmes of the Prophet David.* London: Christopher Barker, 1582.

"Constancy is the foundation on which virtues rest," echoing Gentillet: "constancy is a quality which ordinarily accompanies all other virtues; it is, as it were, of their substance and nature." This idea is also found in *Measure for Measure*: "it is virtuous to be constant in any undertaking"; and *Two Gentlemen of Verona*: "were man but constant, here were perfect." Machiavelli's assertion that "when the deed accuses, the effect excuses," commonly interpreted as "the ends justifies the means," is attacked by Gentillet and strongly condemned in Bacon's "Charge against Owen": "evil is never in order towards good. So that it is plainly to make God the author of evil, and to say with those that St. Paul speaketh of, *Let us do evil that good may come thereof*, of whom the Apostle says excellently *That their damnation is just*."[27] I will here note by the way what appears to be an intentional misprint in the 1606 English edition of Jean Bodin's *Six Books of a Commonwealth*, which reads: ". . . Frauncis Machiauell, and many other following Polybius, have as it were with one consent approoued his opinion. . ." Thus the relationship between Machiavelli and Bacon is more complex than has hitherto been assumed, and might be summarized in what has been said of Shakespeare: "while he clearly rejects the most fundamental tenets of Machiavellian political philosophy as unnatural and therefore destructive, he is not so foolish as to dismiss Machiavelli's other insights out of hand."[28]

~

The infamous Huguenot tract on the right of resistance, *Vindiciae contra tyrannos* (1579), was included as a sort of antidote in several editions of *The Prince*. The *Vindiciae* was first published in Basel with a false imprint of Edinburgh, under the pseudonym Stephanus Brutus Junius — alluding to Marcus Junius Brutus (later in *Julius Caesar*), as well as Lucius Junius Brutus, who deposed Tarquin and established the Roman Republic (later in *The Rape of Lucrece*). Machiavelli advised that "Whoever takes up a tyranny and does not kill Brutus, and whoever makes a free state and does not kill the sons of Brutus, maintains himself for little time." The *Vindiciae*'s account of Tarquin reads:

---

[27] Spedding, James. *The Works of Francis Bacon, Volume XII*, p. 167. London: Longman, Green, Reader, and Dyer, 1869.
[28] Hollingshead (1996), p. 274.

Tarquinius Superbus was therefore esteemed a tyrant, because being chosen neither by the people nor the senate, he intruded himself into the kingdom only by force and usurpation . . . The true causes why Tarquinius was deposed, were because he altered the custom, whereby the king was obliged to advise with the senate on all weighty affairs; that he made war and peace according to his own fancy; that he treated confederacies without demanding counsel and consent from the people or senate; that he violated the laws whereof he was made guardian; briefly that he made no reckoning to observe the contracts agreed between the former kings, and the nobility and people of Rome.

Anti-Machiavel reads:

Tarquin, who enterprised to slay his father-in-law king Servius Tullius to obtain the kingdom of Rome, showed well by that act and many others that he was a very tyrant. . . when he changed his just and royal domination into a tyrannical government, he became a contemner and despiser of all his subjects, both plebian and patrician. He brought a confusion and a corruption into justice; he took a greater number of servants into his guard than his predecessors had; he took away the authority from the Senate; moreover, he dispatched criminal and civil cases after his fancy, and not according to right; he cruelly punished those who complained of that change of estate as conspirators against him; he caused many great and notable persons to die secretly without any form of justice; he imposed tributes upon the people against the ancient form, to the impoverishment and oppression of some more than others; he had spies to discover what was said of him, and punished rigorously those who blamed either him or his government.

The introduction to *The Rape of Lucrece* echoes these passages, and may reflect what Eliot called Shakespeare's "shameless lifting" from Gentillet:

Tarquinius, for his excessive pride surnamed Superbus, after he had caused his own father-in-law Servius Tullius to be cruelly murdered, and, contrary to the Roman laws and customs, not requiring or staying for the people's suffrages, had possessed himself of the kingdom . . . the people were so moved, that with one consent and a general acclamation the Tarquins were all exiled, and the state government changed from kings to consuls.

The *Vindiciae*'s preface, which has been ascribed to Gentillet,[29] includes an edict of Theodosius II and Valentinian III, whereby emperors became subject to Roman law; the edict is also transcribed in full by Gentillet. The *Vindiciae*'s preface challenged, "the Machiavellians are free to descend into the arena: let them come forth. As we have said, we shall use the true and legitimate weapons of Holy Scripture. . ."[30] Gentillet, on the other hand, "must fight against their impiety . . . not by assailing them with the arms of the holy Scripture . . . but by their proper arms and weapons" (that is, pagan authors). However, Gentillet and the *Vindiciae* use many of the same sources, biblical and classical; this in itself is unsurprising, but the similarities are so extensive as to indicate at the least a strong influence.

The *Vindiciae*'s authorship is still unresolved.[31] It was first attributed to François Hotman, author of the *Francogallia* (1573), another Huguenot "Monarchomach" treatise. Hotman's son Jean had been a tutor in the household of English ambassador Sir Amias Paulet, while Francis Bacon happened to be living there. Beza, author of *De jure magistratuum* (Right of Magistrats, 1574), was then thought responsible; his connections with the Bacon family have been noted. Next, attention shifted to Philippe du Plessis Mornay, a Huguenot author and diplomat who fled to England after the St. Bartholomew's Day massacres. During the peace negotiations at Poitiers in late 1577, Bacon met both Mornay and Jean de La Gessée, secretary to the Duke of Alençon. Mornay later invited Anthony Bacon to Montauban, and the two became good friends.[32] Finally Hubert Languet, or a collaboration between Languet and Mornay, was credited with the *Vindiciae*. Languet corresponded extensively with Sir Philip Sidney, a friend of Bacon's who witnessed the St. Bartholomew events and helped try to negotiate a marriage between Elizabeth I and Alençon. Bacon himself has not been proposed as a possible author of the

---

[29] By Mastellone (1969); see Victoria Kahn, "Reading Machiavelli: Innocent Gentillet's Discourse on Method." *Political Theory* 22, no. 4 (1994): 539-60.
[30] *Vindiciae, contra tyrannos*, tr. George Garnett, p. 11. Cambridge: Cambridge University Press, 1994. Other citations are from the 1689 edition, translator unknown, London.
[31] See Barker, Ernest. "The Authorship of the Vindiciae Contra Tyrannos." *Cambridge Historical Journal* 3, no. 2 (1930): 164-81. Also George Garnett, *Vindiciae, contra tyrannos*, pp. lv — lxxvi.
[32] See Daphne du Maurier, *Golden Lads* (1975).

Vindiciae, but it is interesting to note that he had connections to all candidates, a fact that has so far been overlooked.

∼

Numerous parallels with *Anti-Machiavel* are also found in Pierre de la Primaudaye's *L'Academie Française*, published in four volumes from 1578-98. A draft of the first volume had appeared previously in English as *The Anatomie of the Minde* (London, 1576); it resembles the essays of Bacon and Montaigne, but is less aphoristic; as with Shakespeare's Love's Labour's Lost, it features four young French gentlemen secluded for purposes of study. In the dedication to Henry III, Primaudaye (who worked for the Duke of Alençon) speaks of having attended the Estates General at Blois in 1576-77 (as did Bacon). He begins: "Sir, if we credit the saying of Plato, commonwealths begin then to be happy, when kings exercise philosophy, and philosophers reign." Gentillet said: "there cannot come a better and more profitable thing to a people than to have a prince wise of himself; therefore, said Plato, men may call it a happy commonwealth when either the prince can play the philosopher, or when a philosopher comes to reign there." Bacon's *Advancement of Learning* echoes: "although he might be thought partial to his own profession, that said 'then should people and estates be happy, when either kings were philosophers, or philosophers kings'; yet so much is verified by experience, that under learned princes and governors there have ever been the best times." As a recent example Primaudaye cited "Francis I, a prince of most famous memory, [who] so loved and favored letters and the professors of them that he deserved the name of the restorer of sciences and good arts." Gentillet said "the restoration of good letters, which Francis I brought into France, did more to celebrate and immortalize his name in the memory of all Christian nations, than all the great wars and victories his predecessors had."

Primaudaye attributes France's troubles to foreign influence: "the ruin and destruction of this French monarchy proceeds of no other second cause (our iniquity being the first) than of the mixture which we have made of strangers with ourselves. Wherein we are not contented to seek them out under their roofs, unless we also draw them unto us and lodge them under our roofs, yea prefer them before our own countrymen and citizens in the offices and honorable places of this kingdom. . ." An English intelligence paper credited to Francis (or

Anthony) Bacon, "Notes on the Present State of Christendom" (1582), reported "division in [France] for matters of religion and state, through miscontentment of the nobility to see strangers advanced to the greatest charges of the realm, the offices of justice sold, the treasury wasted, the people polled, the country destroyed, hath bred great trouble, and like to see more."[33] Gentillet complains of "all France fashioned after the manners, conditions, and vices of foreigners that govern it, and who have the principal charges and estates." Shakespeare's *Richard II* laments:

> Reports of fashions in proud Italy
> Whose manners still our tardy-apish nation
> Limps after in base imitation.
> Where the world doth thrust forth a vanity-
> So be it new, there's no respect how vile. . .

Primaudaye warns: "It is a hard matter (said Socrates) for a man to bridle his desire, but he that addeth riches thereunto, is mad." Gentillet asked: "Who could then bridle vices and iniquities, which are fed with much wealth, and no less liberty?" Bacon's *New Atlantis* again echoes: "the reverence of a man's self is, next religion, the chiefest bridle of all vices" (Calvin stressed the need to "bridle our affections"). Finally, *The French Academy* echoes the strident tone as well as the content of *Anti-Machiavel*:

> [T]here are a great many amongst us of those foolish men of whom David speaks, *Who say in their hearts that there is no God*. In the forefront of which company, the students of Machiavel's principles and practicers of his precepts may worthily be ranged. This bad fellow, whose works are no less accounted of among his followers than were Apollo's Oracles amongst the Heathen, nay than the sacred Scriptures are among sound Christians, blushed not to belch out these horrible blasphemies against pure religion, and so against God the Author thereof; namely, that the religion of the heathen made them stout and courageous, whereas Christian religion makes the professors thereof base minded, timorous, and fit to become a prey to every one; that since men fell from the religion of the Heathen, they became so corrupt that they would believe neither God nor the Devil; that Moses so possessed the land of Judea as the Goths did by strong hand usurp part of the

---

[33] Spedding, *Works* Volume VIII, p. 27. The same report noted that "the diseased estate of the world doth so concur with [Alençon's] active forwardness, as it give him matter to work upon."

Roman Empire. These and such like positions are spewed out by this hell hound sometimes against true religion, other whiles against the religion and Church of Rome, sometimes also taxing the religion of the heathen of falsehood and cozenage; so that in truth he would have all religion to be of like account with his disciples, except it be so far forth as the pretense and show of religion may serve to set forward and effect their wicked policies. And for this cause he sets down this rule for every Prince and Magistrate to frame his religion by, namely, that he should pretend to be very religious and devout, although it be but in hypocrisy. And to this he adds a second precept no less impious, that a Prince should with tooth and nail maintain false miracles and untruths in religion, so long as his people may thereby be kept in greater obedience.

~

Gentillet's influence, while not so great as to account for "all Elizabethan misunderstanding" of Machiavelli, has not been fully understood. Certainly it is enough to warrant more attention, and I am sure that many more allusions are yet to be found. Though much maligned and seldom studied, recently a few professors have rallied for him; though he speaks for a world long past, many of his arguments are still valid; and even where he is obsolete or unfair to Machiavelli, the historical citations are worthwhile. Gentillet is certainly a reactionary, and he is intemperate and repetative; but he is sincere and learned, and his thinking, as a previous editor said, "always shows itself to be a curious mixture of idealism and common sense . . . it would be quite wrong to see Gentillet as an idealist dreamer combatting the pragmatic scientist, Machiavelli."[34] Leo Strauss, who claimed to hold the "old-fashioned and simple" view of Machiavelli, wrote that "one cannot see the true character of Machiavelli's thought unless one recovers for himself and in himself the pre-modern heritage of the western world, both Biblical and classical."[35] This perspective is best represented by Gentillet, who "was not naïve enough to believe that princes had always been virtuous, but viewing the world as a battle ground between good and evil, he was not prepared to surrender

---

[34] Rathé, Ibid., 220-1.
[35] Strauss, Leo. *Thoughts on Machiavelli*, pp. 9-12. Chicago: University of Chicago Press, 1958. It should be noted, however, that Strauss emphasized the need for "esoteric" writing, whereby philosophers cloak amoral and dangerous views in conventional piety.

without a fight, to accept an amoral standard in personal or political life."[36] Issues raised by Machiavelli will always be with us, and some of his positions will remain controversial; his opponents, even if dated and imperfect, should continue to find readers as well.

---

[36] Rathé, Ibid., 209.

1

*Greek, Latin, and French authors, out of which are
extracted the histories and other things cited in
these discourses against Machiavelli*

Ammianus Marcellinus, Annales of France, Aristotle, the Bible,
Capitolinus, Cicero, Philippe de Commines, Cassius Dio, Dionysius
Halicarnassus, du Bellay, Aeschylus, Euripides, Florus, Jean Froissart,
Herodian, Homer, Horace, Josephus, Juvenal, Jus Civile & Canonicum,
Aelius Lampridius, Livy, Molineus, Monstrelet, Sebastian Munster,
Papon, Paulus Aemylius, Pliny the Younger, Bartolomeo Platina,
Plutarch, Pomponius Laetus, Sabellicus, Sallust, Johannes Sleidanus,
Sophocles, Aelius Spartianus, Suetonius, Tacitus, Thucydides, Trebellius
Pollio, Virgil, Vopiscus, Xenephon

Dedication to the First Edition

To the high and illustrious prince, François, Duke of Alençon, son
and brother of the King.

My Lord,

Being on the point of bringing to light these Discourses against
Machiavelli, to reveal to those of understanding of our French nation the
source and the authors of the tyranny which has been exercised in France
for fifteen years or more, by those who have too much abused the
minority as well as the naive goodness of the Kings; it has come about,
by the grace of God, that your Excellency has undertaken the protection
of the law and the public good of the kingdom against this tyranny.
Which has occasioned me to take the boldness of dedicating to you this
work, and of making it public under the favor of your most illustrious
name, as something wholly according and corresponding to your heroic
and magnanimous designs. For if it pleases your Excellency to have you
read sometimes, by way of pleasure, some chapter of the subjects which
are here treated, you will find many points which not only conform to
your generous and laudable designs, but also approve and authorize
them by several reasons and remarkable examples. You will be able to
see, my Lord, several good examples of the kings of France, your

ancestors, and several great emperors who prospered in their estates, and who happily governed their kingdoms and empires by having had good and wise people in their council. As on the contrary, those who have used bad counselors and governed by flatterers, ambitious and avaricious men, and above all by strangers, have all rushed into great misfortune and have precipitated their whole estate into utter ruin, and their subjects into confusion and misery; which is a fault into which princes often and easily fall, of which nevertheless they should keep themselves from more. It is certain that in all things bad counsel is the cause of infinite evils, and chiefly for a prince and a republic; it is the principal and most grievous malady of which poor France is now afflicted, that your Excellency endeavors to apply the remedies necessary to cure it. You may also see here, my Lord, that the duty of a good prince is to embrace and sustain the Christian religion, and to seek and inquire into the pure truth of it, and not to approve or maintain falsehood in religion, as Machiavelli teaches. And as for policy, your Excellency will also be able to see several notable examples of your royal ancestors of France, and of the greatest Roman emperors, by whom it appears that the princes who governed themselves by mildness, and joined clemency to justice, and who have used moderation and good humor towards their subjects, have always greatly prospered and reigned for a long time. But on the contrary, the cruel, iniquitous, perfidious, and oppressive princes of their subjects immediately precipitate themselves and their states into peril or utter ruin, and have not long prevailed, but most often have finished their days by bloody and violent death. And the examples of good government in the greater part of the noble house of France, from which your Excellency is issued, I am sure, my Lord, that they will always be stronger to revivify you and to make shine in you the heroic virtues of your ancestors, and to drive out from France the infamous vices which are rooted therein; cruelty, injustice, perfidy, and oppression, together with the foreigners who brought them there, and the degenerate and bastardized French, their adherents, who favor their tyrannies and oppressions, which after them follow the subversion of the state of the kingdom. This, too, will cause your Excellency to restore the true manner of French government used by your predecessors, and to banish and send back that of Machiavelli to Italy, from whence it has come to our great misfortune and pity. Wherewith all the kingdom, noblemen, ecclesiastics, merchants, and commoners, even the princes and great lords, will ever be greatly beholden and obliged; as is the poor languishing patient, who is in danger of death, to the prudent doctor who cures him. And posterity will never forget such a great benefit, but will celebrate your heroic and magnanimous virtues by immortal stories and praises. And it seems that God, having pity on poor France and wishing to deliver it from the bloody and barbarous tyranny of foreigners, has aroused you as the final liberator; you, my Lord, who is Prince François, of the house of France, French by nation, French by name, and French in heart and in effect. For who else could better effect the enterprise of freeing France from tyranny, and gain the honor of so high and heroic a feat, than your Excellency, who has nothing that is not French? To whom can poor France best have recourse in her extreme peril and necessity, but to that which is a true stem from the good Louis XII, father of the people, and the great king François, a prince very fond of his subjects, and the debonair king Henri II? We have therefore greatly to praise the goodness of God, which has aroused you and touches the heart, for such an excellent and necessary enterprise; of which everyone must hope, because it is based on so just and reasonable causes as are possible; so that God (who always keeps the party of reason and right) will favor it by his grace. Besides, your Excellency being accompanied by great and illustrious Princes, and so many valiant Knights and wise Lords (who have not defiled the virtues of their ancestors in the stinking smell of Machiavelli and those of his nation), we must hope that our Lord will bring back, by his grace, your counsels and enterprises to a good, successful, and happy outcome.

My Lord, I pray to the Creator that he will give you grace, and that poor France may well feel the deliverance of the tyranny which oppresses it, and the fruit of a good reformation (which we expect from the favorable clemency of God, by means of your heroic and generous enterprise), and that he maintain and increase your Excellency in all greatness and prosperity. This first of March, 1576.

Epistle Dedicatory

To the most famous young gentlemen, as well for religion, modesty, and other virtues, as also for kindred, Francis Hastings and Edward Bacon, most hearty salutations.

After Solon had seen Thespis' first edition and action of a tragedy, and meeting with him before the play, he asked if he was not ashamed to publish such feigned fables under so noble, yet a counterfeit personage. Thespis answered that it was no disgrace upon a stage, merrily and in sport, to say and do anything. Then Solon, striking hard upon the earth with his staff, replied thus: "Yea but shortly, we that now like and embrace this play shall find it practiced in our contracts and common affairs." This man of deep understanding saw that public discipline and reformation of manners, attempted once in sport and jest, would soon quail; and corruption, at the beginning passing in play, would fall and end in earnest. Therefore Tacitus worthily extols the manners of the Germans of his time, among whom vices were not laughed at; for laughters begun of some public shame and dishonesty will assuredly procure some miserable calamity. Hereof France is unto all ages and nations a woeful view, yet a profitable instruction at this day. For when the clear light of the Gospel began first to spring and appear, Satan — to occupy and busy men's minds with toyish plays and trifles, that they might give no attendance unto true wisdom — devised this policy, to raise up jesters and fools in courts; who, creeping in by quipping and pretty conceits, first in words, and after by books, uttering their pleasant jests in the courts and banquets of kings and princes, labored to root up all the true principles of religion and policy. And there were some whom the resemblance of nature or vanity of wit had so deceived, that they derided the everlasting verity of the true God as if it were but a fable. Rabelais among the French, and Agrippa among the Germans, were the standardbearers of that train, who with their scoffing taunts inveighed not only against the Gospel, but all good arts whatsoever. Those mockers did not as yet openly undermine the groundwork of human society, they only derided it. But such Cyclopean laughters in the end proved to be only signs and tokens of future evils; for little by little, what was in the beginning taken for jests turned to earnest, and words into deeds. In the neck of these came new poets, very eloquent for their own profit, who incensed unto lust and lightness such minds as were already inclined to wantonness, by quickening their appetites with the delectable sauce of unchaste hearing, and pricking them forward with the sharp spurs of pleasure. Who could then bridle vices and iniquities, which are fed with much wealth, and no less liberty? Seeing them not only in play, mirth, and laughter entertained, but also earnestly accepted and commended as being very excellent. Yet some trod the steps of honesty, which now lay a dying, and practiced the old manners and fashions which were almost forgotten. For although the secret faults of the court were evil spoken of, yet shame stood in open view; heinous and infamous crimes kept secret corners; princes were of some credit and faith; laws were in reasonably good use; magistrates had their due authority and reverence; all things only for ostentation and outward show, but none would then have feared an utter destruction. Then Satan, being a disguised person amongst the French, in the likeness of a merry jester, acted a comedy; but shortly ensued a woeful tragedy. When our countrymen's minds were sick and corrupted with these pestilent diseases, and discipline waxed stale, then came forth the books of Machiavelli, a most pernicious writer, who began not in secret and stealing manner (as did those former vices), but by open means and by a continual assault utterly destroyed not this or that virtue, but even all virtues at once. It took faith from the princes; authority and majesty from laws; liberty from the people; and peace and concord from all persons, which are the only remedies for present maladies.

For what shall I speak of religion, whereof the Machiavellians had none, as already plainly appears; yet they greatly labored also to deprive us of the same. And although they have wrongfully banished us from our native country, yet still we fight for the church's defense. Moreover Satan uses strangers of France as his fittest instruments to infect us with this deadly poison sent out of Italy; who have so highly promoted their Machiavellian books, that he is of no reputation in the court of France who has not Machiavelli's writings at the fingers' ends, both in the Italian and French tongues, and can apply his precepts to all purposes, as the oracles of Apollo. Truly it is a wondrous thing to consider how fast that evil weed has grown within these few years, seeing there is almost none that strives to excel in virtue or knowledge, as though the only way to obtain honor and riches were by this deceiver's direction.

But now to turn my eyes from beholding so many miseries of poor afflicted France, as often as I see or remember our neighbor countries (which thing I do daily), so often do I bewail our miseries. Yet I am right joyful for your felicities; chiefly because God of his great bounty has given you a most renowned queen, as well in deed as title, even in the midst of so many troubles. For her coming to the crown, even when England was tossed with tempestuous storms, so dispersed those clouds with the brightness of her counsel and countenance, that no civil dissention nor external invasion has disturbed your peace and tranquility these many years, especially with so many wars sounding on every side. For she, by maintaining wholesome unity amongst all degrees, has hitherto preserved the state of her realm, not only safe but flourishing; not by Machiavellian arts, as guile, perfidy, and other villainies, but by true virtue, as clemency, justice, and faith. Therefore when she goes on her progress through the realm of England, she is entertained in all places with happy applause, rejoicing, and prosperity of all her subjects, she being a princess of both nobles and commons, by due desert most entirely beloved. Whereas we against our wills behold our country swimming in blood and disfigured by subversion, which is a joyful object to the eyes of strangers; yea and those labor most to work her destruction, who should be most careful to rescue and deliver poor France out of her long calamities; but the Lord will at length behold our miseries. But O how happy are ye, both because you have so gracious a queen, and because the infectious Machiavellian doctrine has not breathed nor penetrated the entrails of most happy England. But that it might not do so, I have done my endeavor to provide an antidote and present remedy to expel the force of so deadly poison, if at any time it chance to infect you. For when I thought it right, especially in such a confused disorder of matters and times, to impart to our Frenchmen and to other nations these discourses, first written by a man of most singular learning and wisdom, I willingly undertook this labor, which I have performed to the utmost of my power; and now I wholly refer myself and my travail to serve for the benefit of public utility. Yet I properly dedicated and inscribed it to your names, because although I never saw England, yet it might serve as a pledge to testify my thankful mind towards your countrymen, whose singular courtesy and kindness showed to my brethren when they were banished for the profession of the Gospel, has generally bound me to all Englishmen, but privately to you. Also, by way of exhortation I might enflame you (being most virtuous gentlemen), to study and follow the contents of this book, but especially the arts and virtues therein published, and almost in every word thereof so highly commended; which indeed is no other thing than you do already. For beholding your ancestors' monuments of their virtues, which are both many and famous, moves you thereunto more than the directions drawn from all ages and examples here delivered. Therefore my dear friend Francis, among so many notable examples of your realm, tread the steps of your uncle, the Right Honorable Earl of Huntington; a man most admirable and illustrious, as well for godliness and other notable virtues as for noble parentage and honor; that you may show yourself worthy of your place and kindred. And you, good Edward, imitate the wisdom, sanctimony, and integrity of your father, the Right Honorable Lord Nicholas Bacon, Keeper of the broad Seal of England, a man right renowned; that you may lively express the image of your father's virtues in the excellent towardness which you naturally have from your most virtuous father. If you both daily ruminate and remember the familiar and best known examples of your ancestors, you cannot have more forcible persuasions to move you to that which is good and honest. But I will continually pray God to prosper that good hope which your parents and kinfolk have of you, your good studies also; and that he will plentifully bless and beautify you with all the gifts of his spirit, that you may become profitable members of the church, your country, and commonweal, and may live long and happy days. *Kalends Augusti. Anno 1577.*

The first part, entreating what counsel a prince should use

Preface

Aristotle and other philosophers teach us, and experience confirms, that there are two ways to come unto the knowledge of things. The one, when from the causes and maxims men come to knowledge of the effects and consequences; the other when contrary, by the effects and consequences we come to know the causes and maxims. As for example, when we see the earth wax green and trees gather leaves, we know by that effect that the sun, which is the cause thereof, approaches near us; and we come to receive this maxim, that the sun gives vigor and force unto the earth to bring forth fruits. And by the contrary also, when we have knowledge of this cause and maxim, we come to know the effect and conclude the consequence; which is that the sun coming near us, the earth brings forth her fruits, and withdrawing from us, the earth leaves off bringing forth. The first of these ways is proper and peculiar unto the mathematicians, who teach the truth of their theorems and problems by their demonstrations drawn from maxims, which are common sentences allowed of themselves for true by the common sense and judgment of all men. The second way belongs to other sciences, as to natural philosophy, moral philosophy, physic, law, policy, and other sciences, whereof the knowledge proceeds more commonly by a resolute order of effects to their causes, and from particulars to general maxims, than by the first way; although it is certain that sometimes they also help themselves both with the one and the other way.

In the political art then, whereof Plato, Aristotle, and other philosophers have written books, men may well use both these ways. From the effects and particulars of a civil government, men may come to the knowledge of maxims and rules; and on the contrary, by the rules and maxims men may have the knowledge of effects. So that when we see the effects of a political government which is of no value, and which is pernicious and evil, men are hereby brought to the knowledge of the maxims and rules which are of the same sort; and by good and profitable effects, men are also led to the notice of good rules and maxims. And on the other side, good or evil rules and maxims lead to the knowledge of like effects. Yet although the maxims and general rules of the political art may somewhat serve to know well to guide and govern a public estate, whether a principality or free city, yet they cannot be so certain as the maxims of the mathematicians, but are rules rather very dangerous, yea, pernicious, if men cannot make them serve and apply them unto affairs as they happen to come; and not to apply the affairs unto these maxims and rules. For the circumstances, dependencies, consequences, and antecedents of every affair and particular business, are all for the most part diverse and contrary; so that although two affairs be like, yet men must not therefore conduct and determine them by one same rule or maxim, because of the diversity and difference of accidents and circumstances. For experience teaches us that in one same act, that which is good in one time is not in another, but rather hurtful; and that which is convenient for some nations is not good for others; and so of other circumstances. They then who deal in the affairs of public estate need to know not only the maxims and rules of the political art, but also they must have a wise, quick, and sharp wit and judgment, rightly and discreetly to ponder and weigh the circumstances and accidents of every affair, prudently to apply them to the rules and maxims, yea, sometimes to force and bend them to serve the present affair. But this science and habit of knowing well to weigh and examine the accidents and circumstances of affairs, and then to be able to apply unto them their rules and principles, is a science singular and excellent, but rare and not given to many persons. For of necessity he that will come to this science, at least in any perfection to be able to manage and handle weighty affairs, first needs to be endowed with a good and perfect natural judgment; and secondly, he must be wise, temperate, and quiet, without any passion or affection, but all to public good and utility; and thirdly, be must be conversed and experienced in many and sundry affairs. These he cannot have and obtain unless he himself has handled or seen them handled, or else by great and attentive reading of choice histories he has brought his judgment to be very staid and well exercised in such affairs.

We must not then think that all sorts of people are fit to deal with affairs of public estate; nor that everyone who speaks and writes thereof can say what belongs thereunto. But it may be that some will enquire if I dare presume so much of myself as to take upon me effectually to handle this matter. Hereunto I answer that it is not properly my purpose whereunto I tend, or for which cause I enterprise this work; but my intent and purpose is only to show that Nicholas Machiavelli, not long ago a secretary of the Florentine commonwealth (which is now a duchy), understood little or nothing in this political science whereof we speak; and that he has taken maxims and rules altogether wicked, and has built upon them not a political, but a tyrannical science. Behold here then the end and scope which I have proposed unto myself; that is, to refute the doctrine of Machiavelli, and not exactly to handle the political science, although I hope to touch some good points thereof in some places when occasion shall offer itself. Unto my aforesaid purpose I hope to come (by the help of God) with so prosperous a good wind and full sails, as all they who read my writings shall give their judgment and acknowledge that Machiavelli was altogether ignorant in that science, and that his scope and intent in his writings is nothing else but to frame a very true and perfect tyranny. Machiavelli also never had parts requisite to know that science; for as for experience in managing affairs, he could have none, since during his time he saw nothing but the brabblings and contentions of certain potentates of Italy, and certain practices and policies of some citizens of Florence. Neither had he any or very little knowledge in histories, as shall be more particularly showed in many places of our discourse; where (God aiding) we will mark the plain and as it were palpable faults and ignorances which he has committed in those few histories which it pleases him sometimes by the way to touch; which most commonly he cites to evil purpose, and many times falsely. As for a firm and sound judgment, Machiavelli also lacked, as is plainly seen by the absurd and foolish reasons wherewith he confirms the propositions and maxims which he sets down; only he has a certain subtlety (such as it is) to give color unto his most wicked and damnable doctrines. But when a man comes something nigh to examine his subtleties, then in truth it is discovered to be but a beastly vanity and madness, yea, full of extreme wickedness. I doubt not but many courtiers who deal in matters of estate, and others of their humor, will find it very strange that I should speak in this sort of their great doctor Machiavelli; whose books rightly may be called the French Koran, they have them in so great estimation, imitating and observing his principles and maxims no more nor less than the Turks do the Koran of their great prophet Mahomet. But yet I beseech them not to be offended that I speak in this manner of a man whom I will plainly show to be full of all wickedness, impiety, and ignorance; and to suspend their judgment, whether I say true or no, until they have wholly read these my discourses. For as soon as they have read them, I do assure myself that every man of perfect judgment will say and determine that I speak but too modestly of the vices and brutishness found in this their great Doctor.

But to open and make easy the intelligence of what should here be handled, we must first search out what that Machiavelli was, and his writings. Machiavelli then was in his time the secretary or common notary of the commonwealth of Florence during the reign of Charles VIII and Louis XII, kings of France; Alexander VI and Julius II, popes of Rome; and of Henry VII and Henry VIII, kings of England. In which time he wrote his books in the Italian language, and published them about the first beginning of Francis I, king of France, as may be gathered by his own writings. Of his life and death I can say nothing, neither did I, or vouchsafed I once to enquire thereof, because his memory deserved better to be buried in perpetual oblivion than to be renewed among men. Yet I may well say that if his life was like his doctrine, as is to be presumed, there was never man in the world more contaminated and defiled with vices and wickedness than he was. By the preface he made unto his book entitled *De Principe, Of the Prince*, it seems he was banished and chased from Florence; for he there complains unto his magnificence Lorenzo de Medici (unto whom he dedicated his work) of what he endured injuriously and unjustly, as he said. And in certain other places he recites that one time he remained in France, another time at Rome, and another (not sent ambassador, for he would never have forgotten to have said that, but as it is to be presumed) as a fugitive and banished man. But howsoever it may be, he dedicates the said book unto the said Lorenzo de Medici, to teach him the reasons to invade and obtain a principality; which book for the most part contains nothing but tyrannical precepts, as shall appear in the prosecution and progress of this work. But I know not if the Medici have made their profit and taken use of Machiavelli's precepts contained in his book; yet this appears plainly, that since that time they occupied Florence and changed the aristocratic free estate of that city into a duchy, or rather into a manifest tyranny, as will easily appear unto those who are advised and have seen how Florence is at this day governed and ruled. Besides this book of a prince or a principality, Machiavelli has also written three books discoursing upon the first decade of Livy, which (illustrating the other book of the principality) are instead a commentary thereunto. Through all which discourses he disperses here and there a few words out of Livy, neither rehearsing the whole deed nor history of the matter, for which he fishes these words and applies them preposterously after his own fantasy, for the most part forcing them to serve to confirm some absurd and strange thing. He also mixes herewith examples of small and petty potentates of Italy, happening in his time or a little before, which are not worth the recital, but are less worthy to be proposed for imitation. Yet herein is he to be excused, in that he knew no better; for if he had known better, I doubt not but would have brought them to light, to have adorned his writings and to have made them more authentic and receivable. But out of those two books, namely *The Prince* and the *Discourses*, I have extracted and gathered what is properly his own, and have reduced and brought it to certain maxims, which I have distinguished into three parts, as may be seen hereafter. And I have been as it were constrained to do so, that I might revocate and gather every matter to its certain head and place, the better to examine them. For Machiavelli has not handled every matter in one same place, but a little here and a little there, interlacing and mixing some good things amongst them; doing therein as poisoners do, who never cast lumps of poison upon a heap, lest it be perceived, but most subtly incorporate it as they can with some other delicate and dainty morsels. For if I had followed the order that he holds in his books, I must needs have handled one same point many times, yea confusedly and not wholly. I have then drawn the greatest part of his doctrine and of his documents into certain propositions and maxims, and withal added the reasons whereby he maintains them. I have also set down the places of his books, to lead them thereunto who desire to try what fidelity I have used, either in not attributing unto him anything that is not his own, or in not forgetting any reason that may make for him. Wherein so much there wants that I fear that any man may impose upon me to have committed some fault therein; on the contrary, in some places I have better cleared and lightened his talk, reasons, and allegations than they are in his writings. And if any man says that I wrong him in setting down the evil things contained in his books without speaking of the good things which are dispersedly mixed therewith, and might bring honor and grace unto him, I answer and will maintain that in all his writings there is nothing of any value that is his own. Yet I confess that there are some good places drawn out of Livy or some other authors; but besides that they are not his, they are not by him handled fully, nor as they should be. For as I have said, he only has dispersed them amongst his works to serve as an honey sweet bait to cover his poison. And therefore seeing that what is good in his writings is taken from other better authors, where we may learn them better for our purpose, and more whole and perfect than in Machiavelli, we have no cause to attribute honor unto him, nor to thank him for what is not his, and which we possess and retain from a better shop than his. And as for his precepts concerning the military art, wherewith he deals in his books, which seem to be new and of his own invention, I will say nothing but that men do not now practice them, neither are they thought worthy of observation by those who are well seen in that art; as we may see in what he maintains, that a prince ought not to have in his service any foreign soldiers, nor to have any fortresses against enemies, but only against his subjects when he is in fear of them.

For the contrary hereof is ordinarily seen practiced; and in truth it shows an exceeding great pride and rashness in Machiavelli, that he dares speak and write of the affairs of war, and prescribe precepts and rules unto those who are of that profession; seeing he had nothing but by hearsay, and was himself but a simple secretary or town-clerk, which is a trade as far different from the profession of war as an arquebus differs from a pen and inkhorn. Herein it falls out to Machiavelli as it did once to the philosopher Phormio; who one day reading in the Peripatetic school of Greece, and seeing arrive and enter there Hannibal of Carthage (who was brought thither by some of his friends, to hear the eloquence of the philosopher), he began to speak and dispute with much babbling of the laws of war and the duty of a good captain, before this most famous captain, who had forgotten more than ever that proud philosopher knew or had learned. When he had thus ended his lecture and goodly disputation, as Hannibal went from the auditory one of his friends who had brought him there asked what he thought of the philosopher's eloquence and gallant speech. He said, "Truly I have seen in my life many old dotards, but I never saw one so great as this Phormio." So I do not doubt but those who have knowledge in the military art will give the like judgment of Machiavelli, if they read his writings, and will say according to the common proverb, that he speaks not like of clerk of arms. But I leave things touching this matter unto those who have more knowledge therein than I; for it is not my purpose to touch what Machiavelli has handled of the military art, nor such precepts as concern the leading of an army.

By this which we have before spoken, that Machiavelli lived during the reign of Charles VIII and Louis XII, kings of France, and attained the beginning of the reign of Francis I, it follows that there has not been past fifty or threescore years since his writings came to light; whereupon some may marvel why he was not spoken of at all in France during the reign of Henri II, and that after them the name of Machiavelli did but begin to be known on this side the mountains, and his writings come into some reputation. The answer is not very obscure to those who know how the affairs of France have been governed since the decease of king Henri II of happy memory. For during his reign and before, the kingdom was governed after the mere French manner; that is to say, following the traces and documents of our French ancestors. But since, it has governed by the rules of Machiavelli the Florentine, as shall be seen hereafter. From that time until the present, the name of Machiavelli has been celebrated and esteemed as of the wisest person of the world, and most cunning in the affairs of state; and his books held dearest and most precious by our Italianized courtiers, as if they were the books of Sibylla whereunto the pagans had recourse when they would deliberate upon any great affair concerning the commonwealth, or as the Turks hold dear and precious their Mahomet's Koran, as we have said above.

And we need not be abashed if those of Machiavelli's nation, who hold the principal estates in the government of France, have forsaken the ancient manner of our French ancestors' government, to bring France into use with a new form of managing and ruling their country, taught by Machiavelli. For on the one side every man esteems and prizes the manners, fashions, customs, and other things of his own country more than those of another. On the other side, Machiavelli their great doctor describes so well the French government in his time, blaming and reprehending their conducting of affairs of state, that it might easily persuade his disciples to change the manner of French government into the Italian. For Machiavelli vaunts that being once at Nantes, and talking of public and state affairs with the Cardinal of Amboise, who was a very wise man, he plainly told him that the French had no knowledge in affairs of state. And in many places he reprehends the government of our abovenamed kings, Charles VIII and Louis XII; in other places he calls our kings tributaries of the Swiss and of the English. And often when he speaks of the French, he calls them barbarous and says they are full of greed and disloyalty; so also he taxes the Germans of the same vices. Now I beseech you, is it not good reason to make so great account of Machiavelli in France? who so defames and reproves the honor of our good kings and of all our whole nation, calling them ignorant of the affairs of state, barbarous, covetous, disloyal? All this might be borne withal and passed away in silence, if there were not another evil. But when we see that Machiavelli, by his doctrine and documents, has changed the good and ancient government of France into a kind of Florentine government, where we see with our eyes the total ruin of France, it infallibly follows (if God by his grace does not remedy it soon) that now it should be time, if ever, to lay hand to the work, to remit and bring France again unto the government of our ancestors.

Hereupon I humbly pray the princes and great lords of France to consider what is their duty in this case. Seems it, most illustrious lords, seeing at this time poor France, which is your country and mother, so desolate and torn in sunder by strangers, that you ought to suffer it to be lost and ruined? Ought you to permit them to sow atheism and impiety in your country and to set up schools thereof? Seeing your France has always been so zealous in the Christian religion that our ancient kings by their piety and justice have obtained so honorable a title and name of Most Christian? Think you that God has caused you to be born into this world to help to ruin your country, or coldly to stand still and suffer your mother to be contaminated and defiled with the contempt of God, with perfidy, sodomy, tyranny, cruelty, thefts, strange usuries, and other detestable vices which strangers sow here? But rather contrary, God has given you life, power, and authority to take away such infamies and corruptions; and if you do it not, you must make account for it, and you can look for but a grievous and just punishment. If it is true, as the civilian lawyers say, that he is a murderer and culpable of death who suffers to die with hunger the person unto whom he owes nourishment; shall not you be culpable before God of so many massacres, murders, and desolations of your poor France if you give it not succor, seeing you have the means and that you are obliged thereunto by right of nature? Shall you not be condemned and attainted of impiety, atheism, and tyranny if you drive not out of France Machiavelli and his government?

Here if any man will inquire how it appears that France is at this day governed by the doctrine of Machiavelli, the resolution hereof is easy and clear. For the effects which we see with our eyes, and the provisions and executions of the affairs which are put in practice, may easily bring us to the causes and maxims, as we have above said; which is one way to know things, by ascending from effects and consequences to the knowledge of causes and maxims. And whoever shall read the maxims of Machiavelli, which we shall handle hereafter, and descend from thence into the particularities of the French government, he shall see that the precepts and maxims of Machiavelli are for the most part at this day practiced and put in effect and execution, from point to point. Insomuch that by both the two ways, from the maxims to the effects and from the effects to the maxims, men may clearly know that France is at this day governed by the doctrine of Machiavelli. For are they not Machiavellians, Italians or Italianized, who handle and deal with the seals of the kingdom of France? Is it not they also who draw out and stamp edicts? Who dispatch all things within and without the realm? Who hold the goodliest governments and terms belonging to the crown? Yea, if a man will at this day obtain or get anything in the court, for to have a good and quick dispatch thereof he must learn to speak the Messereske language, because the Messers will most willingly hear them in their own tongue; and they understand not the French, no not the terms of justice and royal ordinances. Whereupon every man may conjecture and imagine how they can well observe or cause to be observed the laws of France, the terms whereof they understand not. Moreover, it is plain enough that within these fifteen years Machiavelli's books were as familiar and ordinary in the hands of the courtiers as the breviaries are in the hands of curates of parishes.

And as for the disparity of ancient government which was ruled in following the traces, fashions, and customs of our ancestors, from the modern and present government which is founded upon the doctrine of Machiavelli, it is easily and apparently seen by the fruits and effects which proceed therefrom. For by the ancient French government the kingdom was maintained and governed in peace and tranquility under the observance of ancient laws, without any domestic or civil war, flourishing and enjoining a free traffic, and subjects were maintained in possessing and enjoying their goods, estates, franchises, and liberties. But now, by the Italian government of this time the good and ancient laws of the realm are abolished and suppressed; cruel wars and dissentions are maintained in France; peace always broken; the people destroyed and eaten, and traffic decayed; subjects are deprived of their ancient liberties and franchises, and brought into such confusion and disorder that none knows well what is his own and what is not; but one plows and sows, and another mows and reaps the same. And although this is so true and manifest that it shall not be needful to show more amply that the manner of our ancestors' government was otherwise, and better than the modern which at the present is in use; yet for all that I pretend hereafter upon every maxim clearly to demonstrate by good examples that our ancient Frenchmen guided and governed themselves by good reason and wisdom, clean contrary from the way of Machiavelli's precepts.

Yet I mean not to authorize my sayings by the citation of examples of small potentates and tyrannizers born in one night like toadstools (as Machiavelli does), but by gallant and notable examples of our kings of France, confirmed and fortified; yea by other examples of good and ancient emperors, princes, and Roman captains, and of the Senate of Rome. For I have chosen those two monarchies, the Roman and the French, as the fairest and most excellent, from whence to draw true and good examples which are worthy for a prince to imitate; borrowing but few from other precedent monarchies, as Medes, Assyrians, and Greeks, as less known to us concerning the management and government of their affairs, too far from our time and from our manners and customs. I have lastly chosen the best and most authentic historiographers, and especially those who have written those things which fell out in their own time; and of those affairs, most of which they were spectators and actors therein. Of this sort and order of my own country's historiographers were Froissart, Montrelet, de Commines, du Bellay; and of Romans, Sallust, Tacitus, Suetonius, Dion, Herodian, Lampridius, Capitolinus, Josephus, and certain others who shall be cited hereafter in their places. I also have drawn out some part of my citations out of our

Annales of France, out of Paulus Aemylius, Thucydides, Xenophon, and many other authors, all which are authentic and approved, and by prescript of ancient time and long continuance have gained that praise and reputation to be good witnesses, without reproach or defamation. And for what Machiavelli dares say, that the French have no understanding or knowledge in matters or causes of state, I hope it shall appear clean contrary, not only by the good government which I shall show to have been kept and observed by our ancestors in public causes, but also by the places and examples which I shall bring forth and cite out of M. Philip de Commines, knight and chamberlain of king Louis XI; who lived even in Machiavelli's time, and who understood better how the affairs of a kingdom or commonwealth should be ruled or governed, than ever Machiavelli knew how to guide and rule a simple town. Yet I cannot but confess that for the governing and guiding of a tyrannous state, Machiavelli has more cunning than any other of whom I have read; he so well knew all the points and precepts which were meet and convenient for the establishing of it, as hereafter shall be seen in the handling of his maxims.

Moreover, if in certain places where the matter requires it I speak a little too hardly of Machiavelli's Italian nation, I hope that the good men of that country cannot find it evil; as well because Machiavelli gives me just occasion, having villainously and opprobriously slandered in many ways our French nation, but also because I intend not in any way to blame or reprove the good Italian people. And I will not deny but that among the Italian and Florentine nation there are diverse virtuous people, who are not less than mere Machiavellians, and who detest and abhor his wicked doctrine. For there is not so bad a ground which amongst divers and sundry evil plants brings not out some good. Yet I will give a particular praise and commendation unto such Italians as are virtuous, which more pertains to them than to the virtuous and goodly men of other nations; namely, that as precious stones and some other drugs and spices are esteemed to be most singular as they are most rare, so the good and virtuous are so much the more to be praised and commended because they are rare, and because it is no trivial and common thing in Italy to be a virtuous and good man. There is also another point which excuses me; that is, that the force of truth has drawn and expressed this confession of Machiavelli, when he says that there is no nation or people in Christendom that is more vicious and corrupted than the Italian nation; and that there is no province nor kingdom where there is less care of God and of all religion than in Italy. Although to this last point of religion Machiavelli, who in all his books shows himself a very atheist and contemner of all piety and godliness, meant not to tax nor blame them of his nation of impiety nor of atheism; but only that they are not like the pagans, who so scrupulously observe their superstitions and ceremonies, as we shall more at large set down in the second part of this discourse.

But from whence comes this impudence of Machiavelli to tax and blame the French of disloyalty and perfidy; seeing that he himself also teaches that a prince ought not to keep and hold his faith but for his profit and commodity, and that the observation of faith is pernicious and hurtful? I will not deny but at the present time many Italianized Frenchmen are disloyal and faith-breakers, having so learned by Machiavelli's doctrine; but I deny that in the time of Machiavelli the French nation was contaminated with that vice; as yet there are many good and natural Frenchmen (thanks be to God) who detest all perfidy and disloyalty and are in no way affected to those exploits which the Italians and Italianized do in France, but rather sob and sigh in their breasts to see the French nation defamed with that infamous and abominable vice, detested and hated amongst all countries and nations. And I also hope that the good and loyal Frenchmen will endeavor themselves to recover the good renown and reputation of the French nation, which some degenerated and Italianized have defiled and polluted. But wherefore does Machiavelli so defame and disgrace the French nation for greed? I do much marvel at it, for until the present time the French have always had the reputation to be liberal, courteous, and ready to do any pleasure even unto strangers and those who are unknown to them. And would to God that the French nation had never been of that nature and condition to do well unto strangers, without first knowing and trying their behaviors and manner of life. We should not then see France to be governed and ruled by strangers, as it is; we should not feel the calamities and troubles of civil wars and dissentions, which they enterprise to maintain their greatness and magnitude, and to fish in troubled water. The treasures of France should not be so exhausted and drawn out by their rapines and most insatiable avarice, as they are. What country or nation is there in the world that feels or can justly complain of the covetousness of Frenchmen? Or rather, what nation is there which has not felt the liberality of the kingdom of France? But contrarily we see with the eye and touch with the finger the covetousness and avarice of the Italians who undermine and ruin us, yea, who also suck out all our substance and wealth, and leave nothing at all for ourselves. Some of them are publicans or farmers of the king's revenues or farm-rents; some farmers of the customs and freights of merchandizers and carriages; some farmers of yearly tributes and subsidies; and some of the prince's private rents, yea, of all public and common profits belonging to the

French king, rating them even at what price they will. By that means infinite coin comes into their hands, but there is little which returns again to the public or common good of the prince and country. Others obtain great estates, offices, and benefices, by the means whereof all the treasure and money of the kingdom of France falls into the hands of strangers. And those Italians, who have no means or occasions to deal with the public affairs of the commonwealth, hold and keep banks in good towns, where they exercise most exorbitant and unmeasurable usuries, by the means thereof they wholly eat and consume poor France and bring it unto confusion. And although in Machiavelli's time France was not fallen into that extreme evil and great calamity as it is now at present, yet since that time we have sufficiently felt the greed of the Italians in the wars which our kings of France have made in Italy and Piedmont. For the great store of treasure and money that must needs have been sent beyond the Alps, to satisfy the insatiable and greedy lusts of the Italians, was the cause oftentimes of increasing and raising taxes and tallies upon the people, which little by little rose so high that they exceeded and do exceed many times more than half the revenue of the poor plebian, or common sort of people. But this Italian covetousness which they exercised in France at that time, by their dealings drawing our treasure and money into their own country, was but honey in respect to that which they have exercised and still exercise more and more since they have passed on this side of the Alps; and they come to domineer and perch all over the country of France, and to hold and possess offices, benefices, farms, customs, revenues, and banks, as is heretofore said. And therefore it is clearly and evidently seen that it is (as I may say) against the hair that Machiavelli and the other Italians tax the French of avarice, unless a man will say that the French are more to be blamed and reprehended for passive avarice; that is to say, what they suffer and endure from the Italians, who by their active greed which they practice and put in action amongst us clip the wool on the back, and suck our blood and substance, as men do with sheep. And in this sense to take it, as we should, it is certain and assured that Machiavelli, blaming us of passive covetousness, which we do suffer, shows us briefly that we are beasts who will suffer ourselves to be bereaved and weakened of our wool and our blood (with patience) by strangers. For it may well one day come to pass that they may be made to disgorge their booties and rapines, and that their great heaps of money, gotten by extortions in France, may turn them unto damage; for as the poet Sophocles says:

> Men must not seek, nor love, of all things to get gain,
> For he that draws gain out of that which is naught,
> Before he profit gets, shall sooner loss sustain:

For evil gotten goods are often dearly bought.

And whereas Machiavelli taxes and charges the Germans with greed and perfidy, herein may be seen what an impudent and most wicked slanderer he is. For all men may plainly see that neither in their own country nor in the towns of France where they dwell for their commerce and traffic, they practice no great and execrable usuries as the Italians do; but content themselves with a mean and reasonable profit for their money, as of five or eight percent at the most; whereas the Italians often return their money with the gain of fifty, yea often of a hundredth, for a hundredth. And as for merchandise and traffic, it is well known that no other nation is more plain, faithful, sincere, and loyal than they are in their bargains and traffic. For they do not refresh, polish, and deck up their wares, nor change them and sell one for another; they set not a price for their merchandise more than it is worth, but at the first word they ask what at the last they will have, or not sell it, without seeking any unmeasurable or extraordinary profit upon them who know not what the merchandise is worth. And as for perfidy, deceit, and treason, the Germans have them in so great execration and detestation that they think there neither is nor can be any greater vice or sin than they are. After a man once has forfeited and failed in his faith, contract, and promise, although but in small things and of no great reckoning or value, they will never afterward esteem or account him a good or honest man; so great, I say, is their detestation of all kind of deceit and false dealing. But a man need not marvel that Machiavelli dares so impudently lie upon the Germans, for he has brought forth more strange things than this slander, as we shall show hereafter, both to the good of all others that shall read his writings, and to the manifest and plain laying open of him in his true and perfect colors: for the effecting thereof, let us then now enter into the matter.

1.1
Machiavelli

A prince's good counsel ought to proceed from his own wisdom; otherwise, he cannot be well counseled.

It is a maxim and general rule that good counsel ought to proceed from the wisdom of the prince himself, and not contrary, that the prince's wisdom should proceed from good counsel. For if the prince is not wise himself, he cannot be well counseled. For if he is counselled by one alone in the administration of his affairs, hardly shall he find a man of requisite honesty and sufficiency to counsel him well. And although he should find one of such quality, there is danger that he would take away the prince's estate; for to domineer and reign, there is no honesty or virtue that can keep in the ambition of men. And if an unwise prince takes counsel of many, he will have discordant and contentious counsels and opinions, which he can never accord nor reconcile; meanwhile every one of his counsellors will seek his own profit, of which the prince cannot know or remedy.

Answer

At first this maxim seems to have some appearance of truth; but when it is well examined, a man shall find it not only untrue, but also pernicious and of wicked consequence. I am content to presuppose that it is certain that there cannot come a better and more profitable thing to a people than to have a prince wise of himself; therefore, said Plato, men may call it a happy commonwealth when either the prince can play the philosopher, or when a philosopher comes to reign there. That is to say, in a word, when the prince is himself wise and prudent. For in old time, the name philosopher was taken for a person full of wisdom and science, not for a dreaming unsociable man, as it is commonly taken today. Of old the name of philosopher was attributed for a title of great honor unto the emperor Marcus Aurelius, who in truth was a good and wise prince. But to verify what I say it is not needful to cite many reasons, for it is evident enough that the felicity of a state lies wholly in well commanding and well obeying, whereupon results a harmony and concordance so melodious and excellent that he who commands and he who obeys both receive contentment, pleasure, and utility. But to obey well depends wholly on well commanding, and cannot be without it; so commanding well depends on the prudence and wisdom of him that commands. The emperor Severus, being in wars and his son Bassianus with him, being carried in a litter because he had the gout, saw his soldiers discontented and mutinous, and would have Bassianus for their chieftain. He assembled all the army, but especially his colonels, captains, and corporals, and after having made unto them some remonstrance and oration, he executed all the heads of that mutiny. Afterwards he spoke thus to all the army: "Now know ye that it is the head and not the feet which commands you." And in deed and truth, good commanding proceeds from the prudence and wisdom of he that commands; who remains and has his being not in the feet nor arms, but in a brave mind, well stayed and governed, aided by a good natural towardness, a mature and ripe age, and experience. And the prince who can well command shall also undoubtedly be well obeyed; for a prudent commandment draws after it withal an obedience, because a wise prince will always found his commandments in reason and justice, and to the public utility, not to his own pleasure. By which means they who are to obey shall be constrained by the force of reason and equity, and drawn also by the sweetness of the profit to yield obedience. But if some by these means cannot be induced to obey, as there are always some among many, they will be brought thereunto either by the example of those who let themselves be overcome with reason and public utility, or else by punishment, which is in the prince's hand. He who will show by plurality of examples that prudent princes have always been well obeyed, and that their kingdoms and countries have been happy and full of prosperity, should never be done; but I will content myself to cite only two. Solomon was a king most wise, and a great philosopher; for he asked wisdom from God, who gave it in such abundance that besides being ignorant of nothing a prince should know to govern his subjects well, he also knew the natures of plants and living creatures, and was so cunning in all kinds of philosophy that his knowledge was admired through all the world. His prudence and wisdom made him so respected by all the great kings, his neighbors, that they esteemed themselves happy to do him pleasure and have his amity. By this means he maintained his kingdom in so high and happy a peace that in his time his subjects made no more account of silver than of stones, they had such store. And as for himself, he held so magnificent an estate that we read not of any king or emperor that did the like.

Charles the Wise, king of France, on coming to the crown found the kingdom in great confusion and calamity, for all Guyenne, part of Normandy, and Picardy were occupied by the English. He saw he had king Edward III of England as his adversary, who was one of the most happy and most valiant princes that ever was in England, and who some years before had obtained two great victories in France. One was at Crécy against king Philip of Valois, where France lost eleven princes, twelve hundred knights, and thirty thousand other people of war. The other victory was at Poitiers, by the leadership of the prince of Wales, Edward's son and lieutenant general. King John of France was there taken prisoner, with his son Philip (later duke of Bourgogne), along with many other princes and great lords, all which were taken into England; there was made there a great discomfiture of people. By these two battles lost in France, one after the other in a small time, the kingdom was so debilitated of its forces and goods that it could not stand. Yet for a further heap of mischiefs, at Paris and in many other places of the realm at the same time arose many broils and civil dissentions. But that good king

Charles was so wise and prudent in conducting the affairs of the realm while he was dauphin and regent of France (his father being prisoner), and after when he was king, that little by little he laid to sleep all the civil stirs and discords. Afterwards he did so much that he recovered from the English almost all they occupied; and although he was not so brave a warrior as his father, nor his grandfather king Philip, yet he was wiser and better advised in his deliberations, not hazarding his affairs as they did (fearing to be reputed cowards), nor did anything rashly, without due consideration. He took not arms in hand, but he knew well how and when to employ them to his good; insomuch that king Edward of England, seeing the wisdom of that king, made his arms rebound and become dull, and his victories and conquests were lost. "Truly," said he, "I never knew a king that uses less arms, yet troubles me so much; he is all the day indicting letters, and hurts me more with his missives than ever did his father or grandfather with their great forces and arms." Behold the witness Edward gave of the wisdom of his enemy Charles, which was of so great efficacy that he brought his kingdom into a good peace, by the means whereof his people became rich and wealthy, where before they were poor and miserable. And not only the people became rich, but the king himself heaped up great treasures which he left to his son after him, insomuch that he was not only surnamed the Wise, but also the Rich. I could to this purpose add here many other examples, but in a thing so clear the example of these two kings, Solomon and Charles, shall suffice. These two for their great wisdom have acquired the name of Wise; both were rich in great treasures, both of them maintained their subjects in peace, both left their kingdoms opulent and abundant, and placed the estates of their commonwealths in great felicity.

It is a thing then plain and confessed that it is an exceeding great good to a people when they have a prince that is wise of himself; but thereupon to infer and say, as Machiavelli does, that the government of a prince ought to depend upon his own proper wisdom, and that he cannot be well counselled but by himself, is ill concluded, false, and of pernicious consequence. For a prince, however prudent he is, ought not so much to esteem his own wisdom as to despise the counsel of other wise men. Solomon despised them not, and Charles the Wise always conferred of his affairs with the wise men of his council. And it is so far off that the prince ought to despise another's counsel, that he ought instead to conform his opinion to that of the men of his council who are wise; and ought not stubbornly to resist their advice, but rather to follow it, and hold his own suspected. And therefore that wise and cunning emperor Marcus Aurelius, the philosopher, being in his privy council house with that great lawyer Scaevola, Maetianus, Volusianus, and many other great persons excellent in knowledge and honesty, sometimes took in hand to sustain opinions contrary to theirs. "Well," said he, "the thing then must be done according to your advice; for it is much more reasonable that I alone follow the opinion of so many of my good and faithful friends, as you are, than that so many wise men should follow the opinion of me alone." Unto this opinion agrees also the common proverb, that many eyes see clearer than one eye alone. Experience also teaches us that things determined and resolved by many brains are always wiser, safer, and better ordered than the resolutions of one alone. And we see also that the ancient Romans, and all commonwealths well governed, past and present, have always followed what by plurality of wise men's voices was determined. And truly, the wiser a prince is, the more will he suspect his own opinion. For the same wisdom which is in him will persuade him not to believe himself too much, and to suspect his own judgment, and permit himself to be governed by his council. And contrary, there are no people more presumptuous, nor that think themselves more wise, than those that have no wisdom. If you learn of a prince that thinks himself wise, this principle of Machiavelli, that he ought to govern himself by his own wisdom and counsel, and that he cannot be better counselled than by himself, you shall straight find inconveniences. For then you shall see that he will believe no counsel nor advice but what comes out of his own head; and he will say to those who give him any that he understands well his own matters, and that he knows what he has to do; and so will bring his estate and affairs into confusion, and overthrow all upside down. And from whence comes this evil government and disorder? Even from that goodly doctrine of Machiavelli, which wills that a prince should govern himself by his own wisdom, and maintains that a prince cannot be well counselled but by his own wisdom. The consequence then of this maxim is not small, seeing the public state of a country may stagger and be overthrown thereby. Better then that the prince holds this resolution, to govern himself by good counsel and believe it, and have in suspicion his own wisdom. For if the prince is wise and his opinion found to be founded upon reason, they of his council will easily fall to his advice; seeing also that oftentimes they applaud and like too well the prince's opinions, though they be scant reasonable. And when it happens that they take the hardiness to contradict the prince's opinion, he ought to persuade himself that he strays far from good reason, and in that case he ought to hold his judgment suspected. Contrarily, if the prince be not wise at all — for it is not incompatible nor inconvenient to be a prince and to be unwise with a — yet having this resolution to govern himself by counsel, his affairs will carry themselves better than being governed by the head. But in all cases I presuppose that the prince's council is compounded of good and capable men, who have ever before their eyes the service and utility of their prince, which is no other thing but the common weal. For otherwise, if they are wicked, the prince's affairs cannot but go evil, whether the prince is wise or unwise. For even being wise, he cannot see nor know all, but only considers those things which pass by the relation of his counsellors. And if those of his council are wicked, they may always so handle matters that he shall not be advised but of such things as it pleases them, as soon false as true, to cause him to incline to their pleasure and will. If the prince is unwise, much better those of his council may handle him at their devotion, and in all sorts abuse him.

And therefore the elders have held this maxim, clean contrary to that of Machiavelli; that it is more expedient to the common weal for the prince to be wicked and his council good, than the prince be good and his counsellors wicked. But because the historiographer Lampridius has touched that point very clearly and briefly, I will here recite and translate his own words. He says then in the life of the emperor Alexander Severus, addressing his speech unto the emperor Constantine the Great, in this manner.

"If you ask why Alexander Severus, born in Syria, has been so excellent a prince, seeing that even from the Roman nation and from the other provinces there have proceeded and come men wicked, impure, cruel, contemptible, unjust, and given only to voluptuousness; I may first answer according to the common opinion of good men, that nature (which is everywhere a mother) may in all places and in all nations engender a good prince. I may also say that Alexander was a good prince by fear, because his predecessor Heliogabalus, who was a most wicked prince, was massacred and slain. And to touch the very truth, may it please thy piety to remember what you have read in the historiographer Marius Maximus; that the estate of the commonwealth is better and more assured wherein the prince is wicked, than that wherein the prince's counsellors are wicked. For one wicked man may be corrected by many good men, but many wicked men cannot be surmounted by one good man alone. Alexander had counsellors who were venerable and holy persons, not malicious, not thieves, not partial, not covetous, not consenting to evil, not enemies to good men, not voluptuous, not cruel, not deceivers of their prince, not mockers nor abusers of him as a fool; but persons honorable, continent, religious, loving their prince, who would not mock him nor be mocked by him, who in their estate were no sellers, liars, dissemblers, and who defrauded not their prince of his honor, but loved him. They entertained not eunuchs and flatterers, who serving for news-carriers oftentimes report otherwise than what is said unto them, and who hold their master shut up, providing above all things that he shall know nothing of his own affairs. I know that he brings himself into great danger, who talks to a prince that is a servant and a slave unto such people. But you who have experience of the great mischiefs that such pestilent flatterers bring, and how they deceive princes, you know how to debase and humble them, namely to force them only to deal with the affairs of the house, and not the common weal. Above all, this is most memorable in Alexander, that he would never receive any alone into his chamber but the great master of his household and the great lawyer Ulpian. Neither gave he any man liberty to sell smoke, nor to slander or speak evil of him; especially after he had put to death Euxinus, who often had sold him as a senseless fool. There is more yet; that Alexander spared not his own parents and friends when they deserved punishment, or at least put them from him when they offended, saying that he loved better the commonwealth than his parents and friends. And that you may know what people he had of his privy council, these were they: Fabius Sabinus, the son of Sabinus, an excellent man, a second Cato in his time; Domitius Ulpianus, a learned man and a lawyer; Elius Gordianus, father of that Gordianus who was after emperor, a man very excellent; Julius Paulus, a great person in the law; Claudius Venatus, a great and worthy orator; Pomponius, a very cunning man in the civil law; Alfenus, Africanus, Florentinus, Martianus, Callistatus, Hermogenianus, Venuleius, Trifonius, Melianus, Celsus, Proculus, Modestinus, all excellent doctors of law and disciples of that great lawyer Papinian. All which were great familiars and very private with Alexander. More also he had of his privy council: Catilius Severus, his parent, as learned as any; Aelius Severianus, a person above all others, of greatest sanctity; Quintilius Marcellus, of whom there is not found in history a better man. Alexander then having all those and many other like in his privy council, all which agreed to do well, how could he then either do or think evil? These counsellors at the beginning were put from him out of credit, by evil counsellors who abused Alexander; but afterward, having wisely driven those from him who were worth nothing, he called again his other good counsellors, and loved all well. And these were they who made Alexander a good prince; as contrary, wicked counsellors have made many Roman emperors as wicked as they."

Behold then what Lampridius says touching this question, whether it is better to have a wicked prince who has good counsellors, or a good prince who has evil counsellors; and he resolves what the elders have held, contrary to the new opinion of Machiavelli, who makes no account of a prince's good counsellors if so be it the prince himself is good and prudent; who also says that the affairs of a prince cannot be well conducted unless he guides them himself by his own wisdom. It is then very clearly seen that his maxim is false by the noted reasons of Lampridius; namely, that many good counsellors may well supply the want of wisdom that is in a prince, and moderate his unbridled and indiscreet appetites; but a good prince cannot correct so many evil counsellors, who will feed their prince with smoke and lies, and will hide from him such things as he ought to know for the common weal.

This may yet be better showed by the examples of many princes who have been of small wisdom and virtue, and yet notwithstanding have ruled the commonwealth well by the good and wise counsel of prudent and loyal counsellors wherewith they were served; as did the emperor Gordian the Young, who was created emperor at eleven years of age. Many judged the empire to be fallen into a childish kingdom, and so into a weakness and a bad conduction; but it proved otherwise, for this young emperor Gordian espoused the daughter of a wise man called Misitheus, whom he made the high steward of his household, and governed himself by his counsel in all his affairs; so that the Roman Empire was well ruled so long as Misitheus lived. Likewise Jehoash king of Judah came to the crown a young child, of the age only of seven years; but he was governed by his uncle Jehoiada, a very wise man; while that good counsellor lived, the kingdom was well and rightly administered.

Charles VI of France was but thirteen years old when he came to the crown, and was of small understanding; yet during his minority the kingdom was well and wisely governed by his three uncles, the dukes of Anjou, of Berry, and Bourgogne. There was nothing in their government to be spoken against, but only that they were a little drawing unto themselves the king's treasure; all other affairs were administered well and prudently. Yet true it is that after the king's majority they entered into the government of the kingdom because of a frenzy that took the king, which endured more than twenty years, and then their government was corrupted by ambition, greed, a desire for vengeance, and envy. Yet as I said, during the king's minority they did govern well. The kings of France Clothar IV and Chilperic II were both princes of small understanding, and indeed had no wisdom to conduct the affairs of the realm; but they had for a counsellor and conductor of their affairs that valiant lord Charles Martel, so that during their reign the realm was well ruled, yea with many great and excellent victories.

In our time we know that Charles V was left very young by his father and grandfather; during his minority he could never have known how to govern his affairs, which were great, and in great trouble in many places. His father, foreseeing at his death that his son had need of a good overseer, ordained for that purpose king Louis XII, praying him to accept that charge, knowing well the sincerity and loyalty of that good king, who for nothing would wound his conscience; as he did not, although he might, for thereby he had great occasions for enlarging his limits. The king, to loyally acquit himself of that charge, gave to the young prince for governor a good man, faithful, and of good understanding, called the Lord de Chièvres; by the counsel of whom, and of certain other good counsellors, the affairs of that prince were much better managed (even in that low age) than ever they were in his father's or grandfather's time. This good government in that base age, proceeding from good counsel, gave so great a fame and reputation to that young prince that he was chosen emperor at the age of 20 years.

The emperor Domitian, besides being unwise was wicked and exceedingly cruel; yet during his reign he had the good fortune to light upon such governors and magistrates for the provinces of his empire, being good and wise men, that while he reigned the Roman Empire was well governed, and none but certain particular persons of Rome felt the evil of his vices and cruelty. Charles VIII of France came to his crown at the age of thirteen years, and was a very good prince, but of no great understanding nor wisdom. Yet the Estates that were assembled at Tours gave him a good council, which they chose of fit and capable persons; by which council the affairs of the kingdom were well governed during the king's minority, although there fell out some emotions and stirs of some revolters. I will not here repeat the example of the emperor Alexander Severus, who came to the empire very young, and under whom the affairs of the commonwealth were so well governed, by the means of good counsellors, as above said.

I may also here add many other examples of our kings of France who were not so spiritual, and yet governed well by their good counsel. As also there were many emperors of the Roman Empire, some ignorant and brutish, others voluptuous and effeminate, others cruel and knowing nothing but to handle iron. As were Philippus, Licinius, Diocletian, Maximian, Carus, Carinus, Gallus, Constantius, Aurelianus, Galienus, Leon, Macrinus, Zeno, Justinian, and many others who yet made very good laws, as well for distributive justice as for the policy of the empire, as is seen by the Code of Justinian. Which laws we must attribute to the wise and learned men who were their counsellors, for none of them knew anything, or little (except Macrinus) how to make good laws. Therefore I conclude this point against the maxim of Machiavelli, that a prince may well govern wisely the commonwealth by the good counsel of good and faithful counsellors, though he be ill provided of wisdom.

But here remains a difficulty which is not small; how an unwise prince may provide good and loyal counsellors, seeing that princes who are wise and well advised are therein often deceived. And upon this point I confess, there is nothing harder nor of greater consequence to a prince than to guide himself well in the election of such persons whereof he should compose his council. For there are great hypocrites and dissimulators, and one seems to be a good man, sincere, and continent, who shows himself another man when means come into his hand to corrupt virtue for to make his particular profit thereof. And we see but too much by experience that the old proverb is true, honors change manners. You may see how the most gracious and courteous in the world, the most affable and officious to everyone (that is possible) while they are in base degree, after they are mounted into some high degree of honor and dignity they become rough and haughty, so much that those to whom they showed themselves facile and serviceable, they now seem not to know them, who before were their private friends and familiars. Such people have no good souls, but deserve that their fierceness and pride should dispossess them of that place unto which most commonly their dissembled humility and courtesy has advanced them. This vice is reprehensible, not only in a prince's officers but also in the prince himself, who ought not to put pride and fierceness upon that head whereupon the crown and diadem stands. For this the king Agamemnon is taxed and reprehended by Menelaus his brother, in a tragedy of Euripides, where he says thus:

> Most humble was thou in times past, and kissed each man's hand,
> Most humane, gentle, affable, to none thy gates did stand
> Shut up, to highest honor thou by such means sought to rise:
> But now thou honor has supreme, why proves thou so unwise,
> Another man straight to become, and change thy manners all?
> Yea human duty even to friends, by thee doth not befall.
> To good men that esteem good fame, this is not covenable,
> Chameleon like thy manners changed, thou to be so mutable.

This mutability then of manners, which is seen in many natures of men, is the cause that is so hard for a prince to know how to elect good men for his counsel, and that in that point it is very uneasy to teach a prince how to behave himself therein. Yet I will a little discourse upon that point, how the elders governed themselves in election of prince's counsellors, and then we will return to Machiavelli.

Upon this I first find that our ancient Frenchmen have observed three rules, which I think good enough. The first, that the princes of the blood are always of the king's council; for although it may well come to pass that one of them is not the most resolute nor best garnished with parts requisite to know well to counsel and govern the affairs of the commonwealth, yet seeing they have that honor to be princes of the blood, they may not be excluded unless it be for some great fault and offense. For there may arise (as many times has been seen) great discontentments, troubles, and partialities which often draw after them civil wars and infinite evils. The other rule is that the new king always retains in his service the old counsellors of his predecessor who governed well, especially those who have before acquired the reputation to be good, loyal, and sincere men. The third rule is that the three estates provide good counsellors for the king during his minority, or if by accident he loses the rule of his senses or understanding; as was practiced in both cases during the reign of Charles VI. Which aforesaid rules, as I hope none can deny but they are good and introduced with good reason by our ancestors, so I must needs confess that they are not sufficient in all cases to provide good counsellors for a prince. For it may well happen that a prince of full age may have few or no princes of his blood experienced in affairs, and that the other counsellors who his predecessor left shall either not be good men or not capable, or that they are dead; and therefore he must then come to an election of new counsellors by some other way than by these aforesaid rules.

And upon that point it seems to me that the manner of proceeding which Alexander Severus used to choose his counsellors and his magistrates is very good and merits well to be imitated and drawn into consequence. For first, he never provided any persons for an office in consideration of any favor of kindred or amity, nor in recompense of any service, but only in consideration of the probity and capacity of the persons. If any man was presented to him who was not of good reputation, as well in knowledge and experience as in good life — although otherwise he had done good service in some other charge, or that appeared that he might do well, being of the house and race of wise and prudent people — yet he would not receive him. And the better to be informed of the reputation of persons whereof he had proffers by his wise friends, he caused to be set up in common streets and great public areas where many ways meet, certain posts to fix bills upon them, whereupon was written certain exhortations unto the people, that if any man had anything to say against such and such a man (which he named) wherefore they might not be received and admitted to such and such an office, that he should denounce it. And so made those commands by placards, to the end he might better discover and be advertised of the virtues and vices of persons. "For," said this pagan emperor, "seeing the Christians use well this form to renounce publicly in their assemblies the names of those they will promote unto the order of priesthood, why should not we use it also in the election of our officers and magistrates, into the hands of whom we commit the lives and goods of our subjects?" Moreover, he never suffered offices and estates of magistrates who had power and authority over the people to be sold; nor that any commerce whatsoever should be made of them. "For," said he, "necessarily he that buys, sells; and if I suffer that any man buy an office, I cannot condemn him when he sells it: for it is a shame for me to punish him who sells again that which he buys." Besides all this, in the election of counsellors and magistrates he did ever suspect those who sought offices, and held them for ambitious and dangerous people to the common weal. But they who he could know to be good men and worthy of public charge, and never sought it, these were they who he esteemed most sufficient; and the more they excused themselves from accepting offices, so much the more were they constrained unto them. One day there was one whereof there was good testimony given, unto whom he determined the office of lieutenant general of justice in the town of Rome; but the other excused himself as best he could, saying he perceived himself insufficient and incapable to exercise so great an estate. The more he excused himself, the more Alexander constrained him and commanded him to accept and exercise it; and that he would have it so, being contented with his sufficiency. The other, who in no case would accept that estate, found some light occasion to get from the emperor's presence, and so fled. When the emperor knew he had fled, he searched him out diligently and found him, and caused him to be brought unto him; then he constrained him, whether he would or no, to accept that office. He also had a good grace in the election of the Senate, for he chose not any without demanding the advice of them who were already in that estate, and inquired of the manners, knowledge, and sufficiency of those who were to be senators. And when it came to pass that any man by his opinion did bring any into an office that was not in all points sufficient—as it often comes to pass that those who favor a man make his manners good and his knowledge greater than it is—he thus punished them and brought them to the lowest rung of all their company. Which was a meet punishment; for he that by undue and unlawful means will advance another, merits well to be put from that place himself.

We find in our histories of France that our kings have sometimes imitated the emperor Alexander in the manner of election of counsellors and magistrates. For by ancient ordinances which lately were fresh in the public council of Estates of Orleans (but since unobserved), offices ought to be conferred upon such as were named to the king by other officers and magistrates, and by the consuls and presidents of towns and provinces, who were to make true report of the life, good manners, and sufficiency of those they named. As for the rent and selling of offices, it seems that it has been long tolerated in France. For M. Philip de Commines, in his history of the life of king Louis XI, says that already in 1464 the Parisians made a great traffic and commerce of offices, whereof they are more desirous than any others of the French nation. For (says he) there are some who will give eight hundred crowns for an office that has no wages nor stipend belonging to it; and some will give for an office with a stipend more than it comes to in fifteen years. But it seems to me that Commines touches not the white when he speaks of the cause why the Parisians are so desirous of offices; for the true cause seems to be that by the customs of Paris a father cannot bestow upon one child more than upon another, be they daughters or sons, unless it be in offices. And therefore the Parisians who desire to advantage any of their children above another — as commonly the father who has many children loves one more than another — are as it were constrained to buy offices. And would to God that this custom were yet to invent, and that the Parisians had free dispensation of their goods, and that they had not brought in this villainous traffic of offices. But a strange thing it is which Commines adds, that even in the time of Louis XI the Parliament of Paris maintained that such a commerce and traffic was lawful. But he speaks not of what offices the Court of Parliament tolerates that kind of traffic. It is not credible that at that time offices of judgment were sold, nor that the Court of Parliament approved such a commerce; but rather that they were offices of fines, ushers, castle keepers, sergeants, notaries, offices of waters and forests, and such like, whereof the sale was tolerable; but not of offices of presidents, counsellors, bailiffs, stewards, lieutenants, and other offices of judgment. For it is seen in our annales that king Louis XII, who was called the father of the people, to spare his people and to pay the debts of his predecessor Charles VIII, and to help other great affairs which he had on his hands for the recovering of the duchy of Milan, was the first king who began to sell royal offices, always excepting offices of judgment, which he touched not. This was a very good king, and he did this to a good end, to comfort and help his poor people from taxes and borrowings. He considered that it was more reasonable to take silver for such offices which were not of judgment, as private persons did, upon whom they were freely bestowed; unto whom it was lawful (as is said) by a sufferance already inveterate of the said Parliament, to sell and traffic them. But since, the fact of this good king has been drawn into a consequence and use; the exception of offices of judgment is also clean taken away, in such sort that now all offices indifferently are venal to him who offers most to the last penny. And although we may say still that it is to the same end, namely to help the people, yet it is evident that that end is not sought nor followed. On the contrary, the people are eaten up even to the bones by the buyers of offices, who will draw out of them the money of what they bought. And it seems, according to the saying of the emperor Alexander, that they have reason: for that which may be bought, may be sold.

As for the manner of election of the said emperor, whereby he preferred to estates those who demanded them not, before those who sought them, our kings have sometimes used that also; as Charles the Wise, when he gave the office of constable to that generous and valiant knight Bertrand de Guesclin. For de Guesclin excused himself the most that he could in the world from accepting that estate, showing him that he was a simple knight and that the office of constable is so great, that he who will acquire that office ought rather to command great men than those of low calling; and that he dared not enterprise so much as to command the brethren, cousins, and nephews of his majesty. But the king replied to him: "M. Bertrand, by this means excuse not yourself, for I have neither brother, cousin, nephew, count, nor baron in my kingdom who shall not obey you with a good heart; and if anyone do otherwise, I will cause him to know that it displeases me." So in the end de Guesclin accepted the office as constrained. After the death of this valiant constable, Charles VI, son of Charles the Wise, minding to give that office to the Lord de Coucy, who was a brave and wise knight of a great house, and had performed great services to the crown of France; he refused it, saying that he was not capable for an office of so great a burden, and that M. Oliver de Clysson was more sufficient than he to exercise that estate, for he was valiant, bold, wise, and well beloved by the soldiers. M. Oliver made the like refusal, saying that de Coucy was much more worthy and capable than he. But after great strife thereabouts, in the end Oliver was constrained to accept that office, wherein he acquitted himself well and like a wise and virtuous man. Likewise after the death of M. Louis de Sancerre, Constable of France, the king would needs give that office to M. Charles de Albret, count of Dreux; but he refused it many times, until he was compelled to accept it. Where is now that modesty, to refuse estates and to defer them unto his companion? Where is that time that men esteemed not honors but such as were gotten by true virtue? Where is that happy world, when ambition was so banished from great men? Where are now those good, virtuous and wise princes, who gave no estates and offices but only to them who by virtue deserved them, and who could make so good choice of fit persons? Surely we are come into the time of the emperor Aurelian, when the empire began already to decay, wherein offices were not for men, but for riches; and to the time of Caesar and Pompey, when the commonwealth was altogether ruined and changed into another estate; in which time also offices were not given but for ambition, wealth, and unto those who took part with such great men as sought to carry away the public government. I confess these examples I have rehearsed are but examples; but they may well enough be rules and laws unless we scorn to imitate Alexander Severus, who never gave offices to importunate ambitious men who sought them, but only to those who were modest and desired them not, such as de Guesclin, de Coucy, de Clisson, and de Albret. For they who accept them most hardly are they who will acquit themselves of them most valiantly and wisely.

Now after I have touched the election of a good council and magistrates, I would a little speak of the necessity and utility that comes to a prince, to have good and wise counsellors. And upon this point it seems to me that Plato and the other philosophers have a very proper and fit comparison, when they compared the sovereign authority of a prince to the course and motion of the sun whereby it accomplishes the natural days; and the wisdom of prince's counsellors to the motion and course of the sun whereby it accomplishes the year. For this diurnal motion whereby the sun makes an end of a natural day from one morning to another, is admirable, swift, fearful, and violent; and so it is a sovereign authority of itself, under which men tremble and are dismayed with fear and trouble. We see that the annual motion of the sun opposes itself against this violent and swift diurnal motion, not directly but awry, drawing from the west to the east by the oblique and crooked circle of the zodiac; and by this means tempers the rapacity, violence, and swift diurnal motion, and by its pleasantness distinguishes the seasons of the spring time, summer, autumn, and winter, and nourishes and maintains all living creatures, who otherwise cannot endure. Even so the prudence and wisdom of princes' counsellors, opposing themselves pleasantly and with good grace, by reason and equity, against that sovereign power which of itself is fierce, redoubtable, and fearful, it entertains and maintains public causes and the commonwealth in good estate, which otherwise could not continue. Examples are ordinarily seen in princes that are destitute of good counsel; for straightaway they abuse their sovereign power and authority, and degenerate it into a tyranny, indiscreetly exercising violence, rapines, and injustice. And afterward men shall see it come to pass that it cannot endure, but that they and their estate shall fall into ruin and confusion; for it is a true maxim that no violence can endure long.

Behold then a very great effect of good counsel, that it maintains the prince in his estate and makes him to be obeyed by his subjects. And again, as I may say reciprocally, it maintains his subjects in prosperity under the obedience of the prince. There is yet more, that is, that good counsel obtains honor and good reputation to a prince; for if a prince be not wise himself, nor of great capacity, yet he shall be accounted wise if he provides himself good counsellors. For it is commonly seen that men always attribute the effects of all things unto princes, whether they be victories in war conducted by wise captains, or good rules, ordinances, and provisions which have been laid and built by wise politicians, his counsellors; insomuch that the qualities and conditions of princes' counsellors are always attributed unto him by whose power and authority things are done. And withal, it is impossible that the prince who is provided of good counsellors should never learn with them, and every day be more and more cunning and sufficient to understand and govern his affairs, unless he be exceeding dull and senseless. For however good counsellors the prince has, yet must he not so much repose and trust upon them as he himself will understand nothing of his own affairs. Well to be allowed is the opinion of M. Philip de Commines, who says that God has not established the office of a prince to be exercised upon brute beasts, and to mock and scorn them who speak to them of any affair, answering "I am no clerk, I leave all to my counsellors, in whom I trust," and so go to their pastimes. For (says he) if they have been well nourished in their youth, they will allege other reasons and desire that men should esteem them wise and virtuous.

Moreover, it is certain that the prince who has the reputation and renown to govern himself by good counsel shall always be the more feared and redoubted, both by his enemies and strangers, and they shall not easily get any advantage upon him. Thus it was that Hannibal, a prudent and valiant captain, feared more the wise captains sent against him by the Romans than he did those who were hardy and hazardous. The Roman forces were more feared and doubted by him under the conducting of that wise captain Fabius Maximus than under the other hardy and valiant captains. For when the Romans sent against him the captains Flaminius and Sempronius, one after another, both of them generous and forward, and who desired nothing more than the fight, Hannibal rejoiced thereat. And as he was prudent and hardy, he suffered them to take upon him some small advantages, seeking to draw them unto some place of advantage. They became swelled, for in some light skirmishes they had overthrown some few of Hannibal's soldiers, and thereby thought it was not honorable to recoil, and that men would think their hearts failed them, to fly before such as they had already beaten. They resolved to give battle; and indeed they gave it, but lost it to their great shame and confusion. Seeing this, the Roman Senate sent against Hannibal Fabius Maximus, who was not so forward (and it may be not so hardy) as Flaminius or Sempronius were; but he was more wise and careful, as he showed himself. On his arrival he did not set upon

Hannibal, who desired no other thing, but began to coast him far off, seeking always advantageous places. And when Hannibal approached him, then would he show him a countenance fully determined to fight, yet always seeking places of advantage. But Hannibal, who was not so rash as to join with his enemy to his own disadvantage, made a show to recoil and fly, to draw him after him. Fabius followed him, but upon coasts and hills, seeking always not the shortest way, but that way which was most for his advantage. Hannibal saw him always upon some hill or coast near him, as it were a cloud over his head; so that after Hannibal had many times essayed to draw Fabius into a place fit for himself, and where he might give battle for his own good, and yet could not thereunto draw him, said: "I see well now that the Romans also have gotten a Hannibal; and I fear that this cloud, which approaching us, still hovers upon those hills, will one of these mornings pour out some shower on our heads." Briefly, the prudence and wisdom of Fabius brought more fear and gave more ado unto Hannibal than all the Roman forces, which yet were not small.

I have above recited another example, witnessed of king Edward of England, who said that he feared the missives and letters of Charles the Wise more than he feared the great and puissant armies of 40 and 100,000 men of his father and grandfather; and that wrought him more trouble and broke more of his purposes and enterprises in indicting of letters, than they ever did with their great forces. Which is another witness made for prudence and good counsel, like unto the example of Hannibal; which witnesses are so much the more worthy of credit, as the one proceeded from a most valiant king, and the other from a most noble and hardy captain; both which well knew by long use and experience how to help themselves with force and arms. And if we consider the Roman histories we shall truly find that the ancient Romans made themselves lords and masters almost of all the world, more by wisdom and good counsel than by force; although they used both. Therefore, said Varro (as by a common proverb received in his time) that the Romans vanquished, sitting; as if he would say, as they sit in their chairs in the Senate, they provide so for their affairs by good counsel and wisdom that they get and obtain the upper hand in all their enterprises. Yea, and we see that at this day the Venetians maintain very well their estate, yea, do augment and make it greater, although they understand nothing how to handle arms; and indeed when they must needs go to war, they hire and wage people to do it. But yet notwithstanding are they wise and prudent, keeping themselves as much as they can from war; and when they have war, they do discreetly seek means to quiet and appease it by some other way than by battles, besieging of towns, or any other exploits of war. And assuredly they know better how to finish and bring a war to an end by their wisdom and good counsel, without striking any stroke, than many puissant princes by their forces and arms.

Hitherto we have spoken of a prince's counsel, which in the time of the Roman emperors men called the prince's Consistory, and our French, the king's Privy Council. But now we must know that as well the Roman emperors as the kings of France of old have yet had another council whereunto they had recourse in all their weighty affairs which were of great consequence, as when they stood in need to make laws, ordinances, and rules concerning the universal estate. The Romans called this council the Senate, and the French call it the Parliament. But the name of Parliament anciently signifies an assembly of the three estates, as Philip de Commines says, and as is seen by all our French histories. Our kings also sometimes convocated with their ordinary and privy council some good number of great prelates and barons of the realm, and that assembly they called the Great Council. But afterward men attributed the name of Parliament unto the assembly of judges and senators who judged cases and processes, from whom there is no appeal. And some think that our Parliament is today similar to the Senate of Rome, but they are greatly deceived; for the Roman Senate did not take any knowledge of the processes and cases of particular persons, but only dealt with affairs of the state, of the universal government, and policy, and of matters of consequence unto all the commonwealth. And therefore the assembly of the three estates in France much better resembles the Roman Senate than the Parliaments do at this day, which might better be compared to the Roman Centumvirat, or to their Praetorian government, which dealt in the knowledge of appellations and matters of justice distributive, from which judgment there was no appeal. And as the name of Parliament is at this day otherwise applied than it was anciently, so is the name of Great Council. But to come to our purpose. We read that the good emperors never contemned or thought much in weighty affairs to take the advice of the Roman Senate, and to govern themselves thereby. For although by the change of the state which happened in the time of Julius Caesar, when the commonwealth was changed into a monarchy, the authority of the Senate was much abated and weakened, yet there was never emperor found that dared enterprise altogether to abolish it, but contrary, the good and wise emperors rather helped to establish their authority and power. And the reason why no emperor, good or wicked, dared enterprise to abolish the Senate, was because by the Law Royal (whereby the state monarchy was established at Rome) there was only transferred unto the king the authority and power of the people, and not that which the Senate had.

Which people, although they had sovereign power over every particular person of the Senate, yet had they no power over the whole body of the Senate; for they might punish with death one senator, but they had no superiority over the body of the Senate. So the body of the Senate, and the body of the people, were as it were alike and equal. And the laws of the Senate, which they called *Senatus Consulta*, had as much authority as the laws of the people, which they called *Plebiscita*. And therefore the emperors who by the Law Royal succeeded in the place of the people only (for the Senate never despoiled themselves of their authority to invest the emperor therewith) had never power to decay the Senate, neither dared they enterprise it, although some had a will thereunto, as Nero, Caligula, and their like. But as for the good emperors, besides having no power to abolish the Senate, they never had any desire thereof, but maintained and conserved it, and governed themselves by it, and by it they were better obeyed. For we need not doubt but a people will more willingly obey a law or decree which has been sifted and examined in a great, wise, and notable assembly, such as was the Senate, than when it only passes through the brain of one sole man, or some small number. The emperor Alexander Severus never made law nor edict but when he had on his council twenty great and excellent lawyers, and fifty other great and excellent persons, wise and well experienced. And yet to the end that they might give their opinions more assuredly, he first made them understand the matter upon which they must give their advice, and after gave time to consider thereof, that their opinions might be better digested and resolved. The emperor Theodosius ordained that no law should be available unless it was first concluded and determined with good and assured resolution of all the prince's Consistory, and afterward received and approved by the Senate of Rome. "For," said he, "we know well that the ordinance of good laws and edicts concluded with good counsel and deliberation is the establishment of the assuredness and glory of our Empire." The great and wise emperor Augustus Caesar communicated all the affairs of his commonwealth with the Roman Senate, that as Dion said, he made a sweet and pleasant mingled harmony of the monarchial state with the state of the commonwealth. And he not only did not content himself to confer with the Senate all affairs of importance, and take their advice, but yet he willed that the Senate should give him every year twenty counsellors to be near him, his Privy Council, in which council he had always many men very wise, courteous, and very modest, such as the lawyer Trebatius, and that good and prudent Agrippa his son-in-law, with that so learned and good a pillar of learned men Mecaenas. Tiberius, the successor of Augustus, although he was a prince more abundant in vices than in virtues, not daring wholly to stray out of his predecessor's traces, neither made nor ordained anything of weight without the counsel and advice of the Senate. For this cause also all the good emperors, as Vespasian, Titus, Trajan, Hadrian, the Antonines, and others like, always communicated with the Senate upon all the great affairs of the commonwealth; and they bore themselves not like masters, but like presidents of the Senate. They did not attribute unto themselves any title of honor, nor enterprised to make any triumphs but such as was decreed and ordained by the Senate. And on the contrary, the emperors who were of no account, such as Caligula, Nero, Commodus, Bassianus, Maximinus, Heliogabalus, and others like, extremely hated the Senate, esteeming it as their pedagogue and corrector, and have caused many senators to die, thinking the more easily to command as they would, having no controllers to withstand their wicked actions. But the end was always this, that those who despised and would have annihilated the Senate have ever had an unlucky end, and reigned not long time, but have all been massacred and slain young, and have left unto their posterity an infamy and most wicked memory of them. Herein is shown a continual success of the just judgments of God against them who despised wise counsel; and contrary, a felicity and divine prosperity in other emperors, who governed themselves by the good counsel of the Senate and of the wise men of their privy council. For they reigned and held the empire happily replenished with all goods, honor, and glory, and their subjects under them enjoyed good handling and good repose and tranquility. And we need not doubt that such felicity coming to good princes, the evil haps unto wicked princes, does not proceed from God; for as the wise man says, good counsel comes from God, and he that despises the gift of God, certain it is, that in the end he shall be well chastised.

Our kings of old in France used the same course that these good emperors did; for they often convocated the three Estates of the kingdom to have their advice and counsel in affairs of great consequence which touched the interest of the commonwealth. And it is seen by our histories that the general assembly of the Estates was commonly done for three causes. One, when there was a question to provide for the kingdom a governor or regent; as when kings were young, or lost the use of their understanding by some accident, or were captives or prisoners; in these cases the three Estates assembled to obtain a governor for the realm. Again, when there was cause to reform the kingdom, to correct the abuses of officers and magistrates, and to bring things unto their ancient and first institution and integrity. For kings caused the Estates to assemble, because being assembled from all parts of the kingdom, they might better be informed of all abuses and evil behaviors committed therein, and might also better work the means to remedy them; because commonly there is no better physician than he that knows well the disease and the causes thereof. The third cause why there was made an assembly of Estates was when there was a necessary cause to lay a tribute or tax upon the people; for then in a full assembly the representatives were showed the necessity of the king's and the kingdom's affairs, who graciously and courteously entreated the people to aid and help the king but with so much money as they themselves thought to be sufficient and necessary. And for this reason what the Estates accorded to the king was called by these gracious names, subsidies, subventions, aids, grants; not with these terms, tallies, imposts, tributes, impositions; which were terms more hard and odious. Examples appear of the first case, when the Estates General assembled at Paris after the death of king Charles the Wise, to provide for the government as well of king Charles VI, being under age. Which government they gave unto three of the king's uncles the remainder of all the realm, and the rule of the young king's person was committed to the dukes of Berry and Bourgogne. In like manner the Estates General were held at Tours after the decease of Louis XI, to purvey for the government of king Charles VIII, under age, and of the kingdom. And by the same Estates was established a council of twelve persons, good men and of good calling, to dispatch the affairs of the kingdom, yet in the king's name and under his authority; and the rule of the young king's person was committed unto Madame de Beavien, his sister. When Charles VI was come to the age of 21 years, his uncles were discharged from the government of the kingdom by the advice and deliberation of the king's Great Council. But this good prince by an accident of sickness later fell into a frenzy which sometimes bereaved him of his senses; the Estates assembled at Paris gave the government of the kingdom during the king's indisposition to his two uncles, the dukes of Berry and Bourgogne. In 1356, after king John and his son Philip were taken prisoner and led to England, there remained in France three of John's children; Charles, dauphin and duke of Normandy; Louis of Anjou; and John, duke of Berry. There was a question about providing for the government of the kingdom, because of the king's captivity, but none of them would enterprise the managing thereof himself. The Estates General were assembled at Paris, whereby were elected 36 persons (some say fifty) to govern the affairs of the kingdom with the dauphin, who at the beginning called himself the lieutenant of the king his father, but afterward he named himself Regent.

In 1409, during the reign of Charles VI, the Estates General were held at Paris for the reformation of abuses in the kingdom. And there it was ordained that all accountants for the king's revenues and rents should make their accounts. By the means of which reformation great sums were recovered, and there were also made some good laws and ordinances. In other conventions of Estates the coinage has been reformed from weak and light into thick and of good weight and goodness. Also of late at the Estates General held at Orleans were made many goodly ordinances for the good and comfort of the poor people, reformation of justice, and for the cutting off of many abuses which were committed in plays at cards and dice, in superfluity of apparel, and in matter of benefices. But commonly comes such evil hap, that all good things which are introduced and ordained upon good reason and to a good end, soon vanish away, and wicked examples are always drawn into consequence.

As for the last cause for which we have said the Estates General in old time were called, namely for the grant of helps and subsidies, there are many examples in our histories. As in the time of king John, wherein the Estates accorded great subventions or subsidies to make war against the English, who then held a great part of the kingdom. And after he was taken prisoner and led into England, the Estates agreed to give the dauphin great sums to pay for the king's and Philip's ransom. And it is well to be marked that our histories witness that all the people of France were anguished and grieved with the imprisonment and captivity which they saw their king suffer, but especially the people of Languedoc; for their Estates ordained that if the king was not delivered within a year, that everyone, both men and women, should lay by all colored garments, such also as were jagged and cut, and such as were enriched with gold, silver, or other strange and costly fashion. Likewise to cease all stage-plays, morris dancing, piping, and pastimes, in sign and token of their mourning and lamentation for their prince's captivity. A thing whereby appeared the great and cordial affection of this people towards their king; as truly the French have always been of great love and affection towards their kings, unless they were altogether tyrants. But to make an end of this point: it is certain that before Charles VII no subsidies were imposed without assembling the Estates General. And our kings used to do thus not because they had power by an absolute authority to impose tallages and subsidies without calling the Estates, but to the end they may be better obeyed with a voluntary and unconstrained obedience, and to shun all uproars and rebellions which often happen upon that occasion. And truly the French have always been so good and obedient unto their kings, that they never refused them anything if there were but any appearance of reason to demand it. Yea often the Estates have granted their king more than he would demand or dared look for; as is seen by that which our histories write of the Estates held for subsidies. But because aids and subsidies were customarily granted for making war, M. Philip de Commines says that kings should also communicate and consult with their Estates whether the causes of such wars are just and reasonable; and that the prince cannot nor ought not otherwise to enterprise a war, for it is reason that they who defray the charges and expenses should know something. But yet he passes further and says there is no prince in the world who has power to lay one penny upon his subjects without their grant and consent, unless he will use tyranny and violence. But because those who read this may at first think he seems to limit and restrain a prince's power too much, I will here as it were by an interpretation of his saying, a little clear this point.

You must then understand and presuppose that in a sovereign prince there are two powers; one is called an absolute power, and the other a civil power. The absolute power is that which cannot nor ought to be limited, but stretches itself to all things whatsoever they be, unless it be to the laws of God and nature, and of those laws which are the foundation of the principality and estate. For a prince has not power over God, nor more than the vassal has over his liege lord; but ought himself to obey his commandments and ordinances, so much there wants that he can anything abolish or derogate from them. The prince also cannot abolish the fundamental laws of his principality, whereupon his estate is founded, and without which his estate cannot subsist nor endure; for so might he abolish and ruin himself. As in France the king cannot abolish the Salic Law, nor the three Estates, nor the law of not alienating the countries and provinces united to the crown. For the realm and the royalty are founded upon those three points, which are as three pillars that sustain and hold up both the king and kingdom. Neither can the prince break nor abolish any natural law approved by the common sense of all men. But in all other things the absolute power of a prince reaches without limitation, for it is above all other laws which he may make and unmake at his pleasure; he also has power over the bodies and goods of his subjects, without restriction, purely and simply. True it is that he ought to temper the use of that absolute power by the moderation of his second power, which is civil, as we shall say hereafter. But suppose he will not moderate his absolute power by the civil; we must notwithstanding obey, because God commands us. But before we speak of the civil power, we must a little more amply clear the points to be touched.

The first point then, which is that the absolute power of a prince does not stretch above God, is a matter confessed by all. And there were never found any princes, or very few, who would soar and mount so high as to enterprise upon that which belonged unto God. Even the emperors Caligula and Domitian are blamed and detested by the pagan histories, which had no true knowledge of God, for that they dared enterprise upon God and that which pertained to him. Also it is a maxim in theology that we must obey God rather than men; which maxim has at all times been practiced by all good people and holy persons, who are praised even with the mouth of God in the holy scriptures; as by Daniel and his companions, the Apostles, the Christians of the primitive church, and many of our time. As for the other point, which is that the prince cannot abolish the fundamental laws of his principality, it clear of itself. For if a prince overthrows the foundations of his principality, he ruins and overthrows himself, and his estate cannot endure. For the first senseless and unwise man that comes thereunto will overthrow all upside down. As if in France a king may overthrow the Salic Law, and so subject his crown unto the succession of women, it is certain that long ago the estate of France would have been overthrown. For if kings who have left none but daughters after them, as Philip le Long, Charles le Bel, and Louis XII, had been inclined from natural affection to have the crown fall unto them, the kingdom would have fallen into strangers' hands, and consequently into ruin and dissipation. For the nature of the inhabitants of France, wherein they differ from many nations, is such that they cannot long suffer a foreign prince, as they could not long bear the domination of the Roman emperors. They began to kick against the reign of Tiberius, and became grieved with the rule of princes of another nation than their own; finally they rid themselves of the Romans' yoke, and Gaul was the first province to cut itself from the empire. Neither was there ever found king that dared enterprise to break the Salic Law. It is true that at the instigation of the duke of Bougogne, Charles VI gave the kingdom in dowry with his daughter Katherine, who he married to the king of England, declaring the dauphin to be incapable to succeed in the kingdom. But this donation did not hold, as being made against the Salic Law; after the death of Charles VI, the duke of Bourgogne himself acknowledged the dauphin for king and lawful successor to the crown of France. As for incapacity, it was known there was none, because that duke John, which the dauphin had slain, deserved it well, having killed the duke of Orleans, the king's only brother. Yet because the manner of the execution which the dauphin caused to be made upon John was not by lawful means, he acknowledged his fault in that cause, and made a great satisfaction to Philip. So then the Salic Law has always remained firm, as one of the three pillars of the kingdom and royalty of France, our ancestors never being willing to suffer women to reign and rule over them.

As much is to be said of the Estates General, the authority of which has always remained whole until the present, even from the foundation of the kingdom, as being the second pillar whereupon the kingdom is founded. For if it happens that the crown falls to a king under age, or to one that is not well in his wit and understanding, or if the king is a prisoner or captive, or the kingdom has urgent necessity of a general reformation; how necessary is it in all these cases that the Estates assemble to provide for all affairs, otherwise the estate of the kingdom and royalty would soon fall to the ground. And without doubt it could not long continue in his being if the Estates General were abolished and suppressed. For to say in these cases that the Estates may well order the affairs of the realm, as the princes of the blood and the king's council, is to say nothing, because it may come to pass that the princes themselves are under age, or prisoners, or witless, or suspected, or dead, or otherwise incapable. As also it may come to pass that the king's council shall be dead, or quashed, or suspected, or otherwise unable, so that the estate of the kingdom and the royalty is ill assured upon such foundations. But the body of the Estates General is not subject to a minority, captivity, preclusion of understanding, suspicion, nor other incapacity, neither is it mortal. Therefore it is a more certain and firm foundation of the kingdom's and royalty's estate than any other. For the body of the Estates, which is composed of the wisest and fittest of the kingdom, can never fail, because it does not consist in individuals, but it stands in specie, being a body immortal, as the French nation is immortal. The princes and the king's counsellors are but frail and brittle leaning stocks and means, subject to incapacity, as is not the body of Estates. And therefore the Estates, being the true and perpetual foundation to sustain and conserve the kingdom, cannot be abolished, but ought to be convoked whenever there is to be a provision in the cases above mentioned. Reason wills that the Estates, whom the affairs of the realm touch most, should have a part in the conducting of public things, but most especially in the cases aforesaid, where the king cannot order them. Therefore it is a strange, damnable, and pernicious position which our strangers now governing France dare impudently hold, that it is treason to speak of holding the Estates. But contrary, a man may rather say that it is treason to abolish the Estates, and that they who will hinder them are themselves culpable of treason, being such as overthrow and ruin the realm, the royalty, and the king, in taking away the principal pillar which sustained them. And truly such people merit that processes

and indictments should be laid upon them as enemies of the
commonwealth, who subvert and overthrow the foundations upon
which our ancestors have with great wisdom founded and established
the estate of this goodly and excellent kingdom. The like may we say of
the law whereby the lands and provinces united to the crown are
inalienable; for a king of France cannot abolish that law, because it is the
third pillar upon which the realm and its estate is founded. For proof
hereof I will cite but two examples; one was practiced in the time of
Charles the Wise, and the other in the time of Francis I. By which two
examples may appear not only that this law is a pillar of the kingdom,
but also that the Estates are the very true base and foundation thereof.

King John, having been taken prisoner at the battle of Poiters, was
conducted to England, where he made a treaty of peace with king
Edward of England. But the Estates of the kingdom would not agree to
the treaty, as too prejudicial and to the diminution of the crown of
France. Edward was so angry and spited thereat that he made a great
oath to end and ruin France. And indeed while king John was his
prisoner, he made great war in France and much wasted the flat country,
but he made no great conquest of the towns. In the end the duke of
Lancaster counseled him to make peace with the French, showing him
that he but lost time to run over the fields and spoil the champion
country, and that only soldiers had the profit, and he himself loss of
people and expenses. These reasons could not much move the king to
make peace, he was so sore offended and animated. But God, who had
pity on this poor kingdom in extreme desolation and confusion, wrought
and brought to pass, as it were by miracle, a peace; sending from heaven
a tempest, accompanied with such great lightning over the English camp
that they thought heaven and earth would have met, and the world
finished; such great stones fell with the tempest that they overthrew men
and horses. Then the king of England, seeing God fight against him, in
great fear and distress made a vow unto God that if by his grace he
escaped from that peril he would hearken unto peace, and would cease
to sack and destroy the poor people; as indeed he did after the tempest
ceased. Which peace was accorded to his great advantage; besides the
ransom of three million francs, Guinne remained to him in sovereignty;
also Armagnac, de Albret, de Commines, de la Marche, de Santongeois,
Rochelle, and a good part of Languedoc, which was never before in
peaceable obedience of the English. Unto this peace the French subjects
of that country would not in any sort agree nor condescend, but refused
to obey and yield themselves English. For their reasons they alleged that
the king had no power to dismember and alienate them from the crown
of France, and that they had privileges from Charlemagne whereby they

could not, nor ought to be cut off from the trunk and house of France. After they had long debated and refused to obey, king John, having returned to France, sent into the countries James de Bourbon, his cousin and a prince of his blood, to make them obey the English whether they would or no; those good French subjects should forsake the French obedience and be under the English government. This could not be without great grief of heart, sadness, and incredible displeasure. But above all others, most remarkable for great constancy to remain French were those of Rochelle; for they many times excused themselves unto the king, and stood stiff more than a year before they would let the English into their town. And thinking that their excuses and remonstrances might stand in some stead, they sent to the king their orators; arriving at Paris and being brought before the king, they fell at his feet with weepings, sobbings, and lamentations, making this speech.

"Most dear sir, your poor and desolate subjects of your town of Rochelle have sent us here to beseech your Majesty in all humility, and with joined hands, that it would please you to have pity and compassion upon them. They are your natural subjects, and they and their ancestors have ever been under the obedience of your majesty and your ancestors. Alas, sir, what greater evil hap can there come to us than to now be cut off and alienated from the kingdom and from the crown of France? They are born and have been nourished in the French nation, they are of manners, condition, and language natural Frenchmen. What a strange and deplorable misery should it now be to them, to bend themselves under the yoke and obedience of the English, a foreign nation altogether different in manners, conditions, and language? Shall not this be unto them a cruel and slavish servitude, now to become subjects unto them who of long time have not ceased to vex this poor kingdom with war? For if upon some divine punishment, and for our sins, the poor town of Rochelle must be violently plucked and separated from France, as the daughter dug from the mother, to submit itself unto the sad servitude of a stranger; yet that evil would be far more tolerable in any other nation than that which so long has been a bloody enemy of France, and has shed so much of our blood. Wherefore most humbly we beseech you with tears, that you will not deliver us into the hands of the English, your enemies and ours. If in anything we offended your majesty, for which you will now abandon us, we cry you mercy with joined hands, and pray you in the name of God and of our Lord Jesus Christ, that it would please you to have mercy and compassion on us, and to retain us always under your obedience, as we and our ancestors have always been. We are not ignorant, sir, that your majesty having been prisoner in England, has been constrained to accord with them to their great advantage, and that we are comprehended in the number of towns and countries that must be delivered. But yet we have some hope that we may be taken from that number, by silver; and for that purpose your poor town of Rochelle offers contribution to your Majesty all that it has in its power. And besides that, we offer to pay with a good heart hereafter, for our subsidies and tallies, half the revenue and gains of all our goods. Have pity, then, sir, upon your poor town, which comes to retire herself under your protection in most humble and affectionate obedience, as a poor, desolate, and lost creature to its father, the king, and its natural lord and sovereign. We beseech you, most dear sir, in the name of God and all his saints, that you will not abandon and forsake us; but that it would please your clemency and kindness to retain for your subjects most humble, them who cannot live but in all vexation, languishment, and bitterness of heart, unless we be your subjects."

The king having heard the piteous supplication of these poor Rochellois, mourned and pitied them greatly; but he answered that there was no remedy; that which he had accorded must needs be executed. This answer being reported at Rochelle, it is impossible to speak what lamentations there were through all the town; this news was so hard, that they who were born and nourished French should be no more French, but become English. Finally, being pressed and constrained by the king's commissaries to open the town gates to the English, the most notable townsmen said, "Well, seeing we are forced to bow under your yoke, and that it pleases the king our sovereign lord that we should obey the English, we will with our lips, but our hearts shall remain always French."

After the English had been peaceable possessors of Rochelle and all the other countries named, king Edward invested his eldest son, the prince of Wales, in that government. This prince was valiant and very humble towards those greater than himself, but haughty and proud towards his inferiors. He came and held his train and court at Bordeaux, where having dwelled some years he would have imposed upon the country a yearly tribute upon every fine. But to withstand this new tax, the lords, barons, and counts of those countries went to Paris to offer their appeals against the prince of Wales. Arriving there, they dealt with Charles the Wise, for John was then dead. He answered that by the peace of Brittany, which he himself had sworn to the dead king for him and his successors, he had renounced all sovereignty of the said countries; and that he could not with a good conscience break the peace with the English, and that it grieved him much that with good reason he could not accord their appeal. The counts and barons showed him by lively reasons that it is not in the king's power to release the sovereign power and authority of his subjects and countries without the consent of the prelates, barons, cities, and good towns of those countries; and that it was never seen nor practiced in France, and if they had been called to the treaty of Brittany they would never have consented unto that acquittance of sovereignty. And therefore they humbly prayed his majesty to receive their appellation, and to send the prince of Wales to appear at Paris at the court of France, to quash and revoke the new ordinance for the tribute. Finally, Charles was not offended to hear them speak of a king's power — much unlike our Machiavellians of today, who call them culpable of treason who speak of Estates — neither replied unto them that the power of a sovereign prince ought not to be limited, neither that they spoke evil to revoke into doubt what his dead father had done. But contrary, rejoicing at that limitation, he referred the case to the debate and resolution of the wise men of his council. He was resolved that if what they said was true, he accorded their demand and sent the prince of Wales to adjourn in case of appeal. Which done, the counts and barons easily revolted from the English obedience, and so Rochelle got all Englishmen out of their town and castle. This done, the duke of Berry, the king's brother, would have entered there; but they refused him entry, saying they would send delegates unto the king to obtain privileges, and therefore desired of the duke a safe conduct, which he willingly granted. They sent twelve chosen from among their burgesses, who showed the king in all humility how of themselves they were rid of the English obedience, and that again they would remit themselves into his majesty's obedience, as being their king and natural sovereign prince, but that they besought him humbly to accord them certain privileges. The king asked, what privileges? First, they said, that it would please your majesty to agree unto us that the town of Rochelle may be inseparably united to the crown, so that it may never be separated by peace, marriage, nor by any pact, condition, or misadventure that can come to France. Secondly, that the castle may be thrown to the earth; without which we will keep the town of Rochelle well for your majesty. The king, perceiving their demands and finding them reasonable, and proceeding from a true French heart, accorded their requests; and so the Rochellois returned merrily into the French obedience, from whence they had be separated to their great grief. Here you see how well to the purpose and to the great profit of the king and of the kingdom that law of not alienating the lands, towns, and provinces of the crown was made. But upon this that I have said of the Rochellois, some will say: How does it happen then that the Rochellois are today such bad French subjects? Hereunto the answer is easy and evident; that is, that they are today as good Frenchmen as ever were their ancestors, but they are not good Italians, neither mean to be subject under the yoke of strangers, no more than their ancestors. Let us now come to the other example.

King Francis I, being prisoner at Madrid under the emperor Charles V, there was made a treaty and an accord between the two great princes; whereby among other things the king promised the emperor to grant him all his right and possession of the duchy of Bourgogne, and that he would employ himself to cause the Estates of the country to condescend thereunto. This accord being concluded, the emperor caused the king to be conducted to Bayonne, and there by his ambassadors summoned him to ratify the accord which he had made at Madrid, to make it appear to be made without constraint. The king answered that he could do nothing concerning Bourgogne without first knowing the intent and will of his subjects, because he could not alienate it without their consent, and that he would cause the Estates of that country to assemble, to know their wills therein. Not long after, the king assembled the Estates of Bourgogne, who would by no means consent unto alienation; whereof he advised the emperor, who was content with that answer, upon condition that the king would assure the duchy unto the first male heir which the king should have by Elanor, the emperor's sister, unto whom he was then espoused. So that the law that the king cannot alienate crown lands was then very profitable to the king and the kingdom. And unto this agree the doctors of the civil law, who hold that the emperor cannot alienate anything of the empire, but is bound to increase it to his power. And from thence they draw (but foolishy) the etymology of that name Augustus, saying the emperors are called Augustus because they ought to increase, and cannot diminish the empire; as much they say of other kings and monarchs, for there is therein the like reason.

For a conclusion, no man of perfect judgment can deny but these laws of France, the Salic Law, the law of the Estates General, and the law of not alienating crown lands, are the very true pillars, bases, and foundations of the kingdom and royalty, which none can or ought to abolish. I doubt not but that there will be found many who will be quarrelling at those aforesaid reasons and examples, and will say that to sustain and defend that the king cannot abolish the law is to diminish his power, and to give limitation and restriction to his sovereign authority. But for reply I will only ask if it be not puissance in a prince to conserve him and his estate? If they confess yea — as none can deny it if he is not altogether without judgment — I say, it follows by argument taken from contraries, that it is then impuissance and want of power in a prince, to ruin himself and his estate. And in consequence, it follows that when we say that a prince cannot abolish the fundamental laws of his estate, so much there wants that we diminish his power, that by the contrary we establish it and make it more firm, greater, and as it were invincible. As also on the contrary, those who say that a prince can abolish and change his laws, upon which he and his estate are founded, they establish and place in him an impuissance to conserve himself. For to take it rightly and in good sense, it is an act of impuissance to ruin, destroy, overthrow, and to participate his estate. And contrary, it is an act of power to conserve himself and maintain his estate. No more nor less than when a building falls upon the earth, or when a man lets it fall, these are acts of feebleness, frailty, and impuissance; but when the one and the other hold and stand straight and firm, without cracking or falling, these are acts of force and power.

As for the natural law, it cannot be abolished. For if a prince will authorize adulteries, incest, theft, murder, massacres, and other like crimes which natural reason and common sense cause us to abhor and detest, it is certain and evident that such authorizing is of no value, and that the prince cannot do this. When the emperor Claudius would espouse Agrippina, his brother's daughter, he made a law whereby he authorized the marriage of the uncle with the niece, which was published all over. But Suetonius says that no man would imitate and follow the emperor's example, and everybody so detested and abhorred such marriages as being contrary to the natural law and common sense. And indeed this marriage fell out not well for him; for Agrippina poisoned him to bring Nero to the empire, her son by another marriage; although Claudius had by his first wife Messalina a natural son called Brittanicus, whom Nero poisoned when he came to the empire. So that by the incestuous marriage wherewith Claudius had contaminated and poisoned his house, he and his natural son, who by reason should have been his successor, were killed with poison. We read likewise that Caracalla, beholding one day his mother-in-law Julia with an eye of incestuous concupiscence, she said unto him, "If thou wilt, thou mayst; knowest thou not that it belongs unto thee to give the law, not to receive it?" Which talk so enflamed him yet more with lust that he took her to wife in marriage. Hereupon historiographers note that if Caracalla had known well what it was to give a law, he would have detested and prohibited such incestuous and abominable copulations, and not to have authorized them. For briefly, a prince may well give laws unto his subjects, but it must not be contrary to nature and natural reason. This was the cause why the great lawyer Papinian, who understood both natural and civil law, loved better to die than to obey Caracalla, who had commanded him to excuse before the Senate his parricide, committed in the person of Geta his brother. For Papinian, knowing that such a crime was against natural right, would not have obeyed the emperor if he had commanded him to perpetrate it, nor would obey him so far therein as to excuse it. Wherein the pagan lawyer may serve for a goodly example to condemn many magistrate lawyers of our time, who not only excuse, but also cause to be executed unnatural murders and massacres against all law divine and human. But now we have spoken of a prince's absolute power; let us come to the other.

The other power, which we call civil, is that which is governed and limited within the bounds of reason, of right, and of equity; and which we must presume that the prince will use, and uses ordinarily in all his commands, unless he expressly shows and declares that he wills and ordains this or that from his absolute power and of his certain knowledge. This is that second power which is guided by prudence and good counsel, and which gives a sweet temperature and counterpoise to that absolute power, no more nor less than the second motion of the sun tempers the course of the first, as we have said above. This is that power which establishes and conserves in assuredness kingdoms and empires, and without which they cannot stand, but soon shall be ruined, annihilated, and laid on the ground. This is that power which all good princes have so practiced — letting their absolute power cease without using any, unless in a demonstration of majesty, to make their estate more venerable and better obeyed — that in all their actions and in all their commands they desire to subject and submit themselves to laws and to reason. And in doing this they never thought or esteemed to do anything unworthy of their majesty, but contrary have ever accounted that there was nothing more beseeming the majesty of a sovereign prince than to live and carry himself in all his actions according to right and equity. And that the domination and power of a prince that so governs himself is greater, more secure, and more venerable than his who governs himself after the absolute power. And truly all the good Roman emperors have always held this language and have so practiced their power, as we read in their histories. The emperor Theodosius made an express law for it, which is so good to be marked that I thought it good to translate it word for word. "It is the majesty of him that governs to confess himself bound to laws, so much does our authority depend upon law. And assuredly it is a far greater thing to the empire itself to submit his empire and power unto laws. And that which we will not be lawful unto us, we show it unto others by the oracle of this our present edict. Given at Ravenna the eleventh day of June, in the year of the consulship of Florentius and Dionysius."

To come then to our purpose, you must understand that Commines spoke of this second power in the place above cited, and not of the absolute power of a prince; for by that power it is certain that the prince has good authority to enterprise wars and to levy taxes upon his subjects without their consent. By the royal law mentioned above, the Roman people gave all the like power unto the prince as they had themselves, to use it towards the people and against the people, and gave him absolute power without any restriction or bond to laws, to do what he willed. We also see by the law of God the same absolute power is given unto kings and sovereign princes, for it is written that they shall have full power over the goods and persons of their subjects. And although God has given them their absolute power, as to his ministers and lieutenants on earth, yet he would not have the use of it but with a temperance and moderation of the second power, which is ruled by reason and equity, which we call civil. For God would not that princes use their absolute power so far as to constrain their subjects to sell their goods, as is declared to us in the example of Naboth. For it is most unlikely that God, the great dominator and governor of all princes, would have princes abuse their powers with cruelties, rapines, injustices, or any other unreasonable way of absolute power. But as God by justice punishes the wicked, and by kindness and clemency maintains the good, and rightly and most holily uses his divine power, so would he that princes, his lieutenants on earth, should do the like; not in perfection, for that they cannot, but in imitation.

To conclude our talk concerning the place of Commines, it is certain that a prince may well make war and impose taxes without the consent of his subjects, by an absolute power; but it is better for him to use his civil power, so should he be better obeyed. And as for aids and subsidies, whereof Commines speaks, some say they are not at this day levied by an absolute power, but by the people's consent. Because in the time of Charles VII, who had great and long wars against the English, the Estates General agreed unto him to levy aids and subsidies every year, without calling them together any more, because the wars endured for so long and to assemble every year would come to great expenses; so that if the cause continued, then necessarily the imposition should have continued. But it is certain that this consent concerned only the English wars, which ending, the said consent finished; yet afterward, the accord of the Estates was drawn into a custom. In the time of Charles VIII, the Estates General at Tours were convocated to provide for the government (for his majesty was under age) and for aids and subsidies; which were freely granted by the Estates, although the people of France were then very poor and ruined. And Commines shows one thing that is very true, that the holding of the Estates is very good and profitable for a king of France, whereby he is both stronger and better obeyed; but he complains that in his time there were men, as there are today, unworthy to possess the offices they held, who did all they could to hinder the holding of the Estates, lest their evil behaviors and incapacities should be seen and known. Such men are of like humors as the unworthy emperors Caligula, Maximinus, Commodus, and others whereof we have spoken, who hated the Senate because they would not have such correctors and controllers.

Let us now come to Machiavelli, to prove his maxim, which we have above refuted by good reasons and examples. He alleges two reasons; one, that if a prince govern himself by one counsel alone, it would prove dangerous, for fear that the counsellor seek to occupy the estate. Whereunto I answer that that would be considerable if principalities were today given by tumultuous elections of soldiers, as in times past the Roman Empire was given; For he that could obtain the favor of the men of war either by love or money carried it away. But in our time principalities are hereditary, or are given by grave and deliberate election of more staid and discreet people than were the Praetorian soldiers of Rome. Yet I do not approve that a prince should be governed by one alone when he may have a greater number of good counsellors; for they that have done so in times past have found it evil, and have repented it, as more fully shall be shown in the next maxim. The reason also is evident, because one alone cannot so well by his wisdom examine and search out a matter or cause, nor so well can prevent difficulties, occurrences, and consequences that may happen, as many can do. Therefore also the wise Solomon approves the council which is compounded of many.

The second reason of Machiavelli is that in a council compounded of many there are always discordances and contrary opinions that cannot accord. Whereunto I answer that if a council is compounded of good and fit men, they will always sufficiently agree in their opinions, although they disagree in motives, reasons, allegations, and in other circumstances. These discordances are often very profitable and necessary, if they all look to one end, which is the good of the commonwealth. As happened in the Roman Senate about that horrible and strange conspiracy of Catiline, who with his companions went about to destroy his country with fire and sword. For in that council Caesar reasoned so gently, it seemed he made small account of the matter; and in respect of his authority others after him reasoned in like manner, so mildly and gently that Catiline and his partners were in a good way to have been absolved. But when it came to Cato, he reasoned in another sort, even plainly to rebuke those who spoke before him:

> "Great pity it is that we are in such a time when men attribute the name of wicked things to such as are good. Now is it accounted liberality to give the goods of another man, it is magnanimity to use violence and boldness, it is mercy and clemency to pluck criminal and condemned

persons out of justice' hands. And I pray you, is it so small a thing to have conspired our destruction, and the effusion of our blood? Another crime might be punished after it is committed; but who should punish Catiline after the execution of his conspiracy, and we all be dead? They who before have delivered their opinions seem to be very liberal of our blood, and the blood of so many good men within Rome, to spare that sort of wicked conspirators. If they be not afraid of this conspiracy, so much the more, my masters, have we cause to fear, to watch, and hold upon our guards, without too much trusting them who are in such assurance. For our ancestors have made themselves great by diligence, justice, and by good counsel, free from all covetousness and viciousness. Unto them who are vigilant, take pains and use good counsel, all things succeed; but sluggards and cowards had need to implore aid of the gods, for no doubt they are both contrary and angry with them. And therefore my advice is that they who have confessed the fault should die the death of their desert."

Cato in this manner reasoning against the advice of others who had been before him, greatly to his commendation, drew the rest in the end to his opinion; yet not more to his honor than to the dishonor of Caesar. So then it is not ever evil that in a council there should sometimes be Catos and Appius Claudius and such like persons, who often hold strong against others; for affairs and businesses are so much the better cleared and bolted out. It also holds others better in order, who otherwise by too great facility and fear to contradict suffer themselves to be carried after the first opinion, without debate or due consideration. And truly in all councils there are but too many such as were Valerius Publicola, Manenius Agrippa, Servilius, Pompey, Caesar, and the like, who always reasoned gently and mildly in all things; and too few Catos, Appius Claudius, Quintus Cincinnatus, and such like, who in Senates hold rigorous opinions. For although for the most part such rigorous opinions ought not to be followed, yet being mingled and dispersed among others, they serve well to bring to pass a good resolution, and so make a good and sweet harmony in a council or Senate, as Livy shows in many places. And therefore contradictions of opinions, whereof Machiavelli speaks, are not so much to be feared in princes' councils. Against whose maxim I conclude, that the prince who governs himself by the counsel of men who are wise, honest, and experienced, shall prosper in all good; and he that rules himself by his own head, shall ruin himself; as said very elegantly the poet Horace:

A supreme power, devoid of counsel good,
Falls of itself, as though it never stood.
A temperate power by God exalted is:
The intemperate his hatred does not miss.

1.2
Machiavelli

The prince, to shun and not to be circumvented by flatterers, ought to forbid his friends and counsellors, that they speak not to him, nor to counsel him anything, but only of those things whereof he freely begins to speak, or asks their advice. (*The Prince*, chapter 23)

The means to shun flatterers, who do nothing else but make lies and report leasings, pleasing princes' ears, is to make known that he takes no pleasure in hearing lies, but that it is more agreeable to his nature that men should freely speak the truth. But because the prince should too much debase his majesty to yield an ear to everyone that will utter a truth to him, it is then requisite that he take a third way. Therefore the prince should always hold near him some number of virtuous people, who may have liberty freely to tell him the truth upon all such things whereof he demands advice, and not of any other things, forbidding and inhibiting them to speak to him of anything but that whereof he himself has begun to talk. After having understood their opinions, he ought to deliberate with himself, and choose the counsel that he finds best.

Answer

Machiavelli, making a countenance by this maxim to counsel a prince not to serve himself with flatterers, teaches him the very means to be wholly governed by them. For there is none more truly a flatterer, nor more dangerous, than he who sees before his eyes a thousand abuses, and knows that his prince's affairs go evil, and yet either will not or dares not open his mouth to let him know them; because herein lies the principal duty of a good and faithful counsellor to his prince, to declare unto him the abuses committed by his subjects, be they officers or private persons. And to attend while the prince himself begins the matter first to his council, would be in vain; for he cannot propose what he does not know, and it is a notorious and plain thing that the prince, who is always shut up in a house or within a troupe of his people, sees not nor knows how things pass, but what men make him see and know. This was the cause whereof Diocletian complained so much of the flatterers of his court, who keeping close the truth of things, fed him with smoke, and so by that means made him commit many great faults in the administration of the Empire. But because that history is worth marking, I will recite it at length.

The emperor Diocletian was born in a little village, of base and obscure race; yet in his youth he was so ambitious and covetous of honor that from a young soldier he aspired still higher, so he became a captain, and from a captain to a colonel, and from a colonel to lieutenant general and chief of the army, and finally came to the great dignity of Roman emperor. When he had come to the sovereign degree of all honors, yet was his insatiable ambition and covetousness of glory unsatisfied; for being emperor, he would needs be worshipped as a god, and made his feet to be kissed, on which he wore golden shoes covered with pearls and precious stones, after the manner of the kings of Persia. But who would have thought that he would have given over the imperial dignity, and so many honors as were done to him? Yet in truth he did forsake all this and despoiled himself of his empire, which he resigned to Constantinus, Chlorus, and Galerius, and retired to his house at Salon in Slavonia, where he lived more than ten years a private man, taking his pastime in gardening and rural works, and never repented as a private man that he had deprived himself of the empire. But if this is so strange a thing, that a man so ambitious, who so loved the honors of this world, rid himself of so great a dignity and became a gardener and laborer of the earth; yet more admirable is the cause wherefore he did this. For it was no other cause but the hatred and evil will that he conceived against the flatterers of his court, who abused him in a thousand ways, whereunto he could not well remedy, he was so besieged between their hands. This has been written by many historiographers, including Flavius Vopiscus, who places flatterers among the principal causes of a prince's corruption:

> "A man may ask, what is it that makes princes so wicked and corrupt? First, their great liberty and abundance; secondly, their wicked friends, their detestable attendants, their covetous eunuchs, their foolish and uncivil courtiers, and too plain ignorance of the affairs of their commonwealth. I have heard my father say that the emperor Diocletian, returning to private life, was wont to say that there is nothing harder than to know well how to play the emperor. Four or five will assemble and make a plot together to deceive the emperor, afterwards saying all with one voice what they would have him do. The emperor, who is enclosed in his house, cannot know the truth of things as they pass, but by necessity is constrained to understand nothing but what pleases them to tell him and make him understand. So they cause him to give offices to men who merit them not at all, and cast out those who best deserve them for the good of the commonwealth."

In short, said Diocletian, a good, wise, and virtuous prince is bought and sold by such people. Behold the very words of Vopiscus, who shows that Diocletian was discontented to be emperor because he was governed by flattering courtiers, who caused him to abuse his state. But I leave you to think, if this were not a strange thing to see Diocletian change his imperial estate to a rustic life, for the displeasure he took of his flattering courtiers. For on the contrary we commonly see that princes rather please themselves marvelously to see flatterers, and they cannot go three paces but they have them at their tails, and more willingly do they give their ears unto them than to good people who will tell them the truth of affairs that are important to the state. Tell them this history of Diocletian, and doubt not but they will say he was a sot and a beast to forsake his dignity of emperor for such a cause, and that he better deserved to be a gardener than an emperor. But if they consider what was the end of Galba, of Commodus, of Bassianus, and of many other Roman emperors who by means of flatterers have had fearful deaths, they will not esteem Diocletian such a fool to withdraw himself to a private habitation, there to finish his days otherwise than by the hands of murderers. Yet I must confess that he might have done better, to have put away from him all those pestilent flatterers. And if to rid so many at once from the court there was great peril in so great a change, yet no doubt it was not impossible for him to have dispatched them little by little, one after another, and then to have placed good people about him, thereby to have strengthened himself.

It is then seen by the saying of Diocletian that the maxim of Machiavelli is a true precept of flattery, and that there are no greater flatterers, nor more pernicious than those who keep close from princes the truth of things as they pass. And truly, if the prince has good counsellors and servants, by whom he may be well advertised of all truths which may concern his estate, and where he ought to provide and give rules, although some lies by flatterers be sown amongst them, yet they cannot corrupt the good government of a prince. For truth has always of herself so great a force that she causes lies to vanish as the mists before the sun. And withal, flatterers and liars dare not open their mouths, fearing to be discovered in their evil purposes, when they know that the prince has near him wise and good men, who will freely tell him the truth of all that concerns his state, and who are beloved and credited by him.

By civil law, he that knows any enterprise which tends to the damage of the prince is bound to reveal it unto him, upon pain of being held culpable of treason. They then who are counsellors and most especial servants of a prince, who are in a more particular obligation unto their master's service than other subjects are, ought not they to be reputed for traitors when they conceal the truth from the prince, of such things as pertain to his charge and providence? If any answer that all things for which the prince should provide, import not his ruin, being omitted; I reply that it may not be his present ruin, but yet at length. For one fault and omission draws another after it; after it, another; thus little by little the estate of the commonwealth; consequently the prince falls into confusion. And yet although the omission of providing in such things as the prince is bound to provide does not import his ruin and destruction, either present or at length, yet it must always import damage to the prince or his subjects. And in every case it is the profit and interest of the prince to give provision and rule; for there cannot come but good when subjects are well governed, and when there is good policy in all things.

Here may be demanded, seeing the good counsellors of a prince are so necessary, and flatterers and evil counsellors are so damaging, from whence it comes that yet princes are attended on and garnished with flatterers, and have few good counsellors about them? It seems that master Philip de Commines has well hit this mark; saying that this comes to pass because princes always seek those who feed their own humors and please them best, and contemn those who are contrary, although they may be more profitable. For, said he, those who have been nourished with a prince, or who are of his age, or who can best order and dispose his pleasures, or who apply themselves to his will, are always in his good grace, and the first to whom he disperses his authority and great estates. And a prince never knows how to choose a wise man of good counsel until he finds himself in some great necessity, and often has most need of those who before he despised, as I have seen (said he) of the count de Charolais and king Edward of England.

But upon this point rises yet another doubt; why it is that flatterers rather please princes than wise men? Plutarch seems to me to resolve this question well, when he says it proceeds from this, that naturally men (but especially princes) do too much love themselves. And love of oneself obscures and blinds judgment, so that we can never truly judge of what we love. From hence it follows that when a flatterer tells his prince many good things to his praise, he believes it, and persuades himself that there are many praiseworthy things in himself, although indeed there be nothing. And it helps to this persuasion that the flatterer always takes for the subject of his praises those vices which are in alliance and neighborhood with their virtues. For if the prince is cruel and violent, he will persuade him that he is magnanimous and generous, and such a one as will not put up with an injury. If the prince is prodigal, he will make him believe that he is liberal and magnificent, that he maintains an estate truly royal, and one that well recompenses his servants. If the prince is overgone in lubricities and lusts, he will say he is of a humane and manly nature, of a jovial and merry complexion, and of no saturnine complexion or condition. If the prince is covetous and an eater of his subjects, he will say he is worthy to be a great prince as he is, because he knows well how to make himself well obeyed. Briefly, the flatterer adorns his language in such sort that he will always praise the prince's vice by the resemblance of some virtue near thereunto. For most vices have a likeness with some virtue. The flatterer also on his part will not forget to cover his own faults and vices with the visage and likeness of some virtue near to them. For he will cover his ambition with the zeal of the commonweal, and will say that for the prince's service, and that the affairs of the commonwealth might be well governed, he accepted or pursued such an estate, or took upon himself such a charge, which otherwise he never would have demanded or accepted. His covetousness he will cover with his prince's honor, and will say that it should be no honor to his master, who is so great a lord, to have a servant poor and contemptible. If he is vindictive, he will always cover his vengeances with the prince's mantle, saying that the enmities he has are for the good services he has done for his prince, and that the master is despised and outraged in the person of his servant. And so of all other vices. Insomuch that the prince who yields his ears to flatterers shall always so be dealt with, that they shall believe vices to be virtues. And he will easily believe this, because (as we said) it is the nature of man to love himself too much, and consequently to be blind in judging himself, believing his vices to be virtues. And contrary, if the prince hears a good man speak of an evil thing, telling him the evil, and of a good thing the good, he shall never please him so well as the flatterer. And from hence proceeds the common proverb, which is as true as can be: to follow a man's pleasure and desire, get friends, but the truth, hatred. And this is seen not only in princes but also in particular and private men. For say to a covetous man, or to a wicked usurer who eats up his Christian brother by excessive usuries, that he is a frugal, good, and wise husband; and that he well observes Saint Paul's commandment, who wills every man to care for his family, and if not he is worse than an infidel; certainly you should be accounted for his great friend, and he would take great pleasure to be so tickled in his vice. But if you say unto him that there is no charity in him to destroy and eat up his brother Christian whom he ought to love as himself, and that true charity is joined unto faith, pity, and all other virtues (as Saint Paul says), and that he who is without love, is without faith, without virtue, and is a very infidel; then have you lost him forever, and he will be no more your friend. You have obtained his hatred for telling him the truth.

But good people ought not to desist from that cause, to say truth both to princes and to private persons. For truly, truth is so good and expedient of herself (as Plato said) that not only we ought to prefer her to the good grace, favor and amity of men, but also before all things of the world. A good man then who loves truth will imitate the example of Quintius Capitolinus, who one day making an oration to the Roman people, after he had lively showed them their faults, in that they ceased not in tumult and disobedience of their superiors, whereby some great disorder and confusion might fall to the common weal, added in the end these words. "Masters, I know well that a man may utter more pleasant talk and tell you of things more plausible; but as for me, my nature is not to flatter, and the present necessity causes me rather to tell you true things than pleasant. I have a good mind to please and content you, but I love much better to preserve and guard you from falling into destruction, how little thanks soever I have from you." These remonstrances and words of this good man were of such efficacy by pure and native truth, which he showed to the people without any flattery, that he appeased the tumults and discontentments of the city. And as to the prince's men who ought not to spare to speak truth, and that princes may not take delight to be praised by flatterers, they must show them that whosoever praises any man (be he prince or other) in his presence, is a flatterer. He must set before them the example of that good and wise emperor Alexander Severus, who took pleasure in hearing the praises of great princes who had been seen before him, but would never hear his own. And he greatly praised that saying of the valiant Roman captain Pescennius Niger, who once hearing a certain orator pronouncing a panegyric in his praise, said: "Go thy way and write the praises of Marius and Hannibal, and of other old and valiant captains, that we may imitate them; for it is a pure mockery to praise those who yet live, and especially great princes, of whom there is hope and fear, and who may bereave a man of both life, goods, and liberty. As for me, while I am alive, I will do good and approved things, and after my death, then let me be praised." The emperor Alexander then cited this notable sentence of captain Niger, and would by no means be praised in his own presence. So likewise when men used to salute him, he would not suffer them to use titles and salutations of flattery, such as "God conserve thy divinity, thy sacred majesty, thy clemency," which since have been in use, but they must say only, "God keep thee Alexander." And they who did otherwise, or who would use too many ceremonies in their salutations, were straight mocked and hissed at, and forced out of the emperor's chamber. But indeed he would willingly be saluted by none but good men, and of good reputation; insomuch that he caused an edict to be published, whereby he inhibited and forbade upon great pains that none should dare present himself before his face who knew himself to be, or indeed was of evil fame and reputation. Moreover, they must show to princes that it is the best thing in the world to know himself. For besides that the knowledge of ourselves leads us to the knowledge of God, it makes men (though they be great princes) acknowledge themselves always men, that is to say, subject to fail and to do evil, to follow evil, to leave that which is good, to be ignorant of good things, and to know many evil things and to practice them. For these qualities are common in all men generally. So that he who knows himself a man will also know and acknowledge himself apt to fall and offend, and so will he abate his pride; whereas otherwise it would mount and arise by the foolish and hyperbolical praises of flatterers.

Moreover, as it is very requisite and necessary that wise men who are near the prince should use a free liberty to tell him the truth of all things which concern him, so must they do it with all modesty, accompanied with the honor and reverence that God has commanded us to bear unto princes, as his lieutenants. For that cynical liberty of some philosophers, who knew not how to reprehend and show men's faults but by taunts and bitter biting speeches, are not to be approved; as did that fool Diogenes, who ridiculously and triflingly talked with king Alexander the Great as if he had spoken to some simple burgher of Athens. And Callisthenes, whom Alexander led with him in his voyage into Asia, to instruct him in good documents of wisdom; who indeed was so austere, hard, and biting in all his remonstrances and reasonings, that neither the king nor any others could take in good part anything he taught. It is then very much expedient, if a man means to gather fruit, and do good by his speech, to use gentle and civil talk and persuasions, especially if he has to do with a prince or great man, who will not be gained by rigor (or as they say, by high wrestling), but by mild and humble persuasions. And above all, men ought well to engrave in princes' minds that notable answer that Phocion made unto the king Antipater, who had required something of him which was not reasonable. "I would, sir, do for you service all that is possible for me, but you cannot have me both for a friend and a flatterer." As if he would say that they be two things far different, to be a friend and to be a flatterer, as in truth they are. For the true friend and servant of the prince orders and frames all his actions to the good of the prince, and the flatterer tends and bends all his actions to his own proper good. The true friend loves with a true love his prince, and the flatterer loves himself; the true friend modestly shows his vices in his presence, and praises his virtues in his absence; but the flatterer always exalts the prince in his presence, rather for his vices than for his virtues, and behind his back he blames and defames him, vaunting and saying that he governs him at his pleasure, and that he possesses him, and makes him do what he will. The true friend perseveres in the service of his prince, as well in time of adversity as prosperity; and the flatterer turns his back in time of adversity. The true friend serves for a healthful medicine to his prince, but the flatterer for a sweet poison. The true friend conserves his prince in his estate and greatness, but the flatterer precipitates him into ruin and destruction, as we shall discourse the examples of all these things hereafter.

Moreover, when we say that flatterers are pernicious to a prince, that is not meant of all those who dedicate and give themselves to please the prince. For there may well be gentlemen of his own age about him, to accompany him in his honest pastimes, as to ride, hunt, hawk, to tourney, to play at tennis, to run, and other like pastimes, who do not evil give themselves to please him in such things. But contrary, it is right necessary and requisite that the prince have sometimes such company. For it should not be good nor comely, for want of plays and pastimes, he should procure the habit of a stoic humor; neither that he should get a complexion too severe and melancholic. Hereof we read a very remarkable example above others in Alexander the Great, king of Macedon. When he departed from his country to pass into Asia, to make war upon that great dominator Darius, he had with him first in his love among others, Craterus and Hephaestion, two gentlemen, his best friends and servants. Yet they were far different from each other, for Craterus was of a hard and sharp wit, severe, stoic, and melancholic, who altogether gave himself unto affairs of counsel, and indeed was one of the king's chief counsellors. But Hephaestion was a young gentleman, well complexioned and conditioned in his manners and behavior, of a good and quick wit, yet free of all care but to content and please the king in his sports and pastimes. They called Craterus the king's friend, and Hephaestion the friend of Alexander, as one that gave himself to maintain the person of his prince in mirths and pastimes, which were good for the maintenance of his health. When Alexander had conquered Persia and Media, he began to apparel himself after the Persian and Median manner, the better to gain the hearts of those nations newly conquered. Hephaestion, to please the king, did the like; but Craterus kept his old fashions of Macedonia, and much blamed them for the change of apparel, and said it was even but to barbarize, and began to taunt and gibe at Hepaestion for it. This, their contrariety of manners, was a cause that they entered far into enmity and quarrels; one day they came unto the drawing of swords against each other, and assembled their friends on both sides; and a great mutiny would have fallen out if the king himself, hearing a great noise of people, had not come in good time and separated them, presently and openly rebuking Hephaestion, calling him fool and madman. He took Craterus privately aside and told him that he greatly marveled that he, being a wise man, would so hate Hephaestion for so small a thing. Afterward, he agreed them and publicly declared to them that they were the two gentlemen which he loved most in the world, but if any more they fell to quarrel again, he swore by Jupiter Ammon that with his own hands he would slay him who began it. But after that, they did nothing against each other. Hereupon I say, that it is necessary for a prince to have such as Craterus for his counsel, and it also becomes him well to have such as Hephaestion, to keep him company in his honest pastimes.

But to the end that men may better discern good friends and servants from flatterers, I will now, God willing, discover the examples of many sorts of flatterers, who for the most part have had in singular observation that maxim of Machiavelli, namely to hold close from the prince the truth of things. And the better to distinguish them, I will call them with such names as our ancestors have called them, which are very proper to them. First, there are those our ancient Frenchmen called janglers, which signifies as much as a scoffer, a trifler, a man full of words, or as we call them, long tongues, who by their jangling and babbling in rhyme or in prose give themselves to please great men, in praising and exalting them exceedingly, and rather for their vices than for their virtues. These by their fair language can make of a devil an angel; but in the meanwhile they so enchant men and swell them up with pride, that in effect they make them become even angelical devils. This sort of flatterers were banished and driven out of France in the time of Philip Augustus, as persons serving for nothing but vanities and corruption of manners; unto whom princes and great lords gave gifts which might better have been employed upon God's poor. And therefore that good king made a vow that he would from thenceforth give to the poor all that which before he and his ancestors had given to janglers. And to the end that other lords of the court should follow his example, and that they might have no more occasion to give anything to the said janglers, he banished them all from court.

Such flatterers in truth are very pernicious; for seeking too much to exalt and lift up princes by praises, they are causes to mount them into pride and unmeasurable fierceness, which after brings their destruction. So came it to Julius Caesar. For Lucius Cotta, Cornelius Balbus, and similar janglers persuaded him first to name the month (which was called Quintilis) with and by his name, Julius, which he did; and ever since it is called July. After that, they would make him a temple, to make him be worshiped as a god, and they called him Jupiter in his presence; they also persuaded him to take the name and crown of a king, which he was determined to do, if he had not been prevented by death. When the senators came to speak with him in his house, he would not arise to meet them, but those flatterers hindered him; neither would they permit him to rise out of his chariot to salute him, saying he was Caesar, the sovereign prince of the commonwealth; and that all others ought to honor him, and not he them. These things which Caesar did against his will by the persuasions and constraint of janglers, gathered unto him hatred and evil will of all the Senate; insomuch that some senators conspired against him, and slew him even in the Senate house.

Caligula, for a certain time, was a good prince; but the janglers he had about him, by their unmeasurable praises, made him become (according to Suetonius) a monster. They caused him to take the titles of Pitions, the Son of Camps or Hosts, Most Good, and Most Great Caesar; and in the meanwhile they made him become the most cruel, the most cowardly, and the most wicked tyrant in the world. He took a desire after all those names and titles yet to take the name of a king, and to wear a crown; but his flatterers showed him that the name of an emperor was much more than a king. Therefore from thence forward he attributed to himself a divine honor. So he gave commandment that men in temples should set up images of him through all the world subject to the Roman Empire. The governor of Judea, called Petronius, would have placed an image of Caligula in the great temple of Jerusalem; but the Jews, who extremely detested images, would not suffer him; whereby there was likely to have been a great sedition. But in all other provinces of the empire it was executed without contradiction. Yet not contented that his images should be in all places adored, this detestable monster would often go and place himself in person between the two images of Castor and Pollux in the temple consecrated to them, and have himself worshiped in the midst of the two gods, which he called his brethren. Moreover, he caused a temple to be built and consecrated, where he had an image of him made of gold erected, and had it every day adorned with the same apparel as he wore himself; and founded in that temple priests for his service, who offered up to him rare and precious sacrifices, as pheasants, peacocks, and other like birds and beasts, fetched every day. Sometimes he went into the capitol, to Jupiter's temple, and there would come to the image of Jupiter and make a countenance to talk with him, and speak in his ear, and then would lay his own ear to Jupiter's mouth, as it were to hear his answer. Sometimes he would lift up his voice, and taunt and rebuke Jupiter; and after he departed, he said that he had spoken with Jupiter and had obtained what he asked. I pray you, what will you here say? Is it possible in the world to dream or imagine a more extreme folly, or a pride and arrogance more abominable and enraged? Behold to what point janglers brought him. But this was not all; for seeing himself thus adorned, he was persuaded that no man dared ever enterprise anything against him, and so committed a thousand cruelties, and strange and horrible wickednesses; such as easily a sovereign prince might do who spends his time and power in all excesses, wantonness, and riotousness; wherein he never ceased to wallow and tumble himself, till he was suddenly massacred and slain. Which was a just and merited recompense unto him, because he so lightly believed flatterers and praisers.

You must think that while these janglers handled thus their master, leading him to such follies, that they themselves were merry and joyful to see him governed after their fancy. Yet there was not laughter for them all, and to speak of them who did not laugh, is so much the better fit to make others laugh. First then was one Macro; who seeking to come into favor and good grace with Caligula, not only employed himself to praise and exalt the emperor, but also set on his wife Ennea, to make her fit and handsome to gain the good grace of that young prince, commanding her to refuse him nothing. For such people, to come to the end they purpose, care not therein to employ their honor and that of their wives, even so far as themselves, to be very bawds. She then obeying Macro her husband, did so much by her journeys that she entered into Caligula's amity, and herself discovered unto him how well her husband loved him, and what commandment he gave her. Insomuch that Macro, as well by the means of his wife as by his own jangling, was a good time in credit. But one day he had done something that displeased Caligula, as to break a glass or some other like fault, and this foolish emperor had him called. When he came, Caligula said: "Come hither, gallant, did you not command such a thing to your wife? Do you not know well that it is a thing punishable by our laws to be a bawd to his own wife? You must die." And so constrained him to slay himself, without hearing any excuse or defense.

There are yet two others who received no less, and I will tell you how. Caligula being one day sick in his bed, these janglers came to visit him. The first was one Africanus Potitus, who seemed to be very sad and sorrowful for his disease, and among other adulatory talk, said unto him: "I would, sir, it would please the gods that I might die for the recovering of your health; for I make a vow to the gods that I would die with as good a heart as ever I did anything." The other, called Africanus Secundus, said likewise to the emperor: "O, would that it pleased the gods that I might go skirmish with the sword-players, to be slain by them for your majesty's health; for I swear by the gods that I would willingly employ myself for your recovery." Caligula answered them nothing at that time, but when he was whole, he sent for them both. He said unto them, "Masters, my good friends, I am made to know that you are very devout to the gods. For since the other day when you came to visit me, and you vowed your lives to the gods for my health, I have soon recovered it, as you vowed unto me. But fearing a relapse, and again to fall into my disease if you accomplish not your vow, I have sent for you to make you die, praying you not to take it in evil part." And withal, without attending their answer, he commanded the captain of his guard to dispatch them. This foolish emperor, after those janglers had made him become such a beast and madman, never did good thing but this. But in regard of the execution of these three flatterers, they encountered the best of the world; for they who had made him become a fool, merited well to receive part of his folly.

But it is certain that this sort of flatterers, who are so prodigal of praises, will not spare all honorable titles towards the princes while they are in their presence; but behind their backs they mock them and speak a thousand evils upon them. In the time of Nero, Teridates, brother of Vologases, king of the Parthians, came to Rome with a great retinue. As soon as he arrived, he fell on his knees before Nero, and with his hands towards heaven said thus. "Sir, I who am the nephew of the great king Arsaces, and brother of the king Vologases, am your humble servant and slave, and am come hither to worship you as my god. For I can be nothing but what it pleases you." Nero answered, "You have done well to come unto me to enjoy and have fruition of my sight, and of my presence. For what your predecessors did not leave you, I give it you, and make you king of Armenia; that you may know that it is in me to give kingdoms and to take them away." After this word he put a crown on his head and invested him with the kingdom of Armenia. After that, for a pastime and sport for this new king, plays were appointed wherein Nero had it appear how well he could play upon the cithara, and indeed played among the common players. Also he thrust himself among carters, clothed in green, as they were, to show that in lifts he could also tell how to handle chariot horses. After this Teredates, the new king of Armenia, having retired into his lodging, mocked Nero and spoke infinite evils of him, calling him carter, citternier; and further said that he marveled how they could suffer at Rome such a master and lord. When he was before Nero, he held and respected him as a god; but when out of his presence he detested him as a monster. I ask of you, if such a flatterer deserved at Nero's hand such a present as a kingdom.

Prusias, king of Bithynia, was a flatterer like Teridates. For one day coming to Rome, a little after Paulus Aemilius had vanquished Perseus of Macedon, he made certain senators understand that he desired to enter the Senate, to know his masters and superiors, whose enfranchised slave he said he was, and to congratulate them on their victory. This was granted him; when he approached the place where the senate assembled, he fell on his knees at the door and kissed the lintel. Entering into the hall where the senators sat, he made great reverences, calling the senators his gods and his saviors, and asked leave to go into the temples of the gods, to make offerings and sacrifices to their gods for the victory of Rome over Perseus. This also was granted him. But he was mocked and despised by all the company, for this so great and exorbitant humility and flattering, made to virtuous people who took no pleasure in flattery. This was a king of no worth, a coward and a man full of vices — as commonly all such people are who cover their adulations with so extreme humility — and in the end was slain by his son Nicomedes, who made himself king.

Lucius Vitellius, father of the monstrous emperor Vitellius, was such a flatterer as Prusias. Knowing that the emperor Claudius suffered himself to be governed by his wife Messalina, to gain his good grace and favor he came unto her and prayed her for the honor of the gods, that it would please her to grant him a gift, whereby he should forever feel himself bound to do her most humble service as her humble slave. The empress asked what gift he desired; he said, "Madam, if it would please you to put out your feet, that I may pull off your shoes." It may be supplied in the history that this was at some hour when she meant to put off her shoes, either to go lie down in her bed or to wash her feet, as the elders used much to do. Messalina could not refuse him this so honorable and excellent a demand, proceeding from so generous and heroic a heart, and indeed suffered him to pluck off her shoes. But what did my man? After he had drawn off her shoes, he took one of them smiling, kissed it three or four times in the presence of this madame, and carried it away with him. He ordinarily bore the shoe in his bosom, and wherever he came he showed it to the people, kissing it, saying that the empress had done him the honor and favor to give it him in pure and free gift, and that he bore it in his bosom and kissed it every day in her honor. What should a man say unto this filthy drudgery and slavery?

I will yet set down one other example of janglers, from a senator, and then we pass on. For senators and lawyers may as well be flatterers as others; although they should show better example, because commonly they are wiser. You must then understand that in the time of the emperor Tiberius, many were accused for light matters said or done towards the emperor, because he was known to take pleasure in such accusations. Among others, one day a Roman knight named Lucius Ennius was accused of treason in a full senate, because he had melted a silver image of the emperor to make some other work for his own use. You may think what a huge crime this was, and how men should find it evil for a man to do with his own goods at his own pleasure. Tiberius, seeing that this accusation had no color in it, and that it was but a mockery to call it a crime, much less a crime of treason, forbade that the knight should be criminalized for it. Yet Ateius Capito, a senator and great lawyer (but a very flatterer) rose up, and as upon a free liberty of speech he used these words to the emperor.

> "Sir, we are here assembled in the Senate, where everyone has liberty freely to utter his opinion for the good and utility of the commonwealth. We beseech you not to take from us the power that we have to punish those who commit crimes against the commonwealth; and pardon not you alone that injury done to all. For what a spite and contempt is this, for Ennius to dare cast into the fire the prince's image? Ought he not rather to have kept it by him as a holy and sacred thing, and to have reverenced it for the honor of him whose representation it was? This shows what heart and affection he bears towards his prince, and that if he could, he would do as much to him as he did to his image. For he that reverences the gods also reverences their images. Had he not otherwise enough to make his silver vessel, but to melt for it this sacred image? He would not do so much with the images of Brutus and Cassius; for he honors them in his heart, and would well today find one who might enterprise the same disloyalty against our good prince, as they did against Caesar. Our laws will that in crimes of treason, the least apparent suspicion suffices to condemn the accused. And it is the great interest and profit of the commonwealth to rigorously punish those who never so little attempt against our prince; unless a man will say that the body has not to do, neither to care when the head is wounded and offended. And therefore I conclude that justice be executed upon Ennius as a man tainted and culpable of treason."

Tiberius, although he was cruel in such matters, knew well that this fair opinion of the lawyer Capito was but a mere flattery, which he understood better than he uttered. Therefore, notwithstanding Capito's remonstrance and opinion, he persisted in the inhibitions before made, that the knight Ennius should be no more vexed nor endangered about that matter. And Tacitus says that Capito, by this his goodly opinion, acquired a great infamy and evil reputation, greatly dishonoring both the knowledge of the civil law and the knowledge of letters with which he was excellently endowed. Upon this point I note that which master Philip de Commines well says, that lawyers and great learned men are very fit to be about a prince, and of his council, if they be good men; but being otherwise, they are very dangerous. For they can so well paint and set out their language, alleging laws and histories which not every man understands, that often they take evil conclusions. But when they are good men, they may marvelously order and conduct matters which are handled in council, and bring them to a good resolution; as may be proved by infinite examples out of Livy and other historiographers, which I will not here accumulate, because it is from our determined purpose.

In the rank of janglers may well be placed the poets of our time, who by their poesies full of flatteries and lies seek to hook in some abbotship or priorship, or some other such gift in recompense for their adulations. I confess that a poet may and should take more liberty than an orator or historian to write the praises of some one man, but when praises are so hyperbolical that they fall out rather to the dishonor than the honor of him of whom they are written, then they are not at all tolerable. I will take for example but the epitaphs printed at Paris a little after the death of Charles IX. There those goodly poets say that before he died, the king overthrew more monsters than ever did Hercules, in shedding so much blood of his rebellious subjects; that he died like Samson, who at his death pulled down and overthrew the pillars which he had in his arms, and the house upon himself; so in France, justice, piety, and religion died with him; that France had been his stepmother; that there was in him an exceeding great cunning in all arts and sciences, and that he was also very expert in diverse handicrafts; that Henri, his brother now reigning, succeeded him as Castor to Pollux, as one god to another god; that he died a martyr of Jesus Christ, and that from thenceforth he ought to be invoked as a saint. I pray you is there any man of sober judgment who does not plainly see that such speeches rather become men void of wit and understanding, by some extreme affection of flattery, than these gallant poets, who are led with a generous and right poetic spirit? For meaning to praise unmeasurably, there escapes from them that they speak things redounding to their dispraise; and if the dead king were alive, he would not thank them for such praises. For a good prince, as Horace says of Augustus, ever rejects foolish praises.

> To purpose ill, shall never go my verse
> To Caesar's ear: for if his deeds appear,
> So would he, I his praises to rehearse:
> Too much his praise detests he to hear.

And indeed it is common to all good and virtuous people not only to reject excessive praises, but also to hate as flatterers and liars all those who use them, as Euripides witnesses, saying:

A good man, praise too great cannot abide:
But hates that thing which puffs him so with pride.

If those goodly poets, before they had made their epitaphs, had well read Virgil and Horace, they should have found that these two excellent poets wrote in many places the praises of Augustus. But why do they praise him? Because he established a good peace in all the Roman empire, he caused justice to flourish, he brought the people into a good repose and assurance, and reduced again the golden world. They praise him also because he amplified and enlarged the Roman Empire. But they speak not one word of the civil wars, nor do they praise or dispraise him for overthrowing Cassius and Brutus. And indeed, as Plutarch says, they are piteous triumphs which are made upon civil blood. These epitaphers then should learn to praise a prince as they ought to, and as the elders have done. But when they say that our dead king died like Samson, and that with him also died piety and justice, which he carried in the device of his two pillars, do they not plainly blame the kingdom at present of impiety and injustice? As if justice were not now so good, nor religion in so good estate as in the time of the dead king; or as if they were or could be made worse; yea contrary, everyone sees with his eyes that justice and religion are still in as good estate in France as before the king died, and that they are now so well governed that they cannot wax worse. And when they say that France was a stepmother to the dead king, is not this injuriously to blame the French nation? Wherein has France appeared unto him a stepmother? Because there were rebels against the king, they say. Those who they call rebels deny they are such, and in truth when edicts were maintained and observed, they were seen to be very obedient. But let it be so, that there were in France some rebellious subjects; must therefore all the nation be blamed and called their king's stepmother, seeing there is no nation in the world more obedient to their prince? And as for that great cunning in arts and the meanest mechanical sciences which those poets attribute to our dead king; are they not goodly praises, think you? As if it were some goodly virtue in a prince to make a coffer, or to paint gourds (for which we read the emperor Hadrian was mocked), or to make some similar things. But contrary, the poet Virgil, describing what kind of princes the Roman princes should be, he wills they should have no knowledge in the mechanical arts, but should learn the science to command well, to govern, to vanquish, to pardon, to make laws and edicts, and to establish good manners and customs upon the nations under their governance. In like manner the profane comparison of Castor and Pollux, where one god succeeds another; how unfit a speech is it for a Christian? If princes at this day will believe janglers, they make themselves to be adored upon the altar between two saints, as was Caligula between Castor and Pollux. But enough is spoken of janglers and their janglings, and of their too too impudent and strange praises.

Let us now come to marmosets. A marmoset, according to the language of our elders, is as much to say a reporter, murmurer, whisperer of tales behind one's back in princes' and great men's ears, which are false, or else not to be reiterated or reported. And it seems unto me that this name of marmoset is very proper and fit for such people, and that it merits well to be called again back into use. And I believe it is drawn from hence that such people go marmoting, murmuring and whispering secretly in princes' ears flattering speeches, which they dare not speak clearly and on high before the face of him whom they detract and speak evil of. These people are worse, and far more perilous than plain railers, scoffers, jesters, or janglers; for carrying the countenance of good servants and friends, they make the prince believe that they serve him as spies, to mark and seek out the designs, evil purposes, and carriages of his secret enemies, so that he may not unawares be surprised by them, and that no evil may come unto him. And because, according to Commines, princes are almost all suspicious for doubts and fears that are put into their heads by advisers, they easily believe marmosets and reporters. Yea some princes, he says, promise them that they will say nothing nor disclose anything, which is one of the greatest faults a prince can commit. For besides that, in all men, be they princes or private persons, the ancient proverb has place, which says that the sinews of wisdom is not to believe lightly. Yet it is a thing particularly required in a prince, to stop his ears to all reports unless the reporter will be well known, and sustain the punishment of a slander in case his report be not found true. And thereupon the prince ought to make diligent inquisition to have the truth well averred when the thing is weighty and merits it. And he may not be satisfied with a light information thereof, but he ought to hear him who is charged or blamed before he believes anything. And if the thing be not of great consequence and import, but words spoken lightly in some pleasant talk or at the table, or in choler, the prince ought to despise and make no account of such words but as talk uttered in immoderate babble, without thinking or considering thereof. For there is no man so perfect than can so bridle his tongue, but there will often fall words without consideration, which afterwards when he thinks of them wishes he had never spoken them.

And this imperfection which is in all men ought to be supported by some towards others, and princes ought rather to bear them than particular persons, for two reasons. One, because he is more subject to receive reports than private men; so that if he easily delivers his ear unto them, he shall see a thousand griefs and displeasures, and shall be in continual doubts and fears. The other reason is because all princes ought to consider that men speak more of them than of any private person. For there is neither great nor little but will meddle to speak of princes, yea to judge of their actions, and every man to utter his follies of his good or evil behavior. What should princes then do? It is impossible to bridle their tongues, and if they should be forbidden to speak, they would speak the more. Seeing then both great and small ordinarily speak of princes more than of other things, it is impossible that in such abundance of talk there should not be always much evil; and he that would set foot therein would bind himself to an infinite pain, from whence he would not know how to get out. For the tongues of men are so ready and quick workers in their trade, that they will frame more businesses in a day than a thousand commissaries by their enquiries know how to dispatch in a year. Therefore the prince who contemns words spoken without due deliberation, and such other things as are not of importance, and who forbids that no man shall report unto him such matters, shall in such things do that which is most agreeable to his gravity and majesty, and in so doing he shall show himself more magnanimous, and in heart more generous, neither fearing, distrusting, or doubting anything. Such a one was the great Augustus Caesar; for one day, as one pleaded a criminal case before him against Aemilius Aelianus, the accuser among other crimes maintained that Aelianus was accustomed to speak evil of Augustus, and to detract and slander his majesty. Augustus then making a countenance to be angry, returned towards the accuser, saying, "Is it true that you say Aelianus has spoken evil of me? I wish you could prove it, for I would then cause him to know that I have a tongue as well as he, and would say as much and more evil of him than he has done of me." This poor accuser, seeing Augustus make no more account of it, was much ashamed, and afterward wished that he had never advanced such an accusation. Such also was the emperor Antonius Pius, who would not give place to the murmurs which marmosets blew in his ears, and he made no account of them. As one day Lucilla, the mother of Marcus Aurelius the philosopher (whom Pius had adopted), being in a chapel upon her knees before the image of Apollo, Valerius Omulis, a marmoset, said to the emperor: "Behold, Lucilla makes her prayers to Apollo that you might quickly finish your days, so that her son might reign." But Pius reproved him for such talk and told him that Lucilla and

Marcus Aurelius were too good to think such a thought. So generally we read that all good emperors, such as the abovesaid, and Trajan, Hadrian, Nerva, Alexander Severus, and others have not only hated and detested, but also chased and banished far from the court reporters and relaters of false tales.

But as I before said, it becomes not a prince to make account, but rather to contemn words not spoken by good deliberation. And to that purpose will I rehearse a judgment which was given and recorded in full council of king Charles VI, whereat were his uncle, the duke of Bourgogne, the constable, the marshals of France, and many other great lords of the king's Privy Council. Master Peter de Courtnay, an English knight, being one day at the court of the king of France, offered a challenge unto a French knight called Guy de la Tremouille, by deed of arms to try who was the stronger knight and best in arms. La Tremouille had no desire to refuse him; so that by the consent of the king and of his uncle, the duke of Bourgogne, in their presence and before many other great lords, they ran a lance one against the other and no more, for the king would not suffer them to go any further. The English knight was ill content thereat, but yet without making any other countenance desired leave to return to England, which the king granted, and gave him for his conduct and guide to Calais the Lord de Clary, a French gentleman, one renowned and of great valor. As they went by the way, the English gentleman desired to go by Lucien to salute the countess of St. Paul, the king of England's sister, who dwelled there and who greatly received them and made them good cheer. Talking and speaking of news, as the custom is, this English told the countess that he could not find in France a knight with whom to do deed of arms, and that he would never have thought but to have found in the court great store, covertly taxing thereby the French nobility. Clary, his conductor, marked well his words, but spoke not one word while he came to Calais; being there, he angrily said unto Courtnay:

> "Messire de Courtnay, I have acquitted myself of the charge which the king my lord gave me for your conduction to this town; now that I have no more charge of you, I think good to remember you of certain words you delivered at Lucien, to Madame the countess of St. Paul, where you said you could not find in France a knight with whom to do deeds of arms, thereby taxing the noble knighthood of France. Therefore to maintain with you the contrary, I offer myself to do deeds of arms with you, in what manner you will choose, provided that you can obtain from the governor of this town for the king your master, a permission and place to do them."

The said permission and place was granted, and they so fought that Clary wounded Courtenay in divers places. This came to the king and his uncle's notice; Clary was sent for, who for his defense said that that which he had done was to maintain the honor of France, and cited many fair reasons; whereby it seemed that not only he ought not to be blamed for what he did in that case, but rather he merited to be allowed and praised. The matter was handled in the king's council, and by judgment and decree Clary was condemned to prison for a certain time, and in the meanwhile his goods were seized into the king's hand; and little there wanted he was not banished France. But a certain time after the king pardoned him at the intercession of the duke of Bourbon and of the said countess of St. Paul; and at his deliverance was made known to him the motive of the king's council, which was this: that the king's council thought him worthy of that punishment because a light and rash speech delivered in familiar talk, he would revenge as a serious and weighty matter. If this decree were well observed (as it merited to be) we should not see so many quarrels, murders, and suits for our words rashly and indiscreetly spoken. And it should be a thing much better becoming Christians, not so easily seeking points of honor, to enter into contentions and quarrels; whereby we make demonstration that we are nothing less than that we would appear to be. For we would that by our quarrels and going to law upon an overthwart and rash speech, men should account us of great heart, that we cannot despise and contemn a word of no account pronounced in haste. Was that great emperor Augustus Caesar, and many others, ignorant what were the points of honor? yet were they most magnanimous, and had their hearts so noble and generous that they never took footing upon any words spoken without good consideration, but despised and held them at nothing.

The sentence of the wise man is very true; that slanderers or false reporters are like secret wounds which go down into the bowels. For as we see that wounds within a man's body are almost all mortal, and outward wounds are much more likely to be healed, so words of detraction, of blame, and of slander often bring destruction, either to the reporter or to him whom they are reported, or to him of whom they are spoken, or all together, as I will show by many approved examples. But when such words are openly spoken, either in the presence or with the knowledge of him whom they touch, there is place to purge and justify himself, and to have recompense by justice or by reconciliation, obtained and mediated by friends; so that seldom comes any ruin of either one or the other.

The emperor Claudius was much ruled by his wife Messalina, one of the most intemperate women of her time, and by the high steward of his household, Narcissus, who was too close with Messalina. This good lady was amorous upon a fair young Roman gentleman named Appius Silanus; but fearing the emperor, he would not yield unto the petulance and wantonness of the empress. What did she do? Seeing his refusal, she and Narcissus plotted to separately tell the emperor that they had dreamed of a man very like Silanus entering the emperor's chamber to slay him. And they resolved to tell him this dream at an hour when Silanus should enter the emperor's presence, so that in fear he might command to slay him. This enterprise being made, Messalina sent to Silanus as from the emperor, that he should not fail to come unto him the next morning at his arising, for a certain affair whereof he had to speak with him. Narcissus came the next morning and knocked at the emperor's chamber door, and it was opened unto him; counterfeiting a great astonishment, he approached the emperor's bed and said, "The gods be praised that it has not come to pass what I dreamed in my bed, sir!" "How did you dream?" said the emperor. "Sir, I dreamed that Appius Silanus had slain you about this hour, and awaking upon it I came straight to tell you, for sometimes dreams are images of true things, and not to be despised." The emperor, who was naturally fearful, began to be troubled. Messalina also took her course to his bedside, feigning a great amazement; he immediately told her Narcissus' dream. She, making admirations at it, said "O ye gods, behold a strange thing! All this night I have done nothing but dream that I saw a man very like Silanus, who would have entered here for some wicked enterprise." Seeing the concordance of those dreams, the emperor's fear was redoubled, especially because Messalina told him it was the only reason for her rising so early; for that vision was ever before her eyes, and she could not rest at ease. Upon that talk Silanus came and knocked at the door; the usher who kept the chamber door came to tell the emperor that Silanus was there and would speak with him. Messalina and Narcissus then made a show of fear and great wonder, and told the emperor that it was good to command him slain, lest he were slain himself. Claudius, trembling for fear and exceedingly troubled in mind, believed them and commanded to slay that honest gentleman. Behold how by false reports, even by the report of a dream maliciously devised, this noble person lost his life. And it is to be marked in this history that these false reporters customably have this subtlety, to trouble a prince's senses if they can, either with fear or anger, or by some other means, to bring what they would to their purpose.

The emperor Severus had two sons, Bassianus and Geta, who were instructed as well as was possible. He loved them both equally and ordained them to be emperors together after him; for experience showed that a sovereign principality is not incompatible with two in consort and fellowship, as Marcus Aurelius and Lucius Verus were emperors together in good concord, and Diocletian and Maximian, Maximus and Balbinus, Theodosius and Honorius, Constantius and Galerius, and many others. Severus intending to leave the government of the empire to his two sons together, flatterers about them disposed it otherwise; they made false reports of one against the other, telling him that his brother had such and such talk of him, and that he aspired to be emperor alone, and that it was better to prevent than be prevented. Those two young princes fell into so great and mortal enmity that not only they hated all each other's friends and servants, but also those who would have reconciled them. As soon as their father Severus was dead, Laetus, one of the marmosets of Bassianus, persuaded him to slay his brother and feign that he was assailed by him. This counsel was found good by Bassianus, who was audacious enough and ready to give the blow with his own hand. One morning he entered into the chamber of empress Julia, Geta's mother, and finding him there he slew him between his mother's arms. Bassianus went to find the soldiers of the guard, seeming to be much troubled and narrowly escaped. "Masters," he said, "I have escaped fair; my brother would have slain me, but I am gotten out of his hands. I pray you let us go to the camp, and keep me company, for I am not well assured here." The soldiers, who knew nothing of the blow he had given, believed it was true and followed him, much grieved that his brother Geta had so enterprised upon him. Bassianus gave them all great sums of money, for Severus had left great treasure, and made them swear they would be faithful to him. So that when later they knew the deed done, and found themselves all gained and corrupted with silver, they obeyed him without contradiction as to one sole emperor. And what came of all this? Bassianus, not ignorant that the Senate would find this murder very strange, desired that great lawyer Papinian, his kinsman and Chancellor under Severus, to go to the Senate and make his excuses by an oration well set out: That he had done well to slay his brother, and that he had reason and occasion to do it. Papinian, who was a good man, answered that it was not so easy to excuse a parricide as it was to commit it. Bassianus, grieved at this refusal, had one of his attendants straight cut off his head. After this, willing to show the Senate and the people that he grieved because he had slain his brother, and so they might see it was done by evil counsel, he executed the marmosets who had counseled him in that business, saying that they were the cause thereof. He also killed as many of Geta's friends and servants as he could catch, so that they could enterprise nothing against him; he even slew all those who carried themselves between the two as neutral and reconcilers. I pray you, what was the cause of all this great and horrible butchery? Was it not the mortal enmity which these marmosets had sown between the brethren?

In the time of Commodus there happened a similar thing; and because the history is memorable, I would rehearse it a little at length. Marcus Aurelius was surnamed the Philosopher, because he was wise and studious and a lover of good letters. In his time there were many wise and learned men, because commonly (said Herodian) men imitate their prince and give themselves to such things as the prince loves. There was always about him a great number of good and learned people for his council, which he called his faithful friends, as the king of France does today in his patents. This good emperor, being at war in Hungary with his son Commodus, fell into a disease whereof he died. But before his death he assembled his council and recommended his son unto them, and made a little remonstrance, worthy of such a prince, in this manner.

> "I doubt not, my good friends, that you are anguished and sorrowful to see me in this disposition. For humanity causes that we easily have compassion of men's adversities, but especially when we see them with our eyes. But yet in my regard there is a more special reason; for I doubt not but you bear me good will alike to that which I have ever borne you. But now is the time for me to thank you, that you have always been unto me good and faithful friends and counselors. And I pray you also not to forget the honor and amity which I have borne you. You see my son, whom you have nourished, who now enters into the flower of his youth; who as he that enters into high seas has need of good patrons and governors, lest by ignorance and evil conducting he stray from the right way, and so come into peril. I pray you then, my friends, whereas he had no more fathers but one in me, be you many fathers unto him, that he may always be made better by your counsel. For truly, neither the force of silver and treasures, nor multitude of guards can maintain a prince and make him be obeyed, unless the subjects who owe him obedience bear him good affection and benevolence. And assuredly they only reign long and assuredly who engrave and instill in their subjects' hearts not a fear by cruelty, but a love by bounty. For they ought not to be anything suspected by a prince, drawn to obedience by their own will and not by constrained servitude. And subjects will never refuse obedience unless they are handled by violence and insolence. Very true it is that it cannot be but hard for a sovereign prince, who is at his full liberty, to guide and bridle his affections moderately. But if you always admonish him to do well and to remember the words he now hears from me, I hope you shall find him a good prince towards you and all others. And in thus doing you shall manifestly show that you always have me in remembrance, by which only means you may make me immortal."

Upon this speech his heart and his word failed with languishing, and all his counsellors began to weep and lament; some could not refrain from crying for great sadness and bitterness of heart that they had to see so good a prince fail. After his death, his son and successor Commodus governed himself some little time by the good people and ancient counselors of his father. But this continued not long, for there were marmosets who found subtle means and entries to get into him; when they saw their time, they began to say to him, "Why do you tarry in this base and barren country of Hungary; better for you to be at Rome, to have all the pleasures in the world. You have no cause to believe these tutors your father left you; you are no child, to be governed by tutors. Commodus, a fair young prince who desired nothing but his pleasures, and who yet had no great resolution—although his father had taken great pains to instruct him well—began to let himself be led by marmosets, who never spoke anything to him but of merry and pleasant things. So he made a shameful and dishonorable peace with the barbarians, against whom his father commenced war, and retired to Rome. He began to become cruel, especially against his father's good and ancient counselors, whom he had killed at the instigation of these marmosets, who reported unto him that they bore him no good will, that they blamed his actions and controlled his pleasures. He also executed many senators whom his reporters for the same reason disgraced. Among other marmosets he had one called Perennis, who persuaded him to care for nothing, to take his pleasures and to let him alone with the charge of his affairs. Commodus was glad of this and plunged himself into all lubricity and wantonness; Perennis provided for him three hundred concubines and harlots, and as many slaves. Having cast him into this gulf and destruction, he took upon him the affairs of the empire, and began to confiscate the goods of all whom he bore ill will, and who contradicted his doings; he sold justice for money, and in a little time made himself very rich. But this endured not long, for in a war against the English he replaced the senatorian captains with simple knights, which all the Roman army much disdained; they cut Perennis in pieces as an enemy of the commonwealth.

Cleander was another marmoset who succeeded in his place; who at the beginning made some show that he would do better, but soon did worse. He practiced many cruelties and sold the estates and governments of provinces to those who would offer most. There happened at Rome then a great famine and pestilence. The people, who always lay the cause of public calamity upon the governors, bruited abroad that Cleander was the cause of the plague and the famine, and therefore should die. Cleander, to stop this rumor and cause the people to hold their peace, had the emperor's horsemen rush through the town and suburbs, slaying and wounding innumerable. But the people began to take houses and fight from the windows so well that the horsemen were constrained to retire. Fadilla, the sister of Commodus, seeing this civil war commenced and raised by Cleander, went to find her brother, whom she found among his harlots. All bewept she fell on her knees before him, saying, "Sir, my brother, you are here taking your pleasures, and know not the things that pass, nor the danger wherein you are. For both yours and our blood is in peril, to be altogether exterminated by the war and civil stir Cleander has raised in the town. He has armed your forces and has made them rush against the people, and has brought them unto a slaughter more than barbarous, filling the streets with Roman blood. If you do not soon put to death the author of this evil, the people will fall upon you and us, and tear us in pieces." Saying these words, she tore her garments and was very sad, as it were desperate. Many also who were present increased the fear of Commodus by their persuasions; fearing some great danger to himself, he sent in haste for Cleander, who knew nothing of his complaint. As soon as he arrived, Commodus had his head cut off and carried on a pike through the town, and the sight of the head appeased the people. After this execution Commodus, who had acquired infinite enemies by means of his marmosets, determined at once to cause a goodly execution to be made. He made two lists of the names of those he would execute, one of which was entitled the dagger, and the other the sword. These two lists fell by hap into the hands of Laetus, who was one of his marmosets, and of Martia, one of his courtesans, who found themselves first on the list. Seeing the danger near and evident, they conferred together and resolved rather to slay than be slain. Martia took the charge to poison him, which she did; but Commodus, who had eaten and drunk too much, was provoked to vomit, and cast up the poison. Seeing this, Laetus and Martia had him strangled in his bed. Behold here the end whereunto Perennis, Cleander, and other marmosets brought their masters, and the end they made themselves, and the great evils and slaughters of good people whereof they were the cause. Think you not that this is a goodly example to all kings and princes, to keep them from suffering themselves to be governed by reporters and flatterers? Commodus was of the most noble and illustrious race in the world, as goodly and personable prince as was possible, who was neither subtle nor malicious in nature; the son of the best prince that ever was, who brought him up well and left him a great number of wise and prudent men to govern him well, and towards him had gotten the favor and good will of all the world. Yet these marmosets and flatterers brought him to a miserable end, and reigned but a while, and died young.

The emperor Severus had on his council one Vetronius Turinus, whom he judged to be a good man; but he proved to be a very marmoset. Before the emperor he dissembled well and knew well how to carry his countenance and behavior, but behind his back he vaunted that he governed Severus at his pleasure, and that he caused in the council chamber such resolutions as he thought good. The solicitors of the court who had businesses in the prince's consistory, understanding that Turinus said he had there so great credit, waited upon him to recommend their affairs. What did he then? He trafficked with all the contending parties, and they promised to pay him a good sum to obtain what they sought, yet none knew anything of the others. In the council Turinus gave his own voice without speaking directly for one or the other, as the others did; but it always came to pass that one or the other obtained his cause and paid him the sum he had promised. And as for the other party, he let go, finding some excuse why he did not get his demand. After Turinus had used this occupation some time, to sell the hopes and decrees of the prince's privy council, his dealings were discovered. Alexander immediately sent him to prison; he was condemned as a seller of smoke, tied to a pillar and stifled with the stench of dung and carrion, heaped up near the pillar. Behold the reward that this marmoset Turinus received for the false reports he made against the prince's honor and his counsels.

Enough is spoken of the marmosets of the Roman emperors; let us now speak of our French marmosets. In the time of Charles VI, by marmosets and reporters a great enmity arose between Louis duke of Orleans, the king's brother, and John duke of Bourgogne, count of Flanders, of Artois, and lord of many other lands and territories. Our histories name not these marmosets, but simply say that their household servants incited them to band one against another; the duke of Orleans's servants and favorites said, and said truly, that he was the chief prince of the blood, the king's only brother, also more aged and of riper and more staid wit than the duke of Bourgogne; and that therefore he should not set his foot before him in handling the king's affairs. For at this time, the king having not perfect senses, his affairs were handled with the princes of the blood and the Privy Council; but contrary, the duke of Bourgogne's marmosets said that he was the chief peer of France, and as they call it *le Doy en des Pairs*; that he was more mighty and more rich than the duke of Orleans. And although he was not so near of the royal blood as he, yet he was more near by alliance (for the dauphin, who was yet very young, had espoused his daughter); and therefore he ought in nothing to give place to the duke of Orleans, but that he ought to maintain and hold the same rank that Philip, duke of Bourgogne (his deceased father) did, who while his father lived governed the king and the kingdom at his will. Briefly, these tattlers and reporters caused this duke of Bourgogne to mount into ambition and covetousness to reign, that he enterprised to cause the duke of Orleans to be slain, who hindered his designs and purposes. And indeed he caused him to be most villainously massacred and slain at Paris, near the gate Barbette, by a sort of murdering thieves he had hired, as the duke of Orleans went to see the queen (who had lately been brought to rest by a child). Great damage there was for that good prince, for he was valiant and wise as one might possibly be. Of him descended king Henri II, now reigning, both by father and mother. For king Francis, his father, was son of Charles, duke of Angolesme, who was son also of John, duke of Angolesme, who was son of the duke of Orleans; and Madame Claude, queen of France, mother of the said king Henri, and was daughter of king Louis XII, who was son of Charles, duke of Orleans, who was the son of this duke Louis whereof we speak. I would to God the prince's descendants would well mark the example of this massacre, most horrible, which was committed upon the person of that good duke, their great-grandfather, and the great evil haps and calamities which came thereof, to shun the like miseries which ordinarily happen when such murders go unpunished. For because John of Bourgogne was not punished for this fault, but found people who sustained and maintained it to have been well done (as we shall say more fully in another place) and who followed his part, stirring up civil wars which endured two generations and caused the death of infinite persons in France; and the English got a great part of the kingdom, and the poor people of France fell into extreme misery, poverty and desolation; there were many causes and means of so many evils, for injustice, ambition, greed, desire for vengeance, and other like things might go in the rank of causes of so many mischiefs. But the marmosets of Bourgogne were those who struck the iron against the flint, out of which came the spark of fire (a device fatally taken by the duke) which brought into combustion and into a burning fire all the kingdom for so long time, and at last ruined the house of Bourgogne.

Francis, duke of Brittany (a prince that was a good Frenchman, and affectionate to the king of France, his sovereign) had a brother called Giles, who gave himself to the English when they made war in France, and accepted from the king of England the Order of the Garter and the office of Hight Constable of England. The duke and his brother, much grieved hereat, found means to take him prisoner and put him in a strong castle, where he would never go to hear or see him, he so much disdained him. But yet he sent men unto him whom he trusted, who indeed proved very marmosets and false reporters. For after Giles of Brittany had remained in the castle a certain time, and he had well considered his doings, that he was born a king's vassal of France, and he ought never to have disunited himself from his brother; he then paid his brother's people that came to see him to tell him that he greatly repented what he had done, and that if it pleased him to pardon him, that from thence forward he would follow with a good heart the part of the king of France; and that if it pleased them, he would straight send to the king of England his Order and Constable's sword. What do his marmosets then? They report to the duke that his brother Giles was still obstinate, and so perfect English that no reasons they could make could turn him from that side. The duke sent still many times the same men unto him, but they always made the like or worse report of him; insomuch that this good duke, fearing that his brother was invincible in his obstinance, fearing also that if he should let him loose he would cause the English to come into Brittany to avenge him, commanded the same reporters to strangle him in prison; which they did. Afterward, as God when he sees his time brings the most hid things to light, these murdering reporters could not hold, but discover the truth of the matter, that Giles of Brittany would have done anything that the duke his brother would have had him do; which coming to the duke's ears, he was near out of his wits for his brother's death, and caused the reporters to be hanged and to die with great and rigorous pains and executions. Behold the end of Giles of Brittany, and the reward which such marmosets received, who were the cause of his death. Hereof princes may note a rule: Not to believe too easily reports made of men without hearing them, but especially when it touches life.

One day before the emperor Hadrian appeared one Alexander, who accused one named Aper of certain crimes; and for proof of those crimes he produced certain information in writing against him, which he had caused to be taken in Macedon. Hadrian mocked at it and said to Alexander that these informations were but paper and ink, and might be made at pleasure; in criminal cases we must not believe witnesses in writing, but witnesses themselves, in hearing, interrogating, and confronting them with him that is accused. Therefore he sent the case and the parties to Junius Rufus, governor of Macedonia, commanding him to examine diligently the witnesses and take good notice whether they were good men and worthy of credit; and if Alexander the accuser could not well prove his accusation, that he should banish him to some place. This commandment of Hadrian has since been marked by the lawyers, who since made a law thereof. Behold how men must proceed when it lies on men's lives, and not to believe marmosets and reporters, neither believe papers without seeing or hearing witnesses and the accused, and without searching whether the witnesses be good men or no, as is done at this day. For at this day there is nothing whereof magistrates make a better market than of men's lives. But let us pass on.

I would now rehearse a truly tragic example, of king Richard of England, who was the son of that valiant and victorious prince of Wales. This king came to the crown very young, and had three good uncles about him, the dukes of Lancaster, York, and Gloucester, by whose counsel for a certain time he governed well his kingdom. But the earl of Suffolk, who the king made duke of Ireland, entered so far into the king's favor that he governed him after his fancy. Then he took occasion to talk so of the king's uncles as was very strange; for he told him that his uncles desired nothing but to deal in the affairs of the kingdom, to obtain it for themselves, a thing which they never thought. And he did so much by his reports that the king put his uncles from his council and from dealing with any of the affairs of the kingdom; whereof the people, and especially the Londoners, were so ill contented that they rose up and made war against the king, or rather against the duke of Ireland, and they were at a point to give the battle one against the other. But the duke of Ireland, who was general of the king's army, lost his courage with great fear to be slain or taken, and therefore fled and passed into Flanders, where he finished his days, never afterward returning to England. As soon as he had fled, his army was dissipated and the king's uncles seized upon the king's person, established a new council, and by justice executed some of those who were the duke of Ireland's adherents. A long time after, another marmoset called the earl Marshall gained the duke of Ireland's place, and was so far in the king's good grace that he governed all as he would. One day, this earl Marshall talking with the earl of Derby, eldest son of the duke of Lancaster, the earl of Derby chanced to say: "Cousin, what will the king do? Will he altogether subject the English nobility? There will soon be none; it is plainly seen that he does not desire the augmentation of his kingdom." But he held this talk because the king had put to death and chased away a great number of gentlemen, and caused the duke of Gloucester, a prince of his blood, to die; and yet continued in that rigor to make himself feared, and still revenging what was done in the duke of Ireland's time. The earl Marshall answered nothing to the speeches of the earl of Derby, but only marked them in his heart. Some days after, he reported them to the king, and to make them seem of more credit he said he was ready to enter into the camp against Derby, to aver the said words as outrageous and injurious against his majesty. The king, not measuring the consequence of the deed, in place to make no account of these words, sent for the earl of Derby, his cousin germane; and after hearing before him the earl Marshall speak, his will was that they should enter into the camp and fight it to the utterance. But the king's council conceiving that it might come to be an evil example for such great lords to slay one another, and that the earl Marshall was not of equal quality unto the earl of Derby, they counseled the king to take another course, namely, to banish from England forever the earl Marshall, because he had rashly appealed and challenged unto single combat a prince of the blood; and to banish the earl of Derby for ten years, for speaking the aforesaid words of the king, his lord. The king, following the advice of his council, banished the earl Marshall from England forever, and the earl of Derby for six years only, moderating his council's advice by four years. When Derby came to depart, there assembled in the streets before his gates at London more than forty thousand, who wept, cried, and lamented his departure, and extremely blamed the king and his council. Going away, he left in the people's hearts an extreme anguish and grief for his absence, and a very great amity towards him; yet notwithstanding he left England and came into France. While he was in France, his father, the duke of Lancaster, died. The king, to heap up his evil luck, seized all his lands and goods, because they fell to Derby. Hereby he got great hatred and ill will of the nobility and of all the people. Finally the Londoners, who are a people easy to arise, made a plot against the king and secretly sent word to Derby that he should come, and that they would make him king. The earl arriving in England found an army of the Londoners ready; so he went to besiege the king Richard in his castle, whom he took and imprisoned, and made him resign unto him the realm and crown of England. Richard was put to death in prison, after he had reigned 22 years; a thing very strange, rigorous, and unheard of in England or in any kingdoms near to it. And so the earl of Derby, who had been banished from England, remained a peaceable king, and was called Henry IV. The earl Marshall, who stayed at Venice, knowing this news died ragingly. This was the end of this marmoset, and the tragic evil hap whereunto he brought his master, upon words reported which were never spoken as an evil speech against the king, but only for the grief he had that the council governed so poorly the kingdom's affairs. Which words ought not to have been taken up nor reported to the king, and being reported to him he should have made no account of them, but should have always presumed rather well than evil of his cousin germane.

Herod, born of a low and base race, was created king of Judea, Galilee, Samaria and Edom. He espoused a noble lady of the king's race named

Mariamne, by whom he had two children, Alexander and Aristobulus. But Herod had a sister called Salome, who was a very Tisiphone and served for nothing but to kindle and light fires in the king's court by false reports she invented. This infernal fury did so much that she persuaded Herod that Mariamne sought to poison him by his cup-bearer, and brought out certain false witnesses to prove it. The king believed it and put to death his wife, one of the fairest princesses in the world, and of whose death there was afterward infinite griefs and repentances. But as one sin draws after it another, Salome, fearing Alexander and Aristobulus would feel the outrageous death of their mother, machinated and resolved in her spirit that they must die. So she began to forge false reports, false tokens, and false accusations, and persuaded Herod that his children spoke of revenging the death of their mother, and by the same means intended to usurp the kingdom. Suffering himself to be persuaded by the calumnies and slanders of his sister Salome, Herod journeyed to Rome with his sons and accused them before Augustus Caesar, deducing and setting out the means whereby he pretended that they should go about his death. When it came time to speak for their defense, Alexander and Aristobulus began to weep and lament; Caesar knew well thereby that the poor children were full of innocence. So he exhorted them from thence forward to so carry themselves towards their father, that not only they should do nothing against him unworthy or grievous, but also bring themselves far from all suspicion. He also exhorted Herod to use his sons well and to keep them in his favor. Then the children fell on their knees before their father with great effusion of tears, crying him mercy, by which means they were reconciled with him. But after their return this fury Salome, not content with the reconciliation Caesar had made, began to lay new ambushes by false reports that she made to Herod, wherein she mixed some truth to give the better taste. Herod, who was very credulous in such matters, made Augustus understand that his children had again conspired his death. Augustus answered him that if his children had done against him anything which merited punishment, that he should chastise them as he thought good, and that he himself gave him power and permission to do so. Herod, joyful to receive this power, had the two poor children strangled. Salome aided herself in all this business with another son of Herod's, born of another woman called Antipater. God willed that Herod should discover that the accusations against his two dead children were but slanders, and that Antipater had himself conspired to poison his father. Herod called him before Guintius Varius, the governor of Syria for the emperor. The case being long pleaded and debated, Antipater could not purge himself of the sayings and proofs against him, and did nothing but make great exclamations, irrelevant to the matter, holding that God knew all, unto whom he recommended his innocence. Varus, seeing that he could not well justify himself, wished Herod to imprison him, and so he did. Some days after, Herod fell sick; which coming to the notice of Antipater in prison, he rejoiced greatly. Herod, advised that Antipater wished his death and rejoiced at his sickness, sent one of his guard into prison to slay him, which he did. Five days after, Herod died like a madman; for the evil haps he had in his children, the rage lit a fire in his entrails, which rotted him little by little and engendered worms which ate him alive with horrible languishments before his death. And who was the cause that Herod thus contaminated his hands and all his house with the blood of his own children? Even that most wicked reporter Salome, who devised false accusations and slanders which she blew in the ears of the king.

Besides the flatterers whereof we have spoken above, janglers and marmosets, there is yet a third kind who are greatly to be feared; who under the name and title of principal counsellors, and under the pretext of conducting the affairs by good counsel, they abuse the prince's authority. To shun the mischief that may come thereupon, there is nothing better than to follow the precept of Commines; namely that the king has many counsellors, and that he never commit his affairs to one alone, and hold them equal as nearly as he can. For if he commits much more to one than to another, he will be master, and the others dare not reason against him freely; or else knowing his inclination, dare not contradict him. Therefore in a criminal case handled in the Roman Senate against a gentlewoman of a great house accused of treason, Tiberius, although he was very rude in such cases, would not suffer his adopted son Drusus to reason first, lest thereby had been imposed a necessity for others to have consented to his opinion. And in another case of like matter, where Granius Marcellus was accused to have set his own image above the emperor's, when the case came to handling, Piso, whose opinion the emperor desired first, began to say: "And you, sir, in what place will you reason? For if you reason last, I fear that by imprudence I shall not dissent from you." For that case Tiberius declared that he would not reason at all; and indeed the accuser was absolved, though the emperor had showed a countenance to be angry with him as he heard the accusation. And there is no doubt but that the counsel of one alone is perilous to the prince, because naturally men are divers ways passionate, and that which shall be governed by one alone is often guided by passion. Also the indisposition of men's persons causes that everyone has not always his head well made, as they say, nor are wise at all seasons; and men's spirits as well as their bodies are journals, and have their vicissitudes and changes; for from the wisest sometimes escape absurd and strange opinions.

An example hereof may well be Charles, duke of Bourgogne, then earl of Charolais; having made a peace with the town of Liege, he soon after went to besiege Dinant, a town near the other. The people of Liege, going against the treaty of peace, made ready an army to go succor Dinant, but they arrived after the town was taken. The duke, fierce of his victory, would have rushed upon Liege as peace breakers; but an agreement was made that they should observe the said form of peace, and that for effect they should give 300 men for hostages the next morning at eight o'clock. The next morning came, and eight o'clock, then noon, but no hostages were delivered; so that the duke would gladly have run upon Liege, yet he asked advice of the knights of his council. The Marshal of Burgundy and the Lord de Countay were of advice to fall upon them, and that there was just occasion because they had not held their word to send hostages as promised; and a man might now have them in good case, because they were all divided and dispersed. But the earl of Saint Paul was of a contrary mind, saying that a multitude could not so soon be accorded, and that men must not measure affairs of importance by hours and minutes, but that it was yet good to summon them by a herald. This opinion was followed by most of the men of the council, so that a trumpet was sent to summon them, who met the hostages by the way coming to the duke. Here note, if the duke had had of his council none but the said marshal and de Countay, what effusion of human blood had followed of these poor Liegiois, who would well have kept their word, but they could not so soon effect it. What yet came to pass? Some time after, the men of Liege again broke the covenant of peace; so that the duke would have put to death the 300 hostages, who were not the cause of the peace breaking, but were only pledges and answers of the public faith. The duke asked his council's advice. De Countay was advice they should be slain; but M. de Imbercourt, a wise knight, was of contrary mind, saying it was best to take God on our side and not to slay so many innocents for the fault of their co-citizens; and that their yielding themselves hostages was in part to obey their commonwealth, and partly to employ themselves for the good of their country, but for that cause they did not merit to die. This opinion was followed, and that of de Countay rejected as cruel. A little while after died the said de Countay, as if it were by a judgment of God, although no man had ever before seen him cruel either in deed or in opinion. He was also reputed a very wise knight; but there is not so good a horse but does not stumble sometimes, nor so good a brain but fails. And it is one of the things most proper to men, often and grossly to err. Those who are best in the brain, are not at all hours the best disposed. Men commonly see also that men's spirits never handle a matter after dinner so well as before in the morning. And therefore the prince, to shun such inconveniences, ought to have his council compounded of many.

Scipio the African, being chosen general of the Roman army against Hannibal, reasoned in the Senate that he desired to pass into Africa to draw Hannibal from Italy, and desired permission of the Senate to do so. Quintus Fabius Maximus, an old and wise captain, reasoned first upon that deliberation; he was advice that it ought not to be granted to Scipio, and that by natural reason everyone ought rather to defend his own than to go to conquer others; and that it might come to pass that Scipio would be in Africa and Hannibal would besiege Rome, in which case the forces Scipio took to Africa would little serve the necessity of the commonwealth. He doubted not but that Scipio desired to go to Africa by a boiling heart he had to win honor; but yet he, an old captain who had also assayed what Hannibal was, could not be of that advice. Scipio showed to the contrary that the Carthaginians, seeing themselves in danger, would never leave Hannibal in Italy, for the same reasons that Fabius had alleged, namely, rather to defend themselves than to assail; and that it was more expedient to give battle in another's country, to see if an end can be made of the Punic Wars, than to give it at home. Briefly, he so well debated his opinion that Fabius, however great estimate there was of his wisdom, was not followed. And in truth his opinion was of no value, as by effect appeared afterward; for the Carthaginians revoked Hannibal from Italy, where he had made war sixteen years, to come succor Africa. Scipio gained the battle, and so put an end to the war which Hannibal would have made endure in Italy all his life; because the Romans, after the loss at Cannae, were resolved to give Hannibal no more battle in their country. So then the opinion of Fabius was of no account at this time, although otherwise he was one of the wisest of Rome. I could here yet cite many examples to this purpose, but these shall suffice.

When a prince is governed by one alone, there happens not only the inconvenience that he may be evil counseled, but also it often happens that such counsellors who see themselves alone in credit would master even their master, and often precipitate into ruin themselves and their master with them. After Tiberius had become altogether wicked and plunged in all filthy lubricity — for a long time he had carried himself between good and evil — he remitted his affairs to Sejanus, leaving him all to do and govern, and so loved him that he gave him his daughter in marriage. While the emperor kept in his house of pleasure, Sejanus did at Rome all things which the emperor himself could have done if he had been there. Soon men began to honor him as the emperor himself, and erected images of him before which men sacrificed; and they so accounted of him that happy was he that could have any part in his good grace. Seeing himself so reverenced, he swelled so with pride that he fell to rail of his master, taxing and rebuking his filthy and dissolute life. The emperor was advised of Sejanus' evil words; and as there is no blame nor evil words that touch a man so near to anger as those that are true, so fell it out with Tiberius, who clean cast Sejanus out of his favor, who would master him and speak evil of him. Therefore he had him taken prisoner and put him into prison; as soon as he was there all the world began to cry against him, and even those who before had set up images of him — such is the inconstancy of men — began to detest him and have him in execration. Finally the emperor put him and his children to death ignominiously, and all his goods were confiscated; and yet what is worse, almost all those who had been his friends were also executed. For then it was a deadly crime to have been Sejanus' friend, which before had been held for a great good and felicity.

The emperor Galba was a good and wise prince, but he suffered himself to be so governed and mastered by Titus Junius, Cornelius Lacus, and Icellus Martianus, who were of accord to rob and do evil, and brought upon Galba a common report to be a wicked and unworthy emperor. For his dealings and dispositions were not of one same tenor and constancy as they ought to have been; sometimes he showed himself too sparing, sometimes too prodigal; now remiss and negligent, now too near a taker; often he would refuse things which were not to be refused, or grant that which ought not to have been granted. He condemned noble persons upon simple suspicions; yet he would never accord to the Roman people to punish Tigellinus and Halotus, the ministers of Nero culpable of great wickedness, but contrarily favored them, and advanced Halotus into a high estate. He suffered these three counsellors and governors to sell and give tributes, freedoms, pardons for faults, and all other things. By such means Galba got the evil will of all estates, noblemen, senators, magistrates, and common people; insomuch that he was slain after reigning but seven months. And he received this end because he let himself be mastered by three alone; whereas if he had had a good council, composed of a good number of good and wise people, he would never have fallen into that misfortune; for he himself was good and wise.

And upon the talk I have held concerning Halotus, whom Galba exalted although he was one of the counsellors and instruments of all the wickedness of Nero; I note that a prince who succeeds a good prince whose government has been good, ought to retain his counsellors and officers. But the prince who succeeds an evil prince who has governed evil, and whose government is blamed and cried out on, ought not to retain in his counsellors and servants, but should take others. The reason is because the world always imputes the evil government of a prince unto his counsellors and servants. And if princes could gently and easily rid themselves of their counsellors and ministers, when they see all the world cries out against their government, they would seldom fall into such dangers as they commonly do. Therefore Galba did very evil to serve himself with Halotus and to sustain Trigillinus, who had been ministers of the cruelties and other heinous actions of Nero. For as soon as he did so, his subjects entered opinion and fear that they were again fallen into the time of Nero; and that in place to be better handled and dealt with, they were fallen from a shaking fever into a hot ague, as the French proverb is. For the same reason the emperor Otho, Galba's successor, was evil beloved of all the people, who were in exceeding fear to see about him those who had been the ministers and counsellors to Nero. For although Otho made a good and reasonable entry, and showed himself very kind, courteous, and moderate in all things, seeking by liberality and such other means to obtain every man's good will, yet men could not trust him in any manner, nor hope from him any good as long as he was served by Nero's servants. So that being so evil beloved, he endured not long, but being overcome by Vitellius he slew himself.

Contrarily, Louis XII coming to the crown of France governed himself evil by leaving and forsaking the counsellors and servants of his father, king Charles VII. For he ought to have considered that he succeeded a king who was wise, and who had very well managed and ruled his realm, and in consequence had good counsellors and servants who he should have retained; as indeed he did a good time after he was made king, when he knew by experience the fault he had made. For among other good parts in Louis, he was not proud, but humble, and could well acknowledge his faults and amend them; the fault he made in disappointing the good servants of his father ought no more to be imputed to him for an error, since he corrected and amended it. As said the poet Sophocles:

> To fail and fall a common thing it is
> To all mankind, but he that has the skill,
> Salve to provide to heal what is amiss,
> Astray goes not, as he that stands in ill.

Which never happens to a proud man, who always perseveres in his evils; and if a man will show him anything for his good, he takes it in evil part and instead of amending, he adds more unto them and commits fault upon fault, whereby follows his ruin. The emperor Galba was of that nature; for when a man required anything of him or showed him any faults in the government of the commonwealth, he would provide no remedy for it, fearing to be seen to obey his subjects.

But as for what I have said concerning the change which sometimes ought to be made of the counsellors and servants of a prince's predecessors, it has often happened in France that the king has been forced to change new counsellors to appease the nobility and malcontent people. This happened to Childeric I, son of the valiant king Merovech; for he governed himself by evil counsellors, who the Frenchmen drove from him; whereof he was so afraid that he fled. But some time after, he was called back again and governed well by good and wise counsel, and proved a good and valiant king. The same also came to pass in Charles the Wise, being dauphin; to Charles VI, his son; to Charles VII and Louis XI, and many others, which is not needful to insert here. But I must say that sometimes such changes have been procured upon envy, rather than upon just complaint against those who governed; and such envies often proceed when kings govern themselves by men of base hand, as they call them, for then princes and great lords are jealous. And therefore, to shun such jealousies and just complaints that great men may have to see themselves despised, a prince ought so to advance mean men that he does not recoil great men; and mean men always to acknowledge the place from whence they came, respecting great men according to their degrees without staggering in their duty to their prince and commonwealth. And when they see that by some accident they are evil beloved of great men or of the common people, and that for the good of peace it is requisite to extinguish the envy and jealousy conceived against them, they ought voluntarily to forsake their estate. For willingly to retain it to the detriment and confusion of the commonwealth, therein they evidently show that they are not good servants of their prince. King Charles VII had counsellors both wise and loyal, who had done him great services in great affairs he had, as well when he was dauphin as when he was king. At that time this king had civil war against the duke of Bourgogne, whom secretly the duke of Brittany favored; which war the king would gladly have extinguished. Therefore he himself openly spoke to the said lords and dukes, who answered that they were content to come to some good accord, provided that he would put from him his counsellors and take others. Knowing this, the counsellors said to the king, "Sir, since it holds but thereon to quench civil war, let us all go home again; it shall not come from us that so good a thing shall be hindered." And they themselves desired and counseled the king to accord to that condition. These were good and loyal counsellors; but they are dead, and there are no more such to be found. But such as there are nowadays, who would rather see the commonwealth in combustion and ruin than they would suffer themselves to be removed from their places one pace. Yet these good counsellors withdrew to their houses willingly and without constraint; and soon after, peace was accorded between the king and the duke. These good persons did not allege that men sought to take away the king's faithful counsellors to seduce and deceive him, and that their duty commanded them more than ever to keep near his majesty, seeing the great troubles and affairs of the kingdom, and that otherwise they might be accounted disloyal traitors. No, they alleged no such thing, they looked right upon the white, to keep peace in the kingdom. For they knew well that if they had used these reasons to the duke of Bourgogne, he could have answered that they were too presumptuous and proud to think that in all the kingdom of France there could not be found people as wise and as faithful to their prince as them. For at all times the kingdom of France, more than any other, has been well furnished with wise and virtuous people of the nobility, justice, clergy, even merchants and of the third estate.

To come again to our purpose, it is certain that a prince who commits the government of his affairs to one alone brings himself into great danger, and hardly can such government be without great mischiefs and disorders. For this men commonly hold, that being lifted up unto great honor and dignity, they cannot hold a moderation and mediocrity, which is what gives taste and grace to all our actions. The emperor Severus advanced Plautianus so high, that being great master of his household, the people thought he was the emperor himself, and that Severus was but his great master. He slew, robbed, banished, and confiscated the goods of all such as he would, in the sight and knowledge of Severus, who contradicted him in nothing. So far mounted this great and immoderate license that Plautianus dared attempt the lives of Severus and his two sons. But his wickedness was disclosed by a captain; Severus summoned him, and although by nature he was a cruel prince, yet he was so firmly affected to Plautianus that he never spoke sharp or rigorous words unto him, but only uttered this remonstrance. "I am abashed, Plautianus, how it came in your heart to enterprise this against me, who has so much loved and exalted you, and against my children, whereof Bassianus, my eldest son, has married your daughter, and so is your son-in-law. Truly the condition of men is very miserable, that cannot maintain themselves in such honor and dignity as I have placed you in. I pray you tell me your reasons and defenses to purge you of this act." Bassianus, seeing his father would receive Plautianus' justification, and fearing he would escape, had one of his men slay him in the presence of his father, adding to the saying of Severus: certain it is that great honors attributed to one man alone, as to govern the affairs of a kingdom, not only makes him go out of the bounds of reason, but also subjects him unto great envies, whereby great mischiefs happen unto him.

In the time of Philip le Bel, the count of Longuevile, a valiant and wise knight, governed almost all the affairs of the king and his kingdom, especially of his common treasure, which was distributed by his ordinance. Among other things he caused to be built that great palace at Paris where the court of Parliament is held. After the death of Philip, Charles, count of Valois, began to pursue Longueville before commissions of Parliament delegated for that purpose. Longueville was condemned to be hanged on a gibbet at Paris, as he was indeed; this happened to him by the envy he had procured by his great place and too high credit. For true it is that he was accused of many things, but he was not condemned of any punishable thing. But our histories say that Valois, after the hatred he bore was extinct by Longueville's death, from then on he repented and greatly grieved, and felt his conscience tormented therewith. Falling sick, he had a persuasion that it was a punishment sent him from God; then he began to have many masses said, and great alms to be given for the soul of Longueville and for his own health; but in the end he died of the palsy. So it appears that Longueville was overthrown by his own greatness. We may also well note what a perilous thing it is to wound our conscience to please our affections. For that is to offend the mistress to please the chambermaids; because the conscience, which is the right judgment of reason, whereby we approach unto God and go far beyond beasts, is she who ought to be mistress within us; and our affections ought to be chambermaids. But when we preposterously alter this course and law given from God, we cannot do well.

1.3
Machiavelli

A prince ought not to trust in foreigners. (*Discourses*, book 2 chapter 31)

He who is driven from his country draws to that prince who will receive him, not for any good affection he bears him, but as it were constrained by necessity; and therefore, having no other affection but his own profit, he betrays the prince who has taken him into favor so soon as any other prince offers him more profit, whatsoever he says and promises he has sworn to him.

Answer

I place not here this maxim to refute it; for it is true, in such manner as he deduces and understands it. But because his disciples understand and practice it otherwise, I thought it good not to leave it behind. They say that a prince ought not to give trust to those who are strangers unto him, and who are of another country and nation than he; but if possible, ought to serve himself with those of his own nation, yea, and those in the government of the countries and provinces of another nation that is subject unto him. As the kings of England did in the time when they held Guînes, Normandy, the Isle of France, and most of Picardy; for they gave the governments and offices of all those provinces unto Englishmen, and not to Frenchmen, who were strangers unto them. As also did and does the king of Spain, who being born in Spain yet holds many countries of other nations, as the Low Countries, Burgundy, the duchy of Milan, Sicily, and Naples; but the governors and magistrates there are all or mostly Spaniards. So by those examples the disciples of Machiavelli would say that a prince ought not to serve himself nor trust in those who are not of his nation, although they be of his countries and under his subjection. To the contrary whereof, I will prove that a prince ought to put trust and to serve himself with his subjects, although they be not of his nation; yea that he ought to establish over each nation of his domination governors and officers of that nation itself, as much as he possibly can.

The reason is evident, because naturally every man loves his own country and nation, and consequently a governor or magistrate of the same nation shall be better beloved than a stranger. And being better beloved, he shall also be better obeyed, and shall so bring a better obedience to his prince. For true and assured obedience must proceed more from love than from force or fear, as shall be showed at more length in another place. The other reason is that other nations are different in manners and complexions, whereunto magistrates must accommodate and apply themselves; and if they are strangers, they neither can nor know how to do it. I will not therefore say that magistrates ought to be of the same town or of the same province, but only of the same nation. For contrary, I think that the ordinance of the ancient Romans and of our ancient kings was good, that none should govern in that province where he was born; because having there his friends and parents, he would sooner employ his office to favor them than others. That office also might be more contemptible, being exercised by one of the same place, whose familiar and private knowledge may make him less honored by his neighbors. I will not say also but that a prince who possesses some countries of another nation and tongue than his own ought and may have certain officers and magistrates of his own nation, as a lieutenant general and captains of fortresses; but he should as much as possible serve himself with those of the country. Yea, his lieutenant general ought to often communicate with them and call them to council. For the estate of a prince is nothing else but the estate of a commonwealth; for as much as the power which the people had in and upon themselves, they have transported unto the prince; so that the prince ought to have care, as he has the authority, over all affairs which touch the conservation and increase of the estate and good of the common weal. But although that care truly appertains to the prince, yet his subjects have a great interest that he acquits himself well and duly, because the damage and harm falls upon them if he does evil. And therefore they are always desirous to know how the prince governs himself; and when the prince does them this honor, to call them unto some participation of that charge, they receive a great contentment and greatly love their prince, and more willingly yield him obedience. But if the prince despises them and gives them no offices, but gives them to people who are not of their own nation, they receive a great discontentment, and thereby they presume that the prince distrusts them and does not love them. But it is hard to love where he is not beloved. Hereof arise enterprises, rebellions, revolts, and other broils, which we see always happen sooner or later when subjects are discontented with their prince.

There is yet another reason, which is that naturally men desire honor, which of itself is no evil nor condemnable appetite. For all those who love virtue are touched with that desire, not to be honored themselves, but to the end that virtue may be had in that estimation it deserves. And therefore when the prince shuts the gate to honors from those of his nation, the virtuous people thereof are angry, and grieve that they have not the means to employ and make esteem of their virtue; namely, a good spirit and prudence, which are best employed and shine more in a public, rather than a household government. From hence it also comes that virtuous people become angry and chafed to see themselves despised, as also to see strangers preferred before them, suffering themselves to be governed and guided by turbulent passions, contrary to their natures. Moreover, Hesiod and Aristotle shoot not far from the truth when they say that by right of nature, he ought to domineer and rule who has the abler spirit to know how to command well, because of the difficulty that ordinarily falls in the execution. Yet for all that, that law always sticks naturally in the spirits and minds of men; it seems to those who feel themselves to have some sufficiency, that there is wrong done them when they are passed by, to bring into an office one less capable. By the abovesaid reasons then I hope men may see, and usually we read, how great disorders often come when princes have preferred strangers for public charges, offices, and honors, before those of that nation where such charges and honors are distributed and exercised.

In the year 1158, William, king of Sicily (by birth a Frenchman), gave the estate of the chancellor of his kingdom to a person who was very capable and fit, but not a Sicilian, rather a Frenchman. The lords of the kingdom, grieved to see a stranger constituted in so high an estate within their country, and that the greatest magistracy of justice must be exercised by a stranger's hands, hatched a very cruel conspiracy. For they conspired not only the death of that chancellor, but also all those of the French nation who were dispersed in the kingdoms of Sicily, Calabria, and Apulia. For that purpose they sent secret letters through all the towns and places of the said countries, whereby they advised their friends and adherents, who were already prepared, that they should massacre the Frenchmen of their places and towns on the day and hour assigned. Which was executed, and there was made in the said countries a horrible butchery and exceedingly great effusion of French blood. Behold the mischief that came in that kingdom for having a stranger for a chancellor. True it is, some may say that this massacre of the French in Sicily and other countries of Italy happened not so much because there was a foreign chancellor, but because the Italian race has always been much inclined to shed the blood of our nation. For that same race also made another great massacre in the year 1282, by a conspiracy wherein it was concluded that everyone of the country should slay or cause to be slain his French guest, at the first sound of their Evensong bell on Easter day. Which conspiracy was not only executed, but the rage of the massacres was so great that they ripped the bodies of women of their own nation alive, who were suspected of being with child by Frenchmen, to stifle the fruit they carried. And this cruel and barbarous massacre was called the Sicilian Evensong. By the imitation hereof, the same race plotted and executed not in Sicily, but in France itself, through all the best towns of the kingdom, the horrible and general massacre of the year 1572, which will ever bleed, and whereof their hands and swords are yet bloody. Of which exploit they have incessantly vaunted and braved, calling it the Parisian Matins. M. Martin du Bellay rehearses in his memoirs how the same race murdered a great number of poor soldiers, lame, wounded, and unarmed, slaying them in their highways. But such is this people's generosity of heart, always to be ten or twenty against one, and to brave those who are wounded or unarmed and have no means to resist. This Messeresque generosity is at this day called in France, *Coyonnerie* and *Poltromerie*. But let us come to our purpose touching the disorders that come by foreign magistrates.

By the Peace of Brittany made between John, king of France and Edward, king of England, the country of Aquitaine was acquitted purely and in all sovereignty by France to England. This king Edward, from the first possession of the said country gave it to the prince of Wales, his eldest son, who came and stayed in Bordeaux and kept a great and magnificent court. The gentlemen of Gascoigne and of other countries of Aquitaine, who by the means of the said peace became vassals to the king of England and prince of Wales, came to find this prince at Bordeaux; first, to swear their faith and homage, and secondly to obtain his favor and good countenance, as is the custom of all nobility. The prince of Wales very gently, courteously, benignly, and familiarly entertained them, but in the meantime he gave all the offices and estates of the country—the captainships and governments of the towns and castles, the offices of bailiffs and stewards, and the estates of his court— to Englishmen, although they held no other goods but their estates, spent prodigally, and held as great a train as the lords of the country. And to maintain all that, they committed great extortions upon the people. Hereupon came it that the people, seeing themselves oppressed by the English officers, and the nobility and virtuous people kept from offices, soon revolted from his obedience and caused all the towns of Aquitaine to revolt, one after another. Insomuch that the king of England lost all the country, having procured the evil will of their subjects by giving offices unto strangers.

John, duke of Brittany, because he had taken a wife in England, was marvelously affected to the English, even against the king of France, his sovereign lord. The nobility of Brittany were much grieved thereat; one day the three greatest lords of the country went to him, and after salutations, said to him in this manner: "Sir, we know not upon what thought you show yourself so inclined and favorable unto the English; you know that the king of France is our sovereign lord, and the duchy of Brittany held by the crown of France. We pray you to rid yourself of that affection which you have to the English and show yourself a good Frenchman, such as you ought to be. For we come to declare unto you that if you do it not, we will abandon and leave you to serve the king of France, who is our sovereign lord." The duke was much troubled and could not so much cover his courage, but he said that the king of France did wrong to the king of England to despoil him of Aquitaine. Some time after, distrusting his subjects, he sent into England to have Englishmen for his service, and to give them captainships and governments of towns and castles of Brittany. The king of England sent him people, but the gentlemen of Brittany, thinking that their duke distrusted them and would prefer Englishmen before them, seized the fortresses and towns of the country before the arrival of the Englishmen. The duke, seeing himself brought into a great extremity, abandoned his country and saved himself in England. This came unto him for loving strangers more than his own subjects, and because he desired to give them the charges and estates of the country.

King Charles VIII, in the voyage of Naples, which he made in his own person, conquered the realm of Naples almost without striking a stroke; and was received by all the people, and most of the nobility, as a messiah sent from God to deliver them from the cruel and barbarous tyranny wherein they had long endured under their kings, Alfonso and Ferdinand of Aragon, usurpers of that kingdom from the house of Anjou, to which Charles succeeded. Everyone may judge if it would not have been easy for the king (if he had a good council) to have kept that kingdom in his perpetual obedience. For when a people has been tyrannized by a usurper and recovers its natural prince, who deals with them like a good prince, there is nothing to induce the people to deny him obedience or to revolt. Because on the one side they acknowledge that after God and reason they ought to obey the true and lawful prince, unto whom there is more amity borne than another; and on the other side they see themselves discharged and unburdened of that heavy weight of tyranny and of a usurper. But what came there unto Charles? Thus having conquered that kingdom, he gave all the estates and offices of the country to Frenchmen who were with him in that voyage. Whereof the gentlemen of the country, and especially those who had always either secretly or openly held to the party of Anjou, were so discontented and spited that they cast off all amity and good affection to the king, and immediately entered into practices and plots to make all the country revolt, which they did. Thus for nothing the king lost both his people and his money; who assuredly might well have kept the kingdom of Naples, if he had given the offices thereof to those of the country, and sought means to have maintained them in voluntary obedience.

By this example it appears that the French gained nothing by getting into their hands all the offices and estates of the kingdom of Naples; yet they gained much less in the fact I now come to speak of, seeking to take away the honor of war from the Spaniards at the battle of Aljuberrota. You must then understand that king John of Castile, being an ally with the king of France, demanded succor and aid to make war against king Denis of Portugal. The king of France sent him gallant succors, footmen and horsemen. The French on arriving were very well entertained by king John of Castile. Our French desired the point of the battle, to show both what they could do in war and their good affection to do him service. The Castilians contradicted this, being grieved and envious against the French, who so vaunted and preferred themselves. Notwithstanding all that the Spaniards could do, the king granted them their request, whereof they were very glad, and the Castilians just as sad. What did the Castilians do? Upon spite and envy they plotted to let the French pursue the enemy without following or seconding them, but only made a show of following, so that all the glory might remain to the French, if they vanquished, or all to them, if after the overthrowing of the French they were victors. Upon which resolution it is well to note how envy and hatred blind judgment. For if they had not been very passionate, they might well judge that forces divided might easily be vanquished one after another; as it happened to their ruin and dishonor, and to the ruin of the French; but being joined together they might much sooner have been victorious. Finally the battle was given against the Portugese, who were valiantly encountered by the French; but being abandoned by the Castilians, who held the rearguard, they were found feeble, and were all slain or taken. Which was a thing very lamentable; a thousand gentlemen were taken prisoner, among whom were nineteen great lords, all of whom were slain. For as the Portugese, after the defeating of the rearguard of the French, perceived the arrival of the Castilians, they resolved to slay their prisoners; and did so, lest they either should make war upon them behind, or else escape. So having slain all the prisoners, they marched valiantly against the Castilians, whom they likewise discomfited. If we Frenchmen had not been so ambitious and covetous of glory as to seek glory in a stranger's country above the natives, they would not have fallen into this mischief.

King Ahaziah of Judah was the son of a foreign woman named Athalia, daughter of the king of Samaria. This king governed himself by Samaritans, who were much hated by the people of Judah. At the persuasion of his mother, he gave them the principal charges and offices of his kingdom, despising and casting aside the wisest and most virtuous of his kingdom, by whom he should have governed, after the example of his predecessors. This was the cause of that king's destruction; for as Jehu was destroying the house of Ahab, he also slew Ahaziah, and exterminated almost all his race, as a partner and friend who maintained Ahab. If Ahaziah had governed himself by people of his own kingdom rather than by strangers, that evil hap would not have come to him.

That great king Xerxes, who held the empire of the Medes and Persians and ruled over 127 countries, long governed himself by a foreigner called Haman, who was a Macedonian. Seeing himself in credit, Haman enterprised unjustly to kill Mordecai, who had always been the king's good and faithful servant, under the pretext that he was not of the king's religion. And to cover the enmity he had against Mordecai, and to make it seem he would not harm him alone, he found means for the king to cause a general commandment for the massacring all those of Mordecai's religion. But the king having been advised that Mordecai had done him good services, and that what Haman did was but from envy, revoked the commandment and would not have that massacre executed, but hanged the Macedonian who would have brought his kingdom into combustion by so horrible an effusion of blood.

Alexander, king of Epirotes, had drawn and gathered into his country a great number of Lucanians who had been banished from their country, and used them with such courtesy and hospitality that he not only permitted them to dwell in his empire, but also served himself with them and reputed them for his good and faithful friends, and used them with all the best dealing he could. But it so happened that the king had war against the country of those banished people, and so thought to be well served by them in this war; as indeed they promised him, saying they desired no more than to revenge themselves and bring the country into the obedience of Alexander, and to be afterward established in their goods and in authority under him. But as Livy says, it ordinarily comes that such people have spirits and faith as mutable as their fortune; they used the matter otherwise than what they promised the king. For they made secret pacts to betray this king with their countrymen, who promised them a restoration of the goods and authority they had before banishment, provided they would deliver the king alive or dead. They persuaded this king to give battle against the Lucanians, and brought him into a place near the flooded Acheron River where he could not save himself but by swimming over it. They began to show their treason and turned against the king; seeing the peril he was in, he hazarded himself by swimming to pass over that great flood. As he had almost passed over and recovered the bank on the other side, behold there came one of the banished people, who with a javelin ran him clean through. The body fell in the water and was carried into the hands of his enemies, who cut it in many pieces. Here is the miserable end that came to this poor king for trusting in strangers.

Charles, the last duke of Bourgogne, not being able any way to get his will of the town of Neuss, entered into distrust and discontentment with his own subjects, although in truth they had done all their duties in the siege of the town; yet a prince must do what he will. Upon this mistrust and discontentment of his subjects, he resolved with himself to be served with strangers, and among all other foreign nations he made the choice of Italians. But I leave you to think how good his choice was likely to be; for everyone knows well enough what account Italians make of the observation of their faith, and how Machiavelli teaches that faith is not to be observed but to a man's profit, which they of that nation always well practice. And if sometimes there are found any loyal and good observers of their promise, it is a thing so rare as that rarity should not have anything moved the duke of Bourgogne rather to trust the Italians than his own proper subjects. Yet having taken it in hand, he drew to his service the earl of Campobache, whom he had entertained with four hundred men of arms and more of Italians paid by his hands. As soon as Campobache entered credit with the duke, he began to govern him at his pleasure, so that the duke trusted more in him than in any man in the world. Campobache having gained this point straight began to practice to betray him, and to deliver him to king Louis XI for a recompense of 20,000 crowns and a good earldom. But the king (doing as Fabricius did towards the king Pyrrhus) would not enter into that composition, but advised the duke of Bourgogne to take heed of that traitor and rid himself of him. The duke took this advice in evil part (his senses were so troubled), imagining that the king sent him this word to make him lose his good servants, and therefore more than ever, Campobache. When Campobache saw he could not bargain with the king, he sought a merchant other where; for he was resolved, whatsoever became of his credit, to draw out a profit if he could. Amongst these actions, the duke thought good to besiege Nancy, the principal town of Lorraine. The duke of Lorraine was not so scrupulous to enter into composition with that traitor as the king had been, especially because the duke of Bourgogne made war upon him unjustly and sought to take from him his country. He therefore entered into a compact with Campobache by the means of a gentleman of his named Cyfron, and they concluded and agreed between them secretly. Finally, before Nancy a battle was given by the advice of Campobache, who counselled the duke of Lorraine to levy the siege of the duke of Bourgogne, who was there slain, and his army defeated by the means and treason of Campobache. After this the king took a part of the country of the said duke of Bourgogne, who died in the foresaid battle, because they ought duly for want of male heirs to return to the crown of France; and the rest of his dukedom fell to his only daughter, who was his heir and who was married to the house of Austria. Now you may see how the duke of Bourgogne precipitated himself into ruin, and his countries fell as a prey unto his neighbors, by trusting in strangers and forsaking his good, faithful, and natural subjects and vassals.

The emperor gordian the Young prospered greatly while his affairs were governed by his father-in-law Misitheus, master of his household and his lieutenant general. Gordian made war against Shapur, king of Persia, and drove him out of Thrace and the countries of Syria, and recovered Antioch, Carres [Haran], Nisibis [Nusaybin], and other great towns which the Persians held. So that the name of Gordian was feared and redoubted through all Persia, whereas before Italy itself began to fear the Persians. But upon the course of his victories and prosperities, by ill luck arrived the death of that good man Misitheus; and withal fell yet a worse misfortune, which was that the young emperor gave the estate of his father-in-law to an Arabian called Philippus, who straight began to practice against his master. For the first thing he did was order that victuals would lack in the camp, to make the soldiers mutiny against the emperor; and he sowed defamatory words through the camp against his master: that he was a young man and knew not how to conduct a camp, did not merit to be an emperor, and would cause all the army to be destroyed if they rested upon him. Briefly, he brought the soldiers to what point he would by the means he took. For there is nothing more saucy nor more deaf to hear reasons and excuses than a hungry belly. All the host then were angry against Gordian for the want of victuals, and the principal captains were corrupted by this Arabian who got himself chosen as tutor and governor of the emperor. Having by this means gained the authority to command, he began to enterprise to make his master Gordian die. Which this young prince seeing, offered humbly to receive him into the participation of the empire, and that they two might be together emperors, as but a few years before had been Maximus and Balbinus. But Philippus would not agree to that, perceiving himself strong of the captains which he had gained and corrupted. Then Gordian demanded of him the office which he had given him, of the great master of his household and lieutenant general, and that in place of a master he might so be his servant. But the fierce Arabian denied it him, he was so villainous and ungrateful. Finally Gordian desired him but to save his life; which likewise that wicked Arabian would not accord, seeing that one day he might trouble him, because he was of a very noble race and had many friends all over the Roman empire; and Philippus was of a vile and unknown race. Briefly, this cruel barbarian made forcibly to be brought before his face that young prince, his master, who had advanced him; and there caused him to be stripped and slain. Would any say there could be imagined a barbarousness, disloyalty, or cruelty more strange? A stranger committed it; trust such people who will.

The ancient Romans who were wise took good heed of granting charges and offices unto strangers, nay not to their associates of the same tongue. After they had lost the battle of Cannae, where fourscore senators were slain, the Senate seemed to be utterly overthrown, the number remaining was so small. Then praetor Marcus Aemilius proposed that there should be new senators chosen to supply and increase the ancient number. And upon this proposition, as president of the Senate he first asked the advice of Spurius Carvilius, a senator. Carvilius thought best to choose some good number of the most notable and wise men of the Latins, their associates, because there was a lack of men within Rome, and also to hold the Latins more united and obedient; by the means of which union he said the commonwealth should be much more fortified and increased. But Manlius, who reasoned after him, was of another mind; for he declared high and clear that the fist Latin he saw enter the Senate to sit down as senator, he would slay him with his own hand; and he could never endure that the Senate should be contaminated with strangers. After reasoned that wise lord Quintus Fabius Maximus, who said he never heard nor saw any man argue in the Senate so grossly and to evil purpose as Carvilius had done, especially in the time wherein they were brought to such extremity; and that it was more needful than ever to have in the Senate faithful and loyal persons; and everyone may well know that there can never be good trust and assurance in strangers, who measure faith and loyalty by their profit and loss. "We had need also to take good heed there be no bruit or fame of this foolish opinion of Carvilius, but to let it be trodden under our feet, for fear the Latins take no occasion to lift up their horns if they perceive any wind or breath thereof." Briefly, all the company were of this opinion, and 177 senators were chosen out of the town of Rome, who before had made known their virtue, without more looking into the nobility of their race. And Carvilius was much despised because he would have advanced strangers into the office of senators.

We must not be abashed if the ancient Romans have used this, for even at this day there is not so small a commonwealth that uses it not. See Venice, Gennes, and other towns of Italy; see Strasbourg, Nuremburg, Ausburg, Frankfurt, Magdeburg, and all the imperial towns of Germany, which are governed like commonwealths; and the thirteen cantons of the Swiss; you shall find that they straightly observe this rule, to receive no strangers into offices and public charges. Yea, in many places they will not receive strangers for inhabitants, wherein it may be they hold too much severity and rigor. For hospitality is recommended unto us by God, and it is a very laudable virtue for men to entertain strangers and entertain them well; but strangers also ought to content themselves to be welcomed and entertained in a country or town, without aspiring to master or hold offices and estates. The French nation is that which of all Christendom receives and loves strangers most, for they are as welcome all over France as those of their own nation. Yet we have above showed that our predecessors were sometimes discontented with the English, who would needs have all estates and offices in Aquitaine, as may happen in this time; for nothing has been in times past which may not again be in this time.

The Salic Law, which is observed in France and through all Germany, was not only made to foreclose and bar women from the succession of the crown, and from sovereign domination by reason of imbecility and incapacity to well command, which is in the feminine sex; for in the masculine sex happen often such incapacities. But especially the Salic Law was made to the end that by marriage strangers should not come to the said succession of the crown. For it should be as an intolerable thing to a Frenchman to obey a strange king, as to obey a queen of the French nation, so odious is a foreign domination in France; as also that the consequence thereof with us should ever be evil. For a foreign king would always to estates and offices of the kingdom advance strangers of his own nation; a thing which would always cause in the end disorders and confusion, as is seen by the examples which we have before discovered.

There is also an ancient example of queen Brunehant, or Brunechile [Brunhilda], who advanced to the estate of Maire du Palais de France (which was as much as governor of all the kingdom) a Lombard called Proclaide, who was much in her good grace and amity. This stranger seeing himself lifted up so high, became so fierce and so proud that he made no estimate of the princes of the kingdom, but put them to many troubles and vexations. He became also very rapinous and covetous, as (says the history) is the nature of the Lombards; insomuch that he ate up and ruined the subjects of France. Briefly, his behavior and dealings were such that he got the evil wills of all men, from the nobleman to the carter. At that time there were amongst the children of the queen Brunehant Theodoric, king of Orleans, and Theodebert king of Metz. The barons and great lords, their vassals, desired to make a peace between the two kings' brothers, but this great Maire Proclaide hindered it with all his power; which the said lords seeing, resolved amongst them that it was better that strangers died than for so many gentlemen and subjects of the two kings to slay one another. And so indeed they did slay him as an enemy to peace and concord. The example of this Lombard should be well marked in this time by the Lombards who govern in France.

Louis le Debonance, son of Charlemagne, king of France and emperor of the West, altogether gave the estate of Maire du Palais de France to a Spaniard called Berard, who immediately mounted into great pride. The king had three sons, Lotharie, Louis, and Pepin, who could not support the arrogance and fierceness of this stranger, who as it were would paragon them. This was the cause of an evil enterprise of these three young princes against their own father. For they seized upon his person and brought him into the town of Soissons, and there caused him to forsake his crown and the estate of the empire, and to take the habit of a monk in the Abbey of St. Mark in Soissons, within which they had him kept straightly for a time. But in the end the great barons and lords of France and Germany meddled therein, and dismonked him and restored him to his estate, and agreed the father with the children. This had not happened if that good king and emperor had had that wisdom not to have lifted up a stranger so high; a thing which could not be but unpleasant to his natural subjects, great and little.

For a conclusion of this matter I will here place the witness of M. Martin du Bellay, Knight of the King's Order, a man of quality, virtue, and great experience, who says that he has seen in his time more evil happen to the affairs of king Francis I, by the means of foreigners who revolted from his service, than by any other means. Among which strangers he placed the Bishop of Liege, the prince of Orange, the marquess of Mantua, and lord Andrew Doria, Jerome Moron of Milan (who caused Milan to revolt), and certain others. But because these things are not of very ancient memory, but happened in our world, I will make no longer discourse thereof; seeing these examples and reasons are sufficient to show, against the opinion of Machiavelli's disciples, that a prince cannot do better than to serve himself in offices and public charges with his own subjects of the same countries, as being more fit and agreeable to the people than are foreigners. And as for offices, it has not been seen anciently and commonly that they have been bestowed upon strangers; but within this little space of time they have found means to obtain the greatest and best. For of old there was committed unto them only offices of captainships, so that under that title they might better draw people of their own country to serve the king. But as for benefices, it has long been that the Italians have held and possessed the best in France, which the pope bestowed on them, and our kings dare not contradict. Yet it gave occasion to Charles VI to make an edict in 1356, whereby he forbade that any benefices of the kingdom of France should be conferred upon foreigners; which before and since, by many royal edicts, has often been renewed and reiterated. Which edicts merit well to be brought into use; but it shall not be yet, since they are those who yet govern all.

But I pray here all those who are good Frenchmen, that they will consider a little nearer the wrong they do themselves, to suffer themselves to be reputed strangers in their own country, and by that means recoiled and kept from the charges and estates of the same. For Italians, or those who are Italianized, who have in their hands the governance of France, hold for true the maxim of Machiavelli; that men should not trust in strangers; as it is true. And this is because they would not advance any other but men of their own nation and certain bastardly and degenerate Frenchmen, who are fashioned both to their humor and their fashions, and who may serve them as slaves and most vile ministers of their treacheries, cruelties, rapines, and other vices. As for good and natural Frenchmen, they will never advance them, because they are strangers unto them, and in consequence suspected not to be faithful enough unto them, following the said maxim.

Where is now then the generosity of our ancient Frenchmen, who made themselves redoubted among foreign nations? Where are now our ancestors' virtues, who have caused the Levant to tremble and have sent out their reputation into Asia, and have repulsed and driven back the Goths and Saracens out of France, Spain, and Italy? For it seems that at this day the French hold no more anything of their ancestors' valor, seeing they suffer so few strangers to domineer so imperiously over them, and so to debase themselves to carry on their backs such insupportable burdens, and to suffer themselves to be driven from the charges and estates of the commonwealth. Truly this is far from making us to be redoubted and obeyed in foreign countries, when strangers constrain us to obey them and to take the yoke in our own country. This is to do clean contrary to our ancestors, who subjected strangers unto them, when contrary we subject our own selves to strangers.

The French were reputed to be frank and liberal, far from all servitude; but now our stupidity, carelessness, and cowardice make us servants and slaves to the most dastardly and cowardly nation of Christendom. Our ancestors have vanquished and subjugated in battle great Italian armies; but we suffer ourselves to be overcome by a small number of Italians armed with a rock, a spindle, and a pen and inkhorn. Shall we always be thus bewitched? See we not that by secret and unknown means they overthrow, and cause to die by treasons, poisonings, injustice, now one, now another of the greatest? And that they look to no other mark but to ruin the nobility and all men of valor in France, who are suspected to favor the commonweal, or disfavor them? Be sleepy no longer, for it is time to awake and to think what we have to do, and not to attend till we see all France upon the earth. It is already but too much established, and we have but too long attended to provide for our affairs, and to oppose ourselves against the designs and machinations of these strangers, all which are discovered and known to those who will not shut their eyes. Let us then stir up in ourselves the generosity and virtue of our valiant great grandfathers, and show that we are come from the race of those good and noble Frenchmen, our ancestors, who in time past have brought under their subjection so many foreign nations, and who so many times have vanquished the Italian race, who would make us now serve. Let us not leave off to maintain and conserve the honors, loyalty, integrity, and valiance of our French nation, which these bastardly Italians have contaminated and soiled by their cruelties, massacres and perfidies. We want nothing but courage to effect all this; for these messiers would stand not one whit if they knew once that it is in good earnest and with good accord that the Frenchmen would send them to exercise their tyrannies in their own country, and force them to make account of those they have committed in France.

Here ends the first part, entreating of such counsel as the prince should use

The second part, treating of the religion which a prince ought to hold

Preface

After having before discoursed largely enough what counsel a prince should have and take, it will not be to any evil purpose to handle what religion he ought to hold and cause to be observed in his dominions. For it is the first and principal thing wherein he ought to employ his counsellors; namely, that the true and pure religion of God be known; and being known, that it be observed by him and all his subjects. Machiavelli in this case (as a very atheist and contemner of God) gives another document to a prince; for he would that a prince should not care whether the religion he holds be true or false, but says that he ought to support and favor such falsities as are found therein. And he comes even to this point, as an abominable and wicked blasphemer, that he prefers the religion of the pagans before the Christians; and yet his books are not condemned by our Sorbonne. But before we enter to confute his detestable maxims, I will in manner of a preface demonstrate in few words the true resolution that a prince ought to have in this matter. I presuppose then by a certain maxim, that the prince ought to hold the Christian religion, as it is seen, by all antiquity, simplicity, and excellence of doctrine. For in the first place, none can deny but it is more ancient than any other of all the religions that ever were, because it takes its foundation upon the books of Moses and the promises of God, of Christ and Messiah, contained in those books, which were made to our first fathers from the beginning of the world. But there is no author, Greek or Latin, who was not long after Moses; and it was a thing confessed and held among all learned men that Moses wrote his books many hundreds of years before Homer, Berosus, Hesiod, Manethon, Metasthenes, and others like, which many men hold for the most ancient writers. Moreover, when Moses describes the generation of Noah and shows us that his children have been the first stem and root of divers nations of the world (in token and sign thereof, these nations hold yet at the present the names of such children); doth not this show plainly and truly that Moses began at the world's beginning? Of Madens came the Medes, of Janus the Ionians, of Jobel the Iberians, of Riphat the Riphaeng, of Tigran the Tigranians, of Tharsis the Tharsians, of Cithin the Cyprians, of Canaan the Canaanites, of Sidon the Sidonians, of Elam the Elamites, of Assur the Assyrians, of Lud the Lydians, and others. All these were the children, nephews, or arrear-nephews of Noah, from whence the said nations have taken their names. It follows therefore that they were the first flocks and roots of them. Again, if we look to the ceremonies that in times past the pagans used in their sacrifices, men shall easily know that they are but apish imitations of such sacrifices as were ordained by God, which are described by Moses. For the sacrifice of Iphigenia which the Greeks made in Aulide to prosper them in the war they enterprised against Troy, what else is it than an imitation of Japheth's sacrifice? Who made a vow of a sacrifice to prosper him in the war he enterprised; which sacrifice fell after by the divine will upon his own daughter. The custom of the Gauls and many other people to immolate and offer criminals when they had an opinion that God was angry with them; what other thing was it but a following of the sacrifice of Abraham, and of the sacrifices that God had commanded for the expiation of sins? The pagans also imitated this of Moses' sacrifices, that they immolated the like beasts and reserved also a part of the beast sacrificed to eat. So that thereby also it is clearly seen that the religion of Moses is the primitive and first, and that the other religions are but foul and lazy portraits and imitations thereof. From hence it follows that our Christian religion, which draws its principles from the promises of the Messiah contained in Moses, is the most ancient in the world, yea as ancient as the world itself. For I will not vouchsafe to stay upon the refutation of the strange opinion of Machiavelli and other ancient pagan philosophers, who have maintained that the world had no beginning; but I send them to Empedocles, Plato, and other ancient pagan philosophers who have maintained the contrary. I think that the ignorance of the philosophers who held that the world had no beginning shall excuse them, because they never saw the books of Moses, and in a thing so difficult and hard to comprehend, the spirits of men might easily fail. But the impiety of Machiavelli is no way excusable, who has seen the books of Moses and yet follows that wicked opinion, like a mocker and contemner of the holy scriptures, thinking to show that he knows more than others. He, I say, who is ignorant and full of brutish beastliness, as (God willing) I shall make known.

As for the simplicity of the Christian religion, herein it is seen that the Christians will know God as he wills that we should know him, and as he has manifested himself to us, without passing further. For they are not so presumptuous as were those foolish pagan philosophers who disputed about the essence of God, and disputing on that point fell into opinions, the most absurd and strange in the world. Some, after they had much dreamed in their brains, concluded that the universal world was God; others that it was the soul of the world; others that it was the sun;

and others put forward other like monstrous opinions. They also disputed of his power, of his eternity, and of his providence by natural reasons. In all these they knew not how to resolve themselves therein; for how is man so proud and insensible to think that his brain (which is not half a foot large) can comprehend so great and infinite a thing? It is as great a foolery and grossness as he that in the palm of his hand will comprehend all the waters of the sea. A Christian then has this modesty and simplicity, to know God by those means and according to how he will be known of men, believing that having a will to pass further is to enter darkness and not into knowledge. From hence follows that the knowledge which a Christian has of God is the only true knowledge, and that all the knowledge that others (as pagans and philosophers) ever had, neither was nor is anything but a shadow and imagination, very far from the most part of the truth.

And touching the excellence of the doctrine of true religion, herein it is first seen that it is founded upon the promises of God made to the first fathers from the beginning of the world. Whereby all they that embrace that religion are assured that God is their father, and that he loves them, and that he will give them eternal life by the means of the Messiah. Can there then be anything more excellent than this? Is there anything in the world that can give more contentment or repose to the spirit of man than this doctrine? For when man considers the brevity of his days, the languishing and misery of this world, full of envies, enmities, all vices and calamities, will he not judge himself more unhappy than those beasts if he hoped not for an eternal happiness after this life? The poor pagans having this consideration aspired to an eternity, some in doing worthy acts, whereof there should be a perpetual memory after them; others wrote books that might be read after their death; others persuaded themselves that the gods would send good men's souls into the Elysian Fields, and the wicked into the Acherontic and Stygian darkness. Yet were there some philosophers who disputed that the souls of generous and valiant men after death go to heaven. All these opinions and persuasions of men were but to give rest to their minds, which judged man of all creatures most unhappy without an eternal life after this. But what assurance had they of these opinions, which they gave to themselves? These poor people had none, neither founded they themselves but upon some weak and feeble reasons. For thus they argued that it was not credible that God, who is all good, would create man (who is the most excellent creature in the world) to make him most unhappy, which he should do if he should not enjoy a happy and eternal life after this. They also say that it is not credible that God, who is all just, would equally deal with the good and the bad; which he should do if there were not another life than this, wherein the good might receive a felicity, and the wicked punishment for their misdeeds. But what is all this? These are but feeble and weak, petty reasons, whereupon the spirits and consciences of men can find no good foundation to repose themselves, and to take an assured resolution of a salvation and an eternal felicity. But the Christian has another foundation than this, for he knows that God is of old gone out (if I may so say) from his throne in heaven to communicate and manifest himself to our ancient fathers, to speak unto them, to declare unto them his bounty and love towards mankind. He knows that God has made them promises of the Messiah, which he has since accomplished, and that in him he has promised to give eternal life to all those who lay hold of that Messiah and use his means to come unto it. These promises have been many times reiterated to our said fathers, and in ages well distant from each other, that they might not be forgotten, but that they might be so much the more clear and known by everyone. Insomuch that the pagans themselves (who never read our fathers' writings) have had some knowledge of the promises of God touching the Messiah, they were so clear, notorious and well known, as we shall say more fully in another place. Here therefore a resolution, a great excellency in this doctrine of the Christian religion, viz. that it brings us to a certain knowledge and a firm assurance of an eternal life after this; which knowledge and assurance is not founded upon certain lean philosophical reasons, but upon the promises proceeding from the very mouth of God, who is the truth itself, and cannot lie.

And as for the doctrine of manners, I confess that the pagans and philosophers who have held other religions have spoken and reasoned in reasonably good terms, but yet their doctrine comes nothing near to that which the Christian religion teaches us thereof. True it is that the pagans have spoken something well of justice, temperance, clemency, prudence, loyalty, fidelity, amity, gentleness, magnanimity, liberality, love towards one's country, and such other virtues. He who denies that they have spoken well, and that some have somewhat practiced them, should do them wrong. And the Christians have this in common with them, to approve and follow all these virtues, and for that cause they disdain not to read their books and to learn of them the goodly documents which they have left touching these virtues. But I must say that the Christian religion has launched and entered far deeper into the doctrine of good manners than the pagans and philosophers have done. For proof hereof I will take the maxim of Plato, that we are not only born for ourselves, but that our birth is partly for our country, partly for our parents, and partly for our friends. Behold a goodly sentence we can say no other; but if we compare it with the doctrine of Christians, it will be found maimed and defective. For what mention does Plato make of the poor? Where and in what place of this notable sentence does he set them? He speaks not at all of them; briefly, he would have it that our charity should be first employed towards ourselves, which they have well marked and followed who say that a well ordered charity begins with himself. But this is far from the doctrine which Saint Paul teaches the Christians when he says that charity seeks not her own; and also that which Christ himself commands, to love our neighbor as ourselves. Secondly Plato places our love towards our country, thirdly our love towards our parents, and lastly our friends. And what becomes of the poor? Let them do as they can, for Plato's charity stretches not to them. And indeed a poor person, in the time of the pagans, who had no means to live, had no shorter way than to sell himself to be a slave unto him who bought him, who afterward served himself with him and nourished him. If such a poor man found no man to buy him, he died with hunger. True it is that some were sometimes touched with commiseration of humanity towards poor persons, when they saw them languishing and in misery. But they called not this commiseration a virtue, but only a human passion. Neither had they any hospitals to lodge and nourish the poor in, nor their princes or great lords had their almoniers as Christians have. When a child was born deformed they would kill it, a cruel thing and full of inhumanity, yet it was ordinarily practiced; at Rome it was an express law of Romulus, whereby he commanded to expose and stifle the children who were born deformed. Which not only was a cruelty against nature, but as it were a spite and injury done to the Creator who had created and formed them. They made account of poor men as they did of beasts, for they slew their slaves at their pleasure, and when and for what they would. Vedius Polio, a Roman gentleman in the time of Augustus Caesar, ordinarily caused to slay his servants and slaves, of which he had a great number; choosing always the most profitable, cast the other bodies into his ponds which he had near his house, to feed lampreys. In the pagans' time, to offer pleasure and pastime to the people, they had theaters for combats of poor slaves, who they caused to band in two parts, one against another, furiously setting upon each other with naked swords, and none of them armed with anything for defense. This sport ended when they of one party had slain all the others, or else when all had slain one another to the last. The people laughed and took pleasure to see this, no more nor less than we take pleasure to see cocks fight. Hereby it is seen that the pagans had no pity for the poor, nor of slaves and servants, but regarded them as brute beasts, and made no more account of them than the service they drew from them. Also we never read among all their moral precepts that they ever spoke of the poor, nor that they ever established any good policy to help them. Yet notwithstanding this agrees well with natural reason, to do well to his like. And this so noble a sentence which the emperor Alexander Severus carried for his device: What you would not have done to thee, do it not to another. Which agrees well with common sense and seems well to be a principle of nature, not only in the negative but also in the affirmative. Yet although natural light leads us hereunto, the pagans have not yet come to this point; the historian Lampridius says that the emperor learned this excellent device from the Christians or the Jews of his time. Therefore it appears by the above said reasons that the doctrine of manners taught by the Christian religion is much more excellent than that which the religions of the pagans and philosophers teach, seeing they make no account of the poor, who are recommended to us by so many precepts of religion. Moreover, the Christian religion abases the pride of men's hearts, and so makes them know they are sinners; and the religion of the pagans and philosophers fill men with pride and presumption, persuading them that naturally they are virtuous of themselves, and inclined to do good and virtuous works, which they attribute to their own virtue and not to God. Yet more, the Christian religion teaches us to be patient, to support the imperfections of one another, and to pardon; but contrary, that of the pagans and philosophers persuades to seek vengeance. For a conclusion, none can deny but that the doctrine of Christian religion is in all points more excellent and perfect than that of the pagan religion. But when I speak of the pagan religion, I understand all others. Religions, unless it be the Jewish religion, out of which the Christian takes its origin, I hold for pagans — the Turks, Saracens, and all other barbarous people, who allow neither the Old nor New Testament, and that have no knowledge in them.

But I do not doubt but some will here make a question in this time wherein we are, that is, what religion ought to be accounted Christian, whether the Catholic or Reformed. Hereunto I answer that we ought not to make two of them, and that it is but one same religion, and as the names Catholic, and Evangelist, and Reformed, are all one name, so is the thing itself. For the one and the other acknowledges Christ, which is the foundation, and hold the articles of the faith of the apostles, approve the Trinity and the sacraments of baptism and the holy supper; although there is some diversity in the understanding of certain points, we may not for that make them two separate religions. For in brief, the one and the other is Christian, seeing they take Christ for the foundation. But for this purpose I will here recite a discourse of a learned man which I lately heard at my lodging in my journey from Paris to Basel. By which discourse this good person maintained that the Catholic and Evangelists agree not only in name but in doctrine, although sophists will persuade to the contrary. This proposition at first seemed to me a very paradox, but when I heard and understood the reasons of that good man, his saying seemed very true. There was in the company a Catholic gentleman, not a great talker and babbler but a man very gentle and affable, who took great pleasure to hear this discourse, and asked many questions of this good man, whom I cannot name, for I never saw him before. He was no man of great show, neither was there any great estimation made of him at the beginning, before we heard him speak; but at the end of our table, when we had given thanks, upon certain talk we had of religion he put fort the said proposition. All the company prayed him to clear and illuminate that point, and to speak his full opinion therein; for there was neither Catholic nor Evangelist who did not greatly desire to understand that point. He began then in this manner, after he had prayed all the company to take in good part what he should say, and humanely to excuse his faults, if any escaped.

"Masters, I see well that all this company casts their eyes upon me, attending to hear of me the proof of the proposition which I uttered. To satisfy then your desires, although I have not premeditated all the reasons which might be spoken to maintain that I say: yet I will allege some, which I hope you will not find impertinent. I will then here repeat my proposition, that is, That the Catholics hold the same points of Christian religion that we of the Reformed or Evangelist do. True it is, that the sophisters will needs persuade the Catholics that we hold another doctrine than they do, especially touching the Sacrament of the Altar, or the Supper (for all is one) and touching good works and certain other points. And in verity, the doctrine of our religion differs far from that of the sophisters, yea in principal points, as is seen by the conference of our confession of faith with their articles. But I say and will maintain that most of the Catholics understand not the articles of the sophisters; neither can they comprehend them, because they consist in certain subtle distinctions and sophistical terms. The school doctors, knowing that their doctrine cannot be comprehended by the simple sense and common judgment of men, make the people believe that it makes no matter though they understand nothing, if so be they believe generally that the articles of their faith be true. And this they call an implicit, wrapped, or entangled faith, that is to say, it is so covert and hid that the people understand nothing. But I mean not to speak of the sophists' doctrine, but of such points of religion whereof the Catholics have some knowledge by the apprehension of sense and common judgment. For I maintain, and it is true, that in these points or in the most part, and especially in the chief things they agree with us, although the sophisters make them believe the contrary. And by the way to make it appear, let us a little discourse upon the principal articles of our Christian religion (as of the Sacraments, of justification, of works, and certain other points) and we shall see plainly that the Catholics agree with us.

"First, if you ask a good Catholic if when he receives the Sacrament on Easter day, he crushes and bruises with his teeth the very flesh and bones of our Lord Jesus Christ, he will answer you, he believes it not, and that he detests and abhors that talk of crushing the bruising with the teeth the flesh and bones of our Savior. If you ask of him if he does not believe that when he receives the Sacrament he receives spiritually the body and blood of our Lord Jesus Christ; he will answer, yea, that he believes so. If you yet ask him if when he receives the sacrament of the Host, he believes that he receives and drinks by the same means the sacrament of the blood by concomitance; and that the cup which is given him to drink in is not but for him to rinse his mouth withal; he will say he believes not this, and that eating is not drinking, and that he knows not what concomitance is; and that he believes that receiving the Host he eats the Sacrament of the body, and that drinking on the cup he drinks the Sacrament of the blood. If you demand of him if he believes not that in the holy sacrament there is made a transubstantiation; he will answer you that he believes it not, because he knows not what transubstantiation is, nor what they mean by that long and prodigious word, and that he thinks it is some obscure word invented by sophisters to hide from simple people holy things, and to darken clear things. And truly it is a strange thing, and abhorring from common sense and from all humanity and Christianity, to bruise and burst the human flesh and bones of our Savior Christ between our teeth. And the sophisters would so persuade the good Catholics if they could, that they found this goodly doctrine upon a Canon, which begins *Ego Beringarius*. Where there is this in proper terms. Beringer, unworthy deacon of the church of Saint Maurice of Angiers, knowing the true Catholic and Apostolic faith, detest and anathematize all heresy, even that whereof I have been before defamed. Therefore I confess with heart and mouth that the bread and the wine which are set on the altar after the consecration, are not only the Sacrament but are changed into the body and blood of our Lord Jesus Christ; and that the priest touches not only sensually the Sacrament, but that also he handles with his hands the very body of our Lord, and that he breaks it, and that the faithful break and bruise it between their teeth. Behold the goodly doctrine of this canon, which the sophists would make the Catholics believe; but of five hundred you shall not find one that will believe it. And verily, this canon makes me remember what Archaemenides says in Virgil of the great Polyphemus, who did eat the companions of Ulysses.

> Poor human creatures did he eat, the body, blood, and all:
> My self did see him clasp and grip in his so deep a den,
> Two men of ours in his huge hands, their heads on door lintel
> He knocked so, that blood gushed out, and in my sight those men

He tore and bruised between his teeth, yet dead they were not clean.

"And how should Catholics believe this canon, seeing the priests themselves believe it not? I prove it. For if they believed it they would never say mass upon Fridays, nor in Lent or other fasting days; and the Charterhouse, Celestines nor Enfumine friars and monks would say no masses, for fear to eat flesh. O, but will one say this is a strange reason; I confess it, but the aforesaid Canon is as strange, and how strange soever, yet can it not be overthrown without giving some spiritual interpretation unto the manducation of the Sacrament. But straight as soon as a man comes there, behold we are at an agreement. You see then how the Catholics, yea the priests themselves believe not in that canon which notwithstanding is the only foundation of the mass. Yea, but you will say, the Catholics go to mass and find it good. I confess it, but it is upon custom they go thither, not because they understand or believe any other thing touching the Sacrament, than that we have already said. And therefore seeing they do agree with us in the principal, there shall be no great danger nor loss for them to send away and banish into the Cyclopian Islands or into Polyphemus' den their mass, yea, though but for a time to see and prove whether they might well and commodiously spare it or no. As we read Pope Clement VI did, who excommunicated all the people of the country of Flanders for a certain rebellion that they had made against the king of France, their sovereign; who also interdicted all the priests of the country, upon pain of eternal damnation, to say no masses, nor to administer any Sacraments to the Flemings, till they had obtained absolution of his fatherhood. The poor Flemings seeing themselves without masses (for in no sort would their priests say any), they wrote to the king of England, making unto him great complaints. The king of England sent them word not to be dismayed nor troubled for want of masses, for he would send them priests out of his country to say them enough. But the priests of England went not, fearing to be comprehended in that fulmination of the pope. In the meanwhile the Flemings attending whilst the king of England sent the priests, accustomed themselves so much to be without masses, being merry and making good cheer, that they were well, and no more it troubled them. Many other countries also at this day which have no masses, pass the time well enough to their content, as England, Scotland, and Denmark, and most of Germany. I believe also, if men did assay it in France to obtain peace and union, they would not find it so evil as they think. For already we agree upon the Sacrament, as is abovesaid; we hold also the Epistles, Gospels, and the lessons which are taken out of the Psalms of David, and the Prophets; for we shall always find that in our Bible; yea, far more faithfully enregistred than in the Missal; all the remainder is not worth the holding. For as for their massing garments, men of good judgment know well that apparel adds no holiness to the mass; seeing also that Frenchmen naturally stay not long in one fashion of apparel, but easily change from one to another. I confess in regard of the common people, which only stay upon that they see, that they will take no great lust in a mass without the mass garments; as if the Curate said it in his doublet and hose without more, or in his jerkin, it is certain that commonly the parishioners would greatly scandalize it and would not find it good. And yet a true thing it is that apparel makes not the mass better, neither have they any sanctity in them to deserve to be retained. For if it were true that such garments make the mass better and add any holiness unto it, then it would follow that the better the garments and habits are, so much the better should the masses be; and then would there be found great inequality in the bounty and goodness of masses; and so would it follow that the masses of rich men should be better than poor men's, a thing very absurd and odious. That were also to make village masses of no account, because their mass garments are often tattered and rent. So that we must come to this resolution, to shun these absurdities; that garments bring no holiness to the mass, and that in retaining the holy Sacrament, the Gospel, the Epistles, and the lessons of the Psalms and the Prophets which are in the mass, there would be found no danger to let go of all the rest. Now then if we lay by through all France the superfluous things of the mass, are not all the rest of the exercises of religion alike? The Catholics go to church to pray unto God; so do we also. They go to hear sermons of the word of God; so do we also. They go thither to keep their Easter; and we also. For it is all one to celebrate the Easter and the Supper. Briefly, all our exercises of religion are alike. I know well you will say there is a difference, because the Catholics pray and sing psalms in Latin; and we in French. But I answer you that that is nothing, so that men understand what they say. For God understands well all languages. You will say unto me also that the preachers of the one and of the other preach not the same doctrine. Yet I answer that though it be so, yet do we agree in all the principal points of religion which are necessary to be known for the salvation of our souls. If in any other points our preachers cannot agree, we must let them agree amongst themselves, and content ourselves to know the articles which are necessary for our salvation. For it cannot be said that if we cannot be as subtle and sharp as Saint Thomas Aquinas, Bonaventure, Scot, Bricot, or other like doctors of theology, that therefore we must needs be damned. It were a very strange thing to believe that God would have his holy religion so obscure that none but sophists should think to understand anything of it. But contrary, we must believe that God has given it unto us simple, clear, and intelligible, that even plain people might comprehend and understand it. So if it please God, we need not leave to be saved, although we know not what means transubstantiation, concomitance, and such like terms which are not read in the Bible; and although we be not so sharp and quick to understand the nature of quiddities, the subsistence of accidents separated from the subject, the effects and operations of second intentions, the motion of the Chimaera in Vacuity, and other like deep subtleties of speculative theology. But I have above showed that the Catholics and we do well accord in the

Sacrament of the Altar, or the Supper; so do we in the principal points of Christian religion. Demand of a Catholic, if he does not believe that he shall be saved by the merit of the death and passion of our Lord Jesus Christ; he will say, yea, that he believes it. Ask yet of him if he does not believe that one only drop of the precious blood our Savior, the eternal son of God, is sufficient to save all the world; he will say, yea. Make upon it this consequence, that it follows then that the death and passion of Jesus Christ, who shed all his blood for us, is more than sufficient for our salvation; he will not deny this. Ask him after, if he believes that for our salvation there must be mingled the blood of martyrs, supererogatory works, merits of Saints, and good works, with the blood of Christ, the son of God; he will answer you that he believes not that there must be such a mingle mangle, since the blood of the son of God is sufficient for our salvation; and that that should be to pollute it, and that he knows not what supererogatory works are. And touching good works, which they say we reject; ask of the least child who learns the Catechism, if a Christian ought to do good works to show himself a Christian; he will answer you, yea. Demand of him also if good works be not meritorious towards God; he will answer you that they so please God, that (in regard of them as by merit) an infinite sort of good things are given us, as health, long life, children, and other graces, except eternal life, which he gives us by the only merit of Jesus Christ. I believe there is no Catholic in the world who will say more of good works than this. As for faith in general, we receive but the one and the other, the holy Scripture of the Old and New Testament. Touching baptism, we agree in the substance, namely, that it ought to be done in the name of the Father, the Son, and the Holy Ghost, and with the sign of the water. We differ about spittle, salt, and the conjurations of devils, which the Catholic priests do say to be within the body of little children, and they chase them out; we indeed cast off all this as men's inventions, who would be wiser than God, who prescribes them what they shall do therein. And I assure myself that most Catholics would willingly that those things were rejected; and that priests would not spit in the mouths of their little children; and that they had no salt at all; neither do they believe there are devils within the bodies of their little children. We also differ in certain other ceremonies, which I will not discover now at length. But must we hereupon say that the Catholics are we are of two diverse religions? The Friars and Jacobins, and many other sorts of monks in Christendom, have all different ceremonies, in habits, in rules, in doing their services and in all the exercises of their orders, yet they are all held to be of the Christian religion. Moreover, though there were some difference between us touching doctrine (seeing we accord in the principal points of Christian religion), must there be accounted a plurality and diversity of religion among us for the canon *Ego Berengarius*? Must men make all that stir, to roar out all the cannons and artillery of France, and thunder at all the towns and castles of the kingdom, to fill all places with arms, soldiers, and all the towns with the blood of Christians, and to make red the rivers for such a quarrel as this?

Must brother arm himself against his brother, the father against his son? must needs the nobility ruin itself? must all the people be trodden underfoot, and the whole realm be brought into a combustion? For verily none makes war upon us but because we will not believe in the aforesaid canon, and yet they who do this unto us do not believe in it themselves, as we have before showed. But yet there is a point that seems to be one of the most principal points of religion wherein we differ, namely, touching the pope, in whom we believe not. But I am of opinion that most Catholics believe in him no more than we; and that the matter is not of sufficient weight to make any great contention of. Our ancestors in times past have well passed their time without a pope; and wherefore should not we do so, as well as they. In the time of king Charles VI there were two popes in Christendom, the one at Rome called Pope Urban, and the other at Avignon, who was called Clement. The Christian princes and commonweals at this time knew not which was the better of them; yet some followed the pope of Rome, and they were called Urbanists, and others the pope of Avignon, and they were called Clementines. And when the pope died at Rome or in Avignon, men elected always another in his place; so that it appeared that this plurality of popes would ever endure. The king of France and his counsel were occasioned to exhort both of them to submit themselves to a council which might advise and ordain which of the two should be pope, or if the one or the other ought not to be. The king could never persuade them to come to this accord; and especially the pope of Avignon was more backward than the other. Hereupon the king caused to assemble the University of Paris, and especially our masters of Sorbonne, to have their advice what he should do in this case. At that time was there a learned doctor in theology in Sorbonne College, who was called M. John de Gigenconet, who maintained that the Catholic church might well for a time be without a pope, yea, forever; and alleged many good reasons, which for time's sake I will not here recite. Briefly, the University was congregated, and thereby it was resolved that the king ought to withdraw himself and all his kingdom from the obedience of both the popes until another was legitimately elected. And that there were good means to be dispatched of the pope, viz. to leave the collations of benefices to the ordinary collators, and also to labor unto the prelates of France for dispensations requisite. Hereupon the king made an edict with the advice of his daughter the University (so he names it) whereby inhibitions and defenses were made to all subjects, as well of the nobility and the clergy as of the third estate, no more to acknowledge either of the said popes; for popes neither any more to run either to Rome or Avignon for the obtaining and impetration of benefices, dispensations, or other bulls and provisions Apostolical; but to the ordinary collators and to the prelates of the French church, upon pain to be debarred of their pretended right, and other great punishments. Which edict was observed by the space of three years, at the end of which time a pope was chosen at the Council of Pisa, called Alexander V, under whose obedience the king and his kingdom yielded themselves. But the space of the said three years they did well enough without a pope in France; and so likewise during the said time of plurality of popes, which endured forty years. And there were then many princes who acknowledged neither the one nor the other for popes; as the king of Aragon, the count of Hainaut, the duke of Brittany, the commonwealth of Liege. If then in times past so many could be without popes, why might we not as well spare them now as then? But as I have said before, I see not why the Catholics should so much care for the pope as to travel and journey so far as Rome to kiss his pantophle, nor to spend so much money to buy his pardons, being such vile and base merchandise. To conclude (my masters) it seems unto me by this brief discourse I have made hitherto, that my proposition is sufficiently cleared; that the Catholic and we differ not in religion, but agree in all points necessary for our salvation."

After the good parson had made us the said discourse, truly every one of us thanked him, but especially the Catholic gentleman, saying that as for him he never believed otherwise the points which he had delivered, but even as he had said; and that he would never have thought that they of the Evangelist religion had accorded so well with the Catholics, as he saw they did. "But," said he, "my masters, after so serious a discourse, it should not be impertinent to add another to make us laugh." All the company prayed him to do it; then he began to say in this manner.

"I have above touched how habits and apparel brought no sanctity to the mass; we must also say that they add no sanctity to the persons, neither according to that common proverb, apparel makes not a monk. Yet I find that this question has been sometimes handled with great contention and diversity of opinions, which endured nigh fifty years amongst the friars, because they could not accord upon the color, greatness, wideness, and form of their habits. For you must understand that the glorious Saint Francis, among other articles of his rule he had placed one whereby he ordained that all that were of his order for apparel should clothe themselves with the basest, vilest, and of the lowest price that could be; that they should only have one coat with a hood, and another without; and that they should wear no shoes, nor ride on horseback. Upon the intelligence and interpretation of this article arose great and marvelous altercations and disputations in the order of friars; insomuch that they held a general Chapter to accord those disputations, and to rule themselves all by one sort of habit. For some wore habits of one color, some of another, some short, others long; insomuch that they seemed not to be of the same order. In this Chapter there was a great disputation about the intelligence and interpretation of the said article. About the last two points they were easy to agree; for seeing they were forbidden by the said article to ride on horseback, they resolved to ride but on asses and mules, or on foot, as commonly they do. They considered also that asses were fittest for them in their convents, for being kept with least charge.

As for shoes, they resolved that they would take away the most part of the leather, leaving only a sole with a thong, to go overthwart the foot, to make the sole fast to the foot, and so should they not be shoes, but shoes. But the greatest difficulty and strife was about the fashion of the hood, and of the coat or jacket. For in the said Chapter were moved three principal questions, by certain subtle and cunning friars; the first upon the color, the second upon the quantity, and the third about the form. But to handle these three questions in order, you must understand that about the color there were divers opinions upon which they could not accord. For the blessed Saint Francis had spoken nothing of the color in his rule, but only ordained that those of his order should wear habits of a low price. Then fell out a great question: what color was of the least price, and thought to be most vile. Some reasoned that the green color was the vilest, and might be bought cheaper than any other; and that it was ordinarily seen that people of most vile condition (as carters, mariners, and other mean people) did wear that color in lining to their doublets, as the worst color of all. They said also that the matter wherewith a green color is made is cheaper than any other; for with herbs and leaves green may be made to dye both woolen and linen. Others said the murky or smoky color was the worst and best cheap; for to make that color there need no more but to take white wool and soot. But the third opinion seemed to be best taken with reason and equity; and that was they who said that there was no viler color, nor more meet for their Order, than that which came from the beast's back itself. But it is so, that both white and black came from the beasts' backs; and it is evident that the blessed Saint Francis did so understand it, they should wear the color of the beast in token of humility and patience; saying further that all other colors cost something, if it were but labor; but the color of the beast cost nothing. Therefore they concluded that all the Order of friars ought to wear their garments either of white or black color, and not of green, smoky, or any other colors, and that this was their opinion. Assuredly these reasons of the first disputers were so pregnant that they shaked all the rest of the company; yet notwithstanding those who had disputed for green and smoky colors, thinking it not good to be overcome at the first blow, replied more. They who have disputed of the color of the beast (say they) do show that they hold something of the beast (speaking under the brotherly correction of their superiors, and the Chapter) for that their conclusion is alternative and indeterminative. For they conclude upon white and black, without resolving either upon the one or the other; and that such a conclusion implied evident contradiction. For (say they) there is nothing more contrary than white and black. Moreover, they said that if so be the colors of the sheep be worn by them, men would judge it to be a token of their pride and presumption, which is the greatest of all mortal sins, because for pride Lucifer fell from heaven into hell. For the world may say of them that they cover themselves with the color of the sheep, and notwithstanding are ravening wolves; seeing it is written that men must take heed of them that make outward countenance to be sheep, and yet are wolves, and by that similitude are they noted to be false prophets. They showed also that already other orders of beggars or mendicants have taken possession of those two colors, black and white. For the Jacobins wore white under, and black above. And the Carmelites contrary, black under, and white above; and generally all sorts of other monks who held the rules of Augustine, Bernard, and the blessed Saint Benedict, and others were all monks either white or black. And that it should not be well done to take from them their colors, or to enterprise upon them; for so they might oppose themselves against them, and that that was not the way to draw unto them the devotion of the world. Finally they showed that if their Order of friars took black, there are some countries where there are no black sheep, or very few, as in Berry, Limoges, and Languedoc; then in these countries must they be forced to dye their wool, so would it become dear, and then directly they should do against the rule of blessed Saint Francis that bids them wear clothes of the vilest and cheapest price. This should also be to go against their liberties and privileges, to pay the least they can; for by their rule they are forbidden to handle any silver. And by the contrary, if the order choose a white color, there are other countries where there are no white sheep, or very few; as in Tuscany and many other places, so that the friars there must have their white clothes out of far countries, which will be to their great cost, and so will be directly against the said rule and their liberties. And therefore these disputers persisted still in their first opinion for green and smoky colors. The others who had reasoned for the color of the beast, finding themselves pinched and pricked, replied that that opinion of green and smoky color was the most savage opinion of the world, and according to the reason they had which maintained it. For (said they) green is a color fit for fools. Moreover, in countries where they say there is nothing but coal-black wool, how can they dye that black, green, or smoky? Finally, their disputation became so hot that it was greatly to be feared they would have fallen to fits, if certain ancient fathers sitting in highest places had not imposed silence to the brethren, and made them understand that truly they had well and learnedly debated the matter both of the one part and of the other, and that they thought that the question was weighty, high, and hard, and such as merited the advice and resolution of the holy father the pope, and that therefore they would reserve unto him the determination thereof. As soon as the friars heard speak of the pope, each one held his peace.

"After this, the senior fathers caused to propose the second question of the three for which the Chapter was assembled, touching the quantity of habits, that is, if they should be long, short, wide, or strait. The first disputers, in great number, were all of advice that their garments of order ought to be short and straight, for many good reasons which they alleged. For, said they, habits short and straight are more vile and better cheap than long and large, because they have not so much stuff in them. Therefore since the glorious Saint Francis our founder, willed and ordained that we should wear habits of vile and little price, we cannot better observe that holy rule (wherein consists the estate of perfection) than in making our habits as short and as straight as possible. Moreover (said they) our father and good founder Francis, has he not appointed we should be mendicants, and live upon the alms of good people? therefore we must make account to gather our alms to live, and to seek it sometimes far off, upon pain to endure hunger and want; for we shall have little brought into our convent, then must we trot hither and thither at all times, rain it or hail it, be it hot, cold, dry, or wet, yea in Lent and Advents, to preach, but no kind of habits is more meet to overthwart the fields, than such as are short, for the long are unfit. Contrary, such as reasoned after said that the same opinion was strange and ridiculous; because if friars wore short habits, they would seem more like millers than friars; and it is ordinarily seen that in those countries where friars use short habits, the order was much despised and mocked by the world, and men called them curtal friars; and therefore long and large were most covenable and fit for them; and that (that blessed Saint Francis rightly understood) they should wear long habits; for in the said article he uses the word tunic, which signifies a long robe or garment. Moreover, long habits are more seemly for religious men, and short garments for lay men; and that a long garment makes religious men the most reverenced and honored in the world. They said further that all other sorts of monks wore long and wide habits, and it should be a great novelty if the order of the glorious Saint Francis should take a short habit. Likewise (said they) when we go into the pulpit to preach, or when we go to say mass, it is a goodly sight to have our garments like millers. Therefore they concluded that their habits should be long and large. But the first reasoners replied to this, saying to the first point that the good Saint Francis had taught them the way of humility, and that therefore they ought not to seek to wear long garments, to be therefore honored and reverenced by the world; for that tasted of pride, and not of his humility; and that those who are mocked and despised by the world are esteemed by God; because the wisdom of the world is folly before God. As for the second point, they said that this word tunic in Saint Benedict's rule signifies not a long robe, but a little cloak or cassock; and so is it found in friar Ambrose Calepin's dictionary (who was of our order) not a long robe, but a toga; and that therefore the rule makes for them in that point. So is it best that friars wear short habits, as little cloaks and cassocks, or jerkins. And as for their objection, that other monks wear long and wide garments; so much the better, said they, and the rather should we wear short and straight, that there may be a distinction between us and others. As for their reason, that to wear short and straight garments would make us like lay men; we answer to that (say they) that the hood will make a difference between us and laymen; for the length of garments cannot distinguish us from lay people, for they also wear long robes, as proctors, advocates, counsellors, huishers, physicians, yea even merchants in their shops. We confess (said they) that at the beginning it will be a novelty to see us wear garments short and straight with a hood, but time and custom will take away the strangeness thereof, for in all things there is a beginning.

"The chief and ancient fathers, rulers of this disputation, seeing their friars (who came in place to accord) to enter and grow further into contention and contrariety of opinions, imposed them silence as they had done before upon the first question, and said unto them that they would remit to the holy Father the decision and resolution of this high and hard question, touching the largeness and length of habits; but yet they must advise if at least in this Chapter we may resolve upon the third question, touching the form and fashion of these habits.

"So they began to demand voices for to know whether their habits ought to be single or double; if it be lawful to have some fine and goodly fashion on them, or not; if they should have collars, or none; of skirts, or none; of sleeves, or no sleeves; or if sleeves, whether hanging sleeves; if there must be a hood, whether it were not best to be pointed and sharp, as the Carthusian friars have, or round, as they of other religions have. Upon all those points there was great disputation, and all matters were well and subtly disputed of in this Chapter. It seemed to some that it were not best to have hanging sleeves, for they were not comely, but rather wide and open sleeves, that they might serve for a scrip or pouch. For (said they) since our good father St. Francis has commanded us to beg and live by alms; and that by an article of his holy rule he has forbidden us to carry with us poke, bag, or scrip; as also is forbidden us in the Gospel, it follows well that he would have us to understand that we should have great and wide sleeves for to put our alms in. To this some answered that wide sleeves were dearer than straight; for that they had more matter and stuff in them, and therefore such sleeves are contrary to their rule. And as for the difficulty found out upon the forbidding of bags and scrips, and of the inconvenience that might follow thereof, for want of something to put in their alms; they said, for this there was a help, viz. to take a man with them (which we may call a Judas) who may carry a bag or scrip for that use, yea, he may take silver, if any will give it us.

"Yet were there made many other great arguments and subtle allegations upon this question of the fashion of habits; and some thought it best that that fashion of hoods which the Charterhouse friars used, to be well and best to be imitated. For that the sharp point above might allegorically signify that they had sharp and quick spirits; and having a fame and reputation to be so, their sermons would be more accounted of. But the good fathers considering that nothing could be resolved in that Chapter; and that it was as expedient to send to Rome for three questions as for two, they made the company privy to their advice, namely, that it were best to send to Rome to have the holy father's opinion and counsel upon these three questions; and that some of them present should go for that purpose.

"Certain time after, delegates of their order took their journey to Rome unto Pope Nicholas III, who reigned in the year 1280; which made him understand all the said disputations and the great disorder that was in their order about the said three points. The pope and his cardinals were as much troubled to resolve those high and subtle questions as the said friars had been in their Chapter. Yet the pope, by the advice of the said cardinals, made them upon this matter this resolution; that he ordained and commanded that upon all those questions, that should be straightly kept and observed which should be concluded and determined in a Chapter general, or else in provincial Chapters, which to those ends should afterwards be convocated and assembled; upon condition notwithstanding that always there might be seen shine in the friars and in their works a holy poverty, according to their holy rule. But this was to make them fall into a far greater contention and disputation than ever; so as also in their Chapters which they held afterward, they could never accord, following that ordinance of the pope; but resolved yet again to return to the pope, which they did, but it was about one and thirty years after the former time, during which time they held many Chapters to handle that matter.

"Coming then to no end in their Chapters, they again sent delegates to Rome to Pope Clement V, who then held the Council of Vienna in 1311; who gave him to understand how according to the ordinance of Pope Nicholas, his predecessor, they had done all that which possible they could do to overcome the aforesaid difficulties; which at length they recited unto him, but they could not accord upon any resolution. But contrary, that as they disputed, there arose always new difficulties and doubts in the friars' spirits, and that they therefore came to him as to a very oracle of truth, who could and knew how to resolve all those doubts and many others. The pope having heard them put the patter unto the determination of the cardinals, prelates, doctors, and others assembled in that Council; you must think that this whole Council was greatly troubled, as before pope Nicholas and his cardinals had been. Yet that the said friars might not go away as they came, without having answer from the pope's oracle, there was delivered unto them indeed a true oracle; that is to say, an ambiguous and obscure answer, whereby the pope, by the advice of the said Council, commanded the guardians and other chief ministers of that Order to judge of the vility, color, length, wideness, and fashion of their said Order; the consciences of which commissaries and guardians he burdened, and commanded all the friars that they should obey what their said guardians and ministers should resolve, without seeking out so many scruples and doubts, and without desire to know more than needed, by inventing so many subtleties. These delegates returned home with a fair bull, yet was it not possible by any virtue thereof to set down a rule in habits. For always the friars found to speak against the advice and resolutions of their guardians, saying they understood nothing, and that they had not read the text of the rule of blessed St. Francis, and that they were but beasts. In this contestation of friars against their guardians and superiors, remained their affairs by a long and great space of years.

"Finally, in the year 1323, in the time of Pope John XXII, who held his seat at Avignon, the guardians and superiors of that order went to complain to his fatherhood, showing him that they could not be obeyed upon the resolution they had made in virtue of the power which had been given them by the said bull of pope Clement. So they humbly prayed his said fatherhood that he would vouchsafe to do some good therein. The pope to proceed in this matter more judiciously would hear the party; and therefore sent to those friars who refused to obey their guardians and superiors, that they should either come and make their reasons, or send the cause in writing why they refused obedience. They sent them. The abovesaid pope assembled his cardinals; and being in the conclave, the allegations of the friars' pretended disobedience were read, and no doubt found so great and admirable, so subtle and sharp that a fly could not there have placed her food, and indeed they could never give a resolution thereof. True it is, that the pope could do no less for his honor than to ordain something. Therefore caused he to expedite a bull wherein he exceedingly praised the bulls of his predecessors, popes Nicholas and Clement, and said that he marveled how men cannot be contented with the resolution contained in them. After, he makes declaration that the vility of habits should be measured according to the custom of every country. After that, he gives commission to the guardians and superiors of every order (as did pope Clement) to make a rule for the longitude, latitude, thickness, color, fashion, and vility, as well of the tunics as of the hood, and upon all other accidents, circumstances, and dependences; willing and commanding them to obey the rule that should be made, without any more framing so many objects, arguments, and fantastical contradictions.

"Behold in substance the content of pope John's bull; whereby it appears that neither he nor all the Papal Consistory could ever give a law or a well determined resolution upon the matter of the dispute of friars' habits. I know not how since, they are accorded; but they have taken unto them the white and black color, as it comes from off the beast, and of those two intermingled colors they have made a third color, which of them has taken the name, and at this day are called gray-friars. They have also chosen great side gowns and great hoods, as we see them wear at this day. Briefly, we see them accorded now of all their differences which they had touching the fashion of their habits, except for the sleeves. For there are yet friars with great sleeves, others with straight sleeves.

"This is the discourse touching the friars' contentions, and the three decretals made by three popes upon that matter, whereof the last is called an Extravagant, as in truth it is, and may well be called Extravagant, and the other two also. Praying you, masters, to take it in good part this history; for I have not told it to displease any man, but to pass away the time while our horses eat their provender; I believe it will be now soon time to leap on horseback, every man to draw to his way."

Upon this, each man rose up from the table, everyone contented to hear this discourse which they never heard before, as they all confessed. Then each man took his count, payed, mounted on horseback, and went away. Now let us come to treat Machiavelli.

2.1
Machiavelli

A prince above all things should wish to be esteemed devout, though he be not so indeed. (*The Prince*, chapter 18)

The world looks but to the exterior, and by appearance; and judges actions not by the causes, but by the issue and end. So it suffices for a prince to seem outwardly religious and devout, although he be not so at all. For let it be so, that those who most narrowly frequent his company discover that feigned devotion, yet he or they dare not impugn the multitude, who believe the prince to be truly devout.

Answer

This maxim is a precept whereby this atheist Machiavelli teaches the prince to be a true contemner of God and of religion, and only to make a show and a fair countenance before the world, to be esteemed religious and devout, although he be not. Divine punishment for such hypocrisy and dissimulation Machiavelli fears not, because he does not believe there is a God. He thinks that the course of the sun, the moon, the stars, the distinction of the springtime, summer, autumn, and winter, the political government of men, the production that the earth makes of fruits, plants, living creatures; that all this comes by encounter and adventure, following the doctrine of Epicurus (the doctor of atheists and master of ignorance), who esteems that all things are done and come to pass by fortune and the meeting and encountering of atoms. But if Machiavelli believed that those things came by the disposition and establishment of a sovereign cause, as common sense has constrained Plato, Aristotle, Theophrastus, and all the other philosophers who have had any knowledge to confess, he would believe there is one God who rules and governs the world and all things within it. And if he believed there is one God, he would also believe that men ought to honor him as the sovereign governor, and that he will not be mocked by his creatures. And therefore he would not give such precepts, to make a show to be devout and not to be. For what is it to mock God, if that is not? But those that learn such lessons of atheism, and who put out their eyes that they may not see so clear a light, take pleasure to be ignorant of what (as Cicero says) even nature itself teaches the most barbarous nations; that there is a God who governs all things. Let them know that if they will not know God well, God will well know them, and will make them feel that those who spit against heaven spit against themselves; when they feel how heavy his hand weighs, then shall they know that there is a God, a revenger of those who do not reverence him; but this knowledge shall be to their confusion and ruin. Many atheists have been seen who of a brutish boldness made mock of God; but it was never seen that they felt not the punishment and vengeance of their audaciousness and impiety, as hereafter we will show by examples. Yet we have cause to greatly deplore the misery and calamity of the time wherein we are, which is so infected with atheists and contemners of God and of all religion that even those who have no religion are best esteemed and called in the court language people of service. Being fraught with all impiety and atheism, and having well studied their Machiavelli, which they know upon their fingers, they make no scruple nor conscience at anything. Command them to slay and massacre, they slay and massacre; command them to rob and spoil good Catholics and clergymen, they rob and spoil all. They hold benefices with soldiers' garments and short cloaks, yet exercise no religion nor cares but for the gain thereof. Command them to betray or poison this or that person, they make no scruple at it; yea, they themselves think and devise all wickedness and impieties, as the invention of so many new taxes upon the poor people, who they destroy and cause to die with hunger, without any commiseration or compassion upon them, no more than upon brute beasts. But many years ago, did they not invent the tax of processes and contentions of law in France? By the means of which tax a poor man cannot seek by law to recover his own, unless beforehand he pays the tax and shows his acquittance. But by the means of that generous Prince of Conde it was taken away, by his complaints against these atheists, inventors of such novelties, who both by nation and religion are Machiavellians. Have they not also invented new customs, tributes, and taxes upon paper, inns, the sales of exemptions for lodging soldiers, of wardships, of marriages, of consulships, syndics, and other such like, which cannot be devised but by impious people, who have neither love for their neighbor nor their country? The tax of the small seal, for sealing of contracts, did it not come from the same forge? If it had not been for the Evangelists, who alone dared open their mouths to complain of these bloodsuckers, would they not have made laws and coined edicts to command tributes and sums of money for each child that should be baptized? Likewise to levy the twentieth part of every woman's dowry upon the first conclusion of every marriage, even if they break off again? Have they not established the sale of offices of judgment, and so brought that now into common use which was utterly abolished by the Estates General at Orleans? Have they not devised the offices of counsellors without wages within bayliwicks and stewardships, and all for silver? Have they not, and do they not every day cause the value of money to be augmented for their own profit? For by the means of their banks, firms, and their other dealings in the realm, they have gathered great heaps of money, and can at their pleasure enhance the value thereof, both in their hands and out of their hands. Yet none complains thereof. But in the end it will produce and bring forth some great disorder and confusion, as has sometimes been seen for like actions, for reasons well enough known to wise people. As for peace, these people never like it, for they always fish in troubled water, gathering riches and heaps of the treasures of the realm while it is in trouble and confusion. They always have in their mouths the good maxims of their Machiavelli, to impeach and hinder a good peace. A prince, they say, must cause himself to be feared, rather than loved, and this must be held as a resolved point. But if a peace is accorded to these rebels, such as they desire, then it would seem that the king is afraid of his subjects, whereas he should make himself to be feared. True it is, that if such a peace could be made with them as it might again procure another Saint Bartholomew's journey, nothing were so good and pleasant as that. For that is another resolved point and maxim, that a prince should not hold any faith or promise but so far as concerns his profit; and that he ought to know how to counterfeit the fox, to catch and entrap other beasts, and as soon as he has them in his nets, to play the lion in slaying and devouring them. We have set down unto us that good example of Cesare Borgia, who in our country could so well counterfeit the two beasts. Behold here the language and dealings of our Machiavellians, who at this day men call people of service; for there is no wickedness in the world so strange and detestable but they will enterprise, invent, and put it into execution if they can. From whence comes it that they are thus inclined to all wickedness? It is because they are atheists, contemners of God, neither believing there is a God who sees what they do, nor that ought to punish them. It is that good doctrine of Machiavelli, who among other things complains so much that men cannot be altogether wicked, as we shall touch in its place. These good disciples, seeing that their master found this imperfection in them, that they could not show themselves altogether and in all things wicked, seek by all means to attain a degree of perfect wickedness. And indeed they have so well studied and profited in their master's school, and can so well practice his maxims, that none can deny but they are come unto the highest degree of wickedness. What need men then to be abashed if they see in the world, and especially in this poor kingdom of France, such famine, pestilence, civil wars, father against son, brother against brother, those of the same religion against each other, with all hatred, envy, disloyalty, treasons, perfidies, conspiracies, poisonings, and other great sins to reign? Is there any marvel if the people go to wrack, the clergy impoverished, the nobility almost extinct? For it is the first judgment of the vengeance of God, which he exercises against us because some are filled with all impiety and atheism, which they have learned from Machiavelli. And others who should resist such impieties lest they should take root, suffer them to increase and augment. So that indeed all men are culpable of atheism, impiety, of the spite of God and religion which at this day reigns. Therefore most righteously does God punish us all. For atheism and impiety is so detestable and abominable before God, that it never remains unpunished.

The emperor Caligula was a great atheist and contemner of God, and he was cunning enough to practice Machiavelli's maxims. To counterfeit his devotion, he caused to be bruited that he often spoke with Jupiter; and that he had great familiarity with Castor and Pollux, who he said were his brethren; and that he had good acquaintance with the moon. By this means he not only persuaded the people that he was very devout, but also by means of privacy with the gods that he participated even in divinity with them; and yet never man more boldly despised all divinity than he. But consider what such kind of people these are; there was never cowardly beast more fearful than this wicked atheist; as soon as he heard it thunder (says Suetonius), he would cover and quickly wrap his head and hide himself under his bed. I pray you what other thing was this but an extreme fear of conscience, when he hears the thundering and resounding voice of him whom he contemns? One day being beyond the Rhine with a great and puissant army, as he passed over a little strait on foot, someone near him began to say to him, "Sir, if now the enemy should appear and show himself, we could not be without fear?" What then did this cowardly atheist? At that word he straight mounted on horseback and fled as fast as he could. But as he was cowardly, so was he very cruel; and so shall you almost ordinarily find in these atheists both cruelty and cowardice together. In the end God sent him his due reward; for he endured not long, but was slain by Cassius Chaerea and Cornelius Sabinus, captains of his guard, whereby this wicked contemner of God felt the just divine vengeance, and so he knew he was a mortal man and not God, who caused himself to be worshipped as a god. Dion writes that after his death some ate of his flesh, to prove if the flesh of the gods was of a good taste.

The emperor Phillipus, who reigned in the primitive Christian church, was a wicked Arabian who had no fear of God, but was the most cruel and wicked of the world, as commonly Arabians are. Yet to cover his vices and wickedness he did what Machiavelli commands a prince here; for he feigned to be a Christian, and somewhat favored the Christian religion, which before had been greatly persecuted. But God soon punished this dissimulation and hypocrisy, for he reigned but five years, and by his soldiers was massacred together with his son at Verona.

The emperor Julian, who was called the Apostate, all the time of his youth, in the time of his uncle Constantine the Great, was instructed in the Christian religion; but upon a foolish curiosity he gave himself to diviners and sorcerers, to know things to come, which made him forsake Christianity. Yet he always feigned himself to be a Christian, because for the most part the nobility and the men of war were so; therefore to please them he often went unto the Christian churches, and there used the exercises of their religion. After he was created emperor in Paris and had set a sure foot in the empire, he began to reveal what he had always kept in his heart; that is, to make open the temples for images, and to set up the pagan religion which Constantine had suppressed, and to establish their sacrifices. And although he dared not prohibit the exercise of Christianity, yet underhand he sought by all means to destroy it; for he forbade that any should receive any Christians to be regents or bailmasters, and caused to be sown all manner of partialities and divisions that he could among Christians. Finally after he had reigned for the space of a year and seven months, he was slain at the age of 32 years, making war against the Persians. Some write that as he died he blasphemed spitefully against Christ, crying "Thou hast vanquished, thou Galilean." Behold the unhappy end of this atheist and apostate.

It is commonly seen that such men as have no God give themselves to sorcerers and diviners. For of necessity they must have a master, and after they have forsaken God they must needs take to the devil for their master and governor. The emperor Bassianus Caracalla, being a true contemner of God, fell to delight in magic and witchery; by the art of necromancy he would cause to come to him the soul of his father Severus, and the emperor Commodus, to know of them if he should ever recover from the disease whereof he was sick. The soul of his father (or rather some evil spirit) appeared to him, holding a naked sword in his hand, but spoke not a word unto him; but that of Commodus appearing also, said unto him these words: "Get thee to the gallows." Being at war in Mesopotamia, he had two lieutenants general, Audentius and Macrinus, who he incessantly outraged and mocked, so that neither of them greatly trusted him; he had also at Rome one Maternianus, who executed all his affairs, whom he much troubled. Therefore he sent unto him a command to assemble all the diviners, sorcerers, and necromancers that could be found, to consult together and search out if any secret enterprise was intended or practiced against him. Maternianus executed his commandment, and upon a consultation of them, they answered that Macrinus had determined to slay the emperor Bassianus. Maternianus, who did not love Macrinus, did not fail to advise the emperor hereof; but the packet of letters was presented to him at a certain hour when he was very attentive, and given to take his pastime. Insomuch that he commanded Macrinus, who was nearby, to take the packed and open it, and to tell him the substance of it later, at some hour of council. Macrinus took the packed and opened it, within which he found many letters, speaking of many of his affairs; and among others one was found containing the resolution of the said consultation. Macrinus then was much abashed, and joyful withal; abashed that the diviners and necromancers laid to his charge a thing whereof he never thought, and joyful because the letter did not fall into the emperor's hands; whom he knew to be very cruel, and ready to exercise his choler. Therefore he hid this letter and showed him the other; but thinking of his own cause, he resolved to slay his master rather than to attend while he was slain himself; and the sooner, for fear Maternianus should write again of the same cause. Macrinus then suborned a captain of footmen called Martialis, who also had a quarrel with the emperor, to slay him; who espying one day the emperor going out of the way to empty his body, he slew him with many pricks of a dagger. So that a man may say that it was the devil which played him this part, because he trusted in diviners and necromancers. For had it not been for that consultation, whereby Macrinus was brought in peril of his life, he would have never dared enterprise what he did. But necessity makes men enterprise, even the most cowardly.

The year 1411 the lord de Rays in Brittany, Marshal of France, to come to great estate and honors gave himself to sorcery and necromancy, and caused many little children to be slain for their blood, wherewith he wrote his devilish invocations. The devil brought him to that greatness and height that he was taken prisoner by the commans of the duke of Brittany, who caused his indictment to be made, and he was publicly burned at Nantes.

There may be alleged infinite examples of the judgements of God exercised against atheists, contemners of God and of all religion, yea even in our time, as of that tragical poet Jodelle, whose end was truly tragic, having like an Epicurean eaten and drunk his patrimony, he miserably died through hunger. Lignerolles also, the courtier, who to make it appear that he was a man of service in court made an open profession of atheism: and what was his end? Certain it is, that from whence he looked for his advancement, he receivd his merited ruin and destruction. And la Lande, Bissy Gaiscon, and others (who I will not name for the respect I have of their parents); had they not unlucky ends, after they had emptied and spoiled themselves of all piety and religion? But I will not stay here to make plain so clear a thing of itself; yet would I set down one example very notable for hypocrites who make themselves great zelots of the holy mother church, and under that pretext and color they bring into ruin and combustion their own country, saying that men ought inviolably to keep the religion of his predecessors, and in the meanwhile their hearts tend to no other purpose but to spoil, sack, and enrich themselves with the public ruin.

Josephus rehearses that in the time of Claudius and Nero the Jews raised up many civil wars in Judea and Samaria, so often that they made no account of any other occupation but to live by booties and rapines; so that Vespasian, lieutenant general for Nero, was sent against them with a great army. All the wickedest men of the country, who were worth nothing and who could not live but from the good men, gathered themselves together and called themselves Zealots, saying they would fight for the temple of Jerusalem and for the conservation of their religion, which they had received and learned from their forefathers; and that they would not permit any other religion to be exercised in their countries but their own which was anciently used from hand to hand, since Moses and Abraham. Under the show of this good name of Zealots, and under color of boasting that they would fight and die for the conservation of their ancient religion, they took up arms and elected for captains the worst persons they could find. Vespasian many times had them told (even by Josephus, a captain of their own nation, who wrote this history) that he would change nothing of their religion, but maintain them therein, and in all their liberties and franchises. But like very hypocrites and liars, they thinking one thing with their hearts and saying another with their mouths, would never hearken unto peace in any sort, nor upon any condition whatsoever. Vespasian, seeing their stubbornness, was constrained to war upon them in all extremity, which endured long, even until he came to the empire after the deaths of Nero, Galba, Otho and Vitellius, who did not reign long. Finally these goodly Zealots, who would never hearken unto peace, by their obstinacy came to such an extremity that they themselves set their temple on fire in

Jerusalem (for the conservation whereof they said they fought) and burned it wholly. They overthrew both themselves and their religion, for which they bore arms, and committed a thousand sorts of cruelties and impieties, saying they fought for piety. Briefly, this devout zeal which they bragged of for the ancient religion of their fathers — although they had but a masking and false countenance thereof — was cause of the ruin of Jerusalem and of all the country, and of the death of a million men.

A prince then must take another manner of resolution than what Machiavelli speaks; namely, that he resolves himself to fear God, and to serve him with a heart pure and without dissimulation, according to his holy commandments, in doing the exercises of the true and pure religion of God, which is the Christian. If he does this, God will bless him and make him prosper in his affairs. Hereof there may be cited many examples; I will content myself with a few of the most notable.

The emperor Marcus Aurelius the philosopher, a prince both good and wise, though a pagan, making war against the Marcomanes and Quadiens, people of Germany, was once with all his army in a very great danger and peril. Being enclosed in a withered and dry country, where his soldiers for lack of water died of drought, his enemies, keeping the passage, intended to vanquish them without striking a stroke. By chance, or rather by God's providence, the emperor had in his army a legion of Christians; and it was told him by his lieutenant general that he had heard say that those Christians by their prayers obtained from God whatever they demanded. Which the emperor understanding, addressed himself to that legion — which was a good zeal in the pagan, though without knowledge — and prayed them that they would pray unto their God for the salvation of his army. Which presently they did with a good heart; desiring God, in the name of Jesus Christ our Savior, to conserve that army and the emperor, and draw them from the danger wherein they were. Soon after their prayers, God hearing them sent presently a terrible lightning upon the enemy, and a great rain fell upon the Roman soldiers, who would have died of thirst but that they received the rain upon the hollow bottoms of their targets, bucklers, and morrions. Insomuch that the God of hosts fighting for them, they got the victory without striking a stroke, clean contrary from that the Marcomans and Quadiens looked for. Whereupon the emperor was much ravished with admiration, and afterward greatly honored the Christians.

Constantine the Great, the first Christian emperor, besides overcoming Licinius and Maxentius, great enemies of the Christian religion, also obtained many triumphant victories against the Sarmats, Goths, and Scythians. Happy he was and victorious, because he had the fear of God and the Christian religion in exceedingly great honor and reverence. As much may we say of the emperors Theodosius, Justinian, and other Christians. As much may we say of our kings of France, Charles Martel and Charlemagne, who prospered in the wars they had against the high Germans, Saxons, Frisons, and against the Goths, Huns, Visigoths, Lombards, and Saracens, all of which were then pagans and infidels; from which they obtained great victories and brought them to be subject unto their obedience. This grace came not to them to be such victors by their own forces, seeing their enemies were far stronger than they, considering their forces and number of armed people. But that grace came unto them by the favor of God, whom they served without feignedness and hypocrisy, having the Christian religion in great and singular recommendation and reverence. As much we may say also generally of most of our French kings; for among them we find none such as Caligula, Caracalla, or such other monsters full of impiety and atheism, till lately some few have been found not much inferior to them.

David was marvelously happy in war, and always victorious over his enemies, because he was a good prince, fearing God and honoring his holy religion. Solomon his son, as long as he served God sincerely without feigning and hypocrisy, prospered very well and marvelously in a great and happy peace, and none dared stir him. But as soon as he began to practice the doctrine which Machiavelli teaches, namely to have a feigned and dissembled religion and devotion, straight had he enemies on his head, who rose up against him; as Hadad the Edomite, and Razin, who made war upon him. So generally may be said of all the kings of Judah and Israel, one after another; that God has always prospered those who were pure and sincere in religion, and who have had his service in recommendation; and contrary, upon those impure and hypocrites in religion he has heaped ruins, calamities, and other vengeances.

But I pray you consider a little the reason wherewith Machiavelli proves his maxim. Because (says he) the people look but at the exterior and outward show of things, it is sufficient that the prince show himself outwardly devout, although he be not devout at all. Ought religion then to serve for nothing but to please and be agreeable unto the people? Or ought it not rather to serve to make men agreeable to God? But how would thou that God should take pleasure in your religion — he that sees the bottom of your heart and finds the deepest of your thoughts — if it be simulated and feigned, and that you are a hypocrite? Neither may Machiavelli nor the Machiavellians (that is to say, the atheists of our time) think men so senseless and gross that they cannot soon discover their hypocrisies and dissimulations. Many there are in the world who think by their subtleties and dissemblings to be covered and hid, yet are sufficiently known; and however craftily they do it, all the world knows there is nothing but impiety and wickedness in their hearts. Suppose therefore these simulations and hypocrisies come to be discovered in a prince, I pray you into what honor and reputation will he fall? Shall he not be mocked, blamed, and despised by his subjects, if seeing himself discovered, he makes an open profession of impiety and atheism (as we see many persons do it because they can no longer hide their impiety); shall not this be publicly to authorize all impiety and spite of God and of all religion? For certain it is that men, who are naturally more inclined to evil than to good, when they see their prince follow that course, will do as he does; because ordinarily subjects conform themselves to the manners and conditions of the prince. Behold then the consequence of that most wicked and detestable doctrine of that wicked atheist; which is to bring all people to a spite and a mockery of God and his religion, and of all holy things, and to let go the bridle to all vices and villainies. From which God keep us by his grace, and destroy all them who teach so wicked doctrines, if they will not amend; as certainly he will do, and so let them look for it.

2.2
Machiavelli

A prince ought to sustain and confirm that which is false in religion, if it turns to the favor thereof. (*Discourses*, book 1 chapter 12, 13, 14)

Sage and prudent princes allow false miracles, because they are a means to augment the people's devotion. For when the people see that the prince approves them, none makes any difficulty to believe them after him. Christian princes also should therein imitate the old Romans, who by deceitful miracles feigned false revelations, to encourage their soldiers and to cause their subjects to obey their ordinances. For they caused to publish either what they had read in the books of the Sibyls, or what they had consulted with the Oracle of Apollo, or that they had such and such a revelation, or that the flight of birds or other like tokens had signified unto them a good augury or divination. The people, being persuaded that they were true and pronounced by their gods, obeyed with great good will that which was commanded them by their captains and magistrates, as if the gods themselves had commanded them. In the meanwhile the Roman heads and captains knew of what account this merchandise was.

Answer

This atheist, after he has given the prince a document to hold all religion in his heart as a mockery, and only to show outwardly a fair semblance and countenance of devotion, now passes further and desires that the prince should maintain falseness in religion. I pray you, can there be found in the world a greater impiety and wickedness than this? Are we not beholden to them that have authorized and given countenance unto the writings of this stinking atheist; even unto those who have made two or three translations into French, the better to poison that nation. It is certain that the truth in all things is very commendable, but most especially when it deals in causes and matters of religion. For since religion is the thing which binds us with God, how can falseness bind us with God, who is truth itself? Is darkness compatible with light, or the obscure shadow with the sun? Rather, we always see that darkness vanishes and disperses away by the light, and the shadow also flies from the sun and hides itself behind some opposite. Therefore have the ancient doctors of the Church said and held for a principle of theology, that it would be much better for a scandal and offense to come than for truth to be forsaken. Which sentence even the popes themselves have caused to be placed among their rules of canon law; and would to God they had observed it. But I see well it is to no purpose to cite reasons against this atheist and his disciples, who believe neither God nor religion; wherefore, before I pass any further, I must fight against their impiety, and make it appear to their eyes, if they have any, not by assailing them with the arms of the holy Scripture—for they do not merit to be so assailed, and I fear to pollute the holy Scriptures among people so profane and defiled with impiety—but by their proper arms and weapons, whereby their ignorance and beastliness defends their renewed atheism.

They then took human reason for a foundation, and profane pagan authors; but in truth both one and the other are so much against them that even by them I will prove our Christian religion. For first, if we consider the least creature in the world, and find the causes of its essence and nature, it will lead us by degrees to one God. Take an ant or a fly, and consider the causes which make these little creatures move; you shall find it is heat and moisture, which are two qualities consisting in all living creatures, nourishers of nature; for as soon as heat and moisture fail in any living thing, it can no more live, nor move, and the body is occupied with contrary qualities, coldness and drought, the enemies of nature. Mount and ascend up higher, and consider what is the cause that in the little body of an ant or fly there are found the two qualities of heat and moisture; you shall find that it is because all living creatures are composed of the four elements, fire, air, water, and earth, in which the four qualities of heat, moisture, cold, and dryness consist; and while heat and moisture reign in the body it lives, but when cold and drought domineer it dies. Consider further what is the cause of the heat and the moisture, and the other qualities which we see in the four elements and the bodies made of them; you shall find that the sun is the cause of heat, the moon the cause of moisture, as sense and experience show. Let us yet pass further, and seek the cause why the sun is hot and the moon moist, and from whence come unto them these qualities; we must necessarily now come to a first and sovereign cause, which is one God. For the sun and moon, which are corporal and finite things, cannot be God, who is of infinite essence. Behold then how the least creature in the world is sufficient to vanquish by natural reason the opinion of the atheists; how much more if we come to consider other creatures, and especially the composition of man's body? For there shall you contemplate without going any further, so well ordered a rule, that of necessity must be concluded that there is a most ingenious and excellent workman who has disposed that architecture and building; for within man's body you shall see appear a harmony very like a well governed commonwealth. You see the mind and understanding of man, which is as the king that is set in the highest place, as in his throne, and thence commands all the parts; you see also the heart, the seat of amity, clemency, bounty, kindness, magnanimity, and other virtues, all which obey the understanding as their king; but the heart as the great master has them under his charge. It has also under its charge envy, hatred, vengeance, ambition, and other vices which lodge in the heart; but they are held, mewed, and bridled by the understanding. After, you have the liver, which is the superintendent of the victuals, which it distributes unto all the parts of the body by the means of subaltern and inferior officers, as the belly, veins, and other pores and passages of the body. Briefly, a man may see within man an admirable and well ordained disposition of all the parts, and it brings us necessarily (whether we will or no) to acknowledge that there must be a God, a sovereign architect, who has made this excellent building; and by these considerations of natural things, whereof I do but lightly touch the points, the ancient philosophers, as the Platonists, Aristotelians, Stoics, and others, have been brought to the knowledge of a God and of his providence. And of all the sects of philosophers, there never was any which agreed not hereunto, unless the sect of the Epicureans, who were gluttons, drunkards, and whoremongers; who constituted their sovereign felicity in carnal pleasures, wherein they wallowed like brute beasts. Out of this school Machiavelli and the Machiavellians come, who are well enough known to be very Epicurean in their lives, caring for nothing but their pleasures; who also have no knowledge of good letters, contenting themselves with the maxims of that wicked atheist.

Touching that doctrine of the Trinity which we hold, it must be confessed that the philosophers understood nothing thereof, and that by human reason we cannot well be led to the knowledge thereof. But this knowledge is manifested unto us by the witnesses of God himself, which are so clear and evident in the holy Scripture that nothing can be more. But I have no purpose here to recite them; yet I will say that the doctrine which I hold in this place is not repugnant nor contrary to human reason, but consonant enough, although the ancient philosophers have not penetrated so far. For by their own maxims a very true thing it is that God, an eternal and infinite spirit, cannot possess any qualities or accidents; so that what is a quality in man, as bounty, love, wisdom, is an essence in God. This presupposed as a thing confessed by the philosophers themselves, it follows that the infinite and admirable wisdom whereby God knows himself is an essence and not a quality in God. Yea it is one and the same essence, yet a distinct subsistence or hypostasis from him; for the Wise and Wisdom cannot be without distinction. This wisdom then is the second person of the Trinity; which the Scripture calls the Word, or the Son. Neither is it repugnant to human reason to say that these two persons, in one and the same essence, have an infinite and mutual intelligence together; which intelligence proceeds equally from the two persons, the Father and the Son, as they are of equal essence, yet cannot be confounded with them, although the said intelligence is the same essence. For *Intelligens* (understanding) and *Intelligentia* (the understanding) ought to be distinguished. This intelligence is the third person of the Trinity, which the scripture calls the Holy Spirit. Behold then how man's brain may somewhat comprehend by natural reason the doctrine we hold of the Trinity, by a rude and gross description, which is like to that which the geographers take to portray all the earth; namely, in five or six gross lines, in a paper of a hand's breadth. For the knowledge that our sense can have of so high a thing is far less in comparison with all the earth; and therefore will I confess that we neither need nor ought much to travail to dispute by human reason so high a thing, which of itself is infinite and incomprehensible to our senses and understanding; and that they who least dispute with philosophical reasons are most wise and most modest; and that we ought wholly to hold and resolve upon what is written by and in the holy Scripture. But having to do with atheists, who receive not the witness of the word of God, it has made me show in few words that even by human reason itself they may be vanquished by the truth of that doctrine which we hold. Let us now come to another point.

Natural reason and common sense teach us that there is one God, and that he is perfect in all perfection, for otherwise he could not be God. This is a point resolved. Hereof necessarily follows that God is perfectly just and perfectly merciful. Being perfectly just, by the rule of justice, he must condemn and reject all mankind; for men generally are vicious, and vice merits condemnation. But if God should condemn and reject all mankind, it would be repugnant to his mercy, which also ought to be perfect with effect. How then shall we say that God cannot be perfectly just and merciful together, because it seems that his mercy repugns his justice? God forbid that such blasphemy should proceed out of our mouths. But we say that thereby natural reason leads us to a mediator, who being God and perfect, has satisfied the divine justice; which satisfaction God the creator accepts of mankind, because the mediator is man also. And by the means of this great mediator, God and man, which the creator has given us, he has showed himself perfectly just in receiving of him a satisfaction with dignity to his justice, and perfectly merciful in pardoning us for his sake. Without which mediator we evidently see that God cannot show himself perfectly just and merciful together, that is to say, that he cannot show himself to be God, for the Father cannot be without the Son. It is then a true demonstration drawn from most certain and evident principles; there is one God, therefore he is perfect. If God is perfect, as no doubt he is, he is then perfectly just and merciful; but he cannot be both without a mediator, God and man. Neither Euclid nor Archimedes ever made more certain demonstrations.

But this mediator which the creator has given to men, to make manifest his perfect justice and perfect mercy, is his eternal Son, the wisdom of the Father; in favor of whom, as well before he came into the world and had taken our nature as since, men have enjoyed the mercy and clemency of God, in employing that mediator to satisfy the justice of God. This mediator was promised and established to men from the beginning of the world, and since then his promises have been so often reiterated that not only have they been notorious to the particular people of God, who followed the true religion, but also to other people who follow false religions. The historiographer Suetonius (a pagan who never read any part of holy Scripture) speaking of Vespasian, as though it were a vulgar and common thing, said that through all the East countries there has always been a constant and ancient opinion, as a thing certain, that it was so ordained and foretold by God that from Judea should come the dominator and ruler of the world. As much said the historian Tacitus (another pagan who never saw holy letters) when he said, speaking of the same time of Vespasian: "Many have this persuasion, that within the spirits and writings of the ancient priests was contained, that at that time the East should be in great power, and that from Judea should come the dominator of the world." By which witnesses of these two historiographers it is clearly seen that the promise of the Messiah, the dominator of the world, was known to everyone. But not only the pagans, but also the Jews themselves understand this of a temporal domination; and indeed these two former historiographers, and Josephus himself, a Jew, interpreted this prophecy of Vespasian, who was created emperor of the Roman Empire while in Jewry warring against the Jews. But this foolish and rash interpretation is inexcusable in Josephus, who vaunts that he himself was cunning, foretelling things to come, and in the knowledge of the books of Moses and the other prophets. For all the prophets clearly say that the Messiah ought to be born of the race of Abraham, of Judah, and of David; in Bethlehem, a little town of the tribe of Judah. But Josephus knew well that Vespasian was neither of that race, nor born in the town of Bethlehem; but we must believe that Josephus understood better than he wrote, and that he falsely attributed that prophecy to Vespasian upon a flattering humor, because he had received so many great favors from him.

And as for Tacitus and Suetonius attributing to the emperor Vespasian that prophecy, rather than Christ, men must not marvel thereat; for they were great enemies of Christ, as is seen in many other places of their history. With the same faith Tacitus says that the emperor Vespasian, being in Jewry, healed a blind man with his spittle; and another who had a dry hand, wherewith he could not help himself. For these indeed were the miracles of Christ, which these profane historians would steal from him to attribute unto their emperors. And the better to discover their theft by their own writings, we must first mark what Tacitus himself says; that the blind man coming to Vespasian and falling on his knees before him, declared unto him that he had had a revelation from the god Serapis to address himself unto him. Of which god Tacitus says that even in his time none knew his origin at Rome. But these pagans, who knew not Christ nor any Christian religion but a little by hearsay, thought that the Christians adored that pretended god Serapis, as is seen by a missive which the emperor Hadrian wrote to Servianus, recited by Vopiscus. He says that in the town of Alexandria, those who worshipped Serapis were Christians. So that hereby we may know, even by Tacitus' own confession, that the author of that miracle to heal the blind man was that God which the Christians adored, who was Christ, not Serapis. But as ordinarily it happens, things that are done in far countries are disguised by those who tell them; so we must understand that men spoke well all over the world of the miracles which Christ and his Apostles had done in Judea and in places thereabouts; but they disguised them, attributing them to strange gods and profane men, and never accounted them as the very truth was. Of the same stamp is that which Suetonius writes, saying that Vespasian healed one who was lame and impotent in his thigh; and a blind man also who had a revelation from Serapis, to go for his help to Vespasain. That also which Spartianus writes in the life of the emperor Hadrian, that a blind woman recovered her sight by kissing his knees; and one blind-born recovered his sight by touching him; and by that means Hadrian lost a fever which he then had. For we may easily see that these were Christ's miracles, or his Apostles, which the pagans would steal from them for their princes, as also to persuade the world that there was no divinity in them. For a resolution then of this point, the promises of the Messiah have been known through the world, as also his coming, even to the pagans. For profane authors often make mention of Christ, even Tacitus, who says that Christ was put to death in the time of the emperor Tiberius by Pontius Pilate, his lieutenant in Judea. Behold then how the principal points of our Christian religion may be proved by human reason and profane authors, so great and resplendent was and is that light. For our religion herein may summarily be comprehended: to believe in God and in him whom he sent, Jesus Christ our Savior. If these atheists then will put out their own eyes to the end that they may not know God and the Christian religion, neither by holy Scriptures nor by human reason, nor by the witness of profane authors who speak thereof as of a thing divulged and notorious through all the world; we know not how to do any other thing, but to leave them as desperate persons to welter in their ignorance, brutality, and darkness, till God by his just judgment has sunk them into the bottomless pit.

Now to come to our maxim; we say that to maintain falseness in religion is to tread God and his religion underfoot. Yet true it is that the ancient Romans have approved and maintained the falseness of oracles, although it were not falseness invented by men, but very diabolical illusions, as shall be said in another place. True it is also that they sustained and allowed the books of the Sibyls, and the augurs taken by the flight of birds, and other such follies. But these proceeded from the want of knowledge of the true religion, and because they suffered themselves to be guided by the pagan religion, which consisted in vain ceremonies and foolish lies. Yet notwithstanding, whenever by good reason they could know that any falseness had slid into their religion, they did not maintain it, but took it away. An example hereof is this. The religion of Bacchus was first brought into Rome by a Greek priest, who made sacrifices and ceremonies in the nighttime, and in the beginning only women assisted and were present, who after their sacrifices banqueted together. The Romans, thinking no harm, suffered it for a time; but in succession of time men also resorted there with women, pell mell, and brought there a new ceremony; namely, to put out candles, and ting bells, to the end that none might hear those who cried when they were forced and ravished. There was all villainy committed, not only towards all sorts of women, but also towards young boys. The consuls and Senate having discovered this, proceeded criminally against them who were found in such assemblies, as guilty of ravishing women and sodomy; there were found culpable more than seven thousand, of which most fled, some slew themselves, others were executed by justice. And an edict was made forbidding all sacrifices to Bacchus. Even natural reason made those poor pagans, who were ignorant of religion, understand that that religion could not be true, but is false and rejected when it contains in it any punishable crime. And if they could also have known the other falsities of their religion as well as this, I believe they would have cut it off, whatever Machiavelli says. But in points of religion we may not anything stay ourselves upon that which the ancient Romans have done or said, unless we will seek light in the darkness.

In the year 1509, about 20 years before the canon of Berne had forsaken the papal religion, the Jacobins of Berne would have introduced certain new miracles, devised by apostates, to draw unto them the devotion and offerings of people. But that seignory would not follow the doctrine of Machiavelli, to approve such false miracles, but by burning executed good justice upon the authors thereof. In the year 1534, the Parliament of Paris condemned certain friars of Orleans, who would falsely have made men believe the apparition of a spirit, who desired (they said) that there might be good store of masses said to deliver him from purgatory. For it was found out to be an imposture, deceit, and invention, which the friars had made to abuse the world and to draw water to their mills. There were many judgments of the said court of Parliament, whereby the falseness of relics was condemned and prohibited. As of the image of our Lady which was painted in an old table that had many years remained in a painter's shop for a show; which table a curate near Paris bought cheap, and boring two holes in the eyes, at the time when vines weep placed behind in them two sprigs of the vine tree, so that pitiful Lady wept in the church where she stood, which drew great numbers of pilgrims to that parish. Insomuch that the painter himself and his wife came in great devotion, who had sold it. But this marred all, that they at last knew it to be the old table which had so long kept their shop; by whom the fame of this abuse came to the knowledge of justice, whereby by the said Parliament the curate was condemned and the table burned.

But another time the said court of Parliament of Paris did another thing that seemed to hold of Machiavelli's opinion. For upon a controversy of law which happened between the clergymen of our Lady in Paris, who said they had Saint Denis's head, and the abbots and religious men of Saint Denis, who said they had the whole body of Denis. The court there gave judgment that those of Saint Denis had the whole body of Denis the Athenian; and those of our Lady, the head of Denis the Corinthian. So that they both were content, although before there was never heard of Denis the Corinthian. But that was all one, they provided that their practice diminished not. If they of Ratisbone in Germany had meddled with this strife, it would have been hard to have agreed them, or else there must have been supposed a third Saint Denis; for they say also that they have the whole body of Denis, and have a declarative sentence of a pope and his cardinals to confirm it (as they say). But my purpose here is not to agree them, I only conclude that it is a damnable and detestable thing to sustain lies and falseness in whatsoever things, but especially in religion; for that is to follow the religion of the devil, who is the father of lies.

2.3
Machiavelli

The pagan religion holds and lifts up their hearts, and so makes them hardy to enterprise great things; but the Christian religion, persuading to humility, humbles and too much weakens their minds, and so makes them more ready to be injured and preyed upon. (*Discourses*, book 2 chapter 5)

Entering into consideration what should be the cause that the force and power of Christians is less than that of gentiles, such as were the ancient Greeks and Romans, it seems that it was the difference of religion. For that the Christian religion makes the honor of the world contemptible and of little estimation, whereas the gentiles esteemed honor to be the sovereign good, for which to obtain they had an exceeding great fierceness and hardiness in all their deeds and enterprises. Moreover the pagan religion promises no happiness, but those having fought for the prince, country, and common weal were replenished with glory and worldly honors. So it is plainly seen that the Christian religion has conducted and brought the world unto that weakness and feebleness that we see in it, delivering it as a prey to the wicked and barbarous people, who can deal with Christians as they will, and vanquish and bring them under the yoke. Because all Christians, to take the way of paradise, dispose and arm themselves rather to receive blows than to take vengeance. And it seems that that which makes Christians so effeminate and cowardly proceeds only from this, that they esteem more an idle repose and contemplative life than an active life.

Answer

Behold the maxim and the reasons which this most unhappy atheist has disgorged in his good discourses, to blame and altogether spite the Christian religion, and to bring us unto atheism and despoil us of all religion, fear of God, and of all conscience and loyalty, which are taught by Christianity. But God by his grace preserve us from such a pestilence and contagion, and make us know and shun that execrable poison wherewith that unhappy man has infected the hearts and spirits of infinite, from whence spring the evils and calamities which we see in Christendom today, and especially in France. For without doubt, so many evils and mischiefs as we see and feel at this day and long before, proceed from a just judgment of God, provoked unto wrath against the world for the contempt of his most holy commandments, and of our most holy Christian religion.

True it is that our Christian religion teaches us humility towards God. For we ought to acknowledge before his face that we are poor sinners, and to demand pardon of him, as criminals do, who fall on their knees before a prince, begging grace and pardon. We ought also to acknowledge that the graces we have proceed from God, and that we ought not to be proud of any good thing in us. Moreover, we ought to be modest and gentle towards our neighbor, and to detest all fierceness and cruelty. But do those things debase and disable the hearts of good men to perform and execute their duties of fortitude and valiance in war? Does this Christian humility diminish their generosity? I will ask the resolution of this point of none other but Machiavelli's own nation, which has come into France to make war against the Evangelists. For they have well felt if the humility of Christians has so much abated the Frenchmen's hearts that they dared not well handle them (as they say) both backs and bellies; yet if they will not confess it, the fields, which are white with their bones, will always give good witness thereof. It is strange that this villainous atheist dared utter and send abroad such absurd things, which are so far from all experience and truth. If what he says were the truth, it should follow that no Christian prince could stand against the pagan and infidel princes. But all ancient and modern histories, do they not show us the contrary? The emperor Constantine the Great was a very humble Christian prince, so humble (as some write) that he held the stirrup of the pope of Rome till he got on horseback. Yet he vanquished Licinius, who was a pagan emperor with him, and made him forsake the empire, and besides overcame many pagan nations, as we have said in another place. The emperor Theodosius was so humble that being reprehended for a certain fault he had committed by Saint Ambrose, Bishop of Milan, he debased himself so much to acknowledge his sin that he went upon the ground on all fours from the church door to the place where Ambrose administered the sacrament, and by that means was received into the communion. Yet although he was so humble, he had very great victories against the barbarians and infidels, and against other enemies of the Roman Empire. The emperor Valentinian, who was a Christain, vanquished the Goths in Gaul; and the emperor Justinian overcame them in Italy and in Africa. Charlemagne and many other kings of France, very humble, have notwithstanding gained and obtained good victories against the pagans, as we have otherwise said. The emperor Charles V of late memory obtained in his time victories in Africa against the Turks. Briefly, this point needs no further debate, for it is clearly seen that Machiavelli is a filthy liar to say that the Christian religion is the cause that Christians fall prey to the pagans. For contrary, a small number of Christians have often beaten a great number of Goths, Turks, and other infidels. And it is no more true what the Machiavellians say, that those who horribly swear and blaspheme, with *mortdieu, sangdieu,* and such like, fight better than those who say surely and truly. Because (say they) surely and truly enfeeble and weaken men's hearts; but experience shows in many places that this is false.

When I think upon and consider where Machiavelli has fished this goodly maxim, I can hardly be persuaded but he learned it out of the history of Agolant, a pagan king of Africa, of Mahomet's religion. This king was a great and puissant ruler, who demanded and maintained great wars with Charlemagne; but he was always vanquished, and Charlemagne victorious. So that to escape from Charlemagne by the cheapest and best means, he could devise nothing better than to make Charlemagne understand that he would become a Christian and be baptized. Charlemagne rejoiced thereat and invited him into his lodging, with intent to feast him and give him good entertainment. When he came in to Charlemagne's lodging he saw thirteen poor men, beggarly appareled, eating on the ground without cloth, as beggars used to do; which Charlemagne did to always have before his eyes an image of poverty, to remember Christ and his Apostles, and their humility. Agolant, seeing these poor men, desired to know what they were. Charlemagne answered him, "These be the servants of God"; Agolant said, "Has your God his servants in so evil order, and are your servants so brave? Truly I will never be baptized, to become the servant of your God, for I will never yield to so base an estate as I see God's servants hold." So Agolant would not be christened, for the humility he saw in the estate of God's servants. So Machiavelli rejects the Christian religion because humility is recommended unto us, but loves much better the pagan religion of Agolant, because (says he) it maintains the heart haughty and fierce.

And as for what he says, that the Christian religion promises not paradise but to idle and contemplative people, he shows well that he never knew what the Christian religion meant; for it commands us to travail and not to be idle, and every man loyally to exercise his vocation. Very true it is that among Christians there must be some contemplatives, that is to say, studious people who give themselves to holy letters in order to teach others. But we do not find by the documents of that religion that there is allowed any idle contemplation of dreamers, who do nothing but imagine dreams and toys in their brains; but a contemplative life of laboring studious people is only approved, who give themselves to letters to teach others. For after they have accomplished their studies, they ought to put in use and action that which they know, bringing into an active life that which they have learned by their study in their contemplative life. And those who use this otherwise do not follow the precepts of the true Christian religion.

Touching what he says, that the Christian religion disposes men to receive blows, rather than to vengeance. I confess that is true, that our religion forbids us to take vengeance of our own enmities and particular quarrels, by our own authority; but the course of justice is not denied us. And if it were lawful for everyone to use vengeance, that would be to introduce a confusion and disorder into the commonwealth, and to enterprise upon the right which belongs to the magistrate, unto whom God has given the sword to do right to everyone and to punish those who are faulty, according to their merits. But what is all this to purpose, touching the generosity of heart that men should have in war? For although a man should not be quarrelsome nor vindictive, to find quarrels for needless points, yet he will not cease to perform his duty in warfare for the service of his prince. Yet there is one point in Christians more than in pagans; that is, that a Christian being well resolved in his conscience that he bears arms for a good and just cause, he will less esteem his own life and will more willingly hazard it than a pagan or an infidel will, because he has a firm trust and belief that he will enjoy the eternal life after this frail life. Caesar writes that our ancient Gauls were very generous and warlike, because they held as resolute the immortality of souls, and that those who die, die not at all. How much more then ought Christians to be courageous, who not only are resolved of the immortality of souls, but also allow that God has prepared for them an eternal rest, an immortal glory, and a perdurable beatitude with him and his angels. Surely, as that life and eternal felicity are more excellent than this frail life full of miseries and calamities, so the Christian will never doubt nor fear to change one for the other, but with a magnanimous and generous heart will willingly always bestow his life in a just quarrel. Machiavelli and all his school of atheists, who have nothing that so much troubles their conscience as to think of God, have no such mind. They show themselves generous and valiant to execute some massacre, to slay men unarmed, who have no means to defend themselves; but otherwise they are resolute to hold themselves far from blows.

Finally, when Machiavelli says that the Christian religion teaches us to despise honor, he shows himself a stinking liar. True it is that a man must distinguish the virtue and what is good from vice and the evil which resembles it. For ambition is a vice which comes very near the desire of good reputation, which good men ought to have. If then a man travails and takes pains to come to some estate and greatness by all lawful and unlawful means, and uses it fiercely and to his own commodity, rather than to the profit of the commonwealth, we confess that our religion teaches us to fly and despise such honors. But when a man maintains himself by all honest and lawful means in a good reputation, although by such means he aspires to some estate and dignity whereof he feels himself capable to use it well, and to serve God and the commonwealth therein, we say that by our Christian religion there is not forbidden us such an affectation of honor, and that we may lawfully say we ought to seek and pursue such honor. Briefly, the thing which Christians hold most precious and dear is their conscience towards God, and their honor among men.

M. Philip de Commines, chamberlain of Louis XI, writes that this king was very humble in his habits, in words, and in all other things, and that he could well acknowledge his faults and amend them, and that these virtues were the means whereby he dispatched the great affairs he had on his hands on coming to the crown. So he commonly had this notable sentence in his mouth, clean contrary from Machiavelli's maxim: "When pride marches before, shame and damage follow."

So we must say that humility, kindness, gentleness, patience, easiness to pardon, clemency, and all other virtues which accord with a humane and benign nature, are not contrary to the true magnanimity, but agree thereunto. For magnanimity is nothing but a constant and perpetual will to employ oneself courageously in all good and virtuous things, and to fly, abate, and chase away all vices and vicious things. It is then magnanimity to be humble, soft, gentle, patient, inclined to pardon, and to be far from vengeance, since all those things are virtues, not vices. And on the contrary, it is pusillanimity to be proud, rigorous, sharp, impatient, vindictive, and cruel, because all those things are vices and not virtues. For that virtue of magnanimity is never accompanied with the said vices, neither receives them to wait upon her, only she is waited upon with all other virtues. And for an example, there were never men more moderate, humble, and gentle, nor more inclined to pardon than were Scipio the African, Julius Caesar, Alexander the Great, and great Pompey. Yet were there never in the world men who were more magnanimous.

As much may we say of Charlemagne, Philip, Augustus the conqueror, Saint Louis, Charles the Wise, Charles VII, Louis XII, and many other kings of France who were very magnanimous, yet very soft and gentle. But I shall in another place handle this point more fully, and show that magnanimity has always been joined with humanity, gentleness, and clemency; and contrary, pusillanimity has always been accompanied with cruelty, pride, and vengeance.

2.4
Machiavelli

The great doctors of the Christian religion, by a great ostentation and stiffness, have sought to abolish the remembrance of all good letters of antiquity. (*Discourses*, book 2)

The Christian religion has held this practice to abolish the pagan religion, first to deface the memory of all order and ceremonies thereof, and of all old theology. After that it sought to abolish the poets and historiographers, and to extinguish all knowledge of the deeds of excellent persons and of all antiquity, destroying all old images and all that might represent any sign or trace of the world passed. Yet it could not altogether abolish good letters, because it was constrained to use the Latin language to write her new law, by the means of which language some part of the ancient works yet remained. But if the Christian religion could have formed a new language in a small time, you would have seen all antiquity quite banished and gone. But Saint Gregory and other doctors of that religion, who so obstinately persecuted the letters and writings of the gentiles, were themselves constrained to write them in the Latin tongue. The pagan religion at its beginning did the same to the religion which was before it; for sects and religions change and vary two or three times in five or six thousand years, and the last always makes perish the remembrance of all that had been before it. And if any kept relics of the memory thereof, men held them for fables and gave no credit unto them more than unto the history of Diodorus the Sicilian, who begins a narration of things done forty or fifty thousand years before.

Answer

Machiavelli, desirous to show himself a very atheist without religion, and a man full of ignorance and beastliness, now advances this maxim, the very contrary whereof is plainly seen in the writings of those of our religion, which this impostor and deceiver blames as altogether false and against truth. For so much there wants that the writers of our religion would abolish good letters, the liberal arts, the knowledge of tongues, histories, poetry, and other elder sciences; to the contrary, they have used them to refute the errors of the pagan religion. For they were forced to use them against the pagans to vanquish them, either with natural reason or with citations and authorities out of their own books, because they did not receive the authority of the Bible. And whoever reads the ancient doctors will witness the truth that they have filled their books with citations of profane and pagan authors. And he who will see this more at large, let him read Saint Augustine on the *City of God*, and the Christian institutions of Lactantius Firmian. For he shall see that the purpose of those two authors in the said books is nothing but to refute and overthrow the pagan religion with the falseness thereof, by their own books, and to approve and set out ours. True it is that often they mark the faults and ignorance of pagan authors, and admonish Christians to read them with a spirit of sobriety and not give themselves so much unto them as to leave the holy Scriptures. Which admonitions are good and holy, and are also necessary even in our time; for there are at this day infinite persons who so much please themselves in profane authors, some in poets, some in historiographers, some in philosophy, some in physic, or in law, that they care nothing to read or else to know anything for the salvation and comfort of their souls. Some care not at all for it, others reserve that study until they have ended the studies of other sciences, and in the meanwhile the time runs away, and often it comes to pass that when they leave this world their profane studies are not ended, nor the study of holy letters commenced, and so they die like beasts. Therefore the old doctors are not to be reprehended because they admonish men to read in great sobriety the writings of the pagans, and that men not give themselves so much thereunto, to know human sciences and abandon the divine knowledge, which is as much more excellent as God is than man. Yet there are some pagan authors who ought never to be read by Christians, or at least ought not to come into the hands of youths, who are but too much inclined to vices and lubricities. For a young scholar, can he better learn in a stew among whores and ruffians the terms of all villainy and lubricity, than in that filthy Martial, or in Catullus, or Tibullus, or in certain books of Ovid? And therefore, although we never read any of these poets, if our youths gave themselves only to Virgil to learn all Latin poetry, it is enough; and that author alone, compared to whom all others are but small rivers, might teach them all the poetry that need be known. Yet I will not say but there are many other good poets worthy to be read, as Horace, Lucan, Claudian, and others; but he who well understands Virgil has no need of others for the understanding of poetry. And in every science it seems to be the best, that men may well employ their time, which is dear and short, to read few books, to make good choice of them, and to understand them well. But for proof of what I say, that Machiavelli is a shameless liar in that he dares affirm that the doctors of the Christian religion sought to abolish good letters, I will here set down the advice they have given touching the study of letters of the gentiles. Doctor Bede, as Gratian recites in his decree, says that those who forbid the reading of the gentiles' books hinder men from having apt spirits to comprehend and understand the holy writings, because human sciences fashion our minds and understandings to a better understanding of holy letters; and that Moses and Daniel, who were learned in all the books of the Egyptians and Chaldeans, serve for an example not to utterly reject the books of the pagans. But here I will translate the very words of doctor Bede.

> "He who forbids the reading of secular books, wherein we ought to take what is good for our own, troubles and causes to fail the vivacity of readers' spirits. Otherwise Moses and Daniel would not have learned the wisdom and letters of the Egyptians and Chaldeans, whose superstition they abhorred. Saint Paul would not have cited certain verses out of the gentiles' books in his writings. Why then should we forbid men to read what by good reason ought to be read? But some read secular books for pleasure only, being tickled and delighted with poetical figments and fictions, or else for the ornament of their language. Others read them for erudition, and to detest and refute the errors of the gentiles, and to apply the good things they find there to the use of the erudition of sacred letters; and these merit only praise in studying secular letters. And for this cause Saint Gregory reprehended a certain bishop, not because he had learned

humane letters, but because he expounded them unto the people against the duty of a bishop, whereas he should have expounded the Gospel."

Behold the opinion of this theologian doctor concerning the study and reading of the writings and sciences of the pagans. Speaking upon Luke, Saint Ambrose says that we read the books of the pagans for divers ends; namely, not to be ignorant of what they handle, and to follow the good things in them, and to reject the evil. Saint Jerome, upon the letter to Titus, says that grammar and logic are profitable sciences to know how to speak well and to distinguish true from false, and that secular sciences may serve Christians, to apply them to good uses. And therefore, he said, it is necessary to know them, to the end that we might show that the things said by prophets many hundreds of years before are since come to pass, and described by the books of both the Greeks and Latins. Saint Augustine says against the Manicheans that if the Sibyls, or Orpheus, or other poets or philosophers of the gentiles, have written any true thing of God, men must and may serve themselves therewith to vanquish the vanity of the pagans, but yet we ought not therefore give authority to such authors. By which words he well shows that he approves the reading and study of the gentiles' books, poets and philosophers as well as others. Saint Basil also in the treatise he wrote on the manner of reading the gentiles' books, not only does not reprehend the reading of them, but on the contrary exhorts Christians to read them and to apply the reading of those books to our true end and purpose, which is the piety and edification in the faith and Christian religion. And to conclude, we read that by a council it was ordained that everywhere schools should be established to teach the youth secular letters and liberal arts. The article of the said council, recited by Gratian, is this: "Report is made to us of certain places where they have no care to have schoolmasters for the study of letters. Therefore let all bishops, subjects, and people, in places where there is need, perform their duties in placing masters and doctors who may daily teach letters and liberal arts, for by their means the writings and commandments of God are declared and manifested." What now then will this slanderer Machiavelli say? Can he yet say that the doctors of Christianity have or would have abolished good letters and the writings of the pagans? Will he not hold himself vanquished by so many authorities as we have cited out of Jerome, Ambrose, Augustine, Gregory, Bede, and Basil, who are the principal doctors of Christianity; and the authority of the council, which is an approbation of the universal church? Shall not all this be sufficient to show the impudence of this Florentine?

But now I am desirous to know of this atheist Machiavelli, what was the cause that so many good books of the pagan authors were lost since the time of the ancient doctors of our Christian religion? Was it not by the Goths, who were pagans? For at their so many interruptions and breaking out of their countries, upon Gaul, Italy, and Spain, they wasted and burned as many books as they could find, being enemies of all learning and letters. And who within this hundred years has restored good letters contained in the books of the ancient pagans, Greeks, and Latins? Has it been the Turk, who is a pagan? It is well enough known that he is an enemy of letters, and desires none. Nay contrary, it has been the Christians who have restored them and established them in the brightness and light wherein we see them today. The knowledge of the Greek, Latin, and Hebrew languages has been brought in by others; but in our country of France we may thank king Francis I of happy memory. And since the restoration of languages and secular sciences, men have well experienced that they are requisite and profitable to understand the scriptures of our Christian religion, so far are we off from rejecting them.

And as for what Machiavelli says, that Christianity has sought to abolish all memory of antiquity; how dare he openly impugn the manifest truth? For none is ignorant that the true and primitive antiquity is of the Hebrews, whose books have been conserved, translated, and expounded by the Christians. And as for the antiquity of the pagans, does any man find that the Christians have discarded Homer, Hesiod, Berosus, or any other authors of antiquity? Nay, they are who have conserved them, who have aided themselves with them, and who have interpreted them. Eustachius, the great commentator of Homer, was he not a Christian, even a bishop? But I shame to stay in the refutation of the falsehoods of this atheist; for young and mean scholars may easily impugn his impudent lies.

Machiavelli says that Christianity did not succeed as well as it could have when it went about to abolish good letters, because it was constrained to use the Latin tongue, wherein all secular sciences were written. Herein does he manifestly show his beastliness and ignorance; for who constrained our Christian doctors to write in Latin? The Old and New Testament were first written in Hebrew and Greek; therefore the Latin doctors, if they had wanted to, might have written in these languages, as did Chrysostom, Athanasius, Basil, Cyril, Eusebius, and many others. Yet if writers had used these languages, men would not have ceased to preach in Latin to the Latins, in French to the French, in the German to the Germans, and to other nations, each in its own language. For it has been seen not past threescore years ago that in Italy, France, Germany, Spain, and other places, the Christian religion was not written in the native tongue, yet men held the religion in the said countries. But since then it has been brought into every one of those languages for the commodity of the people, as it was brought into Latin by Augustine, Ambrose, Jerome, Gregory, and other Latin doctors of the primitive church of their time. Yet if they had written in Hebrew or Greek, Christianity would not have ceased to subsist and stand for that. And even if the Latin profane books had perished, the language, which was then vulgar, would not have therefore perished. Therefore does Machiavelli show his beastliness, to say that the Christian religion has been constrained to use the Latin language, and that by that means the profane Latin authors have been conserved. But what means he when he says that if Christianity could have formed a new language, it would have abolished all memory of antiquity? Has there been at any time, in any country, any religion which has formed a new language? And how comes it that a religion can be received by the means of a new unknown tongue? If the Christian religion had invented a new tongue, it could never have been understood, nor received, and in consequence could not have abolished the books written in Latin. Likewise using the Latin that was then in common use, it could no more abolish the books written in that tongue, according to the saying of Machiavelli. Therefore take it which way you will; if Christianity had invented a new tongue, or if it used the Latin tongue (as it did and does), it could not extinguish and abolish the books written in Latin; therefore Machiavelli knows not what he says.

As little knows he what he says when he holds that sects and religions have varied twice or thrice in five or six thousand years, and that the last always causes the remembrance of the first to perish. For who has revealed to him this secret? Who has told him news of things done before Moses' time, if it was not Moses himself? Briefly, there is neither reason nor history whereupon he may found this impudent lie. But hereby he would show that if any doubt whether he is a very atheist, he has no more cause to doubt. For a proof hereof, he makes a declaration that he believes nothing of what is written in scripture of the creation of the world, nor of the religion of God which we hold since Moses. For by the holy Scripture is seen that there are not yet six thousand years since the creation of the world. It is also seen that the Christian religion of Messiah and Christ has not changed since the creation, but has always endured, and shall endure until the consummation of the world. And as for pagan religions, they have changed from one to another in little time, and in the same country, as histories show. At Rome, in the time of Romulus, there was a religion such as it was, which Numa changed; and strange religions of the Greeks and others were received at Rome. Insomuch that about five hundred years after Numa, when his books were found in his sepulcher and men read them, they found no part of their religion in them, as shall be more fully said in its place. Briefly, these pagan religions often changed in regard to their form and ceremonies, but in substance they changed nothing since the children of Cain who began to follow the false religion. For whatever outward change there was, within it was always devilish religion, having for its author the father of lies and falseness. And therefore Machiavelli knows not what he says, but that he is an atheist, and so would manifest himself to be one, by disclosing that he did not believe the holy Scriptures. He thought to have immortalized his name by making himself known to posterity, that he was a perfect atheist replenished with all impiety; as Nero did, who sought means to have men speak of him after his death, in slaying his mother, brother, master, and many good men of his time, and in burning Rome, and such other wicked and detestable cases. As also Caligula wished, so that there might be a memory of his kingdom in time to come, that there might happen some great pestilence and notable mortality, or some exceedingly great famine, ruin, earthquakes, and burning of towns. Because, he said, if my reign passes in peace and tranquility without some great and notable evil luck, none will speak of me in time to come. There are men of such wicked and devilish natures, who are of this humor, who desire to make their renown immortal by vices and wickedness. So has Machiavelli done, who has so well played his part that he has obtained the chief rank of all atheists and impious persons, near Aretino his companion, who lived in his time and has written the praise of sodomy to immortalize his name.

2.5

Machiavelli

> When men left the pagan religion, they became altogether corrupted, so that they neither believed in God nor the devil. (*Discourses*, book 1 chapter 12)

The pagan religion consists principally in the answers of oracles and augurs. And to have good answers of those oracles and augurs, they built to the gods goodly temples and with great ceremonies offered sacrifices to them. And the world was kept in a marvelous devotion by the oracle of Jupiter Ammon, of Apollo in Delos and in Delphi, and like others. But as soon as their trumpery and deceit was discovered, and men knew that the priests of those gods had them make answers after the fancies of those who gave most liberally, they began to despise and contemn those oracles, and no more to believe either in God or the devil.

Then men began to become altogether wicked, pressed, and willing to break, burst, and destroy all like unchained slaves, without any more making conscience of anything. Therefore if princes will be obeyed, they ought to hold their subjects always inclined and devoted to religion.

Answer

Machiavelli still continuing to teach his doctrine of atheism and the spite of our Christian religion, goes about to persuade by this maxim that there was a great loss to men when they lost the pagan religion. But certainly it was the light of the Christian religion which caused the darkness of the pagan religion to vanish, because that religion only depended on oracles, augurs, and other devilish illusions. So that in brief, Machiavelli's mind is that a man should do well to set packing the Christian religion, and that it were a good thing always to live in the pagan religion. What an impiety is this, I pray you? Can any sentence come from the devil of hell more detestable than this? Assuredly it much grieves me to blot paper to write such things, and to expose and lay abroad before the eyes and ears of good men such hard words, which cannot but be found evil in the ears of those who fear God. But the wise man exhorts us to speak to the fool after his folly, that he may not wax proud. Should we suffer such an atheist, who teaches all impiety, to take his course and sow his venom among us, and yet not dare to open our mouths to reveal him as he is? Shall we hold our peace in such a time as is most necessary to speak, to make manifest such wickedness as commonly runs abroad, that it may be shunned and taken heed of? Should this be well done, to meet with common poisoners and firebrands of hell, who run about the country to poison and set on fire all places, and not to stay them, but let them do what mischief they will? I beseech therefore all those who fear God to accept those reasons as lawful excuses that I am so often forced to speak and write so impious and abominable speeches; for although it displeases me to do so, yet I dare not but lay abroad the impiety of this poisoner. He then says that it was a good thing in the time of the pagans to see the world abused with that false opinion, for such he accounts it, of oracles and auguries; but that it was a great mischief and evil luck when the world began to discover that such things were false, feigned, and devised by men; because then the world began to become exceedingly wicked, prompt and willing to all evil, as an unchained slave.

Machiavelli then must note by his own confession, that men then became most wicked as soon as they began to be of the heathen religion, that is, without all religion. What means Machiavelli then openly to teach atheism and the spite of the Christian religion? Yet this he speaks not to bring us unto paganism, which he confesses to be false; but to make men, especially princes and great lords (for whose instruction he wrote his books), utterly to forsake all piety and to bring them to the highest degree of wickedness, whereunto he says they come who have no religion. But when princes or others have taken that good instruction, and offered that mockery unto God and religion, they but advance their own infallible confusion and ruin of their estates, as we have in another place demonstrated by examples.

But to come to the truth of what Machiavelli says, it is certain that as soon as the Christian religion came into light and knowledge, the pagan religion vanished away little by little, as the light also little by little spreads itself. True it is also, that as soon as the falseness of the pagan religion was discovered, there were some who notwithstanding would not be brought to the Christian religion. And as for such, I doubt not but they became always worse, forsaking the pagan religion as false, to follow atheism. No less may we well say of our time, wherein we see many who contemn all religion because they will not enquire and seek after the true religion; whereof they delight to be ignorant, to the end that it may not torment their wicked consciences, nor control their inordinate greed. But as we see many who are not satisfied to know the errors wherein they are wrapped, but also they have desired to know the truth which they ought to hold. So when the pagan religion ended, those who forsook it did not content themselves in knowing it was false, but they also thought good to know the true, which is the Christian, the light whereof made the other vanish away. And indeed, little by little everyone embraced the Christian religion, but there remained certain Porphyrys and Lucians who would be without religion. And would to God that our world were as pure from atheism as that world was; we should not see so many miseries and calamities which are in the world.

And as for what Machiavelli presupposes, that oracles were answers devised at the pleasure of priests, to deceive men in the temples of Apollo, Jupiter Ammon, or any other of the pagan gods; he shows himself to be very ignorant, and to have read little. Yet I will not deny but sometimes the priests intermixed somewhat of their own many times; but it is certain that the said oracles were diabolical answers, which the devil made himself, or caused to be made by some he or she priest who he brought into ecstasies and out of their senses, and so caused them to say what he would; and most often he answered in verses, but commonly ambiguous, in two senses. For how could those priests, who were commonly unlearned and knew nothing, give an answer in verse? It was also impossible that they could have advertisements from regions so far off as men who came to consult those oracles; especially of such particularities whereof answers were demanded of those oracles, to be able to give answers to any good purpose. But I will not stay more amply to prove this point; for those who have read very little of the ancient writings know well how certain it is that these oracles were voices proceeding from devils, which the pagans served under these names, of Jupiter, Apollo, and other like gods.

Plutarch, in a treatise he made of the defects of oracles, shows that the oracles were not things invented by priests; but concerning the failing of oracles, he is found very much distracted and troubled, not knowing how to resolve that question. For it must be presupposed that in his time, that of the emperor Trajan and a good while before, there were no more oracles; insomuch that that good philosopher was much abashed and perplexed from whence it should come. But because that point is well worth knowing, and comes well for our purpose in this place, I will handle it more at large.

You must then understand that Plutarch, who was a great pagan philosopher, to find out the cause of the failing and decay of oracles, entered into a question, whereof he (like a pagan) resolves himself. But to prove his opinion, he uses certain narrations which may well bring us to the truth of the cause of the ceasing of oracles. He then enters into disputation of the nature of the gods; and after many discourses he resolves that there are but one sort of gods, which the elders called demi-gods, which are mortal, though they lived long, five hundred or a thousand years. And he thinks that these demi-gods are those which the gods have engendered with mortal women. For the ancient superstition, to which certain philosophers have been led, believed that the gods sometimes descended below to cohabitate with women, and this served to keep the honor of great ladies who sometimes forgot their duties. Plutarch then would infer that the gods who answered at Delphi, Delos, and other places, were but half gods, and so might be dead, and thus the ceasing of oracles. Yet he held not this opinion nor any other very resolutely, but propounded it for those who would like it, and it seems to be the opinion which he best approves. But I do not think that any at this day will be of this opinion; for in truth it tastes of his paganism, being ignorant and far straying from the true knowledge of God and religion. Yet to prove that the said demi-gods are mortal, he makes a discourse very notable and worth knowing. He says then that in the time of the emperor Tiberius, one Epitherses, a schoolmaster in a town of Greece, sailed to Italy on a ship loaded with merchandise and many people. Making their way, they passed one night near the islands of Echinades, and the sea was so calm that they could perceive no wind, and the ship floating upon the water brought them little by little near Paxo. Having arrived, as some supped and did other things, behold a high and intelligible voice, which cried "Thamus, Thamus." This Thamus was the master of the ship, whose name most of the passengers did not know. This voice cried twice before the master would answer. At the third time he answered, unto which the voice yet cried with a higher sound, that as soon as he should come against the Palodes, he should make known unto the inhabitants there that the great Pan was dead. Epitherses said that at that word all the company of the ship were exceedingly afraid and astonished. So it came into a consultation among them, if the shipmaster Thamus should do what was commanded him by that voice. And the resolution was taken, that if when they came against the Palodes the winds were strong and good for them, they should pass on without stay or saying anything; but if the sea was calm and had no wind, that Thamus should signify unto the inhabitants of Palodes what the voice commanded him. Arriving there and having the sea calm without wind, Thamus got into the stern of the ship, and turning his face towards the land right against Palodes, he began to cry with a high voice, "The great Pan is dead." He had no sooner ended this speech than all the company in the ship heard a great crying and lamentation of many, mixed with a great admiration. Finally, when they arrived at Rome, each of the passengers spread abroad the fame of this thing, insomuch that it came to the notice of emperor Tiberius, who sent for Thamus, who told him all at length. Tiberius, believing it was true that the great god Pan was dead, desired to know what god that was. Some learned people he had about him told him that Pan was the son of the god Mercury and of Penelope. Behold here the account which Plutarch makes of Pan's death, and further says that in his time many heard this history rehearsed by one Aemilianus, son of the said Epitherses. But if we consider the circumstances of this history, we shall find that this voice was a signification of the death of Christ, which caused oracles to fail and overthrew the power of the devil. And it is credible that those lamentations heard at Palodes were complaints of evil spirits, to which were delivered the signification of their kingdom's destruction. And to prove that this history should be so understood, first we must consider that it is reported to be in the time of Tiberius, under whom our Lord suffered death and passion. It is also certain that Tiberius enquired of Jesus Christ, and understanding his miracles, he required of the Senate that they would have him enrolled in the litany of their gods at Rome; but the Senate would not. Moreover, it is credible that in the time of our Lord Jesus Christ, when among the pagans the fame was dispersed of Christ's miracles, as to raise to life the dead from their graves, to make see those born blind, to heal paralytic persons, and such like, that they believed he was God; for upon less reasons they believed others. And because he called himself the true shepherd, and the shepherd of shepherds, it is very likely that the pagans understanding this would divine and gather that it must needs be the god Pan, who they said to be the god of shepherds; and also because he said that he was sent by God his father to preach to men his will, they sometimes also gave him the name of Mercury, whom they said to be the messenger and deliverer of the will of the great god Jupiter. This may be gathered by the historiographer Dion, who said that the emperor Antoninus, warring against the Marcommans, obtained rain from heaven from the god Mercury. And Capitolinus, speaking of the same manner, says that the emperor Antoninus to obtain rain had recourse to a strange religion; but Mercury was no strange god to those pagans, so that we must understand that saying of Dion, of another Mercury than they knew; yet they likely gave him that name because they had heard say he was sent from God, to signify and preach his will. To come again to our purpose, the aforesaid learned men that were about Tiberius, hearing it spoken that so many miracles were done by Christ, easily resolved that he was a god; understanding he called himself the great shepherd, they concluded that he was Pan; hearing also that he said he was sent to deliver the will of God, and that he was born of a virgin, they presumably inferred that he must be the son of Mercury, messenger of the great Jupiter, and of some chaste woman such as was Penelope. For it is likely they could never believe that he was a virgin's son, because it repugned the order of nature that a virgin should bring forth a child. And therefore of all those conjectures laid together, those wise men (or rather ignorant) about the emperor, gathered the answer which they made him, that the god Pan, who died at that time, was the son of Mercury and of Penelope; applying to their gods what they had heard spoken of our Lord Jesus Christ. Behold then how this history, drawn from the pagans, is a perfect witness that by the death of Christ came the failing and ceasing of oracles; and indeed we find in no histories that since his death oracles have been of any account or fame, as they were before. True it is, that the men and women priests of those gods, who answered by oracles, seeing that their master abandoned and forsook them, yet delivered answers themselves of their own devices; but the trumperies, deceits, and fictions were soon discovered by the divulging and dispersion of the Christian religion, in such sort that the oracles and their deliverers were greatly discredited. Nero himself, discovering the abuse, overthrew one of the temples of Apollo wherein were delivered oracles, and slew all the priests belonging to it.

For a resolution then I hold that at the coming of our Savior Jesus Christ oracles failed, as the coming of the son causes darkness to depart from the earth. At his coming he preached the true and pure heavenly doctrine to men, and after him his apostles and disciples preached it also. So that by the doctrine of Jesus Christ, and of his apostles and disciples, all Christians were instructed to fear, love, and honor God above all things, and to serve him according to his commandments in purity and simplicity, rejecting all idolatries, superstitions, and divine services invented by men. Moreover, they in true doctrine taught good manners, to love their neighbors as themselves, and not to do to another what he would not have done to himself; to use towards him the same charity one would have used to himself; to obey superiors and magistrates; to live contentedly everyone in the vocation whereunto God has called him; yea generally Christians were taught in all true virtue, whereas before pagans taught nothing but the mask and resemblance of virtue. For Christ and his apostles taught men to be just, charitable, temperate, gentle, obedient, pitiful, loving good, shunning evil, and they taught not to be outwardly only, but inwardly also without feigning or any dissimulation of heart. Whereas the pagans cared not to be inwardly virtuous and mannerly, if in outward appearance they show so to be, to obtain honor, glory, and advancement unto greatness, which was the mark and end for which they commonly desired virtue, and not for conscience' sake, nor to please God. The examples of Caesar, Pompey, Cicero, and generally of all the old Romans who have had any great reputation of virtue, prove that this is true and that they never aspired to virtue but to obtain honor and to increase their greatness. Cato likewise, who seemed in all his behaviors to despise honor; wherefore slew he himself? Was it to please God, or to satisfy his conscience? Certainly no, for he was not so ignorant but he knew well that murder displeased God, and that no man should murder himself, more than another. Nothing could move his conscience to incite him to slay himself; for he did not feel himself culpable of anything that deserved it. How then? Why should he murder himself? For this, not to receive that dishonor to fall alive into the hands of Caesar; although he knew well enough that there needed no more but a little humiliation to have his life, goods, and dignities saved, as he confessed to his son and his friends before he slew himself. But his heart was so swollen with glory and honor that he loved better to slay himself than to humble himself before Caesar. Here behold how those pagans aspired, not to have virtue but for honor and an outward show; whereas the doctrine of Christ teaches us to desire and lust after virtues, not only to bring them unto outward appearance, but also to adorn our hearts and our consciences inwardly, and so to please God. Moreover, we have also showed that the Christian doctrine comprehends much more perfectly the virtues of good manners than the pagans' doctrine does. How then dare that filthy Machiavelli say that men became wicked, like unchained slaves, when oracles failed? Where did he find this? Where did he read that men were worse and more evil conditioned in that time when oracles failed, than before? Rather contrary we read that when oracles failed, which was in the time of the primitive church, men who gave themselves to the Christian religion were of a holy life and conservation, and those who gave not themselves to that religion, but persevered in their paganism, always learned from the Christians that which made them better and of more account. Let any read the works of Seneca, Plutarch, Pliny the Younger, and of many other pagan authors who were in the time of the primitive church, and he shall find infinite godly and Christian sentences, which the pagans learned from the Christians of their time, as may be necessarily supposed. For such sentences were never borrowed from Plato, Aristotle, or other philosophers who were before the coming of Jesus Christ. As for example when Plutarch disputes of the tranquility of the soul; to fly anger; to shun usury; of the profit that a man may draw from an enemy; that God punishes slowly; and on many other points he utters many sentences which are truly Christian, and hold nothing of the philosophers' doctrine, who were before Christ our Savior. And all the works of Seneca are full of Christian sentences; insomuch that many have esteemed that Seneca himself was a Christian, even that he was well known by Saint Paul; which it may be was not unworthy to be believed. For Seneca, who was in the time of Nero and was a learned man and a lover of the learned, might well have heard Paul speak, who at that time was a prisoner at Rome for the doctrine he preached; and might well have been so curious as to talk with him, to understand what was that doctrine of which all the world spoke. But whatsoever it was, none can deny that the writings of Seneca in many places demonstrate that he learned many things from the Christians. We may then conclude that in the time when oracles failed and Christian doctrine began to be published and divulged through the world, men became better, and not more wicked, like unchained slaves, as this mocker Machiavelli says. For although even in that time there were found certain atheists like himself, men must not therefore infer that all the world, or the most part thereof, became wicked. Neither has Machiavelli uttered this opinion as having read it in any good author, but only thereby to blame the Christian religion as the cause of the corruption of manners. But he impudently lies like a shameless slanderer, who dares to be so bold as to deliver such talk without any proof, and of which the contrary is already clearly proved.

2.6
Machiavelli

The Roman Church is the cause of all the calamities in Italy.

The Roman Church is the cause that Italy, which of old was the most flourishing province of the Roman Empire, is at this day dismembered and cut into petty seignories, as is seen. By the means thereof, she that was wont to subjugate and vanquish other provinces is now exposed as a prey for all foreign kings who will attempt it with a strong arm. And although of all Christianity it be nearest unto the Roman Church, yet has it of all others the least religion; because therein, that most holy court does little else but sow partialities and disorders. And he who will prove whether such evils proceed from the Roman Church, let him procure that she may remove her seat for a small time unto Switzerland, where men live in great rest and unity. For there you would shortly see it fill the whole country with disorder and confusion.

Answer

Although the Roman Church is contaminated with many vices, yet Machiavelli shows himself here a notable slanderer against it; for experience has made us long know that it rather does mischief far off than near at hand, and that it ordinarily enriches the place where it abides. We read that it held its place at Avignon for the space of seventy years, so that by the affluence and plenty of gold and silver which arrived there, the town became so opulent and rich that it yet tastes thereof, and gladly desires it might be always there. As for the Swiss, of whom Machiavelli speaks, I am assured that some would have the seat of the Roman Church among them, even if it cost them much money. And if it were there, the pope should not lack people for his guard, for they would furnish him with as many as he would, and his cardinals also, for their pay. And I am also of the mind that they would accord them letters to be denizens and free burghers in all their towns, though it is contrary to their custom to receive strangers. For so there would every day arrive in their country plenty of silver, which they cannot but love better than either the pope's benedictions or pardons; yet would they also be glad to reap their pardons at a low price. And notwithstanding what Machiavelli says, that if the Roman seat were there placed, there would be no good peace from sowing divisions among the Swiss; that is unlikely, no more than it did so in Avignon or the countries around it. For whereas Machiavelli says it sows divisions and partialities in Italy; that rather happens by the humor of that country's people, who are naturally subject to nourish divisions among both themselves and other nations where they have the credit, as experience is in France. Moreover, the Romans themselves are not of Machiavelli's opinion, neither do they complain that the Roman seat brings them any damage. At the beginning of that great schism of popes, they showed well how greatly they feared to lose their seat. For so much were they afraid that the cardinals should again have a French pope, who might again dwell at Avignon, where the seat had before so long remained, that they constrained the cardinals by force, cries, and popular violence to elect a pope of their own nation. All through the town of Rome, and before the place where the cardinals were assembled to make their election, all the people in a mutiny cried with a high voice, "We will have a Roman, or at least an Italian." This was the cause that the cardinals gave them a Roman, whereof the Roman inhabitants were so joyous that they took him on their shoulders to honor him the more, and carried him so long and so far through Rome that they stifled and smothered him with the great press of their arms. When they saw their terrestrial god dead, they straight returned to the cardinals, saying their pope was dead, and they must give them another. So by their cries and popular tumult, they were constrained to give them a new Italian. But afterwards they made another in Avignon, who was antipope to him of Rome; so that it may well be said that the too immoderate desire of the Romans to have the holy seat at Rome, was the cause of a papal schism which endured near forty years, and was the spring of many evils.

I have before said, and it is true, that the holy seat does more harm far off than near, and it is easy to prove by examples. For by tithes, bulls of benefices, pardons, and other expenses, the holy father has ever had cunning enough to draw store of silver from far provinces, as from France, Germany, England, Spain, and from elsewhere. And all those huge heaps of treasure fell in no other place than at Rome and Italy. So that a good old civilian lawyer was wont to say, the court of Rome has long had good skill to change lead into gold; which act the greatest alchemists and the best exercised Paracelsians of our time could never do. We also see the Romans, by the means of their bullish and leaden art, maintain themselves brave, fine, and in good order; whereas these Paracelsians commonly go all ragged and torn, in great poverty and necessity, having spent their fortunes and patrimonies with blowing the coal, and are by all men a despised people and of no account.

Yet we read in our histories that our kings of France have many times hindered popes from drawing silver out of the realm, by annates, tenths, bulls, and other means; as in the time of Boniface VIII, Benedict XI, Julius II and III. But concerning this matter it is good to mark the determination made in 1410 by our masters of the faculty of the Sorbonne, and by all the University of Paris; who resolved in a general congregation that the French church was not bound to pay any silver to the pope in any manner whatsoever, unless by the way of a charitable subsidy, and that in three cases only. Namely, to employ the said silver to the conquest of the holy land; for the reunion of the Greeks with the Latins; and lastly to preach the Gospel to all creatures. In which cases only, they said, men ought to provide a charitable subsidy for the pope; yet with this condition, that the said pope touch no silver but what the French church appoints treasurers to distribute for the aforesaid purposes, and not otherwise. If this determination were observed, truly the pope would not be contented, but the realm would be much bettered; and if all Christian princes agreed in the observation of this determination, certainly it would come to pass what friar John of Rochetaillade preached in his time against the pope. And because his sermon will not be far from our purpose, I will here briefly rehearse it.

In the time that the holy seat was at Avignon, about the year 1360, there was a Friar Minor called friar John de Rochetaillade, who set himself to preach against the pride, gormandizers, and superfluities of the pope and his cardinals, and generally against all the prelates and clergy; also against princes who too sorely oppressed their subjects. He always took for his text or theme some part of the Apocalypse, and properly applied it to the pope, cardinals, and prelates. Our historians say he was a great clerk, and that he foretold the captivity of king John; and that Pope Innocent VI, much grieved at his sermons, caused him to be imprisoned, fearing that by his great knowledge he caused all the world to err; for the good Saint Peter was of opinion that ignorance preserves men from erring, and that knowledge brings them into error. And indeed, he that knows nothing, wherein can he err? But this good friar John, among other sermons preached one which was the chief cause of his imprisonment, and this was the substance thereof.

> "Masters and ladies, I will tell you a strange case, which in time past of old happened amongst birds, and it is very like that we now see, and hereafter shall see the like happen to our holy Father, the pope. You must understand that in old time a bird was engendered in the world, which was the fairest and most beautiful to see that was possible, but it had no

feathers. The other birds hearing speak of this featherless bird, thought good to go see it; and being all arrived within view of her, they found her most excellent, and pitied her because she could not fly (as they did) for want of feathers. Then they held a council to advise what was best to do, that this goodly bird might not die with hunger, because she could not fly to get her living. They then resolved amongst them that each bird should give her part of their feathers; which they did, and as she took the feathers, she appeared more and more beautiful; insomuch that the other birds gave her still more feathers. As soon as this bird saw herself well plumed and feathered, and that all the other birds honored her, she began to become fierce and proud, and to despise the other birds, and yet not contented with the said contempt and spite, she bucked and contraried them in all she could. Then the other birds again thought it best to advise what was best to do touching this new bird who they had emplumed, and who became so stately and insolent. They concluded in their council that it was best for every one of them to redemand their feathers, by the means of which she was so exalted in pride that she made no account of them. Then all the company of birds finding this new bird, after they had showed her the proud incognizance of herself and them, each one took his feathers; the peacock first, the falcon after, and all the other birds, so that they left her all naked and featherless. So masters (said Frair John to the pope and cardinals) shall it happen to you, and doubt not thereof. For when the emperors, kings, and Christian princes have taken from you the goods and riches that in former times they have given you, which you bestow in extreme pride and superfluity, then shall you remain all naked. Where find you that Saint Peter or Saint Sylvester rid with two hundred horses? Yea, contrary, their estate was very simple, enclosed and hid within Rome."

Thus friar John preaching spoke but the truth; yet this truth, which is so odious to the world, brought him to prison, where he finished his days. I will then conclude this recital, that if all Christian princes would practice the determination of our masters of Sorbonne and the University of Paris, the same would fall unto Saint Peter which fell unto friar John's bird.

Yet it is not only by the change of lead into gold that his holiness does much evil to provinces far from Rome, but also by his interdicts and excommunications. In the time of the schism of popes, he of Rome who was called Urban sent bulls unto king Richard of England (who took his part and was an Urbanist), by which he commanded him to make war upon the king of France, a Clementine, and gave him power to levy silver upon the English clergy. Moreover, he gave so great a quantity of pardons to all those who with a good heart furnished silver for that war, that it seemed he meant clean to have emptied both hell and purgatory of Englishmen; for every man or woman might draw out his father, grandfather, great-grandfather, uncles, aunts, children, nephews, and other ascendants, descendants, and collaterals, by paying so much for every poll. He further promised their souls to be guided right into paradise, who died in this war, or who died the year after they had paid the money for that war; nor that there should be any necessity for the said souls to stray out of their way by purgatory and limbo, but go right into paradise. The said bulls being thus preached and published through England, there was everywhere a great press that year to die, and to give silver, so that in a small time was heaped up the sum of 2,500,000 francs. One part of this silver was given to the Bishop of London, who was chosen general to make war upon the Clementines in Spain; and the other part was delivered to the Bishop of Norwich, who was elected general of another army to make war upon France, which also was Clementine. And indeed these two armies did much harm, as well in Spain as in France; yet the Bishop of Norwich, being a young man and inconsiderate, on entering Flanders met an Urbanist, the king of France, who with 100,000 men constrained him to retire homeward with shame and great loss.

In 1513 great damage happened unto the kings of France and Navarre, by the means of an interdict and excommunication which Pope Julius II cast against all the princes who had sent their ambassadors to the Council of Pisa, whose lands and seignories he exposed and gave as a prey to all men that would invade them. For under color of those wicked and detestable bulls, Emperor Maximilian and the Swiss constrained king Louis XII to abandon Milan and almost all that he held in Italy. And on the other side, the king of England fell upon France with an army of three thousand, assaying to conquer part thereof. But God suffered it not; for in the meantime this wicked pope died, the interdict was revoked, and peace was made with the English. On the other side also, king Ferdinand of Aragon, feigning he would come to prey upon France, entered into the kingdom of Navarre and usurped it from king John d'Albret, who was defeated thereof without being defied, even before he knew the king of Aragon's purpose. Whose successors have since detained the kingdom of Navarre, usurped from John and his lawful successors; yet notwithstanding the said unjust usurpers call themselves most Catholic.

And as for what Machiavelli says, that Italy is the province of Christendom where there is least religion, he says very true; but what would he say now if he were alive? He would find that if in his time they had so well profited in his school as to be very great atheists and contemners of God and of all religion, that now his scholars know far more than their master. And there is no doubt but already long ago all religion was contemned in Italy, even the Roman Catholic. Will you have a better example than what M. Commines rehearses? He says that in the time of Louis XII there were two principal houses at Florence, the Medici and the Pazzi, who were in quarrel and enmity together. Those of the house of Pazzi favored the pope and the king of Naples, by whose counsel and advice they enterprised to slay Lorenzo de Medici and all his race. And to surprise him the better, unprovided and without taking heed, they resolved to massacre him with all his race and sequel upon a solemn feast day, at the hour that the great mass was sung; and that when the priest began to sing Sanctus, Sanctus, it should be the watchword to rush upon them. And indeed they executed their enterprise, except that they slew not Lorenzo, who saved himself in the vestry, but his brother Julian and certain others of his race were slain. I demand of you, if those who enterprised and gave counsel to attempt such an act believed in the mass? We need not doubt but they were very atheists. But if in that time, some forty years ago, Italy was so furnished with atheists and contemners of religion, what think you it is now.

In conclusion, Italy, Rome, the pope, and his seat, are truly the spring and fountain of all spite of religion, and the school of all impiety. And as they already were in Machiavelli's time, as he confesses, so are they far more today. For although the Church of Rome has heretofore made, and yet does, certain demonstrations to sustain a religion, yet in effect it maintains it not otherwise but by subtleties and words. For it commands indeed to fast the vigils and Lent; but is there any place in the world where they care less for fasting vigils and Lent than at Rome? It commands chastity to priests; but is there any place in the world where priests, cardinals, and others are more furnished with whores and bawds? It also commands them to serve their benefices, but of a hundred priests at Rome there is scarcely one that does it. Their religion forbids the sale of benefices, sepulchers, sacraments, and dispensations; but is there any place in the world where there is a greater traffic of them than at Rome? It forbids simony; but where are there any simonacs, if not at Rome and in Italy? I speak only of the ordinances which the Roman Church has made, yet herself does not observe. For if I would cite the ordinances of God, which she observes no more than the other, I should too tediously rehearse them all. But briefly, the Roman Church has invented a thousand traditions wherewith it has burdened the shoulders of poor Christians to their great abashment, but meanwhile the Church itself will keep none of them. Rather that holy seat dispenses with all them of Italy and Rome; and indeed there is no place in the world where the pope's ordinances are less observed, nor where all religion is in more contempt, as Machiavelli himself confesses. Let Christians then make their profit from this confession of Machiavelli, and so let them fly the spring of impiety, of atheism, of corruption of manners, and of the contempt of all religion, lest God punish them and make them perish with such wicked men as make open profession thereof.

2.7
Machiavelli

Moses could never have caused his laws and ordinances to be observed if force and arms had wanted.

The most excellent men mentioned in books who became princes by their own virtue, and not by fortune, were Moses, Cyrus, Romulus, Theseus, and such like; for fortune only gave them the occasion and the matter to execute their virtue. As Moses found the people of Israel in captivity and servitude in Egypt, Cyrus also found the Persians discontent with the proud government of the Medes. Romulus found himself dejected from his birthplace, the town of Alba. Lastly, Theseus found the town of Athens full of troubles and confusions. Without these occasions, coming by fortune, the virtue of their courage would not have appeared; as also without their virtue, such occasions had served them nothing. All those occasions then made these persons fortunate, and their excellent virtue knew well how to make profit of occasions.

Answer

This atheist, always willing to show more strongly that he did not believe the holy Scriptures, dares vomit out this blasphemy and say that Moses by his own virtue and by arms was made the prince of the Hebrews. We see by the books of Moses that he was constrained by God to take charge and draw the Hebrew people out of Egypt, to bring them into the land of Canaan, a place of the primitive of spring of this people. And after he had accepted that charge, we read that God gave him power to do many miracles before Pharaoh and all the people of Egypt, so that the Hebrew people might return in peace to the country from whence they came. Afterwards, having obtained permission to return, we see how the people were guided in the day by a visible and apparent cloud which went before them, and in the night by a pillar of fire. We read so many miracles done by God in their passage through the Red Sea, and in the deserts, and how Moses did nothing but by the counsel and power of God alone. With what boldness then dares this stinking atheist disgorge this talk, to say that Moses was made the prince of the Hebrew people by his own virtue and by arms? Could he by any other means than the Bible know how and what way Moses came to be governor of the Hebrew people? For all pagan authors speak little thereof, and what they speak is but what they read in the books of Moses, or by hearsay from those who read them, seeing it is certain that we have no profane author that was not many worlds after Moses. If then Machiavelli can say nothing of Moses' doings but by his own books, with what impudence dares he deliver the contrary from what is written therein? For to say he was made prince of the Hebrews by his own virtue and by arms, is to deny that God constrained him to accept the charge to conduct the Hebrews, and that they came out of Egypt by the miracles of God, and that they were conducted by the cloud and pillar of fire, and that God nourished them all the way in the desert; which is indeed to deny all that is written in the books of Moses. Assuredly, there is no man of so heavy and dull a judgment but he may well know that this most wicked atheist has taken pleasure to search out the most savage maxims that could be devised, assuring himself that he should ever find monsters of men who would also delight in absurd and bestial opinions, and would give passage and way to his doctrine. And yet the better to show his beastliness, this doctrine may be overthrown even by the writings of the pagans themselves. Trebellius Pollio writes that Moses was alone familiar with God. Tacitus, going about to slander and blame the Jewish religion contained in the books of Moses, confesses that the king of Egypt made the Hebrew people leave his country for sores, rottenness, and other maladies infecting the Egyptians. The poets and philosophers, when they sometimes speak of Moses' doctrine, they call it sacred oracles, showing thereby that they confess that the deeds and writings of Moses came from God, and not from his own virtue.

But with what impudence dares Machiavelli compare Moses to these idolaters, Romulus and Theseus? What similitude had they with Moses in their life or in their death? Romulus and Theseus were two bastards, rude and violent men in their youth, whereof the one slew his brother, and the other his son; the one finished his days slain by his citizens, and the other was banished and chased from his own. Can any find the like in Moses? But this maxim of Machiavelli has no need of a more ample refutation; for the truth is so clear and apparent to the contrary, that a man may manifestly see that this Florentine is a most wicked slanderer and impudent liar.

Yet I think it good to mark another beastliness and ignorance, in that he says that Theseus came to the domination of Athens in confusion. For clean contrary, he came to it because he was acknowledged as the son of

Egeus, king of Athens; and was exceedingly well liked by the Athenians, because he had acquired the reputation of a magnanimous and valiant man, in that he slew and overcame many thieves who robbed the country of Attica and the adjoining countries. And to say the estate of Athens was confused is a jest of Machiavelli's invention. And in what he says, that the occasion and means Romulus had to make himself a prince was because he found himself ejected from his birthplace, the town of Alba; does he not show himself a man of good judgment? For can a man say in good sense and reason, that to be ejected from his country, disavowed by his parents as a bastard, to be put to nourishment among shepherds and beasts, to be impoverished and destitute of all means; that these are means and occasions to be made a prince and to be the founder of a town? If this is true, there will be found men enough who have all those good means to become princes, and so will there be found more princes than other people. But contrary, the means that we read whereby Romulus became a prince and founder of a town, were that he was a strong and violent man, cunning in arms, who gathered together many vagabonds and made them captains; afterwards, he and his brother Remus founded Rome, and to be sole ruler, he slew Remus and made himself king.

2.8
Machiavelli

Moses usurped Judea, as the Goths usurped a part of the empire. (*Discourses*, book 2 chapter 9)

When people are oppressed with famine, war, or servitude in their country, oftentimes they go to conquer other countries, wherein they change their name. As the people of Israel, being oppressed with servitude in Egypt, under the conduct of Moses occupied a part of Syria, which he called Judea; even as the Goths and Vandals occupied the western empire. Likewise the Maurusians, an ancient people of Syria, perceiving the Hebrews coming with great power from Egypt and feeling themselves not strong enough to resist them, abandoned their country and withdrew into Africa, where they conquered ground and chased away the natural inhabitants. This may be proved by the authority of the historian Procopius, who wrote in the life of Bellisarius that he read the inscription on certain pillars written in the country of the Maures in Africa: *Nos Maurisci, qui fugimus a facie Fosu latronis filis*

Nave: that is to say, We are the Maricians who fled before the face of Fosu, the chief son of Nave.

Answer

This atheist, having before said that Moses was made prince of the Hebrews by his own virtue and by arms, will now persuade that he was a thief and usurper of another country, without any title or reason, and that he seized upon Judea as the Goths and Vandals did Lombardy, Spain, and other countries of the Roman Empire. I have before protested, as I do sill, that it grieves me much to defile my paper with such filthy speeches; yet the more am I vexed that the ears and eyes of so many people should be occupied in reading and hearing things evil sounding, and so far from all piety and verity. But it is necessary to discover the doctrine and the doctor of our courtiers at this day, who think that the damnable books of this atheist should serve for rules to conduct affairs of state, as the stern serves to guide a ship. To refute then this maxim, we know that the land of Judea was first called the land of Canaan, having taken that name from Cain the son of Noah, who dwelled there after the deluge and was the first stock of the Canaanites in that country. One part of that land was called Palestine, which name it took from the Philistines, a people coming from Philistim, Noah's nephew, who were a mighty and strong people of that land, and who had the government of the other people of the country. One part also of that land of Canaan was called Judea, of the name of Judah, who was chief of the twelve patriarchs of the children of Jacob, from whence came the people of Israel. We do not read that in the time of Moses this country was called Syria, for at that time the country which afterwards men called Syria was called the land of Aram, who was the son of Shem, the son of Noah. Although those who came after, under the name of Syria, comprised the country of Assyria, which in Moses' time was called the land of Assur, also the son of Shem. And therefore is manifestly seen the beastliness and ignorance of Machiavelli when he says that Moses usurped a part of Syria, seeing the name of Syria was not yet invented, much less comprised the land of Canaan. But what could a simple secretary of the town of Florence either have read or seen except the registers of the town-house? But good authors, Greek or Latin, he never read, as is easy to judge by his writings, wherein he cites no story to enrich his work but the bad and slender examples of the Genoese, the Florentines, the pope, the duke of Milan, and of other such like petty potentates of Italy. He sometimes cites some words out of Livy, but to so little purpose as may be. Moreover it is known that the land of Canaan was promised many times by God to Abraham and his seed, as is seen in Genesis; and that Abraham dwelled there, and his race after him, after he departed from his nephew Lot, unto the time that Jacob and his family were by famine constrained to retire into Egypt. Should we then say that when the Hebrews returned from Egypt to dwell in their original land, which was promised to them by God (master of heaven and earth), that they were usurpers like the Goths and Vandals? Nay contrary, they were the just and true possessors thereof, and with good right expulsed and drove out the Canaanites, occupiers thereof, who usurped from them the land of their education, which God had promised and assigned to them for a heritage.

And as for what he alleges of the Mauritanians, it is a very fable; for the names of all such nations that were vanquished by Moses and Joshua are plainly set down in their books, but there is not found the name of Mauritanians, neither is there found written in any good author that in the land of Canaan there ever dwelled any nation called Mauritanians. And as for that nation of Africa called Mauritania, it never came out of the country of Palestine, but out of Media; by the corruption of tongues these people were called Maures of Medes, as Sallust says, who is a more credible author than this beast Machiavelli, who says that the Mauritanians of Africa came from ancient Syria.

And as for that inscription *Nos Maurusi*, etc., cited by Machiavelli out of Procopius, true it is that Procopius says that in Numidia in Africa the Mauritanians built a town called Tinge, and there set up two pillars of white stone, where they put the said inscription in the Phoenician language. But Procopius does not say that he either saw or read the said inscription engraved on the pillars. And it is not likely to be true that they could have endured entire and whole from the time of Joshua till the time of Procopius, 2500 years or more, seeing the wars and devastations occurring during that time in Africa and all parts of the world. Other authors who speak of the affairs of Africa, far more authentic and ancient than Procopius, do not note the said inscription. It is also absurd to say that the Mauritanians would make known to their posterity that they were cowards, flying before their enemies without any resistance. Absurd also to say that in one town they should set up two pillars for one same thing, but rather to immortalize the memory of their flight they would have erected two pillars in places distant from each other, to the end that if one perished the other might remain. But we need not be abashed by Procopius, who was a rhetorician, a sophist, and a Greek (three qualities yielding to presumption), that he might be too light and forward, and feign too much touching that inscription. For in the same place he says that the Mauritanians, a people of Phoenicia, abandoned their country and went to dwell in Africa, flying before Joshua and the people of Israel; and further, that they were a people composed of the Jebusites, Gessurians, and other people named in the Bible. But the Bible refutes him therein, for it is written that neither the Jebusites nor the other Canaanites were driven out of their country by the Hebrews, but were made their tributaries. And therefore to conclude this point, neither Machiavelli nor Procopius (his great author) is therein more to be credited than the rabbis' dreams, which hold that the Romans sprung from the Judeans, and the Germans from the Canaanites. Yet let this be said, not in any way to diminish the credit and authority of Procopius, who notwithstanding I confess is well to be believed in the history which he has written touching the wars made in his time by the emperor Justinian and his lieutenants Belisarius, Narces, and others.

2.9

Machiavelli

The religion of Numa was the chief cause of Rome's felicity. (*Discourses*, book 1 chapter 12)

During the time of Romulus' kingdom he used the Roman people to make war, which made them martial, rude, horrible, fierce, sanguinary, and without all humility and civility. But on succeeding Romulus in the crown, Numa saw he had to do with a people very hard to govern; and to bring them under policy without softening and mitigating their minds, he thought it best to devise some religion, well adorned and decked with beautiful ceremonies; because without religion he thought it impossible to maintain any policy among men. As soon as he came to the crown, he began to make ordinances concerning priests and the ceremonies of religion, making the people believe they were revealed by the goddess Egeria. And this fell out so well for him that the religion which he instituted was one of the principal causes of Rome's felicity. For it served to give heart and hope to soldiers, to hold them quiet in the field, to maintain good men and to overthrow the wicked, to appease mutinies in the people, and in all things to make them obedient. But a prince ought not to think it impossible for him, what was possible for Numa, nor to be anything discouraged if the subjects he has to deal with be anything witty, that they will not suffer themselves to be carried to a new faith. For I may well say that the Florentine people are not very beastly and rude, yet friar Jerome Savonarola, preaching at Florence, made ten thousand Florentines believe that he privately spoke with God, who revealed unto him such things as he preached in the pulpit.

Answer

Machiavelli having assayed to instruct a prince to reject all religion out of his heart, and to be an atheist and contemn all piety, now would persuade him to invent a new religion that is gallant and beautiful, well farced and stuffed with ceremonies, such as Numa's religion was; yet not to believe therein, but for his subjects to believe, that with the fear of religion they might be better detained in their offices and duties. And that the prince might be more encouraged to procure a new religion, such as that of Numa, he says it is not difficult to do, citing the example of the Florentines, whom Savonarola made believe what he would by feigning a revelation from God. But it is no marvel if this atheist, without religion, thus plays with religions, deriding all, and is willing to persuade a prince to invent a new one. For out of a vessel full of poison, what other thing can come but poison? But it is strange that he proposes Numa for a prince to imitate in the making of a new religion, for the greatest thing Numa invented in his religion was the Temple of Faith, where he established many ceremonies to induce people to reverence their faith and to fear perjury. He also ordained that upon controversies happening among parties, they should be bound to go to the temple and there swear with certain great ceremonies upon the truth of the points of their contentions. Secondly, he persuaded the people that those who usurped upon the limits of others' possessions were predestinate to the gods of hell, to the end that every man might be afraid to take another's goods. But does not Machiavelli teach the plain contrary? Does he not say that a prince nor any other ought to observe his faith but for his profit? Does he not also say that a prince should know the art of trumpery and deceit, and that he should have no scruple to be perjured? Does he not also show that a prince in a conquered country should plant colonies and chase away the ancient natural inhabitants from their goods and possessions? All which things are directly contrary to the religion of Numa, which he commends so much; but it is likely that this ignorant beast praises Numa's religion without knowing that it contained the points of which we now speak.

I doubt not but some will judge at the first sight that this religion of Numa could not be evil, teaching such good things as to observe faith, not to be perjured, nor to usurp others' goods and possessions; but it must not be approved, for one must not by evil and falsity introduce a good thing. This was good, to bring the people to an observation of faith;

but to imagine it was a god or goddess, and to do services and ceremonies unto her, these were damnable and against God's honor, from whom they steal the glory that belongs unto him, when they by form of religion do honor to another thing than him, be it a creature or devised thing. Therefore was not that a Christian oration which was made by Monsieur Capel, the king's advocate in the court of Parliament at Paris? Whereby praising the dead king Francis II of happy memory, because he had care of religion, he showed that realms and commonwealths of ancient pagans, who had good care to observe their religion, obtained prosperity in all felicity. For, he said, although their religion was false and they lived in error and darkness, yet they prospered, because esteeming it good and true, they had it in a singular reverence and observation. This oration of Capel truly had a little of Machiavelli's doctrine, to say that a false religion was the cause that the pagans prospered.

But to show that Machiavelli knows not what he says, I will here recite a history to this purpose. In the year 574 after the foundation of Rome, in the time of the consulship of Lucius Manlius and Fulvius Flaccus, as men dug the earth they found the sepulcher of king Numa, where there were two arches of hewn stone. In one Numa was buried, and in the other were the books he had written, wrapped in wax, in such sort that they seemed to be new. There were seven books in Latin, concerning the ceremonies of the religion which he instituted. Immediately a fame went all over, how the books of king Numa's religion were found, and every man attended that they should be divulged, and by their means all abuses in the Roman religion should be reformed. Yet to do nothing rashly, the consuls gave charge to Quintus Petilius, lieutenant of justice, to peruse those books and report the truth of them to the Senate. Petilius read them from one end to the other, and certified his opinion unto the Senate. And it was found that the religion which was handled in those books was of no account, and that it would be a pernicious and damaging thing to the commonwealth to bring that religion into use. So it was resolved by a decree of the Senate that those books should be burned before all the people, which was done. I would now gladly know of Machiavelli, who so much esteems the religion of Numa, without ever having seen his books, if he can yield a better judgment of them than Petilius and all the Roman Senate. Is not this as a blind man to judge of colors, who speaks of a thing he knows not?

As for Friar Savonarola, the Florentines showed well that he was no such man as would lead them to any new religion; neither did he preach any other religion but the old Roman religion, only denouncing unto them the vengeances and punishments of God which would fall upon them from heaven if they did not repent and amend their sins, and this he assured them as though he had some revelation from God. But among other things he preached and affirmed most that there would come a king out of France to deliver the country from so many tyrants and potentates as then held the country in great servitude and slavery. This talk pleased some who desired change, though others did not delight in it. About the time he made those sermons, king Charles VIII made a voyage unto Naples, and as soon as he was seen in Italy all the world began to say and believe that Savonarola was a true prophet, and that he had well foretold what they saw come to pass. The worst was that the king did nothing worthy of account in the voyage, and the best part of Savonarola's prophecy, which was to purge Italy of so many tyrannizers, remained yet to accomplish. Then the reputation of this good friar began not only to diminish, but also men began to say and believe that he was an abuser; so that in the end he was accused in Florence to be a most wicked heretic, and his enemies said he was worthy to be put into a sack and cast into the river. And he continued to preach that the king of France would come again to perform what he had not executed in the first voyage, and that the will of God was so, and if he did not accomplish it, yet God himself would punish it. The pope and the duke of Milan were troubled by this; for they thought it was but a bait to cause the king of France to come again into Italy, whereof they were greatly afraid. Therefore they joined together against this poor friar, and wrote to the Seignory of Florence, to do justice upon him as a seducer and heretic.

Among others who took Savonarola in hand was a friar (for there was never love between the friars and the Jacobins) who maintained that he was a heretic. And to prove it, he presented to Savonarola a combat, to commit themselves both into the fire; and he who was not hurt by the fire should be held for a soothsayer, and the other whom the fire burned held for a liar and an abuser. Savonarola was sore abashed to hear of such a manner of disputation, and indeed would not accept it, for he was not so learned nor so far a student in logic that he had learned such kind of argumentation, to prove his doctrine by fire. Yet there was found another young Jacobin, a familiar friend of Savonarola's, who accepted the combat to maintain his friend's quarrel. The assigned day having come, behold, the two combatants appeared; but the Jacobin had about him the precious body of the host for his defense, which he took between his hands. The friar and the seignory showed that that was no reasonable defense for the Jacobin, and therefore urged him to let go the host; but he would not for anything depart from it. By that means the combat ended, and those who came to see those valiant combatants go to the fire returned to their houses. But not long after, they were all three indicted, and I know not how nor why (for I find nothing written thereof), they were accused and condemned, and all three were burned. Here behold how the Florentines handled this poor friar, whom Machiavelli reports to have spoken with God. It may be that some at the beginning had a good opinion of him; but in the end they made him know well that he was no such able man as to persuade them either to the religion of Numa, or to any other religion; for most of them cared neither for the one nor the other.

2.10
Machiavelli

A man is happy so long as Fortune agrees with his nature and humor. (*The Prince*, chapter 25; *Discourses*, book 2 chapter 29)

Fortune may be compared to a great flood which nothing can resist, when it overflows its banks with great inundations. But when it remains in its ordinary course, or when it overflows not without measure, the force thereof may easily be resisted by levies, ditches, ramps, and other like obstacles. So Fortune is sometimes so unmeasurable in violence that no virtue can resist her, yet virtue may afterward repair the evils which that overflowing violence of Fortune has brought. It may also very well resist Fortune which is moderate and not too violent, as the forces thereof shall not hurt. I judge therefore that prince happy unto whose nature and manner of doings there happens an accordant and a consonant time; for the diversity of times makes that two, by one same means, come to contrary ends. So that if he who governs himself moderately encounters a time wherein his virtue is requisite, he cannot fail to prosper; yet if the times change he shall undoubtedly overthrow himself if he likewise change not his manners and order of life. Pope Julius II in all his actions proceeded with extreme fierceness and hastiness, yet his actions succeeded well; but many others have fared ill by using too precipitate promptitude and haste. Whereof I conclude that men are happy so long as Fortune accords with their humor and complexion; but as soon as she begins to vary and dissent, then they go fast down the wheel; whom also she determines to overthrow, she blinds them ordinarily; she can likewise choose fit men at her pleasure to cast down the wheel. Commonly she applies and gives herself to young and inconsiderate people, who are most hazardous and prompt in execution;

therein imitating the nature of women, who best love young men, such as to obey them, who must rather be spurred than flattered.

Answer

By this description of Machiavelli is evidently seen that he thinks what the poets wrote for fables concerning Fortune is the very truth. For the pagan poets have written that Fortune is a goddess who gives good and evil things to whom she will. And to denote that she does this inconsiderately and without judgment, they wrap her head in a cloth, lest with her eyes she sees and knows to whom she gives; so that she never knows unto whom she does good or evil. Moreover, they describe her standing upright upon a bowl, to denote her inconstancy, turning and tossing from side to side. Now Machiavelli would make men believe that this is true, and that all the good and evil which comes to men happens because they have Fortune accordant or discordant to their complexions. He says that she commonly favors young people, such as are hazardous and inconsiderate; to the end that thereby men might learn to be rash, violent, and heady, that they may have Fortune favorable to them. But all this doctrine tends to the same end as the former maxims do, to insinuate into men's minds and hearts a spite and utter contempt of God and his providence. For let man have once this persuasion, that no good comes to us from God, but from Fortune, he will easily forsake the service of God. As also when men believe that evil (that is to say, the punishment of vices and sins) comes not from the just judgment of God, but only from Fortune, which inconsiderately and rashly gives evils without consideration, whether or not they merit them, as soon to the good as to the wicked; then we need not doubt but such a man is emptied of all fear of God, and ready to fall into every vice. Here may you see the scope and end whereunto this wicked man tends to bring princes and other men, leaving no manner of impiety behind to infect and sow his poison in the world.

But against this we have good preservatives drawn out of the holy Scriptures, whereby we are assured that nothing falls to us but by God's providence, and that such afflictions as are sent us are for our good, lest the slippery way of prosperity make us fall to our destruction. We praise God for both good and evil, resolving ourselves that that which unto our carnal senses appears to be evil, is not evil to our souls, but very healthful and good; because there is a Christian maxim, that no evil can happen to a Christian from the hand of God our Father. My purpose here is not to handle that point of theology any further, but I will refute Machiavelli even by the pagans themselves.

And first I oppose against him almost all of the ancient philosophers, who have maintained that nothing happens nor is done without some efficient cause, although unknown to us. True it is that they make a distinction of causes, for they say that God is the first cause, who holds in action all other inferior causes (which they call second causes) and makes them work their effects. And although often in this distinction of causes they attribute some things to second causes which they should attribute to the first alone, yet notwithstanding they refer all things to God mediately or immediately. Very true it is that sometimes they use that name of Fortune, applying themselves to the manner of speech used among the people; but there never was philosopher so beastly that ever thought her to be any goddess. But when the ancient philosophers say anything comes by Fortune, or by adventure, or contingency, they mean that the efficient cause of such a thing is unknown. For that is their doctrine and manner of speech, to say that a thing happens or chances by Fortune, and contingently, when they know not the cause thereof.

Plutarch speaks learnedly to this purpose when he says that the poets have done great wrong to Fortune in saying she is blind, and that she gives her gifts to men rashly without knowing them. For, said he, it is we who know it not, for Fortune is no other thing but the cause (whereof we are ignorant) of things which we see come to pass. And therefore the Stoic philosophers, although they knew not the second causes of all things, no more than other philosophers, yet used another manner of speech and attributed the haps and chances of all things unto the ordinance and providence of God, which they called by the name of Fate; yet indeed Fate differs much from the providence of God which the Christians hold. For the Stoics held that God could work no otherwise than the order of second causes would bear and lead him unto; but we hold that God is free in operation and not tied to second causes, without which he can do that which he does by them, and can change them at his pleasure.

Timotheus, an Athenian captain, coming one day from the war, where his affairs had succeeded and sped well, was much grieved at some who said that he was very happy and fortunate. So that one day in a public assembly of all the people of Athens, he made an oration wherein he discoursed all his victories, uttering by the way the means and counsel which he had used in conducting his affairs. And after all this discourse he said, "Masters, Fortune has had no part in all this that I have accounted unto you." As if he would say that it was by his own wisdom that these things had so well succeeded to him. Plutarch says the gods were offended at this foolish ambition of Timotheus, so that he never after did anything of account; but all things he did turned against the hair, till he came to be hated by the Athenians, and in the end was banished and chased from Athens. Hereby we may see that the ancient pagans meant to attribute to the gods that which men in their common manner of speech attributed to fortune; but they never believed she was a goddess.

When de Commines speaks of the Constable of St. Pol, who was so great and puissant a lord, yet in the end such evil luck befell him that his hand was cut off, he makes a wise question and religiously absolves it: What shall we make of Fortune? This man was so great a lord that for the space of twelve years he had handled and governed king Louis XI and duke Charles of Bourgogne; he was a wise knight and had heaped together great riches, and in the end fell into her net. We may well say then that this deceitful Fortune beheld him with an evil countenance. Nay, contrary (said he), we must answer that Fortune is nothing but a poetical fiction, and that God must have forsaken him because he always worked with all his power to cause the war between the king and the duke to continue. For upon this war was founded his great authority and estate; and he should be very ignorant who believed that there was a Fortune therein, which could guide so wise a man to obtain the evil will of two so great princes at once, as well as the king of England; who in their lives accorded in nothing but the death of this constable. Behold the very words of Commines, speaking of Fortune, which sent as much to a good man, and a good Christian, as the maxim of Machiavelli tastes to a most wicked atheist.

And as for what Machiavelli says, that Fortune favors those who are most hazardous and rash; Livy is of another opinion, when speaking of the victory which Hannibal obtained near the lake of Trasimene, against the consul Flaminius. Evil luck, he said, came by the temerity of Flaminius, which was nourished and maintained in him by Fortune; whereas before things had succeeded well with him, but now, he who took counsel neither of the gods nor of men, it was no marvel if suddenly he fell into ruin. This loss of the battle was the cause that Fabius Maximus was elected dictator to go against Hannibal, as indeed after his election he took the field with a new army. And some time after, being sent for by the Senate to assist in certain sacrifices and ceremonies, he left Minutius his lieutenant, saying to him, "I pray you Minutius, take heed you do not as Flaminius did, but trust more in good counsel than in Fortune; better to be assured not to be vanquished than to hazard yourself to be vanquisher." In another place Livy rehearses that Caius Sempronius, captain of the Roman army against the Volsques, trusting in Fortune as a thing constant and perdurable, used no prudence nor good counsel because the Romans had always overcome that nation.

Therefore Livy says Fortune and success follow and abandon rashness, and this happens most commonly. Here you see the opinion of Fabius Maximus, and of Livy, much better than that of Machiavelli, who would persuade us that it is better to be rash than prudent, to have Fortune favorable to us. For certain it is that the haps which men call Fortune proceed from God, who rather blesses prudence, which he has recommended unto us, than temerity. And although it sometimes happens that he blesses not our counsels and wisdoms, it is because we take them not from the true spring and fountain, namely from him of whom we ought to have asked it; and that most commonly we would rather our own wisdom be a glory unto us, whereas only God should be glorified.

Here ends the second part, entreating of such religion as a prince should use

The third part, treating of such policy as a prince ought to hold in his commonwealth

Preface

I have before in order disposed of Machiavelli's maxims touching counsel and religion; and at large I have showed that all his doctrine shoots at no other mark but to instruct a prince to govern himself after his own fancy, not delivering his care to those who would show him the truth, and to void himself of all piety, conscience, and religion. There remains now to handle the third part of his doctrine, which concerns policy; whereof there are many parts, for in it are comprehended such maxims as concern peace, war, faith, promises, oaths, clemency, cruelty, liberality, greed, constancy, craft, justice, and other virtues and vices, considerable in public and political persons. All these things Machiavelli handles in such sort that it is easy to know that his only purpose was to instruct a prince to be a true tyrant and to teach him the art of tyranny; in which art verily he has showed himself a great doctor, far greater than Bartolus. For Bartolus, who was a renowned doctor in the civil law, in his treatise written of tyranny wades not so deep in the matter as Machiavelli does; although reading his treatise it seems that Machiavelli has learned a great deal of his knowledge. But Machiavelli applies it contrary, seeking that men should hold it for good, whereas Bartolus speaks of it as of a damnable thing which men ought to repulse and shun with all their power. And to confer a little thereupon, I will here summarily recite certain points of the doctor Bartolus touching this matter of tyranny, to show what Machiavelli has stolen, yet would apply it to the duty of a prince; whereas Bartolus attributes it to the iniquity and malice of a tyrant.

First, Bartolus constitutes two kinds of tyrants, one in title and the other in exercise. A tyrant in title is he who without any title, or else with a bad title usurps a domination and seignory. A tyrant in exercise is he who having a lawful title to domineer and rule, rules not justly and loyally as a good prince ought to do. After this he numbers ten sorts of actions whereby a tyrant is manifested to be a tyrant in exercise. The first action is when he puts to death the mightiest and most excellent persons among his subjects, for fear they should arise against his tyranny. The second, when he troubles and afflicts good and wise men of his domination, lest they should discover his vices to the people. The third action, when he seeks to abolish studies and good letters, to the end that wisdom may not be learned. The fourth, when he forbids lawful and honest assemblies and congregations, fearing men will rise up against him. The fifth, when he has spies in all places, fearing men speak evil of his evil actions. The sixth, when he maintains divisions among his subjects, to the end that one part may fear another, and so neither one nor the other arise against him. The seventh, when he seeks to hold his subjects poor, to the end that they being occupied in the means to get their living, they may machinate nothing against him. The eighth, when he seeks to maintain war to enfeeble his subjects, and to abolish studies, and to make himself strong when he needs to. The ninth, when he trusts more in foreigners than in his own subjects, and that he betakes himself unto a foreign guard. And the tenth action is when there is partiality among his subjects, and he adheres more to the one than the other. Which ten kinds of action Bartolus proves by reasons of law to be truly tyrannical, by which a tyrant in exercise is known and manifested to be a tyrant, and especially (said he) by these three kinds; when he maintains divisions among his subjects; when he impoverishes them; and when he afflicts them in their persons and goods, so that the most part of the people are discontented. And finally he concludes that to such tyrants by right and reason men ought not to obey nor appear before them, but that they ought to be dispossessed of their estates.

But in all this doctrine of Bartolus can you find one point that Machiavelli would not have applied and taught to a prince? All these ten kinds of tyrannical actions set down by Bartolus, are they not so many maxims of Machiavelli's doctrine taught to a prince? Did he not say that a prince ought to take away all virtuous people, lovers of their commonwealth; to maintain partialities and divisions; to impoverish his subjects, to nourish wars, and to do all these things which Bartolus said to be the works of tyrants? We need then no more doubt that the purpose of Machiavelli was to form a true tyrant, and that he has stolen from Bartolus one part of his tyrannical doctrine, which yet he has much augmented and enriched. For he adds that a prince ought to govern himself by his own counsel, and ought not to suffer any to discover unto him the truth of things; and that he ought not to care for any religion, neither observe any faith or oath, but ought to be cruel, a deceiver, a fox in craftiness, greedy, inconstant, unmerciful, and perfectly wicked, if it be possible, as we shall see hereafter. So that here may apparently be seen that Machiavelli is a far greater doctor in the art of tyranny than Bartolus; yet I compare them not together, for what Bartolus wrote of tyranny was to discover and condemn it, but what Machiavelli wrote was to cause princes to practice and observe it, and to sow in their hearts a true tyrannical poison under the pretext and name of a prince's duty and office. Finally, there is no other cause nor reason to compare this beastly Machiavelli, a simple burn-paper scribe of the town of Florence, with this great doctor Bartolus, who was one of the most excellent lawyers of his time, and as such is yet acknowledged. But now let us enter into the matter.

3.1
Machiavelli

That war is just which is necessary, and therefore arms are reasonable when men can have no hope by any other means.

Machiavelli exhorting the magnificent Lorenzo de Medici to get all Italy, persuades him by this maxim. He shows him that Italy is fit and ready to receive a new prince, because it is now fallen into extreme desolation, more than ever the Jews were in the servitude of Egypt. And that this miserable province has attended to be delivered from her servitude by a prince (meaning Charles VIII) who she esteemed should be sent from God; but that by his acts it appeared that he was reproved and abandoned by Fortune; and that now there was no other hope to be delivered from their misery but in that illustrious house of Medici, which might well enterprise to make itself chief of that redemption, with the church's help, whereupon she ruled (meaning Pope Leo X), with the aid also of his virtue and his own fortune, favored of God. And that the magnificent Lorenzo might well bring it to pass in proposing to himself for imitation the examples of Cesare Borgia and Agathocles; and that Italy delights in nothing so much as novelties, and the Italians surpass other nations in force, agility of body, and spirit. True it is (said he) that when it comes to battles, they will never appear; but men must lay the fault upon the cowardice and little heart of their captains, because they who have knowledge will not willingly obey, and every man presumes to know much. He shows moreover that the magnificent Lorenzo had good occasion to enterprise the taking of Italy, to deliver it from the slavish servitude wherein it is; and that enterprise should be founded upon good justice, because that war cannot fail to be esteemed just which is necessary, and all arms are good and reasonable when men have no hope otherwise but by them.

Answer

This maxim of Machiavelli is a true means to sow both civil and foreign wars all over the word. For if princes had this persuasion, that it is lawful for them to assail any other prince under the pretext and show that he has mishandled his subjects, princes should never want occasions to war against each other. And therefore to say that the magnificent Lorenzo de Medici had just occasion to get Italy, to deliver it from the evil handling of the potentates thereof, who there domineered and ruled; this in no sort could be called a just cause of war, but rather may be called an evil against an evil, and tyranny against tyranny, because the Medici cannot say that they have any right or title to Italy. But if we consider what tyranny is, as the elders have spoken thereof, we shall find that men of old called not only such princes who mishandled their subjects tyrants, as Caligula, Nero, Commodus, and other like; but also those who handled well and kindly their subjects, when without title they usurped domination upon them, as Julius Caesar, Hiero of Syracuse, the governors which the Lacedaemonians set over Athens, and others like. And therefore a prince who has no title over a country cannot lawfully invade it to get dominion there but by tyranny, whatsoever good intent he surmise or has, to use the inhabitants friendly when he has conquered it. Yet he may well aid another prince having lawful title, to oppose against a tyranny, because that is a common duty whereby all good princes are obliged to help those who by title and legitimate cause oppose themselves to resist a tyranny. But if a prince without lawful title goes about to usurp another country, after the counsel of Machiavelli, under a veil to deliver that country from tyranny, this cannot be well and justly done unless a man will say that one tyrant may justly expulse another tyrant.

The Romans have many times by example showed this to be true, and never would they deal in war against any man without just title. The Samnites, who were a mighty people, made war against the Campani neighbors of the Romans, who sent to Rome to ask for reinforcements. They showed that they were the Romans' neighbors, seeing also that by marriages there were infinite alliances between the Romans and the Campanians; and the Romans might always draw great commodities and profits from Campania, which was a fertile and plentiful country. The Romans sent ambassadors to the Samnites, to pray them to cease making war upon the Campanians; then the Campanians' deputies said: "Well, my masters, seeing you will not now defend us against an unjust and tyrannous invasion, yet at least defend what is your own, for we yield and give ourselves to you, yea us and all that is ours." Then the

Senate, taking title and foundation from this dedication, enterprised the defense of the Campanians, which otherwise without title they would never have done.

And truly the saying of the emperor Martian is very memorable and deserves good observation, that a prince ought never to move war while he could maintain peace; as if he would say that arms ought not to be employed by a prince but in the defense of his country, and not to assail another. And indeed a man had need to look about him more than once before he moves war, and well consider and examine if therein there is just cause or not. For wars are easy to commence, as M. Commines says, but very uneasy to appease and finish. And upon this we read that in the Senate of Rome there was once a very notable disputation between Cato (one esteemed the wisest of Rome) and Scipio Nasica (who was reputed the best man of Rome). The matter was this. After the Punic War, the Romans made peace with the Carthaginians, by which peace was accorded that the Carthaginians might not rig any ship of war, nor move war against the Romans or their allies. Some time later the Carthaginians gathered together many ships; which being reported at Rome and the matter propounded in the Senate, Cato and many others reasoned that war should be made upon the Carthaginians because they had gone from the treaty, and that war might justly be offered unto them as breakers of peace. But Nasica was of contrary opinion, that there was yet no sufficient cause to make war; for although the Carthaginians had gone against the peace and violated their faith and promise, yet the Romans received no offense or damage as yet. And therefore he was of advice that the Carthaginians should be summoned to lay down their arms and untackle their ships, and observe peace even in the articles which they had broken. The plurality of voices was of Nasica's opinion, and accordingly men were sent to Carthage to summon them to obey the treaty and to repair contraventions. They would do nothing therein, but prepared themselves more to set upon Masinissa, their ally and friend. But there also were diverse opinions whether they should altogether ruin Carthage from top to bottom after they had taken it, or to let it remain a town. Cato was opinion to totally ruin and destroy it, because it could not be kept in any fidelity, but would break her faith and promise at the first occasion that offered itself. Nasica was of contrary advice, saying it was good that Rome always had an enemy upon whom to make war, that the Roman people might not be corrupted and become cowards by too great peace and prosperity, for lack of whom upon to war. The resolution of the Senate was in a mean between these two opinions, for it was ordained that the Carthaginians should be permitted to remove their town into any other part ten miles from the sea. But the

Carthaginians found this so strange that they preferred to suffer all extreme things; insomuch that by long war they were wholly vanquished, and their town altogether razed and made uninhabitable.

Very memorable also to this purpose is the advice of the Chancellor de Rochefort in the time of Charles VIII. Many counselling this young king to make war against Francis, duke of Brittany, to lay hold of his duchy, this good chancellor showed that the rights the king presented to that duke were not yet well verified; and that it was good to seek further into them before war was attempted, for it would be the work of a tyrant to usurp countries which belong not to him. According to this advice ambassadors were sent to the duke, asking to send on his side men of counsel, and the king would do so on his side, to resolve upon both their rights. This was done, and men assembled to that end; but in the meanwhile Francis died and the king espoused Madame Anne, his daughter and heir, and so the controversy ended.

The same king enterprising his voyage of Naples, assembled all his presidents of his courts of Parliaments, with his Chancellor, his Privy Council, and the princes of the blood, to resolve upon his title and right to Naples and Sicily. These lords visited the genealogy and descent of the kings of Sicily and Naples, and they found that the king was the right heir of these kingdoms; so that upon that resolution this voyage was enterprised. Hereby is seen the vanity of Machiavelli, who presupposes that king Charles had enterprised that voyage to get all Italy, but that Fortune was not favorable unto him. For that was never his design nor purpose; neither did he assay to seize upon anything in Italy, but only certain towns necessary for this passage, in determination to yield them up again at his departure, which he did. And if the king would have enterprised upon Italy, he had a far more apparent title than the magnificent Lorenzo de Medici, seeing all Italy was once by just title possessed by Charlemagne, his predecessor. But this has always been a property in our kings, not to run over others' grounds, nor to appropriate to themselves any seignory which appertained not to them by just title.

We read also of Charles V, called the Wise, that being incited by his nobility and the people of Guines to seize again that country, which was occupied by the English, he would not enterprise it without great and good deliberation of good counsel. And therefore he caused well to be viewed by wise and experienced people the treaty of peace made at Brittany between his dead father and the king of England; for it was told him that the king of England had not accomplished on his side what he was bound to do. After they had (as they thought) well resolved him of this point, yet he was not content to be satisfied himself, but would that his subjects should be also well resolved thereof, and especially such as were under the English obedience. And to that purpose he sent preachers covertly into such good towns as were occupied by the English; by the preachers' inducements there were more than threescore towns and fortresses which revolted from the English and offered themselves unto the king's obedience.

This then is a resolved point, that a prince ought not to enterprise to obtain a country where he has no title, under color to deliver the inhabitants thereof from tyranny. But here may arise a question, if it is lawful for a prince to make war for religion, and to constrain men to be of his religion. Hereupon to take the thing by reason, the resolution is very easy; for seeing that all religion consists in an approbation of certain points that concern the service of God, it is certain that such an approbation depends upon the persuasion which is given to men thereof. But the means to persuade a thing to any man is not to take weapons to beat him, nor to menace him, but to demonstrate to him by good reasons and allegations what may induce him to a persuasion. But he that will decide this question by examples of our ancestors, he shall find divers to be for and against. For to read our French histories in the lives of Clovis I, Charlemagne, and some other kings of France, it seems that their study was altogether bent upon war against pagans, for nothing but to make them Christians with hand-blows and force of arms. But what Christians? When the pagans were vanquished and they could no more resist, they were acquitted upon a condition to be baptized without other instruction. And most commonly, as soon as they could again gather strength, they returned to their pagan religion. And this is well showed us by the history of one Rabbod, duke of Frise; who being upon the point to be baptized, and having his clothes off and one foot in the font, he demanded of the Archbishop of Sens, who should have baptized him, whether there were more of his parents in hell or in paradise. The archbishop answered him that the most must needs be in hell, because his predecessors were never baptized. Then the duke, drawing his foot out of the water, said "Well, I will go to hell with my parents and friends, and I will not be baptized, to be separated from them." And so he withdrew himself, denying to be baptized. Here I leave you to think if this man were well instructed in the Christian doctrine. It seems that at that day, to be a Christian it sufficed to be baptized, and commonly pagans were baptized by force of arms.

We read also that our ancient kings of France made many voyages into Turkey and Africa for the augmentation of the Christian religion, and to revenge (as they said) the death of our Lord Jesus Christ upon the pagans and infidels. But one time the pagans themselves showed them well that they enterprised such wars by an inconsiderate zeal. For the army of France, whereof the duke of Bourbon was chief, warring against the infidels in Africa in the time of Charles VI, the general of the Turks and Saracens sent a herald to the duke, to know why he descended into Africa to make war upon them. The duke assembled the greatest lords of the army to resolve what answer to make to the herald. After, by the advice of all it was answered that they Christians made war upon them to revenge the death of Christ, the son of God and a true prophet, who their generation had put to death and crucified. The Turks, understanding this answer, sent again to the duke and the lords of France that they had received evil information upon that matter, for they were Jews who crucified Jesus Christ, and not their predecessors; and if the children must needs suffer for their ancestors' faults, they should then take the Jews who were among them, and upon them revenge the death of their Jesus Christ. Our Frenchmen knew not what to answer hereunto; yet they continued the war, where was done no notable exploit, but by contagion of the air they were constrained to return after they had lost most of their army.

Likewise, in 1453, the pope having proclaimed a crusade in Christendom to run over Turkey, to avenge the death of our Lord Jesus Christ and constrain the Turks to be christened, the Turks wrote letters to him wherein they signified that the Jews crucified Christ; and as for them, they descended not from the Jews, but from the Trojans' blood, whereof they understood the Italians were likewise descended. And that their duty was not to make war, but rather to help each other restore the great Troy, and to revenge the death of Hector against the Greeks; as they were ready to do, having already subjugated most of Greece. And that they believed that Jesus Christ was a great prophet, but that he never commanded (as he was given to understand) that men should believe in his law by force and by arms; as also on his part, he constrained no man to believe in the law of Mahomet. Behold the substance of the Turks' letters to the pope, which seemed to be as well or better founded upon reasons than the pope's bulls. For verily Jesus Christ willed that his law should be received into the world by preaching, and not by force of arms.

In the time when Christendom was divided into Clementines and Urbanists by reason of a schism of popes, we may well presuppose that the one thought the other to be altogether out of the way of salvation; and our historians say that one side called the other dogs, miscreants, infidels, etc. Their reason was because they said that as there was but one God in heaven, so there ought to be but one on earth; and the Clementines held assuredly that pope Clement was the true god on earth, and pope Urban the false god, and that the Urbanists believed in a false god, and in consequence they all strayed from the faith. For as no religion can stand without believing in God, so they esteemed that those who did not believe in the true earthly god were altogether without religion, as dogs and miscreants; and our historiographers, who held that opinion as well as the other, said that from that time the faith was shaken and ready to fall to the ground. We have before said in another place said that under color of this diversity in religion the king of England, who was an Urbanist, enterprised to make war upon the kings of France and Castile, who were Clementines. Likewise also the Clementines enterprised no less against the Urbanists, even against the pope himself, whom they besieged in the town of Perona, where he was in great danger to have been taken; yet in the end he saved himself at Rome. The king of France determined to destroy the Urbanists by war, but in the end he took another resolution, which was to cause the schism to cease; for he convocated a great and notable assembly in the town of Reims in Champagne, where in person resorted the emperor Sigismund, and there a conclusion was made to exhort the two popes to submit themselves to the new election of a pope, wherein their right should be conserved unto them. And if they would not submit themselves thereunto, that the Christian princes and their subjects should withdraw themselves from the obedience both of the one and the other. After this subtraction was made, because the said popes would not obey the exhortation, there was a new election of a pope in a council held at Pisa by the emperor's and the king's authorities, who was called Pope Alexander V; and the two Antipopes were cursed, as is said in another place. And thus ceased the wars for religion in all Christendom.

To this purpose also you must know that during the said schism of the Clementines and Urbanists, the duke of Brittany had peace with the king of France, and a great assembly was made between them in the town of Tours. The duke appearing there, some of the king's council showed him that he was disobedient to the king, being of another religion than he was — for the king was a Clementine, and the duke an Urbanist — and it was not meet that the vassal should be of another religion than his sovereign lord. The duke answered wisely that it could not be called a rebellion or disobedience, for no man ought to judge of his conscience, but only God, who is the sovereign and only judge of such a matter; and that he believed in pope Urban because his election was before pope Clement's. Some of the king's council, of the meanest sort, made a great matter of this diversity of religion; but the dukes of Berry and Bourgoigne, the king's uncles, thought that it was not a sufficient point to stand upon, to put by an accord with the duke of Brittany. Following their advice, an accord was concluded; a marriage of one of the king's daughters with the duke of Brittany.

This example and advice of these two good dukes, methinks all Christian princes should follow, and not cease to agree together for the diversity of religion, but to remit the judgment thereof unto God, who alone can compound and agree the differences thereof. And not only among princes the bond of amity ought not to be broken for difference of religion, but also princes ought not to use arms against their subjects to force them unto a religion, but they ought to assay by all other means to demonstrate unto them by lively reasons their errors, and so bring them to a good way. And if it appears not that their subjects err and stray, they ought to maintain them and not persecute them at the instigation of flatterers and envious people. An example hereof is memorable of king Louis XII, who was called the father of the people. For in his time certain cardinals and prelates persuaded him to exterminate and utterly root out all the people of Cabriers and Merindol in Provence, telling him that they were sorcerers, incestuous persons, and heretics. They of Merindol and Cabriers, having some scent of the accusation, sent some of their wisest men to remonstrate to the king their justice and innocence. As soon as these men arrived at court the said cardinals and prelates did what they could to hinder, so that they should not be heard, and indeed told the king that he ought not to hear them because the canon law holds that men ought not to give audience to heretics, nor communicate with them. The king replied that if he had to make war upon the Turk, or even against the devil himself, he would hear them. This was an answer worthy of a king, for seeing kings hold in their hand the scepter of justice, it is abuse to condemn any and not to hear them. Louis then hearing the messengers of Cabriers and Merindol, they showed him in all humility that their people received the Gospel, the Bible, and the Apostles' Creed, the commandments of God, and the sacraments; but they did not believe in the pope, nor his doctrine. And that if it pleased his majesty to send to inquire of the truth of their speeches, they were contented all to die if their words were not found true. This good king would needs know if it were so, and indeed deputed his Master of Requests and his confessor to go to Cabriers and Merindol, to inquire of the life and religion of the inhabitants in those places. After they had seen and known all, they made their report unto the king that in those places their children were baptized, they taught them the articles of the faith and the commandments of God; that they well observed their sabbaths, always preaching thereon the word of God; and as for sorceries and whoredoms, there were none among them. Moreover, they found no images in their temples, nor ornaments of the mass. The king having received this report, what judgment gave he of it? Did he condemn them because they had no images nor ornaments of the mass? No, he presently swearing by his oath pronounced that they were better men than he or all his people. Here may princes learn how to use themselves, in supporting against slanderers those in whom there is no appearance of error.

But leaving this question and again taking our purpose; it is certain that a prince ought not lightly to attempt war, as Machiavelli persuades; and upon some necessity, having war at hand, he ought to search out and accept all honest conditions to get out of it. For sometimes the prince who refuses honest and reasonable conditions, upon hope that his forces are great, falls into great distress. And it has been many times seen that petty captains have made head against great and strong powers of mighty princes.

In the time of the battle of Poitiers, where king John was taken, before the battle the prince of Wales offered to yield all that he and his people had conquered since his departure from Bordeaux, and also to yield all the pillage; but the king would not accept this offer, and asked that the prince and four of the greatest lords of his army should yield themselves at his will. The prince, who was generous, chose to fight it out rather than to accept so shameful and dishonorable an accord; so he and his army fought valiantly, and a very small number of English overcame great forces of the French. The king was taken with many other great princes and lords, for which to redeem the kingdom was so emptied of silver that they were compelled to make money of leather, which had only a note of silver. From this battle proceeded infinite evils, miseries, and calamities which would not have happened if the king had been so well advised as to have forgone that war by soft and assured means, rather than by the hazard of battle. But contrary to king John, Charles VII in recovering Guines and Normandy from the English never refused any proffer or compromise, and always sought to recover what his predecessors had lost without effusion of blood.

The Roman histories are full of similar examples. For what overthrew the Carthaginians, Perseus, Mithridates, what abated the pride of Philip of Macedon, of that great king Antiochus and many others, was that they could never accept the good and reasonable conditions of peace which were offered to them by the Romans, but would rather try what force founded upon a good right could do. I say founded upon a good right, because a small force which has right with it often abates a great force which is not founded on a good right. The reason is evident; because he who knows he has just cause to make war, and who sees that his adversary, trusting much in his forces, will not come to any reasonable compromise, redoubles his courage and his heart, and fights more valiantly than he who is driven thereunto rather upon pride than any generosity of heart. But the principal reason is that God, who gives victories, inclines most often to the side of right; and although sometimes it seems that the wrong carries away the victory, yet God always shows by the end and issue, by which we must judge, that he is for the right.

Above all, the prince ought to appease the wars in his own country, whether they are raised by foreigners or by his own subjects; as for such wars he may have in a foreign land, it may happen that they will not prove so evil, but may provide good soldiers in a need. And especially this point is considerable when a prince's subjects are naturally inclined to war, as in the French nation; for then necessarily they must be employed according to their natural disposition, or else they will move war against themselves, as Sallust says in these words:

> If the virtue and generosity of princes, captains, and men of war might so well be employed and show itself estimable in peace as in war, human things would carry themselves more constantly, and men should not see such changes of one estate into another, nor all things mixed in a confusion, as we do see. Therefore a foreign war seems not to be very damaging, but something necessary to occupy and exercise his subjects; but domestic and civil wars must be shunned and extinguished with all our power, for they are things against the right of nature, to make war against the people of their own country, as he that does it against his own entrails.

Therefore says Homer:

> Right wicked are those men who love not parents dear.
> Sottish no less are they who family do hate:
> But most ungodly they their country which do fear,
> With civil wars: so direful to a quiet state.

The prince also ought to consider that by civil wars he more weakens himself and his subjects in one year than by a foreign war he can do in thirty; civil wars also are without comparison more ruinous and dangerous than foreign wars are.

To this purpose there is in Livy a notable oration made by the Roman deputies unto Marcius Coriolanus, who was unjustly banished from Rome and yielded himself to the Volsques, enemies of the Romans. He was elected captain of the Volsques to make war upon his own country; and as he laid siege to Rome, there were sent to him five great Roman lords, including his parents and friends. Marcus Minutius spoke thus for them:

"We are not ignorant, dear lord and friend, that great wrong has been done unto you at Rome, to banish and drive you from your country, for which you have often done so much, and so well fought for it that you may be accounted as a second father or founder. We also know well that by good right you are grieved and spited against us for so unjust a judgment and the wrong done you; for naturally he that is injured is watchful against he that injured him. Yet we cease not to marvel that you do not discern those upon whom you may justly take revenge, from those who have done you no evil or outrage; but you indifferently repute for enemies your friends, as much as those who hate you. Which doing, you violate the inviolable laws of nature; you confound right and wrong, equity and iniquity; you forget yourself so much that you make war upon yourself, in so doing upon your own blood. We who are your friends and of the ancient patricians are sent hither by your country and ours, to complain in her name and pray you cease from this war and hearken unto a good peace, offering to agree unto you all that shall be to your honor and utility. We confess that great wrong has been done you in your banishment; but who has done it unto you? You say the people gave the voice for your condemnation. True it is, we cannot deny but all the people is but one voice, although most were against you. Those then who have given their voices for your absolution, do they merit that you should make war upon them as heretics? And we senators, who have been so sorrowful at your evil, ought you account us as your enemies? But women and children, what have they done to you? Must so many innocents fall into peril and danger to be slain, pillaged and sacked, that have done you no wrong, but rather favored you? If we demand of you why you would raze and destroy our good buildings, framed by our ancestors, where are the statues and images of their victories and triumphs; and will you abolish their memories? What can you answer? Assuredly you can have no color to do this thing unless you will say that friends and enemies are culpable, and innocents living and dead ought equally to suffer vengeance of the injury done you. A thing not meet to be done or even thought on by a man that has never so little reason; you should consider, dear lord and friend, the inconstancy of the affairs of this world, the mutability of men's spirits, and excuse the misfortune which happened to you, to our great grief, and accept an honorable return to your country, which desires you. You may continue to employ your virtue as you have done in times past, and by this means you shall leave after you a good and holy reputation of your virtue to posterity. And if you do otherwise, you shall leave after your death a remembrance that you were an enemy who ruined your poor country, where you were born and tenderly nourished. Yet more, as long as you live you shall be a horror and an execration to all the world, even to the Volsques who are now your friends; all the world will fly your company as a thief and robber. We therefore pray you, dear lord and friend, that you will forget the injury that you have unjustly received, and accept a happy, healthful and honorable return into your country, into your house, where your poor mother is, your dear wife, your friends and children who weep and lament your absence; and especially since it was made known to them that you come with a strong hand to put them to the edge of the sword."

After these ambassadors had thus spoken, Coriolanus' mother Veturia and wife Volumni were sent to him, carrying in their arms his little children, accompanied by a great number of noble women. When Coriolanus saw them arrive, and after his mother and wife fell down on their knees weeping, then nature forced and burst that hard and obstinate courage of his, a peace was made, and he ceased to war upon his own country.

If we know not what mischiefs and calamities come from civil wars, there might be many examples set down thereof; but alas we Frenchmen know too much, and yet many are hardened to persevere therein, and they cannot bow their hard courage to desist from ruining and warring against their mother and country. This pagan Coriolanus may make them ashamed; who did not persevere in warring upon his country, although his courage was rude and full of vengeance, but suffered himself to be vanquished by reason. But they make war in a contrary course, not making any account of reason, love, or piety that they ought to have towards their country, parents, and friends; letting lose the bridle of their passions and vengeances, bursting, ruining, massacring, slaying, pillaging, and destroying from top to bottom their parents, friends, fellow citizens and neighbors, and generally all our poor country which our ancestors have left us so rich and flourishing. I know well that everyone lays the fault upon his adversary, and that everyone says that he fights for his country, who the other party will ruin. But it is easy to judge, for him whose judgment is free from passion, who is in the wrong; for they who seek not another man's, who demand but their own, and that the kingdom be reformed by their own laws and brought into her ancient splendor and renown; can they be called enemies of the country? Is there anything in the world that is more ours than our soul, our conscience, and our lives? That is true, some will say, you may have assurance of your lives, everyone also may have liberty of his conscience; but to speak of reformation is treason. Yea, but what assurance of life will be given us? Even an assurance that shall be under the safeguard and protection of the first wicked man who will conspire a massacre, who shall be invited to enterprise it by the impunity of former massacres. What liberty of conscience can we have, unless it be of Machiavelli's religion, that is to say, to be without religion, without piety, without the power of a frank and free conscience to serve God? Call you it liberty of conscience to be without religion, or without exercise of religion? Nay, it is rather a very slavish servitude. But if it be treason to speak of reforming abuses and corruptions which are in the kingdom, it follows that they are guilty of treason who procure and purchase the commonwealth, against which both reason and all laws do pronounce. If therefore the world at this day esteems enemies of their country those who seek nothing but the good thereof, and that they may have left them their souls, consciences, and lives, God and his verity shall have the victory, and cause those who come after us to judge otherwise.

Although the horrors and calamities of civil wars are sufficiently known in this time, yet will I briefly rehearse two most notable examples. The civil war between Marius and Sulla was a horrible and fearful butchery that filled Rome and all Italy with blood. For both of them were masters of Rome and all Italy, one after another; and so being, they did all they could to massacre one another's friends and partakers, so that all men of quality and all good people were slain, for there was no notable man but held of one or the other. Among other memorable things happening in this war, this especially concerns our cause in hand, which fell in the battle that Pompey, lieutenant of Sulla, obtained against Cinna, the partner of Marius. For one of Pompey's soldiers having struck dead one of Cinna's soldiers, he disarmed him, thinking to spoil him of all he had; but then finding him to be his own brother, this poor soldier fell in a great rage and almost to madness, that he had so slain his own brother. He caused a great fire to be made to burn his brother to ashes, after the manner of the pagans of the time, and making great lamentations and sorrowful exclamations he laid his brother's body upon the wood, then put fire to it. As soon as it was well kindled he cast himself into the fire also, and was burned with his brother's body. Death united the ashes of those two brothers, who the civil wars had separated.

But yet a far worse and greater civil war happened soon after between Pompey and Caesar, and it continued all the time of the Triumvirate of Octavian, Antony, and Lepidus against Cassius and Brutus, and ended between Antony and Octavian. This war endured 32 years and spread itself through almost all the world which was then in subjection to the Roman Empire; even the people of the east, west, north, and south felt their grievous part of this civil war. It was verified that in this unnatural civil war, from the beginning till the fourth consulship of Caesar, 170,000 citizens of Rome died. And you may very well believe that many were slain after, also that ten times as many died in the provinces belonging to Rome; so that these detestable wars swallowed up many millions of men. But the Triumvirate of Octavian, Antony, and Lepidus was a most detestable union, which accorded to take all the government of the commonwealth and to slay all their enemies. But because it often came to pass that a friend of one of the three was another's enemy, when one would have slain him as an enemy, the other would defend him as a friend. Yet the cruelty so surmounted all humanity, and the desire for vengeance so vanquished all amity that these captains entered into a detestable plot to sell their friends to each other in exchange for an enemy. That wicked Antony, to have his enemy Cicero (whom Octavian favored as his friend), was content to deliver in exchange Lucius Caesar, his own uncle on his mother's side; so that the one was exchanged for the other, and they both died. Can there possibly be a more barbarous disloyalty in the world? Is it not a strange thing to hear that a friend should be betrayed to death, to have the cruel pleasure of slaying an enemy? Yet by this course died 130 senators, besides many other persons of quality. Antony, the deviser of this barbarous exchange, received his reward by Octavian himself, whom he induced to commit such cruelties. For in the end they were enemies, and Antony being vanquished in the naval battle at Actium, slew himself, so turning upon himself that barbarous cruelty which he had exercised against Cicero and others.

And it need not seem strange if these civil wars of Rome endured so long as 32 years, for the civil wars between the houses of Bourgogne and Orleans endured sixty years, continuing from father to son for two generations. And as for cruelties, methinks greater cannot be imagined than what were committed at Paris. For they massacred the Constable and Chancellor of France, whom they drew and trailed through the town most filthily; and also murdered many other great lords, archbishops, bishops, prelates, and more than three thousand other persons, gentlemen and other notable people, who by force they drew out of prisons to murder and massacre. The captain of the commons, who committed those barbarous inhumanities, was called Cappeluche, the executioner or hangman of Paris. Those partners of the house of Bourgogne, not contented to instigate such popular commotions and stirs in France, also brought the English into France, who were likely to have been masters thereof. Still not content, they caused Charles VI to war against his own son, who after was called Charles VII. And not to leave behind any kind of cruelty, not even towards the dead, they spread and published all over France certain pope's bulls, whereby they indicted and excommunicated all the house of Orleans and their partakers both quick and dead. When there died any in the hands of the partners of Bourgogne, either by ward, prison, or disease, they buried them not in the earth, but caused their bodies to be carried to dunghills like carrion, to be devoured by wolves and savage beasts. What could they have done more to the execution of all barbarousness and cruelty? Behold what fruits civil wars bring; we see it even today with our eyes, for there is no kind of cruelty, barbarousness, impiety, and wickedness which civil wars have not brought into use.

The prince then who is wise will leave nothing behind to appease civil wars under his own government, but will spend all his care, power, and diligence to hinder it, after the example of that good and wise king Charles VII, and Louis XI, his son. While Charles was yet dauphin, John, duke of Buorgogne, a very ambitious and vindictive man, secretly slew Louis, duke of Orleans, the only brother of king Charles VI. After he had filled the kingdom with wars both civil and foreign, he laid hold of the queen and the king (who by a sickness was alienated from his wits), in order to make war upon the dauphin. These occasions seemed sufficient to those who governed the dauphin, and at last to the dauphin himself, to enterprise a hazardous blow. He then sent word to the duke that he would make peace with him, and prayed him they might appoint a place and day to meet for that purpose. The day was appointed and the place assigned at Mont St. Yonne, where the duke came under the trust of the dauphin's faith and assurance. As soon as he arrived, making his reverence unto the dauphin, he was compassed in and slain, together with certain gentlemen of his train. Philip, son and successor of this duke John, took greatly to heart this most villainous death of his father, and sought all the means he could to be revenged, which continued the civil wars. Meanwhile the English did what they could in France, and conquered Normandy, Paris, most of Picardy, and marched even to Orleans, which they besieged. Charles VI died, so that on coming to the crown his son found himself despoiled of most of the kingdom, and in mockery he was generally called the king of Bourges. This wise king considered well that if civil wars endured, he was in the way to lose all, one piece after another; he therefore laid all his care, power, and diligence to obtain a peace and accord with the duke of Bourgogne. Therefore he sent in embassage his Constable, Chancellor, and his chief counsellors to say that he desired peace, and that he acknowledged that by wicked counsel he had caused the duke's father to be slain; and that if he had then been as advised and resolute as he was now, he would never have committed such an act, nor have permitted it to be done; but he was young and poorly counseled. And therefore in that regard he offered to make him such amends and reparation thereof that he should be contented therewith; yea, that he would demand pardon, not in person but by his ambassadors, and prayed him to forgive that fault in the name of our Lord Jesus Christ, so that between them might be a good peace and love. For he confessed to have done evil, being then a young man of little wit and less discretion, to have slain the duke's father by bad counsel. And besides this he offered to give him many great lands and seignories; and that during his life the king would acquit him and his subjects of the personal service he owed as a vassal of France; and yet made other fair offers unto him. This duke Philip, seeing his sovereign prince thus humiliate himself to him, bowed his courage justly exasperated at his father's death, and hearkened unto peace. The peace was made at Arras, where there was held an assembly of the ambassadors of all Christian princes, of the Council of Basel, and of the pope; there were present more than 4000 horses. All or most of those ambassadors came there for the good of the king and his kingdom, but there was not found one who did not think the king's offers good and reasonable, as also did all the great princes and lords of the kingdom, and all the king's council. So that his majesty's ambassadors, in a full assembly in the king's name, demanded pardon from the duke of Bourgogne for his father's death, confessing that the king had done evil as one young and of little wit, following naughty counsel. Therefore they prayed the duke to let pass away all his evil will, and so be in a good peace and love with the king, their master. And the duke declared that he pardoned the king for the honor and reverence of the death and passion of our Lord Jesus Christ, and for compassion of the poor people of his kingdom of France, and to obey the council's reasons, the pope, and other Christian princes who prayed him to do so. Moreover, besides these things it was accorded to the duke that justice and punishment should be done upon all those who had slain his father, and of those who had given the dauphin counsel to cause his slaughter, and that the king himself should make diligent search through all his realm to apprehend them.

Here may you see how king Charles VI appeased the civil wars of his kingdom by humility and acknowledgment of his faults; and from thence forward he prospered so well that after he had ended his civil wars he also overcame his foreign wars against the English. And this came from God, who ordinarily exalts the humble and overthrows the insolent and proud. For assuredly it does not ill become a great prince to temperate his majesty by a gracious humility, softness, and affability. But, according to Plutarch, it is a very harmonious and consonant temperation, so excellent that there cannot be a more perfect one than this. But if the king had such counselors as many kings nowadays have, what counsel would they have given him? They would have said that to thus humiliate himself to his vassal as to ask his forgiveness, to confess his fault, to acquit him and his subjects of personal service, these are things unworthy of a king; and that a king ought never to make peace unless it is to his honor, but these articles were to his dishonor and disadvantage, and that he ought to have endured all extremities before he made any peace whereby he should not remain altogether master to dispose of persons and goods at his pleasure. For how would they not say thus, seeing they say that it is no honorable peace for the king to accord his subjects any assurances, with the exercises of their religion and reformation of justice. Yet you see that all king Charles VII and his council, all the princes of his blood, all the great lords of his kingdom, and all foreign princes' ambassadors compelled the king to pass more hard and uneasy articles to digest, for the good of peace. Should we say that in so great a number of great personages, there was not any so wise and clearsighted as the counsellors at this day, these Machiavellians? Nay contrary, they were all wise men and of great experience in worldly affairs, they were also of great knowledge, as the delegates of the council of the University of Paris, and of the parliaments; whereas today men know little more than their Machiavelli.

Likewise king Louis XI, as soon as he came to the crown removed from office many great lords and good servants of his father Charles VII, who had virtuously employed themselves in chasing the English out of the kingdom; and in lieu of such persons he placed and advanced men of mean and base condition. Hereupon arose civil dissention against the king; and these men complained that the kingdom was not politically governed, because the king had put from him good men of high calling to advance those who were of small estimation and no virtue. It was not long before the king acknowledged his great fault, and confessed it not only in general, but also in particular to all of them who he had recoiled and disappointed. And to repair this fault, he got again to him all the said lords and ancient servants of his father, delivering them again their estates, or much greater. And in sum, he granted to these all that they demanded, as well for the general as for the particular good of all people, and all to obtain peace and extinguish civil wars. If he had had of his council the Machiavellians of today, they would not have counselled him to do thus, but rather would have told him that it becomes not a king to capitulate with his subjects, nor so to disable himself to them; and that a prince ought never to trust those who once were his enemies, but much less ought he to advance them to estates, and that he should diligently take heed of a reconciled enemy. Yet notwithstanding he did all this, and it fell out well with him, for he was very well served by the pretended reconciled enemies. And to this purpose M. de Commines, his chamberlain, says that his humility and the acknowledgment of his faults saved his kingdom, which was in great danger to be lost if he had stayed upon such impertinent and foolish reasons as those Machiavellians allege. For all things may not be judged by the final cause. What dishonor then can it be to a prince, to use petty and base means, if thereby he makes his country peaceable, his estate assured, and his subjects contented and obedient? What matter for him that is to ascend into a high place, whether he mount by degrees and stairs of wood, or of stone, so that he ascend.

But this is not all, to say that a prince ought to be vigilant and careful to make peace in his country; for after it is made he must observe it well, otherwise it is to no purpose; unless men will say that one ought to make peace so that afterward, in breaking it, he can trap and ensnare whose who trust therein. But those who hold this opinion are people who make no account of the observation of faith, as are the Machiavellians, of whom we will speak upon this point in another maxim. But indeed, that a peace may be well observed, it must be profitable and commodious to those with whom it is made, so that it is agreeable to them, and they may observe it with a good will and without constraint. For if it is damaging and disadvantageous, making their condition worse than that of other subjects and neighbors, it is certain that it cannot long endure. For people that have either heart or spirit in them cannot long endure to be handled like slaves.

Hereunto serves the advice of that noble and sage company, the ancient senators of Rome. There was a neighbor of the Romans who were called the Privernates, upon whom the Romans made war, many times vanquishing them. Seeing that it was impossible any more to make head against the Roman forces, the Privernates sent ambassadors to Rome for peace. Because they had not well observed the precedent treaty of peace, some senators seemed hard to give their cause any hearing, thinking it a vain thing to accord a peace to those who would not keep it. Notwithstanding, some demanded of those ambassadors what punishment they judged themselves to have merited, who had so often broken the precedent peace. One of them speaking for all, and remembering the condition of their birth, rather than their present estate, answered that the Privernates merited the punishment they deserve, who esteem themselves worthy of a free condition, and who have a slavish condition. This answer seemed to some senators too haughty and not beseeming vanquished people; yet the president of the assembly, a wise man, benignly asked them if they were pardoned the invasion of the former peaces, and if now they had a new peace granted them, how would they observe it? The same ambassador, with such like haughtiness of heart as before, said, If you will give us a good peace we will faithfully and perpetually observe it, but if you give us an evil peace it will not hold long. Some of the senators disdained and disliked this answer, saying they spoke too proudly, as it were already threatening a revolt; and that it did not become vanquished people to carry such high minds. But the wisest and most discreet part of the Senate did not think this answer evil or impertinent, but that this ambassador spoke like a frank and free man; and that men should not find it strange if every man detained in servitude would be remitted into his natural liberty as soon as he could, and has means for his purpose. Therefore resolutely they concluded that the Privernates must have such a peace as to be received Roman citizens, enjoying the same liberties and privileges that those of the town of Rome did. This was performed, and very notable is the reason of their motive; for they say, there is the peace loyal and assured where men willingly appease themselves, and a man need not look or hope for an assured peace where men are brought to a slavish subjection.

Here is also to be marked the advice and opinion of the dictator Largius, which he spoke in a full Senate, when the Latins sued for peace after rebelling against the Romans and were vanquished.

> "Masters, my advice is that we ought to use kindly and moderately the victory we have had against the Latins. For it is the most excellent praise that can come, either to public or private persons, not to suffer themselves to be corrupted by prosperity, but to know how to use what is good with a modest and equal courage, because all prosperities are accompanied with envy, even although they come to oppress the vanquished who make no resistance. Moreover, we ought not so much to trust in fortune, which is too inconstant and mutable, as we have often experimented, and therefore ought not to constrain our adversaries to come to the last remedy, that is, despair, which often elevates the heart, yea and often the fortune. We have cause also to fear the evil grace and disfavor of those who we would command, which should come to pass if we should always show ourselves rude and sharp towards those we find faulty. For our ancestors have not obtained the seignory and domination they have left us by showing themselves sharp and rigorous, but rather by appearing gentle, benign, and easy to pardon. Moreover, we must consider that nature has given all men a desire of liberty; insomuch that the faults which men commit, being drawn on with desire, are greatly to be excused; and he that would punish them who desire a good thing, certainly were the next way to overthrow all good order and to bring in among men a confusion, to murder and slay one another. Finally masters, we must consider that the best and most firm domination is that whereby subjects are more detained in obedience by good deeds, than when they are constrained in their duties by punishments. For a good will and well liking accompany the one, and fear the other. But whatever is feared, is also naturally hated. We must also imitate our ancestors, who made themselves great in building of towns, not in ruining them; in drawing their neighbors into their city, not in slaying them. I therefore conclude that we ought to renew and reconfirm the Latins' treaty of peace."

This opinion of the dictator Largius was followed by Servius Sulpitius, who reasoned after him, and generally all the Senate, as full of all reason and equity. And if at this day men are governed by reason, it is certain that the opinion of Largius should be sufficient to show to any prince that to have a good and durable peace, he ought to grant such a one as men will willingly observe, which will be done when they are accorded a reasonable liberty under a good assurance.

And as for assurances of peace, the elders in foreign wars were wont to use hostages, but the principal bonds were public faith and oath, whereof we shall speak in another place. As for civil wars, they had other means besides faith and oath; for they bestowed offices and public estates upon some and the other, if not equally, yet justly, so as to content one and the other. This often happened at Rome, when the commons of the third estate, being oppressed by the greatest and richest, arose in some popular insurrection. For the means they used to appease such stirs was commonly to receive those of the third estate to the consulship, or to be censor, priest, or praetor, or to other offices. And in the end all offices and estates were open to all sorts of people, without distinction of nobles or basest trades, only regarding their virtue and good reputation, until the rich began to buy the voices of election. And truly it seems that when those of one party saw themselves recoiled from the estates and charges of the body of the commonwealth, and rebutted and estranged as suspected, that thereby they have just occasion to distrust themselves, as other men put no trust in them. And to this purpose the answer of Brutus, from the third estate to the nobles and patricians, is well to be marked.

> "Masters, those of the third estate in Rome know well that you lords patricians are indeed men of your word, and that for nothing will you contradict your promises; and that you will very well observe all that you promise, without need of other assurance than your faith and oath. But they further consider that after yourselves presently governing, those who succeed you will not observe what you have promised, but will handle the people tyrannically. And therefore there remains but one sole assurance to the weakest, who fear those stronger than themselves; namely, to find means that the strongest may not hurt them; for so long as there remains any means to hurt, there will never want will in the wicked to execute."

After Brutus had uttered this speech to the ambassadors, the Senate found it was founded upon reason, and they accorded to the people of the third estate magistrates, who were called tribunes of the people. These had the charge to defend the common people against great men, with power to imprison all such as seemed good; and this magistracy proved very profitable while they used it well, but as soon as they abused it, it fell out to be very pernicious. So is it of all other offices.

To demonstrate that men cannot keep a peace when they are handled like slaves, the example of the Saguntines is very notable and admirable. The Saguntines, a people of Spain, were besieged by Hannibal, who held them so straightly in their city that they had no means left to escape or resist. They being reduced to this extremity, Hannibal sent them word to yield themselves to save their lives; for, he said, courage must be vanquished when forces failed. And Hannibal would save their lives if they would yield to him, and of his grace would deal well with them. These poor people well considered the extreme danger wherein they were, and that they had no means to escape Hannibal's hands but by yielding unto him; and to yield they should change their free condition into a servitude. This they feared so much that they preferred to lose their lives; therefore they resolved to deal so that neither their bodies nor their goods should ever come into the power of Hannibal. So they chose certain young men who swore to defend the gates, even unto death, so that in the meanwhile the other townspeople might have time to execute their determination. After this the chief of the town resorted to the common marketplace, and there had all the goods and treasures of the town laid on a heap, and lit a great fire, within which many cast themselves. Others shut themselves up in their houses with their wives and children and burned themselves and their goods; and the young men trusted with the gates made an end of fighting and living together. Was not here, think you, an admirable love of liberty? For if they would have lived but a little while under Hannibal's yoke, there might have been hope that the Romans, their allies, would have delivered them. But yet they rather took choice to lose their lives, even by a most strange and cruel death, than to suffer for a small time a servile subjection under Hannibal.

But as it is rare and unlikely that a servile peace should be long and well observed, so it is a very great fault to break a peace when it is sufficiently commodious and tolerable. This was the only cause of the total ruin of that great and flourishing commonwealth of the Carthaginians. For after they had many times broken the treaty of peace which they had with the Romans, and had been many times vanquished, in the end they were altogether destroyed and their towns razed. And the cause that moved the Romans thus to do, was because they considered that the Carthaginians would never observe faith, nor promise they made, which already so many times they had violated. Especially since they were not at any time bound to any hard condition of peace, but were only hindered to rebel or wax great.

But the example of king Philip of Macedon, and of his son Perseus, is very notable in this matter. Philip, on slight occasion, enterprised war against the Aetolians, allies of Rome. The Aetolians called the Romans to their aid and sent an army into Greece against Philip, to succor the Aetolians and Athenians and to revenge themselves on the king who covertly paid Hannibal to war upon them. After some conflicts this king, fearing the forces and virtue of the Romans, wrought a peace with them. He observed it very well all the rest of his life; and the better to keep it from point to point, he read the articles of that peace twice a day, so that he might not break any point of it. When he was dead, his son Perseus succeeded him. Gathering great store of money and esteeming himself strong enough to war against the Romans, Perseus little by little broke the articles of peace, one after another, and covertly prepared for war. Finally the Romans sent consul Paulus Aemilius with an army, which in less than a month seized upon all Macedonia and brought it into the Roman obedience. Among the prisoners taken were Perseus and his son, who were carried to Rome in a triumph, where they miserably died in a prison. Behold the evil haps of Perseus, for not imitating the example of his father in the observation of the treaty of peace.

Verily, the prince who well considers the good that comes by living in peace will always seek to maintain it, at least within his own domination; for in peace all things flourish, and in war all things are in ruin and devastation. We read that in the time of Antonius Pius all the Roman Empire was in good peace, and all the provinces were rich and flourishing, not only in goods but in virtues and sciences. For at that time good letters flourished all over, and especially the civil law; which was so well practiced, and in all places so good justice administered that the whole empire was a most excellent and admirable thing. Moreover, that good emperor took a great delight to build great works and common buildings, as the amphitheater at Nisme, the Temple of Hadrian's Sepulcher, another amphitheater at Rome, and many other good houses and public buildings most sumptuous to behold. He also repaired bridges, gates, and ways, and furnished many towns with store of money, as well to make new buildings as to renew the old. Herein he imitated the example of his predecessor Trajan, who immortalized his name by his public works and buildings, even building new towns and joining rivers to aid the commerce of all countries. He also dried up great marshes and laid plain rocks and mountains to make fit ways for travelers, and did other notable works. Such actions as these are meet works for peaceable times, and are as honorable and proper to immortalize the name of a prince as to make war in order to have victories and triumphs. We see that the restoration of good letters, which

Francis I brought into France, did more to celebrate and immortalize his name in the memory of all Christian nations, than all the great wars and victories his predecessors had. And truly, princes who love and advance letters merit that learned people should send their honorable memory to all posterity; and those who despise them and hold them underfoot are not worthy that historians and men of learning should bring their words and victories into honor and reputation, much less to immortalize them in the memory of men. For as lawyers say, those who offend and despise laws ought not to enjoy their benefits; so the prince who makes no account of learning ought not to enjoy the benefit thereof, which is to make immortal generous and virtuous men.

But if we make comparison of the magnificence and estate that a prince should hold in the time of peace and prosperity, with what he should hold during war and poverty, there is such difference as between the day and the night. For proof hereof, I will cite but the time of Philip de Valois. For we read that in that time, a time of long peace, the king commonly had four or five other kings residing with him at court, as the king of Bohemia, the king of Scotland, the king of Aragon, the king of Navarre, and many great dukes, counts, barons, and prelates, most of whose charges he defrayed, so that it might appear that the king of France was a king of kings. It is certain that to maintain this magnificent and great estate, there must follow exceedingly great expenses; but he might well do it, for his people being rich and full of peace, they had better means to provide for him a crown than in time of war to give him three and a half pence. At that time a king of England passed into France to do homage to Philip for the duchy of Guines, which the English had long held from the crown of France. When the English king saw the train of the court of France, he was ravished in admiration to see so many kings, dukes, counts, barons, princes, peers of France; constable, admiral, chancellor, marshal, and many other great lords who reputed themselves happy to obtain the good grace of Philip. This moved the king of England far more easily, and he did Philip homage in other means than he thought to have. At his return to England, he said on high that he supposed there was neither king nor emperor in the world that held so magnificent and triumphant an estate as the king of France did. Should we not desire to see such a time again? But we are far from it, and take no course thereunto; for civil wars cannot bring us unto it, only a good and holy peace well and inviolably observed, by a good reformation of justice and of all estates corrupted in France. For without it, the people can never prosper, but shall always be gnawed and eaten even to the bones, and the people being poor, the king cannot be rich, no neither his nobility nor clergy; for all the king's revenues, all tallies, all the nobility's and clergy's rents, proceed from the poor people.

By this which we have above handled, this maxim of war is sufficiently understood; I will add no more thereunto, but that Machiavelli shows himself a man of very good grace when he says that the Italians are a people of nimble and light bodies, for he cannot more properly note them of inconstancy and infidelity; and when he says they never willingly go to battle, he cannot any better tax them of cowardice and pusillanimity. But the reason whereby he would seem to cover this fault is more to be accounted of than the rest, for he says this proceeds from the little heart and cowardice of the captains; as if he said that all Italian captains are fainthearted cowards, who rather discourage than add heart unto their soldiers to fight. And herein I believe he says truth, for so many Italian captains as we have seen in France this fifteen years, there has not been one found that has done any one memorable exploit. They can indeed make many vain and brave shows, and in many subtle stratagems there are found no better warriors; but in battles and assaults of towns, they never come by their wills, as their own Machiavelli bears them witness.

3.2
Machiavelli

To cause a prince to withdraw his mind altogether from peace and agreement with his adversaries, he must commit some notable and outrageous injury against them. (*Discourses*, book 3 chapter 32)

Because men are naturally vindictive and desirous to take vengeance on those who offend them, it consequently falls out that they who have outraged or injured any, especially if the injury be great, can never trust him they have so injured. For every man fears and distrusts his reconciled enemy. And therefore to find means that a prince may never set his heart and mind upon peace, nor reconcile himself to any adversary, he must be persuaded to practice some outrageous act upon his said adversary. So by that means he will never trust him, nor be reconciled with him.

Answer

Behold here the very counsel that Achitophel gave to Absalom, to make him irreconcilable with his father David, and to place a division in all his kingdom. For he advised Absalom to cohabitate and dwell even with his father David's wives, which was the greatest and most villainous injury that he could have done to him. And to this end he did it; that Absalom and all who followed him might be utterly out of hope to make peace with David, and by that means, playing the desperado, they might gather double courage and make themselves possessors of the kingdom. For necessity and despair make men hardy and valiant; but what was the issue thereof? Even this, that Achitophel, the author of this counsel, hanged himself, either out of despair or fear that David would have punished him. Absalom also soon after miserably perished as a reward for his adherence and cleaving to so bad counsel.

The same happened to Tolumnius, king of the Veians, who had caused the Fidenates to revolt from the Romans. For when the Romans sent ambassadors to the Fidenates, to know the reason of their revolt, Tolumnius counseled them to slay the ambassadors, as indeed they did, to the end (according to Livy) that the Fidenates might be more faithful to him, and out of hope of reconciliation with the Romans, perceiving themselves guilty of so strange a crime. So the Romans made war upon the Fidenates, unto whose succor came Tolumnius; and as he was in battle, a Roman named Cornelius Cossus saw him and said, "Behold the breaker of human leagues, the violator of the people's right; now shall thou be sacrificed for the death of our ambassadors." And couching his spear against Tolumnius, ran at him and carried him to the earth, where he slew him, cut off his head, and showed it in front of a number of the enemies, who as soon as they saw the king's head turned their backs and fled.

The Capuans, after receiving many good turns and succors from the Romans, even when they yet had in their town a Roman garrison, enterprised to make their profit of the Romans' calamity in the battle of Cannae. For, seeing that Hannibal had much enfeebled the Roman forces, they revolted from them and joined unto Hannibal. They also sent ambassadors to Rome to tell the Senate that if they would receive the Capuans in equality of government, by according that from thenceforward one of the consuls of Rome should be a Capuan, they would help the Romans against Hannibal. The Roman senators, perceiving a foolish and proud demand of these effeminate Capuans, who were no better warriors than common strumpets, made no answer and chased them out of the Senate. These ambassadors seeing themselves repulsed from their demand, returned to Capua and reported how they sped in their embassage. Then these devilish Capuans, according to the guise and nature of all effeminate cowards, who are always cruel for their own advantage, enterprised in a conspiracy with Hannibal to massacre all the Roman garrison which they had in their town of Capua. The Roman garrison being thus massacred, the Romans sent to besiege Capua. Hannibal, unable to leave without great peril, besieged Rome, hoping thereby to draw their siege from Capua. After Hannibal had removed, the Romans assaulted the town and entered in. Quintus Fulvius, lieutenant general of the Roman army, had a proclamation made that all those of the town who would resort to their camp within certain days would not be held culpable, and not consenting to the revolt and massacre made by the Capuans. But none dared trust this proclamation; not that they doubted the Romans would hold their word, but because they had left no hope to obtain any pardon. Yet most of the senators of Capua concluded to send ambassadors to Rome to obtain grace and pardon, having some hope in the clemency so many times proved in the Roman Senate. And indeed their ambassadors obtained letters of grace. But one Virius, the principal author of the said revolt and massacre, was not of that opinion to have recourse nor any hope in the Senate, judging his crime to be so great that it was impossible to obtain pardon. Therefore he and 27 other senators of his opinion resolved to slay themselves; they prepared a great banquet, furnished with viands and wine, the most exquisite that could be gotten, and drank till their senses were taken from them; and for their last farewell every man drank a glass of poison. Embracing one another, they began to weep and lament the ruin of them and their country, and to detest the wicked counsel they had taken, to use so outrageous a part against the Romans, to take away all hope of peace and reconciliation. So having long wept and lamented, they fell dead upon the earth, one after the other. Is not this a notable example to detest that wicked counsel of Machiavelli, to seek means to be irreconcilable? Is there any prince in the world unto whom a necessity may not sometimes come to be reconciled with his inferior adversary? And if reconciliation may always come in good time and for good purpose, how does this wicked atheist lay down this maxim?

Catiline, a man devoid of all virtue and a bundle of all vice, resolving in his brain to be an exceedingly great man or altogether nothing, devised a conspiracy against his country and drew to his league many Roman gentlemen such as himself. Considering that he could not bring to effect his conjuration without declaring and communicating it to the chieftains of his aid, yet fearing that some of them would disclose it, he made them all take a most execrable oath, that thereby might be foreclosed from them all hope of retiring from his side. So he mixed wine with human blood in pots and made all his companions drink of it, and made them swear with an execration that they would never disclose the enterprise, but employ themselves with all their power to execute it. His partners, already culpable of human blood, were so secret that nothing would have been discovered if God had not permitted a harlot called Fulvia to draw certain words out of a conspirator's mouth, as she demanded of him where he lay the preceding nights. Being drunk, to enjoy his courtesan he disclosed to her that he had been in a company with whom he made an enterprise that would make him rich forever. As soon as Fulvia knew all the conjuration she disclosed it to the consul Cicero. Cicero did what he could to open all the enterprise, but the conspirators held so well their horrible oath that not one of so great a number would ever reveal a word. But yet Cicero found means to know all, by the declaration which the Allobroges made, who Catiline had appointed to furnish him with people for the execution. But the end of Catiline was such that he was slain fighting with a great number of others, and most of his accomplices were executed by justice. Briefly, all who have practiced that wicked doctrine of Machiavelli, to commit outrageous acts to be irreconcilable, their ends and lives have proved very tragedies.

3.3
Machiavelli

A prince in a conquered country must place colonies and garrisons, especially in the strongest places, to chase away the natural and old inhabitants thereof. (*The Prince*, chapter 3)

The best remedy to conserve a newly conquered country or province is to erect colonies, placing strangers there, and from thence banishing all the prince's ancient and natural inhabitants. For by that means the prince should keep that country with a small charge, without troubling the country with great garrisons, only injuring those he expulses from those places to make room for new inhabitants. And as for those who are chased away, he need not fear them, for they will be but some small portion of the inhabitants of that province, who remaining poor and exiled shall from thenceforth be little able to hurt. And as for those who shall be left in peace, it is likely that they will enterprise nothing, fearing by their rebellion to procure a banishment also to themselves as the others have. For men must be tamed by a certain kindness, either in not soiling or altogether discouraging those left in the province; or else he ought to utterly destroy and impoverish them all, as in chasing away and exiling the inhabitants of those places where he will establish colonies. For injuries done to a man ought to be executed in such sort that they may not be subject to fear of vengeance. The Romans knew well how to observe this maxim, sending colonies to all the nations which they vanquished, by the means of which colonies they held the most feeble in their weakness, not suffering them to gather strength; and they also weakened the power of those who were great and most eminent.

Answer

The distinction of the property of the goods of this world, whereby every man ought to be master and assured possessor of his own, has been introduced by the law and right of nature, which wills that to every man be yielded what belongs to him; or else by the right of the nations, which all comes to one end. This distinction of property maintains the commerce and traffic among men; it entertains buying and selling, permutations, loans, and such like, which are the bonds of all human society. And if the distinction of property is not maintained in the world, all commerce is destroyed, and all society decayed and resolved. For although some poets and philosophers praise the community of goods, remembering us of that golden world of Saturn, yet it is plainly evident to all people of judgment that communism induces and brings a carelessness, idleness, discord, and confusion into the commonwealth, as learnedly Aristotle demonstrates in his *Politics*. Therefore it is very necessary that the natural right therein be observed, and every man be maintained in the enjoyment of his own goods, and that to every man be rendered that which is his own. This right ought to be so observed that it is not lawful for the prince to break or violate it, because by reason of natural right it is inviolable, and none can derogate from it. And hereunto agrees the divine right, whereby it is showed to us that king Ahab ought not to take away the vineyard from Naboth his subject. And hereunto also accord the rules of civil right, whereby it is said that the natural right and the right of nations are inviolable, in such sort that the civil right neither can nor ought to derogate anything from them.

Hereby therefore is seen the absurdity and manifest iniquity of this maxim of Machiavelli, who counsels a prince, as soon as he has conquered a new country, to dispossess the masters and right owners of their goods, in towns and places where he knows it to be expedient to make himself strong; and to place there other new masters and possessors of his own nation, in place of those who are dispossessed and banished. For if the prince uses this maxim, certain it is, first that he violates the right and law of nature, which he ought not do; secondly, he acquires the enmity of the inhabitants of that new conquered country, which may be a means to deject him from all. For in the love of subjects and in their voluntary obedience lies the firmness and assurance of a prince's estate, as we shall speak in another place. It is folly to allege that there will be no malcontents but those who are driven away. For Machiavelli says those who remain in the country will be satisfied because they abide still; but I say it is folly to think so. For certainly, people fear what they see happen to their neighbors; and further, not only our own losses engender in us discontentment, but also others' losses, as of our parents, friends, allies, yea, of those not joined to us with any other bond than of our own country, tongue, or religion, although in all these there is a distinction of more and less. Thirdly, those whom the prince chases from their possessions and goods will ever be so deadly enemies that all their lives they will leave no stone unturned to have right and vengeance of such injustice done against the law of nature. And the prince has no cause to think they cannot hurt him because they are poor banished people; for it is certain that there is no little enmity but will be hurtful. Of how small a beginning did Sertorius arise? He was but a simple Roman gentleman, without authority and means; yet with certain troops of barbarians, trained as well as he could, he possessed a good part of Spain. The Romans sent against him Metellus with a great host, which could do nothing to him; they were forced to send Pompey with an army, whom Sertorius braved, calling him the little apprentice of Sulla. And it appeared that if Sertorius had not been slain by his own people, he would sooner have overcome Pompey than Pompey him. Yet Sertorius was a simple soldier, who had neither silver nor treasure; he had no authority to command, neither did any obey him against their will. Spartacus was also but a poor slave, who escaped from his master, gathered together a great number of people and made strong war upon the Romans, who he vanquished many times. But for Pompey and Crassus, with great armies greatly busied to hinder his designs, he would have made himself master of Italy. And was not Cleon another poor slave, yet he gathered an army of 70,000 other slaves, wherewith he almost took all of Sicily? And Viriatus was but a shepherd on the mountains of Spain, and gathering together a great number of shepherds and thieves, he made infinite work for the Romans. Yet in the end certain Roman captains who were sent against him, otherwise unable to overcome him, caused him traitorously to be slain.

This the Senate found not good, but greatly blamed those captains who overcame by such villainous means. After Viriatus was slain his people did not disband, but made full war upon the Romans; the Romans were constrained to give them in appeasement the territory of Valencia in Spain; and so they were satisfied, and gave over their arms. Of late memory, Philibert de Chaton, prince of Orange, Antony de Leva, Andrew Doria, the marquis of Mantua, and many others whereof we have spoken in other places, revolted against Francis I and did him more hurt than all the forces of the emperor Charles V; yet they were no great lords in comparison with the king. Therefore he who is a wise prince will estimate no enemy to be petty and little, but will guard himself from justly offending any man, fearing lest by that means he procure enemies. For enmities will come too fast on a man, before he looks for them.

As for what he says, that the Romans had colonies in countries which they conquered; they did it not to serve for fortresses in that country, as Machiavelli says, but to disburden the city of Rome of their too great a multitude of people, who were still stirring up rebellions and seditions in the town; as in the time of the consulship of Marcus Valerius and Quintus Apuleius. The town, says Livy, was brought to a great quiet and tranquility by discharging it of a great part of the common people, by deduction of colonies. When they were sent into any country that the Romans had conquered, the public and common fields were divided among them; yet the old inhabitants were not chased away, neither were their goods taken from them, but only mingled with the Romans' goods, who dwelled with them in their towns and houses. The Romans also set up colonies as a multiplication of their race, but not to serve them for fortresses in conquered countries. And that it was so appears because they did not erect colonies in all the countries they conquered, not even in the strongest places, but rather in the amplest, fattest, and most fertile places. These said colonies also were no more faithful unto them than other subjects, but often rebelled, as was seen after the battle that the Romans lost at Cannae against Hannibal. For then twelve Roman colonies revolted and entered league with Hannibal. And it is commonly seen that citizens transported into other countries immediately degenerate, taking the manners and conditions of the country, as came to pass in the towns of Alexandria in Egypt, Seleucia in Syria, and Babylon in Parthia, which were colonies of the Macedonians; and to the town of Tarentum, a colony of the Lacedaemonians. All these towns straight despoiled them of the manners, natures, and original generosity of their nation, and they became as soft, effeminate, and cowardly as those into whose countries they removed.

A great and memorable calamity fell to Philip king of Macedonia, by removing to other places the natural inhabitants of the maritime and sea towns of his country. This king, fearing to enter into war with the Romans, because many of his neighbors complained of him to the Senate of Rome, thought it good to stand upon his guard; and distrusting the inhabitants of towns near the sea, he took away their natural inhabitants and gave them land in Emathia to dwell in, and in their places planted the inhabitants of Thrace, in whom he trusted. This caused in all Macedonia a great discontentment, for to their great grief everyone saw their ancient poor dislodged, carrying their children on their shoulders, weeping and lamenting their calamities and making execrations and imprecations against the king, that it might happen to the king and his race to be driven from his kingdom. The king being advised of this universal murmur began to distrust every man, and especially the children of certain gentlemen who he had killed. And he feared that the said children, making use of the people's discontent, would attempt some enterprise against him; therefore he determined to kill the children of the slain gentlemen, for his better assurance. Theoxena, the widow of Herodicus, a great lord who was slain by the king, resolved rather to kill her children than that they should come into the hands and power of the king. So she resolved to save herself and them at Athens, and yet if the worst fell, she provided good swords and poisons. After she had embarked with her children toward Athens, she was followed by another boat of the king's people, and when she saw that they rowed with great diligence to the bark wherein she was, said: "Lo, my children, you have now no other means to shun the tyranny of king Philip but death, which you may see (showing the swords and poison), choose which you had rather die on, either on sharp whetted swords, or to swallow this poison; let the eldest show themselves most hardy and courageous." This exhortation persuaded so much that they slew themselves, some with swords, some with poison. Then she caused them all to fall into the water, even when they yet had breath, and cast herself in after them. The king's people joined to the bark, but they found it empty of the people they looked for. The cruelty of this fact added a new flame of envy and evil will towards the king, so that it seemed to everyone that they heard the infernal furies preparing themselves to bring upon the king and his race the imprecations which all the world made against him. And indeed it came to pass, by the just judgment of God, that as this poor woman had caused her own children to die, so Philip made to die by poison his lawful son Demetrius, a prince of exceeding great towardness, by the false accusation of Perseus, his bastard son. After some time, this king having discovered that by a false accusation he had murdered his own son, he would have disinherited Perseus; and being continually tormented with the shadow and resemblance of his son Demetrius, which his conscience always brought before his eyes, he died desperately, detesting and execrating that wicked Perseus. Perseus, then his only son, who remained to succeed him in his kingdom, after a few years' reign was taken prisoner by the Romans and led in a triumph to Rome, where he miserably died in a prison. So the imprecations and curses which poor people, chased from their country and goods by the king, poured out against him and his race, fell upon him and his. Is this not an example to make the hairs stand upright on princes' heads, when men persuade them to dispossess natural inhabitants of their country and goods? Yet at this day there are too many Machiavellians who say it is good to chase away the natural inhabitants of France, or at least from certain places and corners, and to people them with some race that is good, faithful, and loyal, as Italians and Lombards. But what wants there of an Italian colony at Lyons? A great part of the inhabitants are Italians, and other people of the country conform themselves little by little to their actions, behaviors, manner of life, and language; scarcely shall you find any so vile or paltry an artisan but will study to speak Italian. For these magnificent Machiavellians will give no countenance, nor willingly hear any but those who use their own language; by that means seeking to bring credit both to themselves and their tongue. The towns also of Paris, Marseille, Grenoble, and many others of France, are they not full of Italians?

3.4
Machiavelli

> A prince in a newly conquered country must subvert and destroy all those who suffer great loss in that conquest, and altogether root out the blood and the race of those who before governed there.
> (*The Prince*, chapter 3)

Men willingly change their lords, thinking to amend themselves; this opinion commonly makes them revolt, but most often they are deceived, finding themselves in worse case than before. Therefore, to shun such kinds of revolts a prince ought to take out of the way all those he thinks are displeased with any great loss they have suffered. For I am persuaded that all men of good judgment hold this without doubt, that the estate of a prince or commonwealth cannot long endure in a country unless all those be taken away who, for some great harm they have suffered by the change, are contrary to him. And herein Louis XII dealt unwisely, losing the duchy of Milan as quickly as he had conquered it. For the Milanese found themselves deceived, frustrated of the advantages and commodities which they looked for at his hands, and could not suffer the proud handling of that new prince. Here then was his fault, that he did not take away all malcontents who suffered loss in the change, and especially because he did not utterly root out the race of Sforzas. But Cesare Borgia did not thus; having occupied Romania, of all the lords he dispossessed he left not one alive that he could catch, and very few escaped. Therefore it is better to follow the example of Borgia than of Louis, for sometimes it succeeds not well to imitate the best men; for it was damaging to Pertinax and Alexander Severus to imitate the mildness and bounty of Marcus Antonius; and to Caracalla, Commodus, and Maximinus, that they desired to resemble Severus.

Answer

Machiavelli, meaning to show that his purpose tends and aims only to instruct a prince in all sorts of tyranny, gives him here a precept which Thrasibulus the Milesian gave to Periander, a tyrant of Corinth, and Tarquin the Proud gave to his son Sextus. Periander, having tyrannously obtained the crown of Corinth where he had no right, fearing some conspiracy against him, sent a messenger to ask advice of his great friend Thrasibulus, so to be assured master and lord of Corinth. Thrasibulus made him no answer by mouth; but commanding the messenger to follow him, he went into a field full of ripe corn, and taking the highest and most eminent ears there, he bruised them between his hands and wished the messenger to return to Periander, saying no more unto him. As soon as Periander heard of bruising the most ancient ears of corn, he presently conceived the meaning thereof; to wit, to overthrow and remove all the great men of Corinth who suffered any loss and were grieved at the change of the state; as indeed he did.

As much did Sextus Tarquinius, the son of Tarquin the Proud. Making a countenance of some great argument with his father for his great cruelty, he told the Gabinians (then his father's enemies) that for his safeguard he would fly unto them if it pleased them to receive him, and would bring with him a good troupe of his servants and friends. These poor Gabinians, not suspecting the intelligence between the father and the son, sent him word that he would be very welcome. He went there by stealth with his troupe, and because he gave them to understand that he would make war upon his father to revenge the injury done to them and him, they elected him their captain. As soon as he saw his foot in, he secretly sent a messenger to his father, to tell him what command he had in the town, and to ask what he should do. Tarquin led the messenger into a garden with great store of poppy, whose highest heads he struck with a little staff, making no other answer to the messenger. Returning to Gabium, the messenger told Sextus his father's actions, and it was well understood what he should do. Then he told the people that Antistius Petra, the chief lord and magistrate of the Gabinians, had conspired with certain accomplices to deliver him to Tarquin either dead or alive. He showed letters found in the house of Antistius (where Sextus had secretly put them), written by Tarquin and sealed with his seal, which he read before all the Gabinians. As soon as they heard them they were so angered and moved against good Antistius, who knew not what to say of this thing he never thought of, that they stoned him and suffered Sextus himself to punish the partners of Antistius. Then Sextus having the bridle loose, massacred in their houses all the greatest and noblest of the town of Gabium; and by that means he and his father proved masters of that poor desolate town. But this tyranny and others they committed, caused on the other side the loss of the kingdom and domination of Rome; so that fishing for a frog, they let go out of their net a lamprey. So it happens ordinarily to those who will practice this detestable doctrine of Machiavelli.

If we look into the manner of government practiced by all great conquerors and generous monarchs who became the greatest and noblest in the world, as Caesar, Alexander, Cyrus, Charlemagne, etc., we shall find that they used most contrary means to Machiavelli's doctrine. For they exercised no cruelties towards great or little as they made their conquests, but only so far as the necessity of war carried them. They treated conquered people with all kindness and clemency; they embraced and entertained very well those who were great personages, and altered nothing in the public state, religion, policy, customs, and liberties, but maintained them all, contenting themselves only with sovereignty. And this was the reason why many people desired not to resist them, but to be their subjects; and those who resisted them yielded again easily, without abiding any great battery or assaults. Therefore most generously and nobly dealt king Louis, imitating the kindness and gentleness of those great monarchs when he conquered Milan. For although he later lost it, the fault was not that he would not be so cruel as to exterminate the whole race of the Sforzas, but rather proceeded from the inconstancy of the Milanese and the machinations of Pope Julius II with the Venetians, who thought it not good to have so great a master so near them, as the French and Italian histories evidently demonstrate.

And whereas Machiavelli maintains that it succeeds not well for a prince to imitate the virtuous actions of generous princes, and therefore ought to follow the vicious actions of those who are of no account, he shows that he is both wicked and ignorant. For what more wicked doctrine can be given to a prince, than to say he ought to imitate wicked actions because they sometimes succeed well? This is as much to say that we must be thieves and cut merchants' throats, because thieves gain thereby. But if Machiavelli and all his favorites would judge of the success of all things by their end, as they ought to, they would find that those glorious and good successes that happen to the wicked are but means wherewith God serves himself to bring them into ruin and be utterly overthrown, which they merited, as I have amply showed by many examples. And as for the examples he cites, he shows himself by the application he makes a very beast. It succeeded not well, he says, for Commodus, Caracalla, and Maximinus, in that they would imitate and resemble Severus. O bravely applied and to good purpose spoken! For Pertinax succeeded Commondus and Severus; Commodus never saw or knew Severus, who in his time was yet unknown, being a simple wage soldier of a base unknown race; how should then Commodus propose him for an example to imitate? And as for his son Caracalla, and Maximinus, they were never imitators of Severus but in his vices, namely in cruelty; and therefore we need not marvel if it did not succeed well with them. The emperor Severus had very good virtues, for he was very learned and advanced learned people to estates; he maintained a very good policy in the Roman empire; he made good and holy laws, which are yet in use; he caused good justice to be administered to the people, and kept barbarous nations in a new obedience. His son Caracalla had none of these virtues, although Machiavelli being very ignorant of histories says he was endowed with excellent virtues. For histories attribute no virtue unto him, but that from his youth he was accustomed to live as a soldier; that he was not delicate, but patient of labor; but otherwise the most wicked man in the world in all things. And as for Maximinus, he resembled Caracalla in all things, except that he issued from a base race and a barbarous nation, and Caracalla was an emperor's son. And as for what Machiavelli says, that it succeeded not well to Pertinax and Alexander Severus because of their imitation of Aurelius the philosopher, he shows still more his beastliness, and that he has not read the histories of their lives. For histories show that Pertinax was slain by his soldiers because he appeared to them more greedy than he should have been; so likewise was Alexander slain for the covetousness of his mother Mammea towards the soldiers. But we never read that Marcus Aurelius was ever spotted with that vice of greed, rather contrary that he was a very liberal prince; and that herein, as in all other virtues, he was a true philosopher, that is to say, loving good and hating evil. And therefore Machiavelli knows not what he says when he claims it succeeded not well with Pertinax and Alexander Severus to have a mind to imitate Marcus Antonius. He would better have spoken only of the jests and matters written in the registers of Florence, where he was secretary, than so with a foolish interpretation to corrupt histories he knows not.

3.5
Machiavelli

To be revenged on a city or a country without striking any blow, it must be filled with wicked manners. (*Discourses*, book 1 chapter 35; book 2 chapter 19)

Vanquished cities or provinces revenge themselves marvelously well on the vanquishers, by receiving them gently and filling them with wicked manners. For thus they easily prepare them to be vanquished by whoever assaults them, as it happened to Hannibal's soldiers at Capua. Having long sojourned there at their case in all delights and pleasures, they became so effeminate that they were never after good for anything. This corruption of manners comes ordinarily when corrupted nations frequent amongst others; for they infect them with evil manners. And therefore the German nation remains so entire and constant in its manners because the Germans were never curious to traffic with their neighbors, nor to dwell in other countries, nor to receive foreigners into their country; but always have contented themselves with their own goods, nourishment, manners, and fashion of apparel. Shunning the frequenting of Spaniards, French, and Italians (the three most vicious nations of the world), they have not yet learned their customs and corruptions.

Answer

I have not here set down this maxim to say it is not very true. For besides the examples we read in histories, we know it by experience, seeing at this day all France fashioned after the manners, conditions, and vices of foreigners that govern it, and who have the principal charges and estates. And not only many Frenchmen are such beasts to conform themselves to strangers' complexions, but also to gaggle their language and disdain the French tongue as a thing too common and vulgar. But if we well consider this manner of vengeance taught by Machiavelli in this maxim, we shall find it is a most detestable doctrine, as well for them who practice it as for them against whom it is practiced. The example even of Capua, which Machiavelli notes, proves it. For the Capuans, in receiving Hannibal's army, corrupted and infected the soldiers with all excess and effeminate wantonness; and also by the same means they procured their own ruin and entire destruction, which soon after happened to them. The Persian lords, who with their manners corrupted Alexander the Great, did nothing to their own advantage. For Alexander becoming vicious, they got the evil will of the Macedonians, who took displeasure to see their king corrupted. And finally, after the death of Alexander, which came to him by dissoluteness learned from the Persians, these lords had part of the evil luck whereof they were the cause. And generally we may see that the corrupters of princes and people always take part in the evil whereof they are the cause, as we have showed by many examples of flatterers who have corrupted their princes. We Frenchmen may yield good witness of what account the Italian and Neapolitan nation is, by the frequentation we had with them in the voyage which was made to Naples in the time of king Charles VIII. For from thence brought they this disease, which at this day is now called the French pox, and which we have ever since kept. But yet so, as the Italians and Neapolitans are not exempt therefrom, but both the one and the other have part of that corruption. Briefly, we ought to detest and hate this wicked doctrine of Machiavelli, and reject all vengeance, and follow Saint Paul's lesson, who commands us to converse with good people and of good manners, because the conversation of the wicked not only corrupts good manners, but also sows those that are wicked.

And as for what Machiavelli says of the Germans, we know and see the frequentation of the Germans in France, and yet till this present we have not seen that they have yet gathered corruption of manners. And whereas he sets down the French nation among those most corrupted, we cannot deny it; but we may well say that the doctrine of Machiavelli and the frequentation of them of his nation are the cause of the greatest and most detestable corruption which is today in France. For from whom have the French learned and known atheism, sodomy, treachery, cruelty, usury, and such other like vices, but from Machiavelli and those of his nation? So that they may brag that they are well revenged of the wars which our ancestors have made in Italy.

3.6
Machiavelli

> It is folly to think that with princes and great lords new pleasures cause them to forget offenses. (*The Prince*, chapter 7; *Discourses*, book 3 chapter 4)

During the life of his father Pope Alexander VI, Cesare Borgia usurped the domination of Romania, a land belonging to the church, and was called duke de Valentinois. In making those usurpations he offended many cardinals, and among others the Cardinal of Saint Peter ad Vincula; yet Borgia consented that he should be elected pope after the death of Alexander. Whereof he soon repented; for this new pope, called Julius II, straight betook himself to arms to recover what Borgia had usurped, although Borgia had favored him in his election; which he should never have done, nor suffered any election of a pope who was his enemy. For new pleasures never make men forget old injuries and offenses; and therefore Borgia, who in all other things had governed well, committed a foul fault in the creation of Julius, and himself delivered the means of his final destruction. The same fault was committed by Servius Tullius, king of the Romans, in giving his two daughters in marriage to two Tarquins, who quarreled for the crown and who thought that Tullius would usurp it upon them. For not only this alliance extinguished the envy and rancor which they had to Servius, but what is more, it caused one of the daughters to enterprise to slay her own father.

Answer

It seems that what Machiavelli tells of Borgia bows somewhat from the truth of the history. For Sabellicus writes that during the election of Pope Julius II, Borgia was shut up in the pope's tower to be safe and guarded from his enemies. So there was no likelihood that a man brought into such extremity as to hide himself and be shut up in prison, for the great multitude of enemies he had procured, should have such great credit in the pope's election. But suppose it was true that Borgia helped Julius to the popedom, and that Julius was ungrateful, for the remembrance he had of the old injuries Borgia had done him; what follows hereof? Some Machiavellians will answer that all great lords will always do the like, and that therefore they ought not to be trusted. Is not here a goodly doctrine for a prince? Briefly, it is Machiavelli's mind to teach a prince to trust in no lord who he has once offended; and again, that none who have made a fault or offended him shall any more trust him, whatever reconciliation, peace, concord, amity, pleasure, and good offices may happen since the offence. Here behold a most wicked and detestable doctrine, to say that an offense ought to take so deep root in the heart of the offended that by no pleasures, services, or other means it can be raised out. But Machiavelli seems somewhat excusable to maintain this maxim; for according to the honor of his nation, vengeances and enmities are perpetual and irreconcilable. And indeed there is nothing wherein they take greater delectation, pleasure, and contentment than to execute a vengeance; whenever they can have their enemy at their pleasure, to be revenged upon him they murder him after some strange and barbarous fashion, and in murdering him they put him in remembrance of the offense done unto them, with many reaproachful words and injuries to torment the soul and the body together; and sometimes wash their hands and mouths with his blood, and force him with hope of his life to give himself to the devil; and so they seek in slaying the body to damn the soul, if they could. God by his grace keep all countries — but especially England, which is already so spotted with other vices, and with the doctrine Machiavelli teaches — that they be not soiled and infected with that immortal and irreconcilable vengeance. For how is it possible that man should be without infinite quarrels, and continual and ordinary batteries and murders, even with parents and friends, and with all other persons with whom he has any frequentation, if offenses may never be blotted out but by vengeance? Everyone may well know by experience that those who are among themselves great friends and familiars, yet commit offenses one to another, and sometimes have great stirs, spites, and contentions among them; but must men as soon as they receive any offense at the hand of a parent, friend, or of any other, forget and blot out all amity, Christian and brotherly charity towards his neighbor, and to pardon no faults, but seek the ruin of him that offends us? Surely this is not only far from all Christian piety, but also from all humanity and common sense; even brute beasts, which have no reason, are not so unreasonable. For a dog which we have offended will be appeased with a piece of bread, yea, will fawn upon him who beat him, and as much will a horse do and an ox which has been pricked and beaten, when hay is given them. And as for those who say that vengeance is lawful by right of nature, they are greatly deceived, as the beasts named before show. True it is that nature teaches man and all living creatures to put back violence with violence, when a man is upon the act, and instantly when violence is inferred; but it does not teach that after the act of violence and outrage is committed, a man ought to seek vengeance to put back violence and outrage. For this is not to repel and repulse injury, which already being received, cannot be repulsed; but rather to infer a new injury and violence; and withal that natural right, to repulse violence with violence, it must be understood with reason and equal moderation. That is to say, that such right has place when by no other means in any other sort we can shun the violence which is offered unto us. And indeed, the brute beasts themselves show us we must so use it; for you shall not see a wolf nor a swine seek to put back the violence offered him while they have place to fly, and that they be not brought to a strait. And therefore it is a beastly ignorance to color that detestable vice of vengeance by the right of nature. For it is clean contrary, and especially to the irreconcilable vengeance whereof Machiavelli speaks, which he says cannot be defaced nor forgotten by new pleasures. But I do well know that some Machiavellians will reply upon this doctrine, that Machiavelli speaks only of princes and great lords, unto whom he says that new pleasures cannot extinguish old injuries, and that hereunto accords what Homer says:

> A mighty king that angry is against one less than he,
> Can hide full deep in spiteful heart, that hard it is to see
> His fierce and angry wrathful mood, till he espies his time,
> Revenge to take, according to the greatness of the crime.

But let the case be so, that the wrath and irritations of great princes and lords dwell longer in their hearts than in other persons of less quality, as the meaning of Homer seems to be. It does not follow that a prince is implacable, and that he cannot be appeased by any pleasures or services. It seems that Homer noted no other thing in the particular natures of kings and great lords, but that they know how for a time to dissemble spites and offenses perpetrated against them, and can attend opportunity to revenge them (a thing very true, and that we see often practiced). But it is far from Homer to say that kings and princes cannot be appeased by pleasures and good services that may be done unto them after the offense, yea, in humiliating and reconciling themselves to them. Homer speaks here of choleric kings, who are not masters of themselves, not being able to command their passions and affections which reign in them, and which darken their reason and judgment; such as was king Agamemnon, of whom he especially spoke in the place above cited. For many good and wise kings and princes are seen, who can so well make their passions and affections obey reason, that not only their wise judgment never suffers that a desire after perpetual vengeance shall take root in their hearts, but rather will not leave in their memory the offenses that are done them, but will forget and pardon them of their own motion before any pardon be demanded. For their wisdom judges that those passions of vengeance, besides that they torment and make lean the heart of a prince, are altogether contrary to the principal virtue which ought to shine in a prince; clemency, gentleness, and goodness, a virtue making a prince's estate pleasing and assured, which ought principally to shine in private offenses as justice ought to especially shine in public offenses, as shall be spoken more at large in another place. Although even in public offenses it is sometimes requisite for the public good and utility that the prince use clemency and forgetfulness.

To this purpose is very regardable the opinion that the great and wise Quintus Fabius Maximus held in the Senate. When the Romans began to get up and prosper again after their ruin at Cannae, many of their allies who had revolted to Hannibal proffered to come to them again. Among others there was one Classius Altinius Arpinus, who came to Rome and made the Senate understand that he had means to bring the town of Arpos, where he lived, into their hands. The matter coming to deliberation in the Senate, some argued that it was not good to trust in this Altinius, nor in any other Arpinos, seeing they had violated their faith by revolting unto Hannibal; and that it was folly to make account of such people who have their faith as variable as fortune. And as for his offer to deliver town of Arpos, he did it for no good affection he bore to the Roman commonwealth, but because he saw the affairs thereof dissolve and decay. But Fabius reasoned in another sort.

> "Masters, those who have spoken before seem to give their opinion as if we were already in good peace, forgetting the time lately passed and not considering that we are yet in the heat of war. As for me, I think we stand in need to devise all the means we can find out to contain our allies from revolt. But if recent necessity and their weakness have drawn them on once to a revolt, and if after it is not lawful for them to return and to reconcile themselves, who can doubt but at length all our allies will turn from us to the Carthaginians? My advice then is that we should not reject a reconciliation with such as revolt from us, although they have not been so constant as they should be in a faithful adherence unto us."

The opinion of Fabius was followed by all the Senate, and by the means of Altinius the Romans regained the town of Arpos.

But it seems that the persuasion which Quintus Metellus used in the name of all the Senate unto Aemylius Lepidus and Fulvius Nobilior, censors of Rome, is well worth marking to show that vengeance and enmities ought not to be perdurable in great lords, but ought to appease themselves and be reconciled one to another. The said two censors were two of the greatest princes and lords of Rome, consuls endowed with other great offices and estates, and at that time were censors, which was the greatest office of all; for censors took cognizance of all the abuses of magistrates and senators, and might put them out. These two being enemies, although companions in one charge, the Senate determined to seek means to agree them. So they sent unto them a great number of the principal senators, among them Quintus Metellus, who had the charge to speak for all. In a temple where the censors were, he began to remonstrate and tell them as follows.

> "We know, right honorable censors, that you are now in an estate to reprehend and correct the manners and faults even of senators, yea, it is in you to govern and correct us, and not in us to reprehend you. Yet we have one thing from the Senate to say to you, whereat all good men are offended and scandalized by you. When we consider you apart, we know you to be such that in all the town there cannot be found men more capable and fit to be censors and correctors than you. But when we look on you together, we fear you are not well coupled; neither in that wherein you please us, so profitable unto us, as it may be damaging to us if you two disagree. Therefore we all in general entreat that you will finish in this temple your enmities and rancor, and that in a good union of counsel and amity you will establish elect senators, review our knights, and exercise all other points of your censorship. Titus Tatius and Romulus warred against each other, yet after governed in this city together in good concord and amity. When wars are finished, it is often seen that men become good friends and faithful allies, who before were mortal enemies. There is a common proverb worthy of observation, that amities ought to be immortal, and enmities mortal. Therefore good masters and censors, we beseech you be reconciled together, and hearken unto the Senate's just petition."

Straight after this short oration, although both censors desired to make it appear to the senators that they hated each other with good and just cause, yet they submitted themselves to the arbitrament of the senators. The senators then thought it good that they should give their hands and faith to each other in token of reconciliation and amity, and that both should swear in that temple that earnestly and without all fiction they finished their hatred, and in all true love reconciled themselves. This they did, and solemnly swore that with a good heart and without all hypocrisy they banished and departed from all evil will, and became ever after good friends. According to Livy, all the Roman Senate praised and greatly approved this reconciliation in these censors.

It is then an act of a good man and of an honorable nature to be facile and prompt to reconciliation, and not to engrave in our hearts perpetual enmities and rancors, as Machiavelli teaches. And good men ought not only to be facile in reconciliation, but they ought also to contemn and disdain all revenges by way of action and violence, as being a course unlawful, unfitting, and unbecoming him who would conserve in himself the reputation of an honorable and good man. And this is what the historian Sallust notably says: "A good man loves better to be vanquished than by evil means to do injury. And to vanquish, in whatever sort it be, if on the vanquished there is practiced too bitter a revenge, it is an evil and damaging thing, which often brings the total ruin of commonwealths."

Moreover, generous and virtuous princes ought not only to bury and blot out all old injuries with new benefits, but also even recent and new offenses (which touch the heart more nearly than old) ought to be forgotten in consideration of ancient pleasures and merits. The Caerites, the Romans' allies and neighbors, breaking their faith and treaty of consideration, aided and succored the Tarquinian people, who made war upon the Romans. The Tarquinians and their allies being vanquished, the Caerites could do no better than in all humility submit themselves to the Romans, unto whom they sent ambassadors, who in substance made this oration to the Roman people.

> "Masters, may it please you to remember how in the time of your calamity, when the Gauls took, pillaged, and burned the city of Rome, that you sent into our town of Caeres all your priests, vestal nuns, and all the sacred images of your gods; Caeres was as your holy reverie, the only refuge and safeguard for all your holy things, which were there well received and conserved. We therefore pray you, in favor of Rome, that now in this prosperity you will take pity and be merciful unto us, as we had you in your adversity. If now we have committed any hostile thing against you, it came rather upon fury and folly than of any good counsel. We therefore beseech you not to suffer our ancient good deeds, which we placed and bestowed upon people far from all ingratitude, to perish by a new evil deed, and in your prosperity not to handle as enemies those who in your adversity you elected for friends."

The people (said Livy) were much moved by the ancient merit of the Caerites, rather to forget the new fault than the old benefit, and a peace and remission of their offenses was accorded unto them.

The same moderation of mind was used by Francis I towards the inhabitants of Rochelle in 1541. The Rochelois falling to mutiny against the king's officers over the tax on salt, but acknowledging their fault, they humbled themselves before that good king, demanding pardon; which he granted in an oration with a grave and discreet admonishment, very worthy of a king and Christian prince, in these words.

> "My good subjects and friends, for such I may well call you, since you acknowledge your faults, the office and duty of subjects is so great towards their prince that those who fail in that duty commit so great a

crime that they cannot perpetrate one greater, nor more punishable for the inconveniences which may thereupon follow. For every estate of a well instituted monarch and commonwealth consists in two points; namely, in the just commandment of the prince or superiors, and in the loyal obedience of subjects. If either of these lack, it is as much as the separation of the body and soul; for in man life can no longer endure when the soul desists to command and govern the body, and the body desists from obeying the soul. God grant me grace that I may not fail in the commandment which he has given me over you, which I acknowledge to hold from him as a thing whereof I must make account. And although according to that command I have over you, I may reasonably practice the punishment of justice upon you; yet because it is a thing more fitting for a prince to prefer mercy and clemency before the rigor of justice, but especially towards those who repent and demand pardon; I pardon you with a good heart, seeing likewise that I know you are children of good fathers, whose fidelity has been many times tried by my predecessors, I would rather forget your new misdeed than your ancient merits. I hope also that from henceforth you will as willingly be inclined to obey me as my natural inclination is to pardon you. I will not do to you as the emperor did to them of Ghent, who having committed them under the slavish servitude of a citadel, defiled his hands with their blood. My hands, thanks be to God, are clear from the blood of my subjects; and indeed he lost the hearts and amity of his subjects by shedding their blood; but I hope that my mercy and clemency shall confirm your hearts and love towards me, your king, who kindly handled you as a good father; and that if you and your predecessors have been in times past good and faithful subjects, you will be much better hereafter. I pray you forget this offense which has happened, and for my part, I will not remember it at any time of my life. I pray you also be as good subjects as you have heretofore been, and I hope God will give me grace to be better towards you than I have been. God our Lord and Creator pardon you, and I do heartily forgive you all you have done, without excepting anything."

At this word, proceeding from so magnificent and generous a king, all the Rochelois began to weep for joy, and crying *Vive le Roi*, they prayed God to conserve in all prosperity so good a king, so kind and merciful. Then, upon the king's commandment, all the bells of Rochelle were rung, all their guns were shot off, and bonfires made in sign of great rejoicing.

And so much there wants that good princes have been inclined to vengeance, that contrary, the principality itself makes them forget all affection of vengeance they had before; as we read of the emperor Hadrian, who being come to the empire forgot all his former enemies, insomuch that one day soon after he came to the empire, encountering a capital enemy of his, he said unto him: "Thou art escaped."

Louis XII, before he was king, being but duke of Orleans, had many troubles; for in the time of his predecessor Charles VIII, his enemies thought to have taken him prisoner; but he saved himself in Brittany, where he was persecuted with an army and battle was given him. And the duke of Brittany, who took his part at St. Aubin (where the king's army got the victory), and the said duke of Orleans were taken prisoner and led to the castle Luzignen, and from thence brought to the great town of Bourges. After all this, there was a concord among them, and the said duke came to the crown; being king, they who followed him into Brittany and other places during his adversity persuaded him to be revenged of those who had made war upon him, at the king's command. And they showed to him that the cause of his persecution came not by king Charles' motion, who was then within age, but by his principal counsellors and governors, such as Messire Louis de la Trimonille and others. But that good king Louis shaped them this answer, worthy of so gentle and Christian a king, that could command his choler and passions. "Nay," said he, "a king of France may not revenge injuries done to the duke of Orleans."

King Phillip the Hardy, a gentle prince, was a lover of peace and very easy to grant pardon. The count de Foix in his time rebelled, but at the request of a son-in-law of the count, this good king pardoned him his fault and gave him again certain land which he caused to be seized, and moreover made him knight, and at court retained him into his service. This is far from nourishing enemies and perpetual vengeance, as Machiavelli teaches.

But here I might accumulate and heap up many other examples, of Caesar, Augustus, Trajan, Marcus Aurelius, Constantine, Saint Louis, Charles the Wise, Alexander the Great, Cyrus, and generally of all the good princes who have ever been, all which were endowed with that excellent virtue of clemency, and were far from all vengeance. But these I have recited, I hope may serve sufficiently to show by good reasons and notable examples that the passion of irreconcilable vengeance is unseemly and unworthy of a good prince.

And as for the examples wherewith Machiavelli serves himself, they are but examples of tyrants, and such as were of no account. And of such people I know men had need to take heed; for although for a time they dissemble their choler and their appetite for vengeance, yet they will not fail to discover it as soon as they see a commodious time to be revenged with advantage. But all princes resemble little the Tarquins or pope Julius whereof Machiavelli speaks. For Tarquin, who enterprised to slay his father-in-law king Servius Tullius to obtain the kingdom of Rome, showed well by that act and many others that he was a very tyrant. His end was also such as commonly tyrants have; for he was driven from his kingdom, which he had unduly and unjustly usurped, and was compelled to pass the rest of his days in great poverty as a private person banished from Rome with all his children. And as for Julius, he was known for a true and disloyal tyrant who greatly abused the bounty of king Louis XII; for that good king took Bologna and many other towns from such petty lords as occupied them, and delivered them into the pope's hands because they were lands belonging to the Roman Church. Yet in recompense this good pope, by published bulls, exposed the whole kingdom of France for a prey to whosoever would take it, together with all the countries and lands of the allies of France. And so John de Albert, king of Navarre, lost his kingdom, and king Louis lost Milan and almost all that he held beyond the mountains. And this was the recompense the king received for all his benefits, from this disloyal and wicked pope, of whom in his time was made a pasquil at Rome, and registered in our annals, which in this sort speaks to his holiness:

Of Genoa thy father was, from Greece thy mother came,
A child then born upon the sea, what good in thee can be.
Genoans deceivers are, Greeks huge liars are by fame,
No faith in sea, thou hold'st these points most fully all in thee.

3.7
Machiavelli

A prince ought to propound unto himself to imitate Cesare Borgia, the son of Pope Alexander VI. (*The Prince*, chapter 14)

It is not possible for me to give better precepts to a new prince than to lay before his eyes as an example the acts of Caesar Borgia, duke de Valentinois, son of Pope Alexander VI. And although his affairs little prospered, yet it was not wholly his fault, but rather the malignity of an extraordinary fortune. First then, by the means of the pope he troubled all the states of Italy, that he might more assuredly seize upon part of them. A thing he easily effected; for at the instigation of the pope and the Venetians king Louis XII passed into Italy, and as soon as he arrived at Milan he aided the pope in subjugating Romania, which straightaway was reduced under the hand of Borgia. Secondly, because at Rome there were two mighty factions, the Colonoise and the Ursine, against whose enterprises he feared they would oppose themselves, he got on his side the Ursine faction by fair words and promises, by the means of which he beat down the French forces and overthrew the Colonois. This being done he gained the gentlemen, as well of the one faction as of the other, honestly according them, retaining them in his house, giving them government of towns and other honorable charges after their merits and qualities. So that in a little time the Ursine and Colonois factions remained without chieftains. After this, by fair and sweet words accompanied with good presents, he caused the Ursines to come to him at Sinagallia; which being once together in his hands, he slew them all. Having thus suppressed those two factions, and seeing himself peaceable and all Romania in the duchy of Urbin, to make himself feared and to repress the insolence of the petty lords of that country, he sent there for governor Ramiro d'Orco, a severe and cruel man, unto whom he gave full power. Who exercising his cruelty committed many executions, by means whereof he made all the country tremble with fear, and so as peaceable and obedient as might be. What then did Borgia? To make the world believe that such cruel executions were not done by his command nor consent, suddenly he caused publicly the head of Ramiro to be cut off. After this, being afraid of the French, he refused any more to be served with the French forces; so he put them away, and to assure himself against them, he sought alliance with the Spaniards, who then made war in the kingdom of Naples, and so were farther off to hurt him than the French who abode at Milan. Besides all this, he put to death all the lords who he had wronged, and all their generation, and very few escaped; lest a new pope after his father should take occasion to war upon him, to reestablish those lords or their posterity in their heritage. And as for the lords he had not offended, he drew them almost all on his side to help him bridle a new pope, that he might not enterprise anything against him. His purpose was to make himself lord of all Tuscany, and after lord of all Italy. And already he had under his protection Pisa and Sienna, and Luca inclined to him. But pope Alexander his father died, and failed him in his need, so that his domination being yet as a thing hanging in the air, which was nothing solid, Pope Julius II easily despoiled him. Borgia seeing that fortune, which before had showed him so good a countenance, turned her back and proved so malign and contrary to him, fell sick and died; and upon his deathbed he said he had prevented and thought upon all the inconveniences that might happen to him but death, which he never supposed to have come so soon.

Answer

Is not here a gallant life and a goodly history to propose for princes to imitate; or rather a mark of God's just judgment, which we see he ordinarily exercises against such detestable tyrants who by all manner of cruelties and disloyalties seek to domineer. For God in the end brings all their designs and goodly enterprises into smoke, and makes them die in languishment and confusion, and in displeasure that they have ever lived to see themselves fallen into a mockery and reproach with all the world by their wicked enterprises. Yet this is not all; for dying full of all vices, not grieved for the evils they have done, but rather because they had no means nor leisure to do more mischief, they depart from this languishing life to go suffer eternal pains by the just judgment of God, who yields to the wicked persevering in their vices the reward of their merit. Is not this wicked Borgia a fair example to us—who at his death confessed that he thought not to have lived so little—to admonish us to be always ready prepared to appear before God? Horace himself, a heathen poet, teaches us to make no assurance upon the time to come, neither to set our care and hope thereon, when he says:

> God covers, as with night obscure,
> Always the end of life future;
> And laughs to see afraid the man,
> Of that which no ways see he can:
> Of time present be careful then;
> All other things do flit from men,
> As water in the river.

But to understand this goodly pattern which this atheist proposes here for a prince to imitate, I think it good to discourse a little more amply the life and genealogy of Caesar Borgia. He was a bastard son of Pope Alexander VI, but it is likely he legitimated him; for according to canon law, the pope may legitimate the bastards of other priests, and in consequence also his own. This pope by nation was a Spaniard, and before he was pope called himself Rodrigo Borgia; but coming to the popedom he took the name of Alexander, that he and his son, carrying the names of two of the most victorious monarchs that ever were—Alexander the Great and Julius Caesar—they might make all the world tremble under them. He came to the popedom by the art of necromancy, as some have written, who say he made a compact with the devil, who appeared to him in the form of a protonotary; but others write that he came to it by silver, in buying cardinals' voices. Philip de Commines (one of that time) says that he came to it by silver; as also Pontanus, who wrote this epigram:

> Christ, sacraments, altars are sold by Alexander the pope;
> He bought them very dear, he dear then may sell them I hope.

But it is not much respective I hope, whether he came to the popedom by necromancy of by silver; for it is not impossible but he might come to it by both. This Rodrigo besides the said Caesar had many other bastards, and especially one who in the nighttime during his lascivious whoring in the town of Rome was massacred, and the next morning his body was found in a sack cast into the Tiber, and it was never known who did it. He also had a bastard daughter called Lucrecia, who either because he did not avow her for his or otherwise, was married to one of his bastards, yet entertained by him, as Pontanus wrote:

> Here lies she that Lucrecia is by name,
> But Thaïs is indeed, also by Fame:
> Pope Alexander's daughter in law she is,
> His wife most vile, his daughter eke twice.

But above all his other bastards he most singularly loved that Cesare Borgia, and as soon as he came to the papacy he gave him his bishopric of Valencia in Spain, and made him cardinal, and he was called Cardinal of Valencia. But this cardinal, having the wind in his stern by means of the pope his father, began to cast many things in his head; first to cast away his ecclesiastical state for a temporal and lay state; then he took arms, determining to win all Tuscany or Etruria, then all Italy, and after consequently all the nations which belonged to the empire in the time of Julius Caesar. So indeed he forsook his red cap, and instead of Cardinal of Valencia he was called duke of Valentinois, and immediately by deceits and disloyalties he adventured upon great enterprises. He took for his device, *Ou Caesar ou rein*; as willing to say that he made no account to be less a lord than Julius Caesar was; which device in the end fitted him better than he thought. For where he aspired but to one of the two, that is to be Caesar or altogether nothing, he proved to be both: Caesar by name, and nothing in deed. Moreover, as for the means he took to effect his designs and imaginations, Machiavelli has discoursed them before; but historiographers say that his subtle deceits and devices were at the first suspected and discovered, and that all the potentates of Italy knew straight the intention of him and his father, to tend unto the usurpation and domination of all Italy. Therefore they prepared to hinder them in all they could, and after the pope his father was dead, he was immediately left and abandoned by every man, and had much to do to find where to hide himself; for all his enemies who he had offended arose against him, and especially the Ursins, who straight sought means to massacre him. Fabius Ursin the son of Paul, whom Borgia had caused to be slain, sought him everywhere, and encountering one of Borgia's familiars slew him, cut him in pieces, and washed his hands and mouth with his blood. Hereupon says Sabellicus:

> "I do not think that there can be found a more notable example than Cesare Borgia to admonish us to govern our lives with moderation. He might have been the second after the pope his father in the ecclesiastical order, and have had rich and good benefices, as many as he would; but forgetting himself too much and importuning fortune too much as a mother, he straight experimented her, a most cruel stepmother. He refused to maintain himself in a right high and honorable degree, to be altogether disgraced and brought to nothing. But certainly there is nothing which is of less endurance than an evil counseled prosperity; for it ordinarily rejects great things to bring upon itself calamitous and sad things. Secondly, finding himself destitute of friends and means in the midst of the cruel enmities of men, not being able otherwise to save himself when his father was dead, he reputed it great advantage when he was shut up and guarded in the pope's tower, till there was a new pope chosen."

Behold the censure of this learned Sabellicus touching the life and carriage of this Caesar Borgia, which is full contrary to the mind of Machiavelli. For whereas Machiavelli counsels a prince to imitate the actions of Borgia, Sabellicus discounsels it, and says that his life ought to serve for an example to all men for governing themselves as he did, lest they fall into the same downfall that he did.

To dispute here of the disloyalty, cruelty, and other vices which Borgia used in all his negotiations, and to prove that his life ought not to be imitated, but rather detested, would be superfluous; for the common sense of all men, who have never so little judgment, sufficiently shows to all the world that the said vices are so detestable that the users of them cannot but light on the same end that Borgia did. First, because God customarily so rewards such wicked tyrants; secondly, because it ordinarily comes to pass that they are greatly hated by everyone, insomuch that every man guards himself from them as from a furious beast, and the first who can get him at advantage thinks he does good to the common weal when he rids him from the world; yea, each man watches to catch him in his snare. Therefore no man will give a prince so dangerous and detestable counsel as to use Borgia for a pattern of imitation, unless he would carry him unto the top and fullness of all wickedness and cruel tyranny, which seems to be the end whereat Machiavelli aims, as we shall see at large hereafter.

But whereas Borgia (said he) caused the head to be taken from Ramiro d'Orco, the executioner of his cruelty, I confess it was true, and avow that he did well therein; for if Ramiro would excuse himself and say that his master commanded him to do such cruel executions, that is no good excuse, because he should rather have forsaken his estate and government than commit cruelties without any form of justice, against the law of God and reason. The civil laws themselves will that none should obey his prince when he commands any massacre or unjust slaughter, till thirty days after the command; so that in the meantime either their friends or the magistrate may persuade the prince to pacify his choler and hearken unto reason. And because the law hereupon made by the emperors Gratian, Thesiodus, and Valentinian is worthy to be marked, I translate it thus:

> "If it happens that hereafter we command any rigorous vengeance contrary to our accustomed manner against any, we do not will that they straight suffer punishment, nor that our command is straightaway executed; but that the execution surcease the space of thirty days, and that in the meantime the magistrate keep the prisoner safely. Given at Verona the 15th of the kalends September, in the year of the consulship of Antonius and Syagrius."

It is then seen by that law that Ramiro was justly punished as a man too prompt and forward to execute cruelty. And if this law had been well observed in France, there would not have been found so many and such rash massacres, but the commonwealth would have been in far better state, and the means of peace more facile and easy.

Moreover, the prince who will propose one man alone as his pattern and exemplar to imitate, will find many who have been as virtuous as Caesar Borgia was vicious. But seeing the greatest and most excellent persons at all times were still men, that is to say, not every way absolute but defective and vicious some way, it is best therefore that a prince addict himself to imitate all virtuous men in general, and each of them in their particular virtues. And if we speak of heathen princes, he may propose to imitate the clemency of Julius Caesar in using his victory; for he simply contented himself to vanquish, without cruelty and without bloodshed, as far as he could. He may propose to follow the moderation of Augustus Caesar in the government of the commonwealth, and his diligence to establish peace in the whole Roman Empire. For after the civil wars he never omitted anything which might be a means to bring all the world to peace and tranquility, and he managed the commonwealth with such moderation that it seemed rather a civil government than a monarchy. He had also another virtue, well worthy of imitation; for he was a good justicer, and he not only dealt in making laws and ordinances according to the rules of justice, but also often overheard men's cases and judged them right. He was also a lover of learned men and of knowledge, and greatly rewarded them. And these virtues of Augustus are fit for a prince to imitate. The bounty and lenity of Trajan; the love of peace of Pius; the deep wisdom, the humanity and facility to pardon, and the love and study of good letters in Marcus Aurelius, are also worthy virtues for a prince to follow. But without any longer stay upon pagan princes, who had not the knowledge of Christian religion, a prince shall find sufficient examples to imitate, yea, and not to go farther than the kings of France. Charlemagne was as generous and victorious as ever was Caesar; yet besides this he was very liberal towards good people, a prince continent, gentle, facile to pardon enemies, and endowed with a singular piety and fear of God. For he frequently had the Bible and Saint Augustine read unto him, and nourished poor people in his palace, who sometimes served him at the table. Saint Louis was a good and wise king, fearing God, and a good justicer; for he often sent commissaries into all his provinces to be informed of the abuses, greed, and rapines of magistrates, and had those found faulty well punished. We read one thing of him, not unworthy to be remembered. That one day as he was praying unto God, reciting certain petitions of the Psalms of David fit for that action, a man came suddenly to him to desire a pardon for one that had committed a fault, which was by law punishable by death. He as suddenly granted it, but then falling into a verse of the psalm whish says, *Blessed are those who do justice at all times*, he immediately called the man back and revoked it with this notable sentence. The prince who may punish a crime and does it not, is as culpable himself as he that committed it; and that it is a work of pity and not cruelty to do justice. Besides he was very chaste, far from all lubricity, and never thirsted after revenge. Charles the Wise was a very benign and humble prince, who did nothing but by well digested counsel without rashness, loving the good and safety of his subjects; he was also a prince that very much feared God, he took great delight in reading the Bible, and would have his people read it; to that end he had it translated into French. The prince then who will determine with himself only to imitate those three kings in the aforesaid virtues, certainly shall have for himself a true pattern and example such as a Christian prince ought to have; and not to propose to himself this bastard priest's son, who was a very monster and an exemplar of all wickedness. I name him a bastard because according to the divine and civil law he was not legitimate; although by canon law the pope may legitimate priests' bastards, and in consequence his own, as has been touched above. Yet notwithstanding this question is not without doubt, whether the pope can legitimate his own bastards? And the reason of the doubt is because the doctors of the law hold that legitimation is an act and exercise of jurisdiction; but it is an undoubted maxim that none can exercise jurisdiction in his own deed, and therefore it seems that the illation does not ill conclude, that the pope cannot legitimate his own bastards. But seeing we are entered into this talk, we will look deeper into the matter to draw out some good resolution from this question, by the way only of a tentative and pleasant disputation, and not of a full determination hereof. For as Cato says, amongst serious things joyous and merry things would be sometimes mixed.

Upon this question, namely, whether the pope can legitimate his own bastards, there appear many strong and ample arguments, as well in law as in speculative theology, and as well for the affirmative as the negative. For on the affirmative they allege that by law and right of nature it is given to man to procreate his like; so that when the pope exercises the act of procreation, therein he does nothing which does not agree with the law of nature; this is for the first. Secondly, they allege that popes are called fathers, and therefore they ought to have children, for the name of father is relative to the name of the son, and one of them cannot be without the other. Thirdly, it is a point altogether peremptory and such as no reply can be made against it, namely that by the canons and papal constitutions it is expressly determined that the pope ought to be garnished and furnished with genitories, otherwise he were incapable and unable to be pope by the disposition of law, without any other declaration. Insomuch as if there happen so great a mischief and unhappy hap to Christendom as by adventure they elect a eunuch pope, all whatsoever he does were worth nothing, nor of any value; so that his bulls and collations of benefices, his dispensations, fulminations, aggravations, pardons, legitimations, and other like provisions should have no strength, vigor, nor effect. Which is an admirable point in law, to say that a privation of genitories should induce a nullity of bulls, as if the pope's power depended altogether upon his genitories. But hereof some yield this reason, because they say eunuchs commonly are effeminate, having neither the force nor the power which natural men have, so that it should not be found strange that the canons will that the pope must be accounted without force and power when he is without genitories. Others whom this reason satisfies not, say that the canons in this place contain a positive right; and whatsoever has been constituted by a positive right, a reason cannot be rendered of it; and that we must content ourselves and be satisfied that it has been so ordained, that the pope ought to have genitories, without further inquiring the reason thereof. Yet if it were requisite to yield a reason from that constitution, we must rather say it was ordained to shut the gate of the popedom from papesses or she popes, which otherwise might have crept into that holy seat, as Papess Joan did. But out of this doctrine of the canons, which imports that all popes ought to be furnished with genitories, men draw out corollaries and consequences which marvelously serve to the confirmation of the affirmative of our question. For if it be so, say the canonists, that it is requisite by a necessity that the pope must have genitories, it follows that it is for some end and use. For it were very absurd to say that by the canon law anything has been ordained without any end, because all human actions are done to some end and utility, and in consequence (with stronger reason) the ordinances of the canon law ought to tend to some end; but it is so, that genitories can serve for nothing but for generation; and therefore it follows that the pope ought to use them to that work. And if any object that he ought to use them for generation in the estate of marriage, the reply to overthrow it is very ready, founded upon the universal vow of the Roman Catholic Church, whereby all ecclesiastical persons (and especially the pope, chief of them) have made a vow never to be married. If then it is not lawful for the pope, by the doom of the Roman Catholic Church, to be married; as also by canonical constitutions it is of necessity that he have genitories (which he cannot have but for some use) it necessarily follows that he may and ought to have bastards. This argument may be reduced under the first form of the first figure of the syllogisms in Barbara; which (as the logicians say) of all other are the best concluding arguments. But (say they) taking now this conclusion for a clear and well proved maxim, that the pope by disposition of right ought to have bastards, we shall easily come to the affirmative of our question; for they are called legitimate children who are procreated after the ordinance and permission of law and right, and therefore the pope's bastards shall be found already legitimate from their creation; but much more, when farther the pope himself (who can do all in all) legitimate them. For this legitimation is a superabundant act, which cannot but serve, and at the least cannot hurt; because that which is abundant impairs not the rest, and each act ought to be taken to some end and profitable operation.

Those who hold the negative part of our question have other contrary arguments. The pope, say they, is bound as other ecclesiastical people are to the general vow of the church, and therefore he ought to observe the vows as well as others; especially that he may be a good example to other priests. For if the pope (who commonly is an old man) dispense with himself to have bastards, and breaks chastity and continence required in the priestly order, what an example should that be for a company of young priests, who are idle and at their ease? To say that nature has given men genitories for procreation; it is true (say they), but they must be used in marriage. And if that is a good reason, we may then say that it is lawful for all priests to beak the vow of chastity; but the truth is contrary, for none ought to make himself priest, nor to bind himself unto that vow unless he knows in himself a power to observe it. To say also that popes are called fathers, this is true (say they), but it must be understood spiritual fathers, nor carnal fathers. And whereas by the holy decrees is ordained that the pope ought to have genitories, that is to show (say they) that he is a perfect man, having all his members, as it is requisite he have. And when that decree was made, that the pope should have genitories, we must not understand thereby a dispensation from the vow of the universal church, whereunto he remains always tied and bound. For by the canons the pope cannot dispense against a statute and ordinance of the universal church; so that in consequence (say they) he cannot have bastards, which are not always bastards and illegitimate; and he cannot justly legitimate them because he cannot exercise an act of jurisdiction in his own cause or action. These are the reasons of those who hold the negative part of our question. True it is that they accord well that by plenitude of power the pope may legitimate his own bastards, when he expressly declares that he will have it so of his full and absolute power; and herein all the canonists agree. For when they speak of the fullness of the pope's power, they speak as of a deep pit, which is bottomless, from whence none can come out when they are once in, no more than if a man were sunk into some unmeasurable and infinite deep gulf of the sea. For they hold that it is an infinite thing, which has neither end nor beginning, neither up nor down, neither bank nor bottom, neither middle nor extremity. Yet without wading too far in it, we will speak a little thereof something merrily; for the matter is pleasant enough, as it has been handled by the doctors of the faculty of theology, who do not well accord in this point with the canonists and decretists.

We must then presuppose and understand that there is an old and ancient question, which is not yet decided for want of a judge, that is, which is the great master, the council or the pope. This question had been many times disputed upon, but it could never find a competent judge to dissolve it. For who dares take upon him to judge the pope, seeing kings and emperors are his subjects and vassals (as he says) and owe him obedience, and are bound to hold his bridle and stirrups when he mounts on horseback? The subject and inferior cannot be a judge over his lord and superior, who dares enterprise to end that strife between the pope and the council; so that until this day it remains undecided. Yet during this said strife and contention, the canonists have always firmly held their opinion, which is that the pope is the greatest master; but the doctors of the faculty of theology have held and practiced the contrary, that the council is the chief master. The canonist doctors found upon many reasons, which seem not to be weak, nor evil to those who will not examine things too subtly; for they say the pope and the council represent God and the church; and even as God is above the church, so the pope ought to be above the council. Moreover, it is a certain thing that every council is compounded of men in kind (I discreetly say in kind to cut off an objection, namely that the council might be composed of beasts in wit and knowledge); but the pope is more than a man, and in consequence is greater than the council. As for this point, that the pope is more than a man, there need no doubt be made thereof; for there are express texts enough in the canon law which hold and resolve it in proper terms. These canonist doctors also hold upon this point that the pope is neither God nor man; not that therefore they mean that he is a beast, but that there is a certain thing between them which is more than a man, and less than God. The third argument of the canonists is that they say that the pope represents the great and chief shepherd, and the council the petty and underling shepherds; and that therefore the pope must needs be above the council, as the head shepherd is above inferior shepherds. The fourth argument is because the keys of Paradise were given to St. Peter, who after left them unto the pope's successors, not to the council; so that (say they) if the pope would rigorously deal with them of the council, he would not suffer them to enter Paradise; for to enter into it we must only speak unto him, seeing only he carries the keys thereof; yet he will not do his worst unto them, although they give him great occasions, calling themselves greater masters than he.

The doctors of the faculty of theology, to sustain the contrary and make it appear that the council is greater than the pope, use many subtle and speculative arguments, into which every man cannot enter, for their great subtlety. For when they speak of this matter, they seem to beat into as small dust as Epicurus' atoms the subtleties of St. Thomas Aquinas and Scotus; for they distinguish the pope from the papality, and say that there is a spiritual papality and a potestative papality, and that both of them are not always concurrent in one papal subject. For the spiritual papality may be deficient in the subject, by a defectuosity of science, and the potestative by a defectuosity in the election. After this, they give many limitations to the said double papality, according to which they say the pope's power and actions ought to be governed. But without entering into these so subtle arguments, out of which I cannot dispatch myself with credit, I will only touch such as may best be comprehended by men of mean understanding. The first say that the council may create and depose the pope, as has been seen many times; therefore the council is greater than the pope, for he that has power over another, to make and unmake, must needs be the greater master. Secondly, they say the council represents the universal Church, which cannot err in faith; and the popes have often erred in faith, and among them have been found many heretics, who for such have been condemned in councils. And therefore men ought rather to prefer the council, which cannot err, before the pope, who is subject unto error. They also say that even after the canons themselves, the pope alone cannot decide the articles and differences of faith, but that it pertains to the council; and therefore that the council, which has a more excellent power than the pope, must needs be reputed greater than he. Fourthly, the pope, although he is president of the council, yet he neither has nor ought to have but one voice, no more than a simple bishop; and therefore all the body of the council must needs be more than he, as the body of a court of parliament is more than one of the presidents thereof. Fifthly, they say that when our Lord promised to give the keys of paradise, he said thus: I will give you the keys of the kingdom of Heaven. Here you must note that he speaks in the plural, addressing his speech to many, namely to all his Apostles, not to St. Peter alone, and he speaks also of many keys, which can be in no less number than two, seeing there is a plural number. But these two keys are the key of knowledge and the key of power, whereof the first belongs to the council properly, yet the pope bears them both in his arms. Without the key of knowledge, they say the other is not to be accounted of, neither can in any sort open the gate of Paradise, for the doubtful crooks and bendings of the inward parts of knowledge; insomuch as seeing the council holds the principal key, it follows that it is greater master than the pope. These are in sum the chief arguments of these doctors that I remember at this present; but besides these arguments, there is also a practice held in that case, as well by all princes as universities, which have ordinarily judged and practiced that the council is above the pope. As in the time of king Philip IV, Pope Boniface VIII made a decretal whereby he generally forbade all emperors, kings, and princes of Christendom to levy any tribute upon the clergy, upon pain of a present excommunication, without any other commissance or declaration. The king, because this was against his privileges (by the advice of his council, the prelates of his country, and the faculty of theology of Paris), appealed from the pope, as inferior, to the first future council, as superior. Likewise in the time of Pope Alexander V, who would needs levy tenths upon the French clergy, it was resolved by all the University of Paris likewise to appeal from him and his bull to the first general council. And to be short, appellations have been common from the pope as inferior, to the council as superior; and indeed the doctors in theology all hold determinately this theory, that the council is greater than the pope. Yea, some theologians have gone so far as to say that men may well be without the pope.

By the abovesaid discourse is seen that our masters of theology have desired to circumscribe the infinite plenitude of the pope's power by giving him a master and a superior, namely the council, to keep him within limits. But I find his power cut much shorter by other means; and first, upon this general rule, the pope may do all. They add a condition and moderation thus: *Clave non errate*, provided that the key does not err. This is a moderation right pleasant, which comprehends as much or more than the rule itself. For if you will search the bulls, ordinances, and dispositions of the pope, you shall not find one which does not contain some derogation from law and right; which derogation and repugnancy from right the pope does by virtue of his power, and because it so pleases him. So that according to the said condition laid down by the divines, we may well say such bulls are of no value because they contain an error in law, against which the pope has no strength, according to that saying, *Clave non errate*. Likewise by the same moderation and restriction it may be said that a great part of the canons and decretals are worth nothing; or else, because by these canons and decretals there is added to the holy Scripture, which God has forbidden. The key then of popes being thus falsified in so many sorts and manners (as every day it is), there can remain little good in anything the pope has ever done or yet does, but all or most shall be nothing for want of power, which is the greatest nullity that is.

There is yet another restriction or exemption from the foresaid rule, which St. Thomas Aquinas maintains firmly and stoutly; that is, he says that the pope may do all things, except that he can make no new articles of the faith. This is an exception which stretches far and wide, and much diminishes the infinite power of the pope; for if it is true that he can make no new articles of faith, it follows that we ought not to believe nor give credit to anything the pope has invented himself; and so we ought simply to hold ourselves to the word of God, and not to look to any additions, subtractions, nor multiplications of the pope. Wherefore by Thomas' limitation, what precepts soever are added to the Decalogue, as this: *Dominicis diebus missas audito*, On Sundays hear masses, and such like, are utterly to be rejected. And generally all that the popes have ordained which is contrary, or in any manner repugnant from any place of holy Scripture, must be cast off as a new article of the faith. For we must as well in deed as with the mouth, confess and believe all that is contained in the Old and New Testament, and all the verses generally of the whole Bible ought to be unto us so many articles of the Faith; although there are some more principal and necessary than others.

Insomuch as all the pope's doctrine which repugns the least verse of Scripture is to be rejected as a new article of the faith, by the said exception of St. Thomas.

Besides the two foresaid limitations there is yet another very common amongst the theologians and canonists; for herein they agree, that a heretic pope has no power, nor ought to have any obedience yielded unto him. This has often served for a means to cut off and to limit the pope's power; for even when he waxed too wild, furious, and troublesome to the world, then they would cast him this bone to gnaw on, to say, Thou art a heretic. And so was he often abandoned, so that none made any account of him; as it happened to pope Benedict of Avignon, successor of Clement VI. For this Benedict sent bulls to the king of France whereby he flatly excommunicated the king and all his realm, because the king would not suffer silver to go out of France into Avignon. The abovesaid king had his recourse to the University of Paris, and especially to our masters of the faculty of theology, who straight concluded and resolved that pope Benedict was a heretic unworthy of the name of pope, and that men ought not to obey him, his bulls being of no value as granted by one without all power. And therefore according to that resolution the said bulls were rent and torn in pieces, and all obedience denied the pope. You may ask why this pope was called a heretic; I answer that I know not, for our historians have not set down in what articles of the faith he erred. And it may be that of purpose they imposed the name of a heretic, and not because he was so; for he knew nothing of the Scriptures, neither knew he what the name of heretic meant. Yet for such was he accounted and pronounced, although he knew no theology, nor had ever seen anything of the Bible, but only that which is drawn out of it and inserted in the Missal and Breviary. He was also a reasonably good clerk in the canons, yet not one of the profoundest therein; but he knew sufficient for his provision. Likewise, the pope Boniface, of whom we have spoken before, was declared a heretic by the said University and faculty of theology; not that he erred in the faith (for it was a thing whereof he had little care), but because he would needs enterprise upon the king's privileges. But as soon as he was declared a heretic, all the kingdom of France retired from his obedience. Pope Julius II was not declared a heretic by the University, because they thought it better to prove him in Italy at a council there, so that Italy itself might also withdraw from his obedience. And indeed, do the pope what he could, a council was held at Pisa where he was indicted for a heretic, but he died before the sentence was given. Briefly, of old it was a good and gentle means to bridle the unmeasurable power of the pope, to declare and descry him for a heretic. Our masters also of that time (I know not what they do now) defined a heretic to be he who either in fact or opinion does contrary to the doctrine of the church; so it was very easy to convict popes of heresy, for although they maintained no opinions contrary to the doctrine of the Roman Catholic faith, yet no doubt they did many things reprehensible by that doctrine; and that sufficed straight to make them heretics.

You have heretofore understood the controversy between the pope and the council, and how the council's favorers and partakers have often beaten down the pope's horns, and cut his comb; now I will recite how the pope got a good revenge once. It was in 1437, when Pope Eugenius IV held the Roman seat. At that time a council was kept at Basel, by which among other things it was decreed that Eugenius should lose his popedom, and in his place should come Ame de Savoy, called Pope Felix, who a little before had resigned to his son Louis his duchy, lands, and seignories to become a hermit at Ripaille, a solitary place in Chablais. This pope being chosen, Eugenius began straight to cause very rigorous bulls to be published against him, and anathematized him if he continued to call himself pope. Felix the new pope stood stiff, and all the council for him, which was translated from Basel into the town of Geneva, where this pope held his seat; and from thence dispatched forcible bulls against Eugenius, and made no account of his anathematizations, but hoped well that he should remain master and head of the Church (at least on this side of the mountains) if once he could place his seat at Avignon, as other popes had done. But because he placed his seat at Geneva, the king of France would not depart from the obedience of Eugenius pope of Rome, although he somewhat inclined to the Council of Basel, and approved the resolutions made there. Moreover, he did so much that in the end he agreed pope Felix with pope Nicholas, successor of Eugenius, in the year 1447. And pope Felix contented himself to be the pope's perpetual vicar in Savoy, after he had enjoyed the popedom ten years; having always his seat at Geneva, as well of pope as of the pope's great perpetual vicar. And after this concord made, Felix acknowledged Nicholas for true pope, as also did all those who had elected Felix and remained with him at Geneva. Therefore from that time forward there was no pope at Geneva, neither would those of Geneva receive any into their city again, as I hear. And as for as much as the pragmatic sanction, which were certain articles touching the matter of benefices, which were resolved upon in the said council; they greatly diminished the pope's revenues, and the bullists and datances at Rome. The pope never ceased till he had abolished it in France, by the means of a bishop of Arras, a great favorite of the king's whom the pope made cardinal, giving him a red hat in recompense of his pains. So from that time was abolished the said pragmatic, which had endured and was after a sort observed and kept in France for the space of thirty years, to the great discontentment of the nobles and of those who were rich; who could not so easily and fitly, while the pragmatic lasted, abuse the pope's bulls and indulgences, as they did before and since. True it is that while the pragmatic was in force (which favored learned men) the noble and rich men, by quirks and litigious contentions of law, so troubled the poor graduates that they were commonly repelled from the fattest benefices; for officers of justice have commonly more respect for the money of the rich than the learning of the poor. And they found it an unseemly thing to give some poor master of art, or to some bachelor or doctor in theology, an abbey or bishopric of ten or twenty thousand pounds a year; they thought such fat and pleasant morsels were not for men of base qualities, who had not used to keep abbots' and bishops' tables in Sorbonne or other colleges. Therefore that rule of equity, which wills that poor and base men should not soar and mount so high that they might become too rich and so destroy and corrupt themselves, caused our master of the parliament still to drive away all poor masters of art, bachelors, doctors, and licentiates in theology, and in the decrees, from great and fat benefices, notwithstanding the pragmatic sanction; but they maintained them to enjoy cures, chapels, monarchal portions, and other little prebends of small revenue. And surely this equity of the courts of parliament was great and admirable; for they considered that there is nothing that more corrupts virtuous men, nor that sooner causes them to be idle and given to voluptuousness and other vices, than the great abundance of goods and riches; and therefore they esteemed that it was more expedient to give the good and rich benefices to noble and rich people, than to these poor and base masters of art, and doctors, Sorbonnists, and decritists. For these would but have been corrupted and made proud thereby, and the noble and rich men could not have been more corrupted, neither prouder than they were already. But finally, the pragmatic having been after a sort practiced and used for the space of thirty years, it was quashed and abolished by king Charles VII; and a certain time after, Pope Pius II (who in poesy had before been another Ronsard, and was also called Aeneas Silvius) utterly condemned to all reproach that poor pragmatic sanction, namely, to be publicly trailed and drawn through the streets of the town of Rome, in token and sign of ignominy and infamy thereof, and of the council that made it, which so durst fasten itself unto the pope's sanctity. After sentence was pronounced, this poor pragmatic was ignominiously drawn through the town of Rome; and there might you have seen all the dotaries, bullists, copyists, and notaries about the court of Rome leap, dance, laugh, gibe, and mock at this poor pragmatic, in revenge of the losses and damages which they had by it sustained. And herein truly the council received a great check, which made it well appear to the pope that he was greater master than the council, whatsoever our masters Ockham, Gingencourt, and Gerson have said, written, and maintainted to the contrary, and whatsoever all the faculty of theology had resolved, that the council is greater than the pope.

The pope not only says he is greater than the council, but also than all the kings and emperors of the world, as is proved by many of the pope's canons and decretals; and therefore, upon this point it is not amiss to rehearse the story of Pope Innocent III, and of an emperor of Constantinople who reigned about the year 1200. This pope had written certain letters unto that emperor whereby he rebuked and spoke to him as to his varlet; the emperor made him a modest answer, sending him word that he was much abashed that he should write to him in so lofty and imperious a style, and that therein he did not observe the commandment of St. Peter his predecessor, who wills and enjoins all persons to obey and be subject unto the king as to the most excellent, and unto magistrates under him, his deputies; concluding by this place that the pope ought to acknowledge himself to be subject unto the emperor, and not so bravely to speak to him as to his inferior. But pope Innocent failed not to frame him this answer.

"Thy imperial sublimity marvels that we durst rebuke thee, because thou hast read in St. Peter, prince of the Apostles, that every man ought to be subject unto the king as to the most excellent, and to magistrates established by him. But thou hast not well considered the person of him that speaks: for the Apostle writes to his subjects that in all humility they will yield him obedience; and when he says, to the king as the most excellent, it must be understood of the temporality. For without doubt, the pope in spiritual things is the more excellent, and is so much the more to be preferred before kings and emperors, as the soul is to be preferred before the body. And if thou hadst read that which is written of the sacerdotal and priestly prerogative, thou mightest better have known this; for it is written, behold I have appointed thee over nations and kingdoms, that thou mayst root out, dissipate, build, and plant. Thou oughtest also further to know, that God has placed in the firmament of Heaven two great lights, the sun to lighten the day, and the moon to lighten the night; likewise for the firmament of Heaven, that is, for the universal church, God hath made two lights, that is to say two powers, namely, the papal, which lightens the day, and that is spiritual things; and the royal or imperial, which lightens the night, that is to say terrene and earthly things. If then thy imperial greatness did well understand these things, thou shouldst know as great difference to be between us and thee, as between the sun and the moon; and that kings and emperors are subject under the pope, as the moon is under the sun."

Behold in sum pope Innocent's answer unto the emperor of Constantinople; which contained a profound theological exposition, to make flies laugh. About this time there were also erected and set up in the Church two strong pillars of the papal power and doctrine; namely, the orders of the begging friars and the decretals.

For the last point which we will touch of the pope's power, shall be that which the learned poet George Buchanan, who speaking of this matter touches the white; for he says that the ancient governors of Rome (who were kings, consuls, and emperors) have subjugated and vanquished both earth and sea; but that this was nothing or small in regard of the modern dominators of Rome, as St. Peter, St. Clement, and certain others by their good and holy life gained heaven and paradise, which is already more than the earth and the sea, which the old Romans conquered. But what have the last bishops done, as Pope Gregory VII, Boniface VIII, Sylvester II, Julius II, John XXII, Alexander VI father of Cesare Borgia above mentioned, and other popes their like; they have done more than their predecessor bishops or the ancient kings, emperors, or consuls of Rome; for they have valiantly conquered hell (says Buchanan) and have made themselves masters and peaceable possessors thereof, notwithstanding all the forces and resistance of Pluto and all his sequel, who would not suffer that popes should domineer in hell, but would only receive them as his vassals. But the chance has happened contrary; for the pope is at this day, and has been long time a peaceable dominator and lord of hell, and Pluto is no more but his vassal and the simple executioner of his commandments, and as it were the gaoler of the pope's prisons. Insomuch that when at this day the pope dispatches bulls or pardons, or crusades (as did Pope Leo X in his time), he commands the angels of paradise to go seek the souls of prisoners in hell (after once their ransom be paid) and Pluto and his officers to open their gates and set them at liberty without contradictions, upon pain to lose their charges and estates. And think you that Pluto durst disobey one word of the pope, his sovereign? It is very certain that he dare not once grunt nor contradict him in anything, but (all he possibly can) maintain his amity and do him all the services he can. Here is the substance of that which Buchanan speaks of the pope's power, in these verses:

In older time with iron sharp, and by their naval war,
Old Rome subdued sea and land, though nigh it were, or far:
But after that, the Roman bishops soar'd to heaven on high,
By knowledge, bounty, patience eke, and their humility:

No more remains to their succeeding popes, but only hell,
Whereof possessors are they sure, they have it conquered well.

3.8
Machiavelli

A prince need not care to be accounted cruel, if thereby he can
make himself obeyed. (*The Prince*, chapter 17)

Cesare Borgia was reputed cruel, yet by his cruelty he brought the whole
country of Romania into order and obedience. Wherefore the prince
need take no great care to see himself in reputation to be cruel, if thereby
he maintains his people in a faithful union and obedience. For the cruel
and rigorous executions of a prince do but privately hurt certain
individuals, who ought not to be feared; and the too great lenity of a
pitiful prince is the cause of infinite evils which grow up and engender
in their kingdoms, as murders, thefts, and others like. So that a man may
well say that a pitiful prince is the cause of more evils than a cruel prince.
The example of the emperor Severus may serve us for proof hereof; for
he was very cruel, and by his cruelty overcame Albinus and Niger, and
most of their friends, and so wrought himself a peaceable empire which
he long held, being well obeyed and reverenced by all the world.

Answer

I have heretofore showed how Cesare Borgia by his cruelty obtained for
enemies almost all the potentates of Italy, and thereby so well assured
his estate that immediately when his father was dead he was environed
with enemies, destitute of friends, despoiled of the lands he had
usurped, and constrained to hide himself to save his life. This tragic issue
accords ill with what Machiavelli maintains, saying that the cruelty of
Borgia was the cause that he got the peaceable domination of Romania.
For to say truth, it was not his cruelty — which might easily have been
resisted, Borgia himself being without power — but it was the favor and
fear of his father the pope, who commanded the French powers and
made him feared by all Christian princes. For at that time men feared
more the pope's simple bulls than at this day they fear either the keys of
Saint Peter or the sword of Saint Paul (which he said he had), or all his
fulminations, excommunications, anathematizations, or all the forces
and means he can make. And who would make account of all those at

this day, seeing even the Romans themselves make but a mock of them. But in the time of Alexander Borgia, and the time of Julius his successor, all that the pope willed and ordained was held by Christian princes for an ordinance as from the mouth of God, yea, even when the pope ordained things manifestly wicked; as when Julius delivered as a prey the whole kingdom of France and the lands of the king's allies. For the king of England, the king of Aragon, and the emperor Maximilian all believed that it was a sufficient cause to set upon the king and his allies, and even that it was an express commandment from God. The world then, and even princes, being then overtaken with that beastly superstition and folly, we need not be abashed that Borgia had the means to possess all Romania under the shadow and favor of the pope his father, with the aid of the king of France. And it was plainly seen that the good hap to subjugate Romania proceeded from favor, and not from cruelty (as Machiavelli says), because as soon as that favor ceased all his case was overthrown, and it was straight seen that his utter ruin arrived, as is said. I then maintain clean contrary from the maxim of Machiavelli, and say that cruelty is a vice which ordinarily brings to princes the ruin of them and their estates, and that clemency and gentleness is the true means to maintain and establish a prince firm and assured in his estate.

For proof hereof reasons are clear and manifest. For we call cruelty all executions which are committed upon men, or their lands and goods, without any form of justice, or against all right and equity. Hereupon it follows that as violence is directly contrary to right and equity, so also is cruelty, and that cruelty is no other thing but manifest violence. But according to the maxims of philosophers, no violent thing can long endure; so it follows that an estate founded upon cruelty cannot long endure. Moreover, cruelty is always hated by everyone; for although it be not practiced upon all individuals, but upon some only, yet those upon whom it is not exercised cease not to fear when they see it executed upon their parents, friends, allies, and neighbors. But the fear of pain and punishment engenders hatred; for one can never love that whereof he fears to receive evil, and especially when there is a fear of life, loss of goods, and honors, which are the things we hold most precious. And of that which we hate, we by the same means desire the loss and entire ruin, and search out, procure, and advance it with all our power. But it is impossible, when all a people shoot at the same mark, that a tyrant or cruel prince can long endure, or that he can do so much that there shall not arrive unto him some disaster or evil fortune. And if it sometimes pleases God to suffer him to live long, it is to cause him to take the higher leap, that in the end he may have the sorer fall. As we see it well painted in poets' tragedies, where many tyrants are seen who enduring long have done nothing during the space of their life but knit cords, fasten gallows in some eminent places, whet swords and daggers, and temper poisons for afterward to drink the poison, to stab the dagger in their bosoms, or hang themselves on the gibbet in the sight of all the world; who laughing and mocking them say it is well employed. And we must not say that such tragedies are but poetical fictions, for histories are full of such tragic ends of tyrants who have delighted to shed their subjects' blood and to handle them cruelly.

This vice of cruelty, proceeding from the weakness of those who cannot command their choler and passions of vengeance, and suffer themselves to be governed by them, never happened in a generous and valiant heart, but rather always in cowardly and fearful hearts. Therefore when one advised the emperor Mauricius that the captain Phocas intended and wrought evil against him, and another maintained that he was but a coward, and too fearful to bring anything to pass, Mauricius answered, "So much the more ought I to take heed; for those cowardly and fearful people, when they enterprise a cruelty and have advantage, they can never hold any measure therein." And this vice of cruelty, says Marcellinus, may be called the ulcer of the soul, proceeding from feebleness of the mind and cowardice of the heart. And therefore sick and diseased people are more choleric than those who are in health, and miserable and desperate men more than those who are at their ease and contented. And Marcellinus says that Valentinian was a cruel man because of the choler which so ruled in him that as soon as any spoke unto him any word that displeased him, he changed color, voice, and gait, and could not command himself nor keep from committing many cruelties and injustices, his judgment was so oppressed with choler. Finally it was the cause of his death; for one day the Quadians demanded peace from him, and their ambassadors excusing themselves of a rebellion, he began to speak to them in so great anger, rehearsing his kindness and humanity before used unto them, that at once his voice and words failed him as if he had been struck with a deadly blow, and withal began to send out a mortal sweat. He was immediately carried to a chamber and laid upon a bed, and by the advice of one of his physicians a vein was opened, but it was not possible to draw a drop of blood out, the choler had so burned and dried his inward parts: so he died. A notable example for princes to take consideration of their health, that they never suffer choler nor cruelty to abide in them; for such passions once taking a habit in them, they burn and roast their entrails, and so will not suffer them to live long. But they ought further to consider that such vices also soil and defile the reputation of that generosity and magnanimity that ought to be in a prince. For we have seen, and ordinarily see, that choleric and cruel men have almost always been and are cowards and fearful; but generous and valiant men are gentle and full of humanity. Princes ought further to consider that if they are once spotted with cruelty, they never make good end; and God will have it so, because he who commits cruelty violates the divine law which forbids to shed man's blood and to slay, but by form of justice. He also violates the law of nature; for he destroys his like, which nature has produced, and which has given that instinct even to brute beasts not to destroy beasts of their own kind. There is also a precept of the law of nature, not to offend another. He likewise violates the civil law, whereby is forbidden all murder and homicide, upon pain of death. Is it then any marvel if sanguinary and bloody princes have commonly evil ends, seeing they violate the divine, natural, and civil laws approved by all people and nations.

There was never a more cruel nor a more cowardly man than Caligula; for he quaked and trembled as he went to war to hear of his enemies, without seeing them. Making war in Germany, in a forest near to him he caused certain apostate Germans to lie in ambush, and commanded one of them, when he was at dinner to declare to him that the enemy was discovered in the said forest. As soon as he heard this he immediately sounded the trumpet, and placing his battalion in array, he caused them to assault that poor forest, which he made to be all cut down; and having so obtained this goodly victory against the forest, he came back again with great vaunt and fierceness, taxing and reproaching the cowardice of those who remained behind and were not present at this great overthrow. Was not this an act of a generous and valiant prince? Another time he placed his battalion strong and in good order to fight, and commanded that everyone should march in his rank, and that all their artillery and all other furnishings for an assault should be prepared for a ready fight; yet no man knew what he would do. When his army had marched in order of battle to the shore of the great ocean which was near, he then commanded all his soldiers to fish, and gather as many oysters as they could carry, saying it was the spoil and booty conquered from the ocean; which he then had carried to the Capitol of Rome in sign of that notable victory obtained against that great ocean. Also he caused to be built upon this shore a high tower for a memorial of this happy journey. After, he sent to Rome to prepare for his coming as goodly triumph as could be, to triumph upon the great ocean which he had so valiantly vanquished. Are not these heroic acts, to overthrow a forest and fish for oysters? For cruelty, whereof this monster was full, I will say no other thing but that he always had a servant expert in cutting of heads, who ordinarily at his dinners and suppers beheaded poor prisoners in his presence, and for his pleasure. I leave to speak of so many good people he brought to their deaths; for I should never have done to rehearse all his cruelties. His end was that his people conspired against him, taking for their watchword *Redoubles*, when they all fell upon him and massacred him with thirty blows in his age of 29 years, after he had reigned three years and ten months.

The cruelties of Nero, who caused to be slain Agrippina his mother, Britannicus his brother, Octavia his wife, Seneca his master, and all the most virtuous and good people of Rome, even of the Senate, are notorious enough and would be too long to recite. And never man was more feminine and cowardly than he; for he was never found in any war. But he had good and valiant lieutenants who acquitted themselves well while he played upon the cithara among singers and common players of interludes. His death was strange; for being abandoned by all the world but some four or five servants, he sought to hide himself in a little house of pleasure in the fields, which belonged to Phaon, one whom he had enfranchised. Being there, his men pressed him to slay himself, lest he fall alive into the hands of his enemies; for none of them would do him the pleasure to slay him. Then he commanded them to make for him a grave, and laid down upon the earth for a measure thereof. But while they were making the grave, behold a lackey of Phaon's came, who brought a decree from the Senate whereby Nero was declared an enemy of the commonwealth, with commandment to seek him out and to punish him as a public enemy. After he had read this decree, he took his two daggers and proved whether they were sharp enough; then he put them in the sheath, saying his hour was not yet come. Yet straight he prayed his men that they would begin to weep and lament. Soon after, he desired that some of them would show him by example how he should slay himself. But perceiving knights arriving, he gave himself a stroke with his dagger in the throat, with the help of his secretary Epaphroditus; and he being yet alive there entered a centurion, who feigned that he came to succor him; unto whom he answered that it was too late, and the last word that he spoke was *Viola la foy*; See what faith. He died at the age of 30 years. And it was an admirable thing that he who had caused so many others to be slain in his time, could never find a person that in need would slay him, but was forced to do it himself. A thing also worthy to be marked is that at his last sigh he complained that none kept faith with him; with him, I say, who was full of all disloyalty. And why should they? Do tyrants think that men will keep faith with them, seeing they themselves break it with everyone? If they so think, they are deceived; for to abandon a tyrant and not any way to support him, is to observe faith to his country and to the common weal.

We have before in another place discovered the cruelties and unhappy ends of Commodus and of Bassianus Caracalla, both of whom were fainthearted and cowardly princes, never performing any warlike act, or which tasted of any generosity or courage. We may number with them Didius Julianus, Heliogabalus, Gallienus, Maxentius, Philippus, Phocas, Carinus, Zeno, and many other sluggish and fainthearted princes that never did any good thing, who also by their cruelty brought themselves to miserable ends; for they died violent deaths, and reigned not long. We may also add to those examples that of Herod's cruelty towards his children, whereof we have spoken before. Also the emperor Tiberius, who constrained men to die by languishing in prison, by no means willing to accelerate their deaths, though they prayed him; and he took from them their solace, to study, read, or to talk with any person. The examples also of the emperors Otho, Vitellius, Domitian, Macrinus, and other like, all which were very cruel, and little generosity in them; they all in small time finished their lives, and by the sword. The death of Domitian is worth noting, to show that tyrants cannot shun the divine justice; I will here recite how he was massacred.

First we must understand that this cruel tyrant caused many great lords to die, who were the principal senators of Rome, and even some who had had the consular dignity, yet had done nothing that merited so much as a reprehension. As Cerecalis, Salvidienus, Glabrio, who he caused to die, saying that they were enterprisers of novelties, without either proof or viable conjecture. He also had Aelius Lamia killed, whose wife Domitia Longina he had taken, only because he spoke these words: "Alas I say not a word." And Salvius Cocceanus, because he celebrated the day of the nativity of the emperor Otho his uncle; and Metius Pomposianus, because there was a rumor that he was born in a royal constellation, and because he carried with him a figure of the world and the orations of kings and captains which he found in Titus Livius, and because he named some of his slaves Mago and Hannibal. He also had Salustius Lucullus killed because he had invented a new form of halberds, which he called Lucullienes; and Junin Rusticus, because he had written the praises of two very good men, Taetus Trafea and Elvidius Priscus, whom Rusticus had called most holy persons. And therefore were all philosophers banished from both Rome and Italy. He caused his cousin Flavius Sabinus to die, because the trumpeter or common crier had according to custom openly proclaimed that he was chosen new emperor, and he should have said new consul. He also put to death Flavius Clemens, another cousin, for a light matter of suspicion; and many other great cruelties towards good people and men of quality, which for prolixity I rehearse not. Yet will I say that to make himself be the more feared and reverenced, and to heap up his execrable wickedness, when his officers made any public cry or sent any command to the people, the subscription was always thus: "Your Lord and God commands it so to be done." In the end, feeling himself evil beloved by all the world, he would needs know of the divines and astrologers what should be his end. He sent for a very famous astrologer called Ascletarion, of whom he demanded when and how he should die. Ascletarion answered him, "Sir, not to hide anything I know by art, I find that you shall be soon slain." "And thou," said Domitian, "of what death shalt thou die?" "Sir," answered he, "I find by art, I shall be eaten with dogs." "Well," replied Domitian, "I will keep thee well from that adventure"; and straight to convince him of a lie, he commanded him to be slain and buried, and afterwards his body to be burnt into ashes, according as how the Romans used to bury their dead. But it happened after he was slain, as they thought to have burned his body into ashes in a public place, when the fire was lighted there suddenly arose a great tempest which ejected the body half burnt out of the fire, which immediately was torn in pieces and eaten by dogs. This being reported to Domitian, he was much afraid of this hap; so for what Ascletarion had said to him, as for what other diviners had told him the day and hour he should be slain, he thought it good to stand upon his guard; and the better to see those who came behind him, he had the floor of his gallery where he most often walked set with a shining stone, from which as in a mirror there proceeded such brightness that he might easily see what was behind him. The foretold day being come, and the hour approaching (which was five), he asked what of the clock it was; one expressly answered him that it was six of the clock, to assure him that the danger was past. But about that hour of five there knocked at his chamber door one Stephanus, his chamberlain, who was one of the conspirators against him; his left hand was hanging in a scarf, as if it had been hurt. Stephanus signified to him that he would declare the conjuration intended against him; this was the cause that Domitian suffered him to enter; who straight after his entry, after reverence, presented unto him a request containing the discourse of the conjuration, whereof he let him read a good part. At which, seeing him astonished, he stabbed a poniard in his belly; wounded as he was, he would gladly have revenged himself, but his other household servants entered to massacre him, giving him seven mortal wounds. Behold an admirable example to show that there is no prudence nor human foresight that can hinder the judgments of God be not executed upon tyrants. But if any demand how diviners and astrologers could so justly foretell the death of the emperor Domitian, I answer that we must believe that this said prediction was not by art or science, but the evil spirit would give boldness of enterprising unto Domitian's enemies, in making them know by frivolous divinations his fatal hour, that they might believe the stars of heaven to aid their enterprise. And God above, who serves himself with such means as pleases him to exercise his justice, gives efficacy to the spirit of error. The same effect came of the divination of Caracalla; for it was the cause that Macrinus enterprised to slay him, although he never before thought of it till the astrologers declared their divination; nay he would never have done that enterprise if that divination had not constrained and drawn him unto it.

Master Philip de Commines recites to this purpose a very memorable history that happened in his time. He says there was at Naples a king called Alfonso, a bastard of the house of Aragon, who was very cruel, a traitor and dangerous, for none could know when he was angry, he could so well manage his countenance, and often betray men as he made them good cheer. And he was a man wherein there was neither grace nor mercy, neither had he any compassion for the poor. This king Alfonso had a son as wicked as he, called Ferdinand, who imprisoned many princes and barons of the country, including his brother-in-law, keeping some 25 years. As soon as Alfonso was dead and Ferdinand was king, the first thing he did was to massacre all those princes and barons by a Moor, a slave of Africa, who he rewarded and sent home to his country. When Charles VIII of France enterprised the conquest of Naples, Ferdinand, judging himself unworthy to be king because of his great and abominable cruelties, sent ambassadors to the king to accord with him, offering to yield himself tributary to the crown of France, paying him 50,000 crowns yearly. But Charles, knowing there was no fidelity in the Aragonian race of Naples, would enter into no treaty with him. Ferdinand, despairing to ever hold Naples against the king of France, having his own subjects for his enemies, died for sorrow and despair, and left his son Alfonso as his successor. This Alfonso the new king was as wicked as his father, and had always showed himself pitiless and cruel, without faith, without religion, and without all humanity. Perceiving Charles approaching Rome, and his conscience judging himself to be an unworthy king, he resolved to fly to Spain and to profess himself a monk in some monastery. Before he fled he crowned at Naples a young son of his named Ferdinand, who was not yet hated in the country, his nails not yet either strong or long enough to do evil. This done, he fled into Sicily, and from there to Valencia in Spain, where he took the habit of a monk; and shortly died of an excoriation of gravel. But it was a marvel that this cruel tyrant should be so seized with fear that he should go away in no good order, but left all his moveable goods and almost all his gold and silver in his castle at Naples. And this fear proceeded from a faintness of heart, for never was a cruel man hardy. And when one desired him only to stay three days to pack up his goods: "No, no, let us quickly depart from here; hear you not all the world cry France, France?" Men may see how an evil conscience leaves a man never in quiet; this wicked man, knowing that by his cruelty he had procured the hatred of his subjects, the wrath of God, and the enmity of all the world, was tormented in his conscience as of an infernal fury, which ever after fretted his languishing soul in the poor infected and wasted body. And to end this tragedy, straight after he saved himself the king of France obtained the kingdom of Naples; and a little while after, young Ferdinand died of a fever and a flux. So that within the space of two years, God did justice on four kings of Naples because of their strange cruelties, which were accompanied with disloyal impiety and oppression of subjects; for those always keep company together.

A similar punishment happened by the judgment of God to that cruel king Richard III of England, brother of Edward IV. Edward dying left two sons and two daughters, all young and in the tutelage and government of his brother Richard, duke of Gloucester. This duke, desiring for himself the crown of England, caused his two nephews cruelly to be slain, and made a report that by chance they fell off a bridge. His two nieces he put into a religion of nuns, saying they were illegitimate because Edward could not have lawfully espoused their mother, being previously espoused to a gentlewoman whom he named. The Bishop of Bath being present, protested it was so, and that the promises of marriage were made between his hands. The duke of Gloucester having thus dispatched both his nephews and nieces, caused himself to be crowned king of England; and because many great lords murmured at this cruelty the new king, Richard III, made to die of sundry deaths all those he knew had murmured against him or his tyranny. After all this, when he thought he had a sure estate in the kingdom, it was not long before God raised him up for an enemy the earl of Richmond, of the house of Lancaster; who was but a petty lord in power, without silver and without force, and who but a little before was detained prisoner in Brittany. To whom certain lords of England sent secretly that if he could come into England with two or three thousand men, all the people would come to him and make him king of England. The earl of Richmond hastened to Charles VIII in France, by whose permission he levied people in Normandy, to the number of about 3,000 men. He embarked and took his course to Dover, where Richard attended him with 4,000 men; but God conducted that business, sending a contrary wind which landed the said earl in the northern parts of

England. Marching toward London, Richard met them on the way with 4,000 or 5,000; as they came near to give battle, most of Richard's people turned to the earl of Richmond's side. Yet that king, who despaired otherwise to be maintained in his estate, gave battle to the earl and was slain fighting, after he had reigned about a year. And the earl of Richmond went right to London with his victory, and the slaying of that tyrant; then he took out of the monastery Edward's two daughters, espoused the elder, and was straight made king of England, called Henry VII, grandfather of the most illustrious queen Elizabeth presently reigning.

Alfonso XI, king of Castile, who began his reign in 1310 and ruled forty years, left after him Peter and Henry, his bastard sons. This king Peter was very cruel and inhumane, and among other cruelties he committed he killed his wife Madame Blanche, daughter of Peter, duke of Bourbon, sister of the queen of France and of the duchess of Savoy. He also killed the mother of the said Henry, his bastard brother, and banished and slew many lords and barons of Castile. By his cruelty he acquired the hatred of all his subjects, even of foreign neighbors; so that his bastard brother, being legitimated by the pope as the earnest suit of the nobility of Castile, with the help of Charles the Wise, who sent him a good army, enterprised to eject Peter out of his kingdom and to make himself king, as he did. For as soon as he was entrusted forces in Castile, all the country abandoned that cruel king Peter, who fled and retired to Bordeaux, towards the prince of Wales, praying him to give him reinforcements against his bastard brother. This prince, who was generous and magnanimous, granted his demand under color that the said Peter was a little of his parentage; but in truth he was moved with desire of glory, and to acquire the reputation to have established a lawful king in his kingdom, against a bastard which the French had set in. So he went into Castile with a strong army to establish king Peter in his kingdom; all succeeded well unto him, and he got a battle at Navarre against Henry, who fled into France; and Peter was established in his kingdom. The prince of Wales exhorted him to pardon all such as before had borne arms against him, and from thence forward to become gentle and kind towards all his subjects, which he faithfully promised to be. But he did no such thing, but again exercised his cruelties and vengeances, as well upon the one as the other. In the meanwhile, Henry gathered a new army with the help of the king of France, which was conducted by Bertrand of Guesclin; and unlooked for, they gave an assault and put Peter to flight, with a great overthrow of his people. King Peter saved himself in a castle, which was immediately besieged, and seeing himself poorly provided in it, he by stealth sought to save himself with a few people; but he was encountered by Henry, who slew him with his own hand. By which means Henry with his race remained peaceable kings in the kingdom of Castile, and Peter finished his life unhappy by reason of his great cruelty, whereof he could never be chastised.

By these examples it seems to me that a prince may easily judge, if he is of any judgment, how pernicious and damnable the doctrine of Machiavelli is, to instruct a prince to be cruel. For it is impossible that a cruel prince should long reign, but we ordinarily see that the vengeance of God, by violent means, follows cruelty pace by pace. Machiavelli for confirmation of his doctrine cites the example of the emperor Severus, who indeed was a man very cruel and sanguinary, yet reigned eighteen years and died in his bed. But unto this I answer that the cruelties of Severus seem to be somewhat excusable, because he had for competitors in the empire Albinus and Niger, two of greater nobility than he, and who had more friends. It seemed necessary for him, to weaken the two competitors and to withstand their friends from hurting him, to use that cruelty to kill them; yet he pardoned many Albanians and reconciled himself unto them. Moreover, he exercised part of his cruelties in the revenge of the good emperor Pertinax, which was a lawful cause; yet withal he had in himself many goodly and laudable virtues, as we have in other places rehearsed. So that as his cruelty made him much hated, his other virtues wrought some mitigation thereof. Lastly, he made no other end than other cruel princes; for he died with sorrow (according to Herodian, who was in his time) because he saw his children such mortal enemies one against another; and Bassianus the eldest had enterprised to kill his father, who yet did pardon him. But Bassianus pardoned not his father's physicians, who would not obey him when he commanded them to poison his sick father; for as soon as his father was dead he hanged and strangled them all. Herein also God punished the cruelty of Severus, that having exercised all these cruelties and slaughters to establish the empire in his house, he was frustrated of his intention; for of those two sons Bassianus and Geta, one slew the other; and Bassianus, after he had slain Geta endured not long, but was slain by Macrinus, and left behind him no children. Therefore although it seemed that God spared to punish Severus' cruelty for his other good virtues, yet he remained not unpunished; for seeing his son, who had learned from him how to be cruel, enterprise to slay him, he died of grief and sorrow. And we need not doubt but this conscience assaulted him greatly, for he might well think that it was a just divine vengeance to see himself so cruelly assaulted by his own blood, and to see machinated against himself, by his own son, the like cruelty which he exercised against others. Yet he dissembled and pardoned his son; for how dared he punish that vice that he had taught him? Therefore this example of Severus serves little or nothing to maintain the doctrine of Machiavelli; neither is one example so considerable against a million of others contrary. For men must make a law of that which happens most often, and in many examples, not of that which seldom happens.

When Hannibal began to badly execute his business in Italy, and the Romans having taken courage began to follow him near and hold him short, he took a cruel counsel which much advanced his ruin. For he ruined and destroyed the towns and fortresses which he could not guard, that his enemies after him might not draw any commodity from them, nor make any use of them. This was a cause that they were alienated from him; for according to Livy, example touches men more than does calamity and loss.

It was a great cruelty in the duke John of Bourgogne, when he dared so much enterprise as to cause to be slain the duke of Orleans, the king's only brother; which cruelty cost many heads and was cause of infinite evils in the kingdom of France, and finally was the cause that the duke himself was massacred, in the same manner that he had caused to massacre the duke of Orleans. But yet it is a thing more strange, that this duke dared maintain that he had great need to commit that massacre; yea he found a doctor in theology called master John Petit, who dared affirm in terms of theology that that act was goodly, praiseable, and worthy of remuneration. True it is that in the time wherein we are, there are found many such doctors of the bottle, patrons and defenders of sins and vices, such as this John Petit; but as in the end he was known to be a liar and a slanderer, and his propositions condemned as heretical. So God will cause his imitators of this time, in the end to be found like him; but that the ass may appear by his ears, I have briefly set down his oration.

The duke of Bourgogne, having made himself the stronger in arms within Paris, he took order that there should be held a council and an assembly, therein to propose his justifications. In which council assisted Monsieur le dauphin, the king of Sicily, the Cardinal of Bar, the dukes of Berry, of Brittany, of Lorraine, many counts, barons, and many other great lords, and the rector of the University of Paris, accompanied with many doctors, clerks, and burgesses. There was brought in by an usher master John Petit, a doctor in theology, before all those nobles, to justify the act of the duke of Bourgogne. After then they had given him audience, with both his hands he took off his great square doctoral bonnet from off his head, and began to speak in this manner.

"My most redoubted lords, Monsieur the duke of Bourgogne, count of Flanders and Arthois, twice peer of France, and dean of Peares, is come before the most noble and most high majesty royal, as to his sovereign lord, to do him reverence in all obedience, as he is bound by obligations which commonly are set down by doctors in theology, and of the canon and civil law. Of which bonds the first is of neighbor to his neighbor; the second, of parent towards his parent; the third, of vassal towards his lord; and the fourth will be that the subject not only offend not his lord, but also revenge such offenses as are done against him. There are yet other obligations, that is, that the king hath done much good and honor to my lord of Bourgogne. For it pleased him that Monsieur le dauphin should espouse his daughter, and that the son of my said lord of Bourgogne should marry Madame Michelle, daughter to his royal majesty; and as Saint Gregory says, *Com crescent dona, crescent rationes donorum*, that is, when gifts increase, so do their obligations also. All these obligations are cause that my lord of Bourgogne has caused to slay the duke of Orleans lately dead, which act was perpetrated for the very great good of the king's person, of his children, and of all the realm, as I shall so sufficiently show that every man shall be satisfied. For the said Monsignor of Bourgogne has charged me by express commandment to propose his justification, which thing I dare not deny, for two causes. The first because I am bound to serve him, by an oath taken by me three years ago. The second, because he has given me a good and great portion every year to keep me at school, because he considered I was smally beneficed; which pension did me great good towards my expenses, and yet will so do me long, if it please God and my said lord of Bourgogne. But when I consider the great matter I have taken in hand to handle before this noble company, great fear troubles my heart. For I know I am of small sense, feeble of spirit, and of a poor memory, so that my tongue and memory fly away, and that small sense I was wont to have has now altogether left me, so that I see no other remedy but to commend me to my God and creator, and to his glorious mother, and to Monsignor St. John the Evangelist, prince of theologians. And therefore I humbly beseech you, my most redoubted lords and all this company, if I say anything which is not well said, to attribute it to my simpleness and ignorance; that I may say with the Apostle, *Ignorans feci ideoque miserecordiam consectus sum*, that is, I did it of ignorance and therefore am I pardoned. But some may here make a question, saying it pertains not to a theologian to make the said justification, but rather to a jurist. I answer that then it belongs nothing to me, who am neither the one nor the other, but a poor ignorant man, as I have said, whose sense and memory fail; yet a man may say and maintain that it well belongs to a doctor in theology to defend his master, and to say and preach the truth. Men need not then be abashed if I lend my poor tongue to my lord and master who has nourished me. For it is now in my great need that I lend him my tongue, and those that love me the less for it, I think they commit a great sin, and hereof every man of reason will excuse me. Then to begin this justification, I take my theme upon that which St. Paul says, *Radix omnium malorum cupiditas, quam guidam appetentes, erraverunt a fide*. These words are in the first to Timothy, the sixth chapter, and are thus Englished: Lady greed of all evils is the root, which makes men disloyal. Some may object to me that pride is the first of all sins, because Lucifer by his pride fell from Paradise into hell; and also because it is said in Ecclesiastes, *Initium omnis peccati, superbia*: that is, Pride is the beginning and root of all sin. All men may then argue from this place; then is not dame covetousness. But the answer hereunto is that there are three manners of greed, that is, of Honor, of Riches, and of Carnal delectation; but the first kind comprehends pride, *ergo etc.* This covetousness also of honor comprehends vainglory, wrath, hatred, envy; insomuch that he who his spotted with this kind of greed is inflamed with vainglory, and angry against his lord, whose place and domination he would gladly occupy, and moreover hates and envies him. And all these crimes together, which proceed from covetousness, are called treason, which is the greatest crime that can be. Thus much for the first point of my theme, that dame covetousness is the root of all evils. The second point is that she makes them become disloyal; for with a desire to domineer, they enterprise against their lord, whereas they should be loyal unto him, as I shall show hereafter by many goodly places. But as is fit, to show my lord of Bourgogne's justification, I will take that place of dame covetousness, which I have alleged for my Major, and after I will come to my Minor, and so to the conclusion.

"For proof then of my Major, I will note and propose eight principal verities, by manner of a foundation, out of which I will infer eight conclusions, as it were correlatives, the better to ground the justification of Monsieur de Bourgogne. The first verity is that every subject and vassal who upon covetousness enterprises against the corporal health of his king and sovereign lord, to take away his most noble seignory, commits the horrible crime of treason, and is worthy of double death, that is, of the first and of the second. I prove it, because every disloyal subject and vassal against his sovereign sins mortally. *Ergo, etc.* Also I prove it by St. Gregory, who says thus: *Tyrannus est proprie qui non Dominus reputatur, non juste principatur, aut non principatu decorator*: that is to say, that he that shall have victory upon lady Covetousness and her three daughters, Ire, Hatred, and Envy, shall not need to fear the second death, namely, eternal damnation.

"The second verity is that in the aforesaid case, wherein the subject or vassal is worthy of double death; yet the vassal is more to be punished than the simple subject; and a baron more than a simple vassal; and a count more than a baron; and a duke more than a count; and a king's ally more than a stranger. I prove it, because the obligation of a duke or the king's kinsman towards the king, is by many degrees greater than of a count, baron, or of a vassal. *Ergo*, then the punishment must be in a higher degree. And that my consequence is good, I prove it because the degrees of obligations and prerogatives correspond and fully answer to the degrees of punishment, and so as they are greater, so ought the punishment to be greater, as I have before alleged out of St. Gregory: *Cum crescent done, crescent rationes donorum*. As gifts increase, so ought the reasons of gifts (that is obligations). I prove also my said verity by another argument. It is a greater scandal that a duke or the king's ally should go about to take away the king's seignory, than if it were a poor subject; *ergo* then, the punishment ought to be greater, seeing the scandal is greater. Thirdly, I prove my said verity because there is a greater peril of a great man than of a little; therefore the remedy of punishment ought to be greater to withdraw great men from yielding and obeying the enemy of mankind, and dame covetousness.

"The third verity is that in the case aforesaid, when the vassal commits treason, meriting double death, then is it lawful for every subject, according to the laws moral, natural, and divine, to kill without any command that traitor and disloyal tyrant; and it is not only lawful, but also honorable and meritorious. I prove this verity by twelve reasons in the honor of holy theology. The first of a doctor, which upon the second book of the master of Sentences, says: *Qui ad liberationem patria, tyrannum occidit praemium accipit, & facit opus laudabile & meritorium.* That is: He who slays a tyrant to deliver his country receives a reward, and does a laudable and meritorious work. The second authority is taken out of that excellent doctor Salceber in his book of Policraton, who says: *Amico adularia non licet, sed aurem Tyranni mulcere licitum est, quia ei licet adularia quem licet occidere*: That is, it is not lawful for any to flatter his friend, but with fair words he may well bring a tyrant asleep, for it is lawful to kill him. The third authority is of many doctors in theology, all which I set down but for one, that I may not exceed the number of three, namely of Richard de Mivile, Alexander de Halles, and Astensis, who hold the foresaid conclusion. And for a greater confirmation I add hereunto the authority of St. Peter, who says: *Subditi estote Regi quasi praecellenti.* That is, Let each man obey his king as the most excellent and sovereign. My three second reasons of the twelve are founded upon the authority of three moral philosophers. The first, *Licitum & laudabile est cuilibet subditorum occidere tyrannum*: that is, it is lawful and praiseworthy for every man to slay a tyrant. The second authority is from the noble moralist Tully, who says in his *Offices* that those who killed Julius Caesar were worthy of praise, because he had usurped the seignory of Rome by tyranny. The third authority is out of Bocaccio, who says that men may well conspire and employ arms against a tyrant; and that it is a thing most holy and necessary that a tyrant ought not to be called king nor prince, and that there cannot be a more pleasant sacrifice than the blood of a tyrant. After these authorities cited out of theologians and moralists, I come now to the authority of the legists. And because I am not a lawyer, it suffices me to speak the sentence of the laws without citing them; for in all my life I never studied the canon and civil law but two years, and that was twenty years ago, so that I could learn but a little, and might easily forget that little by the length of time since I learned it. The first authority out of the civil law is that it is lawful to kill forsakers of knighthood; but who can more forsake knighthood than he who forsakes his king, who is the chief of all knighthood? The second authority is that it is lawful to kill thieves and robbers by highways; it is lawful then to kill a tyrant, who continually watches and intends the death of his sovereign lord. I come now to the three authorities of the holy Scripture. The first is that of Moses, who without authority slew the Egyptian who tyrannized over the people of Israel; for at that time Moses had not the authority of a judge over the people of Israel, which was delivered unto him near forty years after he had slain the Egyptian. The second authority is the example of Phineas, who without any commandment slew the duke Zambry, because he allied himself by carnal love with a Saracen woman; whereupon Phineas was commended and reverenced in all three things, in love, honor, and riches. The third authority is that of Saint Michael the archangel, who without the commandment of God or any other fought against the tyrant Lucifer, so disloyal to God his sovereign, who went about to usurp the seignory of God. The said St. Michael was favorably rewarded in three things, that is in honor, love and riches; in love, because God loved him more than any other angel; in honor, because God made him perpetual prince of the heavenly host; in riches, because God gave him riches as much as he desired or could carry away. So it appears that my third verity is well proved by twelve reasons, in the name of the twelve Apostles; of which reasons three are taken from the holy theologians, three from moralists, and three from legists, and the three last from holy Scripture, and they go always from three to three.

"My fourth verity is this: It is more meritorious and honorable that a tyrant be slain by the king's parents than by a stranger; and by a duke than by a count; and by a baron than by a simple vassal; because therein shines more the love and obedience of the slayer, and it is more honorable to the king to be revenged by a great man than a base and mean man.

"My fifth verity is that alliances, promises, oaths, or confederations ought not to be kept, if for keeping them there come any prejudice to the prince or to the commonweal; but to keep them is to do against the moral, natural, and divine laws. I prove this verity by thus arguing: Whenever two contrary obligations are concurrent, a man must keep and observe the greatest, and break the least. But in this case, the bond unto the prince and commonwealth is greater than any other promise or consideration; ergo then we must observe the obligation towards the prince and commonwealth, and break all other obligations, oaths, and confederations. Also in arguing thus, whenever a man does a thing better than that which he swears to do, he is not perjured in doing that better thing and omitting that thing which he swore to do (as expressly the master said of Sentences in the last of the third); but in this propounded case it is better to kill a tyrant, although a man has sworn not to kill him, than to let him live, as has been above showed. Ergo then it is no perjury nor evil done to slay a tyrant against his sworn promise, alliance, or confederation that he has with him. Also Isiodorus in his book of sovereign good says that we must not observe an oath whereby a man shall be forced rashly to commit an evil; but in our case a man shall be forced to an evil by such a promise and oath; ergo he must then not observe it.

"The sixth verity is that if it so happens that the alliances, oaths, or confederations turn to the prejudice of one of the promisers, he is nothing bound to keep them. This verity is proved in thus arguing: The end of every commandment is charity, as the Apostle says, but the chief charity begins at ourselves; ergo the commandment to observe the faith and promise ought not to be observed if it is contrary to the charity which we ought to have towards ourselves, according to that which is said by the Canonists: *Frangenti fidem, fides frangatur eidem*: He that breaks faith, faith ought to be broken to him again. Also in all promises that are made, every man must include, If it please God. But certain it is, it pleases not God that we should do anything against the law and order of charity; ergo etc.

"The seventh verity is that to every subject it is lawful, honorable, and meritorious to kill a tyrant by deceits, speculations, and dissimulations. I prove it first the authority of the moral philosopher Bocaccio above cited. Also by the example of king Jehu, who dissembled to approve the service of Baal, to trap the sacrificers, for which he was praised. Also of Jehoiada, who by treason caused Athalia to be slain, for which he was praised. Also of Judith, who slew Holofernes by dissimulation, whereupon she is praised. And this is the fittest death for tyrants to die on, that is, to be slain villainously by watchings and espyments.

"The eighth truth is that every subject who enterprises and works against his sovereign lord by necromancy and invocation of devils, for covetousness to have the crown, is a violator of the Catholic faith and worthy of double death. For St. Bonaventure (in his second book, sixth distinction) says that the devil never pleases the will of such men, but first idolatry and infidelity are mingled together. For as faith serves much to the operation of the miracles of God, so infidelity is as requisite in the operation of devilish things. The devil also will do nothing for such men unless they agree to yield him the domination over them, whereof he is very desirous. Also that great doctor in the ninth article, in *Secunda Secunde*, says and affirms that invocation of devils never come to effect without a forgoing of a corruption of faith, idolatry, and an express compact with devils. And this opinion do the venerable doctors Alexander de Hales, Richard de Mivile, and Astensis hold, and commonly all the other doctors which have writ of this matter.

"Here you see my eight verities well proved. I come now to eight correlatives. The first is, if it comes to pass that in the case aforesaid, these invocators of devils and traitors to the king be imprisoned, and some of their partakers deliver or cause to deliver them, he ought to be punished with the same punishment as they are themselves, namely, with the first and second death. Secondly, every subject that makes a bargain with any man to poison his sovereign lord, although the enterprise come not to effect, is also well worthy of death. Thirdly, every subject that by dissimulation of pastime causes apparel to be made to put on his sovereign lord, and to put fire therein, thinking to burn him, is also worthy of double death. Fourthly, every subject making alliance with the mortal enemies of the king and the kingdom is also worthy of death. Fifthly, every subject which fraudulently sets dissention between the king and the queen, making the queen understand that the king hates her, and counselling her to go out of the realm, she and her children, offering safely to conduct her out, is worthy of the like death, as above. Sixthly, every subject that gives the pope to understand false things, as to make him understand that his king and lord is not worthy to hold the crown, nor his children after him, is worthy of like death. Seventhly, the tyrant that hinders the union of the church and the deliberations of the clergy, for the utility of the holy mother church, ought to be punished as a heretic and schismatic, and merits that the earth should open and swallow him, as Dathan, Core, and Abiron. Eighthly, the subject who by poison and viands seeks to cause the king or his children to die, is worthy of the aforesaid death. The last is that every subject who with soldiers causes the people and country of his sovereign to be eaten up and exiled, and who takes and distributes his money at his pleasure, and makes it serve his turn to procure alliances with his lord's enemies, ought to be punished as a very tyrant with the first and second death. And here I make an end of my major of the justification of Monsieur the duke of Bourgogne.

"But I come now to declare my minor, wherein I have showed that Louis late duke of Orleans was so much embraced with lady covetousness, of the honors and riches of this world, that he would have taken away the seignory and crown of France from the king's brother and his children, by temptation of the enemy of hell, using the aforesaid means. For he found an apostate monk, expert in the devilish art, unto whom he gave a ring and a sword, to consecrate them to the devil. This monk went into a solitary place behind a bush, where he put off all his garments to his shirt, and fell on his knees, so invoking devils. Straight there appeared two devils appareled in dark green, whereof the one was called Hernias, and the other Estramain. Then this monk did unto them as great reverence and honor as he could do to God our Savior; and one of the devils took the ring, and the other the sword, and after vanished away; the monk went away also. He returned to that place again, and there found the ring, having a red color, and the sword wherewith he sought to have slain the king. But by the help of God and of the most excellent ladies of Berry and Bourgogne, the king escaped. Also the said duke of Orleans made an alliance and confederation with the duke of Lancaster, who in like manner warred against king Richard of England, his lord, as is abovesaid. *Item*, he went about to have carried away the queen and her children, who he meant to have carried into the county of Luxembourg to take his will of her, which the queen would not agree to. *Item*, he practiced to make Monsignor le dauphin eat a poisoned apple, which was given to a child, who was charged to give it to none but to the said dauphin. But it so happened that the child gave it to one of the sons of the said duke of Orleans, who died thereof. *Item*, the said duke has always favored the pope in the extraction of money out of the kingdom, to obtain from him a declaration against the king and his generation, of inability to hold the kingdom, and to give it unto him. *Item*, he has held armed men in the fields for the space of fourteen or fifteen years, who did nothing but pill, exile, rob, ransack, and slay the poor people, and force women and maids. *Item*, he laid tallies upon the king's subjects, and employed the silver in making alliances with our enemies, to come to the crown, and besides he has committed many great crimes, which my said Monsignor le Bourgogne reserves to declare in time and place.

"It follows then by good consequence that my said lord of Bourgogne ought not to be blamed for slaying the said duke of Orleans, and that the king should like that deed well, and to authorize the same as much as were needful. And besides, he ought to be rewarded in three special things, that is, in love, honor, and riches, as were St. Michael the archangel and the most valiant Phineas; that is to say (as I think in my gross and rude understanding) that the king our lord ought more than before to bear amity, loyalty, and good reputation to my said lord of Bourgogne, and to cause to be published letters patents through all the realm. God grant it may be so, who be blessed world without end. Amen."

Here is in substance the oration of that venerable doctor in theology, unto which I have not added one word, only I have shortened certain long and reiterated allegations, whereby might be seen the beastliness of this our master, a man hired to justify one of the most execrable murders that ever was committed. Very notable is the rhetoric and art of this venerable doctor's oration; which in the exordium or beginning to obtain benevolence, confesses that he is an ignorant man without sense or memory. And to make a reason why he has enterprised to be in these causes advocate, he says it is for a pension which the duke of Bourgogne gave him towards his living. After for proof of his major, he cites places of scripture so evil applied that children at this day will discover his folly. And for notable authors he cites a sort of sottish scholastic sophisters of theology, as Alexander de Hales, Salceber, Mivile, and other like. His correlatives and his minor are the false imputations wherewith the duke of Bourgogne charged the duke of Orleans. Moreover, this oration was reviewed by the masters of the faculty of Sorbonne, with the Bishop of Paris and the Inquisitor of faith, and there were condemned for heresies these propositions following. Every tyrant may be slain by his vassal and subject, without commandment of justice. Secondly, St. Michael slew Lucifer without God's commandment. Thirdly, Phineas killed Zimri without the commandment of God. Fourthly, Moses slew the Egyptian without the commandment of God. Fifthly, Judith sinned not in flattering Holofernes, nor Jehu in lying that he would honor Baal. Sixthly, it is not always perjury when a man does that which he has sworn not to do. Which articles having been declared heretical, they were condemned to be burned publicly, as also M. John Petit's bones, who had maintained them (for he was at this judgment dead and buried at Hesdin) and the said articles were executed and put into the fire, but not the doctor's bones, for they could not be gotten, because the duke of Bourgogne then held Hesdin.

Surely it is a strange thing and very deplorable that there should be any such men in the world, who dare maintain with reasons so horrible a crime far from all common sense, and all reason and humanity, as is a massacre done and executed practicedly, without any form of justice. Is not this to call things with contrary names, that is, to call injustice by the name of justice; cruelty by the name of clemency; night by the name of light; evil by the name of good, and the devil by the name of an angel? Is not this to praise that which is despised and detested, to follow that which is to be fled, to love that which is to be hated, to bring into a confusion the distinction of good and evil things. But after I have showed that cruelty cannot be but pernicious and cause of a prince's ruin, whatsoever Machiavelli says to the contrary, it will not be to any evil purpose now to show that kindness, clemency, and goodness are the true means to establish a prince's estate in firmity and assurance. But because we shall handle hereafter another maxim where it shall be more proper to discourse this matter, we will reserve the speaking thereof to that place.

3.9
Machiavelli

It is better for a prince to be feared than loved.

Men love what pleases them, and fear what pleases the prince. Therefore the prince, if he is wise, ought to lean that way which depends upon himself, and not that way which depends upon another. If the prince can have both together, to be feared and loved, that is the best; but it being a very difficult thing to embrace both, it is more assured to be feared than to be loved.

Answer

This maxim is a saying or proverb which our elders have attributed to tyrants, *Oderint dum metuant*; that is, let them hate, so be it they fear. Caligula usurped this ancient proverb, as Suetonius says, and put it in practice during all the time of his reign; and he ended as commonly such princes do who will rather be feared than loved, as in another place we have said. The emperor Tiberius mitigated this proverb, not allowing to make himself feared, and yet disdained not hatred. For he was wont to say, as by the way of a proverb or device, *Oderint dum probent*, that is, let them hate, if they allow. But it seems he made an evil match in coupling hatred with approbation; for what a man hates he does not willingly allow, and that which a man allows, he does not hate. Moreover, all such sayings and proverbs are but tyrants' devices, and our forefathers have so esteemed them, and tyrants have always practiced them. As Nero, when he perceived that by his cruelties he was feared and redoubted, he bragged that none of them who had been emperors before him had any understanding how to command, neither knew the power they had to make themselves be obeyed. But that power was well made known to himself, for men made him well to feel that power evil exercised acquires hatred to him who exercises it, and hatred, ruin, and destruction. So it happened to Caligula, to Tiberius, and so will it always fall unto them who seek to be feared, rather with hatred than with love.

As for what Machiavelli says, that the prince is feared as he will, and as it pleases him; if this were true all should go well for him, for he would always be so feared that none would oppose themselves against his designs and commands, but everyone would come under the yoke and obey him purely and simply. But experience shows us the contrary, and makes us see and know that a prince cannot long be obeyed if his commands are disagreeable and found unjust by those who should obey. At the first occasion that presents itself they unyoke themselves, and their obedience endures no longer than force and necessity endure. And because no force nor necessity can actually endure long, because no violent thing naturally lasts, therefore it follows that disagreeable commandments cannot long be observed, and that obedience founded upon fear is soon broken. For the equity and justice of a commandment is the sinews thereof; and as the body cannot move without sinews, so a commandment which for want of equity displeases the obeyers, shall never be well put in action and practiced, unless it be for a small time and at the beginning.

And as for what Machiavelli says, that it is very hard for a prince to be feared and loved together, it is clean contrary. For there is nothing more easy for a prince than to obtain them both, as reason shows; because it is certain that a prince who maintains his subjects in good peace keeps them from oppressions, causing all those to be punished who would oppress them; and who maintains their liberties and punishes the breakers of them; and who will observe a good policy in his country, that therein may be a free and assured commerce, without imposition of tributes or burdens; and who shall cause good justice to be ministered to everyone; it is certain that such a prince shall be greatly beloved by his subjects, yea and feared thus. When men understand that the prince ministers good justice in every place, without support, favor, or corruption, not leaving punishable faults unpunished, and is not prodigal in granting favors and pardons unless they have a good foundation upon reason and equity, it is certain that he shall be redoubted and feared, not only in his own country but in foreign countries also. For example hereof are all the ancient and good emperors, as Augustus, Trajan, Hadrian, Aurelius, and others who were together feared, beloved, and reverenced. I could here cite almost all our ancestor kings of France, who with good justice were not only redoubted by their subjects, but also by their neighbors. Yea, that good reputation of justice in them was a cause that often foreign princes have submitted their contentions to the judgment of the court of Paris, as we read in histories. And because they ministered good justice, think you they were the more hated? No, not by the wickeder sort, who are forced by their consciences to love and admire the good and virtue, although their lives be contrary. And how should they not be beloved of their subjects, being good kings as they were; seeing Frenchmen are of that nature that they can never hate their king, however vicious he is, but always impute vices and faults to some of his governors and counsellors rather than to him? Truly, if princes had always good men about them, they could never be vicious, at least to the detriment of the commonwealth. Therefore by good right men impute the evil government of a country rather to a prince's counsellors than to himself, as we have proved in another place.

3.10
Machiavelli

A prince ought not to trust in the amity of men. (*The Prince*, chapter 17)

Men generally are full of ingratitude, variable, dissemblers, flyers from dangers, and covetous of gain; and so long as they profit by you, so long you may hold them in your lap, and they will offer you their lives, goods, and all they have, even when there is no need. But in a necessity they will turn their garment and run away; so that a prince who leans upon such a rampart shall at the first fall into ruin. Yea, they will sooner be offended when a man uses love towards them, than if by rigor he seeks to be feared, because men make less account to offend him who uses them gently and lovingly than him of whom they are afraid; because amity is only founded upon some obligation, which easily may be broken, but fear is founded upon a fear of punishment, which never forsakes the person.

Answer

This maxim as well as the former are plainly tyrannous precepts, for as the poet Aeschylus says:

> No friend to trust, what common more?
> Each tyrant has this ill in store.

This is the reason why Denis the tyrant of Sicily dwelled in a strong house, environed with deep ditches full of water on all sides. There was no entry but a drawbridge, which was every night taken in by himself, and certain loose planks of the bridge brought into his bedchamber, which next morning he carried to the bridge again. He also had his daughters learn to be barbers, to pull and trim his beard, and all because he dared trust no man in the world to do those things. Yet Commodus, a cruel tyrant, also used another more sure receipt. For trusting no man with his hair or beard, he himself burnt them with a candle. I leave you to think if such people are miserable, whose consciences are tormented in such sort that they feel worthy to have all the world for a capital enemy, so that they dare put no confidence in any, but are in continual fear and torment.

Far contrary from this doctrine of Machiavelli is the exhortation which Misipsa, the good king of Numidia, gave a little before his death to Jugurtha and his other children, admonishing them to maintain a good amity and concord:

> "It is not puissant armies, nor great treasures, by the means of which a prince ought to conserve and maintain his estate; but by his friends, who are not acquired either by force of arms nor by gold and silver, but by good offices and loyalty. But who ought to be a more loyal friend than one brother to another? Or whom can he trust, who is an enemy to his own blood? I leave you a kingdom firm and assured, if you be good; but feeble and weak if you be wicked. For by concord small things increase, but by discord great things fall to ruin."

Behold a brief exhortation, but very weighty, to show how necessary it is to have good friends and to maintain good amity and loyalty among parents. Like unto this is the oration which Sulla made to king Boccus of Mauritania:

"We are very joyful that you seek to be a friend, rather than an enemy of the Roman people. For even from her birth, the Roman people being poor have always better loved to acquire friends than slaves and servants; and have ever thought it more assured to command voluntary people than any by constraint. King Boccus then cannot chose a better amity than ours, who can both favor you and aid you, and will never hurt you; and to say truth, no one can have too many friends."

The amity and friends which a prince may obtain by a good and just government may serve to assure him of every man in his estate; so he will have need of no guard if he thinks it fit to be rid of them, as did that good emperor Trajan, who often went to visit his friends only accompanied with four or five gentlemen, without any guard or soldiers. The like did the ancient kings of France, who knew not that kind of guard we have now, of gunners and halberdiers, but ordinarily marched without other company than gentlemen, who only bore their swords about them.

Amity, said Cicero, is the true bond of all human society; and whoever will take amity away from among men, as Machiavelli does from among princes, he seeks to take away all pleasure, solace, contentment, and assurance that can be among humans. For the friend is another like ourselves, with whom we rejoice in our prosperity, and our joy increases when we have those to whom we can communicate it. For we are also comforted with him in our adversity and sorrows, and our sadness is more than half diminished when we have one to whom to discharge by amiable communication the bitterness of our heart. Moreover, although we are sometimes blind in our own causes, yet our friend marks our faults and kindly shows them to us, and gives us good counsel in our affairs, which we cannot take of ourselves. Briefly, human life without amity seems no other thing than a sad widow, destitute of the chief sweetness and comfort that can be gathered in human society; as Cicero, Plutarch, and other great philosophers have learnedly discoursed, unto whom I send those who will more amply understand the good and utility of amity.

I will not deny but many such friends may be found like those whereof Machiavelli speaks, who seem to be our friends as long as they hope to draw any profit from us, and who will make us fair offers when they see we have need, but will turn their backs in our necessity. There are indeed but too many such, and we are but too often deceived by them; yet we may not disdain the good for the evil, neither may we defame friendship for the vices and incommodities which accompany it. For among corn commonly grows darnel, and among wholesome herbs some are venomous, which in outward show seem to be fair and good; yet men may not cast away a thing so necessary as corn for fear of finding darnel in it, nor the wholesome herbs for such as are venomous; but we must seek as much as may be, to know and to separate that which is evil from that which is good. And here that manner of electing friends which Augustus Caesar observed is worthy of observation. For he did not easily retain every man in his friendship and familiarity, but took time to prove and find their virtues, fidelity, and loyalty. Those he knew to be virtuous people, and who would freely tell him the truth of all things (as did that good and wise Maecenas), and who would not flatter him, but would employ good will sincerely in the charges he gave them – after he had well proved them, then would he acknowledge them his friends. But as he was long and difficult to receive men into familiar amity, so they who he had once retained for friends, he would never forsake them, but always continued constantly in his friendship towards them. Adversity also is a true touchstone to prove who are feigned or true friends; for when a man feels labyrinths of troubles fall on him, dissembling friends depart from him, and those who are good abide with him, as said the poet Euripides:

Adversity the best and certain'st friends doth get,
Prosperity both good and evil alike doth fit.

3.11
Machiavelli

A prince who would put any man to death must seek out some apparent cause thereof, and then he shall not be blamed, if he leaves the man's inheritance and goods to his children. (*The Prince*, chapter 17)

When a prince will pursue the death of any man, he ought to color it with some justice, and when he puts him to death he must abstain from the confiscation of his goods. For the children who abide behind will sooner forget the death of their father than the loss of their patrimony; for nothing makes a prince so hated than when he comes to touch the goods and wives of his subjects.

Answer

This is also another tyrannical precept, like the former. For it is a custom with tyrants to impose false accusations and blames against those they will kill, sometimes before the execution, sometimes after. We have showed the example of Domitian, who without cause took occasion to kill many great Roman lords who were suspected by him, as ordinarily all good and virtuous men are, who are better than themselves. The emperor Tiberius, according to Tacitus, at the beginning of his reign hated men of eminent virtue, and also those who were extremely vicious; suspecting the virtue of some and fearing to be dishonored and despised by the vicious. But after he came to the fullness of all vices and loved most those who were most vicious, he practiced too much this principle of Machiavelli against many virtuous and honorable men. For he killed a learned and most excellent man called Cremutius Cordus, because he wrote a history wherein he praised Cassius and Brutus. He slew also Aemylius Scaurus for writing a tragedy which displeased him, and many other railers, whereby he sought to cover his tyranny. Nero likewise, after he had slain his mother wrote lies to the Senate, to be published all over how he had discovered a great conspiracy that his mother had intended against him, and that he was constrained to slay her to prevent her from doing so. In like sort Caracalla, after he had slain Geta his brother, caused a fame to be spread all over that he escaped fairly, for his brother would have slain him. Briefly, all tyrants did so, practicing their cruelties and vengeances under some pretext or false color, as Machiavelli teaches. And there are none at this day who cannot exemplify this position with many late and fresh examples in our time. For the massacres of Paris executed on Saint Bartholomew's Day, and the execution made after of many great lords, were all colored with false imputations by these Messiers Machiavelli and by wicked judges, their slaves, as everyone knows.

And as for what Machiavelli says, that the children of those unjustly killed do not care so long as their goods are not taken; I believe few men will accord with him on this point, for everyone who has a good man's heart will sooner make account of honor and life than of goods. But it is certain that if the successor, his son or other kinsman, makes no account to pursue justice by lawful means, he loses his honor and by civil law is culpable and unworthy of succession. Moreover the injury done in the person of his father is reputed done to the son himself; and the contrary, every man esteems himself to suffer injury when any of his parents or friends suffer it. Such violent executions are without doubt more intolerable than loss of goods, and do much more strongly wound the hearts of men who are not destitute of natural love towards their blood, and have honor in any recommendation, than all other losses and damages that they can suffer. And although Machiavelli holds for a maxim that a dead man bites not nor makes no war, yet the death of a man is often the cause of many deaths and of great effusion of blood, as more at large shall be said in another place.

3.12
Machiavelli

> A prince ought to follow the nature of the lion and of the fox, not of the one without the other. (*The Prince*, chapter 18, 19)

You must understand that men fight in two manners; one with laws, when matters are handled by reason, the other with force. The first is proper to men, who have the use of reason, the second pertains to beasts, which have neither reason nor intelligence. But because the first is not sufficient to keep men and to maintain them, enjoining things belonging to them, one must often have recourse to the second, which is force. Wherefore it is needful that a prince can well play the beast and the man together, as our elders have taught, when they wrote that Chiron the centaur, half man and half beast, was given as an instructor to the prince Achilles. For hereby he gave to understand that a prince ought to show himself a man and a beast together. A prince then being constrained to know well how to counterfeit the beast, he ought among all beasts to choose the complexion of the fox and of the lion together, and not of the one without the other. For the fox is subtle, to keep himself from snares, yet he is too weak to guard himself from wolves; and the lion is strong enough to guard himself from wolves, but he is not subtle enough to keep himself from nets. A man must then be a fox to know all subtleties and deceits, and a lion to be stronger and to make wolves afraid. The emperor Didius Julianus knew well how to play the fox, in promising soldiers great sums of money to obtain the empire. For after he was chosen he then played a fox's part, deceiving them in giving them much less than he promised; but not knowing withal how to play the lion, he was soon overthrown. For Severus, who was cunning to play both, came against him with great force, and he was slain by his own soldiers of his guard, who went to Severus' side. Meanwhile Severus, seeing the captain Albinus was in Gaul with a puissant army, and the captain Niger in the Levant likewise with a great army, he played the fox to allure them by fair words, so they would not hinder him in obtaining the empire; for he feared them because they had great forces in their hands, and because they were more noble and of more ancient houses than he. He made them great promises, especially to Albinus to associate him the in empire, and to give him the name and authority of Caesar, which was the like title as at this day is King of the Romans. And as for Niger, he held his children in hand as hostages, under color of honor and favor, so that he feared him less. As soon as he had thus by playing the fox with deceit stayed Albinus and Niger, he ended his enterprise to make himself known a peaceable emperor; but after this, taking unto him the nature of the lion, he turned his forces against Albinus and Niger and overcame them both, one after another. So that by knowing well how to play these two beasts, the lion and the fox, he made himself a peaceable emperor without competitor. Contrarily, the emperor Maximinus, after he was elected emperor by the soldiers of his host, could not play the part of the fox, but only that of the lion; which was the cause that he endured not, and that many were elected to hinder his quiet possession of the empire, and in the end he was overthrown and slain by his own soldiers.

Answer

Machiavelli has not yet handled a discourse more worthy of his sufficiency than this. For he teaches by this maxim the manner to be a beast, and especially how a prince should in all his behavior use himself like a beast. Think you, I pray, that to teach how being a man, you may imitate a beast, is a small matter? I know well that our Machiavellians will say that herein is hidden a secret of philosophy, and that Machiavelli means that a prince should be as subtle as a fox and violent like a lion; not that he must go with four feet, or that he must dwell in the deserts of Arabia or in holes in the woods, or commit other such like actions as the fox and lion do. I am content to agree to them this moral sense, and that their master meant here to declare some singular and memorable doctrine; let us now come to examine it. He says then, when a prince cannot fight like a man, that is, by reason, he ought to fight like a beast, that is, to use force and subtlety. To this I answer that a prince in his quarrel has either reason or right on his side, or else he has them not. If not, he ought not to fight against any man, for each war ought to have its foundation upon reason, as elsewhere we have showed. If the prince has reason on his side, and his opponent refuses to come to reason, then the prince may justly constrain him by force of arms. And this is not called fighting like a beast, or a lion, but as a man using reason; who employs his own corporal force and the force of his horses, of his armies and walls, and of all other things offensive and defensive, to serve for instruments and means to execute what reason commands and ordains. So that force employed to its right use is nothing but a servant of reason, which obeys her in all her commandments; and therefore therein there is nothing of a beast, and those who thus employ their forces do nothing that holds of a beast. As for guile and subtlety I say likewise, that in war a man may lawfully use subtleties against his enemies, if his faith and the rights or war are not violated; and this is not called foxlike subtlety or unlawful deceiving, but it ought to be called military prudence. And therefore in war to use subtlety, fraud, and military sharpness of wit (for all those names may be well used), is not to counterfeit the beast, nor to play the fox. But I know well that Machiavelli is of another mind, namely, that a prince is not bound unto right, faith, or religious promise, to hinder him that he may not use now force, now subtlety, according as the one or the other may best serve him, to come to the end he pretends. For of faith and promise, or of right and reason, men may not speak in Machiavelli's school unless to mock those who esteem them most holy bands of human society. But concerning faith and promises, we shall have another maxim wherein we shall rip up this matter to the bottom; but here I will only show that these foxlike subtleties and deceits whereof Machiavelli means in his speech, do not ever succeed well to those who use them, but most commonly they fall into their own nets.

When Hannibal by means of an ambush had entrapped the captain Marcellus, lieutenant general of the Roman army, who was there slain, he found on him his sealing ring. He considered a subtle device, namely, to write to the Salapians in the name of Marcellus, by which he sent them word that the next night he would come into Salapia, and that they should hold the garrison of the town ready. Crispinus, the lieutenant of Marcellus, knowing Hannibal to be a master of subtle inventions, sent through all the towns word that Marcellus was dead and his ring in Hannibal's hands, and that they should believe no letter under the name of Marcellus. The Salapians, having received this notice and Hannibal's letters, also put their garrison in arms; and as Hannibal approached the town, he put in the first ranks those who could speak the Roman language. As soon as they arrived at the gates, they called the guards; who playing their parts, took up the portcullis and let about six hundred of Hannibal's soldiers in. Then they let fall the portcullis and cut in pieces all who entered; which caused Hannibal thus to be taken in his own net. Thus was he discovered for a fox, and often they turned his own nets upon him, as they do upon foxes by bending their nets backward. And truly it is most often seen that such subtleties as taste of treachery and disloyalty succeed not well. For as captain Quintius said to the Aetolians: "Subtlety and audacious counsels are at first very agreeable and pleasant; but to guide they are difficult and hard, and full of sorrow in the end."

Concerning this subtlety and perfidious deceit, a notable advice is given by the Senate of the ancient Romans. The Romans being upon the point to move war against Perseus of Macedonia, they first sent ambassadors unto him, and among them Martius Phillipus, to know the designs of the king and to try if he would repair the faults and injuries which he had committed against the Romans. The ambassadors found the king slenderly prepared for war, and altogether indisposed to acknowledge or repair his faults. Therefore making him understand that he need look for nothing at the Romans' hands but amity, and that he might easily look for a good peace or truce, with this hope they left him and returned to Rome. Soon after they arrived, they declared to the Senate all that they had done in Macedonia, and especially how they deceived king Perseus in making him believe that he might at his pleasure have peace or truce, wherein they thought to have done well. But the old senators answered them that they did not like nor would they countenance such treaties as not beseeming the Romans; and that their ancestors did not vanquish their enemies by deceits and subtleties, nor by battles at night, nor by feigned flight, nor by other deceits, but by true and perfect virtue. For their custom was ever to announce war before they began it, sometimes even assigning the place of battle. Our ancestors, moved with this sincerity and loyalty, would not employ the physician of their enemy king Pyrrhus, who offered to poison his master for a certain sum of silver, but they revealed to the king the disloyalty of the physician. Also by this sincerity they would not take the children of the Falisques, who were delivered by their own schoolmaster, but sent the schoolmaster bound and all his scholars back again to the Falisques. And such doings become the Romans well, and not to use the subtle deceits of the Punics or the craftiness of the Greeks, who esteemed it more honorable to deceive their enemy than to vanquish him. And that although for the present time subtlety has profited, yet the enemy vanquished by deceits never holds himself for vanquished, but only acknowledges himself surmounted by true virtue without any subtlety or deceit. Behold what was the opinion of these old and wise senators, who rejected and despised the foxlike subtleties whereof Machiavelli makes such great account.

In 1383 the duke of Anjou, brother of Charles the Wise, went into Italy with a puissant army to conquer Naples and Sicily. Among other lords who accompanied him in this voyage was the earl of Savoy, who led a good company of knights. As they were in Poville and Calabria, seeing none to resist them, they began to devise a place where they might assuredly have resistance; and it was made known to the duke of Anjou that the strongest place in the country was the egg-castle of Naples, which is built in the sea, within which Charles de la Paix, a competitor for the said kingdom of Naples, remained. The duke enquired by what means he might come to have it; then came to him an enchanter, who said he would help him get it in the way he helped Charles. "And how is that?" answered the duke. "Sir," said the enchanter, "I will cause a gross and thick cloud to arise out of the sea, which shall have the form of a bridge, whereof your enemies shall be so afraid that they shall yield themselves to you." Replied the duke, "Yea but can men pass upon that bridge?" "I will not assure that, for as soon as any make the sign of the cross as they pass, or in any way cross their legs or their arms, all will fall to the ground and go to nothing." The duke began to laugh, and sent to the earl of Savoy to have counsel upon this matter. The earl asked the duke to send the enchanter to his chamber; next morning the duke sent him. When this enchanter arrived, Savoy said to him: "Well, sir, you say you will make us enjoy the egg-castle?" "Yes, sir, for Charles, who now possesses it, obtained it by my means; and I know he fears me more than all the forces that can come against it." "Well," replied the earl, "I will deliver him from that fear, and I will not have him say that so many brave knights as we are could not vanquish so weak an enemy as Charles de la Paix but by means of an enchanter." He called the hangman and had the enchanter's head cut off; for this wise earl had no mind to vanquish by deceits and enchantment, but by true and natural virtue. And surely generous hearts always disdain crafts, subtleties, and deceits, which cannot last long; for after a prince or captain has a name to use it, and when a thing is to be done seriously and plainly, men always think they intend some subtlety or deceit. And if it succeeded well for Severus' deceit, so it does not for all men, nor for most. And Severus was greatly defamed for such frauds, but his other virtues made him prosper.

But should we call this beastliness or malice, what Machiavelli says of Chiron? Or has he read that Chiron was both a man and a beast? Who has told him that he was delivered to Achilles to teach him that goodly knowledge to be both a man and a beast? Xenophon says that Chiron was Jupiter's brother (so great a man he makes him), full of great knowledge and of all virtue, generosity, piety, and justice. Nay he says further, that Asclepius, Nestor, Amphiaraus, Peleus, Telamon, Theseus, Ulysses, Castor, Pollux, Aeneas, Achilles, and almost all great persons who the Greeks place among their gods learned from him the virtues whereby they have obtained immortal praise and the reputation to be gods. He also says that Chiron was not in the time of Achilles, but long before; but because Achilles was instructed and nourished in his discipline, virtue, and manner of life, men say he was Achilles' instructor. True it is that the poets have called him a centaur, because he took great pleasure in riding horses and in hunting, which are exercises well befitting a prince. Although he loved horses and the exercise of knighthood, yet he was never esteemed to hold anything of a beast, but rather of the divinity, as being endowed with all excellent virtues which bring men near God and take them farthest from beasts. And therefore the beastly malice of Machiavelli is seen in perversely abusing the example of that valiant and generous prince Achilles, to persuade a prince not to stick to govern himself after the imitation of beasts; this is false and devised, for Chiron rather held of divinity than of a beast, neither was Achilles instructed but in all heroic virtues. And we do not read that he ever used any foxlike subtlety or unlawful policy, or any other thing unworthy of a magnanimous prince well nourished and instructed in all high and royal virtues.

But since Machiavelli travails so much to persuade princes to learn how to play the lion and the fox, why does he not persuade them also to carry those two beasts in their arms? We see many which bear lions, because it is in some things a generous and noble beast, but there are seldom seen in any arms any foxes portrayed; because every noble and generous man who loves virtue disdains and hates all deceit, falsehood, and foxlike dissembling, as things very unfit for gentlemen. The Machiavellians who esteem it so fit that a prince should know how to play the lion and the fox together, should carry foxes in their arms, the more to authorize this maxim; but they would not be known to be what they are, so they might the better deceive the world, and lest men cry after them, "The fox!"

3.13
Machiavelli

Cruelty which tends toward a good end is not to be reprehended. (*Discourses*, book 1)

Romulus at the beginning of his kingdom slew Remus his brother, and afterward consented to the death of Tatius Sabinus, king of the Sabines, whom he associated in his royalty, that he might unite together in one same city the two people, the Romans and Sabines. It would seem to many men of gross conceit that Romulus proceeded evilly, to begin his kingdom with the murder of his own brother, and that it was an act of evil example. But as for me, I am of a far other opinion; for it is a general maxim that the state of the commonwealth cannot be well lead and compounded of new laws, if the lawmakers and judges be many; but there ought to be no more than one person and spirit to do, rule, and ordain all. And therefore the prince who desires to come to that point is not worthy of any reprehension if he commits any extraordinary exploit to come thereunto. For that violence which destroys all is greatly to be reprehended, but not that which tends to make things in a better state. Therefore Romulus is worthy of praise in that he slew his brother and caused to slay Tatius his companion, so that he alone might establish a good policy at Rome; as after he did, erecting there a Senate by which he was counseled in all his affairs both of peace and war, and they made also good rules and ordinances. A like praise is due to Agis, king of Sparta, who sought to conform the corrupted state of the Lacedaemonians, and to establish in use the ancient ordinances of Lycurgus. Knowing that the Ephori might hinder and contradict him in his designs, he caused them all to be slain; whereby he got great renown, as much or greater than Lycurgus himself, the first author of such laws. True it is that Agis could not make an end of his good intents and purposes, because of the unlucky designs of the Macedonians, who vanquished him to the hindrance of his gallant enterprises.

Answer

There was never murder nor cruelty which was not colored with some pretext or show of good. Some cover themselves with justice, affirming all they do to be founded upon a good reason and equity; and that justice would have done no less than that which they have executed; and that their execution is the shortest way of justice, which would otherwise have been too long. So that in place of murderers, cutthroats and massacres, they are not ashamed to call themselves abbreviators of justice. And why should they be ashamed, seeing that justice at this day is so practiced as to make her serve but as a palliation or coverture for all assailments, murders, and vengeances? Every man's eyes see that in many places justice serves no other turn but to lend her name to those who seem to do well, when they do evil against their own consciences, therein following the doctrine of Machiavelli. Murderers therefore and massacrers may well from henceforth cover themselves with the name of abbreviators of justice without reprehension, seeing officers of justice take also that trade upon them and cause unjust and wicked executions to be done. Both of these truly (according to this maxim of Machiavelli) pretend for their mischievous wickedness a laudable end, and say it is to minister and exercise justice when they do the aforesaid executions. Others cover their murders with another end, namely the public good, saying that their murders and massacres are done to shun a greater evil which would have come by him or them they have slain or murdered. There are some who make a covering of peace and tranquility, and so will say that the murders which they did or caused to be done were executed to establish peace and to make troubles cease. Briefly, after Machiavelli's doctrine, there cannot be found so cruel a tyrant and murderer but he should be justified, praised, and remunerated; because all murders, massacres and assassinations are always found done to a good end, and the most cruel hangman and executioners will never want a color for their most detestable and sanguinary actions. Notwithstanding what palliations and shows soever that take, the work always shows who was the workman; and in the end their colors will deceive them like the deceitful painting of harlots. Their mask or visard taken from them, murder will always be found murder, and theft theft, and wicked men as they are; although most subtly they play the fox, according to their master's doctrine, yet in the end they will always be known for foxes. And though they sometimes deceive before they are known, they are therefore after double punished in regard of the profit they get by deceiving, when none will believe or trust them in any manner, no not even when they have no intention or will to deceive at all. For always men presume of them as men ought to presume of deceivers and wicked men who are without faith and promise; for men hold them for such, and they can be held for no other in regard of their actions and behaviors in the past. This then is the first evil proceeding from Machiavelli's doctrine, which is that they themselves who practice it bring evil to themselves, and are decried, hated and evil beloved of all men.

The other inconvenience which follows this maxim is that if the prince permits men to commit murders under color of a good intent and end, he shall break the order of justice which he ought to observe in the punishment of offenders, and so shall turn all upside down and bring his estate and country into confusion and peril. For when justice goes evil, all goes evil; and when well all goes well, as in another place shall be showed more fully. Murders and massacres also never remain long unpunished, for God sends them their reward, as came to Romulus (Machiavelli's own example), who was an unjust murderer, and in the end was murdered himself. And in our time we see examples enough, and I believe we shall see more in those who the hand of God has not touched. But among these evils and inconveniences which ordinarily lay hold of these murderers and follow them even to their graves with furies, fears, and torments which vex their consciences, I could here cite for confirmation of this maxim what Saint Paul says, that we must not do evil that good may come thereof. But I have already said in another place that I will not employ the sacred armor of holy Scripture to fight against this profane and wicked atheist; but I will still give him this advantage, to contend with his own arms, namely with profane authors who were not Christians, herein alone resembling him; for in other things he holds nothing of them, and especially in the matter whereof we speak they have been most far from his detestable doctrine.

When Tarquin the Proud saw that he had so behaved himself as to utterly lose the amity of his subjects, he then resolved to cause himself to be obeyed by fear. He took to himself the knowledge of capital cases against great men, which before pertained to the Senate, to make himself the better feared and obeyed; and so he put to death those he thought good under certain pretexts and colors, thinking thereby the better to assure his estate. But how did he assure it? Thus, he so practiced this doctrine of Machiavelli that he became extremely hated by all men, in such sort that his subjects not being able to bear his tyranny, drove him out of his kingdom, where he miserably died.

And so much there wants that the ancient Romans delighted in massacring and slaying, that they hated even the too rigorous punishment of offenders; as the punishment of Metius Suffetius Albanois, who was with four horses drawn to death, for a strange and damnable treason intended by him. For although he merited to be so handled, yet the Romans had the cruelty of the punishment in so great disdain and detestation that everyone turned his eyes away (said Livy) seeing so villainous a spectacle. And it was the first and last time that they ever used that rigorous punishment. Likewise it greatly displeased the Romans that some, thinking to do well, caused to be slain a tribune of the people, a very seditious man called Genutius, who ceased not to trouble the commonwealth by divisions whereby he stirred the common people to uproar. If Genutius had had his lawful trial it is likely he would have been condemned. But therein there was mischief, that none dared lay hold upon him for the reverence of his estate during that year, but he must be suffered either to do what he would, or else to resist his designs by other means than accusation, and not at all to condemn him before he was out of office. This seemed a good color to dispatch him, to shun the seditions and troubles which this tribune raised; yet the execution which was made without course of law was found naught, and of an evil example and consequence, and was the cause of great mischiefs and broils which followed after.

And as for what Machiavelli writes, that Romulus slew Tatius his companion in the kingdom the better to govern the town of Rome, this is false. For histories witness that after he had caused this execution to be made, he became cruel and proud towards the senators, exercising tyranny in many things. The senators themselves slew him, even in the Senate house, and cut him in little pieces, whereof every man took one piece in his bosom, so that the body of Romulus was not found. For they hired one to say that he saw the body fly into heaven, and the senators helping this rumor placed him in the litany of their gods, and persuaded the people that he ascended to heaven both in body and soul. But they gave Romulus his reward for the murder of his brother Remus and his companion Tatius, and they murdered him as he had done them. For briefly it is a general rule that murderers are always murdered, which rule has seldom any exceptions.

But whereas Machiavelli says that to rule and govern a commonwealth well, there should be but one person to meddle therein, there has always been the contrary practiced. When the Romans thought it good, by good laws and ordinances to govern the estate of their commonwealth, they considered that the number of two consuls (who were their sovereign magistrates) was too few; and therefore they abrogated and took them clean away, and elected ten men in their places, unto whom they gave the same authority which the consuls had before, and especially gave them power and express charge to make laws and ordinances for the policy, government, and justice of the commonwealth. They made the Laws of the Twelve Tables, which endured long after them, yea even at this day some of these are in good use and observance. Natural reason also shows us that a law and rule made and examined by many brains must be better than when it is made by one alone; but because I have touched this point more at large in another place, I will wade no further therein.

As touching what Machiavelli says of Agis, Plutarch speaks otherwise thereof. For he says that he was the most meek and quiet man in the world, who sought to reform the state of Sparta by all good and honest means, and to bring into force and use the ancient laws of Lycurgus. And because the Ephori opposed themselves against his designs and purposes, he had Lysander and Agesilaus advanced to the estate of Ephori. But Agesilaus, overtaken with avarice, refused to stick to this good purpose of king Agis, so that he could not in any way bring to pass that good reformation which he intended. Here is all which Plutarch says; he speaks no word that Agis should cause the Ephori to be slain, but contrary that the Ephori brought Agis to his death; neither speaks he of any enterprise of the Macedonians. And I know not where Machiavelli has fished for what he here writes, unless he takes it out of his own brain, and then he owes nothing to any man, seeing it is his own. But howsoever it is, he can learn it from no author who shall not be always convinced of a lie by that learned Plutarch, who speaks as I have set it down.

3.14

Machiavelli

A prince ought to use cruelty all at once, and do pleasures little by little. (*The Prince*, chapter 17)

He who will invade a principality, if it is to be sharply and cruelly practiced, should at the first entry be dispatched with all expedition, that there may be no occasion to return often to business; to the end that afterward by gracious and good dealing he may sooner bring under and tame his subjects. For injuries and offenses ought to be committed all at once, that being the less time felt by subjects, they may stir and anger them less. And contrary, pleasures must be done little by little, that by often iteration thereof, those upon whom such benefits are bestowed may the more desirously and pleasantly drink them up and imprint them within their hearts. It is true indeed that many who were cruel could not long continue their principalities in peace; but that happened to them because their cruelties were not handsomely and well exercised. But they may be accounted well exercised when they are committed but once, as it were upon a necessity to assure himself and to avoid and shun a greater inconvenience, for augmentation of the commonwealth. Agathocles the Sicilian by practice of this maxim became king of Syracuse. This gallant was but a potter's son, and all his life wicked and full of vices; yet those vices were accompanied with a great braveness of courage in arms. Little by little he did so much by his battles that he became Praetor of Syracuse; and being in that estate, desirous to make himself king and to usurp the tyranny, he caused the people and the Senate to be assembled, making them understand that he would execute some great matters of importance before them. The people and the Senate being assembled, at a watchword he had given his soldiers, they put to death all the Senators and the most noble of the people, and so made himself sovereign lord of the town without any impeachment. Whosoever then considers the prudence of Agathocles, and the greatness of his courage, to enterprise and execute so great a thing, I would not judge him inferior to any other captain before him. In our time during the reign of Pope Alexander VI, Oliver de Fermo was educated and brought up by his mother's brother, called Giovanni Fogliani, who sent him to learn the military art under captain Paulus Vitellius, thereby to come unto some honorable estate. This Oliver, being a gallant and personable man and of a quick wit, after a time as mercenary scorned this base manner of life and determined, with the help of certain citizens of the town of Fermo, to get possession and to make himself master and lord of the town. To obtain this he wrote a letter to his uncle Fogliani, saying that having long been out of his country, unable to see his parents and friends, and now coming to visit them, so that those of the town might think he had been honorably employed in his pursuit of war, desired his uncle to find means that he might honorably enter with a hundred horse of his friends and servants; and that he would in good order meet him, which should be not only to his honor, but also to his uncles that had nourished him. Fogliani greatly rejoiced at this news, and failed in nothing to prepare all that was possible to honor his nephew. The whole town celebrated and rejoiced at his coming, conducting him with all honor agreeable to his descent, unto the townhouse where he abode certain days, while he made all things ready for the execution of his enterprise. At the last he prepared a great banquet, unto which he invited his uncle and all other most noble persons of the town of Fermo. At the banquet's end, he began to talk of weighty matters concerning pope Alexander and his son, the duke of Valentinois. His uncle making a certain answer, Oliver began to smile, and told him that such an answer should have been made more private, as also their whole talk of that matter. Giving them to understand that he would discover unto them certain secrets of that matter, he drew them apart into a chamber; and as soon as his uncle and the noblest and greatest of the company were sat down, suddenly entered a great company of soldiers he had hired and hid someplace nearby, who put to death in a moment his own uncle and all the others in his company. This murder being executed, Oliver and his soldiers overran the town, besieged the sovereign magistrate in his palace, and did so much that finally everyone was constrained to yield him obedience. This done, he made himself sovereign lord of the town, and he there established a certain government, but yet caused all such to be slain as might be malcontent with that change, or could hurt him in any way. And within a little while after, by good, civil, and military ordinances, he not only made himself assured in the seignory of the city of Fermo, but also made himself redoubted by all his neighbors. Yet the evil luck was that he suffered himself to be deceived by Cesare Borgia, who by fair words drew him to Senigallia; where catching him he caused him to be hanged. And if not for this evil adventure, he was a man likely to have done great things.

Answer

Machiavelli persists in giving tyrannical precepts unto a prince, teaching him by this maxim a very exquisite means to tame a people newly reduced into his obedience, and to obtain their grace and favor. That is, that a prince at his first entry and at once should make a horrible slaughter of all such as he suspects might hinder his designs and purposes; the others who remain he may bring on with gentleness, and assure them unto him by bestowing pleasures upon them little by little. But I pray you, is there so brutish a man in this world who sees not the absurdity and wickedness of this doctrine? How is it possible that a prince should make himself either loved or obeyed in a newly conquered country by such barbarous usage, seeing those who use all the kindness they can have much ado to obtain it? Assuredly there is no nation so effeminate and servile that will not suffer themselves to be cut in pieces before they will subject themselves under such a prince whose entry has been so cruel and sanguinary, as Machiavelli counsels. Yet if it so falls out that for a time a people are forced under such a yoke, it is impossible that such a subjection should longer endure than that force continues. The example alleged of Oliver de Fermo shows it well, for he continued not long, no more than did Cesare Borgia, who by similar means had usurped the domination of Romania. But can a man imagine a more cruel and detestable act than what Machiavelli rehearses of Oliver de Fermo? Who under the pretext of amity massacred most wickedly his own parents, and those who had given him so honorable an entertainment as was possible? Yet Machiavelli proposes this gallant example for a prince to imitate, as he had with the example of Cesare Borgia. And as for Agathocles, true it is (as Suidas and others write) that he usurped the tyranny of Sicily by causing with treason and treachery the chief rulers of Syracuse to be slain. But what end made he also? Even such as he merited; for being desirous to make great his domination over Italy, he thought best to practice with spies, who kept not their word with him; his purpose being broken by the same means of treason and unfaithfulness, by which he made himself great, he died with grief and heaviness of mind. And still are not these judgments of God, who ruins tyrants by the same ways which he suffers them to get up and come to advancement? And although Agathocles had so bad an end, as his life also had been very wicked, yet Machiavelli dares to compare him with the greatest and most virtuous captains of times past, and offers him as an example for a prince to imitate. So that men may well say that this wicked atheist has no other purpose in his books than to persuade a prince to become a tyrant and most wicked, by embracing all vices and chasing away all virtue. But heretofore I have sufficiently discoursed upon the effects of cruelty, and therefore need speak no more hereof.

But is this not a wise reason, to say that cruelty ought to be exercised all at once, that it may not be too often felt, as that which is done little by little at many times? And why? That which is done all at once is not felt but at the instant it is practiced. Nay contrary, we commonly see that such great cruelties as men commit against a great number of persons, so wound and irritate the hearts of all the kinsfolk and friends of those murdered, that they feel it during their lives; sometimes the wound bleeds even to the third generation. But the cruelties which are committed at many and divers times do not so far penetrate the courage, nor prick men so lively to the quick, although continuance increases discontentment. No man can deny but that it is a thing far more fearful and horrible to our senses to see a great slaughter, and a great heap of murdered persons, than to see only one or two. And no man can promise himself that the prince will handle him kindly who commits such a general massacre, as Machiavelli counsels, whatever good countenance he afterwards shows of his gentle and kind carriage. For the first apprehension of his cruelty will be found so fast sticking and engraved on the hearts of men, that no demonstrations of gentleness and humility can abolish or raise it out.

3.15

Machiavelli

A virtuous tyrant to maintain his tyranny ought to maintain partialities and factions among his subjects, and to slay and take away those who love the commonwealth. (*Discourses*, book 2 chapter 2; book 3 chapter 3)

It most commonly happens that what is profitable to a prince is damaging to his subjects, and what is profitable to his subjects is damaging to him; which often causes princes to become tyrants, better loving their own profit than that of their subjects. As also the contrary makes subjects often arise against the prince, not able to endure his tyranny and oppression. To keep subjects then, so they do not conspire and agree together to arise against his tyranny, he must nourish and maintain partialities and factions among them. For by that means you shall see that distrusting each other and fearing that one will accuse and disclose another, they will not dare to enterprise anything. But here withal he must cause all to be slain who love liberty and the commonwealth and who are enemies to tyranny. If Tarquin the last king of Rome had well observed this maxim, and had caused Brutus to be slain, no man would have been found that dared enterprise anything against him, and then might he always after have exercised his tyranny at his pleasure without control.

Answer

Machiavelli has showed how a prince should best become a tyrant, namely by exercising all manner of cruelty, impiety, and injustice, after the examples of Cesare Borgia, Oliver de Fermo, and Agathocles; now he shows how he may maintain and conserve himself in his tyranny by feeding and maintaining partialities and divisions among his subjects, and putting to death those who appear to be curious lovers of the common weal, because none can love the good and utility of the common weal but must be an enemy of tyranny. As contrary, none can love tyranny but must be an enemy to the common weal. For tyranny draws all to itself and despoils subjects of their goods and commodities, to appropriate all to itself, making its particular good from what belongs to all men and applying to its own profit and use what should serve for all men in general. So it follows that whoever loves the profit of a tyrant consequently hates the profit of his subjects, and he who loves the common good of subjects hates the particular profit of a tyrant. But thus speaking I do not mean of tributes which are lawfully levied upon subjects; for the exaction of taxes may well be the work of a prince and a just ruler; but we speak of the proper and particular actions of tyrants.

Surely indeed, if there is any proper and mere means to maintain a tyranny, it seems well that what Machiavelli teaches is one, to maintain subjects in partialities and divisions. For as Quintius said when he exhorted the towns of Greece to accord among themselves, "Against a people who are in a good unity among themselves, tyrants can do nothing; but if there is discord among them, an overture is straight made for him to do what he will." I freely then confess, and if I would deny it, experience proves it, that in this point Machiavelli is a true doctor who well understands the science of tyranny, and no man can set down more proper precepts for so wicked a thing than what this maxim contains, namely, to slay all lovers of the commonwealth and maintain partialities among other subjects. Surely if anything serves to maintain a tyranny, these seem most proper and fitting; for they are made from the same mold that tyranny itself is, and drawn from one same spring of most execrable wickedness and impiety.

But yet I will hold that neither these tyrannical precepts nor any others can long maintain a tyrant or a tyranny. For the ordinance of God, being far stronger than any detestable precepts of Machiavelli, repugns them, and never suffers tyranny to be of any long endurance; as we have before showed by examples of Nero, Caligula, Caracalla, and Domitian. Sophocles says, "No man did ever see a tyrant once to prove godly." And because tyrants are always full of impiety, God, with whom they strive, brings his justice upon them; yea he commonly makes them pass the edge of the sword, or else to die from some other strange and violent death. For as Juvenal says, "A tyrant seldom life doth end, but by the sword, which God doth send." And besides that, God brings them to a tragical and miserable end; even during their lives they are continually tormented in their consciences with fears, distrusts, and furies, which so trouble them day and night that they obtain no rest. To this purpose Tacitus rehearses that when Tiberius was come to the highest degree of his tyranny, remaining in a place near Rome called Chevrieres, he wrote a letter to the Senate which showed that he felt himself every day more and more tormented and troubled in conscience, because of the cruelties and injuries which he exercised. This is then not without cause, added Tacitus, that an excellent wise man (meaning Plato) affirms that if tyrants' souls might be seen uncovered, a man should see them torn and wounded with blows of cruelty, riotousness, and wicked counsel, as we see bodies ulcerated with rods and cudgels. What pleasure could Denis the tyrant of Sicily have, who trusted none? When one day a certain philosopher told him that he could not be but happy who was so rich, so well served at his table, and had so goodly a palace to dwell in, and so richly furnished. Denis answered him, "Well, I will show you how happy I am." And withal he led that philosopher into a chamber gallantly hanged with tapestry, and laid him on a gilded rich bed; there were brought exquisite and delicate viands and excellent wines. But while the servants made these provisions for Monsieur the philosopher, who was so desirous of a tyrannical felicity, another varlet fastened by the hilts to the upper bed a bright shining sharp sword, and this sword was hung only on a horse's hair, the point of it right over the philosopher's face so newly happy; who immediately as he saw the sword hang by so small a thread, and right over his visage, lost all his appetite to eat, drink, or to muse at or contemplate the excessive riches of the tyrant, but continually cast his sight upon that sword. And in the end he prayed Denis to take him from the supposed beatitude wherein he was laid, saying that he would rather be a poor philosopher than in that manner to be happy. "Did I not then say well to you," answered the tyrant, "that we tyrants are not so happy as men think, for our lives depend always upon so small a thread?"

What repose could Nero have, who confessed that often the likeness of his mother, whom he slew, appeared to him, which tormented and afflicted him; and that the furies beat him with rods and tormented him with burning torches. What delicateness or sweetness of life could Caligula and Caracalla have? who always carried coffers full of all manners of poisons, as well to poison others as themselves in case of necessity, for fear they should fall alive into the hands of their enemies. Heliogabalus also, what comfort had he in the world? who provided always cords of silk to hang himself, and brave poinards and golden swords, exceedingly sharp, in like manner at a need to slay him. And indeed it is one of the greatest wisdoms that can be in a tyrant to take a good course for his death, when it is necessary and expedient for him. For they are often troubled and come short therein, as we see of Nero, who in his need could find no man who would slay him, but was forced to slay himself. True it is that his secretary held his hand, that with more strength and less fear he might dash the dagger into his throat, yet neither his secretary nor any other person would of themselves attempt it. If this secretary had been one of Machiavelli's scholars, it is likely he would have proved more hardy.

But we have to note, upon this maxim as well as the former, that by his precepts here Machiavelli tends and goes about to form a tyrant; and that we ought to hold for a true tyrant every prince and ruler who uses these precepts and practices them. That is, he who uses the cruelties commended by Machiavelli, who maintains his subjects in division and partiality, and who seeks to slay all those who love the commonweal and desire a good reformation and a good policy in it. There are also other tokens and marks whereby to know a tyrant, as those which we have before cited out of doctor Bartolus, and those also which historiographers have marked to have been in Tarquin the Proud. For they say that when he changed his just and royal domination into a tyrannical government, he became a contemner and despiser of all his subjects, both plebian and patrician. He brought a confusion and a corruption into justice; he took a greater number of servants into his guard than his predecessors had; he took away the authority from the Senate; moreover, he dispatched criminal and civil cases after his fancy, and not according to right; he cruelly punished those who complained of that change of estate as conspirators against him; he caused many great and notable persons to die secretly without any form of justice; he imposed tributes upon the people against the ancient form, to the impoverishment and oppression of some more than others; he had spies to discover what was said of him, and punished rigorously those who blamed either him or his government. These are the colors wherewith the histories paint Tarquin, and these are ordinarily the colors and livery of all tyrants' banners, whereby they may be known. It seems that Tarquin forgot nothing of all that a tyrant could do, but that he did not slay Brutus, which was a fault in the art of tyranny (as learnedly Machiavelli notes it), which fell out to be his ruin. But the cause hereof was that Brutus in the court counterfeited the fool, and Tarquin had no suspicion of him. For none but wise men and good people are suspect and grievous to tyrants; but as for counterfeiting fools, spendthrifts, flatterers, bawds, murderers, inventors of imposts, and such like dregs and vermin of the people, they are best welcome in tyrants' courts. Yet even among them, tyrants are not without danger; for among such fools sometimes it happens a Brutus will at last play out their ends. So that their lives ever hang by a small thread, as Denis the tyrant said.

But the example of Hieronymus, another tyrant of Sicily, is to this purpose well to be noted. This Hieronymus was the son of a good and wise king called Hiero; whom they also called a tyrant, because he had no legitimate title, though he exercised it sincerely and in good justice. When Hiero died he left his son very young, and gave him fifteen tutors to govern his affiars; among them Andronodorus and Zoilus, his sons-in-law, and one Thraso, who he charged to maintain Sicily in peace, as he himself had done for the space of fifty years. Especially he charged that they should maintain the treaty and confederation with the Romans, as he had all his reign. The said tutors promised to perform his request, and to change nothing in the estate, but altogether to follow his footsteps. Straight after Hiero was dead, Andronodorus being angry because of so many tutors, caused the king (who was but 15 years old) to be proclaimed of sufficient age to be dismissed of tutors, and so dispatched himself and others of that dutiful care they ought to have had of their king and country. After, he got to himself alone the government of the kingdom; and to make himself feared under the king's authority, he took to him a great number for his guard, wore purple garments and a diadem upon his head, and went in a coach drawn with white horses, altogether after the manner of Denis the tyrant, and contrary to the use of Hieronymus. Yet this was not the worst; for besides all this, Andronodorus caused the young king, his brother-in-law, to be instructed in pride and arrogance, to contemn every man, to give audience to no man, to be quarrelous and to take advantage at words; of hard access, given to all new fashions of effeminacy and riotousness, and to be immeasurably cruel and thirsty for blood. After Andronodorus had thus framed to his mind this young king, a conspiracy was made against him (unto which Andronodorus was consenting), to dispatch and slay him; it was discovered, but still executed, which was strange. For one

Theodorus was accused, and confessed himself to be one of the conspiracy, knowing he must die; and desiring to be revenged of that young tyrant, he accused the most faithful and truest servants of the king. This young tyrant, rash and inconsiderate, straight put to death his friends and principal servants by the counsel of Andronodorus, who desired nothing more because they hindered his designs. This execution performed, immediately the young tyrant was slain by the conspirators themselves; which was made easier by the discovery of the conspiracy, because the tyrant's most faithful friends and servants were slain. Soon after the tyrant's death, Andronodorus obtained the fortress of Syracuse; but the tumults and stirs which he raised in the country (as he thought for his own profit) fell out so contrary to his expectation that finally he, his wife, and all their race were exterminated, the innocent as well as the guilty. And so does it ordinarily happen to all young princes who by corruption are degenerated into tyrants; so falls it out also unto them who are corrupters of princes, to draw them into the habits of wickedness.

Lastly, here should not be omitted this wickedness of Machiavelli, who confounding good and evil together yields the title of virtuous unto a tyrant. Is not this as much as to call darkness light, vice good and honorable, and ignorance learning? But it pleases this wicked man thus to say, to pluck out of the hearts of men all hatred, horror, and indignation which they might have against tyranny, and to cause princes to esteem tyranny good, honorable, and desirable.

3.16
Machiavelli

A prince may be hated for his virtue as well as for his vice. (*The Prince*, chapter 19)

Pertinax was elected emperor against the will of his men of war, who before had by custom lived licentiously in all vices and dissoluteness under his predecessor Commodus. So that Pertinax, a wise and virtuous prince, was hated by all his men of war, because they feared he would reform them and bring them into their old military discipline. The like happened to the emperor Alexander, a prince endowed with many good virtues. Hereupon you may note that malice and ill will are acquired among men by virtue as well as vice. And therefore if a prince will conserve himself in his estate, he must accommodate and apply himself to the humors of those who can hurt him; he must also imitate and follow their vices and corruptions, for in such cases good works and virtues are pernicious and contrary to them.

Answer

So that a prince, if he has any love and inclination to virtue, may utterly despoil himself of all, and make no account of it but as a thing unprofitable and damaging, Machiavelli here proposes this maxim. As though he would say that between virtue and vice there is no difference, and that it makes no matter which of them a prince follows, provided that he follows what will be most profitable to maintain him. And because vice seems to be most fit to maintain a tyranny, his counsel is that a prince should follow it. And if any reply that vice will make a man hated and evil beloved by all the world, yea, and by his own subjects; he answers that so will virtue, and cites the examples of two emperors, Pertinax and Alexander Severus, who he says were hated by their soldiers for their virtues. I pray you is there any devil in hell that could sow and maintain a more wicked doctrine than this? If we take away the difference of vice and virtue and make them one, wherein do we differ from brute beasts? Surely herein only, that we shall be more full of vices and wickedness than they are, because the spirit of man is more ready to invent all sorts of vices and deceits than the nature of beasts. But the common sense, reason, and judgment of all men, and the daily experience which we perceive with our eyes, manifestly show us that in this maxim and others Machiavelli is a most impudent liar. For not only have all good and virtuous princes always been well beloved and liked, but also the vicious and wicked princes have always been and are evil beloved and hated by all the world except their flatterers, who make a show of love while they have means to draw any profit from them. But because I spoke of the friendship of flatterers, I need not again here repeat it.

Yet I must say and confess, touching men with excellent virtues, that sometimes it falls unto them as it does to men who are weak-eyed regarding the light of the sun; for as they cannot bear nor endure the light and brightness of sunbeams, so men of small virtue cannot abide and endure men of great and excellent virtue. As many times it fell out among the Athenian people, who could not suffer men in whom appeared virtues greater and more eminent in comparison with the common virtues of other men. They had a law in their commonwealth whereby every ten years they banished forever some of the most excellent persons of their city, and they called that the Law of Ostracism.

And their reason was suspicion that people of high virtue would seize upon all the domination of the commonwealth if they should be always suffered to increase. And it may be this reason was not altogether impertinent in the popular estate of the commonwealth of Athens, where there was some likelihood that a great man endowed with great virtues might little by little steal away the people's hearts and favor, and afterward take to himself sole domination and authority. And notwithstanding this law in Athens, which they often practiced against the greatest and most virtuous persons, as against Pericles, Themistocles, Alcibiades, and other such like great and good men; yet this was not because they hated their great virtues, but contrary they greatly admired them; yet they were greatly suspected, and the people could not endure them by comparison, no more than men that are blear-eyed can abide the sun. And men must not think that when they banished them by ostracism, that therein they imputed to them any villainy or dishonor; but rather this kind of banishment was honorable, and those who were banished were esteemed men of great and excellent virtue. True it is, they could have been content to escape that honor; as also many persons of base virtue would have been glad to have been banished by ostracism, as it happened to Hyperbolus, a man of small virtue; but they never showed the like favor to any other of his quality. Neither was this because Hyperbolus had committed any fault which merited banishment, but because at the end of ten years, the Athenians having need of their good and greatest men, knew not upon whom better to practice it than upon this bad companion, who with his audaciousness and popular sermons had gathered great riches. Hyperbolus then, long known to the Athenians by his orations, received this honor and recompense, the greatest honor that he ever had in his life.

At Rome likewise all the world had in great honor and admiration the great honesty, plainness, and severity to maintain laws in Cato the Younger; yet the people never employed him in any great charges or estates, but rather bestowed their likings upon men endowed with meaner virtues. And the Romans could not persuade themselves that it was expedient for them to elect into the consulship or into any other supreme magistracy any man of excellent virtue, such as Cato was, yet they could not but admire and highly praise him. Livy also witnesses that the great virtues of Furius Camillus, Paulus Aemylius, and of Scipio Africanus were much admired by that people, yea, praised and exalted even to heaven. But yet they were suspected, and for such accused and rejected. Their accusers could say nothing against them but that they were too much honored and esteemed because of the great victories and magnificent triumphs which they had. Petilius, the accuser of Scipio, said it was a great shame that every man esteemed that the city of Rome, governess of the whole world, was as it were hidden under the shadow of Scipio; as though he alone should and ought to have all the honor and credit of the whole commonwealth, and to hold it covered under his shadow. Scipio replied nothing to this accusation, neither knew he indeed what to reply, unless he had said that there was no reason his virtue should hurt him; but knowing well that his citizens could not abide him, he banished himself from Rome and withdrew himself to a rural house which he had in Liternum, where he finished his days. Briefly, then, it may be said that men are sometimes suspected, especially by the common sort of either base or no virtue, because of their great and eminent virtues; but yet neither hated nor despised.

But in a prince this ought to have no place; for the more virtuous men are, the more the prince ought to love and honor them, and to serve himself with them. For in so doing the virtues of good and virtuous servants are imputed unto the prince himself, as we have before showed. Neither can a prince ever draw any great services from men of small virtue, for good services are the effects of virtues; and as no man gathers from a bush or bramble good pears or other pleasant fruits, a prince cannot look for gallant and good services from vicious men of base virtue. A prince also can have no just occasion to suspect men of great virtue, for many reasons. First, because such persons have in greater recommendation the integrity of their fame and honor than men of mean fortune, or (as they say) of a base hand; and therefore will not easily attempt any filthy or wicked thing which may turn to their dishonor. Secondly, seeing themselves beloved, honored, and recompensed for good services by their prince, their love and desire to serve him will more and more increase, and so prove a means directly contrary to all evil enterprises. Thirdly, because men of excellent virtue are always generous and of great courage and mind; but it is a thing altogether repugnant to all generosity to commit wicked enterprises against a good prince, or a work of fainthearted villainies. Finally, in the time wherein we are, principalities and kingdoms being bestowed either by hereditary succession or by the election of certain nobles, and not by a tumultuous election by corrupted persons, they would be very mad to aspire to his place or to enterprise any evil against him, to deprive themselves of that good they already enjoy, without any likelihood to attain unto better. And if with all this a virtuous man has any fear of God, he will enterprise no evil against his prince, if only for this cause, that God wills and commands that we obey our prince and that we honor him above all things in the world. So that he who disobeys him, disobeys God, and who despises him despises God also. So, more than any other reason, all

those who account themselves Christians ought to have special regard
to deliver faithful and voluntary obedience, seeing God commands it, to
their lawful prince.

And as for what Machiavelli says, that the emperor Pertinax was hated
by his soldiers for his virtue, it is very false. For although in all other
things he was a notably good and virtuous prince, he was soiled with
that filthy vice of greed and illiberality — which Machiavelli teaches to be
a notable virtue for a prince — so much that being come to the high
degree of Roman emperor, yet he commonly dealt in the traffic of
merchandise, for the inordinate desire of gain. And as soon as he was
created emperor, even by his people of war, yet he was so far from being
bountiful in recompensing them that he cut off the soldiers' pensions
which his predecessor Trajan had provided for their nourishment and
maintenance. This greed was the cause he was despised by them and
slain. And as for Alexander Severus, it was also the greed of his mother
Mammea which was the cause that the soldiers hated them, and slew
them both together, as Herodian witnesses, who lived at that time. And
therefore the examples of Pertinax and of Alexander are alleged by
Machiavelli to no purpose, to show that princes are hated for their
virtues. Yet even if it were true that the soldiers who slew Pertinax were
people hating virtue, as also those who slew Alexander Severus (who
had gathered all corruption of vices under his predecessor
Heliogabalus); it does not follow that of such examples we must make a
rule and maxim. For thieves and murderers hate justice and magistracy,
yet it does not follow that a prince is not always more loved than hated
by doing good justice. Briefly, such examples are exceptions of the rule,
which notwithstanding does not cease to remain always true and certain;
no more no less, as philosophers say, that the rule is true that summer is
hotter than winter, although some days in winter are more hot than
some days in summer.

3.17
Machiavelli

> A prince ought always to nourish some enemy against himself, so
> that when he has oppressed him he may be accounted the more
> mighty and terrible. (*The Prince*, chapter 19)

Princes make themselves great when they overcome weighty and
difficult things which hinder their designs. Therefore a good and wise
prince with a certain ingenious care will nourish some enemy against

himself, to the end that happening to oppress him, his riches and greatness may the better increase. For such an enemy shall serve him as a sufficient matter to increase his greatness, and as a ladder to ascend higher.

Answer

Behold a maxim of the same note as the former, hereunto tending, that a prince should always seek means to make himself feared rather than loved. But a prince who observes the doctrine of Machiavelli needs take no great care to seek means to nourish an enemy against himself; for there will be enough, and more than one would wish, both within and without his country, even in his own house. But to say that he can oppress them all to make himself feared and redoubted, that is no assured thing; rather contrary, he may assure himself that in the end either one or the other will oppress and ruin him. When Milicus disclosed to Nero a great plot practiced against him, he performed what Machiavelli prescribes; for by oppressing and putting to death all the conspirators and enemies, and all their friends and allies, he made himself so feared and redoubted that there was not in Rome great or little but trembled for fear at the name of Nero. Such great men, whose friends and parents were put to death, came and fell down on their knees before him, and thanked him for the good and honor he had done them, to have purged and cleansed their parentage and alliance from so wicked men as those he had slain. Others, in sign of joy for the death of their friends and parents, caused their houses to be hung with laurel, made sacrifices to the gods to give thanks for so great a good, and celebrated feasts as if there had been marriages. The Senate also in a great terror ordained processions and public sacrifices to give thanks to the gods that this plot was discovered; they even built and consecrated a chapel to the sun in the house where the plot was made, because it shined to the discovery thereof. They also built a temple to the goddess of health. Nero, thinking that all these joys were true and unfeigned, exercised more and more his butchery, and in the end made himself so assured that he was feared by all the world, that he thought he had the upper hand of all his enemies. But it was clean contrary; for by this strange slaughter with so much other wickedness, of which he was full, he brought himself into a deadly hatred of all the world. Insomuch that the provinces of the empire revolted one after another, and in the end he was abandoned by every man except four or five of his meanest servants, who kept him company in his flight until he had slain himself. Therefore Nero needed to take no thought how to nourish enemies against himself, as Machiavelli teaches in this maxim; for he never lacked a great number, as all tyrants have ordinarily.

And how should not tyrants have good store of enemies, seeing even good and wise princes do not want them? To this purpose master Philip de Commines makes a very good discourse, saying that it pleased God to give to all princes, kingdoms, and commonwealths an opposite and contrary unto them, that both the one and the other might be held in their duties; as England has France, Scotland has England, Portugal has Castile, Grenada has Portugal; the princes and commonwealths of Italy are contrary to each other, and so it is of all countries and seignories of the earth. For if there is any prince or commonwealth which lacks its opposite to hold it in fear, it shall fall into a tyranny and luxuriousness. Therefore God by his wise providence has given to every seignory and to every prince his opposite, that one for fear of another might be stirred up to a modest and temperate carriage. And there is indeed nothing that better holds a prince in his duty, nor which causes him to walk more upright than the fear of his opposite and contrary. For the fear of God, nor the love of his neighbor, nor reason (whereof he commonly has no care), nor justice (for there is none above himself), nor any other thing can hold him in his duty, but only the fear of his contrary.

After Commines had dispatched this question he entered into another, which depends hereof. What is the cause that commonly princes and great lords have not the fear of God, nor love to their neighbors? He answers, the lack of faith; for if a prince believed verily the pains of hell to be such as indeed they are, he would do no wrong to any man, nor retain others' goods unjustly. For if they believed assuredly (as it is true and certain) that they are damned in hell and are never likely to enter paradise, who retain other men's goods without making satisfaction, or that do any wrong to any without amends unto him, it is not likely there would be found a prince or princess in the world, or any other person who would withhold another's goods in good earnest, whether his subjects, vassals, or neighbors; or would put to death any wrongfully; not to hold them in prison, nor take from one to give to another, nor procure any dishonest thing against any person. If then they had a firm faith, and believed the pains of hell to be horrible and great, without end or remission for the damned, knowing again the shortness of this life, they would not do what they do. And for example when a king or a prince is a prisoner, and he fears to die in prison, is there anything so dear in the world he would not give to come out? Certainly he would give both his own and his subjects' goods altogether. As we have seen king John of France, being taken prisoner by the prince of Wales at the battle of Poitiers, paid three million francs for his ransom and acquitted to the English all Aquitaine, or at least as much as they then held; and many other cities, towns, and places, all of which came to a third part of the kingdom, which was thereby brought into great poverty, such that no coin was current but it was made of leather, with a little nail of silver in the middle of it. And all this gave king John and his son Charles the Wise for his deliverance out of prison. And if they would have given nothing, the English yet would not have put him to death, but at the worst kept him in prison; and yet if they had caused him to die, the pain that he had suffered would not be comparable to the thousandth part of the least pain in hell. Why then did king John give all that has been said, and so overthrow his children and the subjects of his kingdom? Because he believed what he saw and knew well, that otherwise he could not be delivered. But you shall not find a prince, or very few that if he had a town of his neighbors, would yield it for the fear of God or the pains of hell. It is then the want of faith, because princes believe not that God will punish the wrongs they do to another, and that they do not also believe that the pains of hell are horrible and eternal, as they are. Yet this is certain, that God will punish them as well as other men, though not in this world, yet assuredly in the other. Yea will some say, but who will inform against them, or dare stand before God for that purpose? I answer that the complaints before God against princes, the dolor and sorrowful lamentations of orphans and widows whose fathers and husbands they had killed, shall stand as complainants before God; and generally all those who they have afflicted and persecuted in their persons or in their goods, shall present themselves before our Lord, the true judge, with piteous tears and dolors, and shall serve for witnesses and accusers. And God, who is a just judge, shall punish such princes as do not fear him, and it may be will not attend to punish them in the other world, but in this world. But let them know that when it pleases God to punish princes, as they are greater than simple people, so he will bring them to a greater fall. And a true token that God begins to ruin a prince is when he so diminishes his senses that he makes him fly the counsel of the wise, and elevates into credit with him new people, violent, unreasonable and foolish, slothful and flatterers, who do and speak all things to please them. For when we see this happen to a prince, we may well say that God prepares his ruin.

Behold in sum, in its proper terms, the opinion of that wise knight Commines, of the cause why God raises enemies unto princes; which opinion is truly very Christian, and proceeding from a man of a wise judgment, and well experienced in affairs of state, wherein he was exercised for the space of thirty years in the time of king Louis XI and Charles VIII, in embassies and other great and honorable charges. He was no such petty burnpaper as Machiavelli, who dealt in nothing but in registering and writing of the small broils and troubles of one house of the town of Florence; and coming out of no better school dares to give lessons and documents to princes and mighty kings, to teach them how they should govern, or rather how they should become tyrants. But contrary, he who will read the history of Commines shall find many good precepts which that good knight has marked by experience in his time, which indeed are good and proper, as well to inform and instruct a good prince as those of Machiavelli are to inform a most wicked tyrant.

Upon this speech above cited of Commines, that God diminishes the senses of such princes as he will ruin, I will add for a confirmation the saying of an ancient wise man, cited by the poet Sophocles:

> Agreeing well to verity,
> The saying of the wise man is:
> That which most evil you do true,
> Most good it seems to you twice.
> Thus when we stir up God to ire,
> He plagues us much for our desire.

3.18
Machiavelli

A prince ought not fear to perjure, to deceive, and to dissemble, for the deceiver always finds some who are fit to be deceived. (*Discourses*, book 2 chapter 13; *The Prince*, chapter 18)

The prince who will become great and make great conquests needs to learn well the occupation and art of deceiving; as John Galeazzo did, who by that art took the duchy of Milan from Messire Bernard his uncle. The Romans also, under that name of allies and confederates, so deceived the Latin people and many others that they reduced them into a servitude and subjection; yet they never espied it until the end. True it is, in this art of trumpery and deceit men must use great feignedness, dissimulations, and perjuries; and the prince who shall be hereunto made by nature and art shall always obtain prosperous success in his affairs. For men are commonly so simple, and so soon bend to present necessities, that the deceiver always finds some who will suffer themselves to be deceived. Hereupon we may allege infinite examples of peace, truce, and promises which have been broken by princes, yet have had good event. And hereof we may allege one example of fresh memory, of Pope Alexander VI, who never did otherwise but made an art of abusing men; neither ever applied his mind to other study; neither was there ever found a man who would confirm his promises with more horrible oaths, nor that less kept and observed them. Yet his trumperies and perjuries succeeded all well unto him, for he knew well enough therein how all sorts of men must be handled.

Answer

In this maxim is an amplification of what has been before set down by Machiavelli, when he said that a prince ought to know how to play the fox. For now explicating what it is to play the fox, he says it is to know how to deceive, to dissemble, and to be perjured; and that a prince ought to be adorned with these goodly virtues of trumpery, dissimulation, and perjury. But as for trumpery, which men call subtlety, we have sufficiently spoken of it; and of perfidy and perjury we shall afterward speak in another maxim. Therefore here we will make no long discourse, because we will not often repeat the same thing. And withal there is no man in the world of so small judgment who does not see that this maxim contains a detestable doctrine, altogether unworthy not only of a prince, but of every man, of whatever condition. And I do not believe that the Bohemians, who go from country to country telling good fortune; jugglers, or rather rogues who make an occupation of deceits and abusing the world, will not condemn this maxim as wicked and abominable if they are made judges.

And as for what Machiavelli says, that the deceiver will always find some who will suffer themselves to be deceived, I confess there will always be found some idiot fools and sots that he may deceive, and that sometimes he may deceive sharp witted and wise men; yet notwithstanding it is as certain that there is not so great a deceiver but sometimes he is deceived. For as soon as a deceiver is discovered to be one, every man takes heed to negotiate and traffic with him, or if they are forced to have to do with him, for fear of being deceived they will do their best to deceive him. And herein most of the world make no conscience, and think it not only lawful but praiseworthy to deceive a deceiver. He who has once a name to be a cozener and deceiver, all men will dispose themselves to deceive him if they can; and by that means the deceiver having cause to take heed of many sundry persons, it is impossible but he should be often deceived, and be often caught in his own nets. Therefore Machiavelli's reason does not so well conclude as it seems; for if the deceiver always finds some to deceive, he shall also find some who will deceive him. And it may be sometimes, for one that he deceives he may find six who will deceive him; because none can be so perfect in the art of trumpery (which art Machiavelli so much recommends to a prince), but also he shall always find others who know more than himself in some points; and many together know more than one alone, in all points of that art, one in one point, and another in another. So that in the end he himself shall always see, according to the common proverb, the deceiver shall be deceived.

As it happened even to Pope Alexander VI, whose example Machiavelli here cites; for the end of all his trumperies and perjuries was to make his bastard Cesare Borgia lord and king of all Italy, and afterwards of all Christendom if he could. But the issue of his designs and purposes was a tragical act, as we have before said in another place. Moreover, the cause why that pope deceived Christian princes many times, and even Louis XII, was that in that time men so greatly feared the pope's bulls and interdictions, and that they believed him to be a true lieutenant of God on earth, so that they dared not discredit anything he did, but rather believed all his words as oracles. But today children would mock at his actions, and few men would be baited with his allurements.

But for what Machiavelli says, that the ancient Romans under the deceit of those names, allies and confederates, brought into their subjection and servitude their neighbors, it is a plain and pure lie. For they subjugated all men by war, at divers times, as we read in histories. True it is that once they vanquished and brought them under, they then made treaties of peace and confederations which were not greatly to the advantage of those who were overcome; as in reason they might. For if by the right of nations, those who are vanquished by wars may be bond-slaves of the vanquishers, by a stronger reason may the vanquishers reserve to themselves some preeminence over the vanquished. But the preeminence which the Romans commonly reserved to themselves in all their treaties, was that the allies and confederates should not make war upon any without their consent, and that they should contribute unto their soldiers in their wars. Moreover they left to all people their franchises, liberties, goods, religion, magistrates, and all other things, without altering anything, and without imposing upon them tributes of money or such like. This cannot be called a servitude, as Machiavelli calls it; or if it is a servitude, there are no people in Christendom, whether subjects of princes or commonwealths, which are not in a double and quadruple servitude.

And whereas Machiavelli says that a prince ought to know the art of trumpery and deceit, some will ask, to take heed of it, what are the precepts of the art. Whereunto I answer for Machiavelli that no man can give precepts, practical or singular, which may be applied to every business, to avoid deceit and fraud. But the general precepts, which the philosophers call axioms, are these: boldly to forswear themselves; subtly to dissemble, to insinuate into men's minds and to prove them; to break faith and promise; and such like as heretofore we have handled, and shall hereafter. But here we must note one thing, which is that one well experienced in the art of trumpery will not always practice that principle, to break faith; for if he ordinarily does it, he shall reveal himself to be a manifest deceiver; whereas he ought to dissemble and not make an outward countenance to be so, but rather to be a good and honest man. And therefore to observe all the principles of that art together, without breaking one in observing another, he shall in small matters keep his faith, to break it in great things and matters of consequence. Hereof Fabius Maximus admonishes Scipio to take heed:

> "You desire to make war upon the Carthaginians in Africa, under the hope to have the favor of king Syphax and the Numidians, who have promised you aid and succor. But take good advice how you trust in the barbarous nations, who commonly make no account to break their faith and deceive. True it is, in small matters they will keep their faith with you, well to assure you in their promise and loyalty, that they may afterward break it to their great profit and advantage, as soon as they see they have means and occasion in their hands altogether to ruin you."

What then should a man do to guard himself from such deceitful faith of deceivers, which appears and shows itself in little things, and is defective in great matters? A man must do what Scipio answered to Fabius: "I know well how a man must lean upon the evil assured faith of Syphax and the Numidians. I think so much to lean and rest myself upon them as may serve my turn, so that yet always I may hold myself upon my guard, to warrant myself from all perfidy and treachery."

Moreover there is yet another remedy against such deceivers and dissemblers, who promise much and in their hearts have no other intention but to break their promises. That is to shun and fly from them as from hell, and from more than capital enemies, as Homer teaches us:

> He that one thing in heart, another in mouth doth bear:
> Fly him an enemy thine, and as hell-fire him fear.

3.19
Machiavelli

A prince ought to know how to wind and turn men's minds, that he may deceive and circumvent them. (*Discourses*, book 1 chapter 42; *The Prince*, chapter 18)

In our time we have seen princes knowing how to cavalier the spirits of men; who had the cunning subtlety to handle and prove men's minds, and who have surmounted and gone beyond such men as stood upon their simple loyalty. And this is done when a prince marks the virtue or vice of him whom he means to undermine and deceive, by giving him a bait fittest to deceive and entrap him; as did Appius Claudius, one of the ten sovereign potentates that were created at Rome. Meaning to lay hold forever of the sovereign domination of the Romans, he drew to his league and devotion all the principal men he could gain. Knowing that Quintus Fabius, who before was as good a man as can possibly be, had a spirit inclined to ambition and honor, Appius gained him by promises of great estates and honors. In the end Fabius became as wicked as Appius himself. Knowing also many young Roman gentlemen, otherwise well born and well instructed, were desirous of wealth and riches to fulfill their lusts, he gave them great gifts and promised them much more if they always followed him at the tail wherever he went, as his guard and vassals of his tyranny. Even so, a prince who will thus handle and toss men's minds shall easily with deceit catch whom he will, and always obtain the upper hand on them.

Answer

Ah poor Frenchmen, too simple, you see the nets and snares which so often catch you; you speak freely, you brag and vaunt, you disclose your hearts and will unto the Machiavellians, who can cavalier your spirits and discover the bottom of your hearts, and afterwards bring you into their nets at their pleasure. But they are not such; they are slow and prolonging, secret, close; they suffer not a word to fall from their mouths without premeditation in what sense you may take them, and so make you serve their end, which is ordinarily contrary to what you think. They can also say that these Frenchmen are light and inconstant; they cannot keep their secrets, they abound in words and are indiscreet; they have no retention in their mouths, but disclose their thoughts to every man. And in truth we must confess that France has no neighbor nation whose spirits are so easy to cavalier. And certainly this maxim is one of the greatest secrets of the Machiavellian Cabal, wherewith they aid themselves most to execute in France what they do. And if Frenchmen could break their practice, it would be easy to overthrow all their designs and purposes, where little by little they ruin all those they fear and suspect, drawing them into a slavish and Turkish servitude and placing among them Italian colonies.

But this maxim is practiced many ways, by marking the vices as well as the virtues of men. For if he sees a man's mind addicted to ambition, he needs but an office with greater promise, and then may they do all he wills. Having thus cavaliered and captivated his mind, he brings them into his net, to make him serve his turn in all manner of wickedness that he will command him to do. For as Sallust says, ambition, because it has some resemblance of virtue, is often the cause of great evils, even the ruin of great cities and commonwealths. And indeed we see, both by old and modern examples, that this detestable ambition has often drawn men to bandy and arm themselves, to the ruin of their own country; most wickedly forgetting the duty they owe to the conservation thereof by divine, natural, and human right; to enjoy only the smoke of honor, which often brings the ruin of their goods, loss of their lives, and destruction of their souls. Such may we call all those who make war upon their own nation, to deprive them of the enjoying of their goods, lives, conscience, and religion, and all other things which are theirs, and which they cannot take from them but by injustice and iniquity. But behold, they are blinded with ambition and are slaves to those who have brought them into their snares, who could so well cavalier their spirits, and even by that vice which they have noted in them. In like manner, if these Machiavellians mark the mind of a man to be given to lubricity and Venus' delights, they will prepare for him delicate and bravely adorned courtesans who will soon take him in his own lust with the fish-hook of his own vice. If they discover him to be covetous, they will bestow some gift upon him, as some benefice or other thing, and will promise him a hundred times as much; but withal, behold the man cavaliered and entrapped. Likewise if they note a man virtuous, that he is loyal and constant in his word, they will seek to draw out of him some word and promise, and thereupon lay an ambush for him. If they see him of a mind inclined to the commonwealth, they will get him some charge, that thereby he may be in some way entrapped. Briefly, in thus cavaliering men's minds, and by discovering their virtues, vices, courages, affections, and passions, they frame crafty engines fit to make men fall into their devotion, or else altogether to take them out of the way, or to make them serve their designs and purposes. Lastly, the means to shun their frauds and subtleties are not difficult to wise men; for such cavaliering merchants are sufficiently known at this day. And therefore to cause them to fall into their own snares and ambushes, men must antecavalier them; that is, men must work against them.

3.20
Machiavelli

A prince who uses clemency and lenience advances his own destruction. (*Discourses*, book 1 chapter 32)

In a hundred times it will hardly happen once that the good and comfort which a prince does to his subjects, when he sees himself as it were forced to do it, for fear of rebellion or otherwise, is gratefully received by them; but they rather think themselves beholden to those who draw their prince unto the bestowing of such benefits upon necessity and constraint. And this is often the cause that the people seek occasions and means to draw the prince into that necessity. Therefore a prince ought never to attend that extreme necessity, to show himself kind and liberal; for there is likely to be so little help therein, that it will rather advance his ruin.

Answer

It should be best and most expedient for a prince to prevent all his subjects with good and courteous dealings, than to attend till he sees himself constrained to diminish his rigor, and (as the common proverb says) to bend or break. Notwithstanding the counsel given here by Machiavelli is altogether wicked, and cannot but bring into ruin a prince and his estate. For in sum, his counsel is to hold hard against his subjects, not abating his rigor nor using any kindness or graciousness, unless he sees himself constrained and pressed thereunto. If a prince then will stand stiff, always rigorously handling his subjects and oppressing them without abating, although he hears of their grievances and complaints, and sees them prepared to rebellion and denying their obedience; what other thing can follow but the entire ruin of him and his estate? For wherein consists the estate of a prince, but that his subjects agree together to yield him obedience? If then by his obstinate rigor and evil dealing he brings his subjects into that necessity to deny him obedience, will not that be the ruin of him and his estate? There is no man of good judgment but knows this. Therefore said the poet Sophocles:

Even as hard steel in fire we see
In pieces break most easily:
So minds too hard and fierce which be,
Most oft with fall on ground doth lie.

This precept, whereby Machiavelli would make a prince stiff and inflexible against his subjects, can bring to him but his own ruin; as it happened to Rehoboam when his people humbly desired an ease of their tributes, and he obstinately and proudly denied them. Following such counsel as Machiavelli gives here, this king answered his subjects that he had no intent to abate his former dealing with them, but contrary he determined to augment rather his rigor towards them. And for this cause did the greatest part of his kingdom cut themselves from his rule and obedience.

And to say that the people are unthankful to their prince for benefits accorded as it were by constraint, this is false, and experience shows us the contrary. For the people are not so speculative that they will seek out and examine the impulsive cause which moved the prince to commit or ordain anything, but hold themselves contented with the good and profit which redounds to them by that ordinance. And the enjoying of the good they receive brings to them such a pleasure and contentment that it moves them to thank their prince for that good, and to praise and bless him, yea, to pray unto God for his conservation and prosperity. In all the peace that was made in France since the civil wars, there has always been seen an experience thereof. For a man may well say that the king accorded peace to the Protestants as it were by constraint, which indeed is contained in the edicts of peace. For the king himself so declared it in other edicts which he made when the war was renewed, as he declared by an edict in 1568, wherein he said that he had always had in his heart to abolish the religion of the Protestants, and the cause of his suffering it before had been by constraint, and to accommodate himself to the time. The courtiers also have always called it the suffered religion, and the Roman Catholic the authorized religion. Although these good edicts of peace were accorded by the king against his heart, yet the people did not cease to be thankful unto their king, to praise and exalt him as a lover of the good, and to bless and praise God for him both publicly and privately.

But put the case that it were true what Machiavelli says, that the subjects of a prince cannot be thankful for a benefit accorded by constraint; it does not follow that such a benefit and a better handling must be unprofitable and without fruit. For it is certain that this will always cease the complaints of the people and cause them to desist from all rebellions and whatever enterprises are intended and machinated against him. Livy shows us by many examples that this happened often in Rome, where the commons entered into seditions against the patricians and great men in authority; but they were appeased as soon as the great men granted what they desired. And yet we do not find that the great patricians and nobles of Rome accorded unto the commons except when constrained against their will. There were among them men of as good wits and judgment as Machiavelli, such as Coriolanus, Appius, Cato, Fabius, and others, who cried that they must not accord to common people what they demand, because it is an evil example and gives the people occasion to rebel and be seditious, causing their faults to turn to their profit. But notwithstanding all these reasons, most of their wise senators found it more expedient to bow and give place to the tumultuous people than to resist them. There have been many times seen in France rebellions and stirs of the people over new taxes, who straight were stayed by taking them away. And indeed natural reason well shows that it ought to be so, for in all things, whatever they are, as soon as the cause is taken away, men also take away the effect thereof. Moreover, I will not deny but this is of very evil consequence, that profit should come from rebellion and sedition; but upon this point it is worth noting that seldom or never people arise without some great, just, and urgent occasion; and therefore if the prince has not done his duty to cut off that occasion before, and thereby arises rebellion and sedition, he may not find it strange or evil to remedy it rather late than never, and so to purge his negligence. A prince instead to harden his heart against his subjects, as Machiavelli teaches, shall do better not to be so obstinate, but to ply and bow his courage when the good of the commonwealth and his own requires it, following the admonition which that wise knight Phoenix gave to the prince Achilles, his disciple:

Appease thyself Achilles strong, thy hardened heart abate,
A mortal man it not becomes implacable to be:
Though power most, and honor eke on gods attend and wait,
To prayers of us mortal men, yet yield they, we do see.

Good princes have ever done so, and never were hindered by Machiavelli's subtle distinctions, that he who owes obedience ought to humble himself first, and that the prince ought to accord nothing to his subjects but from his own proper motion, lest he be seen to receive a law from them unto whom he should give laws; and that he ought not to capitulate to them, and that it would be a very dishonorable thing for a prince to be seen doing anything by constraint and against his will; with many other such speculative, frivolous, and foolish reasons. For we see by the historiographers that wise princes never regarded such childish reasons, but bowed and mitigated themselves as they saw the safety of their subjects and the conservation of their own estates required. And they never esteemed a healthful and good counsel dishonorable, neither such means and conditions to be wicked or disadvantageous, when thereby they might conserve the love and obedience of their people.

3.21
Machiavelli

A wise prince ought not to keep his faith when the observation thereof is hurtful to him. (*The Prince*, chapter 18; *Discourses*, book 3 chapter 42)

A prudent and advised lord neither can nor ought to keep his faith when such observation is prejudicial to him, and when the occasions and necessities which caused him to make his promise are already past and extinguished. If all men of the world were good, this precept were to be blamed; but seeing the ordinary wickedness of men, who themselves keep no faith, neither is the prince also to be bound to observe it towards them. Neither is it to be feared that a prince cannot always find sufficient reasons to cover and color that violation and breaking his faith. Likewise it must considered that all forced promises may be broken, especially when they concern the commonwealth, as soon as the force is passed. Hereof we read many examples, and this is every day seen and practiced in our time, that not only forced promises are not kept among princes after the force is gone, but also other promises are no more observed after such occasions fail which were the cause of making such promises.

Answer

Although the other maxims of Machiavelli may be called wicked and detestable in the highest degree, yet this one carries away the prize above all others which concern duty among men. For whosoever will take away faith and loyalty from among men, as Machiavelli would do, he withal takes away all contracts, commerce, distributive and political justice, and all society and frequentation with one another; none of which can stand but by the observation of faith. But if it were so, that for lack of observation of faith towards each other, men dared not sell, buy, exchange, lend, or make other contracts, and that men dared not make any commerce of merchandise with each other, nor observe any public policy, wherein should we differ from brute beasts? In nothing but that we should be worse than they; for then every one must dwell by himself; there should need no towns nor boroughs to dwell together, but men might be vagrant and separated one from another, taking by force the goods from each other. Insomuch that a man might say that to take away faith from among men, as Machiavelli does, is to bring them into a brutish estate wherein they cannot live, nor subsist, nor enjoy the necessary commodities which one receives from another, and in consequence it is to induce and to bring a ruin and universal deluge to all mankind. Yet if any Machiavellian will reply that the intent of their master is not to take away all faith from among men, but only to break faith when there is profit in doing so; I will answer that in effect that is all one, and that these two things are almost equal, to take faith altogether away, and to break it whenever there is an appearance of profit. For he that buys and promises to pay, may say after he has received the merchandise that by this doctrine he is dispensed withal to pay nothing, because it is for his profit to have both silver and the merchandise. He also unto whom a man lends anything, may say he has a dispensation from Machiavelli not to yield again what was borrowed, because it is for his profit to keep it. And so in all contracts and commerce, men may cover the breach of faith with the veil of utility and profit, and by that means banish and chase away all faith from men. Behold the effect and consequence of this detestable and wicked doctrine of Machiavelli.

Which to refute might well suffice the apparent evidence of evil, and the absurdity which follows thereupon, whereof the most rustic idiots of the world may judge. Sufficient also is one place of holy Scripture, whereby God commands us to hold our faith and promise, even to our damage. But as I have said before, I will combat this profane Machiavelli by pagan and profane authors, and show him that he has but slenderly read his Livy, upon whom he has written his discourses full of ignorance and wickedness. Sextius and Licinius, tribunes of the Roman people, to obtain the favor and grace of common people in debt, would have a law pass whereby all debtors might preaccount in payment of their debts to their creditors, all the interest which they had before paid; and that the rich landowners should be constrained to release the land they had over five hundred acres, to be divided among the poor. Appius Claudius Crassus, patrician, opposed himself against this law, and showed that it was pernicious and damaging, because by such a law public faith, which is the bond of all human society, is broken. For the goods and possessions which the rich men hold, they or their ancestors have obtained them by contracts of buying, selling, exchanging, and other like wherein there always passed faith and oaths. And therefore they who will take from the rich what they have gotten by a good and lawful title, confirmed by that bond of faith and oath, would be to take away all faith from among men, without which no human society can stand. And likewise to make creditors lease their debts by imputing unto them interest long before payed in satisfaction of the debt, that should also be to break faith and promise of obligations, and to make an overture to all deceit and distrust, in such sort as the contract of love and such like should be abolished. By those remonstrances, founded upon good and solid reasons, Appius Claudius hindered that law from passing or being authorized; there was then such an account made of faith, which they preferred before all difficulties and particular necessities. And afterward many times, that law of taking away from rich men what they possessed more than five hundred acres, was refreshed and brought into question by other tribunes; but it never came to effect, yet there arose from it infinite seditions, murders, pillages, and other innumerable evils. A thing which well shows that the violation of public faith draws always with it a great tide of evils and calamities.

The Romans, seeing themselves one day lacking money for the maintenance of their armies and payment of soldiers, the Senate consulted what provision to make. None of them thought it good to impose a tax or tribute upon the people, which would prove very grievous in many sorts. At last they all agreed that soldiers must needs be paid; for, they said, if the commonwealth stands not by faith, it cannot stand by riches. It was therefore better to spend the good of the commonwealth in loyally paying soldiers' wages, and so acquit themselves of their faith towards them, than to spare the commonwealth by the failing of faith and word. All the Senate being of this advice, they thought it expedient to find money, and therefore a charge was given to praetor Fulvius, in an oration to the people, to show them all their public necessities and to exhort those grown rich by farming grounds belonging to the commonwealth to lay out some silver for the maintenance of the army in Spain. Fulvius so well persuaded that the farmers accorded to lay down a certain sum of money, as much as was demanded, upon condition to enjoy their farms for three years, and that the commonwealth would take upon them the perils of the sea which might come unto them in their commerce by shipwrecks and hostile incursions. For they were certain that such money as they lent to the commonwealth was assured to them, as in their hands, upon the public faith. And if the Romans had not had that good reputation, they would not so soon have found money for their need. But those who have that virtue well to observe their word, shall never want those with whom to contract.

King Perseus of Macedonia, determining to make war upon the Romans, sent ambassadors to the Achaeans, a people of Greece allied to the Romans, to draw them to his side. But Callicratides, a notable man among the Achaeans, was of advice that they should give no ear unto Perseus, nor to his ambassadors, because the Achaeans had already confirmed an alliance by faith and oath with the Romans, and that upon that faith was founded all the assurance of their estate; and that faith had that property, that it would not be violated nor suspected in any sort whatsoever. And therefore it was a breach of faith only to afford audience to that king whom they saw plainly prepared to make war upon the Romans. This reason, founded upon the authority of public states, was the cause that nothing was accorded to Perseus. And likewise hereunto accords the saying of the emperor Aurelius, that the most lamentable thing in this world is when faith is broken and violated by friends, and without the same no virtue can be assured.

To this purpose, that faith cannot be suspected, it is notable what the dictator Fabius Maximus did. Hannibal, being in battle array near Rome, conceived this subtle device, to ruin and utterly destroy all the houses in the fields belonging to Fabius. And he did this to bring a suspicion upon Fabius, that he had made some secret pact with Hannibal against his faith and duty. Fabius knowing well that it was not sufficient to perfectly observe his faith, but that also he must be exempt from all suspicion, straight sent his son to Rome to sell and rid him of all he had without the town, which he did; and so assured his public faith by his particular damage, taking from the people all sinister opinion they might take of him. And assuredly there is nothing in the world more pleasant than when faith is sincerely kept, even in adversity and when men have most to do. Therefore the Romans esteemed those their good and loyal allies who kept their faith loyally during the time they had wars in hand. As did Ptolemy, king of Egypt, when the Romans had to do with Hannibal and the Carthaginians; for he was always firm in the consideration and alliance which he had made with them, insomuch that when their war with Hannibal was finished, they sent ambassadors to Ptolemy to thank him that in their so doubtful and hazardous affairs his faith had not altered, and to pray him to continue.

Attalus, king of Pergamus in Asia, came to the degree of royalty by his virtue; for he was neither son nor successor of a king, neither had he the heroic virtues of Hercules, Alexander, or Caesar, to conquer a kingdom. Briefly, according to Livy he had nothing in him that could either aid or bring hope unto him at any time to be a king, but only riches, which he bestowed and used so well that by their means, and by his fidelity towards the Pergames, he became king of Pergamus after he had once vanquished the Gauls of Asia. As soon as he was come to this degree, he allied himself by considerations with the Romans, and always kept his faith perfect and entire; insomuch that by the integrity and constancy of his faith, and by good justice, he reigned 44 years and left his kingdom stable and firm to his son Eumenes, whose domination the Romans greatly augmented because he continued in his father's loyalty, who at his death charged him to repute that fidelity to be the best heritage he left him.

There was nothing in the world which the old Romans had in greater reverence and observation than their public faith; therefore they had a temple of faith where men swore and solemnly promised all their treaties of peace, truces, confederations, alliances, and other such like; and those who first did violate it were esteemed dedicated to the gods of hell. And with a like sincerity did they also observe their faiths in particular contracts; so that everyone thought they could not better assure a debt than in lending to the commonwealth. Yea, when by reason of great wars their treasuries were empty, such as had the custody of pupils' and widows' portions, and other like, would bring all to the treasurers of the commonwealth. For every man, says Livy, thought he could not better place his silver, nor better assure it than under the public faith.

When Scipio the African entered into Sicily with his army to pass into Africa, because he entered as a friend he would suffer no man to take anything from the Sicilians. But, according to Livy, thinking that the first thing he should do was to maintain and defend the public faith, he by a proclamation commanded every man in his camp to yield and give to the Sicilians all their own whatsoever. He also deputed judges to hear and determine all complaints touching such causes. This so pleased the Sicilians that from thence forward they showed themselves very affectionate to aid the Romans in their African war.

While Hannibal was in Italy, Valerius Levinus being consul, there was a loan of money made of the Roman people. Afterward it came to pass that Scipio having passed into Africa with his army, the Carthaginians sent to Hannibal to come and defend Carthage and the countries of Africa, and he was constrained against his will to return. As soon as he voided Italy, although the Romans had not ended their war, neither were out of great affairs, yet Levinus certified the Senate that during the time of his consulship there was a great sum of money borrowed from the people; that it was time to pay it, and that he in particular was bound in this case to acquit the public faith. Therefore he desired that the borrowed money might be restored; the Senate liked well of his speech, and it was decreed that the said money should be paid at three payments, the first immediately, the other within two years, and the last within two years after that. When it came to the third payment, there was no money in the treasury to pay it, because of the great affairs that the commonwealth had in their wars. Upon this necessity the Senate resolved that whatever came of it, they must acquit their public faith; and therefore they gave to particular persons the lands and possessions belonging to the commonwealth, in payment for every man's debts, retaining only upon every acre three half pens to rent, to show that that land had been the commonwealth's; with this covenant, that such debtors should have their payment in money as soon as the commonwealth had silver, if they would rather have money than land.

This Roman virtue straightly to observe faith was not only resplendent in the body of the commonwealth, but also among particular persons, who never had regard to anything in the world so much as in keeping their faith. When Scipio was in Africa warring upon the Carthaginians, he accorded a truce with them, if they would for that purpose send ambassadors to Rome, which they did. While the said ambassadors made their voyage to Rome, Asdrubal, a Carthaginian captain, breaking the truce, distressed and took 230 Roman ships. Whereof Scipio being advised, sent ambassadors to Carthage to show the Senate that breach of the peace, so unfit for people that demanded peace. But these Roman ambassadors were so evil entertained at Carthage that the common people would have stoned them, and they were forced to go back again. Not long after, the ambassadors which the Carthaginians had sent to Rome returned and passed through the camp of Scipio. Scipio sent for them and showed them how their people had violated the public faith by breaking the truce, and offended the right of nations by the violent repulsing of his ambassadors; yet, said he, I will do nothing against the custom of the Romans in the holy observation of the public faith, neither anything uncomely to myself. And after this speech he sent them away, not doing them any harm. Hereby men may know that at that time the scoff and jest so much used by the canonists was not in use: Faith must be broken to him that breaks faith. Caesar also had this property, that he would never imitate the treachery and disloyalty of his enemies, nor break his faith unto them, although they broke theirs. And indeed, as that wise captain Cincinnatus said, natural reason shows us that we must not sin for others' example, nor break a law because others have already broken it, nor commit that fault which we reprehend and condemn in others.

These ancient Romans were so scrupulous and exact observers of their faith, that not only they esteemed that a man violated it when he did anything against it, but also whenever he suffered anything to be done by others which seemed to be to the detriment of that faith. As when Hannibal besieged and ruined the town of Saguntum in Spain, an ally of the Romans; because they could not give reinforcements to the Saguntines before the taking of their town, they thinking that herein their faith was engaged, never ceased till they had rebuilt and repopulated it. And therefore they warred in Spain for the space of fourteen years, at unspeakable charge; and vanquished the Turditans, who brought in Hannibal against the Saguntines; and drove the Carthaginians wholly out of Spain, and redeemed all the Saguntine slaves which Hannibal had sold after taking the town. So well affected were these old Romans to leave nothing behind whereby they might make known that a public faith was the one thing in the world they had in most singular recommendation.

Jugurtha, king of Numidia in Africa, wickedly slew his two brothers, the natural and legitimate children of good king Micipsa, who left his kingdom to the said brothers and Jugurtha, his nephew and adopted son. The Romans, who greatly loved that good king Micipsa, where much grieved that this adoptive had dealt so wickedly with those unto whom the kingdom better belonged. Notwithstanding, they gave him safe conduct to and from Rome because he made the Senate believe that he would justify himself. When he arrived at Rome he sought for his justification to obtain friends by great presents; but he could in no way cause this fact to be approved. Yet he returned to his kingdom in all assurance; for although he merited by reason and justice to have been stayed, seeing the execrable act he had committed, and because it pertained to the Romans to do justice thereof, because they had the protection of the children of Micipsa; yet notwithstanding (according to Sallust) the public faith got the victory.

After Nerva was chosen emperor, he entered into the Senate, and after he made them understand how kindly and temperately he meant to behave himself in the government of the empire, he added for a conclusion an oath and promise that never by ordinance and command would he put to death any senator. A thing which greatly pleased all the company, especially because that cruel emperor Domitian, his predecessor, had caused a great number to die, often for frivolous and trifling causes. What followed? It happened that certain senators conspired against that good emperor, and that the conspiracy was discovered; but that good prince seeing that the conspirators were senators, having given to them all his faith and oath that he would cause none of them to die, loved better to observe his faith than to punish with death those senators which well merited it. What will our Machiavellians say here, who most cruelly put to death and massacre against public faith even those who in no way have deserved any punishment?

But it is time to leave those ancient Roman examples, for we should never have done to rehearse them all; now let us come to domestic examples. In 1508 Louis XII, who held the duchy of Milan, made a league at Cambrai with the emperor Maximilian and Pope Julius II, to expulse the Venetians from the firm land they held, as usurpers upon the empire, the Church, and the duchy of Milan. And it was accorded that in the following year, at a convenient time, the three princes should appear upon the place with their armies, and each should regain what was his own after they had conquered the lands the Venetians held. The king came with his army and many great princes and French lords, but the emperor and the pope failed; yet the king, seeing himself strong enough alone, gave battle to the Venetians and got the victory. Their chieftains were taken, 2,000 troops were slain, and almost all the towns the Venetians held on firm land were yielded unto him. What then did this good king? Although the other two did not hold their faith unto him, and though he might easily have kept all he had conquered, yet notwithstanding he voluntarily yielded to the emperor Verona, Vicenza, Padua, and other places belonging to the empire; and to the pope he yielded Rimini, Faenza, Cervia, Ravenna, and other church towns. Hereby this good king, showing in what great recommendation he had of the observation of his faith, maintained whole and perfect his promise. For if with excuses he would have dealt deceitfully, to have broken his faith as Machiavelli says he ought to have done, did he not have a fair pretext, to say that others did not hold promise with him? Might he not have said that he was not bound to reconquer theirs at his own charge, by the tract of their league? Might he not well have beaten the pope with his own canons, alleging as before, *frangenti fidem, fides frangatur eidem*? But he was a plain man, without guile, and sincere; he sought no evasions or refuges, but was an upright observer of his faith and promise. Yet Machiavelli reprehends him because he did not use deceits and trumperies as the popes Alexander and Julius did.

The memory is yet fresh of the great wars which the emperor Charles V and Francis I of France had together; as also how they objected to each other's observation of faith in their public writings. Yet whatever imputations were laid by one to the other, experience manifested the truth in 1539 when the emperor, under word of the king, passed through France on his way from Spain to Flanders, where the people of Ghent had risen up against him. In that passage the emperor showed well that he believed the king was a prince who would keep his faith unviolated, notwithstanding all the wars, enmities, hostilities, and other differences which had so often happened between them, and were still alive. And it is certain that if the emperor, who was a wise prince, had the least doubt in the world of the king's faith and loyalty, he would never have put himself in his hands, and especially for so small an occasion as to go in haste to build a citadel in the town of Ghent. The fact even contradicted his word, for he had many times before given an intimation to the king that he would not hold and observe sincerely his faith; but by the fact he showed that he believed the contrary of what he had said, and so found by experience that the king was a prince who had in greater estimation his faith and promise than anything in the world. For he not only gave to the emperor an assured free passage through his kingdom, but also did it with all the honor and good entertainment that was possible. To obtain this passage, the emperor had promised and liberally offered to invest the king or one of his children with the duchy of Milan, as appertaining to him by good title. So that if the king would have observed the precepts of Machiavelli, and had broken his faith, he would have had a good pretext and color to have arrested the emperor until he had effected his promise in making the king a full possessor of Milan. But that wise and generous king, who knew that public faith ought to be observed uprightly, without any addition of glosses or restrictions — herein using the wise counsel of his constable Montmorency, who was no Machiavellian — thought it good, purely and sincerely, first to observe faith on his side. And although the emperor did not accomplish his, but having passed into Flanders fed the king with words of hope and of no effect, yet never a man of noble heart and good judgment will condemn what the king did here. For whatever profit the violation of his faith would have brought to him, yet the fruit of that profit could not have endured long; for the emperor would have left nothing untried to regain what by such craft was extorted from him, and would have brought the whole empire into the quarrel. The king also would have incurred the blame and defamation of a faith-breaker before the world, but instead left his adversary that reputation, and obtained forever the title and honor of a loyal king for keeping his faith sincerely, without in any way disguising or offending it.

But now let us discover the evils which proceed from disloyalty and breach of faith. First, the violators reap this punishment, that men no more trust them. The Samnites, having often broken their faith and their treaties of peace and alliance with the Romans, sent ambassadors to Rome to renew them. After these ambassadors were heard in the Senate, they received this answer:

> "Masters ambassadors, if the Samnites who sent you had always kept their faith well, we could willingly have hearkened unto you and

renewed our alliance; but because we have often perceived that you prepare for war even while demanding peace, reason wills that we should no more rest upon your words, but rather respect the effects. We therefore make you know that shortly we will send an army into your country, to prove whether you love war better than peace."

After this answer the ambassadors returned to their country; the Romans sent the then consul with an army, who found all things peaceable and received an amiable entertainment, with a full furnishing of all necessary victuals. The Romans, knowing that the Samnites desired to live in peace and that their hearts agreed with their words, renewed the ancient treaty of consideration.

When Hannibal was at the point of being vanquished by Scipio, and knew that the Carthaginians imputed their ruin to him, he withdrew to Antiochus in Syria, to invite him to make war upon the Romans. He found this king already willing to do so, because he thought the Romans grew too great and approached too near his border. Hannibal, seeing Antiochus ready to war upon the Romans, thought he had found a master under whom to employ himself, to make some show of his valor in his trade of war, and that he would yet work much trouble for the Romans, his sworn enemies. But he was greatly deceived in his hope; for that king would never give him any charge in his army, however brave and valiant a captain he was, but always suspected him because he practiced that doctrine of Machiavelli, to keep no faith but for his profit and advantage. And but for this Punic treachery, which was well known in Hannibal, he would have been employed in some great and honorable charge, since he knew better how to war upon the Romans than any of Antiochus' captains. And Antiochus needed not doubt that Hannibal would fight well against the Romans, his mortal and irreconcilable enemies; but he doubted that Hannibal, obtaining the love of the soldiers (who willingly love old captains), might attempt some enterprise against him, to take his kingdom or to play him some other Punic trick of cunning. Briefly, that faith and disloyalty of Hannibal was so suspected by Antiochus, that not only would he give him no charge in his army, but also would never believe his counsel, though Hannibal gave him the best counsel in the world for the conducting of his war. Which is a point very notable to be marked, that a man should so much distrust a perfidious person as to think he would ever use perfidy and disloyalty, even when he uses the office of a faithful counselor and good friend. But it came to pass that when Antiochus had been vanquished by the Romans, Hannibal was constrained to seek out another master, and fled towards Prusias in Bithynia, who received him into his safeguard. But then he met with as perfidious a person as himself, who determined soon after to deliver him to Quintius, captain of the Roman army. Hannibal perceiving this, and seeing all passages shut up from saving himself, took the poison he always carried with him in case of necessity; for he did not trust in any man, as it is the nature of perfidious persons to esteem every man like themselves, and not to trust in any. After making great imprecations and execrations against Prusias for betraying him, he drank that poison and died miserable. Whereupon it is a thing worthy to be noted, that perfidious persons and faith-breakers ordinarily find their like, who bring them into the necessity of detesting and execrating even perfidy itself, which before they made a virtue. A true sentence which they pronounce against themselves, and whereby they condemn themselves, leaving an example and judgment after them to detest perfidy as a contagious pestilence to those who use it.

The emperor Bassianus Caracalla showed many examples of his perfidy; but among all he committed three most notable, which so descried him that none would ever again trust him. The first was that which he used against Abgar, king of the Osrenians, when he came to see Caracalla under the word of safe conduct. Caracalla broke his faith and put him in prison, and seized his goods and his country. In this fact he might cover himself with that doctrine of Machiavelli, and say he did well because it was for his profit. But the part he played with the king of Armenia succeeded not as well. Which king he sent for, making him understand that he would agree him with his children, with which the king then had some dissention. As soon as he came Caracalla cast him into prison, as he had done with Augarus. But the Armenians, having discovered this perfidy and disloyalty, rose up in arms and would not submit themselves to the obedience of that perfidious Caracalla. He also played another part of treachery, under the pretext and show of marriage, with Artabanus, king of the Parthians. For he wrote letters to him whereby he signified that their empires were the two greatest empires of the world; and that being the son of a Roman emperor, he could not find a better wife than the daughter of the king of the Parthians. He therefore asked her hand in marriage, to join the greatest empires of the earth and to end their wars. The king at first denied Caracalla his daughter, saying that such a marriage was very unfit because of the diversity of their languages, manners, and habits; also because the Romans had never before allied or married with the Parthians. But upon this refusal Caracalla insisted and pressed him more strongly than before, and sent to Artabanus great gifts, so that in the end he gave to him his daughter. Caracalla, assuring himself that he would find no hostility in the Parthian country, boldly entered far into it with his army, saying he went but to see the king's daughter. On the other side, Artabanus prepared himself and his retinue in as good order as was possible, without any army, to go meet his new son-in-law. What did this perfidious Caracalla? As soon as the two parties met, and Artabanus came near to salute and embrace him, he commanded his soldiers to charge upon the Parthians. The Romans attacked as if there had been an assigned battle, and there was a great slaughter made of the Parthians; but the king, with the help of a good horse, escaped with great difficulty and danger. He determined to revenge himself of that villainy and treachery; but Macrinus relieved him of that pain, and soon slew that monster Caracalla, who was already detested through all the world because of his perfidy.

Besides that perfidy and violation of faith is the cause that none will believe nor trust those who have once done it, there yet proceeds another upon it; which is that breach of faith is commonly the cause of the total destruction and ruin of the perfidious and disloyal person. The example above noted of Hannibal may well serve to prove it; for his treachery was first a cause that none would trust him; secondly, it was the cause that another perfidious person, seeing him without friends or means, played another part of perfidy and forced him to poison himself. We have also recited the example of Virius and the Capuans, who desperately slew themselves because they had broken their faith with the Romans. But among other examples, that of king Syphax of Numidia is most illustrious and memorable. This king promised Scipio that he would provide reinforcements against the Carthaginians. The Carthaginians knowing this, found means to lay a bait for the king by a fair damsel named Sophonisba, who by her enticements drew him into her nets and caused him to break with Scipio and make an alliance with the Carthaginians. The king married Sophonisba, who was of a great house, and it was accorded that they would have the same friends and enemies. Scipio being advised of this was much astonished and grieved; yet he thought it good not to attend while the two powers were joined together. He then placed his army before Syphax, who was going with 30,000 troops to help Carthage, and overcame all those succors. Syphax himself was taken prisoner, his horse having been slain under him, and was brought alive to Scipio, who asked why he had broken his faith with the Romans, which he had solemnly sworn with his hands. This poor captive king confessed that an enraged folly had drawn him unto it, by means of that pestilent fury Sophonisba, who by her flatteries and enticements had bereaved him of his understanding. Afterward he was led in a triumph to Rome by Scipio, and died miserably; his kingdom brought under the obedience of the Romans, who gave a good part of it to Massinissa, another king of Numidia, who had ever been loyal and faithful in the observation of his faith. So that Syphax lost himself and his kingdom by his perfidy and breach of faith, and Massinissa acquired great reputation and honor, and greatly enlarged his kingdom by rightly observing his faith and loyalty.

Charles the Simple, king of France, made strong war upon Robert, duke of Aquitaine, and vanquished him in a battle near Soissons, where Robert was slain. Heber, count de Vermandois, brother-in-law of Robert, was so grieved and displeased at the overthrow that he enterprised a part of perfidy and villainy to catch the king's sovereign lord. Therefore with a show of amity he invited the king to a great feast in the town of Perona, where the king came with many other great princes and lords. But the count had them all taken prisoner and shut them up within the castle of Perona. Afterward he enlarged all the said princes and lords, upon condition never to bear arms against him; but he kept the king, who died within two years. Louis III, his son, succeeded him in the crown; he did not immediately revenge the death of his father, fearing an insurrection because of the count's great kindred and friends. Later he made a great and solemn feast and invited the great lords and barons of his kingdom, including count Heber and his friends and kin. As they were all assembled at the feast, behold, there arrived out of England a courier (a thing feigned by Louis), who booted and spurred fell upon his knees before the king and presented letters from the king of England. The king took the letters and had them read low by his Chancellor, the better to deceive. As soon as he had read them, the king began to smile and say on high to the company: "Truly men say true, that the English are not wise. My cousin of England sends me word that in his country a rustic and clownish man had summoned his lord to a dinner at his house. And as soon as he came there, he took him prisoner and strangled him. Therefore he sends me word to have the opinion of the princes, barons, and lords of France, to know what justice should be done upon that subject. I must make him an answer; and therefore, my masters, I pray you tell me your advices. What think you," he said to the count de Blois, the most ancient. The count answered that his opinion was that the said rustic fellow should die ignominiously, and that according to his desert. All the other princes and lords were of the same opinion, even Heber. Then the king said, "Count de Vermandois, I judge you and condemn you to death by your own word; for you know that in the show of friendship and under the shadow of a feast in your house, you invited my father and retained him and brought him most villainously to his death. Therefore by your own confession you merit a most ignominious death." Straight after, the king commanded that he should be hanged, which was done. So this perfidious and disloyal Heber received the reward of his perfidy and breach of faith, as he himself judged to have merited.

Edward II of England was much governed by the house of the Spensers, who took upon themselves the handling of all the affairs of the kingdom, and despised far greater lords than themselves. The king having lost a battle against the Scots, all England imputed the evil luck of that loss to the evil government of the Spensers. Believing that the great lords of England who envied them had caused this rumor to be sown, they resolved to take vengeance by a most perfidious and disloyal means. For they persuaded the king to convoke a general assembly of states, ostensibly to advise and provide for the affairs of the kingdom. The princes and lords of the kingdom, not doubting anything, assembled at the king's command. But the Spensers had persuaded Edward that they meant to get his kingdom from him; and as soon as they were assembled, he commanded them to be arrested. Without any knowledge of case, he executed 22 of the greatest lords and princes of the realm, among them Thomas, duke of Lancaster, the king's uncle and a good and sage prince, who after was canonized and sainted. This perfidy joined with cruelty — for commonly one goes with the other — was the cause that the king was deprived of his royalty as unworthy to carry the crown, and was confined to prison, where he finished his days. And the Spensers, authors of such disloyalty, were executed and rigorously punished according to their merits. For after they had been drawn on hurdles through the streets of Hereford, their privy parts were cut away and cast into the fire; then their hearts; their heads were cut off and carried to London; their bodies were quartered, and the quarters were carried to towns and set on the tops of the gates, in detestation of their great perfidy and disloyalty.

It was also a great perfidy in Charles the last duke of Bourgogne, in that he gave safe conduct to the count of St. Pol, constable of France, to come to him with good assurance; and then took him prisoner and delivered him to king Louis VII; making their progress at Paris, his head was cut off in the place de Greve. True it is that the said count had committed great faults, as well against the king as against the duke; he had also always studied to nourish war between the said two princes; yet notwithstanding it was a very dishonorable and infamous thing for the duke to take him prisoner after he had given him his faith and assurance by the safe conduct which he granted him. For if he had not been taken, he would have fled into Germany with his silver, and from thence in time he might have made his peace and again have come into the king's favor. But he was deceived as before; and the said perfidy was so much the more infamous and dishonest because it was perpetrated by this duke of Bourgogne for the covetousness to gain the towns of St. Quentin, Han, and Bohain; which belonged to the count, and which the king gave to the said duke to deliver and betray him. But behold the just judgement of God, who permitted that this Bourgogne was in the end beaten with the same rods wherewith he had beaten the count of St. Pol; for being twice overthrown at Granson and Morat by the Swiss, the siege of Neuss ill succeeding unto him, and also having lost the duchy of Lorraine (which before he had unjustly occupied upon the duke of Lorraine, who conquered it), all these traverses and troubles engendered such grief, sadness, and confusion in his spirit, and great indisposition in his person, that he was never after whole either in body or mind. His wits thus coming into decay, there came into his brain a distrust of his own subjects, and he therefore thought good to serve himself with strangers; and to chose a loyal and faithful nation he addressed himself to a count de Campobache, an Italian, and gave him charge to bring with him many Italians to his service, as he did. This was the last act of the tragedy of his life; for this Campobache ceased not till he had betrayed him unto the duke of Lorraine before Nancy, which the said Bourgogne held besieged, and there was slain in an assault which the duke of Lorraine gave him to constrain him to raise the siege. And so in like sort, as by perfidy and violating of his faith, he had caused the constable of St. Pol to lose both life and goods; so by the treason and perfidy of Campobache, he both lost his life and his house was ruined and rent in pieces, which was the greatest house in Christendom next to that of France.

He that would set down all the calamities and mischiefs proceeding from perfidy and breach of faith, would never finish. It caused the ruin of Carthage, which for a long time was one of the greatest and most flourishing commonwealths that ever was in the world. It was the ruin of Corinth, of Thebes, and of Chalcis, which were three of the greatest, fairest, and richest cities of Greece. It was the cause of Jerusalem's destruction, and of all the country of Judea. Briefly, there never happened any great subversion or desolation in the world, whether of city, commonweal, kingdom, empire, great captain or monarch, or of strong and flourishing nation, but it came upon perfidy and breach of faith. True it is that it draws behind it cruelty, avarice, and other like companions; but yet perfidy is the mistress and governess of all. She breaks peace; renews civil and foreign wars; she troubles people and nations that are quiet, destroying and impoverishing them; she profanes and defiles holy and sacred things; she banishes and chases away all piety, justice, and fear of God; she brings in atheism and contempt of all religion; she defaces all amity and natural affection towards parents, our country, and nation; she confounds all political order; she abrogates good laws and customs. Finally, what mischiefs have there ever been in the world which that hideous monster perfidy has not engendered? Assuredly it is an Alecto, an infernal fury, excited and called lately from hell to the vexation and utter overthrow of this poor world.

And as for what Machiavelli says, that a man may find reasons and covers to cloak and color the breach of faith; this has no place among good men who respect their honor, who also repute palliations but trumperies and frauds that make men's perfidies the worse and more damnable. After the first Punic War, the Carthaginians made a treaty of peace with Caius Luctatius, lieutenant general of the Roman army, who made the reservation, Under the pleasure of the Senate and Roman people. The treaty displeased the Romans, and therefore as soon as they were advised thereof, they told the Carthaginians that they would not ratify it. Soon after, Asdrubal, lieutenant general of the Carthaginian army, made another treaty with the Romans wherein the Saguntines were comprehended. This treaty was long observed on both sides, yet the Carthaginians only secretly ratified it. Eventually the Carthaginians sent Hannibal to besiege Saguntum, which they took and ruined. The Romans then sent ambassadors to Carthage, to know why they had violated the treaty regarding the Saguntines. The Carthaginians in their Senate would have colored this fact with fond subtleties, saying that they never ratified the treaty made by Asdrubal, and that it was as lawful for them to disavow that treaty as it was for the Romans to abrogate the truce of Luctatius. This color seemed to have some appearance in it, but being more narrowly entered into, nothing will be discovered but deceit and fallacy. For there must be made a greater estimation of a ratification by deed than by word, as the assurance of deeds is far greater than that of words. So that the Carthaginians, who for many years had effectually approved the treaty of Asdrubal, could by no means afterward reprove it; as also because in that truce there was no reservation contained, as there was in the treaty of Luctatius. The Roman ambassadors, seeing the palliation and quarreling deceit of the Carthaginians, gave them no reply but to present their choice of peace or war. The Carthaginians left that choice to the Romans, who chose war, by which the Carthaginians lost themselves and their country. And this came from their deceitfulness and breach of faith.

Not unworthy of rehearsal are the subtle distinctions of king Antiochus' ambassador to Titus Quintius, lieutenant general of the Roman army then resident in Greece to defend the Greek towns from that barbarous king. This king, perceiving his affairs could not well succeed against the powers of the Romans, sought peace without any further hazard. Quintius made the king's ambassadors understand that the only means of peace was that their king should avoid Europe and leave Greece at liberty. Menippus, one of the ambassadors, replied by goodly distinctions well trussed together, whereby he showed that there are three kinds of considerations and treaties of peace. One, with those who are vanquished by war, unto whom the vanquishers may give law. The second, when two enemies equal in forces make peace without battle; in which kind, as they are like in force, so ought the conditions of peace be alike and equal. And the third is when those who were never enemies before are brought to amity and confederation, in which kind neither ought to give law to the other. He added to this distinction that their master Antiochus was of this third kind, and therefore they were abashed that Quintius would give a law saying he must avoid Europe. Quintius, who was not expert in making distinctions, unless with the sword—although otherwise of good natural sense—said: "Well, you have made me a distinction, and I will make you another. There are two kinds of wars; the one may be made in Asia, the other may be made in Europe. Touching the last kind, the Romans have just cause for war against your master for the guard of the towns of Greece, lest they should fall into the hands of Antiochus; just as they have preserved them from the hands of Philip of Macedonia. And as for the first kind, the Romans are content not to deal at all. And if Antiochus will make war in Asia, let him do it, we will not hinder him." The ambassadors, who accounted to have brought much to pass by their subtle distinctions, were much astonished when they heard this contradiction of Quintius; for they could not reply one word. And in the end there was no remedy but for Antiochus to pass from Europe. Hereby is seen that such subtleties and palliations, in treaties of peace and observation of faith, are but ridiculous things. For the affairs of the world ought to be governed by a common sense and solid judgment, and not by subtleties and distinctions, which should be sent to sophists and logicians, to maintain their arguments in schools.

The Greeks have always been great masters in subtleties, as their writings show, yea, too much. For it has often happened that determining to govern their affairs by subtle reasons, rather than by arguments founded upon good judgment, they have overthrown themselves into utter ruin and confusion. Hereof there is a very memorable example in the Peloponnesian War described by Thucydides, which endured 28 years and nearly ruined all Greece from top to toe; for it was founded upon a subtlety of small importance. This was the matter. Two of the greatest commonwealths of all Greece were Athens and Lacedaemonia; for all the rest were small in comparison, and except for a few were in association with one or the other. These two great commonwealths had a treaty wherein among other articles it said that any of the cities of Greece might lawfully associate with one or the other. But it happened that the Corcyreans, who were not allied with either state, had war against the Corinthians, who were associated with the Lacedaemonians. The Corcyreans, feeling themselves weak, entered into league with the Athenians, showing them that they might receive them into their society. The Corinthians, on the contrary, demonstrated to the Athenians that if they aided the Corcyreans in this war it would be against the treaty, which was to be understood in the wholesomest and best sense, and not to the detriment and ruin of the confederates. Therefore the treaty must be understood in such a way that the reception of new associates would be without damage and prejudice to the parties. The Corcyreans replied that although it was not expressed that it would be lawful to receive associates to make war against confederates or others, yet it must be so understood, especially when new associates make war for a good right and just quarrel, as is ours (they said) against the Corinthians; and that the treaty could not be violated, neither is the interpretation contrary to equity when men will maintain right and reason. The Athenians made no account of this interpretation, though it was conformable and agreeing to the sense and equity of the treaty, but rather held it better to stick to the Corcyreans. On the other side, the Lacedaemonians banded themselves for the Corinthians, as reason required; and by that means those two great commonwealths were brought to the skirmish of war against each other. They drew after them all the rest of Greece, or most of it; and this Peloponnesian War was great, cruel, long, and almost utterly overthrew the estate of Greece upside down. And all this came upon the captious interpretation, contrary to all equity and reason, which the Corcyreans made of the treaty of confederation.

In like manner was the subtle disputation of those who caused the famous captain Pompey to die. After he lost the battle of Pharsalia against Caesar, he embarked on the sea with his wife and friends, hovering about Egypt, hoping to be entertained by the young king Ptolemy in consideration of the pleasures he had done to his father. At his approach he sent a messenger to know if Ptolemy would receive him in assurance; but the king's affairs were then managed by three base persons who understood nothing less than how to govern affairs of state. They were Theodotus the rhetorician, his schoolmaster; Achillas, his domestic servant, and a chamberlain. These three venerable persons fell to counsel, to deliberate what answer the king should make to Pompey. At the beginning they differed in opinion, one saying it was good to receive him, the other not. But in the end all three accorded in the worst opinion they could have taken, which was to receive Pompey and slay him; which opinion this goodly rhetorician Theodotus persuaded to the other two by his subtle reasons. He said, "If we receive Pompey, it is certain we will have Caesar for an enemy and Pompey for a master. If we do not receive him, they will both be our enemies, Pompey for rejecting him and Caesar because we have not stayed him. But if we receive him and put him to death, Caesar will thank us and Pompey cannot revenge himself upon us; for a dead man is no warrior." Upon these goodly reasons of that subtle rhetorician, the conclusion was taken by these three bad people to put to death this great person Pompey, who had had so many triumphs and victories in his life, and who had sometimes seen five or six great kings wait on him at once, as an arbiter of their contentions and differences. If these bad counselors had considered the greatness of Pompey, who had so many virtuous and great lords as parents and friends, as also the magnanimity of Caesar, who would vanquish by true force and not by perfidies and treasons, they would never have stayed upon the cold and foolish subtleties of this gentle rhetorician, and they would not have concluded the death of so great a man. But yet they concluded it and executed their conclusion, putting Pompey to death as soon as he had taken port in Egypt. But it was not long before they received the reward of their perfidy; for Caesar soon arrived, unto whom Pothinus and Achillas presented the head of Pomey, thinking to please him greatly. Caesar turned his face away and began to weep, and commanded Pothinus and Achillas put to death. And that subtle reason of Theodotus, who persuaded them that Caesar would thank them for their murder, was not found true. Seeing this execution and finding himself very culpable, Theodotus fled and lived some years miserably wandering and begging here and there, fearing to be known by the world which everywhere had him in execration. But in the end, after the death of Caesar, Brutus found him by chance and caused him to die miserably, after he had made him endure infinite torments. Behold the end of those three counsellors of that young king Ptolemy, who also by their evil conducting made a poor end; for he was slain in a battle near the Nile, and none could ever find his body. Would to God those who today resemble these three counsellors might receive similar guerdon and reward as they did, to teach them to conclude the committing of massacres and the use of perfidy and treason, which will not fail them in the end: for God is just.

But the scoff which Theodotus alleged in this counsel, that a dead man makes no war, is at this day ordinarily in the mouths of our Italianized courtiers, and thereupon they ground their counsel to slay and massacre all those they hate. We must, they say, slay this and that man, it is good to dispatch them, for a dead man makes no war. But if a man replies to them that a dead man may yet be cause of war, although he can make no war, what would they answer? Dare they deny so apparent a thing as we see with our eyes, and whereof histories furnish us with infinite examples? Louis, duke of Orleans, brother of king Charles VI, made no war indeed after he was slain by the duke of Bourgogne; yet he was the cause of a civil war in France which endured more than sixty years. Pompey, after he was slain, made no war, but his death was the cause of a great and long civil war in the Roman Empire. The violating and death of a Levite's wife, was it not the cause of a war wherein there died more than sixty thousand men? Those slain at Vassy in 1562, did they not draw on a civil war which endured too long? Those also slain in August 1572, in the great towns of France and especially Paris; were they not the cause of great wars? It is therefore a foul and an inconsiderate saying to allege that a dead man makes no war, thereupon to found their massacres and slaughters, without considering the consequences thereof. Hereupon is very memorable the speech that the young prince Geta made to his father Severus. Having vanquished Albinus and Niger, his competitors to the empire, Severus began to make a great slaughter of those who had sided with them because they were of a more noble house. He said to his children Bassianus and Geta, "I shall by this means ease you of all your enemies." Hereupon Geta demanded of him, "My lord and father, those who you mean to put to death, are they a great number?" "Yea, many." Geta asked, "Have they neither parents, allies, nor friends?" "Yea, they have many," replied Severus. "Then you will leave us more enemies than you take from us." This wise speech of the young prince so touched the heart of Severus, although he was cruel, that he would have ceased from his slaughter if not for Plautianus and other courtiers, who intending to enrich themselves by confiscations, incited him to continue. Let murderers, then, hold themselves assured that for every one they have slain, they stir up ten enemies. And yet this is not all; for all the rest of their life they have souls and consciences tormented with the remembrance of those they have most wickedly murdered; and the shadows and remembrances of them shall always be before their eyes as a fear and terror unto them. O how the shadow of that great admiral shall strangely torment these great enterprisers of massacres! It will never leave them at rest, but shall be a burning flame that will aghast and fearfully accompany them even to their sepulchers. Let them then hearken unto the menace and threatening he makes in his tomb against them:

Although the soul from body my cold death has ravished,

Yet absent I will follow thee, yea, with a flame full black
My shadow always shall appear about thee as one dead,
Which shall revenge on thee my blood, thou who no ill dost lack.

I thought good by the way to touch what war the dead make or what cause of war they are, to refute that saying of the Machiavellians, that a dead man makes no war. Let us now come where we left off, of subtleties, which we say ought not to be practiced in the government in the affairs of state, and that thereby none may cover any perfidy.

When Hannibal won the battle of Cannae against the Romans, he took a great number of prisoners; he sent some of them to Rome to work their redemption for ransom, making them swear to return upon their faith. But one of them advised himself of a subtle device to stay without breaking his faith; having passed a good part of the way towards Rome, he suddenly returned to Hannibal, saying he had forgotten something, then went back to Rome. But the affair coming to debate in the Senate, none would yield to redeem the prisoners; those who came to Rome for that purpose returned very sad to Hannibal, except the one who had returned before, who remained in his house, thinking he was well discharged of his faith and oath. But when the Senate heard of the fallacious and deceitful return of this soldier, so unworthy for a Roman, they commanded him to be drawn out of his house and led by force to Hannibal. Hereby you may see that no wise people of good judgment, such as were the ancient Romans, can approve such subtle palliations and covertures of an infraction and breach of faith, such as Machiavelli persuades to a prince.

A similar deceit was in Philip VI of France. He had made an oath, as almost all his predecessors had done, never to run over, or attempt to besiege, or take anything belonging to the empire; yet desiring the castle of Tin, the bishops near Cambrai, which troubled him much, caused his son, the duke of Normandy, to besiege it. He went there as a simple soldier, without any command at all; by which subtlety Philip could not save his oath, for he who does anything by a mediator is as much as if he had done it himself. Neither did the deceit succeed well unto him, for the duke of Normandy was constrained to raise his siege, and soon after the king lost the battle of Crécy.

The emperor Valentinian was cruel in his actions and dealings, and had many officers like himself. Among these was a criminal judge called Maximus, who when examining criminals promised them if they would confess the truth they would suffer no punishment, either of sword or fire. These poor accused persons, as often men do, confessed things they had never perpetrated, trusting his faith and promise. But this wicked judge had them beaten down and slain with hammers, thinking by this caviling to save his oath. God willed that for a recompense he should be hanged under emperor Gratianus, a gentle and kind prince. For it often happens that such cruel judges, who have bestowed great pains to make their diligence allowed by cruel princes, have been afterward paid their wages and received their due recompense from some good prince succeeding.

Nabis was a tyrant who without right or title got sovereign possession of the commonwealth of the Lacedaemonians, and there committed many cruelties and indignities. The Aetolians, a furious and cruel kind of people, esteemed that it would be a great glory and honor to them if they could slay this tyrant in any way; and that all Greece, especially the Lacedaemonians, would thank them. So they enterprised to join themselves to him under a pretext and show of faith and society, the better to overthrow him. Alexamenes was deputed captain of the Aetolian forces, and entered into league with Nabis, who at that time greatly feared the Romans. Alexamenes persuaded Nabis that they must often exercise their soldiers together, by bringing them into the fields to wrestle, leap, skirmish, and practice other military exercises. One day in the field Alexamenes came up behind Nabis and threw him clean off his horse with a blow, and then slew him. This done, Alexamenes and his people returned to Sparta, thinking to seize upon the castle to guard themselves from the assaults of the tyrant's friends. But they could not obtain it, for the Lacedaemonians were so grieved at that most perfidious and villainous part of the Aetolians against their king—although they desired nothing more than his death—that they furiously rushed upon the Aetolians, who were dispersed through the town. The Lacedaemonians slew almost all of them, and among them Alexamenes himself; those who escaped the sword were taken prisoners and sold.

For the last example of this matter, I will set down that of Joab, David's nephew and constable, unto whom he did great services. Yet David commanded his son Solomon that he should put to death his cousin Joab because of his perfidy; for he had slain Abner and Amasa, two other great captains, traitorously and under the color of amity. Joab seemed to have great causes to justify his act, for Abner had slain Asahel, Joab's brother, and therefore Joab could not but receive just sorrow and feeling thereof. Moreover Abner had followed the contrary part to David, standing for the house of Saul. Amasa was a rebel and a seditious person against David, and had followed Absalom's part; so it was evident, if Joab had had our Machiavellians as judges, they would not only have judged him innocent, but for a remuneration they would have made him some great amends with the goods of Abner and Amasa. But the judgment of David, which he made at his death, against his sister's son, who had done him infinite good and great services, showed well how execrable and detestable Joab's perfidy was to him. And hereby princes must learn to imitate this holy and wise king, by whose mouth God teaches them that they ought to observe faith and promise, even to their damage; a doctrine fully contrary to the doctrine of this filthy and wicked Machiavelli.

To conclude, perfidy is so detestable a thing both to God and the world, that God never leaves perfidious and faith-breaking persons unpunished. Oftentimes he waits not to punish them in the other world, but plagues them in this one, often strangely and rigorously, by exterminating in a moment all their race, wives, and children; as the poet Homer (although a pagan) has wisely taught us, saying:

> Though straight the God of heaven lay not his punishment divine,
> At all times on the perfidious for his great perjury:
> Yet neither he himself, nor child can scape his ire in fine,
> No nor his wife, but all destroyed by hand of his shall be.

3.22
Machiavelli

Faith, clemency, and liberality are virtues very damaging to a prince, but it is good that he has some similitude and likeness thereof. (*The Prince*, chapter 18)

There is no necessity that a prince should be garnished with all these virtues, but it is requisite that he has an appearance of them. For I dare well say this, that having and observing them in all places, they will fall out very damaging to him. And contrary, the mask and semblance of them is very profitable, and indeed we see each day by experience that a prince is often constrained to go from his faith, and from all charity, humanity, and religion, to conserve and defend his own; which verily he shall soon lose if he exactly observes all points which make men to be esteemed virtuous.

Answer

Machiavelli here sets down three virtues, Faith, Clemency, and Liberality, which he reproves in a prince as damaging and pernicious. But whosoever can recover the masks and similitudes of them as they are naturally portrayed, will do well to adorn and deck himself with them as whores and courtesans do, who apparel themselves like women of honor to make men believe that they are honest and good women. But I will not stand here upon invectives to refute or cause men to detest such a filthy doctrine. For what man is so brutal or ignorant, that sees not with his eye how Machiavelli delights to mock and play with the most excellent virtues among men? As for the faith which is and ought to be among men (for Machiavelli speaks not of the faith towards God), we have discoursed upon it in the former maxim. And as for liberality, we shall speak upon it in another place. Here we will speak of clemency, and examine Machiavelli's doctrine, whether this doctrine can be damaging to a prince or not.

To show that clemency cannot be damaging, but is profitable to him unto whom God imparts that grace to be endowed therewith, an argument from the contrary concludes well and evidently for this purpose. For if cruelty, which is directly contrary to clemency, is pernicious and damaging to him that is infected therewith, as we have above showed, it follows that clemency and gentleness are both profitable and honorable to him that is adorned therewith. And indeed it is a virtue both agreeable and admirable with every man, which brings to whatsoever person it dwells in favor, grace, amity, honor, and good will of every man to do him pleasure. All which are affections that can never be idle, nor without some operation of their natural effects, as the fire cannot be without heat, nor light without shining. So that a man debonair and gentle (I speak of men generally, but especially of a prince), being the chief means to obtain the favor, grace, amity, and reverence of the people, he cannot help but feel great utility, agreeable contentment, pleasures, benefits, great assurances far from all fear, and most exceeding great repose and tranquility in his soul and conscience. But in order to deduce the good effects and utilities which proceed from clemency, I advise the reader that I speak of that virtue in its most ample signification, according to which it comprehends not only mercy and kindness towards offenders, but also bounty, goodness of nature, mansuetude of manners, facility to accommodate himself to the people's humors and to all such a man has to command, also humanity and officious affability towards all men. For briefly, all these aforesaid virtues are like the honey and sweetness of a well-complexioned and settled soul; which sweetness may well be called in one word clemency, although according to its diverse effects and respects, men give it diverse names.

This natural kindness and bounty of the soul then, being in a prince, first produces this effect; that it will soften and mitigate the punishments of offenders, yea sometimes will forgive and altogether acquit them, according as the circumstances of the fact and of the person require. For a prince ought well to consider when, how, to whom, and why he pardons a fault, because it is not clemency but cruelty when a prince may do justice and does it not, as Saint Louis said. But as equity is the soul of justice, which often is repugnant and contrary to the rigor of laws and ordinances, therefore a prince must employ his clemency to bring equity in use, by dispensing with the punishment of offenders who should suffer by the rigor of laws. But if there is no equity nor available reason to persuade a prince to dispense with the law, then he is bound to do justice, otherwise he merits to be reputed not clement, but cruel and culpable of the crime which he would not vouchsafe to punish. And in this point it is very necessary that a prince is wise and vigilant to guard himself, that he be not surprised nor deceived, and that he use not cruelty instead of clemency, by the ordinary opportunity of those who sue for pardons. And not to fall into this inconvenience, when the fact is of evil example and the commonwealth has interest therein, the prince ought not to use remission and grace without knowledge of the cause, and without good counsel.

The emperor Marcus Aurelius governed himself very wisely in his use of clemency to those who committed crimes. For as to those who had not perpetrated great and erroneous faults, and had not taken a custom therein, he mitigated such punishments as were ordained by laws by some other lighter punishment; so in weighty crimes of evil consequence he was inexorable and for them had no favor, much less pardon. And in regard to offenses committed against himself particularly, he was as prompt and voluntary to pardon as was possible, and so it appeared in the case of Avidius Cassius. For Cassius being in Esclavonia with a Roman army, hearing a false report that this good emperor was dead and believing it to be true, he enterprised to make himself emperor, and as such made himself known and saluted by his army. After, having notice that Aurelius was in good health, he was much abashed and troubled that he had so rashly enterprised upon his master's estate. Yet notwithstanding he did not desist from holding and carrying himself as an emperor, fearing that some would slay him as soon as he forsook his forces, having so far embarked and engaged himself therein. Yet he could not shun what he so much feared, for he was slain by some of his captains who thought thereby to please Aurelius, and carried to him his head. Aurelius, seeing the head of Cassius, was exceedingly grieved and sorrowful, and said to them who brought it that they should not have slain him, since he had not so commanded, for so had they taken from him the use of mercy. He rather desired they had brought him alive, that he might have reproached the benefits received at his hands, and with reason showed him how little cause he had to conspire against him, and might have showed himself a better friend to Cassius than Cassius had been to him. "Yea but sir," replied one of the captains, "what if by sparing the life of Cassius, he had gotten the victory of you?" Answered the emperor,

> "We do not fear that, for we have not so honored the gods, nor lived in such sort that Cassius could have vanquished us. No good princes, or very few were at any time vanquished or slain, or despoiled of their estate, but only those who well merited it; as Nero, Caligula, Otho, Vitellus, and the like, who were cruel and full of vices; and like Galba and Pertinax, who were exceedingly given to greed, than which vice nothing becomes a prince worse. But Augustus, Trajan, Hadrian, our father Antonius Pius, and such that moderately governed, so deceased they honorably and without violence. Cassius was a good and valiant captain, whose fault we desired to have pardoned, because it rather proceeded from temerity than evil will against us, being persuaded when he made his enterprise that we had been dead. And although he could never have excused himself because he had greatly injured our children, who by right and reason ought to succeed us in our estate; yet we would not have had him die for that, for if our children merited to succeed us in the empire, Cassius could not have overthrown their estate. But if contrary, Cassius better deserved than they to govern the commonwealth, and had been better beloved, it would have been reasonable and just for him to be emperor."

By this answer of that good emperor a man may see how facile and easy he was to pardon offenses against him, which is a very fitting virtue in a prince. For a prince can hardly rigorously punish faults committed against himself, but he shall be taxed and blamed for rigor and cruelty, although the fault merits grievous punishment; as the same emperor witnesses by his missive unto the Senate, who made too rigorous a pursuit against the accomplices of Cassius. And because the letters contain notable sentences worthy of such a prince, I will here translate them.

> "Masters, I pray and require you that in regard to the Cassian conspiracy you will depose and lay aside your censure, and conserve my piety and clemency, yea, your own, and let none die that are culpable. Let no senator be punished, nor noble blood be shed; let those who are banished be called again, and let their confiscated goods be yielded unto them again, and would to God that I could revoke and call again to life those who are dead. For there was never found that a prince committed a good vengeance of his own grief, but it was always thought too rigorous and sharp, though never so just. How should I not say pardon, since they have done nothing; let them live in all assurance, and so know that they live under the empire of Marcus. Let them enjoy their father's patrimony, his gold, his silver, and other goods, that they may be rich, assured, and

free; and let them be examples of our piety and clemency, also of yours, in the mouth of all the world. Neither is it any great clemency to pardon the children and wives of those who are banished and condemned, since I demand and pray you for pardon even of the guilty themselves, whether they be senators or knights, that you may deliver them from death, from confiscations, from infamy, from fear, from envy, and from all injury; and that you will do this while we reign, that they who were slain in the tumult for enterprising against us be not defamed."

After this missive was read in the Senate, all the senators with an honorable acclamation began to cry, "The gods conserve Antony the clement, Antony most pitiful, Antony most merciful! The gods perpetuate thy empire into thy race; we wish all good to thy wisdom, to thy clemency, to thy doctrine, to thy nobility, and to thy innocence." This acclamation declares well how amiable and acceptable clemency makes a prince, for there is nothing in the world that better gains the hearts of men, nor that bring to a prince more reverence and love than this gentleness and lenity of heart. And indeed this good emperor by his clemency got this much, that after his death all Rome made a certain account that he ascended into heaven, as to the place of his origin. Because, they said, it was impossible that so good a soul, endowed with so excellent virtues, should come from any other place but heaven, neither return again to any other place. The very name of Antoninus was also so reverenced and loved by all the world; from father to son in generations after him many successive emperors caused themselves to be called Antonys, that rather they might be beloved of the people, though that name did not belong to them, nor were of the race or family of Antoninus; as did Diodumenus, Macrinus his son and companion in the empire, and as also did Bassianus and Geta, Severus' children, and Heliogabalus, they were all surnamed Antoninus. But as this name appertained not to them, so they held nothing of the virtues of that good emperor, with whose name they decked themselves. Yet many reprehended in Aurelius his great clemency, whereby he so easily pardoned such as conspired against him; saying that he provided ill for the safety of himself and his children, to suffer conspirators to live. This was but a means to embolden wicked people to enterprise conspiracies; and among others the empress Faustina, his wife, found it evil and of bad consequence that he did not rigorously punish the partakers of Cassius; whereupon he wrote a very memorable letter to this effect.

"Very religiously dost thou, o Faustina, my dear companion, have care of the assurance of us and our children. But whereas you admonish me to punish the accomplices of Cassius, I advise you that I had rather pardon them; for nothing more recommends a Roman emperor among all nations than clemency. That was it which placed Julius Caesar in the number of the gods; which has consecrated Augusts; which gave that most honorable title of Pius, that is, gentle and godly, to thy father. Finally, Cassius himself had not been slain if my advice had been demanded in the slaying of him. I pray thee therefore, my dear companion, be not afraid, but hold thyself assured under the protection of the gods, who no doubt will guard us, because piety and clemency are so pleasant and agreeable unto them."

For a resolution then, it is certain that nothing can so become, or is so worthy of a prince to practice as clemency, by pardoning those who offend him, and even those who have committed some fault that may be excused by some equitable reason, and by mitigating the punishments of the law to those who upon custom commit no excess, and who otherwise are virtuous and valorous people, and their offense not exceeding great and heinous. For if otherwise a prince uses clemency, without having these considerations before his eyes, his fact will rather hold of cruelty and injustice than of clemency. But for a man to practice it with a counterpoise and equal balance of equity, justice can be nothing interfered, but rather shall be reduced and applied to its true rule.

But assuredly, as a prince's clemency brings to his subjects the fruit of a good equity, so does it also acquire unto himself this inestimable good, to be beloved of everyone, as was Aurelius. The like happened to Vespasian, who was greatly beloved for his great clemency and gentleness. For he was so gentle, kind, and clement that he easily forgot offenses committed against him; yea, he would do good to his enemies, as when he married and endowed very richly and honorably the daughter of Vitellius, his enemy who warred upon him. Moreover he would not suffer that any were punished who did not well deserve it. Likewise his son Titus was so good and clement that he was never blamed for bearing evil will to any man, and often he had this word in his mouth, that he had rather perish himself than lose any. He was of the people surnamed the delights of mankind, for his kindness and clemency. In like sort Trajan, Hadrian, Pius, Tacitus, and many other Roman emperors were so beloved and reverenced by their subjects for their natural humanity and clemency, that they are placed after their deaths in the roll of their gods.

Moreover, whenever a prince is soft and clement, there is no doubt but his subjects will imitate him therein; for it is the people's nature to conform themselves unto their prince's manners, as the proverb says:

The example of the prince's life in all things commonly
The subject seeks to imitate with all his possibility.

But whenever subjects imitate that most excellent virtue of debonairity and clemency, it is also certain that the whole body of the commonwealth is much better composed, more quiet, and better governed. For when men are given to that virtue, they will addict themselves to justice, temperance, charity, piety, and all other virtues which ordinarily accompany clemency, from whence cannot but arise the estate of a most perfect commonwealth. Therefore we read that in the time of Aurelius the world was commonly well reformed in good manners; for every man studied to imitate him in his virtues, and especially in his moderation and gentleness; insomuch (says Capitolinus) that he made many good men of such as were bad before, and such as were good, he made them better. This is also the cause why debonair and gentle princes are always so praised and esteemed, not only by men of their time, but also by all historiographers and all posterity, because they are ordinarily the cause of many goods to all their subjects; as by contrary cruel princes are always defamed during their lives and after their deaths, because of great mischiefs whereof they are cause, authors, and executors. This is well painted out by Homer, when he says:

A wicked man, full of fierce cruelty,
Behind his back by all accursed shall be;
Both during life, and after death also,
Defame on him in every place shall go:
But contrary, the good and sincere man
Will grave in mind his praise all that he can.
How all men in each place set forth his praise
To borders even of nations strange always.

But I well know that hereupon the Machiavellians will say and reply that if a prince will be so facile to pardon and practice clemency, he will thereby incite men to take experience of his virtue, and consequently provoke them to commit evil and excess under the hope of impunity. Hereunto I answer in a triple sort: First, I say that if a prince uses clemency without derogating from his justice, there will follow no impunity of a punishable crime, nor by consequent any provocation to commit any punishable excess. For justice shall always have her course, although by clemency it may be moderated. Secondly, suppose that the clemency of a prince might be a means or occasion unto men to take more license to do evil; yet this could not take place but in persons of evil nature. For men of good natures and disposition will rather be incited by a prince's clemency to be good like him, by following his virtues, than to be wicked and ungodly thereby. The prince endowed with clemency will love and follow other virtues, and hate vices, and consequently will honor and advance virtuous people, and hate and recoil from those who are vicious. This will cause the wicked, who are inclined to vices, to guard themselves from committing punishable faults; for although they promise to themselves an easiness to entreat pardon for their faults by the prince's clemency, yet they cannot promise to themselves to be beloved and entertained by him, but rather evil liked and unadvanced. Thirdly, although clemency cannot but draw with it some iniquity and injustice — as verily a prince cannot so evenly poise and weigh his affairs in the practice of clemency, but there will always be found in them some injustice — yet that evil which follows clemency is not so great that we ought therefore to altogether take away clemency from a prince, from whence proceeds infinite goods, profitable and commodious, as well to the prince and his estate as to his subjects and the whole commonwealth; as may easily be collected out of that which has been already said, and shall be spoken hereafter.

The ancient Romans confess that their facility to pardon has many times brought wars upon them, as also revolt of their allies and confederates. But what then? Lest they therefore always show themselves prompt and voluntary to use clemency towards those who offend them? Nay rather it was the virtue whereof they made greatest estimation, and which they most practiced, knowing well that clemency was the true foundation of the greatness and estate of the commonwealth. And this is it which the ambassador of the Romans spoke in an assembly of the Aetolians, who were solicited to ally themselves with Philip of Macedonia against the Romans, rather than to renew their alliance.

"Our ancestors have often experimented, and we also have seen that because we have ever been easy to pardon, we have occasioned many to experiment our clemency; yet we were never so discouraged as not at all times use equality to those who have broken their faith unto us, and such as holily observed them, as also reason wills that the loyal and faithful be better beloved, favored, and respected than others. Have we not warred upon the Samnites for the space of seventy years? And during this time, how many times have they broken their faith? How many times have they risen up against us? Yet we have always received them for our allies; by marriages we have come to an affinity with them; and finally, we have received them for citizens into the town of Rome. The Capuans revolted from us to ally themselves with Hannibal; but after we had besieged them, there were more in the town who slew themselves, pressed with an evil conscience, than we caused to die after we had taken the town by force, and left them their town whole with their goods. Having also vanquished Hannibal and the Carthaginians, who had done us so many mischiefs and so often broken their faith, yet we left them in peace and liberty. Briefly, o Aetolians, you should know and believe that the Roman people will always have clemency in most singular recommendation, and you shall do far more for yourselves to replant yourselves into our amity and alliance, unless you love better to perish with Philip than to vanquish and prosper with the Romans."

Unto this remonstrance of the Roman ambassadors, the Aetolian states would deliver no answer; but among themselves resolved secretly neither to be on one side nor the other, and that at the end of the war they would join themselves to the strongest; which in the end was their bane, yet they found refuge in the Romans' clemency. And verily clemency is such a virtue that a prince may never despoil himself of it, although sometimes it seems he gets harm thereby. For clemency is not cause of any evil, but only the malice of men abuses it; yet it does not therefore follow that it is to be rejected because a man may abuse it, no more than to cast away all wine as a pernicious thing because many therewith are drunk. But let us now come to the other effect of clemency.

Besides the effects whereof we have above discoursed, which are to temper the rigor of justice, to make the prince beloved, reverenced, and praised by all the world, and to fill his subjects with good manners, there are yet three other effects worthy of note in a prince's clemency; that thereby he may be better obeyed, more assured in his estate, and may augment his domination. And to touch those three points in order, one after another, I will presuppose for the first point that a prince makes himself easily and well obeyed when the wills of his subjects are of themselves well disposed to yield obedience. But it is certain that when a prince is debonair and clement, his subjects will be well disposed to obey him, for two reasons; one, because he shall be beloved, and the amity which his subjects bear him shall incite and stir them more willingly to obey him. The other reason, being soft and gentle his commands are sweet and gracious, founded upon reason and equity; and this will cause them to easily yield obedience, because there is nothing that more induces a subject to render his prince obedience and to obey his command, than when they see and judge that the commandment is both reasonable and equal. For equity is the sinew of the commandment and the law, which makes it forcible and brings it into action, and without this equity the law cannot endure nor long be obeyed.

Therefore the laws and ordinances which the Romans gave to the Macedonians after they had brought them under their obedience endured very long before they were in anything changed or corrected. For they were so upright and convenient for that nation that their usage—according to Livy, the true corrector of laws—found nothing to reprehend or correct by the experience of many years. Very memorable also is the manner of the Romans' use to make laws, and especially those which they gave to the Macedonians. For they were not contented to handle and deal with them in their Senate, to cut and stretch them after their fancies as some do today, who make laws in their chambers with such as themselves; but elected ten delegates or deputies, wise and honorable men, who went all over Macedonia to inquire of the manners and conditions of the country people, and of their ancient customs and liberties, and to have the people's advice of such laws as were fittest for them. By this means they made very convenable laws for the nation of the Macedonians, which they found good, holy, and equal, and they willingly obeyed and observed them with good hearts and without any constraint. And assuredly this is the best means when men make new laws and ordinances, that is to have the advice of those who are to have and obey them, to know of them the discommodities that by them may fall out, which they must needs know better than any other. And for this reason the ancient kings of France made their laws and ordinances by the advice of the Estates General, or at least by the assembly of a great number of barons, prelates, and wise people of each great town of the kingdom, which assembly they called the king's Great Council. And the Roman emperors made their laws by their Senate's advice, as we have in another place said. And indeed it is a rash presumption of one man alone, or a few men, to think they can make laws of themselves, and fitting ordinances for a people and a nation, without having the advice of those of that nation, yea of many and divers countries. The ancient Romans were of a better judgment than such presumptuous persons, and they never received a law till it was well tossed and handled, and till everyone spoke that would either persuade or dissuade the law which was to be enacted. Therefore, according to Livy, it often came to pass that the tribunes, whose office it was to cause the law to be received or rejected by the people, desisted from the receipt of a law, being moved to do so by the reasons and remonstrations of those who dissuaded it. And often opposing themselves against the reception of a law, they departed from their opposition, being moved thereunto by the reasons of those who persuaded; and truly if the laws and ordinances which are made for the government of a kingdom or other principality were so well examined before they were concluded, and every man were heard in a general assembly to persuade or dissuade them, so many absurd and weak laws would not be made as are, neither in consequence would they be so poorly observed as they are. For they should be made equal and commodious for those who should obey them, and so would each man obey them with good will; because as is said, equality is what holds law in action and observation.

Moreover none need doubt but when he who has authority to command is beloved, by that means he shall be better obeyed. Lucullus was a valiant and wise captain who executed great matters against Mithridates and Tigranes, two of the greatest kings of the Levant and of all Asia; but in the end, not being able to obtain the love of his soldiers, he was in hazard by their disobedience to have overthrown all the glory and honor which he had acquired. This disobedience of his army was the cause that the Romans called him from the Levant before he had altogether ended the subjugating of those two kings, and sent in his place Pompey, who did nothing else but gather the fruit that Lucullus had sown, and carried away the honor and triumphs of his pains and travails. For the necessity was such that Pompey must necessarily be sent in Lucullus' place, because Lucullus was not obeyed by his soldiers because they did not love him, he was so stern and uncourteous. And as soon as they had obtained Pompey for their captain, they greatly obeyed him because he was gentle, clement, and affable, insomuch that he did with them what he would, and by their forces and valor he brought all the East under the Romans' obedience. This then was a great evil hap for Lucullus, who otherwise was endowed with excellent virtues; that he could not use softness, clemency, and kindness towards his soldiers, and have gotten love, and to have contained them in his obedience, but so to lose the fruit of his travails and victories, not wholly finishing that whereof he had taken charge.

But yet greater evil luck happened to Appius Claudius, who was so exceedingly rigorous and imperious that he caused his soldiers rather to hate than to love him. Being consul and captain of the Roman army against the Volsques, he practiced towards the soldiers the same rigor and severity he did against the common people at Rome, and cared not to be beloved, but only sought to make himself to be feared. This was the cause that his soldiers would not obey him, but when constrained they executed their charges cowardly and negligently. When he commanded to march quickly and swiftly, his soldiers would go slowly and softly; when he came towards them to command them anything, they would not regard him, but fixed their eyes on the ground and cursed him as he passed by. He once went about to assemble them all in one place, to persuade them to perform their duties in battle; but they scattered themselves hither and thither. When he saw this manifest disobedience, instead of correcting his rigor he augmented and redoubled it, causing them to be whipped with rods and putting to death the captains who dispersed themselves, and at last he put to death one out of ten in the army by lot. Yet for all this he did nothing of account or to his honor. Returning to Rome, he was accused by the tribunes of his great severity and inclemency, and by not getting the love of his soldiers, he effected nothing but dishonor and shame. But fearing to be condemned, he procured his own death in his house; and this evil hap, accompanied with great opprobrium and ignominy, would not have happened to him if he had been of a gentle and good nature, to have obtained love.

The bounty, clemency, and gentleness of a prince manifest themselves by many means towards his subjects; as by good tractations and comforts, far from oppression; by maintaining their liberties and franchises; by making edicts and equal ordinances; and in observing and causing good justice to be observed. But the pleasantest means, which most contents the subjects, is when the prince does them this honor, to communicate himself to them, deal in public affairs with them, and asks their advice, aids, and means. For subjects, seeing themselves on the one side so much honored by their prince as to be called into the participation of his counsel, and seeing and understanding on the other side the urgency of public affairs, and just reasons why the prince demands such or such a thing, it is certain that they will obey much more voluntarily than when they know nothing of his affairs, and they know not why nor wherein money should be employed that is demanded. This was seen and practiced at the beginning in a parliament held at Tours during the reign of Charles VIII in 1483, as M. Philip de Commines witnesses; for the poor people of France were before vexed and eaten up for more than 20 years with great taxes and civil wars, which never come without a great ruin. Yet notwithstanding, seeing themselves so much honored by their prince as to be convocated together with the Estates to understand public affairs, and therein to give their aid and advice, not only did the Estates accord the tax which the king demanded, but also humbly besought his majesty that it would please him to assemble them again within two years; and that if the king had not enough money to dispatch his affairs, they would at his pleasure furnish him; and that if he had any war, or that any would offend him, they would employ their persons and goods for his service, and never would deny him anything whereof he had need. Behold then how this soft and sweet manner of a prince's actions, to confer of his affairs with his subjects, makes him so obeyed that by this means he may sooner obtain a great thing than by rigor a small thing. And to this purpose he asks certain questions with good grace:

> "Might it not be accounted a far more just thing before God and the world, to levy money by such force as this, than upon an inordinate will? For no prince cannot otherwise levy it but by tyranny; would privileges

to take it at their pleasure be alleged against so good subjects, who so liberally give what is demanded? Was such an assembly dangerous and treasonable? According as some men of base condition and baser virtue say, alleging that to congregate the Estates is to diminish the king's authority and to commit treason. But rather those commit treason towards God, the king, and the commonweal, who hold estates and offices which they never merited. Neither serve they to any other thing but to whisper and tattle in princes' ears things of small account. And they fear nothing more than great assemblies, so that they may not appear and be known as they are."

These words of Commines are very notable to be applied to our time.

Let us now come to the other effect of the clemency of a prince, which concerns the assurance of his estate. Hereupon I think every man will confess unto me that there is nothing that better assures a prince in his estate than when he has no enemies. But a debonair and gentle prince shall never lightly procure enemies, but rather daily friends; because that virtue of clemency is of itself so amiable and attractive that those endowed with it are always loved. And if sometimes enemies arise against a good and gentle prince — as envy and desire to make themselves greater sometimes causes ambitious and covetous men to enterprise upon such clement princes — yet very hardly shall such enemies shake their estates or prevail against them, and especially if that prince with his clemency has about him a good council. For his virtues will procure him many friends of his neighbors, and make his subjects voluntary and obedient; insomuch that it shall be very easy for him to resist the enterprises of those who will invade and set upon him. We read that the emperor Alexander Severus was very modest, soft, clement, and affable towards his subjects, wherewith Mammaea his mother was not content; so that one day she said unto him that he had made his authority disregarded and contemptible by his clemency. He answered, "Yea, but I have made my estate so much the longer and more assured." And in truth he had in likelihood lived longer, but she so ruled him that he and his son got the evil will of his subjects by the extreme avarice and arrogance that was in her, which caused the death of them both. The same notable speech of Alexander is attributed to Theopompus, king of Sparta, who knew that the puissance of a king is good and excellent when kings use it well; but because there were far more kings who abused their powers, he provided for himself and his successors certain censors and correctors, which were called Ephori. Some said to Theopompus that by this establishment of Ephori he had lessened and enfeebled his power; "Nay then," he said, "I have fortified it and made it perdurable." Meaning to say, as true it is, that there is nothing which better fortifies nor which makes more firm and stable a prince's estate, than when he governs himself with such a sweet moderation that he even submits himself to the observation of laws and censures. The emperor Severus, otherwise endowed with many great virtues, had not this good, to be debonair and clement, but rather was rigorous and cruel. Yet he knew well and confessed that clemency is a virtue most worthy of a prince, and he much desired to be so esteemed, although his actions were contrary. I know well that here the Machiavellians may reply upon me that he feigned and only made a show to esteem of clemency, upon a certain kind of playing the fox, and dissimulation, which Machiavelli holds to be convenient for a prince. Hereunto I make double answer; first I say, suppose in this place Severus meant to play the fox, yet when he so much praises clemency and so fain would seem clement, he thereby seems to approve that virtue as both loveabe and good. Secondly I say that it is credible that Severus, although he was exceedingly sanguinary and cruel during his reign, yet in the end found that it would have been better for him if he had been clement. For with his own eyes he saw Plautianus, his greatest friend, and Bassianus his eldest son who ruled with him, both (though not together) conspire to slay him; insomuch that he dared not punish them, because they had learned from him to be sanguinary and cruel. And at the end of his days, the last words he spoke were that he left the empire firm and assured to his Antonines — meaning Bassianus and Geta, which he named Antonines so that they might be beloved — provided that they proved good princes. But if they were wicked and cruel, then he left them weak and poorly assured. And indeed these last words were as a prophecy to his children; for Bassianus was as cruel as he, and began to exercise his cruelty in slaying with his own hand Geta his brother; and after continued it upon his friends and other notable people, a great number of whom he brought to their deaths. And therefore his foot was not long in the empire, but as his father prophesied he was soon despoiled thereof, slain by his lieutenant Macrinus, having reigned six of his twenty-nine years. Domitian was also a very cruel prince, yet he greatly praised clemency; and when he reasoned upon any affair in the Senate he often interlaced among his speeches some commendations of his own clemency, although he was most cruel and wicked. And briefly, we may say and conclude that this virtue of clemency is so excellent and loveable of itself, that even the wicked who reject it are constrained to have it in estimation and to confess it is a virtue worthy of a prince.

From the beginning when Rome was reduced into the form of a commonweal and delivered from the tyranny of the Tarquins, the people were sent to war without wages; and while they were at war the interests and usuries which they owed to the rich (for the poor are always debtors to the rich) left not to increase and multiply; insomuch that when the soldiers returned, some being maimed and wounded, instead of having rest in their houses they had the usurers on their backs, who demanded interest for the time of the war. Hereupon arose a great sedition, for the poor could not suffer this rude handling, that they should thus be tormented with seizures and pawning their goods, and with imprisonment for the interest growing during the war, being in the commonwealth's service. This cause finally coming to deliberation in the Senate, Valerius Publicola, who was one of those who helped away the tyrant from Rome, spoke thus: "This, the usurers' rigorous dealing, is but a new tyranny; and it is but a small thing for us to have expelled the tyranny of the Tarquins, if now we will establish another; and it is too unreasonable that soldiers should pay interest while they served the commonwealth, since they also served without wages." Therefore he exhorted the Senate to relieve the people of those interests, that afterward they might with better will serve the commonweal at a need. "For otherwise," he said, "it is certain that if there is a continuance of this rigorous dealing, it will bring the people into a greater disobedience and a sedition into the commonwealth, and by this means the state may be shaken and hazarded. But if the people are kindly and graciously used in acquitting them of the said interests, by this means you shall make the city most assured." The Senate followed the advice of Publicola, knowing well that the firmness and assuredness of the public state is founded upon clemency and gentleness.

Hannibal at war in Italy, meaning to go to Capua, commanded one of the prisoners he held to guide him to a place called Casin, which was on the way. This prisoner, supposing Hannibal had asked to go to Casilin, because Hannibal spoke poor Latin, conducted them to Casilin, far from the way to Capua. Hannibal, perceiving he was misguided, caused to whip and hang the prisoner before he would hear any excuse. This rigorous execution and other cruelties that he used never caused the Romans' allies to break with them, although on every side they saw themselves in great peril, because, according to Livy, they knew that they were commanded by a just and moderate government, and by good people that hated cruelty; therefore they did not refuse to obey the best, most prudent, and humane.

When Antiochus, king of Syria and a great dominator in the Levant, was at war against the Romans, they sent against him Lucius Scipio as general, though he was no great warrior, because the great Scipio Africanus, his brother, declared that if Lucius was chosen general, he would be there as his lieutenant. When they were both in Greece it happened that the only son of Scipio Africanus was taken prisoner by

Antiochus' soldiers. Antiochus having this young lord in his hands, entertained and used him honorably, knowing that the great Scipio was of such clemency that he would never forget that the pleasure and amity of so great a personage might stand him in good stead in necessity, as the loss of a battle, or of captivity, or such like. Not long after, Scipio fell sick; whereof Antiochus hearing, sent him his son without ransom, fearing Scipio would die with grief and melancholy, by whose death he doubted to lose a good refuge. For that king, according to Livy, trusted more in the clemency and authority of Scipio alone, for the uncertain and doubtful haps of war, than in his army of 60,000 footmen and 12,000 horsemen. Is not here, think you, an admirable effect of clemency, that an enemy better assures his estate upon his enemy's clemency than upon his own forces?

But what need we any more to amplify by examples or authorities this point? Does not ordinary experience show, as it ever has, that good and clement princes have always been very assured in their estates? Augustus, Vespasian, Trajan, Hadrian, the Antonines, and many other Roman emperors; and most of our kings of France, who were clement and debonair, fully proves this; for they reigned very peaceably, died natural deaths, and after were greatly lamented by the people. Here I may not forget a notable sentence of the emperor Antonius Pius, which he received from Scipio the African, which was this: That he loved better to preserve one of his subjects than to slay a thousand of his enemies. Assuredly a sentence of a good and clement prince, who delighted not in shedding of blood, as our Machiavellians do at this day; who are so covetous of this blood that when one of their enemies falls into their hands, they will not give him for a hundred pounds. They may well say, contrary to Scipio and Pius, that they would rather slay an enemy than save five hundred friends. Are not these people worthy to command? Neither do they make any more account of their prince's subjects than of slaves, which men may beat, scourge, or slay at their pleasure, as beasts. As indeed there has been lately a burn-paper fellow, a writer for wages, one of these Machiavellians, who dared publish in writing that the authority of a prince over his subjects is like that which a lord has over his villain and slave, having power over death and life, to slay and massacre them at their pleasure without form of justice, and so to despoil them of their goods. And how comes this? Does this sot think that the office of a king is like that of a galley captain, to hold his subjects in chains and every day to whip them with scourges? Surely those who hold this opinion merit to be so handled, yea, that some good galley captain would twice or thrice a day practice that goodly doctrine upon their shoulders. But how much more notable and humane is the doctrine we learn of in the life of Augustus, who so much feared that men thought he would diminish the liberty of the people, that he could never abide to be called *Dominus*, that is, Lord, but abhorred it as an injurious name full of opprobrium, because it has some relation to *Servius*, which is to say, servant or slave; he being far from the affectation of such great and magnificent names, as many great men have since well liked of without showing the effect of them.

The third point now remains, which is to show that the clemency of a prince is the cause of the increase of his domination. Hereupon we read a memorable history of Romulus, who was so clement, soft, and gentle towards the people he vanquished and subjugated, that not only many individuals but the whole multitude of people submitted themselves voluntarily and unconstrainedly under his obedience. The same virtue was also the cause that Julius Caesar vanquished the Gauls; for he was so soft and gracious to them, and so easy to pardon, and used them every way so well, far from oppression, that many of that nation voluntarily joined themselves unto him, and by them he vanquished the others. When Alexander the Great made great conquests in Asia, most commonly the citizens of all great cities met him to present him with the keys of the towns; for he dealt with them in such clemency and kindness, without in any way altering their estates, that they liked better to be his than their own.

Hannibal, having taken the town of Saguntum in Spain, was so feared and redoubted that most of Spain submitted themselves to his obedience and abandoned the Roman society, because they had not aided Saguntum against Hannibal. The Romans, to repair their fault whereat they took much grief, sent great forces into Spain under the leadership of Publius Scipio, father of the African, and Cneius his uncle. Hannibal, to contain the Spaniards, took in hostage the children, brethren, and parents of all the nobility of the country, and the most notable citizens of the good towns, and set them under guard at Saguntum, under the charge of a small number of soldiers. God willed that those hostages should find some means to escape from their prison, yet they happened to fall into the hands of the Scipios. The Scipios, having possession of them, in place to revenge themselves for the fault they and their parents had made by revolting from the Romans, welcomed and dealt with them very graciously, and sent them all to their parents and houses. This clemency and kindness of the Scipios was the cause that soon after all Spain forsook the obedience of Hannibal and the Carthaginians, and fell under the government of the Romans, which they never would have done if these hostages had been dealt with after the counsels and precepts of Machiavelli.

Yet the example of clemency in Scipio Africanus is more notable than this of his father and uncle. After the deaths of his said father and uncle, this young lord full of all generosity and hardiness came to besiege New Carthage in Spain, and got it by assault. Besides the great riches which he found within the town, he found there also a good number of Spanish hostages which they had regained upon the Romans after the death and overthrow of the Scipios and their host. As soon as the town was taken, Scipio had all the hostages brought before him, and wished them to take good courage, and said that they should fear nothing because they were fallen into the power of the Roman people, who loved better to bind men to them by good deeds than by fear, and to join all foreign nations unto them rather by a society than by a sad servitude. After he had thus encouraged them, he dispatched messengers through all Spain, to the end that every man might come there to seek his hostages, and in the meanwhile gave express charge to his treasurer Flaminius to handle them well and honorably. Among other hostages there was a young lady of a great house brought to Scipio, who was of so great beauty that as she passed by she drew each man's regard upon her. This lady was affianced to one Allucius, prince of the Celts. Scipio, taking knowledge of her parents and to whom she was affianced, and that Allucius extremely loved her, sent for them all. Her parents came with a great quantity of gold and silver for her ransom; Allucius came also. They all being present before Scipio, he said to that young prince Allucius:

> "My dear friend, understanding that you ardently love this young lady, as her beauty well merits it, I thought it good to keep her for you, as I would my affianced should be kept for me, if the affairs of the commonweal permitted me to think upon the action of legitimate love. In favor then of your affections, I have preserved your loves inviolate; in recompense whereof I only desire and pray you that henceforth you will be friends unto the Roman people. And if you will credit me as a good man, desirous to follow the traces of my father and uncle, whom you knew, know that in our town there are many like us, and that there is no people in the world which you ought less to desire for your enemies, nor more for a friend."

After Scipio had thus graciously entertained this young prince, he was so filled with shame and joy that presently he prayed the gods that they would acquit to Scipio that great benefit, for he could never do it. The said lady's parents stepped forward and presented to him a great quantity of gold and silver for their daughter's ransom, which though Scipio refused it, they pressed it so sore upon him that he accorded to take it, and bade them lay it before him. Scipio called Allucius and said to him, Good friend, besides the dowry which your father-in-law will give you, my desire is that you will take this silver at my hands as an increase of her dowry. Allucius, very joyful of so great a benefit, thanking him greatly, returned with his lover in great contentment unto his country; where as soon as he came he sowed the fame of those things though all Spain, saying that there was come into that country a young lord like the gods, who vanquishes all men by arms, by clemency, and by magnificence. Within a small time after, he came into the service of Scipio with 1,400 horses; not long after came also to Scipio the parents of the other hostages which he had taken at New Carthage, all which he yielded unto them conditionally to be the Romans' friends. He gave also to a great lord called Mandonius his wife, the sister of another great lord named Indibilis, who were exceedingly joyous thereof, and promised to Scipio all fidelity. Among those prisoners also there was found a young prince called Massiva, the nephew of Massinissa, king of Numidia, whom he sent to his uncle after he had honorably appareled, mounted and accompanied him. This was the cause that Massinissa stuck so firmly to the Roman party, wherein he constantly persevered all his life, and greatly aided Scipio to the overthrow of the Carthaginians. And as for the Spaniards, whose hostages Scipio had sent home without ransom, they performed many great favors to him in all his Spanish wars. Briefly, this great clemency, kindless, and gentleness of Scipio, were the cause that all his high and mighty enterprises were ever facile and easy unto him. But herein appeared in him a double clemency, namely that the two lords abovenamed revolted, and caused all their country to revolt also, upon a false fame of Scipio's death. But after finding the report false, they resolved yet once again to prove his clemency as an assured refuge, and so went and fell on their knees before him, desiring pardon and confessing their faults. Scipio, after he had rebuked them, said unto them:

> "My friends, by your merits you shall die, but you shall live by the benefit of the Roman people; and although the custom is to take all arms from rebels, yet I will not take them from you, but if you fall any more into such a fault, I shall have reason with arms to disarm you. Therefore seeing you have many times experimented with the Romans' clemency, take heed also you prove not their vengeance and wrath."

By this example of Scipio it appears that a prince ought always to be inclined to clemency, whereby he may obtain friends, augment his domination, shun God's indignation, the envy of men, and to do to another what he would have done to himself. This is it which Romulus said to the Antenates and Caeninians, who he had vanquished and subjugated.

"Although you have merited to suffer all extreme things, because you rather loved war against us than our amity, yet many reasons move us to use our victory moderately, in respect of the indignation of the gods, unto whom pride is odious; the fear of the envy and evil will of men; and because we believe that mercy and clemency is a great release and remedy for the miseries and calamities of mortal men, which we would gladly entreat of others in our own distress and calamities. We therefore pardon you this fault, and leave you in the same enjoying of your goods as you were before."

The Roman Senate always had clemency in great recommendation, even towards those who had often rebelled. The Ligurians rose up against the Romans many times, insomuch that they sent against them Marcus Popilius, consul, with a puissant army. Popilius having subjugated and vanquished them, he took their arms from them, dismantled and destroyed their towns, and sold the goods and persons of those who were taken in war. The Senate thought this very hard, to sell so many men who implored the Romans' mercy, and took it to be an evil example to cause their enemies thenceforth in desperate sort to have recourse to arms, rather than to their clemency. So it was ordained that they should be redeemed who were sold, and also that their goods could be recovered; that the Ligurians should also have their arms; and withal Popilius was commanded to return and give over the government to another of Liguria.

Camillus, a Roman general, besieged the town of Falisques, the Romans' enemies. The schoolmaster of Falisques enterprised a great wickedness and villainy; for making a countenance to lead, for sport and pastime, the youth of that town who were committed to him to be instructed, he straight brought them to Camillus' camp, hoping he would give some good recompense, speaking in this manner. "Lord Camillus, I yield into your hands the town of Falisques, for I here bring you their dear and loving children, which to recover they will easily yield themselves to you." To whom Camillus answered,

"Wicked wretch, you do not address yourself to your like. We have by compacts no society with the Falisques, but by nature we have; we are not ignorant of the right of war and of peace, which we will courageously observe. We make not war upon young children, for even when we take towns, we pardon them, so do we also to them who bear arms against us. You would vanquish the Falisques by deceit and villainy, but I will vanquish them by virtue and arms, as I overcame the Veians."

After this, Camillus commanded to bind the schoolmaster's hands behind him, and to give all the scholars rods in their hands, who whipped him naked into the town. As thus in this sort the children brought their master to the town, all the people ran to see the spectacle; which so changed their courage, before full of wrath and hatred against the Romans, that they straight sent delegates to Camillus to desire peace, admiring the Roman clemency and justice. Camillus, knowing that he alone could not enterprise to conclude a peace, sent the delegates towards the Senate of Rome, where on arriving they made this speech.

> "My masters, having been vanquished by an agreeable victory both to gods and men, we yield ourselves to you, knowing that our estate shall be better under your domination than in our own liberties and customs. The issue of this war will serve hereafter for a double example to all mankind, for it seems you better love loyalty in war than present victory. And we, being provoked by your kindness and loyalty, gladly and willingly yield you the victory. We offer ourselves your subjects, and we shall never repent ourselves of your domination, nor you of your loyalty."

The peace and alliance accorded to the Falisques, Camillus entered Rome in triumph, and was more esteemed to be a victor by clemency than if it had been by arms.

He who would here collect so many examples as histories furnish us concerning this matter, would never be done; but I satisfy myself with the most memorable among them. For in a notorious and evident thing, there is no need to insist more amply.

3.23
Machiavelli

A prince ought to have a turning and winding wit, with practice made fit to be cruel and unfaithful, that he may show himself such when there is need. (*The Prince*, chapter 18)

It is good that a prince should appear to be loyal, piteous, liberal, and effectually to be so whenever he sees it is profitable to him. But yet a prince's spirits must be so flexible, so ductile and easy to be led, so handsomely and naturally fitted, and with custom used, that he can do the contrary at all times as needed. For often necessity requires that a prince should show himself disloyal, cruel, fierce, and niggardly.

Answer

The philosophers call habit that promptness and exactness which men acquire by frequent exercise of the actions of every art. As a tailor, by customary exercise of cutting and shaping, obtains a habit and dexterity to know well how to make garments. As an archer in a crossbow or gun, by the frequent exercise of shooting, obtains that habitude to draw well, and to shoot nigh the white. And so it is in all other actions and sciences, every man may get a habitude by frequent exercise. Machiavelli's mind is that it is not sufficient for a prince sometimes to be cruel, perfidious, fierce, covetous, and illiberal; but by frequent exercise of cruelty, perfidy, and greed, he must obtain a habit, promptly, dexterously, and handsomely at his pleasure to practice these goodly virtues at a need; even as an archer or gunner cannot know how handsomely to handle his bow and gun to come near the mark, who has not once or twice before handled them. Because as Aristotle said, one sole action makes not a habitude, no more than one swallow brings a certain assurance of spring's coming. But I pray you, is not this a triumphant doctrine for a prince to be taught? Nay, rather to teach some devil of hell. For since the nature of devils cannot but tend to evil, a man may say that it should be very fit that they had (as I believe they have) Machiavelli to teach them the precepts of the art of wickedness; as this maxim must be one of those whereby he wills that these vicious qualities of cruelty, perfidy, and niggardliness should be in a prince, not as in a habit and perfection. But I will not stand to refute here this maxim, for we have before sufficiently spoken of cruelty and perfidy, and at large demonstrated how unworthy they are for a prince. And as for greed, we shall have occasion to speak of it in another maxim; yet I would desire all persons who have in them any piety and love of virtue, to learn to detest so abominable a doctrine as this which Machiavelli here teaches. For there never was Arabian, Scythian, or Turk who ever taught a more strange and barbarous doctrine as to persuade men to make habitudes of vices. Let us also learn to discern spirits before we believe them; if Machiavelli had been known to be such a man as I hope he shall be deciphered by this discourse, it is likely he should not have done so much harm as he has. And finally, let us thank our good God, who has not permitted that our spirits should be infected with such a corruption as to approve or follow such abhorrent doctrine from piety and reason, and such monstrous and savage opinions. For as Thucydides calls them servants and slaves of absurd opinions, who follow evil counsel sooner than good, as the Athenians often did; so do I believe them to be double, yea centuple slaves and miserable, who suffer their spirits to be persuaded and deluded with the doctrine and impiety of Machiavelli.

3.24
Machiavelli

A prince desirous to break a peace promised and sworn with his neighbor ought to make war against the neighbor's friend. (*Discourses*, book 2 chapter 9)

The prince having made certain capitulations with his neighbor, long established and well observed, fearing to break them directly lest he fall into open war, he must stir his neighbor by taking arms against his neighbor's friend, knowing that the other will feel himself touched when the assault is delivered to his friend and confederate, and will sustain and revenge him, and so shall it seem that he himself is the first provoker of war and breaker of peace.

Answer

Machiavelli, because he has above taught that a prince may always find colors enough to palliate and cover the infraction of faith, now gives a rule saying that to palliate a rupture of peace or confederation, he must assail his confederate's friend. We have before amply disputed against these subtle palliations, and have showed by many examples that the issue has always proved evil to those who use them. And surely such subtleties are not only most unworthy of a generous prince, but also of all other men; and by laws he is no less punishable who has done wrong to a man by subtlety than if he had done it by force.

The ancient Romans, by the form and course they had to make considerations and peace with their neighbors, showed well how far they were from this doctrine of Machiavelli. For the Pater Patratus, who was the stipulator or master of ceremonies or arbiter of peace, after all articles accorded and oaths taken, pronounced at great height these words: "The first of the two people who breaks the peace, be it by deliberate counsel or by subtle deceit, grant O Jupiter that the same day he may be bruised and beaten, as now with this flint stone I bruise this pig." Briefly, they no less detested the rupture of a peace made by a subtlety than if it had been made by an open war. They also held it for a certain thing that always the evil fortunes of a renewed war fell upon them who had broken the peace. But because we have above discoursed upon this matter, we will pass on to the next maxim.

3.25
Machiavelli

A prince ought to have his mind disposed to turn after every wind and variation of fortune, so he may know to make use of a vice when needed. (*The Prince*, chapter 18, 25)

A good thing is not always profitable nor in season, and often a prince who would practice it shall thereby draw on his own destruction. For sometimes it falls out that necessarily he must use vice and that which is evil. Therefore a wise prince ought to take great heed to the time and to the wind-like variation of fortune, and ought to know how to serve himself with a vice for his profit and advantage, when times require it. Otherwise, if he always follows virtue and the good, there are seasons so contrary, by the chance of fortune, that immediately he will fall into ruin.

Answer

Because a prince who has been nourished in virtue, as he reads Machiavelli might find some difficulty in believing him, and esteem that it should evil become him altogether to despoil himself of virtue and put on vice; for this cause Machiavelli, desirous to resolve this doubt, shows here that it is not uncomely for a prince to change from virtue to vice. And to encourage him to make this change, he says that sometimes such a time and season may happen when it is necessary for a prince to know how to use a vice to serve fortune's turn, which commonly opposes virtue. Yet there is no man of so small judgment that sees not with his eyes that this doctrine contains two points altogether wicked. One, to say it is necessary to a prince, for the conservation of his estate, to use vice. The other, to approve and allow lightness and inconstancy of manners, by changing good into evil. As for the first point, we have heretofore amply handled it, where we have showed that good princes, given to virtue, have always prospered in their estates; but contrary the wicked, who exceeded in vices, have always had hard fortunes and evil haps in their kingdoms, and have come to unlucky ends. As for the other point, inconstancy, we must here touch in a few words.

I will then presuppose that constancy is a quality which ordinarily accompanies all other virtues; it is, as it were, of their substance and nature. Therefore justice is defined as a constant will to yield to every man that which belongs unto him. And temperance may also be defined as a constant moderation to use well all things; and prudence may also be defined as a constant provision in all affairs, and so of all other virtues. Hereupon I make this illation, since constancy is of the nature and substance of all virtues, and as it were mixed among them, it follows that he who is inconstant can have no virtue in him, for virtue goes not without constancy. Machiavelli also, as beastly as he is, so understood this, for by degrees going about to lead a prince and all who follow his doctrine to a sovereign wickedness (as philosophers lead men to a sovereign good), he has considered that he must make his foundation inconstancy. For an inconstant man disposed to turn with all winds can never be but full of all forms of vices, and void of all virtue; because in virtue there can fall out no change nor variation, since all virtues accord and agree among themselves. But among vices there may be changes, inconstancies, and variations, because often they are contrary and hold the places of extremes. As for example, avarice and prodigality are contrary vices, as also are temerity and cowardice, ignorance and malicious subtlety, cruelty and dissolute lenity, ambition and spite of honor, and so of other vices. Inconstancy then may well perch among vices, flitting and moving from one to another; but among virtues she can find no place, because as I have said, they all naturally so hold on constancy, that without it they cannot be virtues. Machiavelli then was not anything deceived, when thinking to lead a prince unto a sovereignty of wickedness, he furnishes him with inconstancy and mutability as the winds. For as soon as the prince shall clothe himself with Proteus' garments, and has no hold nor certitude of his word, nor in his actions, men may well say that his malady is incurable, and that in all vices he has taken the nature of the chameleon. At the hands of such a prince who is inconstant, variable in his word, mutable in actions and commands, there is nothing to be hoped for but evil, disorder, and confusion.

How much the more notable and worthy to be engraved in princes' hearts is that sentence of Scipio the African; that they are vanquishers, who being vanquished give place to fortune. But the better to understand this, I will set down the occasion of this notable speech. After Scipio, his father, and uncle were overthrown with most of their army in Spain, the day having come when they elected their magistrates in Rome, none dared hazard himself to demand the government of Spain. And because none did it, they esteemed the affairs of the commonweal to be in a deplorable and desperate state. Young lord Scipio, only 22, arose and demanded the government of Spain, showing by a grave oration full of magnanimity and assured constancy that his carriage would be good, and that they need not fear that in regard of his young age there should be found in him any temerity, for he would do nothing but by good counsel. And although the name of Scipio might seem unlucky in that his father and uncle had been vanquished and slain in Spain, he doubted not but to turn the chance of fortune. Briefly, by a great and favorable consent of all the people he was chosen governor of Spain and general captain of the Roman army. As soon as he was in this estate and well assured of his virtues, he began to speak with such a majesty and constancy that all men became fully resolved that he would well acquit himself of this charge, to the honor and benefit of the common weal. In Spain he convocated the old bands which remained after the defeat of his father and uncle, giving them thanks for the fidelity they had borne and for receiving him joyfully as their captain, although he was young of age; for the good hope they had of him, who was of the race of their dead captains; and that he would so well perform his duty that they should truly know that he was of the race of their dead captains. The public fortune (said he) of the Roman commonweal and your virtue must keep us from all despair of our affairs. For this good luck has ever been fatally given us, being vanquished in our great war, yet ever notwithstanding to remain victors, by resisting by constancy and virtue all malignity of fortune.

Another time long after, speaking to Zeusis and Antipater, ambassadors of the king Antiochus, who demanded peace from him after he had been vanquished, Scipio used these words full of gravity and wisdom.

> "The peace which you demand now that you are vanquished, we agree unto you, with like conditions as you offered before our victory. For in all fortune, good or evil, we have always the same courage; neither can prosperity exalt us, nor adversity humble us too much. And if you yourselves were not good witnesses thereof, I would cite no other testimony than that of Hannibal, who is in your army. Therefore make known unto the king your master, that we accord unto him the same peace which we offered him before our victory."

Here may you see how constant the Romans were in virtue, without any change either in prosperity or adversity. Here is no Machiavelizing, we must not go to the school of Scipio, nor of the ancient Romans, nor of any other valiant princes to learn Machiavelli's doctrine of having an inconstant and mutable courage, to change and to turn as the wind. This must be learned in the school of a sort of Italian Machiavellians, resembling harlots who love every man yet love no person, and who with doubtful and unstayed minds run here and there like tops.

We commonly say that the king is the living law of his subjects, and that the prince ought to serve for a rule to his people. But is it not a ridiculous thing to say that the law ought to be a thing inconstant and mutable with every wind? On the contrary, the law ought to be firm, constant, permanent, inviolable, and inviolably observed, else it is not law. And therefore among all mortal men the prince is he who ought to be most constant and firm, to show that he is the true and living law of his people and subjects, unto whom his carriage and actions ought to serve for a rule. A prince then must be of one word, and take heed that he be not mutable nor double of his promises, and that he always have a magnanimous and generous courage, tending to virtue and the public good of his kingdom and principality, and that no trouble nor adversity may abate that generosity and constancy of courage, nor any prosperity make him swell with pride, whereby to draw him from virtue. In a constant course he must show himself grave and clement, and these two should be in him with a temperature. Such gravity is requisite for the majesty of his calling, with such clemency and affability as his subjects desire in him. In all his actions he must always show himself to be one man, loving and amiably entertaining men of virtue and of service, and always rejecting vicious people, flatterers, liars, and other like, from which he can never draw out good services. Finally, he ought to be constant in retaining his good friends and servants, and not take a sinister opinion of them without great and apparent causes, and in all things govern himself constantly, by good counsel, and be master of himself, that is to say, of his affections and opinions, to direct them always to good and sage counsel, such as were those great Roman monarchs Augustus Caesar, Vespasian, Trajan, Hadrian, the Antonines, Alexander Severus, Constantine the Great, Theodosius, and other like. Such before them were the great Darius, king of the Persians and Medes, conqueror of the monarchy of Africa; the great king Cyrus, and Alexander the Great. Such also were the ancient kings of France; the great Clovis, the generous Charlemagne, the good Saint Louis, Philip August the conqueror, Charles the Wise, Charles VII, the victorious Louis XII, Francis the great reformer of letters, Henri II, and many others. These are they that a prince must propose to imitate, not those of no account, who do not deserve a place among princes, such as Agathocles, a potter's son and usurper of the Sicilian tyranny; or Oliver de Fermo, a barbarous and most cruel soldier who massacred his own parents and friends to usurp the tyranny of the place of his nativity; or that Cesare Borgia the pope's bastard, full of all disloyalty, cruelty, inconstancy, and other vices, and far from all royal virtues, who Machiavelli proposes for patterns to be imitated by princes. Reasonless creatures themselves, do they not show that a prince ought to be constant, to maintain his subjects in peace and tranquility, without stirs or motions? The king of honey bees, is he not always resident and abiding in his hive with constancy, to keep his little subjects in tranquility? And whenever among these small creatures there are found some inconstant and straying kings, who cannot abide in their hives and within the circuit and limits of their power, do we not see that they bring all their little people out of order? For straight as their king begins to stir and go out, his subjects remove withal; so that often by the removing of the king, he himself is lost with all the troupe of little subjects; by precipitation and headlong casting himself, by his inconstancy, into marshes and pools where both he and his are lost. Princes, then, and all others must learn from these petty creatures how necessary constancy is to them; that being inconstant and variable (as Machiavelli teaches) they cannot fail to destroy and ruin themselves and others.

Hereupon is very worthy to be noted what Euripides said, that a good and virtuous man never changes his manners for the change of either air or country, neither for prosperity nor adversity; his verses Englished are these:

> An evil ground under a heaven serene,
> good store of corn ofttimes doth bring, we see:
> good ground also, with a sharp air I ween,
> bad store of fruit produces unto thee:
> yet by the heavens a good man or an ill,
> his nature change will not for any hap:
> for always wicked, wicked prooveth still,
> and good men, good will prove, for evil clap
> in good men's hearts there's no adversity,
> in life of his can breed diversity.

And assuredly this fashion of the Machiavellians, to change manners with each wind, cannot be found any way good by good and virtuous men who have their hearts in a good place; no more than they can approve the rhyming verses which the Machiavellians always have in their mouths: "When thou at Rome, a Roman life then must thou lead; when other where, do as they do, in the other stead." For these manners are proper to the chameleon, which takes all colors of the place where he is, and of the polypus, which always seems to be of the color of the earth whereupon it shines. But this is not convenient nor comely for a good man, who ought always to be constant in virtue, without changing or varying, no not though the heavens should fall upon him. But because the poet Horace very elegantly describes what kind of person a constant man ought to be, I will set it down as an end of this maxim.

> So constant is a good man always in his life,
> that he stirs not for all the people's rage and strife:

The tyrants fierce cannot move him, nor boisterous wind
which all the sea doth turn: nor thunder claps I find:
His constant virtue cannot alter any way,
No though the heavens should fall upon his head, I say
No fear could touch his haughty heart, by night or day.

3.26
Machiavelli

Illiberality is commendable in a prince, and the reputation of a
tradesman or handicrafts man is a dishonor without evil will. (*The
Prince*, chapter 8, 16)

If the prince will be liberal, he soon impoverishes himself, and being
poor shall be despised by every man. And if he will repair and help his
poverty by pilling his subjects, he shall make himself hated by them and
will be reputed a tyrant. But contrary, being greedy he shall be judged
puissant, and having wherewith to furnish any affair when it happens,
he shall be honored and esteemed. And if the reputation of a tradesman
or illiberal person be dispersed of him, this cannot be hurtful, seeing he
seeks nothing at his subjects' hands by force. Yet a prince may well be
prodigal of another's goods, as of booty acquired by war, as Cyrus,
Alexander, and Caesar; but of his own he ought to be a holder and
illiberal. For there is nothing that more consumes itself than largesse and
freeness of giving, which by the practicing thereof loses the means to be
practiced. In our time we have seen so many great matters effected, but
by such men as had the reputation to be greedy; all others have come to
nothing. Pope Julius was liberal till he obtained the popedom, but as
soon as he had gotten it he forsook that trade, to the end to make war
upon Louis XII of France, as he did. The king of Spain likewise
understood that king Ferdinand (grandfather of the emperor Charles V)
had not so happily achieved so many great enterprises, if he had affected
to be esteemed liberal.

Answer

In my opinion this maxim should not please courtiers, either
Machiavellians or others; who like best that a prince be not only liberal,
but rather profuse and prodigal, so far are they from the opinion that he
should be covetous. But certainly as illiberality and greed is damnable
and no way beseeming a prince, so also is profusion and prodigality; but
most praiseworthy it is that he hold a course between both, and that he

be liberal, acknowledging the services done to him, and to be bountiful toward good and virtuous people, and for the advancement of the commonwealth. For that is true liberality when men employ to good uses the goods and gifts dispensed, and not when they employ them to evil uses. But to show how liberality ought to be exercised in a prince, we will first speak of illiberality and prodigality, its two extremes.

As for greed, which Machiavelli holds to be fitting for a prince, it is certain that there is nothing in the world which makes him more contemptible and spited than it does. For of itself it is odious in all men, because it is filthy and mechanical; but especially in princes, who being constituted in a more ample and opulent fortune than other men, ought also to show themselves more liberal, and further removed from illiberality and greed. The emperor Galba, otherwise a good and sage prince, but suffering himself to be governed by some about him who were ravenous and covetous, always being too hard to his soldiers, thus destroyed and defiled all his virtues. But what is more, the greed and rapines of his officers brought him into contempt and caused him to be slain by his soldiers. The emperor Pertinax was one of the most wise and moderate princes that ever was, and who a man might say was irreproachable and a very father of the people. He always studied every way to comfort his subjects; but he was so spotted and defiled with that vice of greed, that he thereby became so hated and contemned by his soldiers that they slew him. The emperor Mauricius was a very niggard; so great was his greed that he delighted in nothing but heaping up treasure, and would spend nothing. Whereby every man took occasion to blame and despise him; his great store of treasure made his lieutenant Phocas, otherwise a man of no account and a coward, but as greedy as his master, slay him to obtain the empire. But yet Phocas coming to the empire continued in greed more than ever was found in Maruicius, and respected nothing but heaping up treasure by rapines and extortions, without any care of the government of the empire. This miserable greed and carefulness was the cause of his own ruin and the entire dissipation of the Roman Empire; for during his government were cut off Germany, Gaul, Spain, most of Italy, Slavonia, Mesia, most of Africa, Armenia, Arabia, Macedonia, Thrace, Assyria, Mesopotamia, Egypt, and many other countries. Some cut themselves from the empire, others were occupied by the king of Persia and other potentates; which was an exceedingly evil hap, and very memorable, that thus the Roman Empire should fall in pieces by means of this emperor's greed.

This happened not alone to Phocas, for the like fell to king Perseus of Macedonia. This king, having enterprised war upon the Romans, gathered together great store of treasures; but when it came to be distributed to have soldiers, he showed himself as holding and greedy as was possible. Having asked the Gauls for soldiers, for a certain sum of money, he refused to deliver them silver when they came; excusing himself among his people that it was dangerous to receive so many strangers in his country, for fewer would serve him. The Gauls seeing themselves thus mocked by this king returned, spoiling all his country as they passed; and after, the Romans vanquished Perseus and got all his treasures, which he lost along with his crown and his life; and all this fell unto him by his greed.

Marcus Crassus, a Roman citizen worth 350,000 crowns per annum, was yet so greedy that on seeing Lucullus enriching himself in the Levant war, never ceased till he had obtained commission to make war upon the Parthians. And what incited him most to purchase that charge was that he heard say that Pompey (who had made war there not long before) had good means to heap up great treasures, if he had wanted; that he might have pillaged the temple of Jerusalem, where the treasures of the sacred vessels and of the widows and orphans amounted to the sum of two thousand talents, or five million crowns. So Crassus resolved to rob that temple to redouble his riches, and therein not to be so scrupulous as Pompey had been. And so indeed, Crassus passing by Jerusalem against the Parthians pillaged the temple, and to himself appropriated all that treasure, which was partly the goods and substance of poor widows and orphans. Crassus going on came to Armenia, and from thence came to the Parthians, where he gave battle to king Herod, or rather to his lieutenant Surena. But Crassus losing the battle, where his only son was slain, escaped on foot, thinking to save himself; which he could not do, but in the end was overtaken and slain. His head was carried to Herod, who with it served himself in a tragedy played before him, where they talked of a hunter who had slain a great savage beast. Here may you see the tragic end of this insatiable greedy wretch Crassus, who was justly and soon punished for this great and horrible sacrilege which he had committed in the holy temple of Jerusalem.

By these examples then it is evidently seen that greed is customarily the cause of the ruin of such princes and great lords as are infected therewith; so far is it off that it is profitable, as Machiavelli says. Yet true it is that there have been some, but very few who being covetous yet have not been ruined by that vice, as the emperor Vespasian; but the reason why his covetousness was not the cause of his destruction is because he exercised it not else but upon his ravenous magistrates, and because he employed on good uses and for the utility of the public good such money as his avarice heaped up; yea, he even practiced great liberalities towards good people, and ruined cities to rebuild them.

Surely if those reasons are well considered they will serve Vespasian for an allowable excuse, if it so be that a vice can be anything excused; for first there was no great harm that he should draw water from such sponges, who had sucked up the substance of the people, and to cause them to disgorge and cast up the booties whereof they were full. And in my opinion there would be no harm if they did the like today, for what harm is there to take from a thief? The other excuse is yet more considerable; that Vespasian did not employ the silver which his greed had collected upon his own pleasures and delights, but bestowed it on good uses for the good of the commonwealth. And certainly there is nothing that more troubles subjects who pay tributes than when they see that the prince spends badly the silver levied upon them; who would more liberally furnish him with a crown than they would with a penny, if they saw their money well bestowed. Our king Louis was herein something like Vespasian; for he levied much money upon his subjects, even triple what his predecessors had, but he spent it not upon his pleasures and delights, nor other dissoluteness, nor in practice of liberality upon unworthy people, but upon good things about the affairs of the kingdom; as to buy peace with his neighbors, and to corrupt foreigners who might serve therein or in others' affairs. Moreover, he did not as the emperor Mauricius, or as king Perseus, who heaped up great treasures and then dared not touch it; for as Commines says, he took all and spent all.

Princes then who levy money upon their people are somewhat excusable when they employ it upon good uses; and especially when they have that discretion to pill the pillagers, and to ransack thieves and eaters of the poor, and spare other good subjects who are not of that sort. But such as make great levies and bestow them badly, they cannot be anything excused in their greed and prodigality. The emperor Caligula on succeeding Tiberius found an inestimable treasure, even 67,500,000 crowns. To calculate this unmeasurable sum after the proportion of 1,240,000 crowns, which made the 32 mule loads which were sent for the ransom of Francis I, it should be found that the 67 million of Caligula should make about 1,800 mule loads, which is a huge and most admirable treasure. Yet this monster spent all this in less than a year. But was this possible, you will say, that such great heaps should be laid out in so little space? Yea, I say, for this brainless fool caused houses to be built upon the sea, and only where men said it was deepest. To make good foundations there, he was forced to cast in great heaps of stones, as great as high mountains; for so much as anything was impossible, so much the more he loved to do it. Moreover, he delighted to bring down mountains and rocks, to equal them with flats and plains, and in plains to erect mountains; this must be done even the very day he commanded it, upon pain of life. He also had baths to be made in waters of very precious scents; he would make prodigal banquets served with excellent pearls and other precious stones, which he had liquified and dissolved so that they might be drunk. He had ships made of Lebanon cedars, whose sterns were all covered with pearls, and within them were built baths, galleries, halls, and orchards; and there sitting among dancers and players of instruments he had himself carried about the coasts of Campania. By these unmeasurable and monstrous expenses, he saw the end of that great treasure in less than a year. Hereof came it that lacking silver he converted himself to rapines, and to lay great and new taxes upon victuals, processes, laborers' salaries, harlots' gains, players' gains, and upon many such like things. And so having again gathered huge heaps of crowns, upon a covetous pride to touch and handle money he delighted to walk barefoot and tumble upon it. By this means and with cruelty and other vices he was hated by all the world, and soon slain. And in truth he was inexcusable for inventing new and great taxes upon his people, seeing he so badly employed the money.

Nero likewise laid great taxes and levies of money upon his subjects, and quashed and voided the wills of those who would not make him their heir. As an ingrate person this prince by force took treasures out of temples and committed infinite other extortions; but how did he spend all this money? In making sumptuous banquets, as Caligula did; in giving unmeasurable gifts to flatterers and bad people, and upon other strange dissoluteness. He always appareled himself with exceeding rich and precious habits, yet he never wore a garment twice; he played away great sums of money at once; he fished with golden nets with purple and scarlet cords; he never went abroad with less than a thousand coaches or litters drawn with mules, whose shoes were of silver, and muleteers gallantly and costly appareled. His wife Sabina Poppea had her coaches drawn with gold cords and filled with furniture of gold; whenever she went abroad she bathed in the milk of five hundred she-asses. Briefly, Nero made so great and riotous expenses that no silver could suffice; spoiling his provinces of their goods and riches by rapines and taxes, and practicing great cruelties (for rapine and cruelty are always companions), he brought upon himself the hatred of all the world, and came to a miserable end, as we have above said.

The like happened to emperor Vitellius, who in a year spent in banquets nine million crowns. Dion says that in a vessel served at his table he had so many tongues, brains, and livers of certain strange and exquisite fishes and birds, as cost ten thousand crowns. Suetonius says that his brother bestowed a supper upon him whereat was served two thousand exquisite fishes, and seven thousand precious birds, besides all other services. These so exorbitant and unreasonable expenses drew him into greed, rapine, and cruelty, which was the cause that he was slain, having reigned but a year and ten days.

Here might I add to these the examples of Domitian, Commodus, Bassianus, and many other Roman emperors who held the two extremities of liberality, covetousness, and prodigality, using rapine to heap up silver and profusion to spend it; all which had the same end as Nero, Caligula, and Vitellius had. But hereby is sufficiently showed in those examples the contrary of the maxim Machiavelli says is true; and that a prince who is covetous and hard cannot prosper, but especially when he naughtily bestows the treasures and money which he heaps up. Now there remains to show that liberality is profitable and necessary for a prince, when he applies it to good uses.

When Alexander the Great departed from Macedonia to go to the conquest of Asia, he had all the captains of his army appear before him and distributed to them almost all the revenue of his kingdom, leaving himself almost nothing. One of the captains, named Perdicas, said to him: "What then will you keep for yourself?" "Even hope," answered Alexander. "We then shall have our part thereof, since we go with you." Thus Perdicas and others refused the gifts which their king offered them, and were as thankful as if they had accepted them. They accompanied him in his voyage into Asia full of good will to serve him, as they did. For he was so well served by these valiant Macedonians, his subjects, that with them he conquered almost all Asia. So the liberality of Alexander was very profitable unto him.

The ancient Romans customarily increased the dominations of their allies, as they did to Massinissa, king of Numidia, to whom they gave a great part of the neighboring kingdom of Syphax and some part of the country of the Carthaginians, after they had vanquished them and Syphax. As also they did to Eumenes, king of Pergamus in Asia, unto whom they gave all they conquered from king Antiochus beyond Mount Taurus, which came to more than four times as much as all Eumenes' kingdom. They also practiced great liberalities towards Ptolomeus, king of Cyprus; towards Attalus, another king of Pergamus; towards Hiero, king of Sicily, and many others. And what profit they got by all this — even this, that in the end all the countries and kingdoms fell into the Romans' hands, either by succession and testamentary ordinance of those kings, or by the will of the people, or otherwise. And this reputation of liberality which the Romans acquired was the cause that the kings and potentates of the world affected and so greatly desired their amity and alliance. Sulla's lieutenant Marius, making war upon

king Jugurtha, persuaded Bocchus, king of Mauritania, to take part with
the Romans against Jugurtha, because (said he) the Romans are never
weary with vanquishing by beneficence, but always enrich their friends
and allies.

Augustus Caesar, seeing the many enemies he had gotten by civil war,
knew not whether he should put them all to death, or what to do. For on
one side he considered that if he caused them all to die, the world would
think that either he was entering into the butchery of a civil war, or else
to usurp a tyranny. And on the other side he feared that some mischief
would happen unto him if he suffered them to live. His wife Livia, a
good and sage lady, showed him that he ought to gain his enemies by
liberality and beneficence. He followed this counsel and began with
Cornelius, the nephew of Pompey, whom he advanced into the office of
consul; and in like sort to others whom he took to be his enemies, he was
so bountiful that he gained all their hearts. But because the remonstrance
which Livia made to Augustus is very memorable, I will here summarily
recite it.

"I am very sorrowful, my most dear lord and spouse, to see you thus
grieved and tormented in your spirit, so that your sleep is taken from
you. I am not ignorant that you have great occasions, because of many
enemies still lamenting the deaths of friends and parents slain during
those civil wars; and that a prince cannot so well govern but there will
always be malcontents and complainers. Moreover, the change of estate
you have brought to the commonwealth by reducing it to a monarchy,
means that a man cannot well assure himself of those he esteems his
friends. Yet I beseech you, my good lord, to excuse me if I am a simple
woman to take the hardiness to tell you my advice upon this matter;
which is, that I think there is nothing impossible to repress by soft and
gentle means. For the natures of those who are inclined to do evil are
sooner subdued and corrected by using clemency and beneficence
towards them, rather than severity. For princes who are courteous and
merciful make themselves not only agreeable and honorable to them
upon whom they bestow mercy, but also towards all others. And on the
contrary, those who are inflexible and will not abate their rigor are hated
and blamed not only by them towards whom he shows himself such, but
by all others also. See you not, my good lord, that seldom or never do
physicians cut sick members off the body, but seek to heal them by soft
and gentle medicaments. In like sort are maladies of the spirit to be
healed; and the gentle medicaments of the spirit may well be called
affability and soft words of princes towards everyone, his clemency and
placability, his mercy and debonairity, not towards wicked and bad
persons who make an occupation to do evil, but towards those who have
offended by youth, imprudence, ignorance, by chance, by constraint, or
who have some excuse. It is also very requisite in a prince not only to do
no wrong to any person, but also to be reputed such a man as will never

do wrong to any man; because that is the means to have the amity and benevolence of men, which a prince can never obtain unless he persuades them that he will do well to the good, and that he will do wrong to no one. For fear may well be acquired with force, but amity cannot be obtained but by persuasion. So that if it please you, my lord, to use benefits and liberality towards those you esteem your enemies and those who fear you, you will easily gain them and others henceforth for your friends."

This remonstrance of Livia was the cause that Augusts let loose and set at liberty all them who were accused to have enterprised anything against him, satisfying himself with the admonishments he gave them, and besides gave great goods and benefits unto some of them, so that as well those as others of his enemies became his friends and good subjects. Behold here what good came to Augustus by his beneficence and liberality.

Marcus Aurelius feared nothing more than the reputation of a hard and greedy man, and always wished and desired that such a spot of infamy might never be imposed upon him. And indeed all his carriage and actions were such that none could impute to him any spot of greed, but all liberality worthy of a good prince; for first he established public professors of all sciences in Athens, unto whom he gave great wages, which proved a most profitable act to the common weal, worthy of such a prince. And this was partly the cause that in his time there was so great a store of learned people in all manner of sciences; insomuch that the time of his kingdom was and has since been called the golden world. In our time Francis I imitated the example of this great and wise emperor, establishing public lectures at great wages in the University of Paris, a thing whereof his memory has been and shall be more celebrated through the world than for so many great wars he valiantly sustained during his reign. Secondly, Aurelius forgave the people all the fiscal debts and arrears which they owed him going back fifty years, which was a huge and unspeakable liberality. But he did this to take away all means and matter from officers and fiscal procurators, of molesting and troubling his subjects afterward with researches and calling of old debts. Thirdly, he never laid a tax or extraordinary exaction upon his people, but handled them in all kindness and generosity; he never made profuse and superfluous expenses, but held an estate both at home and in the court, sober and full of frugality. And finally, to show how he delighted in liberality, he had a temple built to Beneficence.

Behold here a true pattern after which princes should conform themselves to know how to practice that goodly virtue liberality. And very notable is that point that Aurelius held the estate of his house ruled by frugality and sobriety, and far from the strange profusions of those monsters, Caligula, Nero, and Vitellius. For he considered that it was much better to employ revenues for the public wealth of his empire, rather than in riotousness and vanities; and that such unmeasurable profusion constrained a prince to rapines, and to deal evil with his subjects, because (as the common proverb says) unmeasurable largesse has no bottom. Therefore did that great emperor Trajan also hold his estate soberly governed, and he maintained no unprofitable persons in his service. No more did the emperor Severus, who would not suffer in any offices any persons to be placed who were not necessary. They also had good salaries and rewards from him; he would often rebuke them for not demanding gifts from him. "And why," said he, "would you have it that I should be your debtor, seeing you ask me nothing." Hadrian also had this prosperity, that he gave great gifts to his good friends and servants, and made them rich before they demanded anything. And above all, he was liberal towards professors of letters and learned men, who he enriched; but he much hated those who by evil means became rich; and generally all good emperors were adorned with the virtues of liberality and munificence, which they practiced with such moderation and prudence that they were never spotted, neither with Machiavelli's greed, nor his prodigality. And therefore they flourished and prospered during their reigns, and left after them a perpetual memory to posterity of their virtues and praises.

Our kings of France, as Clovis, Charlemagne, Louis the Piteous his son, Robert, Henri I, Louis le Gros, Louis VIII, Saint Louis, and many others were very liberal, but they exercised their liberality and principality upon the Church and churchmen, who they too much enriched. Yet we read that Charlemagne was also very liberal towards learned men, and that he spent much in founding and maintaining the University of Paris. And a man may generally mark in our kings of France a Christian liberality which they have always had, that is, that they have been great almoniers, exercising their liberality upon poor people, which is an exercise of that virtue worthy of a Christian prince, which he should never forget.

By this I hope the maxim of Machiavelli is sufficiently refuted, and that it evidently appears by our examples and reasons that greed is damaging and dishonorable to a prince, as also is its contrary, profusion, and that liberality is profitable and honorable unto him. And as for the reasons which Machiavelli alleges, they are as foolish and false as his maxim. For to say that a rich prince shall be esteemed puissant because he has great treasures is a bad conclusion. King Perseus of Macedonia had great treasures, yet was esteemed pusillanimous and of small valor, and such was his reputation in his own country and among his own subjects.

Crassus also was known to be richer than Pompey, but he was not esteemed so valiant nor so good a man, neither in his life had he the tenth part of Pompey's honors. Maruicius and Phocas by their greed heaped up great treasures, but were they therefore esteemed puissant and valiant? Nay contrary, they were esteemed cowards, and in the catalog of such emperors as held the most abject and infamous places.

But I pray you let us come to the reason. When a prince has the fame to be a great treasurer, does he not give his neighbor occasion to seek means to enterprise upon him to obtain those treasures? Why is it that the Venetians, who if they wanted might be the greatest treasurers in the world, have made a law among them to have no treasure in their commonwealth other than of arms? It is because they know well (as they are wise) that if they heap up treasures of money, they shall but prepare a bait to draw their neighbors on to make war upon them. But wars come too soon, and under the pretext of more occasions than we would, therefore we need no baits to draw them upon us. It is not then best for a prince to be reputed a man full of treasures and silver, as Machiavelli thinks; for money of itself cannot but serve us for a bait to attract and draw upon us those who are hungry and desirous of it. And although commonly money is thought to be the sinews of war, yet it is not so necessary that without it war cannot be made. I will not here cite the poor Huguenot soldiers, who most commonly warred without wages; I will only cite the military estate which was in the Roman Empire in Valentinian's time, and ever since. For in that time the military art was so policied that every soldier took for a month so much bread, so much wine, so much lard, and so much of other necessary things. His habits also were new from term to term, and all other things necessary, so that he touched little or no money, yet had all he wanted. And indeed money serves but for commutation; for men cannot eat it, nor apparel themselves with it, nor if he is sick can it heal him. Wherefore then serves it? For a prompt, quick, and easy commutation. For if you have money, you straight have whatever you need. If then by other means and policy order be taken that a soldier have all he needs, it will be found that money makes not a prince puissant. Moreover, I confess that it is certain that in the military policy which we have at this day — which is that a soldier shall receive in money all he needs — that money is very necessary, and that without it a man can do no great thing; and it is as sinews, or as the maintenance of the sinews of war, but yet by good husbandry a prince may have enough of it, and without covetousness.

As for what Machiavelli makes no account of, that a prince be reputed to be a tradesman, I leave it to them who have (I will not say) the heart of a prince, but only of a simple gentleman, that has honor but in little recommendation, if they would not be grieved to be reputed a tradesperson. I know well that the nobility of Italy, who more commonly trade and deal with merchandise than with arms, care not for that name of tradesman, if so they may get money. But the gentlemen of France, of Germany, of England, and of other countries of Christendom are not of the humor of that mechanic nobility, neither would they for anything in the world be so reputed, as Machiavelli would persuade them.

And as for the examples which Machiavelli cites of pope Julius and Ferdinand of Spain, who he says were covetous yet effected great matters; I answer him in one word, that it proves nothing of what he says. For Julius made no great prowess nor conquests, as every man knows; and Ferdinand in his exploits and enterprises of wars was not covetous, from anything we read in histories. And if that were true which Machiavelli says of those two, I will oppose against those two obscure examples the ones above cited, which are far more illustrious and notable, and by which I have showed that greed has always been pernicious to princes, and liberality without profusion profitable and honorable.

For a resolution then of this matter, I say that the vice of ingratitude ordinarily accompanies greed, and that none can be covetous and illiberal unless he prove ingrate to his friends and good servants, which is one of the greatest vices wherewith a prince can be noted. For it is impossible that his affairs can be well governed without good and loyal ministers and servants, such as he never can have being ingrate. Therefore a prince ought well to engrave perpetually in his memory the sentence of king Bochus, who said it was less dishonorable for a prince to be vanquished by arms than by munificence. And therefore that good emperor Titus, whenever he passed a day without exercising some liberality and beneficence, said to his friends: "O my friends, I have lost this day"; meaning that it was the chief mark at which a prince should shoot, to wit, beneficence, and that otherwise he employs his time badly.

3.27
Machiavelli

A prince who will make a straight profession of a good man cannot long endure in this world, in the company of so many others that are so bad. (*The Prince*, chapter 15)

Many have written books to instruct a prince and to bring him to perfection in all virtues, as Xenophon did at the institution of Cyrus.

There are also philosophers and others who have formed ideas and figures of monarchies and commonwealths, whereof there were never seen the like in the world, because there is a great difference between the manner in which the world lives and the manner in which it ought to live. He who will amuse and stick upon the forms of philosophers, monarchs, and commonwealths, by despising what is done and praising what ought to be done, shall sooner learn his own ruin than his conservation. Leaving behind all that can be imagined of a prince's perfection, and staying ourselves upon that which is true and subject to be practiced, by experience I say that the prince who will maintain himself ought to learn how he may sometimes not be good, and so ought to practice according to the exigencies of his affairs. For if always he will hold a straight profession of a good man, he cannot long endure in the company of so many others who are of no value.

Answer

This maxim merits no other refutation than that which results from the points handled before; for we have at large demonstrated that the truth is clean contrary to what Machiavelli says here, and that princes who have been good men have always reigned long and peaceably, and have been firm and assured in their estates. And the wicked have not reigned long, but have violently been deposed from their estates. And as for ideas and forms of perfect monarchs and commonwealths, whereof some philosophers have written, they handled not that subject by saying there were any such, but proposed a pattern of imitation for monarchs and government of commonwealths. For when a man will propose a pattern to imitate, he must form it the most perfect and make it the best he can; and after, every man who gives himself to imitate it must come as near it as he can, some nearer, others less. But a prince who proposes to himself Machiavelli's patterns, such as Cesare Borgia, Oliver de Fermo, Agathocles, how can he do any good thing or approach to any good, seeing the patterns hold nothing thereof? Patterns then which men propose to imitate must be set down as best as can be, so that if in our imitation we happen to err from a perfect image of virtue, yet we may in some sort express it in our manners. But what means Machiavelli when he says that men must leave behind what authors have written of a prince's perfection, to draw us unto that which is nowadays practiced? What is this but in a word to tell us we must leave the good precepts of virtue, to abide and stay ourselves upon vices and tyranny. For those who have written of a prince's perfection have set down nothing which may not well be practiced, and if a prince cannot fully do and practice all the precepts which are written, he may at least practice part of them, one more, another less. But we must not say that if a prince cannot be perfect, that therefore he must altogether forsake and cast off all virtue and goodness, and take up tyranny and vice. For as Horace says:

> He that in highest place cannot abide,
> Let not the meanest place him be denied.

So that it seems Machiavelli knows not what he should say, when he holds that we must not stay upon what authors have written of a prince's perfection, but upon what is practiced and in use. For if he means that vice alone is in use, he then gives wicked counsel and advice; and if he will confess that good and virtue is in use and practice, then it will follow that we must not reject what is written of a prince's perfection, although a man cannot come to the perfection thereof; for always it is good and praiseworthy to come as near thereunto as we can.

And touching what Machiavelli says, that a prince who is a good man cannot long endure among so many others that value nothing; I see well that he means hereby to persuade a prince to apply himself to the wicked, and do as they do, and be wicked with them who value nothing. But if Machiavelli had well considered that goodness and virtue are always in price and estimation, even with men of no value, who are constrained to praise that which they hate; and if he were resolved, as it is certain, that subjects commonly apply themselves willingly to imitate their prince — Dion witnesses that in the time of the emperor Aurelius, a philosopher, many studied philosophy to be like him — he would never have given this precept to a prince, to accommodate himself to the vices in fashion and use. Contrary, he would have taught him to follow goodness and virtue, to draw his subjects thereunto, and to receive honor and good reputation in the world. But in truth we need not marvel if Machiavelli holds opinions so discrepant from the way of virtue, for that is not the path whereby he pretends to guide and conduct a prince. His way is that which leads to all wickedness and impiety, as we have in many places demonstrated.

The ancient Romans one day found certain verses of their prophetess Sibylla, where it was said that the Romans would always chase out of Italy every foreign enemy, if the Mother of the Gods were brought to Rome. The Romans, who were very superstitious in a vain religion, sent ambassadors to the oracle of Apollo at Delphi, to know where they might find the Mother of the Gods. The oracle sent them to king Attalus of Pergamum; Attalus led them into Phrygia and showed them an old image of stone, which in those quarters they had always called the Mother of the Gods. The ambassadors brought the image to Rome, and the Senate fell into deliberation who should go to the gates to receive the Mother of the Gods; it was concluded that it must be the best and most virtuous man in the city. When then it came into question, who was the best in all the town, every man (according to Livy) desired the lot might fall upon him; and there was not any but loved better to be elected the best man of the city, than to be chosen either consul or dictator, or into any other great estate. The election fell upon Scipio Nasica, cousin of the African, who was a young man but very good, and the son of a good father; he went out to receive that old goddess of stone, Mother of the Gods. But I demand of you, if those good Romans had been instructed in the doctrine of Machiavelli and had learned of this maxim, that it is not good to make a straight profession of a good man, would they have so much wished that this election had fallen upon them, and preferred this title of a good man before so high dignities of a consul or dictator? Certainly no; but they who hold contrary to the doctrine of Machiavelli make more estimation of goodness and virtue than of the greatest riches and dignities.

And indeed there is nothing more certain but that it is the best and most honorable title that a man can possibly have, to be a good man. And let it not displease great lords who are embarked in the highest title of honors, of constables, marshals, admirals, chancellors, presidents, knights of the order, governors, and lieutenants of the king, and other like great states. For all those titles without the title of a good man are worth nothing, and indeed are but smokes to stifle those who have them. But I confess that if they have the name of a good man, along with these titles, then they are worthy of double honor, and to be beloved and respected by all the world.

3.28
Machiavelli

Men cannot be altogether good nor altogether wicked, nor can they perfectly use cruelty and violence.

John Pagolo usurped Perugia, which was Church land, by murdering his cousins and nephews to come to the seignory. This was a man accomplished in all vices, without conscience, who kept his own sister. In 1505 Pope Julius II, going about to reunite to the Church lands separated from it by the usurpation of many particular lords, took his journey to Perugia accompanied by many cardinals, with but a simple unarmed guard; yet this train was garnished with baggage and movables of inestimable value. Pagolo knew well that they came to dispossess him of his seignory, yet did not have the courage to slay both him and his cardinals; although he might easily have done it and enriched himself with the booty. So he suffered himself to be taken and carried away by the pope, his enemy. It was not any remorse of conscience that made Pagolo commit the fault, but it was because he knew not in a need to be altogether wicked. Hereupon I conclude that men leave to lose great fortunes and occasions which happen to them, because they know not how in need to be altogether wicked.

Answer

This maxim is a true end and scope whereunto Machiavelli would lead a prince, and all such as follow his doctrine; namely to be altogether wicked, in all perfection of wickedness. The degrees to come to this so high and sovereign wickedness have for the most part already been declared. For Machiavelli has showed that cruelty, perfidy, impiety, subtlety or deceit, greed, and other like — which are the degrees whereby men mount the top of all wickedness — are very fit and meet for a prince, and that he ought to be decorated and adorned with them. But now he complains that men, although otherwise full of vices, yet cannot use them so dexterously and handsomely that they may mount to the highest, greatest, and sovereign wickedness; and that it is a great fault and brings to them great damages in their affairs. I pray you, can there be found among the Scythians, Arabians, or any other barbarous nation which lives without law or policy, a more detestable and infamous doctrine than here is taught in Machiavelli's school? May not any man see that he builds by his precepts a true tyranny? Yea that he uses the like method to teach his sovereign wickedness that philosophers do to teach the sovereign good? For as Aristotle, Plato, Cicero, and others who dealt in writing of the sovereign good, first showed the virtues and good manners whereby they must ascend thereunto, as by degrees, so this stinking doctor Machiavelli uses the same manner, teaching a prince all kinds of evil and wickedness, which may lead to the highest degree and top of all vices, and of all evil.

But I will not long stay in refuting this maxim, for I think I have before so well beaten down those degrees whereby he would have princes ascend to that height of wickedness, that he who follows the way which we have showed shall not need to fear mounting thither, but rather not doubt the contrary. We have also made appear by reasons and notable examples that those who give themselves to the vices of perfidy, impiety, cruelty, and other vices which Machiavelli teaches, ordinarily come to evil ends; so far is it off to be damaging that a man cannot be perfectly wicked, as he most impudently affirms. And as for the example of Pagolo which he cites, it is a strange thing how this gallant should not attain to the full top of all wickedness, since they of his nation have commonly their spirits so prompt and quick to all evil and corruption. But it is credible that he was some fainthearted fellow, who wanting no good will to slay the pope, only wanted courage to enterprise and perform it. But some may say that Pagolo feared to do well, if he had slain the pope Julius, and therefore he would not do it because he would not do good, but only apply himself to evil and vice, as Machiavelli teaches. And indeed if he had slain this pope, he had done great good to all Christendom of that time, for Julius lighted and stirred up wars among Christian princes, and delighted in nothing so much as to sow trouble everywhere, yea he vaunted that he would do more with Saint Paul's sword than all his predecessors had done with Saint Peter's keys. Pagolo then, who had sworn to the doctrine of Machiavelli, as is to be presumed, would not be the cause of so great good as by slaying that monster, to do so much good to Christendom. But Machiavelli found he did evil in that he did not slay the pope, and speaks thereof as a man passionate. For there was never a greater enemy to the pope than Machiavelli; I therefore do greatly marvel how papists can esteem of Machiavelli. But indeed they who esteem so much of him are not papists, although they say they are, but are a people who in their hearts make no care either of God or of the devil, nor of the pope, nor of the popedom, no nor of any religion, but are very atheists full of impiety, like their master. Yet indeed they go well to mass, and there is good policy in it; for therein they make it appear that they have so well profited in their Machiavellian philosophy, that they are come to the perfection that their master taught them in this maxim.

3.29
Machiavelli

He who has always carried the countenance of a good man, and would become wicked to obtain his desire, ought to color his change with some apparent reason. (*Discourses*, book 1 chapter 42)

When a man desires to change from one quality to another, as when he will become wicked for some cause, having always before carried the countenance of a good man, he must do it discreetly and seek occasions to lean upon new friends in place of the old, who abandon him. Herein a great fault was committed by Appius Claudius, who was one of the ten sovereign potentates of Rome. Having always showed himself a lover of the people, humane, kind, communicative, of easy access; and going about to usurp the sovereign domination of Rome, he too suddenly changed his qualities into those clean contrary, turning his robe from white to black; which was why the world discovered his hypocrisy and malice, and pointed at him with their fingers. So he could not attain his purposes, which he might have if little by little he had changed, always seeking some apparent occasion to become cruel, fierce, rigorous, and unsociable; and had provided himself friends of like qualities to maintain him, as is said.

Answer

This maxim is like that of foxlike deceit, whereof we have spoken before. For this is a precept for a good man to become wicked while the world does not perceive it. And (says Machiavelli) he must not be so gross as to change from good to evil at the first arrival, as from white to black, because this change may be perceived by the world; but he must proceed unto it by a subtlety, seeking palliations and colors to hide his change, and to give apparent reason thereof. As if a man will become cruel, he must cover his cruelties with some appearance of justice. If he will become ravenous and a catchpoll, he must cover his rapines with some appearance of necessity and public utility. Thus he changes himself little by little, and so from good shall he become wicked, and none perceives it. And it is good to be noted, the comparison which Machiavelli makes of the change and variety of manners, by the change of colors. For as black never takes white well, unless first white be tainted with some other color, as blue or red, so the change from good to wicked is never made to any good purpose without some pretext and show, which gives to a man an appearance between good and evil.

Here is a singular precept in the art of wickedness, to become wicked while the world does not perceive it. For if the world knows it, then it is an ignorance of the art which wills a knowledge to dissemble well, and that a man should be apt to know handsomely to feign and deal, with his visage and countenance, to deceive men. By joining then together these two precepts, to be a dissembler and to be wicked, to do evil, it will follow that this maxim is very proper for this art. For it teaches how to become wicked yet not to discover himself to be so, but always to observe the pretext of dissimulation.

You see then—and he who sees is not very blind of sense and understanding—that this abominable Florentine perseveres still to teach a prince the art of wickedness. But because we have before disputed against all the kinds thereof, as likewise against hypocrisy and dissimulation, I will speak no more hereof. And as for the example of Appius Claudius, one of the ten potentates of Rome, it serves nothing for Machiavelli's purpose. For Appius, exercising an office which endured for but a year, carried himself well for that first year; which was the cause that he and his companions were continued in their estate another year. But with great difficulty they obtained that continuation, for it was as it were a breach of their law to continue an office to any person more than a year. Seeing that it would be impossible to obtain from the Roman people a continuation for a third year, Appius thought it good now to make himself feared, by seeking to obtain his estate by force. And likely enough he would have gotten again his office had there not happened a war against the Romans. Appius and his companions could do no less, if it were but to defend themselves, than levy an army; but none would obey them, because the time of their offices was expired, and they no longer acknowledged them for lawful magistrates. For want of obedience they were constrained to forsake their offices, and to submit themselves to the people's mercy; Appius Claudius and Spurius Oppius were set in prison, where they died, and the other eight were banished and their goods confiscated. The cause then why Appius could not obtain the tyranny he had enterprised was not that he had changed too suddenly from good to wicked, but because the time of his office being expired, he could not be obeyed. And herein all the dissimulations and foxlike dealings of Machiavelli could have done him no good; for as soon as any man's office was expired in Rome, he who held it must come out, whether good or wicked, because such was the law.

Moreover, this maxim here is not only wicked, but also hard to practice. For it is very difficult for a man to change from good to wicked and not be perceived, though in his actions he uses many palliations and dissimulations. For among people there is always someone who is not a beast, but (as the proverb is) can know flies in the milk; and who straight can discover the dissimulations of those Machiavelizing foxes, and can cry, the fox! that men may take heed of him.

3.30
Machiavelli

A prince in time of peace, maintaining discords and partialities among his subjects, may more easily use them at his pleasure. (*The Prince*, chapter 20)

Our ancient ancestors, especially those who were esteemed the wisest, have always held that people must be held in obedience by the means of partialities. And for that cause they nourished discords in certain towns, the more easily to govern them. The Venetians also, moved with the like opinion, maintained in the towns of their government the factions of the Guelphs and Gibelines, that their subjects' minds being occupied with such studies might have no leisure to think upon rebellion. Yet a prince who has any blood in his nails will not nourish such partialities in time of war, for so may they bring him hurt; but in time of peace he may by such means handle his subjects much more easily.

Answer

Whenever the commonwealth is governed by a good prince, who uses good counsel in the conducting of his affairs and gets the love of his subjects, it is certain that both in time of peace and war he shall always be obeyed. For most of the people will obey him voluntarily and without constraint; some for love, others for fear of his justice, which he shall have well established in his domination. And therefore this maxim cannot be but damaging and pernicious to a good prince, for it alienates him from the love of his subjects. For if he nourishes partialities among his subjects, he cannot possibly carry himself so equally towards both parties, but in them both will be jealousy and suspicion. Each party will esteem the other to be more favored, whereupon he will hate his prince, and by that means it may come to pass that the prince shall be hated by both parties; and so both the one and the other shall machinate his ruin, which he can hardly shun, having all their evil wills. And suppose he had but the evil will of one party; yet he could not be assured, seeing men are naturally inclined to desire to ruin and destroy what they hate; and that not only many, but even one alone may well find and encounter means to bring to pass his purpose, and to execute an enterprise, as before we have demonstrated by many examples. Therefore this maxim cannot but be very pernicious and very perilous for a prince who will use it. But it may be a tyrant may make use of it to hider a concord of the people, which may prove ruinous and perilous unto him. For when a people accords, a tyrant's nails have no great power upon them; neither can he easily introduce or practice tyrannical actions upon a people in good concord, because it refuses the yoke and denies obedience unto wicked ordinances and new burdens, and without obedience nothing by him is brought to effect. Therefore those who mean to introduce a tyranny first cast this foundation of partiality as the most certain means to establish and build it; although no tyranny is ever firm or assured, and we seldom or never see tyrants live long, because all tyranny comprehends violence, and by nature violent things cannot endure; as also that God sets in foot and exercises his justice upon them. Yet for all that, there is not a better nor more expedient means to establish a tyranny than to plant a partiality among the people. And this is the mark and end whereat Machiavelli shoots, to establish a tyranny, as we have before showed in many places.

It may be Machiavelli learned this maxim from Claudius Appius, who was a man of courage and very tyrannical towards the Roman people. And if all other senators had been of his humor, assuredly the Senate would have usurped a tyranny in the city and changed the aristocratic estate into an oligarchy; but most often he remained alone in his opinion. But we must understand that at Rome there were ten tribunes of the people, who were magistrates established to conserve the liberties and franchises of the common people against the tyrannical enterprises of the great men of the city. They had power to oppose themselves against all novelties, as new laws, new burdens and taxes; and after a firm opposition, none might pass any further. They also had power to propose and pursue the reception of new laws, as they knew it was requisite and profitable for all the people; whereby it often came to pass that the tribunes sought to pass laws to the great dislike of the patricians and senators, and to the utility of the common people. Appius always gave the Senate advice to sow a partiality among the ten tribunes, so that they might oppose themselves against a law which otherwise they would have to pass. For, said he, by this means the tribunes' power shall ruin itself without us seeming to have meddled therein, and without the people knowing that any of our action is in it. This counsel of Appius was many times followed, but in the end they found it did them no good; for after the tribunes were partialized against each other, and nothing could pass nor be concluded by way of deliberation and accustomed voting, they then fell to arms and seditions. So that in the end the people were constrained by force to pluck from the patricians what they would not permit to be handled and disputed by the accustomed way of good deliberation and conclusion by plurality of voices. Thus the patricians were often constrained, to appease the people, to grant them things which by reason they might have persuaded them to leave. For it is the nature of men to always desire what is denied them, as the poet Horace says very well, expressing what ordinarily happens in the world:

> That which denied is most commonly,
> Desired is by us most ardently.

Moreover, it often came to pass that the patricians desired to pass some law which seemed to them profitable for the commonwealth, but they could not come to the sentences because they had fashioned the tribunes to a contradiction of each other. And of those tribunary partialities arose great insurrections of the people, and great murders and effusion of blood, as there did when the two Gracchi brothers were slain. And therefore that good counsel of Appius, whereupon Machiavelli has made his maxim, was cause of great evils and calamities; as surely it is easy to judge that all partialities and divisions are cause of ruin and desolation among a people. Whereof we are also advised by him who is truth itself, our Lord Jesus Christ, who says that every kingdom divided in itself shall be desolate. And if there be any Machiavellian so gross-headed that he cannot comprehend this in spirit, yet he may see this by experience in France if he is not altogether blind. And if he is French, he cannot but palpably touch it in the loss of his goods and in the death of his parents and friends, unless he is a lazer or without sense. For all the late ruins of France, from where have they proceeded but from the partialities of papists and Huguenots, which foreigners sowed and maintained thereof. It is folly to say that the diversity of religion was the cause thereof. For if men had handled all controversies of religion by preaching, disputes, and conferences, as at the beginning they did, they would never have fallen into partiality. But since men came to arms and massacres, and by constraint would force men to believe, partialities sprung up, which was the only mark whereat all foreigners shot, that thereby they might plant in France the government of Machiavelli.

The Chalcedonians were well advised not to believe the counsel of the Aetolians, which resembled this doctrine of Machiavelli and the counsel of Appius. For when the war was open between the Romans and king Antiochus, the Chalcedonians, allies and friends of the Romans, assembled the states of their countries to resolve upon what Antiochus made them understand; that he came into Greece to deliver them from the subjection and servitude of the Romans, and therefore required them to ally themselves with him. The Aetolians — who were very inconstant and mutable people with each wind, as are the Machiavellians — chanced to be in that assembly, and persuaded the Chalcedonians that Antiochus had passed from Asia into Europe to deliver Greece from Roman

servitude; and that they thought it best that all the cities of Greece ought
to ally with both the two parties, the Antiochs and the Romans. For, they
said, if we ally ourselves with both parties, when one offends us the
other will avenge us. The Chalcedonians found this counsel not good,
knowing well that none can serve two contrary masters, neither could
they ally themselves with two nations' enemies, and that those who will
entertain two contrary parties shall often fall into the bad graces of both.
And therefore Mixtion, one of the principals of the Chalcedonians, made
to the Aetolians a very wise and notable answer:

> "Masters Aetolians, we do not see that the Romans have seized upon any
> town in Greece, neither that they have placed any Roman garrison
> thererin, nor that any pays them tribute; neither do we know any whom
> they have given any law, or in any way changed their estate. And
> therefore we do not acknowledge ourselves entangled in any servitude,
> but in all ways are in the same liberty we have always been. Being
> therefore free, we stand in no need of a deliverer, and the coming of
> Antiochus into Greece cannot but hurt us, and he can perform no greater
> good unto us than to withdraw himself far from our country. And as for
> us, we are resolved to receive none within our towns but by the authority
> of the Romans, our allies."

The Chalcedonians then governed themselves after this answer, and it
happened well unto them. But the Aetolians were almost all ruined and
lost by practicing their foolish opinion, to entertain both the Romans and
Antiochians together. For so were they of necessity forced to seek
practices maintaining war between that king and the Roman
commonwealth, to the end that the two powers might always stand on
foot, without the ability to overthrow the other; because otherwise they
could not attain to their design and purpose, which was to keep
themselves in friendship with both parties. Yet thus seeking to sustain
them both and maintain them enemies, they made themselves hated by
both; so that after the retreat of Antiochus these miserable Aetolians fell
into a desperate case, likely to have torn each other in pieces, accusing
each other as the inventors of that wicked counsel. Yet in the end, by the
Romans' clemency and bounty, which pardoned them, they had a
certain subsistence, though in a mean sort.

In the town of Ardea, a neighbor of the Romans, there was a like
partiality as there is at this day at Genes; for now at Genes the people are
banded against the nobles, and they will by no means receive any of the
nobility for duke of Genes; insomuch as all dukes of Genes must needs
be villains and base men of race, and it may be there will be found in
France of the like race as at Genes. The like partiality (I say) being in the
town of Ardea, between the nobility and the people, it it happened that

two young bachelors, one of the people and another of the nobility, fell at debate against each other about obtaining in marriage a young maid of excellent beauty, but of a base and carterly race. Great bandying fell out about this marriage, they of the nobility all casting their heads and employing their abilities for their gentleman, who loved and desired the maid. And they obtained so much that they got the maid's mother on their side, who affected that her daughter might be placed in a noble house; but contrary, the people who were for the other young man of their own race and quality did so much for him that they gained the maid's tutors, who thought that it was more reasonable that their pupil should espouse a husband of her own quality than to mount into a higher degree; for that equality ought as much as might be, to be observed in marriage. Upon altercation of this marriage the parties were drawn into justice, and the maid was adjudged to the gentleman, after the advice of the mother. Yet although by law the gentleman got the cause, by force he could not; for the tutors with strong hand forced the maid from her mother. The gentleman to whom she was adjudged, being almost enraged at this rape and injury that was done him, gathered together a great company of other gentlemen, his parents and friends, and gave charge upon those who had taken away his betrothed wife. Briefly, there was a great stir and noise through the town, and a great number slain on both sides; and at last the gentlemen remained masters of the town, and the people were driven away. The people, straying about the fields, ruined the houses and possessions of the nobles; the nobles sent to Rome ambassadors for aid, and the people likewise sent to the Volsques (people of Tuscany) for their aid. By this means the Romans and Volsques fell to war against each other; but the Romans carrying away the victory beheaded the principal authors of the insurrection, which happened for this marriage in the town of Ardea; and confiscated all their goods, which were adjudged to the communality of the Ardeates. Here you see how the partiality which was in the town of Ardea was the cause of that great calamity and combustion; and therefore well to be noted are these words of Livy: "The Ardeates were continually in an intestine war; the cause and commencement whereof proceeded from the contention of partialities, which always have and will be ruinous and damaging to people, far more than external wars, than famine, than pestilence, or than all other evils which the gods send upon cities, which they will altogether destroy." These words are full contrary to the Machiavellian doctrine, as indeed they are the words of another manner of author than Machiavelli; at whom I much marvel that he dare attempt to write discourses upon Livy, since any may see he understands him not, and his doctrine is also clean contrary to that of Livy. Unto the said sentence of Livy I will add that which he recites from Quintius Capitolinus, who admonishing the soldiers of his army:

> "Our enemies come not to assail us upon any trust they have in our cowardice or their own virtue, for many times already they have assayed both the one and the other; but it is for the confidence they have in our partialities and contentions which now are between the patricians and the people. For our partialities are the venom which empoisons and corrupts this city, because we are too imperious, and you too unmeasurably desiorous of liberty."

The partialities of the Carthaginians, were they not the cause of their utter ruin? There were two factions at Carthage, the Barchinian (whereof was Hannibal's house), and the Hannoenne. As soon as Hannibal's father Hamilcar was dead, the Carthaginians elected as general of their army Asdrubal, one of the Barchian faction, who they sent to make war with Spain with a great army. This Asdrubal had learned the art of war under Hamilcar, which was the cause why he sought to have young Hannibal near him, to administer unto him the same benefit which he had received at his father's hands. Therefore he wrote to the Senate of Carthage, who brought this to deliberation; Hanno's advice being demanded, he reasoned in this way.

> "Masters, I think the demand of Asdrubal is very equal, yet I do not think his request should be granted. For it is equal in that he desires to restore a like benefit to the son which he received from the father; yet we ought not to accommodate ourselves to his will, and give him our youth to nourish after his fancy. I am then of advice that this young Hannibal be nourished and educated in this city, under the obedience of laws and magistrates, and that he be taught to live after justice, and in equality with others, lest this little fire one day raise up a far greater."

The wisest and best advised of the Senate were of this opinion, but the plurality (which was of the Barchian faction) was to send young Hannibal into Spain; who as soon as he arrived was much beloved by the soldiers, as well because he resembled his father Hamilcar as for his military virtues. Not long after, he was chosen general of the Carthaginian army. But as soon as he was settled in that estate, he accomplished the prophecy of Hanno; for he lighted the great fire of the Punic Wars against the Romans, whereby in the end the Carthaginians were utterly ruined. All this proceeded but from the partiality which was at Carthage; for as soon as the Hannonians reasoned one way, the Barchinians reasoned to the contrary, and they studied for nothing but to obtain the upper hand without care or consideration what opinion was best. And thus ordinarily it happens where there is any partiality; for then men give themselves more to contradiction than to judge after a wholesome sentence, and without passion of what is profitable and expedient.

The partialities of the houses of Orleans and Bourgogne (in our grandfathers' memory), were they not cause of infinite miseries and calamities, wherewith France was afflicted for the space of more than threescore years? And of the entire ruin of the Bourgognian house? Louis duke of Orleans, the only brother of king Charles VI, took for his device *Mitto*. duke John de Bourgogne took for his *Accipio*, challenging as it were thereby an egality with the only brother of the king, under color that he was richer than he. This commencement of contrary devices, which they had painted in their banners of their lances and on their servants' livery coats, erected a great partiality; insomuch that the duke of Bourgogne enterprised to cause the duke of Orleans to be slain (as he did). The children of the duke of Orleans, because justice was not executed on their father's massacre, levied arms; duke John also by arms resisted them, and all the realm was partialized about the quarrel of these two great houses. After, duke John was slain at Monterean-sante-Yonne in a strange manner; whereupon his son Philip, willing to revenge himself, sent for the English, whom he caused to pass through France, and occupied at least a third part of the kingdom. This duke Philip made peace with the king; but he had a son Charles, his successor, who would never put trust in the king of France, fearing himself because of the wars which his father and grandfather had raised in his kingdom, but would needs grapple with king Louis XI. This king, who was too good for him, raised him up so many enemies on all sides that the house of that duke came to ruin. Behold the fruits of partialities, which Machiavelli recommends so much to a prince! And hereupon should well be noted the saying of master Philip de Commines: That divisions and partialities are very easy to sow, and are a sure token of ruin and destruction in a country when they take root therein, as has happened to many monarchies and commonwealths.

To prove his saying Commines sets down other examples; the partiality of the houses of Lancaster and York in England, whereby the house of Lancaster was altogether ruined and brought down, and the one house delivered to the other, seven or eight battles between three and fourscore princes of the royal blood of England, and an infinite number of people. This here is no small thing, but it is rather an example which should make us abhor all partialities. He further says that by the means of the said partiality between these two houses, many great princes and lords were banished and chased from England, and among others, that he saw a duke of the house of Lancaster, the chief of the league of that house and brother-in-law of king Edward IV, who saved himself in Bourgogne, yet in so poor estate that he went barefoot and without hose after the train of duke Charles of Bourgogne, demanding his alms from house to house. He after recites the tragic acts of the duke of Warwick, of the kings Edward and Henry, of the prince of Wales, of the dukes of Gloucester and Somerset; which are strange histories that cannot be heard or read without great horror, and cannot but make men detest all partialities and divisions.

During the Punic Wars there were created consuls Marcus Livius and Claudius Nero, who bore great enmity towards each other of long standing. The Senate, fearing that this enmity should cause some partialities in the administration of their estate, which might turn to the damage of the public good, admonished them to be reconciled. Marcus Livius answered that it was not needful, and that their enmities and partialities should cause them with envy to seek to do better than the other. But the Senate was not of that advice; for they remembered that in the time of the proconsulship of Quintius Paenus, Caius Furius, Marcus Posthumius, and Cornelius Cossus, the Roman army had been vanquished by the Veians because of the partialities of the chieftains, who could not accord in their counsels and designs, but always tended to contrary ends. The like also happened in the proconsulship of Publius Virginius and Marcus Sergius. But the most memorable and latest example which the Senate had before their eyes was the loss of the battle at Cannae, where the Romans lost 50,000 men; which loss happened by the discord and partiality of two chieftains, Paulus Aemylius and Terentius Varro. These examples moved the Senate to exhort these two consuls, Livius and Nero, to a reconciliation, not believing that their partiality could serve them for anything but evil to conduct the affairs of the commonwealth. Being constrained by the Senate's authority, they accorded and reconciled themselves, and very well acquitted themselves in their charge, and overthrew 50,000 men which Asdrubal brought into Italy to Hannibal his brother. In this defeat Asdrubal was slain, and his head secretly carried and cast into Hannibal's camp, who yet had no news of that journey. When Hannibal saw the head of his brother he deplored his fortune and despaired of his affairs, knowing that the Roman virtue would never bow nor stoop for either misfortune or calamity.

The reconciliation and concord of Marcus Livius and Claudius Nero, then, were the cause of a great good and utility to the commonwealth, and remounted the affairs thereof into a great hope, and abated the pride that Hannibal had taken from the battle of Cannae; as also by the contrary, the partiality of Paulus Aemylius (who was a wise captain) and of Terentius Varro (who was very rash and heady) was the cause that the Roman commonwealth was almost utterly overthrown, and that Hannibal was mounted into so great pride and hope to be master thereof.

Concord then, and not partiality, is profitable and healthful to a commonwealth; and to this purpose is very memorable, the oration of Fabius Maximus to the Roman people. Fabius being elected consul five times, and twice having had for his companion Publius Decius, the people at this time would have for his companion Lucius Volumnius. But Fabius arose upon his feet, and turning himself towards the people said:

> "My masters, I have already had in two consulships Publius Decius for a companion, and we have carried ourselves together in a very good concord; therefore I pray you to give me him yet this time again, in favor of my age, which can hardly now accustom itself to any other companion. You know that there is nothing more firm for the tuition of the common weal than magistrates who accord well; for every man will communicate his counsel more privately with him he knows, and who is of manners and conditions accordant with his own, than with another."

At this request of Fabius, the people accorded unto him Decius for his companion, with such joy and comfort that each man thought that from so good concord of two consuls, there could not proceed anything but good and profit to the commonwealth.

The Romans one day having no silver in their treasury for a war which was on their hands, the Senate gave charge to certain senators to remonstrate to the people that each man should make them ready to do their best for the defense of the commonwealth, and that none ought to abandon the defense of their country for want of food and payment of wages. This was so well done that first the knights offered to serve for nothing; then great troupes of people ran to the palace to have themselves enrolled to march without wages. The Senate ordained that the colonels assemble their regiments, and by orations give them great thanks in the name of the Senate and of the commonwealth, for their goodwill in freely serving the common weal. Which commission they all executed, highly praising the generosity of Roman soldiers. All the world was taken with such joy for this great concord and unanimity of great and small to conserve the commonwealth, that everyone wept for joy and cried on high that assuredly the city of Rome was most happy, invincible, and eternal by this concord; that the knights were most brave men, worthy of praises; that the people were good and loveable, and that the debonarity and kindness of the Senate had been vanquished by the prompt and voluntary obedience of the people. Here you may see what opinion the Roman people had of concord, so far were they from thinking that partialities were good.

But when we say that concord is good, necessary, and profitable for the conservation of the public good, I do not mean that all persons who deal in the commonwealth ought of necessity to be of one humor, of one voice and complexion. For rather contrary, they must needs be gentle and sharp, affable and fierce, severe and pitiful, such as Appius and Publicola, Cato and Caesar. For as in the lute, if all strings were of one sound, the harmony would be worth nothing; but being of diverse sounds, tending to one melody, it proves a pleasant and agreeable harmony. So in a commonwealth or in a prince's council, if all were of one humor and inclination their advices and government could not be good. But being of divers natures yet tending to one end, which is the common good, their opinions shall always be better debated by divers and contrary reasons, and conclusions better taken and better digested. This is what Tullius Hostilius, king of the Romans, said to Sussetius, dictator of the Albanois:

> "The partialities which you reproach us with are profitable, and not damaging to the commonwealth, as you say; for we contend together who shall most profit it, great or young, old or new citizens. And because to maintain a public estate two things are necessary, force in war and prudence in counsel, we will contend and debate upon them both who shall do best, and who shall show himself most virtuous in war and most prudent in counsel. This partiality in counsel then, when all men tend to the public good, are well according dissonances, which in the end makes a very sweet harmony."

I conclude then this matter with the saying of Commines, that if a prince is in peace, maintaining partialities among his subjects will bring him into war; and if he is at war they will bring him into ruin and confusion. I conclude then that a prince above all things ought to take heed that he nourish no partialities, unless among women. For a prince may take pleasure in maintaining a partiality among the ladies and gentlewomen of his court, and so may always have some pleasant news to laugh at and take his pastime. But yet I could like better that among the ladies of a prince's court there should be such a partiality as there was in times past among the Roman ladies. The patrician ladies had a chapel dedicated to chastity, where they often went to make devotions in a great troupe. These ladies being one day in their chapel, there arrived Virginia, a patrician married to Lucius Volumnius, who was of the third estate, although also a great lord. These patrician ladies would by no means suffer Virginia to enter into their chapel, because she was not married to a patrician, but thrust her back. Virginia said she was by race a patrician, a chaste wife without reproach, and married to a lord who had received great honor and estates in the commonwealth, although by race he was but of the third estate. Notwithstanding whatever she could say, these patrician ladies would not suffer her to enter the chapel. Virginia seeing this, to show that she was a chaste lady had an altar erected to Pudicity, and dedicating it in the presence of a great troupe of other patrician ladies, said: "I dedicate this altar to the patrician Chastity, and admonish you all that the same contention which is among our husbands, of who shall be most valiant and virtuous, may also be among us, who shall be most chaste; and that you may so do and behave yourselves, as this altar may be more holily and chastely reverenced than this chapel here." Behold here a contention worthy of virtuous and sage ladies! But at this day ladies contend who shall best dance, paint, and deck themselves, and to do such like things as do not lead them into the chapel of the Roman patricians, nor to the altar of Virginia's chastity, but rather lead them clean contrary.

3.31
Machiavelli

Seditions and civil dissentions are profitable and blameless.

I say against the advice of many that dissentions and civil seditions are good and profitable, and that they were the cause that Rome is mounted into the lofty degree of empire wherein it has been. I know well that some hold that it was rather her valiance in arms and her good fortune which had lifted her up. But they who hold this do not consider that deeds of arms cannot be conducted without good order and good policy, and that it is policy which commonly leads to good fortune. But certain it is that seditions have been the cause of good order and of the good policy which was established at Rome. And in sum, all the good acts and examples of the ancient Romans have proceeded from this fountain of seditions. For good examples proceed from good nurture and education; good nurture proceeds from good laws and policies; and the mother of good laws is sedition and civil dissentions, which most men condemn without consideration.

Answer

It were to be desired that Machiavelli and his nation, who esteem seditions and civil dissentions so profitable, had reserved them for themselves, with all the utility and profit that is in them, and not have participated them with their neighbors. As for France, they might well have spared the seditions and partialities which the Italian Machiavellians have sown on this side of the mountains, which cause so much bloodshed, so many houses destroyed, and so many miseries and calamities, as every man feels, sees, and deplores. Would to God then all civil dissentions had remained among the Florentines and other Italians, who love them and find them good, so that the French had been without them; then France would not be so rent and torn in pieces, as it is, and it should not be enfeebled of more than half its forces. The people would not be so poor as we see them, nor so naked of substance and all good means. For civil dissentions have brought to the realm such a ransack and discomfiture of goods, and have so abandoned and overthrown all free commerce and good husbandry (which are the two means to store and fill a country with abundance of goods), that at this day there are seen no good houses, but those which were wont to be are ruined and altogether impoverished and made barren. And truly it is as in a forest, when a man sees all the good oaks hewn down, and there remains nothing but thorns, shrubs, and bushes. For even such a forest which has few or no trees in it merits the name of a bush, rather than a forest; so the kingdom or commonwealth whose good and ancient houses are impoverished deserves rather to be named a desert than a kingdom or commonwealth.

Moreover, the reason which Machiavelli alleges, whereby he would prove seditions to be good, is very gross and foolish. For follow with this: Because seditions are sometimes not the cause but the occasion that some good laws and rules are made, they are therefore good. This reason is like the argument of a certain philosopher whom Aulus Gellius mocks, who would maintain that the fever quarantine is a good thing because it makes men sober and temperate, and to guard themselves from eating and drinking too much. Philosophers who broach such absurd opinions deserve to be left without answer, with their seditions and fever quarantines, to draw out such profit from them as they say proceeds from them. Does not the common proverb say that from evil manners proceed good laws? And does it therefore follow that evil manners are good? That is, does it follow that white is black, and black white? The grossest headed fellows know well that lawmakers never set down laws but only to reform vices and abuses which are in a people. So that indeed no laws would have been made if the people walked uprightly and committed no abuses, nor had any vices. For laws are not set down but for transgressors, and to hold intemperate persons within limits and bounds. Hereof it follows that abuses, vices, strayings, and lusts are occasions of good laws, and prudent princes and lawmakers are the efficient causes of them; but it does not therefore follow that vices, abuses, and straying lusts are good things.

Moreover it is not always true what Machiavelli says, that seditions are causes or occasions of having good laws and rules. The seditions which were raised up at Rome by Tiberius Gracchus and his brother Caius, tribunes of the people, which were so great and sanguinary, were not the cause of any good laws. They were the cause that they both were massacred, as they merited, but they were neither cause nor occasion of any good law or rule. And how should they be the cause thereof, seeing they tended to authorize and pass wicked laws, and despoil true masters and proprietors of their goods? For Tiberius Gracchus pursued by his seditious faction that a law called Agraria might be received and authorized, whereby it was not lawful for a Roman citizen to possess above ten acres of land; which was as much to say, to take away the more from them who had more. And because Marcus Octavius, his companion in the tribunate, opposed the law as both wicked and unjust, Gracchus would needs have him dispatched of his estate; and sought to make a Triumvirate of himself, his brother, and his father-in-law, to divide among the people rich men's goods. This was the cause that the great lords of the city, by the advice and counsel of Scipio Nasica (who was accounted the best man thereof), slew him in the Capitol and cast his body into the Tiber. His brother Caius Gracchus being tribune of the people, later sought again to bring up that law Agraria, and would needs devise one out of his own brain; whereby it was ordained that in all judgments and conclusions of affairs there should be 600 knights and 300 senators, all having voices. This he did to have the plurality of voices at his command, knowing that the knights would always easily incline to his pursuits; and so he could not fail to obtain what he wanted, if at all deliberations there were twice as many knights as senators. But this was a wicked law, tending to overthrow and weaken the authority of senators, and therefore they hindered it. Lucius Opimius, consul, by decree of the Senate, caused the people to arm themselves and assail Caius Gracchus and the seditious of his troupe. And in the conflict Gracchus was slain, with Flacchus his fellow in the Triumvirate. Finally, the seditions of these two brethren Gracchus tended to bring forward wicked laws, and hereof came to no good, but they were the cause of infinite murders and of great effusion of blood.

The seditions which were raised up at Rome by the triumvirate of Octavius, Antoninus, and Lepidus, what good did they bring to the commonwealth? They were the cause of infinite mischiefs; of great and long civil wars; of the death of infinite persons; of the ruin, impoverishment, and pillage of the provinces of the empire; and finally of the change of state from a commonwealth into a monarchy. And although the subjects of the Roman Empire did not then feel any harm by that change, lighting on a good prince, Augustus, yet afterwards they felt it under five or six emperors, all which successively followed: Tiberius, Caligula, Claudius, Nero, Otho, and Vitellius, all which were bad emperors and governed very tyrannically.

Herodian writes that the Greeks were first subjugated and brought under subjection by the Macedonians, and after by the Romans, because of their accustomed seditions, whereby they banished or put to death the most valiant and generous persons they had in their commonwealth. And yet after they were brought under the Romans' yoke they could not hold themselves from being seditious, even when there were many competitors to the empire. For they banded with those who often caused the ruin and destruction of their best towns, as happened in the time of Severus to those who partialized for Niger.

Before the Romans had subjugated the Gauls, Gaul was divided into petty commonwealths (as Julius Caesar says in his commentaries), which notwithstanding were leagued together, and held a diet once a year at Dreux to parley and confer of the whole country's affairs. But at last there fell a partiality among them, and a great war arose between the Sequanois and the Autunoys. The Sequanois drew to their succors the Germans, under the leadership of Ariovistus; and the Autunois the Romans, under the conduction of Caesar. Caesar arriving in Gaul to succor the Aurunois, did so well that he planted greater division and sedition through all Gaul, and by that means subjected it to the Roman Empire. And it was a province which the Romans esteemed most opulent and rich of all them under the empire, so they made their account to draw ordinarily out of it great store of silver. And indeed after Gaul was made subject to the Romans, it was always much vexed with taxes and tributes, and with the extortions and pillages of governors; who, to cover their robberies with some color, said that it was needful to hold the Gaulois poor lest they rebelled against the Romans, against whom they had anciently made war and obtained so many victories.

The ten potentates who were created at Rome in the place of consul would usurp a tyranny and continue in their estate beyond the time established by laws. But what means did they use? Even sedition; for so long as they could maintain sedition between the people and the patricians, their tyranny was in some assurance; but as soon as the great and the small of the city were in accord, the ten potentates were ruined and overthrown. But this example is very fit to confirm the maxim of Machiavelli, according to the end whereunto it tends, which is to establish a tyranny; for seditions and civil dissentions may serve a tyrant's turn to maintain him in his tyranny. But because we have sufficiently parleyed of tyrannical actions and cited many examples, which in their places may be found, we pass on.

3.32
Machiavelli

The means to keep subjects in peace and union, and to hold them from rebellion, is to keep them always poor. (*Discourses*, book 1 chapter 22; book 2 chapter 7; book 3 chapter 16, 25)

The towns which are placed in lean and barren soils are customarily united and peaceable, because the inhabitants there, being ever occupied in plowing and laboring the earth, have no other means nor leisure to think upon seditions and rebellions. And contrary, towns situated in fat and rich countries are easily inclined to stirs and disobediences. For truly, strife and debates which arise every day among men proceed only from riches and abundance of goods, and rich people will not suffer themselves to be handled as we commonly see. Therefore the Romans maintained their colonies in poor estate, and assigned them small possessions, lest they should rise up against them. Yea even within their own town a long time reigned very great poverty; notwithstanding which the citizens left not to be virtuous people, employed in great public charges, as were Quintus Cincinnatus, Marcus Regulus, Paulus Aemilius, and many others who were very poor yet executed great things. And surely we have ever seen that poverty has produced better fruits than riches, and that a people being rich and fat have always been more prompt to rebellion and disobedience. Therefore it is a healthful and good remedy to hold subjects poor, to the end that by their riches they neither may corrupt themselves nor others.

Answer

Here may a man see the very counsel which Guiemand gave to Giles, governor for the Roman emperor in the town of Soissons and neighboring countries. Chilperic IV, king of France, had for one of his closest friends this Guiemand, who was a valiant and sage French baron. This king sometimes led a slippery and inordinate life, so that to furnish his pleasure and unmeasurable expenses he was constrained to impose upon the people great taxes, and to commit great extractions. The

French, who at that time were of an austere courage (according to the history), began to hate him and bear him evil will, and to resolve among themselves to seize his person and appoint a tutor for him, and so to take from him all his young and bad counselors about him. Which he perceiving asked Guiemand's advice, what he should do. Guiemand counseled him to fly and to give place to the French ire, which in his absence he would appease; and as soon as they were quieted, he would recall him. He also parted a gold ring in two, and gave one half to the king, saying, "Sir, when I send you this other half, which I keep, it shall be to you a certain token that you may boldly come again, and without fear." Chilperic then retired towards the king of Thuringe, and in his absence the French elected for their chieftain the said Giles, governor of a great part of Gaul, which the Roman emperor then held. This Giles called Guiemand to be about him as one of his council, because he was reputed a wise man. Guiemand dissembled the best he could for the space of nine years, all which time he was about this Giles, yet never forgetting the amity and fidelity which he bore to his king. But among other things which he counseled this governor, this was one, that he gave him to understand that the Frenchmen's nature is to be rudely handled in great subjection, and to take great heed they do not enrich themselves; for they are far better poor than rich, and when they are rich and at their ease, then they immediately rebel against their prince. Briefly, by this goodly counsel, whereof he desired such issue as afterward happened, he put in that Roman governor's head to lay great taxes and exactions upon the French people, and withal to practice cruelties. This was the cause that the Frenchmen, by the advice and secret handling of Guiemand himself, called again their king Chipleric, unto whom Guiemand sent the half ring which he had. The king returning, the French gentlemen met him even at Barres, where they dealt with him most honorably. The king also forgave them all new tributes and taxes, and from thence forward governed himself wisely; and of a Sardanapalus, which he had been before his flight, he became after his return a noble and valiant prince, and chased the Romans from a good part of Gaul which they held, and greatly enlarged the limits of the realm of France. Therefore it is evidently seen that the maxim of Machiavelli, or the counsel which Guiemand gave to Giles (which is one same doctrine), is not very good, and that the issue thereof cannot be but evil.

And to argue this point by reason, I think every man will confess that it is more expedient for a prince to be king and lord of a rich and plentiful country than a poor and barren one. For a withered and poor country cannot nourish any great people; moreover, a poor and barren country cannot produce and bring forth things necessary for the tuition thereof, as abundance of corn, wine, fodder, money, and other things. Finally, to make a kingdom strong and puissant, to maintain and augment it, there is a necessity that it be copious and rich of all things. And although Machiavelli in a certain place where he speaks of war, maintains that the common saying is false, that money is the sinews of war; this hinders not, but what we say may be true. For suppose it is true, as Machiavelli by his foolish subtlety maintains, that it is the good soldiers which are the sinews of war, and not money; yet these sinews cannot stir, nor be brought to any great actions without clapping upon the cataplasm of money. So that if money is not the sinews of war, because it has not of itself either motion or operation, yet at least it is the means which cause the sinews to move, and without which soldiers can do nothing, or at least without payment and victuals, apparel, and armor. And if it is objected that there are some poor nations which notwithstanding are puissant and warlike, as were the Macedonians in the time of Alexander the Great, who were poor in regard to the Greeks, Persians, and Medes; and as are at this day the Tartars and Scythians, and as the Swiss were within this hundred years; hereunto I in many ways answer. Frist, I will not deny that the poor countries cannot be but naturally good warriors, as commonly all northerly nations are, as the Macedonians, Scythians, Tartars, Swiss, and Germans. But this martial virtue proceeds not from their poverty; for in Africa, America, and in many other places of Asia, and in many islands there are many poor nations, yet nothing warlike. But if poor nations which are naturally warlike become rich, they will not therefore lose their warlike virtue; as the Swiss today are very opulent and rich, yet are they nothing less valiant in war than they were in the time of the battle of Morat, about a hundred years ago, which they got against the duke of Bourgogne. In which time they were so poor that many of them could not discern vessels of silver from pewter, as M. de Commines says. The Macedonians also became very rich after Alexander conquered Asia, yet they always remained generous and valiant. The Romans also in the time of the foundation of Rome were very poor, but within a small time they became very rich, yet did not lose their valor and generosity. It is not then the poverty of the country which makes a warlike people, but rather the nature and inclination of the heaven, which likewise is much aided when the country may become rich.

If it is objected that we see many princes and private persons who abuse their riches, as Caligula did the 67 million in gold which Tiberius left him, and as Caesar did the great treasures he heaped up in Gaul, and as many others did, hereunto I answer in two ways. First, I say it does not follow that riches and treasures are evil because some abuse them, no more than wine is to be condemned because many are drunk therewith. And although there are some princes and other persons who have abused their riches, there are also many who use them well. Moreover, I say that the consequence is not good in this case, from the particular to the general. For I confess that it would be better and more profitable for the commonwealth, that there were many houses meanly rich than some few excessively rich; because often that excess proves very pernicious to him who enjoys it, who is thereby sometimes incited to stray out of the limits of laws and temperance. But suppose it true that great riches are most commonly damaging to individuals; it does not therefore follow that they are so for a country in general. For the more rich a country is, so much more is it strong and puissant, if it is well governed and the individuals do not abuse their richness. Which they will not do, especially under the yoke of good laws and good magistrates, if every man has not too great abundance, but in a mediocrity according to their qualities and degrees. For such a mean seems very requisite and profitable, because it is an aid to come unto virtue and to be exercised therein; but excess is often pernicious, as it was in many particular Romans in Caesar's time, who were so exceedingly opulent and rich that their excessive riches drew them out of the limits of virtue, to give themselves unto all luxury and to enterprise novelties and changes.

But when I say that unmeasurable riches are most often pernicious to individuals, I mean also the person of a sovereign prince. For it is neither good nor profitable that a prince treasures up heaps of riches; for it serves for a bait to draw unto him enemies, or to engender quarrels and divisions after him; and we often see that princes' great treasures are causes of more evil than good. The treasure Tiberius left after him, for what good purpose did it serve? It served to commit a thousand villainies and unprofitable expenses, full of corruptions, which Caligula would never have made if he had not found that treasure. And the treasure which Charles the Wise left behind him, wherefore served it but to sow enmity and division among brethren; Louis, duke of Anjou, got it, for which the dukes of Berry and Bourgogne bore him evil will; and on their sides also, to get treasures they caused great exactions to be laid upon the people. And what good did this treasure to the duke of Anjou? It tended to the destruction of him and his treasure, in the conquest of Naples and Sicily. The great treasures of king Croesus of Lydia incited him to war against king Cyrus of Persia and Media, to his own destruction. The treasures of Perseus, king of Macedonia, made him put such great confidence in his forces that he would needs have war with the Romans, and so lost all, together with himself. Briefly, it is neither good nor profitable for a prince to heap up great treasures and riches enclosed in one place. And what then? must a sovereign prince be poor? No, but contrary, he has need to be rich and very opulent, for otherwise he shall be feeble and weak, and cannot make head against his enemies; but his riches and treasures must be in the purses and houses of his subjects. That is to say, a prince must so deal that his subjects by good handling and maintenance of good peace may abound and be rich, that their towns may be maintained in their liberties and franchises, and in free commerce; and that the laborer and all others may be comforted and preserved from extraordinary and excessive taxes, and from exactions and pillaging of magistrates, and of a company of ruffians and violent persons who under color that they hold the place of an archer or horseman in the king's military will eat and ruin the poor laborer; and others under color of a commission to receive tenths, and of others under divers other pretexts. For to say true, the petty and inferior people are as much or more soiled and spoiled by magistrates, and those who usurp the office of magistrates, as by the taxes which are destined for the prince. If a prince then shoots at this mark, that through all his country and lands of his obedience, his subjects be rich and abundant, and that there is the greatest number possible of rich houses, then shall there be so many treasurers for him, and he shall never want in his need. For the nobleman shall serve in good order, even at his own expense if need be in affairs of war; the merchant and laborer shall furnish him with silver and soldiers; the clergy will willingly contribute their tenths. Briefly, the prince shall find ordinarily good and assured recourse in his subjects' purses, which will be the best treasuries he can have; for in place of great wages to other treasurers, who can often subtly steal from their price without being perceived, these treasurers will take no wages from their prince, nor steal from him, neither will his treasure perish in their hands. And truly, the true and assured riches of a prince, which he cannot lose and which cannot fail him, is the richness of his subjects; for other of the prince's treasurers may be undone by the poverty of collectors of debts, or by some other chance of war or shipwreck; but the treasure that is in all the people's hands is not subject to hazards. And therefore the prince cannot better treasure up wealth and enrich himself than by growing rich by good dealing with his subjects. The Venetians, who are wise politicians, use this; for it is a capital crime in their commonwealth to speak of gathering money for a public treasure. But their individuals are so rich that the public cannot be poor.

By these reasons it seems to me that the maxim of Machiavelli is sufficiently refuted; and that it is seen that a prince, for the good of his estate, ought to maintain his subjects rich and not poor. For to say that poor subjects will be more tractable and obedient, and will more easily thrust their heads under the yoke, and will better bear burdens when they are laid upon them, it is rather contrary. This was the opinion of the emperor Galba, who when Vitellius enterprised upon the empire said that there were no people less to be feared than those who are every day in thought to live; and therefore Vitellius being such a one was not to be feared. But Galba knew well in the end, to the loss of his life, that his saying was not true, and that a person in necessity will seek all means, good and bad, right and wrong, to obtain his purpose. The same cause of poverty made Otho aspire to the empire; for he himself said that he would rather die in war, in hazarding himself to come to an empire, than to die in prison for his debts. Therefore Julius Caesar said to those who were poor and great spenders, or who were loaded with crimes, that they stood in need of a civil war; meaning that the best means to put away their poverty was to see pillages and thefts permitted, as they are in civil wars, to gather silver and other goods cheap, with little labor. And to this purpose is very notable the sentence of Sallust: "Always men of one city, who have no goods, envy good people; make account of those who are naught; hate the present government, and desire a new; and disdaining their own affairs study for a change, because poverty cannot incur any hazard of loss."

If it were needful to confirm this by examples, to show that poverty has many times been cause of great insurrections and civil wars, we read that at Rome there were many stirs and seditions against usurers, who eat up and impoverish the people, and cause great faintness. The like happened often in France; for in the time of king Philip Augustus, Saint Louis, king John, and many other times, the Jews and Italians who held banks and practiced usuries in France, whereby they ruined the people, were chased and banished from the kingdom. The factions of Mailotins, and of those who carried cowls and hoods of diverse colors, and other similar popular inventions tending to seditions and civil wars, were not founded upon any other foundation than that; for poor people of base estate are always the authors and executioners of such factions and seditions. In the time that France was under the obedience of the Roman Empire, we read that the Gauls rose up often, when they sought to impoverish them by undue exactions. As in the time of Augustus there was in Gaul one Licinius, a tax collector who practiced great and undue exactions upon the people, unknown to Augustus; and because at that time part of Gaul paid tributes, each chief of every house a certain sum by month, this master deceiver, to swell his profit, made a week but six days, and a month but 24; so that in a year were fourteen months. Augustus being advised hereof was much grieved, yet did no justice thereon. Not long after, Augusts sent Quintilius Varus into Gaul for governor, who was a great lord and before had governed Syria, where he had filled his hands. Arriving in Gaul, he sought to do there as he had done in Syria, and began to commit great exactions upon the people, and to deal with them after the Syrian manner, that is, like slaves. Seeing this, the Gauls made a countenance to voluntarily accompany Varus and his army against the high Germans, upon whom he made war. Bur after they had conducted him and his army into a strait, whence he could not save himself, they set upon him and defeated and cut his army in pieces. Varus and the other great lords of his company slew themselves in despair. And hereupon the Gauls rebelled against the Romans many times; as under Nero, under Galien, and under many others; and at last freed and cut off themselves altogether from the obedience of the empire. Whereupon I conclude that to go about to hold the people poor, as Machiavelli counsels, there can arise nothing but insurrections, seditions, and confusions in the commonwealth.

But the means a prince ought to hold to enrich his subjects without weakening his own power, is first to take away all abuses committed upon the people in the collection of ordinary tributes. For a prince most righteously may levy ancient and accustomed tributes to sustain public charges, otherwise his estate would dissolve. And he ought not to follow the example of Nero, who once thought to abolish all tributes and taxes; and because the Senate showed him that he ought not to do it, he imposed other new ones without number. For a good and wise prince will do neither the one nor the other, but without inventing any new tributes will maintain himself in the exaction only of the ancient; and it seems requisite that such taxes and imposts be duly laid without favor or respect of persons; which in times of old was a reformation that king Tullius Hostilius made at Rome, whereupon he was much praised, and his poor people comforted. Men must also imitate the ancient Romans, who excepted no person from patrimonial tributes; for there was neither senator nor bishop but he paid as well as those of the third estate. There must also be a provision made that the receivers and treasurers, who are those which do most hurt to the people, may no more pillage and spoil the world. There must also be held that such excessive usuries are no more practiced under the name of pensions and interests; and that it be permitted to deliver silver to a certain moderate profit, which upon great pains it is unlawful to exceed. For so to forbid at once all profit is to give occasions to seek out palliations in contracts, by sales of pensions, by letting to hire fruits, by selling to sell again, feigned remunerations, and such like colors. There must be a provision made that foreign bankers may no more make themselves bankrouts. And here would be brought in use a law, made in the time of the emperor Tiberius, whereby it was ordained that no man might hold a bank, upon great pains, who had not two thirds of his goods in ground of inheritance. Moreover, there must be expressed the superfluities of apparel, of banquets, and other like, whereby men so impoverish themselves, so that poverty is more tolerable. For a Cato the Elder said, in an oration for the Law Oppia against the great estates and luxuries of women:

> "It is a great evil and dangerous shame, the shame of poverty and parsimony; but when the law forbids superfluities and excesses of apparel and other vain expenses, it covers that shame with an honorable mantle of living after laws, seeing that it is a most praiseworthy thing, and the contrary punishable. And assuredly, it ordinarily comes to pass that when we are ashamed of what we should not be, we will not be ashamed of what we ought to be."

Finally, a prince must be a good justice, ever respective of the meaner and poorer sort; be not oppressed by the greatest, neither by those who are violent or evil. All those things shall be no charge to the prince to bring to pass; yet by these means he may greatly enrich his subjects, who then will never spare anything they have at the prince's demand. The people of the earldom of Foix are of their own natures rude and stubborn enough, yet we read that in the time of Gaston, count of Foix (the time of Charles VI), his subjects paid him such great taxes that he held a king's estate, though he was but a count. They paid him very liberally, without constraint, and bore unto him great amity and benevolence. And whereupon came this? Because he maintained them in peace when all his neighbors were in great war, and he maintained such good justice among them that he alone pilled and vexed them. And it is certain that if men must be robbed and spoiled, they would rather be so dealt with by one man alone than by many; and that subjects will bear it better at their prince's hands than at those of individuals; but especially when extreme and hard taxes are laid upon subjects, if they are seen to be employed for the public good, and there is good peace and justice, it is somewhat softened and sweetened. And therefore Commines together praises and reprehends Louis XI, his master, saying that he pillaged and oppressed his subjects, but yet he would never suffer anyone to do them evil, or any way to rob and spoil them.

To many it may seem that what we have said tends too much unto the dispraise of poverty, which notwithstanding seems to be praised and recommended by our Christian religion. But hereunto I answer that poverty of itself is neither praiseworthy nor worthy of vituperation, but men must judge of them according to circumstances. For if it is suffered with holy patience by a Christian man who takes it in good part, and contents himself with the vocation whereunto God has called him, and with the means he has given him, and if it is accompanied with a simple and gentle spirit, assuredly such poverty may be placed in the rank of the greatest virtues. For it is no small virtue to be able well and constantly to bear poverty without straying out of the path, but rather a very difficult and rare thing. Therefore the pagans themselves praised and admired Aristides, Phocion, Lysander, Valerius Publicola, Fabricius, Curius, Quintus Cincinnatus, Menencus, Agrippa, Paulus Aemilius, and many other great persons who have carried themselves like good and virtuous people, though they were very poor, because they suffered poverty with a great and constant courage, and without straying from virtue. Yet so much there wants that Christian doctrine approves this poverty of begging, that contrary it forbids us plainly that none should be suffered to beg. And likewise the word of God witnesses to us that good men will not willingly suffer their children to beg for their bread, for always God assists and gives them means. Therefore monks called mendicants have gone too far in praising, extolling, and exalting poverty, not taking it as it must be understood by the word of God. And so it is likely they will soon repent that from the beginning they have made so deep a profession of poverty, against which they have many times since pleaded, kicked, and spurned, yet never could be rid of it, but always have been compelled by popes and parliaments to observe it as a thing wherein lay all the perfection of the orders. But because this account and narration is pleasant to tired and wearied readers, I will a little discourse upon the wars of these mendicant friars.

You must then know that these mendicants at their first entry into the world (to renown their names) proposed to themselves straightly to follow the estate of perfection, that by their own merits they might enter Paradise and cause others to enter into favor of them, and with their authority. This estate of perfection they constituted in three points, chastity, obedience, and poverty; of the two first points we will not speak here, but only of the last point, which is poverty. Of this poverty they have made three kinds, high, mean, and base; high poverty (which the Franciscan friars attribute unto themselves) is that which has nothing in this world, neither in proper nor in common any way; that is, neither fields nor house, nor possession, nor rents, nor pension, nor beasts, nor movables, nor apparel, nor books, nor rights, nor actions, nor fruits, nor any other thing in the world. Behold here indeed a sovereign, pure, and exceeding near poverty, wherein there neither wants anything, neither is there anything to be reproved, since it has nothing at all. The second kind (which is for the Dominicans and Jacobins) is a mean poverty, which has nothing particular or proper, but only some things in common, as books, apparel, and daily victuals. The third and last kind (which the Carmelites and Augustines have retained for themselves) is base poverty, which may have proper, common, and in particular whatsoever is justly necessary to life, as apparel, books, certain pensions, and some lands, for help of their kitchen and necessity of their living. And it is good to note in those good brethren the Carmelites and Augustines, how humble they show themselves, to be contented with so base a kind of poverty, without any desire to mount higher, as acknowledging themselves unworthy and incapable to ascend into so high and superlative a degree.

These mendicants then, being obliged and restrained unto poverty by a solemn vow which they made at their profession in their orders, they are so annexed, united, and incorporated in it and with it, that never after they could be never so little separated or dismembered, what diligence or labor soever they used to do it. Hereof they have found themselves much troubled and sorrowful, for howsoever gallant and goodly the Theorique of Poverty is, yet in practice they have found it a little too difficult and hard. And indeed, if you consider more nearly the theory thereof (especially of that high and sovereign poverty), I know not whether you can find anything in the world more excellent and more admirable; for they who make profession thereof, in my opinion come something near an angel-like nature; because the angels have no need of the use of the earthly and corruptible goods of this miserable world, but only take care of divine and spiritual things. More also, they who make profession of this high poverty have this advantage over the rich men who possess the goods of this vale of miseries; that they are not wrapped in so many mischiefs and travails which accompany those goods, but are frank and free, taking no care nor thought for plowing, manuring, sowing, reaping, grape-gathering, lopping of trees, grafting, eradicating, cutting, planting, building, selling, buying, or doing any other like things which concern the affairs of the world. From all these things they are free and exempted, having nothing which hinders them to be in a continual contemplation and meditation of divine things, to come in time unto a great and deep wisdom, yea to approach the angelical nature of the Cherubim and Seraphim, which have no other occupation than to contemplate and exalt the Divinity. But also if on the other side you consider the great difficulties in this so strict and straight use of poverty, you shall find it verily a sad and unpleasant thing; for it is an approved maxim as well of the mendicants as of all other monks, yea of all men in general, that every man must live. But a man cannot well live with contemplations and meditations; for the belly is not satisfied with such viands, but it must needs have bread and victuals, which grow and proceed from the earth and possessions of this world. Whereof it follows that they must needs have possessions to obtain victuals, or at least they must buy and obtain from them unto whom possessions do belong.

But the profession of poverty (especially of that high one) repugns and contraries all this; for thereby it is not lawful to have any possessions, nor to acquire corn, wine, or other victuals, for as much as by the acquisition thereof, whether it be by sale, donation, exchange, or the like, the acquirer and obtainer thereof makes himself a proprietor and master of the thing which he obtains; which is not lawful to do for those who make profession of high poverty, which can no way be proprietors of anything, be it moveable or unmovable, victuals, apparel, or any other thing whatsoever, as is said. Therefore you see that the practice of poverty is something grievous and troublesome, and not so pleasant as the theory; for as for theory, you cannot find a thing more pleasant nor facile, nor which less hinders a man in worldly affairs, nor which merits more to be practiced and esteemed in all good companies, and especially in great feasts and banquets, after the old proverb, which says

He that implete is of viands,
Fasting, to others recommends.

But upon these difficulties touching the practice of poverty, the mendicants have made many great questions and scruples of conscience, which many popes have sought to resolve, yet could never satisfy nor content those brethren. Among others, the Friar Minors were greatly troubled in their spirits upon this; that by their rule which the blessed St. Francis left them, it is said by an express article that the brethren of that order can have nothing proper in any manner, neither may they have any means to live, but to beg hard and without shame. For there are among them who think that this may be understood of simple property, and not of usufruct or use thereof; so that retaining the usurpation only of possessions and other things granted unto them, rejecting the property of them, they think not to violate any part of their rule. But those who give this interpretation of the rule dare not justify their interpretation thereof, lest they contradict the testament and last will of blessed St. Francis, their founder; whereby he had ordained and expressly forbidden that none should gloss upon his rule; and that none should say that it ought to be understood thus or thus; and that none should obtain Apostolical letters from the pope, either to add thereunto or to declare. Insomuch as on the one side, not daring to adventure to give declarations and new sense to the rule, and on the other side being held so short thereby that they dare neither have nor acquire anything, their consciences are marvelously troubled and tormented; and especially since some of their adversaries call them thieves, proving it by this argument. *Whosoever possesses or eats another man's goods, whereas he has nothing, nor can have anything of his own, he is a thief.* But the mendicants, and especially the Friar Minors do possess habits, books, movables, chambers, bribes, asses, and other movable goods, and do eat bread and pittance, in all which goods they can have no right of property, nor other; ergo then, etc. Unto which argument assuredly they cannot answer; for if they reply that in these goods by them possessed, they have the use simply without any property; besides that they have given an interpretation to the said rule against the testamentary prohibition of their glorious founder, a man may reply upon them that if they will say they have a right of use in the said goods, it will then follow that that right should be to them in propriety; and that therefore having the propriety of that right, they should always find themselves breakers and gainsayers of their rule, which prohibits to have anything proper, whether possessions, rights, or other goods. Hereat let every man think if it must not needs be very grievous to those good Friar Minors, that men should thus argue against them by subtle arguments to prove them thieves, as living on other men's goods and of that which was not theirs, like birds of prey. And so much the more this pinches them, because they see that high poverty (whereby they pretend to mount to the degree of perfection) is the cause whereupon this blame and defamation comes. But they dare not well complain nor speak a word, but only tolerate all things in all patience and humility, not without great scruple of conscience, which many among them make whenever they think in their spirits that that which they eat is not their own, neither the apparel that they wear; and that they have not nor can have in them any property, any right, any usufruct, nor any simple usage. Yet could they not so repress this their grief of mind, but it would by many tokens break out; yea, and that meat which with sad minds and striving consciences they had crammed into their belies withal, was again disgorged and vomited. Finally, after they had remained a long time in that anguish and perplexity of spirit and of conscience, it happened that they created a pope at Rome who in his youth had been a Friar Minor, who was called Pope Nicholas III. The friars seeing that such a pope, who once was one of theirs and who knew the difficulties which were in the practice of this high poverty, could not he be but favorable unto them, held a Chapter general where they resolved to send certain delegates and ambassadors to this pope, humbly to beseech him to do them this favor and grace, as to take away and cut off all the said difficulties. These delegates then in 1280 hastened towards the paternity of this pope, and showed him from the Chapter general of their order, the great and indissoluble difficulties wherein they were, for the intelligence of the rule of blessed St. Francis, and for the observation of the prohibitions contained in this testament, and generally for the whole practice of that high poverty; humbly beseeching his said paternity to provide therefore, as he knew to be requisite. Yet they most humbly showed unto him by form of advice (without any mind of presumption to give any interpretation to the said rule) that it seemed unto them that the glorious St. Francis neither understood nor willed that they should be left naked of all goods. For by the same rule he had commanded them to observe the Gospel, and to follow the traces of Jesus Christ; but Jesus Christ (said they) had a purse and silver in it, as we read in the Gospel, and that therefore they thought it should be permitted unto them so to have also. Moreover, they said, by rejecting the goods and testamentary legacies that good Christians would give them, that they so should be homicides of themselves and tempters of God, because they deprived themselves of things necessary for the conservation of their lives. Also, that this great and high poverty leads to the estate of bestiality; because we can obtain no knowledge without having books either in propriety or in use. Also, suppose they ought to have nothing at all proper in particular, it does not therefore follow that they ought to have nothing in common; and therefore that his holiness might well permit them to have goods under the common name of the convent. And that the blessed St. Francis having commanded them by his rule to beg hardly and without shame, in consequence has permitted them to take whatsoever any man gives them in alms, be it movable or unmovable, silver or cloth, to enjoy or use as their own. Moreover, they humbly remonstrated unto him that often in cases of maladies and other necessities they were forced to borrow, which they could not repay unless they had whereof to do it; and that therefore it was necessary unto them to be permitted to acquire and heap up, to satisfy those who had lent them in their necessity for their credit's sake. Upon this supplication and remonstrance pope Nicholas assembled the college of cardinals, who in their conclave examined well this great case; and by their advice he ordained and declared that Friar Minors could have nothing in propriety, neither in particular, nor in common, because the true perfection of the order consists in this point, to be disappropriated every way of all goods, without having or retaining in them any right. But he reserved unto them the fact (and not the right) of the usage of goods, which by legacies or otherwise might fall and appertain unto them, retaining to himself and to the Roman Church the propriety of those goods. Conditionally also, that this fact and deed of usage be not excessive, and that in the said friars there always shine a notable and apparent poverty. And answering to their reasons, he said that our Lord Jesus Christ desiring to yield to our infirmities, and to condescend to our imperfections, thought it good to have a purse and silver in it, but yet that notwithstanding to have a purse and silver is of itself an action of human infirmity and imperfection. And as for what they say, that the abdication and rejection of all propriety of goods may prove an homicide to himself and a temptation of God; he answered no, but that the true way to perfection is altogether to commit himself to the providence of God, without having any care to provide for living; and that the means of begging (which by their rule was permitted them) could never fail them; and that also neither was it needful to have store of victuals, that they might the better observe the said rule, but especially in that article whereby they are enjoined to fast every Friday, the Vigils, Advent, and Quadragesima, which comes to half the year or thereabouts. And that as their poverty ought to be straight, so their victuals also ought to be straight and sober, and that they ought to eat little; for it agrees best with that so high poverty. And as for what they say, that it may be lawful for them to have goods in common; he answers that it is very evident, no, because the rule restrains them to a rejection and abdication of all property; and that which is common to many, may well said by right to be proper to all in general, and to everyone *in specie* or particular. And finally, upon that last point wherein the friars understand that in cases of necessity they are forced to borrow, and that therefore they desire permission to acquire, to repay; pope Nicholas answered them that they have not well proceeded therein, to contract either borrowing or lending, because in that kind of contract there is a translation of propriety from him that lends, in him who receives; and as the legists say, *Mutuum est cum fit de meo tuum*, that is, A thing is lent when that which is mine is made thine. To shun therefore this inconvenience, he gave them an acute and ingenious counsel; which was to procure and find means that those who had devotion to give their convent should appoint for them principal payers in their place, of things which were necessary to them in their maladies or otherwise, towards them who would furnish them thereof; or that they should name someone (of whom they might be assured, to him that would give them any legacy) to be executor of his will, by employing the legacy to satisfy the furnitures made, or to make, for the friars. Upon condition notwithstanding, that the property and possession of the silver or other thing bequeathed be in no sort transferred unto the said friars, but always to remain with him that bequeathed it. Behold in sum how pope Nicholas resolved the difficulties of the mendicants touching the practice of their poverty; for he permitted to them the use of goods which fell unto them, and reserved the propriety of them to the Roman Church, and besides permitted them to accept testamentary legacies by persons interposed. Wherein he well showed what a good friend he was of that order, and that he forgot not the place wherein he was nourished in his youth; yet he left a scruple in this bull, whereupon there fell out no less contentions than before, because he circumscribed his permission or indulgence with this condition: that always there should shine in these friars a holy and manifest poverty. This was a condition which touched them very near, as shall be said hereafter.

Yet the mendicants, seeing themselves to have a permission by this apostolical bull of pope Nicholas, to cause legacies and foundations to be given unto them, immediately began to practice themselves diligently to have them. And because they considered that by sermons they might easily draw the devotion of the people towards them, they rushed upon that practice with all their might; which so well succeeded unto them because the bishops and curates of that time (as for the most part they were at that day) were but beasts, and could not preach at all, neither well nor ill, but the most sufficient only knew their mass at the most. The sermons then of these mendicants being of great estimate and credit with the people, they straight drew unto them store of legacies, pensions, and foundations, they never forgetting (either at the beginning or end of their sermons) to recommend the works of charity towards their convents, deciphering their necessities at large, and very eloquently assuring the good people that they might thereby gain Paradise for them and theirs by doing good to their said convents. By this means also they drew to them the practice of burials and confessions, insomuch that every man and woman went to the mendicants to be shriven; who failed not, but always enjoined them for penance to give something to their convents, and to cause masses to be said for them. And whensoever it came to the extreme confession in the article of death, they exhorted the diseased to elect their sepulcher in their convents, and so to give them good legacies and benefits. Briefly, they wrought so well and diligently by practice upon practice, that legacies and benefits even rained on all sides upon them, to the great prejudice of curates, who lost almost all their ancient and accustomed oblations, and who saw their offertories and suffrages go to nothing in their open sight, to their great grief.

This was the cause that about the year 1311, the curates (being countenanced by bishops) complained much to Pope Boniface VIII, saying that the mendicants troubled them in their ancient possessory of sermons, confessions, and sepulchers, and that they thought it was most reasonable that they to whom appertained the charge of souls, should also have the bodies of the dead to bury, and that they should hear them in confession, unto whom they administered the sacraments. Moreover they showed that the mendicants invented many novelties, as to preach within their convents at the same hour that the curates said their parochial masses, and that they also preached without their convents, without either the bishop's license, or the curate of the place. And by such practices and novelties the said mendicants had taken away from the curates most of their obventions and revenues, and so brought their estates almost to nothing; therefore most humbly they besought his paternity to remedy those abuses, and to maintain them in their ancient possessions. Pope Boniface upon this complaint of the curates (for which all bishops and prelates entered) would give provision, and by his ordinance which he made, with the advice of his brothers cardinals, he exhorted the curates to take patiently, that the mendicants have right and authority to preach, confess, and bury, showing them that it was free to the people to go hear a sermon, to confess themselves, and to choose their sepulcher where they thought good. Moreover, to do them right in this, that the mendicants frustrated the said curates of their practices and obventions, he ordained that from thence forward the said curates (lest they carried the name of curate in vain and without profit) constituted by Apostolical authority, that they should levy and retract a fourth part from all legacies, foundations, and other obventions which the said mendicants could obtain, and might any way fall and come unto them by means of the said sermons, confessions, sepulchers, or otherwise; forbidding the said mendicants for no cause to preach in their convents at the hour that parish masses, or at the hour that bishops or their vicars preach; and not to preach out of their convents without the permission of the bishop or the curate of the place. Exhorting moreover the said curates and mendicants respectively to live and carry themselves together from thence forward in good peace and concord, and by no means to suffer that the spirit of division (the enemy of human nature) be so familiarly acquainted with them.

The pope Boniface having made this ordinance and rule between the curates and mendicants, soon after they entered further than ever into contentions and debates. For when curates went into the mendicants' convents to ask their fourth part of the practices and obventions, they would straight join all together and make such a shouting, braying, and hissing at the poor curate, calling him beast, idiot, ass, and saying he could not well read his mass, nor decline their name. And further would ask them certain petty questions out of grammar, and bid them turn something into Latin, to shame them. "And thinkest thou beast" (said they) "that we have taken pains to prepare meat to put in thy mouth? Belongeth it unto the ass, to reap that which we sow; go, go beast to thy

Breviary, if thou canst read it, and come not into our convent to beg anything, unless thou wilt have our discipline. Go and study thy *Dispauterie*, and *Amo, Quae Pars*, and come not hither to trouble and defile the pure fountain of holy theology, wherein thou understand nothing." Some others cried come, come unto our refectory, and we will lay the trebelliane fourth part on their shoulders. These poor curates then, seeing the said mendicants approach them, in a great fear retired out of their convents. And knowing no way possibly to obtain their due which had been granted them by pope Boniface, they offered their griefs and sorrowful complaints to Pope Benedict XI, in the year 1304 or thereabouts. But the mendicants were not cowards to remonstrate also their good right on their side; and among other reasons especially showed that as by good right none will withdraw a Falcidie or fourth part from devout and godly legates, so none ought to take a fouth trebellaine from their practices and obventions, seeing they were bestowed on them for godly causes also. Pope Benedict, after good deliberation upon this weighty matter, with the advice of his cardinals and of certain other good old doctors of law, found that the mendicants' reasons were well founded in right, and that there was no apparent reason wherefore they should pay to the curates the fourth part. For although there was some color in what the curates said, that they ought to have the fourth part because they had the name and title of curates, even as an heir ought to have the fourth trebelliane free because he has the name and title of heir; yet in this rule there is a fallacy (said these old doctors) in regard of legates for godly and devout causes. For legates are exempt from delivering of fourth parts; such like as those which mendicants take of godly Christians. And for confirmation of their opinion, they cited Godfredus in Summa, Azo, Huholinus de Fontana, Guilliermus de Cuneo, Rainerius de Foro Livio, Hubertus de Bobio, Petrus de bella Pertica, Oldradus de Ponte, and many other old doctors of law. They also cited certain strong pillars out of Bartolus and Baldus, upon which they said their opinion was founded. And therefore pope Benedict, moved with their allegations and with equity, razed and made of no validity the ordinance of pope Boniface in that case, taking away and utterly abolishing the said fourth part; yet something to content the curates, he ordained that they should have the half of the funerals of those who were buried with the mendicants, that is to say, half of the spoiled things which served for the conduction of the body (as torches and cloth about the coffin), which was no great booty in comparison with legacies, obits, foundations of masses, and other obventions; yet there was no help, the curates must needs be contented with this sanction and decree for this time.

Yet hereof engendered a greater quarrel than ever between the curates and mendicants. For the curates said high and clear that Benedict had done them wrong to take from them the said trebelliane of mendicants, and that those new come beasts would have all, and would spoil all curates of their goods and revenues. And that under the title and name of mendicants and contemners of the goods of this world, they manifested themselves to be rapinous hypocrites who will needs have all by right or wrong. These curates so cried and complained, and so well remonstrated their right unto Pope Clement V at the Council of Vienna, Anno 1311, that the pope razed the ordinance of Benedict, and again brought into force that of Boniface.

Moreover, in the said Council of Vienna there was demonstrated unto pope Clement that the mendicants had greatly abused the commission of pope Nicholas, who had reserved that always in the order of the mendicants there should shine a holy and apparent poverty; yet already the said mendicants so well practiced and profited in their trade that there was no more amongst them any appearance of poverty. For each day they instituted heirs, they gave legacies, pensions, and revenues; vines, gardens, and other possessions; also they built their convents like royal palaces, insomuch that there appeared in them nothing but richness and opulence, so much there wanted that in them appeared any sign or token of holy poverty, as should shine in them according to their rule, and the reservation and condition which pope Nicholas set down in his bull. Pope Clement having understood all this by the advice of the said council, declared the mendicants (although he himself had been one) incapable to be heirs, to receive testamentary legacies, or to have possessions, rents, or pensions, yea, to have barns of corn or cellars of wine, unless in time of great necessity, or to have precious church ornaments or houses sumptuously built. Briefly, this pope to their great grief brought them again to their first practice of high poverty, mean, and base, and cut near their wings, that they might not forsake and abandon it from thence forward. Yet he took not from them their usage of fact, of some small and few goods, as many as might be necessary for their simple nourishment, therein comprehending the youth of the order, and without anything departing from their poverty; so that always there might remain something unto them justly whereof to live.

But Pope John XXII, in 1324, took yet from them the said usage of fact, and sent them purely and simply to their clap-dish, and begging for their living, saying that the said usage of fact reserved to mendicants imported and attributed to them a propriety; because the act of use is proper to them who exercise it, and therefore whoever has that act of use, he in consequence has something proper; which after he concludes by his bull that all that goodly subtlety and invention of pope Nicholas, to leave the use of goods to mendicants, and to reserve the property of these goods to the Roman Church, was but a simulation and hypocrisy wherewith the mendicants seek to cover themselves, and abandon fairly that holy poverty wherein they have constituted the estate of perfection, and whereunto he sent them.

When the mendicants saw themselves thus disgraced and remitted as deep as ever into their poverty, they were much offended, but then there was no order nor means to remedy it, but for a long time made the best of it they could. About threescore and sixteen years after this ordinance of pope John (that is 1490) there was a pope created called Alexander V, a Candiot by nation, who had been a Friar Minor in his youth; unto whom these mendicants resorted and showed him that they were the true curates and pastors of the people, because they had right and privilege from the Apostolic seat to confess all people and to bury their bodies; and that those whom they confess were held and reputed both well and duly confessesed, without need to be again confessed to the curates; and those who they bury were known and reputed to be well and duly buried. They further said that they had privileges to preach to the people and to say masses, as good and available (at the least) as them of curates; yea the people liked them better and said they were devout, and frequented them more than those curates said. And withal they said that in their convents there was great store of masses, and at all times, to the great profit and commodity of every man. For they who for their breakfast in the morning, or when they were to ride forth, had need of a morning mass, they should find there some ready said, at three or four o'clock. They likewise who rise late, as good old and devout women, found masses at nine, ten, and eleven o'clock, yea as many as they would between five o'clock in the morning until dinner time. They further remonstrated to the paternity of this holy father that the said curates were asses and shod beasts, who could not acquit the due of the least sermon which was made in all the year, and who lived not upon their cures and benefices, but suffered them to be seved by as ignorant vicars as themselves, who cared not for anything but to make profit by farming the said cures, whereby they commit infinite abuses, seekinig only to clip their sheep without giving them any spiritual food. But as for us (said they), we distribute unto them spiritual meat in all largesse and abundance, as well by celebration of masses and other divine services, as by multiplication of sermons within and without our convents. Wherefore it evidently follows (said they) that we are the true and actual curates of the people, performing and executing all the acts of legitimate curates, and that they who say they are curates are so but in a shadow and fantasy only, and that they are unworthy to carry the name and title they have, and thereby to enjoy the fruits, designs, oblations, obventions, and other revenues and practices which said curates possess. So they concluded in this that it would please his paternity to create, establish, and constitute them the alone and true curates, and put them in real and actual possession of the said cures, and of the revenues and dependences of them, with inhibitions to those who called themselves curates, and to all others not to trouble, molest, nor hinder them in any sort, by themselves or by interposed persons, upon pain to incur the indignation and malegrace of St. Peter and of St. Paul, and of perpetual damnation, without any hope of grace, pardon, or appeal. Upon this goodly remonstrance, containing so ponderous and considerable reasons, pope Alexander referred the matter to council, and by the advice of his cardinals granted to mendicant friars all that they demanded, and caused with great expedition to go out fair and ample bulls, and well leaded. These good mendicant friars, as soon as they had got out their bulls, came straight from Rome to Paris to cause them to be received and registered in the court of Parliament. But before they presented them to the said court, they advised and concluded that it was most expedient to have the people favorable and on their side. Therefore through all a whole lent, they preached at Paris in all their convents the contents of their bulls, saying that they only were the true curates and pastors of souls, by the ordinance and creation of the pope, God's lieutenant on earth, of whose power none ought to doubt; and exhorted the people from henceforth to acknowledge them, to the end to shun the pains set down in our holy father's bulls, against all contradictions thereof. And in their sermons they did not forget to make invectives against a company of curates who knew nothing but to take the revenues of their cures without deserving them, neither spared they also to tax and detest their beastly and too notorious ignorance. But yet they were something deceived in their opinion, for at Paris many cures were held and possessed by doctors, theologians of Sorbonne; these doctors then fearing the consequence of these bulls of the mendicants, and that thereby they might be disposed of their cures, immediately mounted also into pulpits to counterpreach and blazon the said bulls and those who had obtain them. Therfore they showed to the people that from all times, exceeding all memory of any man living, curates were in actual and legitimate possession to take and receive tenths, oblations, obventions, and other fruits and revenues affected and dependants to cures. And the mendicants, contrary to the proper professioin of mendicity, were in possession, season and enjoyance of poverty, mean, and base, respectively without any trouble, hindrance, or contradiction, in the knowledge and view of all the world. And that therefore everyone ought to be maintained and guarded in his possession, without any innovation, that is, all curates of the goods and revenues of their cures, and mendicants of their poverty and begging. And for proof thereof they cited many good places, saying it is written that man must give to Caesar that which is Caesar's, and to God that which is God's, which is to say that we must needs yield to every man that which belongs to him, to curates tenths and oblations, and to mendicants their begging and alms. They further said that it was reasonable that the name should answer to the thing, and that since the Friars, Jacobins, Carmelites, and Augustines have chosen the name of mendicants, that really and in effect they ought to be beggars, and not curates. A short time would not serve to set down and discover all the reasons and allegations which the curates preached and blazed abroad against the mendicants, and the mendicants against the curates. For neither the one nor the other ever studied better sermons than they did in this contestation and contention; the curates defended themselves by their long possession, and by the ancient and modern canons which assigned them their charge of souls, and which compare them to Levites; yea even in taking their tithes. The also cited, *Non alligabis &c.* that is, Thou shalt not bind the throat of the ox which treads out the corn; and *Dignus est operarius &c.* that is, The workman is worthy of his salary or wages, and many other like places which they had at their fingers' ends. And to confute those mendicants' bulls they said they were but new come, wherewith they do trouble the world; and that before they were born the people were as well preached unto and instructed, and masses, confessions, and other divine services as well done and exercised, as since they came into the world; and that they had nothing in them but babble and certain subtlty, wherewith they brought the people asleep and persuaded them that they are learned, although they know nothing; and that they are full of hypocrisy and simulation, making an outward profession of poverty, yet tending in effect to no other end but to have and heap up goods and revenues. They moreover said that it was a mortal sin to give anything to these mendicants, unless some few bribes and alms, because those who gave them either silver or possessions, or rents, or revenues, made them to be condemned in hell by causeing them to break their vow of poverty, and by making them break their rules which they had sworn to observe. And that they who are the cause that any other does evil and sin, are as culpable as he that does it. The mendicants to the contrary alleged their apostolic bulls, and the pope's power, and said it was a heresy of the greatest and most insupportable that could be in the world, to say that the said bulls ought to have no place; because that was as much as to revoke into doubt the high and unmeasurable power of the great vicar of God; and that those who preach against the said apostolic bulls should feel the smart of it. They also took the places of scripture before cited, *Non alligabis, Et dignus est mercenarius, &c.* saying that they formally made for them; for they were the true oxen which tread out the grain, and the true workmen who travail in divine service; and that they say more masses in a month in one of their convents, than there is said in all the cures of Paris in a year. And that for one man and one woman which those curates confess, they confess a hundred, and therefore for curates to cite these places they but cut themselves with their own knives. And as for their sermons (said they) these masters curates will be so proud, to compare them with ours. Do not all men see that commonly they can do nothing but at the offertory speak a few words which they have learned by heart from their master, to get their offerings in? Do they not likewise see that everyone mocks them because of their ignorance and evil life, and that commonly there is no good play that has not a curate in it? But as for us, you see how we preach (said they) in pulpits, our sermons are other manner of things than their proems, and there is no more comparison to be made between their speeches and our sermons, than to compare a calf to an ass. Moreover if we should come to a disputation to speak Latin, were these curate to be compared with us? The least novices in our convents shall always say a lesson more sufficiently than these curates, if they will but learn it. Finally, all this Lent passed in sermons and countersermons of the said mendicants and curates, all which of the one part and the other sought to win the people's favor and devotion, to enjoy the fruits and revenues of cures. After the Lent was passed they came to justice, for the mendicants pursued the reception and enrolling of their bulls, entreating the cout of Paris to admit and allow them, whereupon the said curates of Paris formed an opposition. As the parties proceeded in their causes, they respectively alleged by intendits, replies, duplications, triplications, the reasons and means touched before, and far more reasons which touched the quick. But the evil luck was for the mendicants, for upon the point of their good hope to obtain the cause on their side, pope Alexander died. Then the curates began to oppose against them that the said bulls had no force nor vigor in them unless they were confirmed by Pope John XXIV, successor of the said Alexander. The mendicants, much grieved hereat, sought to obtain a confirmation, but could not; for the curates got before them, and the poor mendicants seeing themselves out of hope to obtain the reception and enrolling of their said bulls, resolved to leave the pursuit thereof; and the Jacobins first left the cause, and the others consequently. So that the curates were maintained definitively in the possession and enjoyance of their cures, and of the revenues depending thereunto; and the mendicants were maintained in their possession and season of their beggary, with express inhibitions (accorded by the consent of the said curates) not to trouble nor molest them in any sort, and each to bear his part of the law charges.

These mendicants seeing themselves fixed and fastened to their poverty, more than ever took it with the best patience they possibly could, for so were they forced to do. Yet notwithstanding some individuals among them, who were the most angry and had most credit, did so much that they obtained for them provisions and reservations from the pope, of certain cures and other benefices, with dispensation to hold and possess them, notwithstanding their vow of poverty. The curates of France, fearing the consequence, made their complaints to king Charles VI, then reigning. The king by the advice of his council made an ordinance in the year 1413, wherein he much praises the rules of the mendicant's founders, in that by them it is ordained that they ought to live in poverty and mendicity, without having anything in common or in particular, saying that such and ordinance is both salutary and good. And that poverty is so annexed to the monarchal profession of mendicants that the pope himself cannot separate them; which considered, he forbids expressly that none shall have regard to the said provisions obtained by any mendicants upon cures or other benefices, and if any be in possession, that he be taken out, and they who are not yet received, that none should receive them in. And commanded all bailiffs, stewards, and other officers of the realm not to suffer so pernicious, yea so superstitious a thing to have place, but rigorously to punish those who stand against this ordinance, notwithstanding all bulls, provisions, and dispensations of the pope to the contrary. So that by this, the king's ordinance, the mendicants were more strongly tied to the possession and enjoyance of their poverty and beggary, as well in general as particular; this happened at the pursuit of the said curates, their adversaries.

But yet a strange case it is, that the passions and hatred of men should be such as they have no end. The said mendicants were so far from contentment at this ordinance that they bore great malice to all curates, yea the one beheld the others with an evil eye, and could not hold themselves from reciprocal detractions and evil speeches, and from blazing one another in pulpits, taxing the abuses and heresies of each other and describing one another's merchandise. When Pope Sixtus IV came to his papacy, in the year 1472, the mendicants became very proud because he was a Friar Minor, and waxed insolent and audacious against curates, assuring themselves that the pope would support them in all things. The curates then not being able to suffer the detractions, scolding, and insolences of these mendicants, complained to the pope, who could do no less than seek than to accord them. For this elect he deputed four cardinals to hear the differences of the said curates and mendicants, and in quietest manner to compound them. The cardinals heard the parties in their allegations, and did so much with them that they submitted themselves to their final judgment. After this, to set a firm and final peace between the said parties, they pronounced for them an amiable sentence, which was authorized by the pope in 1478, and contains the articles following. That curates from thence forward should no more say that the mendicants were authors of heresies, seeing that the faith has been greatly brought to light by them. And likewise the mendicants shall preach no more that parishoners are not bound to hear the parochial mass, their curate on Sundays, and solemn feasts, seeing that by the canons they are thereunto restrained and obliged. *Item* that neither the one nor the other shall any more solicit persons to choose a sepulcher in their churches, but shall leave it at the free election of every man. *Item* that the said mendicants shall preach no more that the parishoners are not bound to confess themselves to their own curate, at the least at Easter, since by right they are bound thereunto, and that every good parishioner ought to make his Easter with his own curate, without anything derogating by that article from the privilege mendicants have to hear confessions, and to enjoin penance to confessed and repentants. *Item* that the mendicants, in their actions of preaching, of saying Matins, and ringing their bells, do not enterprise upon the hours that curates say their service, unless it be by consent of the parties. *Item*, that the mendicants shall no more turn away the persons and parishoners from their parish masses, neither shall curates take away the devotion of parishoners from the mendicants, but rather aid and succor them. Behold in sum the articles of this peace, and arbitrary sentence between the mendicants and curates, which the pope Sixtus greatly approved, and generally exhorted them all to concord and union, in the name and as vicar of him who said *Pacem meam do vobis, Pacem meam relinquo vobis*, I give you my peace, I leave you my peace. By which articles of the said arbitral sentence is seen how these curates and mendicants publicly blamed one another; and all this proceeded not but from the ardent zeal they all had, not to the edification of the people, but to have their offerings and oblations. For since that time, they could so well manage and deal with the poor ignorant world that they made them give them whatsoever they would, especially those who were sick, when they were at confession, and asked absolution from purgatory and hell, they would never absolve them unless they gave to their convents and churches whatsoever they desired.

This conclusion here is also clean contrary to the maxim of Machiavelli, that poverty cannot be a cause to hold a people in peace and obedience, seeing it was cause of so many discords and dissentions, even amongst them who made profession thereof, and who constituted their perfection therein. By this discourse also we may note the sanctity of the mendicants (wherewith this poor world has been so much ravished), who from the beginning of their birth in this world have raised up so many riots and strifes against curates, and all for the paunch. For they began and flourished in the time of Pope Gregory IX, Anno 1230, which pope was then much troubled with resolving the hard points about their poverty, and amongst other points resolved them that it ought to be understood not only in the abdication of all propriety to particulars, but also to the general, as pope Nicholas recites it in his abovesaid decretal. For that of pope Gregory is not found printed in the body of the canon law, as the others are, whereof before we have made mention. But herein is no great loss, no not though all the canon law were lost with it; for although some thing be good in it, yet most of it is good for nothing but to maintain wickedness, abuses, and Romanish superstitions; that it were expedient to bury that little good in it so that all the evil might be choked with it. For from hence there is come into the world infinite (both spiritual and corporal) calamities.

3.33
Machiavelli

A prince who fears his subjects ought to build fortresses in his country to hold them in obedience. (*Discourses*, book 2 chapter 24; *The Prince*, chapter 20)

The prince who has more fear of his own people than of foreigners must build fortresses; but he who doubts foreigners more than his subjects need not. For the best fortress that is, is not to be thought evil by subjects; and if a prince is once thought so, there is no fortress that can save him. It is true that fortresses may be profitable to a prince in time of peace, to give more courage to him and to his governors established in them, to hold the people in subjection, and to use against them greater audacity and rigor. But yet this shall be but weak assurance, unless the prince has means to raise up a good and strong army to tame his subjects if they rebel. For to think to tame them by reducing them to poverty, *Spoliatis arma supersunt*: arms remain yet to the unarmed. Also to disarm them, *Furor arma ministrat*: fury administers arms enough. Likewise, to slay the chief heads of the people, more heads would arise, as of the Hydra. The Sforzas built the castle at Milan and judged that by the means of that fortress they might with assurance handle their subjects at their pleasure, and therefore spared no kind of violence. Thus they acquired the hatred and evil will of their subjects, which was the cause that the French, their enemies, carried away Milan at the first assault; and the Sforzas had no good by their fortress, but were spoiled of all the duchy.

Answer

Although Machiavelli has not dealt with the art of tyranny in his writing by a method, yet he has not left behind any part of that art. For first he has handled how a tyranny ought to be built; that is, by cruelty, perfidy, craft, perjury, impiety, revenges, contempt of counsel and friends, entertainment of flatterers, trumpery, hatred of virtue, covetousness, inconstancy, and other like vices; whereby he has demonstrated that men must ascend by degrees to come unto a sovereign wickedness. Secondly, he has showed how one ought to be maintained and conserved in that high degree of wickedness and tyranny; namely, by maintaining among subjects partiality and seditions, and in holding them in poverty and necessity. Now he adds another means, namely to build fortresses against his subjects, as by making citadels in good towns, and by building forts upon bridges and common passages, and other like castles and fortresses. And Machiavelli thinks this means ought to be practiced, and that other aforesaid means are not sufficient to establish a tyranny. For poverty, he says, is no sufficient means to contain a people in obedience, for they are never without arms. And though they should disarm them and slay their chieftains, yet that would not suffice, because the anger and fury of the people would furnish them with sufficient arms, and chieftains would arise unto them like the heads of a Hydra.

But I will not stay long in the refutation of this maxim; I will only say this, that experience makes us wise, and that the invention of the citadels, which in our time princes have built against their subjects, has been the cause of infinite evils. For all commerce and traffic has been and is greatly diminished in towns where they have been built, and there have been and are committed infinite insolences by soldiers against citizens; and no good has come to their princes but great expenses and the evil will of their subjects. For this construction of citadels is an apparent show that the prince does not trust his subjects, especially when they are built anywhere but at the borders of countries. When the subjects know that their prince distrusts them, they also esteem that he does not love them. And when the subject is not beloved by his prince, he cannot also love him; and not loving him, he obeys him not but as constrained, and in the end will get his head out of the yoke, as soon as there falls out a fit occasion. Here is the profit of citadels.

Yet I will say this by the way, that our Machiavellians of France, who were authors and enterprisers of the massacres of Saint Bartholomew, read not well this place in Machiavelli. For they said that men must not stay upon fishing for frogs, but must catch in their nets great salmons; and that one salmon's head was worth more than ten thousand frogs, and when they had slain the chieftains of pretended rebels, they should easily overthrow the rude and rascally multitude, which without head could enterprise nothing. These venerable enterprisers should have considered what their doctor Machiavelli says here, which they have since seen by experience: that a people cannot want heads, which will always rise up, even those heads which are slain. If they had so well noted and practiced this point of Machiavelli as they do others, so much blood would never have been shed, and their tyranny may have longer endured. For the great effusion of blood immediately cried for vengeance to God, who according to his accustomed justice has heard the voice of that blood; and for the cry of the orphan and the widow, he has laid the axe to the root of all tyranny, and already has cut away many branches thereof; and if it please him will not tarry long to lay all on the ground, and so establish France in its ancient government.

As for fortresses in frontiers of countries, they have long been practiced, and are profitable to guard from incursions and invasions of enemies, that those who dwell near borders may the more peaceably enjoy their goods. We read that the emperor Alexander Severus gave his frontier fortresses to good and approved captains to enjoy during their lives, to the end (according to Lampridius) that they might be more vigilant and careful to defend their own. And afterward the emperor Constantine ordained that the said fortresses, with their grounds and revenues, should pass to the heirs of the said captains, who held them as a heritage. And hereupon, some say, has come the civil law called *Feudi*.

3.34
Machiavelli

A prince ought to commit to another those affairs which are subject to hatred and envy, and reserve to himself those that depend upon his grace and favor. (*The Prince*, chapter 7, 14)

A prince who will exercise some cruel and rigorous act ought to give the commission thereof unto others, to the end that he may not acquire evil will and enmity by it. And yet if he fears that such a delegation cannot be wholly exempted from blame, having consented to the execution which was made by his commission, he may cause the delegation to be slain, to show that he did not consent to this cruelty, as did Cesare Borgia and Remiro d'Oorco.

Answer

This maxim is a dependency of that good doctrine which Machiavelli learned from Cesare Borgia, who although was very cruel, yet appearing so soft and gentle, following the maxim enjoining dissimulation, committed the execution of his cruelty to Remiro d'Oorco, as we have said before. And because we have fully shown that all dissimulation and feignedness is unworthy of a prince, we will stay no longer upon this maxim. I confess that there are many things which seem to be rigorous in execution, although they are most equal and just, which it is good for a prince to commit to others, to give judgment and execution by justice, as the case merits. For as the emperor Marcus Aurelius said, it seems to the world that what the prince does, he does by his own absolute authority and power, rather than by his civil and reasonable power. Therefore to shun that blame and suspicion it is good for the prince to delegate and hand over such matters to judges who are good men, not suspected nor passionate; and not do as the emperor Valentinian did, who would never hear nor receive accusations against judges and magistrates he had established, but constrained the recusators or refusers to cause before the judges. Whereby he was much blamed, and his honor impeached and disgraced. For the chief point which is required to cause good justice to be administered is that judges are not suspected nor passionate, because the passions of the soul and heart obfuscate and trouble the judgment of the understanding, and cause them to step aside and stray out of the way. It is also a thing of very evil example when a prince with an appetite for revenge, or to please the passions of vengeful men, elects judges and commissaries that are passionate, and which have their consciences at the command of those who employ them. As was done in the time of king Louis Hutin in the judgment of Messire Enguerrant de Marigni, great master of France; and in the time of Charles VI, in the judgment of the criminal process of Messire Jean de Marests, the king's advocate in the Parliament of Paris. And a man may put to them the judgments given in our time against Amie du Bourg, the king's counsellor in the said parliament, and against captain Briquemand, and M. Arnand de Cavagnes, master of the requests of the king's household, and against the count Montgomery and many others. For the executions which followed manifested that the judges were passionate men, their consciences being at the command of strangers who governed them.

3.35
Machiavelli

To administer good justice, a prince ought to establish a great number of judges. (*Discourses*, book 1 chapter 7)

To have prompt and quick expedition of good justice, many judges must be established, for few can dispatch few causes, and a small number is easier to gain and corrupt than a great number. And withal, a great number is strong and firm in justice against all men.

Answer

Experience has made us wise in France that this maxim of Machiavelli is not true; for since they multiplied the officers of justice in the kingdom, by the increase of counsellors in parliaments, by erection of presidents' seats, and by creation of new or alternative officers, we have processes and law cases more multiplied, longer, and worse dispatched than before. By good right and reason the last Estates General held at Orleans complained to Charles IX of the multiplication and multitude of officers, which served as it still does, to multiply law cases, to ruin and eat up the people; and yet no better expedition of justice than before, but rather worse and notoriously longer, and of greater charges to the parties. Upon which complaint it was holily ordained that offices of justice which became vacant by death should be suppressed, and that none should come in their place until these offices were reduced to their ancient number, as it was in the time of Louis XII. And by the same means it was also ordained that the said offices should be no more sold, but conferred and bestowed by the king at the nomination of notable men of quality, to persons having good reputation of honesty, and whose ability in knowledge would be examined extemporarily before their reception. But the Machiavellians have razed and quashed these two articles, to have silver for the sale of offices and to bring abundance of merchandise; for the greater number of offices, so much the better is the traffic and commerce, because there are every day more times of respite whereof to make money. And we must not think that the abundance of offices has brought a low price and cheapness to their merchandise; for contrary, it has made them dearer by a third or half within this ten years. Insomuch that an office of a counsellor in Parliament, which was not wont to cost more than three or four thousand francs, will now cost two or three thousand crowns; and the offices of presidents and procurers, which were not wont to be sold, are within this little time sold as all other offices, at the price of ten, twelve, even twenty thousand francs, according as they are, and according to the greatness of the parliaments. For they are not all at once price. But I pray you, upon whom do our Machiavellians of France bestow these offices? Upon beasts or ambitious men, for learned men will not buy them if they are not drawn on by ambition, but they would rather be reputed worthy to be presidents or counsellors than to be so in effect by the price of silver. As for those who are beasts and ignorant, they have some reason to make provision for that merchandise, to get the means to live and pay their debts; otherwise they should die of hunger, or else be despised and pointed at, for by reason of their ignorance they shall be employed in no affairs of justice, and shall have no practice. And truly they are those who within this little time have made this kind of merchandise so dear; for because they are in great number, they run thither fast with great desire to have; which is the cause that the Machiavellians, seeing so many merchants arrive, so exceedingly eager to buy, hold up without all reason the price of their merchandise, and will by no means part with it but to him who offers most. But I will not here stay to dispute against these buyers and sellers, for I am of opinion that all their processes shall be made at the first Estates held.

By the resolution then of the Estates of Orleans, it is seen that this maxim of Machiavelli was reproved and condemned, and that it is neither good nor profitable for the commonwealth that there should be a great number of officers of justice, but better a mean number of them. And this might easily be judged and known by natural reason. For the prince who shall establish a great number of officers to administer justice, either he must make a multiplication of degrees of officers, or he must establish many in one same degree. If he makes many degrees of officers, then justice shall be more prolonged and pernicious, because those who plead must pass through the hand of many officers, by many instances from one degree to another. And therefore it is evident that the multiplicity of officers in degree cannot be but damaging and pernicious. If the prince makes a multitude of officers in one same degree — as was done in France when presiding seats were instituted, when new counsellors of parliament were added to the old, and when many lieutenants and other officers were newly created — the great number will not cause justice to be better nor more promptly ministered, but contrary shall be the cause of great charge and procrastination. For much time goes away while many judges are gathered together to reason one after another, and after, as the proverb says,

Affairs to many committed,
are always carelessly regarded.

Moreover, suitors always desire to inform the judge of the principal points of their case with their own mouths, fearing something should be left out either by negligence or by too much haste. And withal, what is said in a common proverb, that the lively voice touches better than the writing, and better engraves a thing in the spirits of men. This desire of the parties to cause the judge well to understand their right is not reprehensible, but just and reasonable, and ought not to be denied them; yet in the meantime the multiplicity and great number of judges makes this point very difficult and uneasy. For men have not so soon spoken to all, and finding one he straight finds now another. Moreover, if the matter to judge is easy and without difficulty, wherefore serves it to assemble a great sort of judges to decide the case, since one alone can as well dispatch it as many? And withal, that one alone can rid more matters in his study in a day or two than an assembly can do in a month; for a man may labor his case at all hours, in the morning, all the day, at night by candle light, on holy days and working days; whereas the body of an assembly will not travail nor sit but certain hours and on certain days. If the matter to be judged is difficult and hard, it may seem at first that many can better judge of it than one alone, because many eyes see clearer than one eye alone; and withal, there is not so great appearance of corruption in many as in one alone; but for these difficulties, there are other easier provisions than by multiplications of officers. For there needs but good consideration to establish in every subaltern seat one officer alone, a good man of good knowledge and well paid; for being a just man and well paid, he will not be easily corrupted, much less than a great number are at this day. And being learned and of good knowledge, he will easily resolve difficulties; and in a case of difficulty he may take for an assessor some one of the most sufficient advocates of his seat, and privately hear in his study the parties and their counsel, and upon their hearing resolve with wise inspection into all things with the help of his books, may dispatch and rid himself of all difficulties. Moreover, inferior judges can hardly judge poorly unless they err either in fact or right; from which they shall guard themselves if supreme judges perform well their duties by not sparing the personal adjournment against those who by gross ignorance err in right, or who by negligence err in fact. And assuredly, if such judges have good censors who will mark their faults, reprove and correct them, judges shall be as well administered by one alone as by many. But our sovereign judges are glad of the faults of their inferiors; for their evil judgments bring the greater practice unto them, to fill their purses, to pay for their offices, to glut their avarice, and to furnish the unmeasurable pomp of themselves and their wives. So that the same happens to justice as to the human body; for when the head is whole, it will purvey and provide for the necessities and maladies of the members, and seek out all things fit for that purpose; but when the head is diseased, all the members feel it. So the corruption which is in parliaments makes all justice in inferior courts depraved and corrupted.

I resolve then against the saying of Machiavelli, that it is better that there were but one person in every estate or degree of justice, than a great multiplicity of officers. But my meaning is not to stretch this unto sovereign justice, but contrary I think that it is good and necessary that judgment be executed by more than one person; namely, by a mean number of good and well chosen men. For a judgment given by a notable company has more weight and gravity, as a sovereign judgment ought to have, than that which comes from one alone. Also because a sovereign judgment may sometimes take its foundation upon the pure and simple equity — which sometimes directly repugns the local customs, ordinances, and laws — it is good and necessary that equity be judged to be equity by the judgment of many. And it is not meet that one alone should take upon him that great license to depart from authentic and received laws to follow his own opinion, which he will call equity. For that should be to give power to every particular judge to judge after his fantasy, against received and approved right, and so to suffer to pass under the name of equity, huge iniquity. Since then none may easily and without great reason depart from received and approved laws, it follows that none may easily induce an equity against the said laws, unless to induce it he uses great and deliberate consideration and examination, and well ponders the circumstances and consequences by a good and experimented judgment, which one alone cannot do except he be of some exceeding invention, knowledge, and experience, and of a good and sound judgment; such a one as can hardly be found. Therefore it is much better to commit to many — not to everyone, but to such as are well chosen — that power to induce equity against received laws, and not to one alone. Besides this, it pertains to sovereign judges to examine the new edicts and laws of princes, to mark and note if there is anything hard in them which would be good to mitigate and lenify; which they must either themselves do before they allow or divulge them, or else they must signify to the prince a cause why they do not approve them. This, one alone can never so well do as many, how great and wise so ever he may be, because the spirit of one man alone is not capable to see and comprehend all the particular cases which may be applied to the matter of an edict, neither in memory or cogitation can he comprehend whatsoever absurdity, incommodity, or iniquity can be in a law. But many, casting and discoursing in their minds everything, one foreseeing one thing and another another, by examining and disputing upon the matter may the better perceive and comprehend the law and the inconveniences thereof. For it is not to be doubted but that by the dispute of learned and sufficient men, who examine by a good judgment contrary reasons, conjuncts, and adjuncts of everything, may far better comprehend the difficulties and incommodities of an edict, than by the reasoning of one alone. The manner which the Romans anciently observed in the making of new laws shows this, for those who proposed and preferred them were commonly men of good spirit, great judgment, and experience in the affairs of the common weal; but yet every man great and small was heard to contradict the law proposed, and often a base person of small estimation, who had neither great knowledge nor experience, yet noted in the law absurdities and inconveniences which were causes of rejecting it, or at least moderating and correcting it. Again, because sovereign judges are censors and correctors of inferior judges, it is very requisite that they be many in number, because it will seem hard for a magistrate to be corrected by one alone, unto whom (it may be) he would not give place in anything, either in good knowledge or experience. Finally, because corruption is more to be feared in sovereign judges, who have none above them to correct their faults, than in subaltern and inferior judges, who themselves may be corrected, it is requisite that sovereign judges be in number; for it is harder to corrupt many than one alone. I confess then, in the sovereign degree of justice of a prince, it is good and expedient that he have a sufficient number of persons to exercise it, always provided the number not be too great; and unbridled, for the quality is therein more requisite than the quantity. The like is to be of the king's council, where it is good and requisite that there be many heads, as we have said in another place. For confirmation of my saying, I will cite no other thing than the example of our ancestors. For in the time of Louis XII, inferior officers were not many in one seat and degree of justice, for there was but one in every seat thereof to administer it; namely, a provost, or ordinary judge, in the first degree; a lieutenant general, or bailiff or steward in the second degree; but in sovereign courts of parliaments, and the Great Council, there were many, yet not in so great number as they are today.

But seeing we are in hand with means to establish a good justice, I will touch therein some small points which I have marked in histories. We must then presuppose that to cause good justice to be administered, a prince must have good laws and create good magistrates and officers. As for laws, some concern the decision of matters, and others the formality of process; touching those concerning the decision of matters, it seems well that there has been sufficiently provided by the local custom of every country, and by the right or law written. Well might it be desired that the doctrines of the doctors of civil and canon law were well chosen, and the good set apart and authorized; for though in judgments we can hardly lack them, yet are they so confused and wrapped with contrary opinions, that those who hope to find in the doctors' glosses and commentaries the solution of some doubtful question, often fall into inexplicable labyrinths, and for treasure instead find coals. Which would not come to pass if the good doctrines which often come in use, and which are founded upon reason and equity, were separated and distinguished from the troupe and mixture of those doctors' writings. And touching laws which concern the formality and conducting of process and litigations, it seems to me that there has been sufficient provision in France by royal ordinances. But it seems not to be sufficient that a prince make good laws, well and rightly to conduct the processes and contentions of subjects; but it will be very requisite and necessary that he make laws to prohibit and hinder the birth of these processes and contentions. For otherwise good justice and ready expedition of cases shall indirectly serve for an occasion to increase and multiply, because men will be made prompt to move actions when they are assured to have speedy and good justice. So that to shun this, and to make sure that the thing which of itself is good and holy, is neither cause nor occasion of evil, it shall be (as I have said) very requisite to have good laws to hinder the birth and origin of contentions, wherein it seems to me that the said royal ordinances are defective and maimed. So is there great need of some Lycurgus or Solon to make those laws, men's wits are so wild, and their spirits so marvelously plentiful and fertile to bring forth contentions and differences, and so easily to dissent from each other. Yet notwithstanding I do not think it impossible to repress, somewhat though not altogether, this arising and fecundity of law cases; but because it will be too long now to discourse, we will reserve it for another time.

But it is nothing to have good laws if there are not good magistrates for their execution. For the magistrate is the soul of the law, who gives it force, vigor, action, and motion, and without whom the law is but a dead and unprofitable thing. A good magistrate then is a most excellent thing, yea the most excellent in the world; a very rare thing, at least in his time; yet there might be sufficient in a mediocrity, if they were well chosen and sought for. But now the first that pays most is received without any care to choose the fittest. Dion writes that the emperor Caligula had a horse called Velocissimus, which he so much loved that he made him often dine and sup at his table, and caused him to be served with barley in a great vessel of gold, and with wine in great caldrons of gold also. Not contented thus to honor his Velocissimus, he determined to advance him unto estates and offices, and to the government of the commonwealth, and so resolved to make him consul of Rome, and would have done so if he had not been prevented by death. The Machiavellians of today who read this in Dion can well say that this was an act of a senseless madman, to give such an estate to a beast. Yet do they find it good at this day to give estates to just as senseless beasts, more dangerous than Velocissimus was? For if the worst had fallen out, if Velocissimus had been created consul, he could have done no other harm to the commonwealth, nor to individuals, unless it had been a blow with his foot to those who saluted him too near; but he would never have made any extortions, pillages, or other abuses, which the beasts placed in offices in our time commit. And Horace says that we mock him who wears a torn shirt under a silk cloak, or that has a gown on the one side too long, and on the other short; but he is not mocked who wastes great goods riotously, who overblows right, and commits infinite sins and abuses in his charge; men will say he does evil, but not that he ought to be punished.

How many offices there are in France more fit for Velocissimus than for those who hold them; and what is least perilous every man laughs at, but what is most dangerous to a commonweal, no man dares so much as say it ought to be amended, much less corrected. For there is a simple beastliness and ignorance, and a malicious beastliness and ignorance. The simple ignorance is like to that of Velocissimus, who can do neither good nor evil; but malicious beastliness and ignorance is a beastly ignorance of all good and right things, but of a great capacity to hold all vices and wickedness, such as our Machiavellians. If then a man must choose one of the two, who sees not that it is much more expedient to choose a simple beastliness? Can any then deny but it were better to have for a magistrate Velocissimus than some of our Machiavellians, or our office-chasers, who come by retail unto that which they bought in gross.

But if the prince resolves to establish good magistrates, without which he can have no good justice, though his laws be the best in the world, he must consider and note many things both in particular persons and in bodies in general. For he should take notice of the office for which he seeks to provide an officer, and accordingly seek a person whose virtue and sufficiency may be correspondent and equal to the functions of that estate. For a far greater sufficiency is required in a president than in a counselor; and in a counselor than an inferior judge; and in a judge than in a castle guard. Here it is where ought to be observed the geometric proportion whereof Aristotle speaks, by giving to the fittest the greatest estate, and to those who are meanly fit, mean offices and estates, and the least to such as are least sufficient. This is what Fabius Maximus showed to the Romans during the war with Hannibal, when two young lords were created consuls; that is, Titus Octacilius (the nephew of Fabius), and Aemilius Regillus.

> "Masters, if we had peace in Italy, or if we had war against a lesser captain than Hannibal, so that there were place to amend and correct a fault when it was made, we would not hold him well advised who would hinder your election and withstand your liberty. But in this war against Hannibal we have made no fault, yet it has cost us a great and perilous loss; therefore I am of advice that you elect consuls who match Hannibal. For as we would have our people of war stronger than our enemies, so ought we to wish that our heads and chieftains were equal to those of our enemies. Octacilius is my nephew, who espoused my sister's daughter and has children by her, so that I have cause to desire his advancement; but the commonwealth's utility is more dear to me. And withal, no other has greater cause than my nephew, not to charge himself with a weight under which he should fall."

The Roman people found his reasons good, therefore revoked their election, and by a new suffrage elected Fabius himself, and gave him for a companion Marcellus, who assuredly were two great and sage captains.

This rule, to elect magistrates equal to every charge, above all ought to be well practiced in the election of sovereign judges, so that after they have judged, if they have committed a fault it cannot but very hardly be repaired. So that the reason which Fabius alleged, having place in the election of sovereign judges, the provision which followed it merits well to be drawn into an example and consequence for the good and utility of the prince's subjects.

The particular qualities required in a magistrate cannot better nor more briefly be described than by the counsel which Jethro gave to Moses. For he advised him to elect people fearing God, true and hating greed. Surely this counsel is very brief for words, but in substance it comprehends much. For first, the magistrate who fears God will advise to exercise his office in a good conscience and after the commandments of God, and above all things will seek that God be honored and served, according to his holy will, and will punish those who do the contrary. If the magistrate fears God, he will love his neighbor as himself, because God so wills; and in consequence he will guard himself from doing anything against his neighbor which he would not have done to himself. Briefly he will in a book, as it were, write all his actions, to make his account to that great Lord and master whose fear he has in him. Secondly, if the magistrate is veritable and a lover of truth, it will follow that in the exercise of his office, in civil as well as criminal matters, he will always seek out the truth and shut his ears to impostures and lies of slanderers; which is no small virtue, wherein judges often err. Also, a magistrate that loves truth will be of sufficiency, knowledge, and capacity to exercise his estate; for ignorance and truth are no companions, because truth is no other thing but light, and ignorance darkness. And for the last point, if the magistrate hates greed, he will not only guard himself from practicing it, but will also correct it in others; and by cutting off this detestable vice, the root of all evil, he shall keep down all other vices, which are like rivers proceeding from this cursed and stinking spring. And as we see that the greed of wicked magistrates is cause of the length of law cases, because they desire that the parties who plead before them should serve their turn as a cow for milk, it follows that the poor people are pillaged and eaten to the bones by those horseleeches. Also contrary, when the magistrate hates greed he will dispatch and hasten justice to parties, and not hold them long in law, neither pillage and spoil them; a thing bringing great comfort and help to the people. Briefly then, if these three qualities which Jethro requires in magistrates and officers of justice were well considered by the prince, in such a way that he would receive none into office who feared not God, loved not truth and hated greed, certainly justice would be better administered, to his great honor and the utility of his subjects.

I will not say that among the pagans there were magistrates who had the true fear of God, for none can have that without knowing him, and none can truly know him but by his word, whereof the pagans were ignorant; yet there were pagans who had the two other parts which

Jethro required in a magistrate. When Cato the Elder was sent governor and lieutenant general to Sardinia, he found that the people of the country had an old custom to bestow great charges at the reception of governors sent from Rome. He also found all through the country a great company of bankers and usurers who ruined and ate up the people; as soon as he was in his government he cut this off, and would not suffer them at his arrival to be at any charge for his entertainment. He also drove from the country at once all the bankers, without any liberty to stay upon condition to moderate their usuries; which some found hard and evil, thinking that it would have been better to have given them a mean to their usuries beyond which they might not pass, rather than taking from them the means to give and take money for profit, a thing seeming prejudicial to commerce and traffic. But so much there wanted that Cato stayed not upon these considerations, believing that the permission of a certain rate might easily be disguised and perverted, and that men who are subtle in their trade might easily in their contracting and accounting make them lay down eight for ten, or twelve for fifteen. Briefly, Cato governed himself so in his estate and government that the fame of his reputation was of a holy and innocent person.

He was in all matters assuredly a brave man; he was a good soldier, a good lawyer, a good orator, cunning in both town and rural affairs, proper in time of peace, and as proper in time of war; a man of severe innocence, and who had a tongue that would spare no man's vices, even publicly to accuse them, as indeed in all his life he never ceased to accuse vicious and evil living people, to make them condemned by justice; and especially in his age of 90 years he accused one Sergius Galba. Cato stepped forward one day to demand the office of censor, which was an office very meet for him, because he delighted more to blame and reprehend the vices of men than to praise their virtues. In the pursuit of this office he had many competitors who also demanded this estate; not so much for the desire to have it, but they foresaw that if Cato were censor he would practice a rigorous censorship, and that he would degrade many officers and magistrates who were far from good. And what they feared most was that Cato himself, as he sued for that office, said openly that if he were chosen censor he would bring to trial a heap of vicious corrupted magistrates, and would reform offices by reducing them into the first form and degrading inculpable and unworthy officers. Those who opposed themselves to his pursuit hereof did it for no other cause but because they feared his touch. Briefly, he did so much that not only was he elected censor, but also got for companion in his censorship Lucius Valerius, whom he demanded because he was of the same humor. These two being censors, they did not fail to remove many from their places, including many senators and magistrates of great houses and nobility. They caused their houses, built on public land, to be demolished and overthrown; they caused ponds and lakes to be paved which were full of mud and dirt, and purged all the gutters, sinks, and jakes of the city. They greatly heightened and raised the farms of the commonwealth lands, which before had been held at a low price by persons who by plots had let them out far dearer. Briefly, they administered a very profitable censorship, whereupon Cato was surnamed *Censorius*. Would to God we had at this day such men, and that princes would employ them; for the commonwealth stands in great need to be purged of so many evils and corruptions that infect and ruin it.

King Charlemagne and Saint Louis may in this place serve for examples to all kings and princes. For we read that these two good kings, true lovers of good justice performing the office of good censors, sent often in their time commissaries through all the provinces to be informed of the abuses of magistrates, and such as they found in fault, and did not well observe all edicts and ordinances, were rigorously punished. During their reigns justice was exceedingly well administered, to the great help and comfort of the people. The prince ought also, in his election of magistrates, to advise himself well and choose officers who in judgment will have no respect of persons. For the magistrate ought to yield equally to the poor as to the rich, according to the merit of the case and not after the desert of the persons. From the beginning of the Roman commonwealth, they had few or no laws written to end contentions and differences among them; but they were ended as seemed good to magistrates, who always gave a color to their sentences by certain decrees and judgments which they said had before been given in similar cases. By this palliation and deceit, saying that they had been before so judged, they administered justice after their own fantasies, so that they almost always carried away the gaining of the case; for magistrates who were at their command supported and favored them. The meanest sort of people, perceiving that under color of former judgments they were abused, and that they almost always lost their cases against the great men of the city, many began to quarrel and complain. The tribunes publicly proposed that it was necessary to elect ten potentates in place of the two consuls, to administer the commonwealth and write laws and ordinances; whereby from thence forward the differences and law controversies might be decided, and not after the fantasies and former judgments of judges and magistrates. The great men, after their custom, opposed themselves against this. Hereupon there arose a great stir and sedition within the town of Rome, which neither the consuls nor the senate could appease. But at the new creation of consuls it happened that Lucius Quintius, who dwelled in the fields in a little farm, was elected; when they sent for him they found him at his plow's tail, plowing his final possessions. This good person was honorably brought as sovereign magistrate into the town; as soon as he arrived, he began to exercise his estate and to administer justice to every man, poor and rich, without respect or exception of persons. He in a little time dispatched all old cases which had long hanged in suspense, and behaved himself so discreet and just in the handling of all cases that he was generally esteemed a good and equal judge. He abode all day in the palace to hear and dispatch cases, and he gave audience to every man very patiently and benignly, and used speedy and good justice to all indifferently, having no regard to persons, but only to the merits and the justice of the case then in question. By this means Quintius brought to pass that not only the great men were no more suspected by the common, but also justice was so agreeable and plausible to the people that the sedition ceased, and all the people were appeased, so that none demanded any more to have new laws, but every man greatly contented himself to have so good and equal a judge and magistrate. And surely there is nothing in the world which sooner ceases seditions and stirs, nor that better maintains public peace and tranquility, than a good justice administered by good and equal magistrates. But on the contrary, a wicked justice is often cause of uproars, insurrections, and civil wars, as poor France can say at this day.

The example of both these cases appeared some years after Quintius was out of his magistracy, for those who succeeded him did not have that grace nor dexterity to administer justice well. The tribunes took up again their determination to create ten potentates to write laws and ordinances, after which men might be judged in all cases. And indeed the Senate, as it were constrained, accorded to this creation; and there were chosen ten potentates, who with great deliberation composed the Laws of the Twelve Tables, which were found very good and equal. And not only they proposed and made in public places the said laws, and engraved them in tables of brass, but what is more, they administered justice to every man after these laws, with great uprightness and equity. And among other potentates there was Appius Claudius, who showed himself very soft and affable to the common people, heard them patiently and did them very good and speedy justice; so that people made no account of the tribunes, thinking they needed not to run to them for help, since Appius alone performed not only the office of a good judge, but also of a tribune, to sustain the good right of the common people. But this good justice endured but a year; for the second year, the said potentates being made to continue but a year in their estates, they resolved altogether to remain without despoiling themselves of that office. And to gain people to their faction, they began to do justice clean contrary to that of the first year, using favor and subordination, always giving sentence to the profit of those who were on their side, to sustain their tyranny. By this means they drew many persons to be of their faction and wrought a great partiality within Rome, some holding for the ten potentates, others against them. But in the end their imperious and tyrannical arrogance was the cause that the partialized people accorded, and great and small set themselves all on one side against them, whereupon fell their total ruin. The first year of their estate, by their good justice they brought and maintained a good peace in the city; but in the second year, by their evil and wicked justice they reduced all into troubles and confusions within the city.

Unto this example of the ten potentates might we compare the wicked, partial, and venal justice which has reigned in France fifteen years (which is and has been the principal cause, and as it were the nurse of all troubles and seditions), and that little of good justice which we see to shine (as lightning, which soon passes away) after the first troubles in Provence, when the President de Morsen and certain other counsellors were sent there. For the little good justice which they did in that quarter, in so little time as they remained there, was the cause that the people of Provence (who naturally are very hot and furious) carried and guided themselves in the other following troubles more modestly than any other of the French nation.

We have before said that Quintius patiently heard all who demanded justice from him; which is a point that all justices and magistrates ought well to observe. For according to the right of nations and of natural equity, none ought to be condemned without being heard. In the time that the Tarquins were chased from Rome, they underhandedly practiced with many citizens, by promises and otherwise, to commit a treason to the commonwealth and to establish Tarquin the Proud in his estate. The corrupted citizens procured many slaves of the best sort of citizens, by promises of liberty and other good recompenses. All the hired people, a very great number, concluded secretly that they should one night seize upon the strongest places of the town, and that the slaves should slay their masters in their beds as soon as they heard the watchword; and this being done, some should go and open the gates to the Tarquins. There were two brothers, Marcus and Publius Laurentius, who were of the conspiracy; they were many times tormented in their sleep with hideous and fearful dreams, and this made them go to their divines to know from where these dreams proceeded. The divines told them they proceeded from some wicked enterprise which they had in their heads, which they could not well bring about, and that it were good they left off, that they might be tormented no more with such dreams. This was the cause that the two brothers revealed the conspiracy to Servius Sulpitius, one of the consuls. Sulpitius saw an evident and near peril to the commonwealth; yet he did not think it good to deal in the punishment of the culpable before they were well vanquished, and plain matters averred against them — as our Machiavellians of today do, who take the law against men after they have slain them — but secretly communicated the fact to the Senate. The Senate referred to him to proceed in that matter as he though fittest for the utility and conservation of the commonweal. Sulpitius, considering that among the conspirators there were many great persons well allied, and that he might reap great envy and hatred if he caused any to die without an open conviction of the fact, resolved to bring the case to a clear and evident proof. He then took order that the strong places of the city were guarded by good men on a certain night assigned, and sent to Tullius Longus, his companion in the consulship, who then was besieging the town of Fidenes. He had him come to Rome with a good part of his army, and remain at the gates on the night assigned, till Sulpitius sent him word. This done, he gave charge to the two brothers Laurentines to advise their accomplices to execute their design that night, and that they should all meet in the marketplace to discuss what to do. The conspirators being assembled there, the consul Longus was assigned to enter the town with all his forces, and so in the marketplace they were wrapped in by the good order that Sulpitius had taken. So that by this means they were all convicted of the fact, and none of their parents or allies could deny the crime. This was the cause that every man said afterward, when it came to the punishment of the conspirators, that it were a good deed to punish them, and that Sulpitius had performed his duty well. Briefly, by this clear and evident proof which Sulpitius drew out of this conspiracy, he obtained great honor and praise; whereas he should have heaped upon himself great envy and evil will of the allies and parents of the guilty if he had caused them to be executed without great and evident verification of the crime.

Helpidius also, lieutenant of justice at Rome in the time of the emperor Constantine, showed himself a good and sincere judge. For, being commanded by the emperor to rack and torment a poor accused person, he would never do it, because he found no matter nor sufficient proofs against him, but humbly asked the emperor to discharge him from office rather than constrain him to do a thing against his conscience.

The prince then who will make a good election of magistrates ought to take care to choose persons who, like Cato, will not wink at vices; and who will patiently hear parties and judge equally, as did Quintius; who will be diligent to draw out the truth before giving judgment, as did Sulpitius; who fear to offend their consciences, like Helpidius. And briefly, that they fear God, love truth, and are not greedy, according to Jethro's counsel. Thus doing, he need not fear to have his justice well ruled and holily administered. He must take heed he not do like the emperor Tiberius, who gave his offices to great drinkers and gormandizers, who took pleasure to see a man give up much wine and viands into their bellies. Neither ought he imitate the example of Julian the Apostate, who gave Alexandria a most cruel and turbulent man for a judge. And when it was told him that this judge was a man very unworthy of such an office, he said, "I know not how unworthy he is; but because the Alexandrians are turbulent and greedy persons, I will give them a like judge, who may deal with them after their merits." This was a very inconsiderate part of this emperor, to give a wicked magistrate to a corrupted people for their amendment; for that is as if one should give to a diseased person a wicked physician to heal him. There was a similar act committed in our time by the Machiavellians; but no marvel if atheists follow the traces of an apostate, for the one is as good as the other. Neither ought the prince also do as the emperor Valentinian, who constrained parties to subject themselves to the judgment of judges who were their enemies. For all these said emperors were greatly blamed by authors of their time, and are yet by all histories, for their poor choice of unworthy men in offices, who they ought rather to have repulsed as many other emperors did, dismissing them from office for far less causes. As some have written that Augustus Caesar dismissed a magistrate as ignorant and incapable for writing *Ixi* in place of *Ipsi*. And Vespasian fired another because he perfumed himself and smelled of musk, saying he would have loved him better if he had smelled of garlic. And Domitian another because he delighted in dancing and puppet plays; for Domitian, although otherwise very wicked, had this good in him, that he well chastised all such as our Machiavellians are today. Likewise also the censor Fabricius dismissed the senator Cornelius Rufinus for having vessels of silver weighing ten marks, which today comes to forty crowns. But I leave you to wonder if they would not have rigorously punished those who spoil and eat the people, who sell justice or commit similar abuses which today are manifestly tolerated in France; since they dismissed men from office for far lighter causes, as failing in spelling a word, smelling of perfume, dancing, or having plate worth ten pounds. For these things seem not to be great faults, but today men rather make virtues of them.

But it is not enough for a prince to make good election of his officers and magistrates by the consideration of each man's particular virtues; but also, in seats where he must establish many judges together, he must compose that body by considering the qualities required to give a good harmony and temperature to all the body. And for this purpose he ought to compose and temper it of persons of diverse estates and countries; as for example, a parliament and judgment seat composed of many should not be made all of the nobility or clergy, or of the third estate, but some of every estate. Likewise, it should not to be composed of men all of one town, but ought to be taken from divers jurisdictions or dioceses. And those two points have anciently been observed in France, according to the royal ordinances so enjoining. But today we may add that a parliament should not be all Roman Catholic, and none of the reformed religion; for if the estate of the clergy, for the conservation of its privileges, has obtained that in all such places there are magistrates of the clergy, why should they deny it to men of the profession of the Gospel? To this purpose we read that at Rome there was a time wherein there were many more knights than senators in the sovereign assembly of judges. Publius Rutilius, a good and sincere man who had obtained the ill will of the knights, was condemned to banishment because he had repressed the excessive and undue exactions of publicans in Asia. The senators, disdaining and grieving at this wicked judgment, stirred up Livius Drufus, tribune of the people, at whose instigation a law was made that the senators and knights should be of the same number in the judgment of cases. Which law was found good and profitable to the commonweal; as contrary they found the law bad which Caius Gracchus would have passed, whereby he sought to have two knights for every senator in judgments. For herein there is no equality nor equity; and therefore by good reason that law was rejected, to the ruin of Gracchus, who was slain in the too earnest pursuit of that law.

Josaphat, king of Judah, after establishing good magistrates enjoined them to execute good justice to every man, without regard to the riches nor the dignity of a person, but only to the fear of God. He established a seat like a parliament in Jerusalem, composed of persons elected from all the lines and families of his kingdom, holding the degree of supreme jurisdiction, unto which men might only appeal from the sentences of inferior judges. The same method also kept the ancient Romans in all sorts of their magistrates; for they not only had of their nobility, but also of their knights and of their third estate, to the contentment of everyone. And the magistrates being so tempered, they so might be suspected neither by great nor little. This is what was said by Marcus Valerius, that valiant and wise senator and great captain of war, persuading the Senate to receive the people into offices and the administration of the commonweal.

"Masters, all who will well establish a public estate ought to consider not only the present, but also what may come. But certainly, if the whole administration of the commonweal always remained in the hands of the rich, it might come to pass in time that some small number of them would usurp a tyrannous domination over the people. But when some of the people are mixed among the rich, they dare enterprise no tyranny, fearing to be punished by the laws whereof the magistrates of the people may pursue against them. Finally, so much the greater terror and fear we propose before the eyes of transgressors and corrupters of manners, by putting against proud and greedy men many observers and watchers in their heads, so much the better shall the estate of our commonwealth be established and assured."

A prince, having by good election well ordained the magistrates of his justice, ought to consider how he may maintain them in their duty to walk upright and to keep themselves from corruption. To do this he must observe two things; dismiss those who deal evil in their charge and punish them according to the greatness of their faults, and recompense and remunerate those who deal well in their charges. We have above set down some examples of emperors who chastised their vicious magistrates, which examples merit well to be drawn into a consequence, at least for great faults of magistrates. But above all, a prince ought to have before his eyes the example of the king Saint Louis, who often sent commissaries through his provinces to get information of the abuses of magistrates, that he might do justice thereof. For this example merits well to be practiced in the time wherein we are. Moreover, the emperor Alexander Severus practiced very well these two points, punishing evil magistrates and remunerating the good. For on the one side, he so hated wicked magistrates who abused their offices that when Arabinus was reported to have committed thefts in his office, he said in great choler, "O gods immortal! Arabinus not only lives, but dares appear in the Senate, and before me." On the other side, Alexander would remunerate and bountifully reward good magistrates who acquitted themselves in their charges well. For, he said, good magistrates who are good men must be bought and enriched; but wicked men of no value must be impoverished and driven away. We may also cite the example of most of our ancient kings of France, who paid well their officers of justice. For although it seems that their wages at present are little, yet at the time when their wages were first constituted and set down, they were great and sufficient enough to maintain them. And there is no doubt but a man might as well and honorably maintain himself some 60 years ago with 300 pounds a year, as now for 1,000; for truly since that time all things have proved four times dearer. Whereupon it follows, since expenses are quadruple and the wages of magistrates are not raised, that it is requisite they were augmented, the better to encourage them to do their duties, and to take from them all occasion and excuse of abuses.

Hereupon some have thought that to shun abuses and corruptions of magistrates it is good and expedient to make them temporary, as for two or three years; or else to make them ambulatory, by moving them from time to time from one province to another. This opinion, which seems to be founded upon many good reasons, has been held by a great person of our time. For if magistrates were temporary, in consequence they should be subject to the syndics and have to give account of their administration. And if they were ambulatory, they would not know the persons subject to their jurisdictions; neither could they contract with them any inward familiarity, which often causes judges to stray from the right way and draw the curtain from the eyes of justice. And both by the laws of the Romans and the ordinances of Louis, and many of the king's successors, the magistrates of provinces could neither be perpetual, nor could they govern in the provinces where they were born. Yet if we consider that France is composed of divers provinces, which each have different courses of law, we see that it is impossible to find magistrates fit to administer justice in every province, for lack of knowledge of the different styles, customs, and manners of every country, which are not well learned but by use and practice. And also, old men and many persons very capable to exercise offices, neither can nor will subject themselves to an uncertain removing from one province to another. For the affairs of their families could not well bear it, and every man must have care of his family. We see also that men advanced to offices, although learned and capable, yet at first have not had the dexterity to apply their knowledge, for it is obtained by the handling of matters and experience. Whereupon it follows that if magistrates were temporary, they should be at the end of term when they began to understand how they ought to handle their offices; and by appointing deputies, the same would come to them. And so it would come to pass that in offices there would more often be placed new men than experienced, a thing neither good nor profitable to the commonweal. And for this reason we read that the emperor Antonius Pius always continued his magistrates who had acquitted themselves well. And in the time of Severus and the emperors after him, for the office of the Praetorian prefecture they always provided one who before had served as an assessor, and therefore knew how to handle that office. And certainly in the Romans' time there was this incommodity in the matter of magistrates, that often they were at the end of their time before they understood how they should administer. But that incommodity was much more supportable in that time than it is today in France, for the Roman magistrates seldom decided private and particular cases; but in France magistrates must deal in all cases.

After the prince has well established his justice by the publication of laws and the institution of good magistrates, he is yet not discharged, for he ought himself to deal therein. And this is another point of the counsel Jethro gave to Moses. For after he had counseled him what magistrates he should establish, he added more, that Moses ought to reserve to himself the knowledge and decision of great affairs. And assuredly this is a point very necessary, and which a prince ought not to leave behind; for he is debtor of justice to his subjects, and ought to give them audience in things whereof he is to have necessary knowledge. For all things are not proper to be handled before magistrates established by the prince, but many things pertain to the prince alone; as when a common man will complain against some great lord or magistrate, or against publicans and tax collectors, or when a man labors for a pardon, gift, recompense, and similar cases. The prince then ought himself, either alone or in his council, give audience often to his subjects. For we read that by the creation of kings and monarchs, the authority attributed to them by the people consisted in three very notable points: the first, to minister good justice unto their subjects by causing them to observe the laws and customs of the country, and to take knowledge of the injuries which are great and of consequence. The second, to convoke an assembly of a Senate to handle the affairs of the commonwealth. And the third, to be the chieftain and sovereign of war. And as for the first duty, the ancient Greeks (even Homer) call them distributors of justice. This is why almost all good princes have had their ordinary days of audience, wherein they took knowledge of the complaints and grievances of their subjects, and administered justice unto them. Julius Caesar took great pains to hear cases and administer justice, and to cause them to observe laws which concerned the commonwealth; as especially the law Sumptuariam, which would permit no excess in banquets nor apparel. Augustus Caesar likewise kept an ordinary audience, which he continued till night; being ill at ease, he would even hold audience in his house. Claudius also, though he was of a heavy and dull spirit, yet he held his audience and administered right to parties. So did Domitian, however wicked he was in other deportments, yet with great industry and diligence administered good justice, often revoking decrees given for favors by the Centumvirate seat, and did not spare to punish corrupted judges. Galba likewise, although he was 72 when he came to the empire, yet dealt with audience of parties and administered justice. So did Trajan, Hadrian, the Antonines, Severus, Alexander, and many other Roman emperors. And very memorable is what is written of Hadrian; that one day as he went into the fields, he was asked by a poor woman to do justice upon a complaint she made to him. The emperor very kindly said to her that it was no place for her to require justice, and sent her away till another time. The woman replied to him, "Sir, if you will not do me justice, wherefore deal you to be emperor?" Hadrian stayed and heard her, and did her justice.

If we read the histories of France, we shall find that it has yet been more common for our ancient kings to hold audience than it was for Roman emperors. Charlemagne, besides taking care that stewards, bailiffs, and their deputies should walk upright without abusing their offices, would also reserve to himself all great cases, or those among great lords. Then he had the parties appear before him, heard them patiently, and agreed them amiably if he could by any means. And so he gave his sentence, and good and prompt justice. King Louis I, following the traces of his father Charlemagne, held a public audience in his palace three times a week, and heard grievances and complaints of everyone, executing to all quick and right justice. But what good came there hereof? Even this, says the history: that all public good in this good king's time was so well governed and administered that there was almost none among his subjects that complained of wrong or injury, but all men lived in great peace and prosperity; one not daring to offend another for fear of the good king's justice. So much could that royal virtue of justice do for the maintenance of peace and prosperity in a kingdom. King Philip Augustus, surnamed the Conqueror for his great prowess and conquests, was also a good justicer and willingly heard the complaints of his subjects. One day, understanding that the count of Auverne greatly pillaged his subjects and neighbors, exacting great sums without the king's consent, and having found him guilty thereof, condemned him on the advice of the barons of the realm to lose his land and seignory, which from that time was united to the crown. We may also place here the good justice of the kings Charles the Wise, Charles VII, Charles VIII, Louis XII, and many other kings of France who gave audience to the complaints of their subjects. But it shall suffice to close up this matter with the example of that good king Saint Louis, who among other virtues was a very good and upright administer of justice. This good king, having a great zeal to establish good justice in his kingdom, first ordained that the good and ancient laws and customs should be well and straightly observed, upon the pain he would take of his magistrates if they caused them not to be observed. And so that the magistrates might carry themselves well in their offices, he chose the best men he could find to secretly inquire of their virtues and vices. And so that they might administer good and brief justice to the poor as to the rich, without exception of persons, he forbade them to take presents, unless some present of food not exceeding ten shillings a week; nor any other benefits for them or their children, neither from them who were in contention. For this good king considered that presents, benefits, and desire of gain are the means whereby magistrates may be corrupted; and therefore to shun all corruption, he must cut off the means of it. Moreover he very rigorously punished officers of justice who abused their estates, and spared not even great lords themselves, but punished them after their merits. As happened to the lord de Coucy, who strangled two young Flamins when he found them hunting in his woods. The said lord, fearing to be handled as he had dealt with the Flamins, would have taken the hearing of the case from the king, saying he was to be sent for before the peers of France. But the king forced him to abide his judgments, and indeed would have had him killed if great lords (parents and friends of the said lord de Coucy) had not importuned so much for his pardon. The king accorded that he should have his life, but yet condemned him to the war against the Turks and infidels in the holy land for three years, a sort of banishment, and fined him 10,000 Paris pounds. This king did not pardon easily, nor without great deliberation; and he often had in his mouth that verse of the psalm of David: Happy are they who do judgment and justice at all times. He said also that it was no mercy, but cruelty, not to punish malefactors. Moreover, he was a king full of truth, chaste, charitable, and fearing God; which are virtues exceeding worthy for a good prince, and which commonly accompany good justice. But the godly precepts he gave near the end of his life to Philip the Hardy, his son and successor, well merit to be written in gold upon the lintels of doors, and the houses of all kings and Christian princes, to have them always before their eyes.

"My son, since it pleases God, our Father and Creator, to withdraw me now from this miserable world to carry me to a better life than this, I would not depart from you without giving you for my last blessing the doctrines and precepts a good father ought to give to his son, hoping you will engrave in your heart these your father's last words. I command you then, my dear son, that above all things you have always before your eyes the fear of God, our good Father; for the fear of God is the beginning, yea the accomplishment of all true wisdom; and if you fear him, he will bless you. Secondly, I exhort you to take all adversities patiently, acknowledging that it is God who visits you for your sins; and not to wax proud in prosperity, accounting that it comes to you by God's grace, not by your merits. Thirdly, I recommend to you charity towards the poor, for the good you do to them shall be yielded unto you a hundredfold, and Jesus Christ our Savior shall account it done unto him. After this, I recommend to you very straightly, my dear son, that you cause to keep well the good laws and customs of the kingdom, and to administer good justice to your subjects; for happy are those who administer good justice at all times. And to do this, I enjoin you that you be careful to have good magistrates, and command them not to favor your procurators against equity, and that you rigorously punish those who abuse their offices; for when they make faults, they are more punishable than others, because they ought to govern other subjects and serve them for an example. Suffer not in judgment a respect of persons, and favor the poor only as the truth of the fact appears, without favoring him as to the judgment of his case. Moreover, I command you that you be careful to have a good council of persons staid and of good age, who will be secret, peaceable, and not greedy; for if you do this you shall be loved and honored, because the light of the servants makes their masters shine. Also more, I forbid you to take tallies or tributes upon your subjects but for urgent necessity, evident utility, and just cause; for otherwise you shall not be held for a king, but for a tyrant. Further, I command you that you be careful to maintain your subjects in good peace and tranquility, and observe their franchises and privileges which they enjoy, and take heed you move no war against any Christian without exceeding great occasion and reason. I exhort you to give the benefices of your kingdom to men of good life and good conscience, not to luxurious and greedy wretches. My dear son, if you observe these my commandments, you shall be a good example to your subjects, and you shall be the cause that they will accustom themselves to do well; because the people will always give themselves to the imitation of their prince. And God by his bounty maintain you firm and assured in your estate and kingdom."

Thus finishing this good king's last words, full of holy zeal and correspondent to his life, passed and yielded his soul to his creator who had given it him. His son, king Philip III, called the Hardy because of the valiance he showed against the infidels and other enemies, made good profit of these excellent commands, and maintained the kingdom in good peace and great prosperity during his reign.

For an end hereof, I note in this good king Louis that it is very true what the scripture witnesses unto us; that the just shall spring up and receive from God the blessing of a good and long generation. For over three hundred years the descendants of this good king held the crown of France, and there was no more any other race of royal blood but his. For the house of Valois and the house of Bourbon have issued from this good king. God by his mercy grant grace to princes of this time, who are descended from so good a root, that they may engrave in their hearts the godly commandments of this king, whose meaning truly was not only to prescribe to his son Philip, but generally to all his posterity.

3.36
Machiavelli

Gentlemen who hold castles and jurisdictions are very great enemies of commonwealths. (*Discourses*, book 1)

The leagues and cantons of Germany live very peaceably and at their ease, because they observe an equality among themselves and suffer no gentlemen in their country. Those few they have, they hate so much that when by adventure any of them falls into their hands, they put them to death and take no mercy, saying they destroy all and hold schools of wickedness. I call them gentlemen who live on their revenue without giving themselves to any trade. These in a country are very dangerous, and above all, high justices who hold castles and fortresses, and who have a great number of vassals and subjects which owe them faith and homage. The kingdom of Naples, the land of Rome, Romania, and Lombardy are full of such manner of men, and they are the cause that hitherto no good political state can be constituted in those places; for they are formal and capital enemies of the civil estate of commonwealths.

Answer

Those who have frequented the countries of Germany and Switzerland may well give Machiavelli the lie for what he says in this maxim, that in those countries may be found many gentlemen having under them men, jurisdictions, and castles, who were not only maintained in their nobility and authority, but were also greatly respected and employed in public affairs. And so much there wants that they should hold a school of wickedness, but contrary, they alone hold the countries in peace and see justice administered to their subjects. I will not deny but there are gentlemen in Germany, Switzerland, France, and otherwhere, who are bad enough, and who are violent and vicious; yet for some few we must not condemn all in general, as Machiavelli does here, who says they are dangerous people in a country, and that they are enemies to a political state. I know not if those he named are such (the gentlemen of Naples, of Romania, of Lombardy, and of Rome), and I am content to confess unto him, because I will not contest and strive against him upon a fact which has some appearance of truth. But I deny that on this side of the mountains they are such, but contrary we see that it is only the nobility of France and other neighboring countries who authorize and protect justice, and who make it to be obeyed. Yet I will also confess that the gentlemen on this side of the Alps are very dangerous, and great enemies to such a political state as Machiavelli has built by his writings, that is, a tyrannical state. For histories tell us that our ancestors, especially the barons, lords, and gentlemen, have always vigorously opposed themselves against tyrannies, and would never suffer them to grow up or take root. Which is a natural thing in the French nobility, and good, though evil for the Machiavellian foreigners who are come into France to practice their tyrannies; for by God's grace, they shall (with much ado) not take any deep root there.

3.37
Machiavelli

The nobility of France would overthrow the estates of that kingdom if their Parliaments did not punish them and hold them in fear. (*Discourses*, book 1 chapter 1)

The kingdom of France is a kingdom living under laws, more than any other, whereof their Parliaments are the guardians and maintainers, especially that of Paris. And hitherto that kingdom is maintained because the Parliaments have always been obstinate executors and resisters against the nobility, without which the kingdom would come to ruin.

Answer

Machiavelli would have done much better to have meddled only with the estate of Florence; for he shows his ignorance, and that he never knew the estate of France, nor how it has been governed by our ancestors. For I pray you, where has he found this, that the kingdom of France would dissolve and come to ruin, except that the Parliaments are executors against the nobility? Is not this as much to say that the French nobility will ruin the kingdom if not bridled and held short by Parliaments, and that it would be better if there were none? I doubt not but that Machiavelli thought thus; for we see it by the practice of the Machiavellians, who never shot at any other mark than to ruin the nobility in France, the better to establish their tyranny without contradiction. And for this effect they have violated and overthrown all the good laws of the kingdom, by the means of which it has always hitherto been maintained. And Machiavelli confesses the truth, which his disciples having well marked, and desiring to ruin the said kingdom, have not failed to begin by the laws thereof, knowing well that having ruined her foundations, she will be easily dissolved and overthrown.

But to refute this maxim I will cite no other thing but what we see in our French histories, that our kingdom was as much or more flourishing, and better governed, before there were any Parliaments in France. For the Parliament of Paris, which is the oldest, was established and constituted in the time of king Philip le Bel, in 1294; that of Toulouse during the reign of Charles VII, in 1444; that of Bordeaux in 1451; that of Daulphin, 1453; the Parliaments of Dijon and Provence during the reign of Louix XI; that of Rovan in the time of Louis XII, in 1499; and that of Brittany was erected only in the time of Henri II, in 1553. But before there was any news of all those Parliaments, was not the kingdom large and flourishing, rich in peace, flourishing in war? None can deny this without giving the lie to all our histories, which witness that in the times of Clovis, Charles Martel, Charlemagne, Philip August, Saint Louis, and of many other kings of France, the kingdom greatly flourished in peace and war; yet there was no news of all the Parliaments abovenamed. And so much there wanted that the gentlemen troubled or ruined the estate of the kingdom when there were no Parliaments, that contrary they were those who exercised in person the estates of bailiffs and marshals, and ministered justice to every man through the provinces, and when they were constrained to travel they appointed lieutenants to exercise their offices. And as for appellations from their sentences, they were discussed by a general meeting of the deputies of provinces and good towns of the kingdom, which congregated at a place assigned by the king once a year. Which assembly men well called a Parliament, in the old French tongue. But those assemblies were not formed offices, neither in anything were like the Parliaments at present, but rather were like the assembly of our Estates General. There sat the deputies of the short robe, whereof most were gentlemen, who they called laymen; and the deputies of the long robe, who we call clerks (although since then only counsellors' clerks are called clerks, and laymen those who are married); with the peers of France, when they would sit with them. Therefore gentlemen were employed to do justice to the people, not only in offices of bailiffs and marshals, but also as delegates of towns and provinces to assist in the assembly of Parliament, which otherwise men called the Court of Peers. It is therefore seen that the saying of Machiavelli is a mere slander, and that the nobility of France is not such as he makes it —

although in all states there are both good and evil — and that of all times, even before there were any Parliaments, the nobility were employed to maintain the kingdom in peace and repose by their exercise of the charges and offices of justice.

And would to God that yet at this day gentlemen would not give themselves so much to arms, but that some of them would study the civil law, that they might exercise offices of justice. The ancient Romans made no less account of a civil virtue, whereby a man knew how to maintain peace and justice in his country, than of the military virtue whereby we are defended from foreign oppression. And indeed it is a small thing, according to Sallust, to be puissant in arms without, when within we have no counsel. For the barbarians, as the Scythians and the Tartars, are great warriors against their enemies and neighbors; yet among themselves they have no counsel, no good policy, no well-governed justice, no letters, sciences, nor schools; and in sum they are barbarians, though they are warlike. Whereby appears how much it serves to the public estate of a country to have within it a good justice and a good policy, and fit and capable people to manage it well. But our gentlemen at this day (at least the many) have letters and sciences in too great contempt, and think it derogates from their gentry and nobility if they know anything, and make mock at those who deal with a pen and inkhorn, which is one of the greatest vices which at this day reigns among the nobility. And if they delighted not in ignorance, but would vouchsafe only to read histories, they should find that Julius Caesar, Augustus, Tiberius, Claudius, Hadrian, Marcus Aurelius, Severus, Macrinus, and many other emperors were very learned in letters and sciences, yea themselves wrote books. We also read in our histories that king Charlemagne, Robert, Charles the Wise, and of recent memory Francis I, were princes endowed with good knowledge, for their times. I say for their times, for the time of those ancient kings, except Francis, was full of barbarousness and ignorance, and far from the learned world of the emperors named. I will also note another notable vice which runs current among gentlemen at this day, which is that they make so great account of their nobility of blood that they esteem not the nobility of virtue; insomuch that it seems to some that no vices can dishonor or pollute the nobility and gentry which they have from their ancestors. But they ought well to consider that to their race there was a beginning of nobility, which was attributed to the first that was noble in consideration of some virtue that was in him. If, then, the nobility and gentry of a race took its origin and spring from virtue, it follows that as soon as it holds no more of the said spring, it is no more nobility, nor gentry; no more nor less than the water which springs from a neat and clear fountain, when it pollutes and corrupts itself in filthy bogs and miry sinks, shall be called the fountain water, but shall be accounted corrupt and stinking water, though it runs from a most pure and clear spring. We read that the emperor Marcus Aurelius made so great account of the nobility of virtue, although he himself was most noble and of an ancient race, that in comparison to it he made no estimate of nobility of race; therefore he married his daughters to persons who were not of great ancient nobility, but were wise and virtuous, such as none were found among the most illustrious races of Rome. Maecenas also was a great lord in the time of Augustus, issued from a royal race, yet he made no account of that nobility of blood in comparison with that true nobility, which is of virtue. He loved, honored, praised, and enriched learned men, yea was very familiar with them, and had them ordinarily at his table, although otherwise they were of base race. This, his love and favor which he bore to learning, was the cause that his name by them was immortalized, and hereupon those who are liberal and who love learned men are called Maecenates. The poet Horace greatly praises him because he preferred the nobility of virtue before that of race, when he says:

Thou say'st true Maecenas, what matters it to thee:
On what blood he is born, so that born he be free.

Therefore gentlemen of race ought not to despise those who by their virtue may boldly say and carry themselves for nobles, but ought to respect them and acknowledge in them the cause from whence their nobility of blood took its origin and commencement. Those also who are noble, not only of race but of virtue, ought verily to be respected and double honored; for as the poet Euripides says:

At the good accounted is, of noble blood to be:
But double is his honor, whom we virtuous do see.

Here will I end these present discourses, exhorting and praying the French nobility and all other persons who love the public good of France, to mark and earnestly consider the points which above we have handled against Machiavelli. For so may they know how wicked, impious, and detestable the doctrine of that most filthy atheist is, who has left out no kind of wickedness to build a tyranny accomplished by all abominable vices. They who know this, I believe will courageously employ themselves to drive away and banish from France Machiavelli and all his writings, and all those who maintain and follow his doctrine and practice it in France, to the ruin and desolation of the kingdom and of the poor people. I could have much more amplified this discourse if I would have examined all the doctrine of Machiavelli; for he handles many other very detestable and strange things, as the means to make conspiracies, and how they must be executed as well with sword as with poison, and many other like matters. But I abhor to speak of so villainous and wicked things, which are but too much known among men, and have contented myself to handle the principal points of his doctrine which merit to be discovered and brought to light.

I pray God our Father and Creator, in the name of our Lord Jesus Christ our only Savior and Mediator, that he will preserve his church and his elect from the contagious and wicked doctrine of such godless and profane men as are too common in the world; and that he will not suffer his flock to be tossed and troubled by a sort of turbulent and ignorant spirit; but that he will grant us grace always to persevere in his holy doctrine, and in the right way which he has showed us by his word; and well to discern and know abusive, lying, and malicious spirits, to detest and fly them and continually to follow his truth, which will teach us his fear and his commandments, and by his grace will bring us unto eternal life. So be it.

FINIS

Appendix A: Parallel Passages in Francis Bacon and *Anti-Machiavel*

Bacon, *Advancement of Learning*:

As for evil arts, if a man would set down for himself that principle of Machiavel, "That a man seek not to attain virtue itself, but the appearance only thereof; because the credit of virtue is a help, but the use of it is cumber"... or that other protestation of L. Catilina, to set on fire and trouble states, to the end to fish in droumy waters, and to unwrap their fortunes...

Anti-Machiavel:

As for peace, these people never like it, for they always fish in troubled water, gathering riches and heaps of the treasures of the realm while it is in trouble and confusion.

We should not then see France to be governed and ruled by strangers, as it is; we should not feel the calamities and troubles of civil wars and dissentions, which they enterprise to maintain their greatness and magnitude, and to fish in troubled water.

Bacon, *Advancement of Learning*:

Machiavel had reason to put the question, "which is the more ungrateful towards the well-deserving, the prince or the people?" though he accuses both of ingratitude. The thing does not proceed wholly from the ingratitude either of princes or people; but it is generally attended with the envy of the nobility; who secretly repine at the event, though happy and prosperous, because it was not procured by themselves.

Anti-Machiavel:

But I must say that sometimes such changes have been procured upon envy, rather than upon just complaint against those who governed; and such envies often proceed when kings govern themselves by men of base hand, as they call them, for then princes and great lords are jealous.

Bacon, "Of Seditions and Troubles":

Also, as Machiavel noteth well, when princes, that ought to be common parents, make themselves as a party, and lean to a side, it is as a boat that is overthrown by uneven weight on the one side... For when the authority of princes is made but an accessary to a cause, and that there be other bands that tie faster than the band of sovereignty, kings begin to be put almost out of possession.

Anti-Machiavel:

For if he nourishes partialities among his subjects, he cannot possibly carry himself so equally towards both parties, but in them both will be jealousy and suspicion. Each party will esteem the other to be more favored, whereupon he will hate his prince, and by that means it may come to pass that the prince shall be hated by both parties; and so both the one and the other shall machinate his ruin, which he can hardly shun, having all their evil wills.

Bacon, *Advancement of Learning*:

But that opinion I may condemn with like reason as Machiavel doth that other, that moneys were the sinews of wars; whereas (saith he) the true sinews of the wars are the sinews of men's arms, that is, a valiant, populous, and military nation; and he voucheth aptly the authority of Solon, who when Croesus shewed him his treasury of gold said to him, that if another came that had better iron he would be master of his gold.

Anti-Machiavel:

And although Machiavelli in a certain place where he speaks of war, maintains that the common saying is false, that money is the sinews of war; this hinders not, but what we say may be true...

The great treasures of king Croesus of Lydia incited him to war against king Cyrus of Persia and Media, to his own destruction.

Bacon, *Advancement of Learning*:

So in the fable that Achilles was brought up under Chiron the Centaur, who was part a man and part a beast: expounded ingeniously but corruptly by Machiavel, that it belongeth to the education and discipline of princes to know as well how to play the part of the lion in violence and the fox in guile, as of the man in virtue and justice.

Anti-Machiavel:

But should we call this beastliness or malice, what Machiavelli says of Chiron? Or has he read that Chiron was both a man and a beast? Who has told him that he was delivered to Achilles to teach him that goodly knowledge to be both a man and a beast?

Bacon, *Advancement of Learning*:

Concerning want, and that it is the case of learned men usually to begin with little and not to grow rich so fast as other men, by reason they convert not their labours chiefly to lucre and increase; it were good to leave the common place in commendation of poverty to some friar to handle, to whom much was attributed by Machiavel in this point, when he said, that "the kingdom of the clergy had been long before at an end, if the reputation and reverence towards the poverty of friars had not borne out the scandal of the superfluities and excesses of bishops and prelates."

Anti-Machiavel:

These mendicants then, being obliged and restrained unto poverty by a solemn vow which they made at their profession in their orders, they are so annexed, united, and incorporated in it and with it, that never after they could be never so little separated or dismembered, what diligence or labor soever they used to do it. Hereof they have found themselves much troubled and sorrowful, for howsoever gallant and goodly the *Theorique* of Poverty is, yet in practice they have found it a little too difficult and hard.

450

Bacon, *Advancement of Learning*:

> And therefore the form of writing which of all others is fittest for this variable argument of negotiation and occasions is that which Machiavel chose wisely and aptly for government; namely, discourse upon histories or examples... And it hath much greater life for practice when the discourse attendeth upon the example, than when the example attendeth upon the discourse. For this is no point of order, as it seemeth at first, but of substance. For when the example is the ground, being set down in an history at large, it is set down with all circumstances, which may sometimes control the discourse thereupon made and sometimes supply it, as a very pattern for action; whereas the examples alleged for the discourse's sake are cited succinctly and without particularity, and carry a servile aspect toward the discourse which they are brought in to make good.

Anti-Machiavel:

> Yet although the maxims and general rules of the political art may somewhat serve to know well to guide and govern a public estate, whether a principality or free city, yet they cannot be so certain as the maxims of the mathematicians, but are rules rather very dangerous, yea pernicious if men cannot make them serve and apply them unto affairs as they happen to come; and not to apply the affairs unto these maxims and rules. For the circumstances, dependencies, consequences, and antecedents of every affair and particular business, are all for the most part diverse and contrary; so that although two affairs be like, yet men must not therefore conduct and determine them by one same rule or maxim, because of the diversity and difference of accidents and circumstances.

Bacon, *Novum Organum*:

> There are and can be only two ways of searching into and discovering truth. The one flies from the senses and particulars to the most general axioms, and from these principles, the truth of which it takes for settled and immovable, proceeds to judgment and middle axioms. And this way is now in fashion. The other derives axioms from the senses and particulars, rising by a gradual and unbroken ascent, so that it arrives at the most general axioms last of all.

Anti-Machiavel:

Aristotle and other philosophers teach us, and experience confirms, that there are two ways to come unto the knowledge of things. The one, when from the causes and maxims, men come to knowledge of the effects and consequences. The other, when contrary, by the effects and consequences we come to know the causes and maxims... The first of these ways is proper and peculiar unto the mathematicians, who teach the truth of their theorems and problems by their demonstrations drawn from maxims, which are common sentences allowed of themselves for true by the common sense and judgment of all men. The second way belongs to other sciences, as to natural philosophy, moral philosophy, physic, law, policy, and other sciences...

Bacon, "Of Discourse":

It is good, in discourse and speech of conversation, to vary and intermingle speech of the present occasion with arguments, tales with reasons, asking of questions with telling of opinions, and jest with earnest...

Anti-Machiavel:

For as Cato says, amongst serious things joyous and merry things would be sometimes mixed.

Bacon, *New Atlantis*:

The reverence of a man's self is, next religion, the chiefest bridle of all vices.

Anti-Machiavel:

Behold then the consequence of that most wicked and detestable doctrine of that wicked atheist; which is to bring all people to a spite and a mockery of God and his religion, and of all holy things, and to let go the bridle to all vices and villainies.

Bacon, *De augmentis scientiarum*:

Constancy is the foundation on which virtues rest.

Anti-Machiavel:

I will then presuppose that constancy is a quality which ordinarily accompanies all other virtues; it is, as it were, of their substance and nature.

Bacon, "Of Adversity":

Prosperity doth best discover vice, but adversity doth best discover virtue.

Anti-Machiavel:

Adversity also is a true touchstone to prove who are feigned or true friends, for when a man feels labyrinths of troubles fall on him, dissembling friends depart from him, and those who are good abide with him, as said the poet Euripides: Adversity the best and certain'st friends doth get, prosperity both good and evil alike doth fit.

Bacon, "Of Great Place":

It is much true which was anciently spoken: A place showeth the man, and it showeth some to the better, and some to the worse.

Anti-Machiavel:

And we see but too much by experience that the old proverb is true, honors change manners.

Bacon, "Of Suspicion":

But this would not be done to men of base natures; for they, if they find themselves once suspected, will never be true.

Anti-Machiavel:

For the best fortress that is, is not to be thought evil by subjects; and if a prince is once thought so, there is no fortress that can save him.

Bacon, *Apophthegms New and Old*:

> Mr. Bettenham used to say, that riches were like muck: when it lay upon an heap, it gave a stench, and ill odour; but when it was spread upon the ground, then it was the cause of much fruit.

Bacon, "Of Riches":

> Of great riches there is no real use, except it be in the distribution; the rest is but conceit.

Anti-Machiavel:

> Briefly, it is neither good nor profitable for a prince to heap up great treasures and riches enclosed in one place. And what then? must a sovereign prince be poor? No, but contrary, he has need to be rich and very opulent, for otherwise he shall be feeble and weak, and cannot make head against his enemies; but his riches and treasures must be in the purses and houses of his subjects.

Bacon, "Of Riches":

> Men leave their riches either to their kindred, or to the public; and moderate portions prosper best in both. A great state left to an heir, is as a lure to all the birds of prey round about to seize on him, if he be not the better stablished in years and judgment.

Anti-Machiavel:

> For it is neither good nor profitable that a prince treasures up heaps of riches; for it serves for a bait to draw unto him enemies, or to engender quarrels and divisions after him; and we often see that princes' great treasures are causes of more evil than good.

Bacon, *Advancement of Learning*:

> It is true, that taxes levied by public consent, less dispirit, and sink the minds of the subject, than those imposed in absolute governments.

Anti-Machiavel:

It is certain that a prince may well make war and impose taxes without the consent of his subjects, by an absolute power; but it is better for him to use his civil power, so should he be better obeyed.

Anti-Machiavel:

[T]rue charity is joined unto faith, pity, and all other virtues...

Bacon, *Advancement of Learning*:

But these be heathen and profane passages, having but a shadow of that divine state of mind which religion and the holy faith doth conduct men unto, by imprinting upon their souls Charity, which is excellently called the bond of Perfection, because it comprehendeth and fasteneth all virtues together.

Anti-Machiavel:

But I must say that the Christian religion has launched and entered far deeper into the doctrine of good manners than the pagans and philosophers have done. For proof hereof I will take the maxim of Plato, that we are not only born for ourselves, but that our birth is partly for our country, partly for our parents, and partly for our friends. Behold a goodly sentence we can say no other; but if we compare it with the doctrine of Christians, it will be found maimed and defective. For what mention does Plato make of the poor? Where and in what place of this notable sentence does he set them? He speaks not at all of them; briefly, he would have it that our charity should be first employed towards ourselves, which they have well marked and followed who say that a well ordered charity begins with himself. But this is far from the doctrine which Saint Paul teaches the Christians when he says that charity seeks not her own; and also that which Christ himself commands, to love our neighbor as ourselves. Secondly Plato places our love towards our country, thirdly our love towards our parents, and lastly our friends. And what becomes of the poor? Let them do as they can, for Plato's charity stretches not to them.

Bacon, Speech on taking his seat in Chancery:

> I will promise regularly to pronounce my decree within few days after my hearing and to sign my decree at the least in the vacation after the pronouncing, for fresh justice is the sweetest, and to the end that there be no delay of justice, nor any other means-making or laboring, but the labour of the counsel at the bar.

Anti-Machiavel:

> And as we see that the greed of wicked magistrates is cause of the length of law cases, because they desire that the parties who plead before them should serve their turn as a cow for milk, it follows that the poor people are pillaged and eaten to the bones by those horseleeches. Also contrary, when the magistrate hates greed, he will dispatch and hasten justice to parties, and not hold them long in law, neither pillage and spoil them; a thing bringing great comfort and help to the people.

Bacon, "Of Counsel":

> The wisest princes need not think it any diminution to their greatness, or derogation to their sufficiency, to rely upon counsel. God himself is not without, but hath made it one of the great names of his blessed Son; The Counsellor. Salomon hath pronounced that "in counsel is stability."

Anti-Machiavel:

> For a prince, however prudent he is, ought not so much to esteem his own wisdom as to despise the counsel of other wise men. Solomon despised them not, and Charles the Wise always conferred of his affairs with the wise men of his council.

Bacon, *Advancement of Learning*:

> But this appeareth more manifestly, when kings themselves, or persons of authority under them, or other governors in commonwealths and popular estates, are endued with learning. For although he might be though partial to his own profession, that said "then should people and estates be happy, when either kings were

philosophers, ore philosophers kings"; yet so much is verified by experience, that under learned princes and governors there have ever been the best times.

Anti-Machiavel:

I am content to presuppose that it is certain that there cannot come a better and more profitable thing to a people than to have a prince wise of himself; therefore, said Plato, men may call it a happy commonwealth when either the prince can play the philosopher, or when a philosopher comes to reign there.

Bacon, *Advancement of Learning*:

For howsoever it hath been ordinary with politic men to extenuate and disable learned men by the names of *Pedantes*; yet in the records of time it appeareth in many particulars, that the governments of princes in minority (notwithstanding the infinite disadvantage of that kind of state) have nevertheless excelled the government of princes of mature age, even for that reason which they seek to traduce, which is, that by that occasion the state hath been in the hands of *Pedantes*. For so was the state of Rome for the first five years, which are so much magnified, during the minority of Nero, in the hands of Seneca, a *Pedanti*: so it was again for ten years space or more, during the minority of Gordianus the younger, with great applause and contentation in the hands of Misitheus, a *Pedanti*: so was it before that, in the minority of Alexander Severus, in like happiness, in hands not much unlike, by reason of the rule of the women, who were aided by the teachers and preceptor.

Anti-Machiavel:

This may yet be better showed by the examples of many princes who have been of small wisdom and virtue, and yet notwithstanding have ruled the commonwealth well by the good and wise counsel of prudent and loyal counsellors wherewith they were served; as did the emperor Gordian the Young, who was created emperor at eleven years of age. Many judged the empire to be fallen into a childish kingdom, and so into a weakness and a bad conduction; but it proved otherwise, for this young emperor Gordian espoused the daughter of a wise man called Misitheus, whom he made the high steward of his household, and governed himself by his counsel in all his affairs; so that the Roman Empire was well ruled so long as Misitheus lived... I will not here repeat the example of the emperor Alexander Severus, who came to the empire very young, and under whom the affairs of the commonwealth were so well governed, by the means of good counsellors, as above said.

Bacon, *Advancement of Learning*:

[T]he writing of speculative men of active matter for the most part doth seem to men of experience, as Phormio's argument of the wars seemed to Hannibal, to be but dreams and dotage.

Anti-Machiavel:

Herein it falls out to Machiavelli as it did once to the philosopher Phormio; who one day reading in the Peripatetic school of Greece, and seeing arrive and enter there Hannibal of Carthage (who was brought thither by some of his friends, to hear the eloquence of the philosopher), he began to speak and dispute with much babbling of the laws of war and the duty of a good captain, before this most famous captain, who had forgotten more than ever that proud philosopher knew or had learned. When he had thus ended his lecture and goodly disputation, as Hannibal went from the auditory one of his friends who had brought him there asked what he thought of the philosopher's eloquence and gallant speech. He said, "Truly I have seen in my life many old dotards, but I never saw one so great as this Phormio."

Bacon, *Advancement of Learning*:

For Machiavel noteth wisely, how Fabius Maximus would have been temporizing still, according to his old bias, when the nature of war was altered and required hot pursuit.

Bacon, *Apophthegms New and Old*:

Fabius Maximus being resolved to draw the war in length, still waited upon Hannibal's progress, to curb him; and for that purpose, he encamped upon the high grounds. But Terentius his colleague fought with Hannibal, and was in great peril of overthrow. But then Fabius came down the high grounds, and got the day. Whereupon Hannibal said, *That he did ever think, that that same cloud that hanged upon the hills, would at one time or other, give a tempest.*

Anti-Machiavel:

Seeing this, the Roman Senate sent against Hannibal Fabius Maximus, who was not so forward (and it may be not so hardy) as Flaminius or Sempronius were; but he was more wise and careful, as he showed himself. On his arrival he did not set upon Hannibal, who desired no other thing, but began to coast him far off, seeking always advantageous places. And when Hannibal approached him, then would he show him a countenance fully determined to fight, yet always seeking places of advantage. But Hannibal, who was not so rash as to join with his enemy to his own disadvantage, made a show to recoil and fly, to draw him after him. Fabius followed him, but upon coasts and hills, seeking always not the shortest way, but that way which was most for his advantage. Hannibal saw him always upon some hill or coast near him, as it were a cloud over his head; so that after Hannibal had many times essayed to draw Fabius into a place fit for himself, and where he might give battle for his own good, and yet could not thereunto draw him, said: "I see well now that the Romans also have gotten a Hannibal; and I fear that this cloud, which approaching us, still hovers upon those hills, will one of these mornings pour out some shower on our heads."

Bacon, "Of the True Greatness of Kingdoms and Estates":

A civil war, indeed, is like the heat of a fever; but a foreign war is like the heat of exercise, and serveth to keep the body in health.

Anti-Machiavel:

Therefore a foreign war seems not to be very damaging, but something necessary to occupy and exercise his subjects; but domestic and civil wars must be shunned and extinguished with all our power, for they are things against the right of nature, to make war against the people of their own country, as he that does it against his own entrails.

Bacon, "Of Unity in Religion":

> But we may not take up the third sword, which is Mahomet's sword, or like unto it; that is, to propagate religion by wars or by sanguinary persecutions to force consciences...

Bacon, "Advertisement Touching a Holy War":

> I was ever of opinion, that the Philosopher's Stone, and a Holy War, were but the *rendez-vous* of cracked brains...

Anti-Machiavel:

> But here may arise a question, if it is lawful for a prince to make war for religion, and to constrain men to be of his religion. Hereupon to take the thing by reason, the resolution is very easy; for seeing that all religion consists in an approbation of certain points that concern the service of God, it is certain that such an approbation depends upon the persuasion which is given to men thereof. But the means to persuade a thing to any man is not to take weapons to beat him, nor to menace him, but to demonstrate to him by good reasons and allegations what may induce him to a persuasion.

Bacon, "Of the Vicissitude of Things":

> Surely there is no better way to stop the rising of new sects and schisms, than to reform abuses; to compound the smaller differences; to proceed mildly, and not with sanguinary persecutions; and rather to take the principal authors by winning and advancing them, than to enrage them by violence and bitterness.

Anti-Machiavel:

> It is then very much expedient, if a man means to gather fruit, and do good by his speech, to use gentle and civil talk and persuasions, especially if he has to do with a prince or great man, who will not be gained by rigor (or as they say, by high wrestling), but by mild and humble persuasions.

Anti-Machiavel:

> For that cynical liberty of some philosophers, who knew not how to reprehend and show men's faults but by taunts and bitter biting speeches, are not to be approved; as did that fool Diogenes, who ridiculously and triflingly talked with king Alexander the Great as if he had spoken to some simple burgher of Athens. And Callisthenes, whom Alexander led with him in his voyage into Asia, to instruct him in good documents of wisdom; who indeed was so austere, hard, and biting in all his remonstrances and reasonings, that neither the king nor any others could take in good part anything he taught.

Bacon, "A Proposal for Amending the Laws of England":

> Callisthenes, that followed Alexander's court, and was grown in some displeasure with him, because he could not well brook the Persian adoration; at a supper, which with the Grecians was ever a great part talk, was desired, because he was an eloquent man, to speak of some theme; which he did, and chose for his theme the praise of the Macedonian nation; which though it were but a filling thing to praise men to their faces, yet he did it with such advantage of truth, and avoidance of flattery, and with such life, as the hearers were so ravished with it that they plucked the roses off from their garlands, and threw them upon him; as the manner of applause then was. Alexander was not pleased with it, and by way of discountenance said, It was easy to be a good orator in a pleasing theme: "But," saith he to Callisthenes, "turn your stile, and tell us now of our faults, that we may have the profit, and not you only the praise"; which he presently did with such a force, and so piquantly, that Alexander said, The goodness of this theme had made him eloquent before; but now it was the malice of his heart, that had inspired him.

Anti-Machiavel:

> When Alexander the Great departed from Macedonia to go to the conquest of Asia, he had all the captains of his army appear before him, and distributed to them almost all the revenue of his kingdom, leaving himself almost nothing. One of the captains, named Perdicas,

said to him: "What then will you keep for yourself?" "Even hope," answered Alexander.

Bacon, *Advancement of Learning*:

Lastly, weigh that quick and acute reply which he made when he gave so large gifts to his friends and servants, and was asked what he did reserve for himself, and he answered, "Hope."

Anti-Machiavel:

Hereof we read a very remarkable example above others in Alexander the Great, king of Macedon. When he departed from his country to pass into Asia, to make war upon that great dominator Darius, he had with him first in his love among others, Craterus and Hephaestion, two gentlemen, his best friends and servants. Yet they were far different from each other, for Craterus was of a hard and sharp wit, severe, stoic, and melancholic, who altogether gave himself unto affairs of counsel, and indeed was one of the king's chief counsellors. But Hephaestion was a young gentleman, well complexioned and conditioned in his manners and behavior, of a good and quick wit, yet free of all care but to content and please the king in his sports and pastimes. They called Craterus the king's friend, and Hephaestion the friend of Alexander, as one that gave himself to maintain the person of his prince in mirths and pastimes, which were good for the maintenance of his health.

Bacon, *Advancement of Learning*:

For matter of policy, weigh that significant division, so much in all ages embraced, that he made between his two friends Hephaestion and Craterus, when he said, "that the one loved Alexander, and the other loved the king"; describing the principal difference of princes' best servants, that some in affection love their person, and others in duty love their crown.

Bacon, "A Proposal for Amending the Laws of England":

For the laws of Lycurgus, Solon, Minos, and others of ancient time, they are not the worse because grammar scholars speak of them.

Anti-Machiavel:

So is there great need of some Lycurgus or Solon to make those laws, men's wits are so wild, and their spirits so marvelously plentiful and fertile to bring forth contentions and differences, and so easily to dissent from each other.

Bacon, "Of Anger":

Anger is a kind of baseness, as it appears well in the weakness of whose subjects in whom it reigns…

Anti-Machiavel:

This vice of cruelty, proceeding from the weakness of those who cannot command their choler and passions of vengeance, and suffer themselves to be governed by them, never happened in a generous and valiant heart, but rather always in cowardly and fearful hearts.

Bacon, "Of Revenge":

Revenge is a kind of wild justice, which the more a man's nature runs to, the more ought law to weed it out.

Anti-Machiavel:

And if it were lawful for everyone to use vengeance, that would be to introduce a confusion and disorder into the commonwealth, and to enterprise upon the right which belongs to the magistrate, unto whom God has given the sword, to do right to everyone and to punish those who are faulty, according to their merits.

Bacon, "Of Revenge":

Public revenges are for the most part fortunate; as that for the death of Caesar; for the death of Pertinax; for the death of Henry the Third of France; and many more.

Anti-Machiavel:

Moreover, he exercised part of his cruelties in the revenge of the good emperor Pertinax, which was a lawful cause; yet withal he had in himself many goodly and laudable virtues, as we have in other places rehearsed.

Bacon, *History of the Reign of King Henry VII*:

After that Richard, the third of that name, king in fact only, but tyrant both in title and regiment, and so commonly termed and reputed in all times since, was by the Divine Revenge, favouring the design of an exiled man, overthrown and slain at Bosworth Field; there succeeded in the kingdom the Earl of Richmond, thenceforth styled Henry the Seventh.

Anti-Machiavel:

A similar punishment happened by the judgment of God to that cruel king Richard of England, brother of Edward IV… Yet that king, who despaired otherwise to be maintained in his estate, gave battle to the earl and was slain fighting, after he had reigned about a year. And the earl of Richmond went right to London with his victory, and the slaying of that tyrant; then he took out of the monastery Edward's two daughters, espoused the elder, and was straight made king of England, called Henry VII, grandfather of the most illustrious queen Elizabeth presently reigning.

Bacon, "Of Friendship":

The like or more was between Septimus Severus and Plautianus. For he forced his eldest son to marry the daughter of Plautianus; and would often maintain Plautianus in doing affronts to his son; and did write also in a letter to the senate, by these words: "I love the man so well, as I wish he may over-live me."

Anti-Machiavel:

The emperor Severus advanced Plautianus so high, that being great master of his household, the people thought he was the emperor himself, and that Severus was but his great master.

Bacon, "Of Friendship":

> Augustus raised Agrippa (though of mean birth) to that height, as when he consulted with Maecenas about the marriage of his daughter Julia, Maecenas took the liberty to tell him, that "he must either marry his daughter to Agrippa, or take away his life: there was no third way, he had made him so great."

Anti-Machiavel:

> And here that manner of electing friends which Augustus Caesar observed is worthy of observation. For he did not easily retain every man in his friendship and familiarity, but took time to prove and find their virtues, fidelity, and loyalty. Those he knew to be virtuous people, and who would freely tell him the truth of all things (as did that good and wise Maecenas), and who would not flatter him, but would employ good will sincerely in the charges he gave them — after he had well proved them, then would he acknowledge them his friends.

Bacon, *De augmentis scientiarum*:

> When the prince is one who lends an easy and credulous ear without discernment to whisperers and informers, there breathes as it were from the king himself a pestilent air, which corrupts and infects all his servants. Some probe the fears and jealousies of the prince, and increase them with false tales...

Anti-Machiavel:

> A marmoset, according to the language of our elders, is as much to say a reporter, murmurer, whisperer of tales behind one's back in princes' and great men's ears, which are false, or else not to be reiterated or reported.

Bacon, "Of the True Greatness of Kingdoms and Estates":

> And, certainly those degenerate arts and shifts, whereby many counsellors and governors gain both favour with their masters and

estimation with the vulgar, deserve no better name than fiddling; being things rather pleasing for the time, and graceful to themselves only, than tending to the weal and advancement of the state which they serve.

Anti-Machiavel:

First, there are those our ancient Frenchmen called janglers, which signifies as much as a scoffer, a trifler, a man full of words, or as we call them, long tongues, who by their jangling and babbling in rhyme or in prose give themselves to please great men, in praising and exalting them exceedingly, and rather for their vices than for their virtues.

Bacon, "Of Friendship":

So as there is as much difference between the counsel that a friend giveth, and that a man giveth himself, as there is between the counsel of a friend and of a flatterer; for there is no such flatterer as is a man's self, and there is no such remedy against flattery of a man's self as the liberty of a friend.

Anti-Machiavel:

And above all, men ought well to engrave in princes' minds that notable answer that Phocion made unto the king Antipater, who had required something of him which was not reasonable. "I would, sir, do for you service all that is possible for me, but you cannot have me both for a friend and a flatterer." As if he would say that they be two things far different, to be a friend and to be a flatterer, as in truth they are.

Bacon, *Ornamenta Rationalia*:

The coward calls himself a cautious man; and the miser says, he is frugal.

Anti-Machiavel:

And it helps to this persuasion that the flatterer always takes for the subject of his praises those vices which are in alliance and neighborhood with their virtues. For if the prince is cruel and violent, he will persuade him that he is magnanimous and generous, and such a one as will not put up with an injury. If the prince is prodigal, he will make him believe that he is liberal and magnificent, that he maintains an estate truly royal, and one that well recompenses his servants. If the prince is overgone in lubricities and lusts, he will say he is of a humane and manly nature, of a jovial and merry complexion, and of no saturnine complexion or condition. If the prince is covetous and an eater of his subjects, he will say he is worthy to be a great prince as he is, because he knows well how to make himself well obeyed. Briefly, the flatterer adorns his language in such sort that he will always praise the prince's vice by the resemblance of some virtue near thereunto. For most vices have a likeness with some virtue.

Bacon, *Ornamenta Rationalia*:

He that injures one, threatens an hundred... he of whom many are afraid, ought himself to fear many.

Anti-Machiavel:

Moreover, cruelty is always hated by everyone; for although it be not practiced upon all individuals, but upon some only, yet those upon whom it is not exercised cease not to fear when they see it executed upon their parents, friends, allies, and neighbors. But the fear of pain and punishment engenders hatred; for one can never love that whereof he fears to receive evil, and especially when there is a fear of life, loss of goods, and honors, which are the things we hold most precious.

Bacon, *Ornamenta Rationalia*:

He conquers twice, who restrains himself in victory.

Anti-Machiavel:

The clemency of a prince is the cause of the increase of his domination. Hereupon we read a memorable history of Romulus, who was so clement, soft, and gentle towards the people he vanquished and subjugated, that not only many individuals but the whole multitude of people submitted themselves voluntarily and unconstrainedly under his obedience. The same virtue was also the cause that Julius Caesar vanquished the Gauls; for he was so soft and gracious to them, and so easy to pardon, and used them every way so well, far from oppression, that many of that nation voluntarily joined themselves unto him, and by them he vanquished the others. When Alexander the Great made great conquests in Asia, most commonly the citizens of all great cities met him to present him with the keys of the towns; for he dealt with them in such clemency and kindness, without in any way altering their estates, that they liked better to be his than their own.

Bacon, *Advancement of Learning*:

When Periander, being consulted how to preserve a tyranny newly usurped, bid the messenger report what he saw; and going into the garden, cropped all the tallest flowers; he thus used as strong an hieroglyphic as if he had drawn it upon paper.

Anti-Machiavel:

Periander, having tyrannously obtained the crown of Corinth where he had no right, fearing some conspiracy against him, sent a messenger to ask advice of his great friend Thrasibulus, so to be assured master and lord of Corinth. Thrasibulus made him no answer by mouth; but commanding the messenger to follow him, he went into a field full of ripe corn, and taking the highest and most eminent ears there, he bruised them between his hands and wished the messenger to return to Periander, saying no more unto him. As soon as Periander heard of bruising the most ancient ears of corn, he presently conceived the meaning thereof; to wit, to overthrow and remove all the great men of Corinth who suffered any loss and were grieved at the change of the state; as indeed he did.

Bacon, *Advancement of Learning*:

And the virtue of this prince, continued with that of his predecessor, made the name of Antoninus so sacred in the world, that though it were extremely dishonoured in Commodus, Caracalla, and Heliogabalus, who all bare the name, yet when Alexander Severus refused the name because he was a stranger to the family, the Senate with one acclamation said, *Quomodo Augustus, sic et Antoninus*: in such renown and veneration was the name of these two princes in those days, that they would have had it as a perpetual addition in all the emperors' style.

Anti-Machiavel:

The very name of Antoninus was also so reverenced and loved by all the world, from father to son in generations after him many successive emperors caused themselves to be called Antonys, that rather they might be beloved of the people, though that name did not belong to them, nor were of the race or family of Antoninus; as did Diodumenus, Macrinus his son and companion in the empire, and as also did Bassianus and Geta, Severus' children, and Heliogabalus, they were all surnamed Antoninus. But as this name appertained not to them, so they held nothing of the virtues of that good emperor, with whose name they decked themselves.

Bacon, "Charge against Somerset":

So it appeareth likewise in Scripture, that the murder of Abner by Joab, though it were by David respited in respect of great services past, or reason of state, yet it was not forgotten.

Anti-Machiavel:

For the last example of this matter, I will set down that of Joab, David's nephew and constable, unto whom he did great services. Yet David commanded his son Solomon that he should put to death his cousin Joab, because of his perfidy.

Bacon, *Advancement of Learning*:

So likewise in the person of Solomon the king, we see the gift or endowment of wisdom and learning, both in Solomon's petition and in God's assent thereunto, preferred before all other terrene and temporal felicity. By virtue of which grant or donative of God

Solomon became enabled not only to write those excellent parables or aphorisms concerning divine and moral philosophy, but also to compile a natural history of all verdure, from the cedar upon the mountain to the moss upon the wall (which is but a rudiment between putrefaction and an herb), and also of all things that breathe or move. Nay, the same Solomon the king, although he excelled in the glory of treasure and magnificent buildings, of shipping and navigation, of service and attendance, of fame and renown, and the like, yet he maketh no claim to any of those glories, but only to the glory of inquisition of truth; for so he saith expressly, "The glory of God is to conceal a thing, but the glory of the king is to find it out"; as if, according to the innocent play of children, the Divine Majesty took delight to hide His works, to the end to have them found out; and as if kings could not obtain a greater honour than to be God's playfellows in that game; considering the great commandment of wits and means, whereby nothing needeth to be hidden from them.

Anti-Machiavel:

Solomon was a king most wise, and a great philosopher; for he asked wisdom from God, who gave it in such abundance that besides being ignorant of nothing a prince should know to govern his subjects well, he also knew the natures of plants and living creatures, and was so cunning in all kinds of philosophy that his knowledge was admired through all the world. His prudence and wisdom made him so respected by all the great kings, his neighbors, that they esteemed themselves happy to do him pleasure and have his amity. By this means he maintained his kingdom in so high and happy a peace that in his time his subjects made no more account of silver than of stones, they had such store. And as for himself, he held so magnificent an estate, that we read not of any king or emperor that did the like.

Bacon, *Advancement of Learning*:

Dramatic poesy, which has the theatre for its world, would be of excellent use if well directed. For the stage is capable of no small influence both of discipline and of corruption. Now of corruptions in this kind we have enough; but the discipline has in our times been plainly neglected. And though in modern states play-acting is esteemed but as a toy, except when it is too satirical and biting; yet among the ancients it was used as a means of educating men's minds to virtue.

Anti-Machiavel:

After Solon had seen Thespis' first edition and action of a tragedy, and meeting with him before the play, he asked if he was not ashamed to publish such feigned fables under so noble, yet a counterfeit personage. Thespis answered that it was no disgrace upon a stage, merrily and in sport, to say and do anything. Then Solon, striking hard upon the earth with his staff, replied thus: "Yea but shortly, we that now like and embrace this play, shall find it practiced in our contracts and common affairs." This man of deep understanding saw that public discipline and reformation of manners, attempted once in sport and jest, would soon quail; and corruption, at the beginning passing in play, would fall and end in earnest.

Bacon, *Advancement of Learning*:

So again we find that many of the ancient bishops and fathers of the Church were excellently read and studied in all the learning of the heathen… it was the Christian Church, which amidst the inundations of the Scythians on the one side from the north-west, and the Saracens from the east, did preserve in the sacred lap and bosom thereof the precious relics even of heathen learning, which otherwise had been extinguished as if no such thing had ever been.

Anti-Machiavel:

But now I am desirous to know of this atheist Machiavelli, what was the cause that so many good books of the pagan authors were lost since the time of the ancient doctors of our Christian religion? Was it not by the Goths, who were pagans? For at their so many interruptions and breaking out of their countries, upon Gaul, Italy, and Spain, they wasted and burned as many books as they could find, being enemies of all learning and letters. And who within this hundred years has restored good letters contained in the books of the ancient pagans, Greeks, and Latins? Has it been the Turk, who is a pagan? It is well enough known that he is an enemy of letters, and desires none. Nay contrary, it has been the Christians who have restored them, and established them in the brightness and light wherein we see them today.

Bacon, "Of the Colours of Good and Evil":

So the Epicures say of the Stoics' felicity placed in virtue; that it is like the felicity of a player, who if he were left of his auditory and their applause, he would straight be out of heart and countenance; and therefore they call virtue *bonum theatrale* [public good].

Anti-Machiavel:

Briefly, a man may see within man an admirable and well ordained disposition of all the parts, and it brings us necessarily (whether we will or no) to acknowledge that there must be a God, a sovereign architect, who has made this excellent building; and by these considerations of natural things, whereof I do but lightly touch the points, the ancient philosophers, as the Platonists, Aristotelians, Stoics, and others, have been brought to the knowledge of a God and of his providence. And of all the sects of philosophers, there never was any which agreed not hereunto, unless the sect of the Epicureans, who were gluttons, drunkards, and whoremongers; who constituted their sovereign felicity in carnal pleasures, wherein they wallowed like brute beasts.

Bacon, "Of Custom and Education":

And therefore, as Machiavel well noteth, though in an ill-favoured instance, there is no trusting to the force of nature, nor to the bravery of words, except it be corroborate by custom. His instance is, that for the achieving of a desperate conspiracy, a man should not rest upon the fierceness of any man's nature, or his resolute undertakings, but take such a one as both had his hands formerly in blood.

Anti-Machiavel:

Catiline, a man devoid of all virtue and a bundle of all vice, resolving in his brain to be an exceedingly great man or altogether nothing, devised a conspiracy against his country and drew to his league many Roman gentlemen such as himself. Considering that he could not bring to effect his conjuration without declaring and communicating it to the chieftains of his aid, yet fearing that some of them would disclose it, he made them all take a most execrable oath, that thereby might be foreclosed from them all hope of retiring from his side. So he mixed wine with human blood in pots and made all his companions drink of it, and made them swear with an execration that they would never disclose the enterprise, but employ themselves with all their power to execute it. His partners, already culpable of human blood, were so secret that nothing would have been discovered if God had not permitted a harlot called Fulvia to draw certain words out of a conspirator's mouth, as she demanded of him where he lay the preceding nights. Being drunk, to enjoy his courtesan he disclosed to her that he had been in a company with whom he made an enterprise that would make him rich forever. As soon as Fulvia knew all the conjuration she disclosed it to the consul Cicero. Cicero did what he could to open all the enterprise, but the conspirators held so well their horrible oath that not one of so great a number would ever reveal a word. But yet Cicero found means to know all, by the declaration which the Allobroges made, who Catiline had appointed to furnish him with people for the execution. But the end of Catiline was such that he was slain fighting with a great number of others, and most of his accomplices were executed by justice. Briefly, all who have practiced that wicked doctrine of Machiavelli, to commit outrageous acts to be irreconcilable, their ends and lives have proved very tragedies.

Bacon, "Of the Colours of Good and Evil":

The ill that a man brings on himself by his own fault is greater; that which is brought on him from without is less. The reason is because the sting and remorse of the mind accusing itself, doubleth all adversity... So the poets in tragedies do make the most passionate lamentations, questioning, and torturing of a man's self... where the evil is derived from a man's own fault, there all strikes deadly inwards, and suffocateth.

Anti-Machiavel:

Men may see how an evil conscience leaves a man never in quiet. This wicked man, knowing that by his cruelty he had procured the hatred of his subjects, the wrath of God, and the enmity of all the world, was tormented in his conscience as of an infernal fury, which ever after fretted his languishing soul in the poor infected and wasted body.

Bacon, "Notes on the Present State of Christendom":

The division in his country [France] for matters of religion and state, through miscontentment of the nobility to see strangers advanced to the greatest charges of the realm, the offices of justice sold, the treasury wasted, the people polled, the country destroyed, hath bred great trouble, and like to see more.

Anti-Machiavel:

Besides the examples we read in histories, we know it by experience, seeing at this day all France fashioned after the manners, conditions, and vices of foreigners that govern it, and who have the principal charges and estates.

Appendix B: Parallel Passages in *Vindiciae contra tyrannos* and *Anti-Machiavel*

Vindiciae contra tyrannos:

Notwithstanding, the Machiavellians are free to descend into the arena: let them come forth. As we have said, we shall use the true and legitimate weapons of Holy Scripture, of the philosophy of ethics and of the laws of the commonwealth, of customs of nations, and of historical examples; then we shall boldly join battle with them on foot.

Anti-Machiavel:

I see well it is to no purpose to cite reasons against this atheist and his disciples, who believe neither God nor religion; wherefore, before I pass any further, I must fight against their impiety, and make it appear to their eyes, if they have any, not by assailing them with the arms of the holy Scripture—for they do not merit to be so assailed, and I fear to pollute the holy Scriptures among people so profane and defiled with impiety—but by their proper arms and weapons, whereby their ignorance and beastliness defends their renewed atheism.

Vindiciae contra tyrannos:

As for the characteristics of the method of teaching (I address myself to philosophers and disputants): from the effects and consequences he inferred the causes and major propositions or rules, in order to demonstrate the matter more clearly and definitively. He rendered it visible and comprehensible, as if ascending through certain degrees to the peak: so that in the manner of geometricians—whom he seems to have wanted to imitate in this matter—from a point he draws a line, from the line a plane, and from the plane he constitutes a solid.

Anti-Machiavel:

Aristotle and other philosophers teach us, and experience confirms, that there are two ways to come unto the knowledge of things. The one, when from the causes and maxims, men come to knowledge of the effects and consequences. The other, when contrary, by the effects and consequences we come to know the causes and maxims... The first of these ways is proper and peculiar unto the mathematicians, who teach the truth of their theorems and problems by their demonstrations drawn from maxims, which are common sentences allowed of themselves for true by the common sense and judgment of all men...

Vindiciae contra tyrannos:

In treating these questions we will bear in mind this old and, to be sure, perfect image of the governance of kingdoms, as a legitimate, chaste, and blameless matron without any excessive adornment; in its place these Machiavellians do not hesitate to present us with an illegitimate, painted, lewd, and wanton harlot. This ancient method of administering provinces, kingdoms, and empires was that of your ancestors; and princes who were well endowed with every sort of royal virtue carefully kept to it for as long as they lived, as something passed on from hand to hand.

Anti-Machiavel:

And we need not be abashed if those of Machiavelli's nation, who hold the principal estates in the government of France, have forsaken the ancient manner of our French ancestors' government, to bring France into use with a new form of managing and ruling their country, taught by Machiavelli.

Vindiciae contra tyrannos:

And clearly, in order that this majesty of the king and the ancient rights of the peoples should be restored in their entirety amongst the Gauls, some of your own compatriots have, as generals, led armies against that nation which, despising both God and man and buoyed up by the strengths and artifices of cunning and perfidy, wholly concentrated its talent, power, and force on reducing the Gauls — who are free by nature and entirely autonomous in their way of life and the laws and practices of antiquity — to a servitude of barbarous cruelty.

Anti-Machiavel:

The French were reputed to be frank and liberal, far from all servitude; but now our stupidity, carelessness, and cowardice make us servants and slaves to the most dastardly and cowardly nation of Christendom… Let us then stir up in ourselves the generosity and virtue of our valiant great grandfathers, and show that we are come from the race of those good and noble Frenchmen, our ancestors, who in time past have brought under their subjection so many foreign nations, and who so many times have vanquished the Italian race, who would make us now serve.

Vindiciae contra tyrannos:

A tyrant subverts the state, pillages the people, lays stratagems to entrap their lives, breaks promise with all, scoffs at the sacred obligations of a solemn oath, and therefore is he so much more vile than the vilest of usual malefactors… Therefore as Bartolus says, "He may either be deposed by those who are lords in sovereignty over him, or else justly punished according to the law Julia, which condemns those who offer violence to the public."

Anti-Machiavel:

All these ten kinds of tyrannical actions set down by Bartolus, are they not so many maxims of Machiavelli's doctrine taught to a prince? Did he not say that a prince ought to take away all virtuous people, lovers of their commonwealth; to maintain partialities and divisions; to impoverish his subjects, to nourish wars, and to do all these things which Bartolus said to be the works of tyrants? We need then no more doubt that the purpose of Machiavelli was to form a true tyrant, and that he has stolen from Bartolus one part of his tyrannical doctrine, which yet he has much augmented and enriched. For he adds that a prince ought to govern himself by his own counsel, and ought not to suffer any to discover unto him the truth of things; and that he ought not to care for any religion, neither observe any faith or oath, but ought to be cruel, a deceiver, a fox in craftiness, greedy, inconstant, unmerciful, and perfectly wicked, if it be possible, as we shall see hereafter.

Vindiciae contra tyrannos:

Let us then reject these detestable, faithless, and impious vanities of the court-marmosets, which make kings gods, and receive their sayings as oracles...

Anti-Machiavel:

And it seems unto me that this name of marmoset is very proper and fit for such people, and that it merits well to be called again back into use. And I believe it is drawn from hence that such people go marmoting, murmuring and whispering secretly in princes' ears flattering speeches...

Vindiciae contra tyrannos:

It may be the flatterers of the court will reply, that God has resigned his power unto kings, reserving heaven for himself, and allowing the earth to them to reign, and govern there according to their own fancies; briefly that the great ones of the world hold a divided empire with God himself... This discourse, I say, is worthy of the execrable Domitian who (as Suetonius recites) would be called God and Lord. But altogether unworthy of the ears of a Christian prince, and of the mouth of good subjects, that sentence of God Almighty must always remain irrevocably true, "I will not give My glory to any other," that is, no man shall have such absolute authority, but I will always remain Sovereign.

Anti-Machiavel:

The first point then, which is that the absolute power of a prince does not stretch above God, is a matter confessed by all. And there were never found any princes, or very few, who would soar and mount so high as to enterprise upon that which belonged unto God. Even the emperors Caligula and Domitian are blamed and detested by the pagan histories, which had no true knowledge of God, for that they dared enterprise upon God and that which pertained to him.

Vindiciae contra tyrannos:

> Seeing then that kings are only the lieutenants of God, established in the Throne of God by the Lord God himself, and the people are the people of God, and that the honour which is done to these lieutenants proceeds from the reverence which is born to those that sent them to this service, it follows of necessity that kings must be obeyed for God's cause, and not against God, and then, when they serve and obey God, and not other ways.

Anti-Machiavel:

> We also see by the law of God the same absolute power is given unto kings and sovereign princes, for it is written that they shall have full power over the goods and persons of their subjects. And although God has given them their absolute power, as to his ministers and lieutenants on earth, yet he would not have the use of it but with a temperance and moderation of the second power, which is ruled by reason and equity, which we call civil.

Vindiciae contra tyrannos:

> The Emperors Theodosius and Valentinian to Volusianus, Great Provost of the Empire.

> It is a thing well becoming the majesty of an emperor, to acknowledge himself bound to obey the laws. Our authority depending on the authority of the laws, and in very deed to submit the principality to law, is a greater thing than to bear rule. We therefore make it known unto all men, by the declaration of this our Edict, that we do not allow ourselves, or repute it lawful, to do anything contrary to this. Dated 11 June at Ravenna, under the consuls Florentius and Dionysius.

Anti-Machiavel:

This is that power which all good princes have so practiced — letting their absolute power cease without using any, unless in a demonstration of majesty, to make their estate more venerable and better obeyed — that in all their actions and in all their commands they desire to subject and submit themselves to laws and to reason... And truly all the good Roman emperors have always held this language and have so practiced their power, as we read in their histories. The emperor Theodosius made an express law for it, which is so good to be marked that I thought it good to translate it word for word.

"It is the majesty of him that governs to confess himself bound to laws, so much does our authority depend upon law. And assuredly it is a far greater thing to the empire itself to submit his empire and power unto laws. And that which we will not be lawful unto us, we show it unto others by the oracle of this our present edict. Given at Ravenna the eleventh day of June, in the year of the consulship of Florentius and Dionysius."

Vindiciae contra tyrannos:

Now, if they were true friends indeed, they would desire and endeavor that the king might become more powerful, and more assured in his estate according to that notable saying of Theopompus, king of Sparta, after the ephores or controllers of the kingdom were instituted. "The more" (said he) "are appointed by the people to watch over, and look to the affairs of the kingdom, the more those who govern shall have credit, and the more safe and happy the state."

Anti-Machiavel:

We read that the emperor Alexander Severus was very modest, soft, clement, and affable towards his subjects, wherewith Mammaea his mother was not content; so that one day she said unto him that he had made his authority disregarded and contemptible by his clemency. He answered, "Yea, but I have made my estate so much the longer and more assured." ...The

480

same notable speech of Alexander is attributed to Theopompus, king of Sparta, who knew that the puissance of a king is good and excellent when kings use it well; but because there were far more kings who abused their powers, he provided for himself and his successors certain censors and correctors, which were called Ephori. Some said to Theopompus that by this establishment of Ephori he had lessened and enfeebled his power; "Nay then," he said, "I have fortified it and made it perdurable." Meaning to say, as true it is, that there is nothing which better fortifies nor which makes more firm and stable a prince's estate, than when he governs himself with such a sweet moderation that he even submits himself to the observation of laws and censures.

Vindiciae contra tyrannos:

But we see in many places, that when the people has despised the law, or made covenants with Baal, God has delivered them into the hands of Eglon, Jabin, and other kings of the Canaanites. And as it is one and the same covenant, so those who do break it, receive like punishment... Thou hast neglected the Lord thy God, He also has rejected thee, that thou reign no more over Israel. This has been so certainly observed by the Lord, that the very children of Saul were deprived of their paternal inheritance, for that he, having committed high treason, did thereby incur the punishment of tyrants, which affect a kingdom that in no way pertains to them. And not only the kings, but also their children and successors, have been deprived of the kingdom by reason of such felony. Solomon revolted from God to worship idols. Incontinently the prophet Ahijah foretells that the kingdom shall be divided under his son Rehoboam.

Anti-Machiavel:

David was marvelously happy in war, and always victorious over his enemies, because he was a good prince, fearing God and honoring his holy religion. Solomon his son, as long as he served God sincerely without feigning and hypocrisy, prospered very well and marvelously in a great and happy peace, and none dared stir him. But as soon as he began to practice the doctrine which Machiavelli teaches, namely to have a feigned and dissembled religion and devotion, straight had he enemies on his head, who rose up against him; as Hadad the Edomite, and Razin, who made war upon him. So generally may be said of all the kings of Judah and Israel, one after another; that God has always prospered those who were pure and sincere in religion, and who have had his service in recommendation; and contrary, upon those impure and hypocrites in religion he has heaped ruins, calamities, and other vengeances.

Vindiciae contra tyrannos:

Ahab, king of Israel, could not compel Naboth to sell him his vineyard; but rather if he had been willing, the law of God would not permit it.

Anti-Machiavel:

For God would not that princes use their absolute power so far as to constrain their subjects to sell their goods, as is declared to us in the example of Naboth... And hereunto agrees the divine right, whereby it is showed to us that king Ahab ought not to take away the vineyard from Naboth his subject.

Vindiciae contra tyrannos:

The queen Athalia, after the death of her son Ahaziah king of Judah, put to death all those of the royal blood, except little Joas, who, being yet in the cradle, was preserved by the piety and wisdom of his aunt Jehoshabeah. Athalia possesses herself of the government, and reigned six years over Judah... Finally, Jehoiada, the high priest, the husband of Jehoshabeah, having secretly made a league and combination with the chief men of the kingdom, did anoint and crown king his nephew Joas, being but seven years old. And he did not content himself to drive the Queen Mother from the royal throne, but he also put her to death, and presently overthrew the idolatry of Baal. This deed of Jehoiada is approved, and by good reason, for he took on him the defence of a good cause, for he assailed the tyranny, and not the kingdom.

Anti-Machiavel:

King Ahaziah of Judah was the son of a foreign woman named Athalia, daughter of the king of Samaria. This king governed himself by Samaritans, who were much hated by the people of Judah. At the persuasion of his mother, he gave them the principal charges and offices of his kingdom, despising and casting aside the wisest and most virtuous of his kingdom, by whom he should have governed, after the example of his predecessors. This was the cause of that king's destruction; for as Jehu was destroying the house of Ahab, he also slew Ahaziah, and exterminated almost all his race, as a partner and friend who maintained Ahab. If Ahaziah had governed himself by people of his own kingdom rather than by strangers, that evil hap would not have come to him.

Vindiciae contra tyrannos:

For the wisdom of a senate, the integrity of a judge, the valour of a captain, may peradventure enable a weak prince to govern well.

Anti-Machiavel:

Contrarily, if the prince be not wise at all—for it is not incompatible nor inconvenient to be a prince and to be unwise withal—yet having this resolution to govern himself by counsel, his affairs will carry themselves better than being governed by the head.

Vindiciae contra tyrannos:

There is, therefore, both truly mildness in putting to death some, and as certainly cruelty in pardoning of others.

Anti-Machiavel:

For a prince ought well to consider when, how, to whom, and why he pardons a fault, because it is not clemency but cruelty when a prince may do justice and does it not, as Saint Louis said.

Vindiciae contra tyrannos:

> If the prince has committed some crime, as adultery, parricide, or some other wickedness, behold amongst the heathen, the learned lawyer Papinian who will reprove Caracalla to his face, and had rather die than obey, when his cruel prince commands him to lie and palliate his offence; nay, although he threaten him with a terrible death, yet would he not bear false witness.

Anti-Machiavel:

> For briefly, a prince may well give laws unto his subjects, but it must not be contrary to nature and natural reason. This was the cause why the great lawyer Papinian, who understood both natural and civil law, loved better to die than to obey Caracalla, who had commanded him to excuse before the Senate his parricide, committed in the person of Geta his brother. For Papinian, knowing that such a crime was against natural right, would not have obeyed the emperor if he had commanded him to perpetrate it, nor would obey him so far therein as to excuse it…

> Bassianus [Caracalla], not ignorant that the Senate would find this murder very strange, desired that great lawyer Papinian, his kinsman and Chancellor under Severus, to go to the Senate and make his excuses by an oration well set out: That he had done well to slay his brother, and that he had reason and occasion to do it. Papinian, who was a good man, answered that it was not so easy to excuse a parricide as it was to commit it. Bassianus, grieved at this refusal, had one of his attendants straight cut off his head.

Vindiciae contra tyrannos:

> And instead of approving that which that villainous woman said to Caracalla, that whatsoever he desired was allowed him, we will maintain that nothing is lawful but what the law permits. And absolutely rejecting that detestable opinion of the same Caracalla, that princes give laws to others, but received none from any; we will say, that in all kingdoms well established, the king receives the laws from the people; the which he ought carefully to consider and maintain; and whatsoever, either by force or fraud he does, in prejudice of them, must always be reputed unjust.

Anti-Machiavel:

> We read likewise that Caracalla, beholding one day his mother-in-law Julia with an eye of incestuous concupiscence, she said unto him, "If thou wilt, thou mayst; knowest thou not that it belongs unto thee to give the law, not to receive it?" Which talk so enflamed him yet more with lust that he took her to wife in marriage. Hereupon historiographers note that if Caracalla had known well what it was to give a law, he would have detested and prohibited such incestuous and abominable copulations, and not to have authorized them.

Vindiciae contra tyrannos:

> Julian the apostate, did cast off Christ Jesus to cleave unto the impiety and idolatry of the pagans: but within a small time after he fell to his confusion through the force of the arm of Christ, whom in mockery he called the Galilean.

Anti-Machiavel:

> The emperor Julian, who was called the Apostate, all the time of his youth, in the time of his uncle Constantine the Great, was instructed in the Christian religion; but upon a foolish curiosity he gave himself to diviners and sorcerers, to know things to come, which made him forsake Christianity… Finally after he had reigned for the space of a year and seven months, he was slain at the age of thirty-two years, making war against the Persians. Some write that as he died he blasphemed spitefully against Christ, crying "Thou hast vanquished, thou Galilean."

Vindiciae contra tyrannos:

> Tarquinius Superbus was therefore esteemed a tyrant, because being chosen neither by the people nor the senate, he intruded himself into the kingdom only by force and usurpation.

> The true causes why Tarquinius was deposed, were because he altered the custom, whereby the king was obliged to advise with the senate on all weighty affairs; that he made war and peace

according to his own fancy; that he treated confederacies without demanding counsel and consent from the people or senate; that he violated the laws whereof he was made guardian; briefly that he made no reckoning to observe the contracts agreed between the former kings, and the nobility and people of Rome.

Anti-Machiavel:

Tarquin, who enterprised to slay his father-in-law king Servius Tullius to obtain the kingdom of Rome, showed well by that act and many others that he was a very tyrant... For they say that when he changed his just and royal domination into a tyrannical government, he became a contemner and despiser of all his subjects, both plebian and patrician. He brought a confusion and a corruption into justice; he took a greater number of servants into his guard than his predecessors had; he took away the authority from the Senate; moreover, he dispatched criminal and civil cases after his fancy, and not according to right; he cruelly punished those who complained of that change of estate as conspirators against him; he caused many great and notable persons to die secretly without any form of justice; he imposed tributes upon the people against the ancient form, to the impoverishment and oppression of some more than others; he had spies to discover what was said of him, and punished rigorously those who blamed either him or his government. These are the colors wherewith the histories paint Tarquin, and these are ordinarily the colors and livery of all tyrants' banners, whereby they may be known.

Vindiciae contra tyrannos:

Besides all this, anciently every year, and since less often, to wit, when some urgent necessity required it, the general or three estates were assembled, where all the provinces and towns of any worth, to wit, the burgesses, nobles, and ecclesiastical persons, did all of them send their deputies, and there they did publicly deliberate and conclude of that which concerned the public estate. Always the authority of this assembly was such that what was there determined, whether it were to treat peace, or make war, or create a regent in the kingdom, or impose some new tribute, it was ever held firm and inviolable; nay, which is more by the authority of this assembly, the kings convinced of loose intemperance, or of insufficiency, for so great a charge or tyranny, were disthronized.

Anti-Machiavel:

Our kings of old in France used the same course that these good emperors did; for they often convocated the three Estates of the kingdom to have their advice and counsel in affairs of great consequence which touched the interest of the commonwealth. And it is seen by our histories that the general assembly of the Estates was commonly done for three causes. One, when there was a question to provide for the kingdom a governor or regent; as when kings were young, or lost the use of their understanding by some accident, or were captives or prisoners; in these cases the three Estates assembled to obtain a governor for the realm. Again, when there was cause to reform the kingdom, to correct the abuses of officers and magistrates, and to bring things unto their ancient and first institution and integrity. For kings caused the Estates to assemble, because being assembled from all parts of the kingdom, they might better be informed of all abuses and evil behaviors committed therein, and might also better work the means to remedy them; because commonly there is no better physician than he that knows well the disease and the causes thereof. The third cause why there was made an assembly of Estates was when there was a necessary cause to lay a tribute or tax upon the people; for then in a full assembly the representatives were showed the necessity of the king's and the kingdom's affairs, who graciously and courteously entreated the people to aid and help the king but with so much money as they themselves thought to be sufficient and necessary.

Vindiciae contra tyrannos:

About the year 1300 Pope Boniface VIII, seeking to appropriate to his See the royalties that belonged to the crown of France, Philip the Fair, the then king, did taunt him somewhat sharply: the tenor of whose tart letters are these:

"Philip by the Grace of God, King of the French, to Boniface, calling himself Sovereign Bishop, little or no health at all. Be it known to the great foolishness and unbounded rashness, that in temporal matters we have only God for our superior, and that the vacancy of certain churches belongs to us by royal prerogative, and that appertains to us only to gather the fruits, and we will defend the possession thereof against all opposers with the edge of our swords, accounting them fools, and without brains who hold a contrary opinion."

In those times all men acknowledged the pope for God's vicar on earth, and head of the universal church. Insomuch, that (as it is said) common error went instead of a law, notwithstanding the Sorbonists being assembled, and demanded, made answer, that the king and the kingdom might safely, without blame or danger of schism, exempt themselves from his obedience, and flatly refuse that which the pope demanded; for so much as it is not the separation but the cause which makes the schism, and if there were schism, it should be only in separating from Boniface, and not from the church, nor the pope, and that there was no danger nor offence in so remaining until some honest man were chosen pope.

Anti-Machiavel:

Yet we read in our histories that our kings of France have many times hindered popes from drawing silver out of the realm, by annates, tenths, bulls, and other means; as in the time of Boniface VIII, Benedict XI, Julius II and III. But concerning this matter it is good to mark the determination made in 1410 by our masters of the faculty of the Sorbonne, and by all the University of Paris; who resolved in a general congregation that the French church was not bound to pay any silver to the pope in any manner whatsoever, unless by the way of a charitable subsidy…

As in the time of king Philip IV, Pope Boniface VIII made a decretal whereby he generally forbade all emperors, kings, and princes of Christendom to levy any tribute upon the clergy, upon pain of a present excommunication, without any other commissare or declaration. The king, because this was against his privileges (by the advice of his council, the prelates of his country, and the faculty of theology of Paris), appealed from the pope, as inferior, to the first future council, as superior.

Likewise, the pope Boniface, of whom we have spoken before, was declared a heretic by the said University and faculty of theology; not that he erred in the faith (for it was a thing whereof he had little care), but because he would needs enterprise upon the king's privileges. But as soon as he was declared a heretic, all the kingdom of France retired from his obedience.

Appendix C: Parallel Passages in *The French Academy* and *Anti-Machiavel*

French Academy:

Sir, if we credit the saying of Plato, commonwealths begin then to be happy, when kings exercise philosophy, and philosophers reign.

Anti-Machiavel:

I am content to presuppose that it is certain that there cannot come a better and more profitable thing to a people than to have a prince wise of himself; therefore, said Plato, men may call it a happy commonwealth when either the prince can play the philosopher, or when a philosopher comes to reign there.

French Academy:

It is a hard matter (said Socrates) for a man to bridle his desire, but he that addeth riches therunto, is mad.

Anti- Machiavel:

Who could then bridle vices and iniquities, which are fed with much wealth, and no less liberty?

French Academy:

He that has but half an eye may see that there are a great many amongst us of those foolish men of whom David speaks, *Who say in their hearts that there is no God*. In the forefront of which company, the students of Machiavel's principles and practicers of his precepts may worthily be ranged. This bad fellow, whose works are no less accounted of among his followers than were Apollo's oracles

490

amongst the heathen, nay than the sacred Scriptures are among sound Christians, blushed not to belch out these horrible blasphemies against pure religion, and so against God the author thereof...

Anti-Machiavel:

For what shall I speak of religion, whereof the Machiavellians had none, as already plainly appears; yet they greatly labored also to deprive us of the same... he is of no reputation in the court of France who has not Machiavelli's writings at the fingers' ends, both in the Italian and French tongues, and can apply his precepts to all purposes, as the oracles of Apollo.

French Academy:

For the ruin and destruction of this French monarchy proceeds of no other second cause (our iniquity being the first) than of the mixture which we have made of strangers with ourselves. Wherein we are not contented to seek them out under their roofs, unless we also draw them unto us and lodge them under our roofs, yea prefer them before our own countrymen and citizens in the offices and honorable places of this kingdom... they have left us nothing but new manners and fashions of living in all dissoluteness and pleasure; except this one thing also, that we have learned of them to dissemble, and withal to frame and build a treason very subtly. Such is the provision wherewith our French youth is commonly furnished by their Italian voyages.

Anti-Machiavel:

For besides the examples we read in histories, we know it by experience, seeing at this day all France fashioned after the manners, conditions, and vices of foreigners that govern it, and who have the principal charges and estates. And not only many Frenchmen are such beasts to conform themselves to strangers' complexions, but also to gaggle their language and disdain the French tongue as a thing too common and vulgar.

French Academy:

> This is that which at length (as Crates the philosopher said very well) stirs up civil wars, seditions, and tyrannies within cities; to the end that such voluptuous men, and ambitious of vainglory, fishing in a troubled water, may have wherewith to maintain their foolish expenses, and so come to the end of their platforms.

Anti-Machiavel:

> And would to God that the French nation had never been of that nature and condition to do well unto strangers, without first knowing and trying their behaviors and manner of life. We should not then see France to be governed and ruled by strangers, as it is; we should not feel the calamities and troubles of civil wars and dissentions, which they enterprise to maintain their greatness and magnitude, and to fish in troubled water.

French Academy:

> But whatsoever my speech has been hitherto, my meaning is not to find fault with the right use of hospitality, which ought to be maintained and kept inviolable in every well-established commonwealth. In this respect France has been commended above all nations for entertaining and receiving all sorts of people; provided always that they be not preferred before our own children, and that they be contented to obey and live according to the common laws of the country.

Anti-Machiavel:

> For hospitality is recommended unto us by God, and it is a very laudable virtue for men to entertain strangers and entertain them well; but strangers also ought to content themselves to be welcomed and entertained in a country or town, without aspiring to master or hold offices and estates. The French nation is that which of all Christendom receives and loves strangers most, for they are as welcome all over France as those of their own nation.

French Academy:

What ought they to do, that say they are all members of that one head, who recommends so expressly unto them meekness, mildness, gentleness, grace, clemency, mercy, good will, compassion, and every good affection towards their neighbor? All which things are comprehended under this only sacred word of Charity...

Anti-Machiavel:

True charity is joined unto faith, pity, and all other virtues...

French Academy:

Notwithstanding, wisely applying themselves to places and persons, they can in their serious discourses intermingle some honest pastimes, but yet not altogether without profit. As Plato in his foresaid feast interlaces certain comical speeches of love, howbeit all the rest of the supper there was nothing but wise discourses of philosophy.

Anti-Machiavel:

But seeing we are entered into this talk, we will look deeper into the matter to draw out some good resolution from this question, by the way only of a tentative and pleasant disputation, and not of a full determination hereof. For as Cato says, amongst serious things joyous and merry things would be sometimes mixed.

French Academy:

Kings, princes and magistrates, who because they see and hear for the most part by other men's eyes and ears, ought necessarily to have such friends, counsellors, and servants about them, as will freely tell them the truth, as hereafter we may discourse more at large.

Anti-Machiavel:

And to attend while the prince himself begins the matter first to his council, would be in vain; for he cannot propose what he does not know, and it is a notorious and plain thing that the prince, who is always shut up in a house or within a troupe of his people, sees not nor knows how things pass, but what men make him see and know.

French Academy:

Francis I, a prince of most famous memory, so loved and favored letters and the professors of them that he deserved the name of the restorer of sciences and good arts, sparing neither care nor means to assemble together books and volumes of sundry sorts and of all languages for the beautifying of his so renowned a library, which was a worthy monument of such a magnifical Monarch; whose praiseworthy qualities we see revived in our king, treading in the selfsame steps.

Anti-Machiavel:

We see that the restoration of good letters, which Francis I brought into France, did more to celebrate and immortalize his name in the memory of all Christian nations, than all the great wars and victories his predecessors had... In our time Francis I imitated the example of this great and wise emperor, establishing public lectures at great wages in the University of Paris, a thing whereof his memory has been and shall be more celebrated through the world than for so many great wars he valiantly sustained during his reign... You have gloriously crowned that work, which that great king Francis your grandfather did happily begin, to the end that arts and sciences might flourish in this kingdom.

French Academy:

It is a usual speech in the mouths of men altogether ignorant of the beauty and profit of Sciences, that the study of letters is a bottomless gulf, and so long and uneasy a journey that they who think to finish it, oftentimes stay in the midway, and many being come to the end thereof find their minds so confused with their profound and curious skill, that instead of tranquility of soul, which they thought to find, they have increased the trouble of their spirit.

Anti-Machiavel:

For there are at this day infinite persons who so much please themselves in profane authors, some in poets, some in historiographers, some in philosophy, some in physic, or in law, that they care nothing to read or else to know anything for the salvation and comfort of their souls. Some care not at all for it, others reserve that study until they have ended the studies of other sciences, and in the meanwhile the time runs away, and often it comes to pass that when they leave this world, their profane studies are not ended, nor the study of holy letters commenced, and so they die like beasts.

French Academy:

Through want of skill and ignorance he falls into a worse estate than he was in before, and as we commonly say, from a gentle ague into a pestilent and burning fever...

Anti-Machiavel:

They were fallen from a shaking fever into a hot ague, as the French proverb is...

French Academy:

Whereunto also the precepts and discourses of learned and ancient philosophers may serve for our instruction and pricking forward; as also the examples (which are lively reasons) of the lives of so many notable men, as histories, the mother of antiquity, do as it were represent alive before our eyes.

Anti-Machiavel:

And you, good Edward, imitate the wisdom, sanctimony, and integrity of your father, the Right Honorable Lord Nicholas Bacon, Keeper of the broad Seal of England, a man right renowned; that you may lively express the image of your father's virtues in the excellent towardness which you naturally have from your most virtuous father. If you both daily ruminate and remember the familiar and best known examples of your ancestors, you cannot have more forcible persuasions to move you to that which is good and honest.

French Academy:

If we compare worldly goods with virtue (calling that good which usurps that name, and is subject to corruption); first, as touching those which the philosophers call the goods of fortune, and namely nobility, whereon at this day men stay so much; what is it but a good of our ancestors?

Anti-Machiavel:

I will also note another notable vice which runs current among gentlemen at this day, which is that they make so great account of their nobility of blood that they esteem not the nobility of virtue; insomuch that it seems to some that no vices can dishonor or pollute the nobility and gentry which they have from their ancestors. But they ought well to consider that to their race there was a beginning of nobility, which was attributed to the first that was noble in consideration of some virtue that was in him.

French Academy:

Ambition truly is the most vehement and strongest passion of all those wherewith men's minds are troubled; and yet many notable and virtuous men have so mastered it by the force of their temperance that oftentimes they accepted offices and estates of supreme authority, as it were by compulsion and with grief; yea some altogether contemned and willingly forsook them.

Anti-Machiavel:

Besides all this, in the election of counsellors and magistrates he did ever suspect those who sought offices, and held them for ambitious and dangerous people to the common weal. But they who he could know to be good men and worthy of public charge, and never sought it, these were they who he esteemed most sufficient; and the more they excused themselves from accepting offices, so much the more were they constrained unto them.

French Academy:

The custom that Aurelius Severus used is much more praiseworthy. For when he sent governors into the provinces, he caused their names to be published many days before, to the end that whosoever knew anything in them worthy of reprehension, he should give notice thereof; and they that reported truly, were promoted to honor by him and slanderers grievously punished.

Anti-Machiavel:

And upon that point, it seems to me that the manner of proceeding which Alexander Severus used to choose his counsellors and his magistrates, is very good and merits well to be imitated and drawn into consequence... And the better to be informed of the reputation of persons whereof he had proffers by his wise friends, he caused to be set up in common streets and great public areas, where many ways meet, certain posts to fix bills upon them, whereupon was written certain exhortations unto the people, that if any man had anything to say against such and such a man (which he named) wherefore they might not be received and admitted to such and such an office, that he should denounce it. And so made those commands by placards, to the end he might better discover and be advertised of the virtues and vices of persons.

French Academy:

Caligula, a most cruel emperor, never had secure and quiet rest, but being terrified and in fear awoke often, as one that was vexed and carried headlong with wonderful passions. Nero, after he had killed his mother, confessed that while he slept he was troubled by her, and tormented with Furies that burned him with flaming torches.

Anti-Machiavel:

What repose could Nero have, who confessed that often the likeness of his mother, whom he slew, appeared to him, which tormented and afflicted him; and that the furies beat him with rods and tormented him with burning torches. What delicateness or sweetness of life could Caligula and Caracalla have? who always carried coffers full of all manners of poisons, as well to poison others as themselves in case of necessity, for fear they should fall alive into the hands of their enemies.

Anti-Machiavel:

The governor of Judea, called Petronius, would have placed an image of Caligula in the great temple of Jerusalem; but the Jews, who extremely detested images, would not suffer him; whereby there was likely to have been a great sedition.

French Academy:

Caligula, a Roman emperor, sent Petronius into Syria with commandment to make war with the Jews if they would not receive his image into their temple. Which when they refused to do, Petronius said unto them that then belike they would fight against Caesar, not weighing his wealth or their own weaknesses and inability.

French Academy:

Alexander the Great, being by the states of all Greece chosen general captain to pass into Asia and to make war with the Persians, before he took ship he inquired after the estate of all his friends to know what means they had to follow him. Then he distributed and gave to one lands, to another a village, to this man the custom of some haven, to another the profit of some borough town, bestowing in this manner the most part of his demeans and revenues. And when Perdicas, one of his lieutenants, demanded of him what he reserved for himself: he answered Hope.

Anti-Machiavel:

When Alexander the Great departed from Macedonia to go to the conquest of Asia, he had all the captains of his army appear before him and distributed to them almost all the revenue of his kingdom, leaving himself almost nothing. One of the captains, named Perdicas, said to him: "What then will you keep for yourself?" "Even hope," answered Alexander.

French Academy:

Fabius the Greatest comes first to my remembrance, to prove that the resolution of a courageous heart, grounded upon knowledge and the discourse of reason, is firm and immutable. This captain of the Roman army being sent into the field to resist the fury and violence of Hannibal, who being captain of the Carthaginians, was entered into Italy with great force, determined for the public welfare and necessity to delay and prolong the war, and not to hazard a battle but with great advantage.

Anti-Machiavel:

Seeing this, the Roman Senate sent against Hannibal Fabius Maximus, who was not so forward (and it may be not so hardy) as Flaminius or Sempronius were; but he was more wise and careful, as he showed himself. On his arrival he did not set upon Hannibal, who desired no other thing, but began to coast him far off, seeking always advantageous places. And when Hannibal approached him, then would he show him a countenance fully determined to fight, yet always seeking places of advantage. But Hannibal, who was not so rash as to join with his enemy to his own disadvantage, made a show to recoil and fly, to draw him after him. Fabius followed him, but upon coasts and hills, seeking always not the shortest way, but that way which was most for his advantage.

French Academy:

Scipio Africanus, general of the Romans, at the taking of the city of Carthage had a young damsel taken prisoner, of rare and excellent beauty. And when he understood of what great calling she came, and how her parents not long before had betrothed her to a great lord of Spain, he commanded that he should be sent for, and restored her unto him without abusing her in any respect, although he was in the flower of his age and had free and sovereign authority. Moreover, he gave for a dowry with her the money that was brought unto him for her ransom.

Anti-Machiavel:

Yet the example of clemency in Scipio Africanus is more notable than this of his father and uncle. After the deaths of his said father and uncle, this young lord full of all generosity and hardiness came to besiege New Carthage in Spain, and got it by assault... Among other hostages, there was a young lady of a great house brought to Scipio, who was of so great beauty that as she passed by she drew each man's regard upon her. This lady was affianced to one Allucius, prince of the Celts. Scipio, taking knowledge of her parents and to whom she was affianced, and that Allucius extremely loved her, sent for them all... The said lady's parents stepped forward and presented to him a great quantity of gold and silver for their daughter's ransom, which though Scipio refused it, they pressed it so sore upon him that he accorded to take it, and bade them lay it before him. Scipio called Allucius and said to him, Good friend, besides the dowry which your father-in-law will give you, my desire is that you will take this silver at my hands as an increase of her dowry.

French Academy:

Camillus, a Roman dictator, is no less to be commended for that which he did during the siege of the City of the Fallerians. For he that was schoolmaster of the chiefest men's children among them, being gone out of the city, under color to have his youth to walk and to exercise themselves along the walls, delivered them into the hands of the Roman captain; saying unto him that he might be well assured the citizens would yield themselves to his devotion, for the safety and liberty of that which was dearest unto them. But Camillus, knowing this to be too vile and wicked a practice, said to those that were with him, that although men used great outrage and violence in war, yet among good men certain laws and points of equity were to be observed. For victory was not so much to be desired, as that it should be gotten and kept by such cursed and damnable means; but a general ought to war, trusting to his own virtue, and not to the wickedness of others. Then stripping the said schoolmaster, and bending his hands behind him, he delivered him naked into the hands of his scholars, and gave to each of them a bundle of rods, that so they might carry him back again into the city. For which noble act the citizens yielded themselves to the Romans, saying that in preferring justice before victory, they had taught them to choose rather to submit themselves unto them, than to retain still their liberty; confessing withal that they were overcome more by their virtue than vanquished by their force and power.

Anti-Machiavel:

Camillus, a Roman general, besieged the town of Falisques, the Romans' enemies. The schoolmaster of Falisques enterprised a great wickedness and villainy; for making a countenance to lead, for sport and pastime, the youth of that town who were committed to him to be instructed, he straight brought them to Camillus' camp, hoping he would give some good recompense, speaking in this manner. "Lord Camillus, I yield into your hands the town of Falisques, for I here bring you their dear and loving children, which to recover they will easily yield themselves to you." To whom Camillus answered, "Wicked wretch, you do not address yourself to your like. We have by compacts no society with the Falisques, but by nature we have; we are not ignorant of the right of war and of peace, which we will courageously observe. We make not war upon young children, for even when we take towns, we pardon them, so do we also to them who bear arms against us. You would vanquish the Falisques by deceit and villainy, but I will vanquish them by virtue and arms, as I overcame the Veians." After this, Camillus commanded to bind the schoolmaster's hands behind him, and to give all the scholars rods in their hands, who whipped him naked into the town. As thus in this sort the children brought their master to the town, all the people ran to see the spectacle; which so changed their courage, before full of wrath and hatred against the Romans, that they straight sent delegates to Camillus to desire peace, admiring the Roman clemency and justice. Camillus, knowing that he alone could not enterprise to conclude a peace, sent the delegates towards the Senate of Rome, where on arriving they made this speech. "My masters, having been vanquished by an agreeable victory both to gods and men, we yield ourselves to you, knowing that our estate shall be better under your domination than in our own liberties and customs. The issue of this war will serve hereafter for a double example to all mankind, for it seems you better love loyalty in war than present victory. And we, being provoked by your kindness and loyalty, gladly and willingly yield you the victory. We offer ourselves your subjects, and we shall never repent ourselves of your domination, nor you of your loyalty." The peace and alliance accorded to the Falisques, Camillus entered Rome in triumph, and was more esteemed to be a victor by clemency than if it had been by arms.

French Academy:

Caracalla the emperor, traveling with his army towards the Parthians, under pretense of marrying the daughter of Artabanus their king, who came for the same purpose to meet him, he set upon him contrary to his faith, and put him to flight with an incredible murder of his men. But within a while after, being come down from his horse to make water, he was slain by his own men; which was noted as a just punishment sent from God for his unfaithfulness.

Anti-Machiavel:

[Caracalla] also played another part of treachery, under the pretext and show of marriage, with Artabanus, king of the Parthians. For he wrote letters to him whereby he signified that their empires were the two greatest empires of the world; and that being the son of a Roman emperor, he could not find a better wife than the daughter of the king of the Parthians. He therefore asked her hand in marriage, to join the greatest empires of the earth and to end their wars. The king at first denied Caracalla his daughter, saying that such a marriage was very unfit because of the diversity of their languages, manners, and habits; also because the Romans had never before allied or married with the Parthians. But upon this refusal Caracalla insisted and pressed him more strongly than before, and sent to Artabanus great gifts, so that in the end he gave to him his daughter. Caracalla, assuring himself that he would find no hostility in the Parthian country, boldly entered far into it with his army, saying he went but to see the king's daughter. On the other side, Artabanus prepared himself and his retinue in as good order as was possible, without any army, to go meet his new son-in-law. What did this perfidious Caracalla? As soon as the two parties met, and Artabanus came near to salute and embrace him, he commanded his soldiers to charge upon the Parthians. The Romans attacked as if there had been an assigned battle, and there was a great slaughter made of the Parthians; but the king, with the help of a good horse, escaped with great difficulty and danger. He determined to revenge himself of that villainy and treachery; but Macrinus relieved him of that pain, and soon slew that monster Caracalla, who was already detested through all the world because of his perfidy.

French Academy:

Antoninus and Geta, brothers and successors in the empire to Severus their father, could not suffer one another to enjoy so large a monarchy; for Antoninus slew his brother Geta with a dagger, that himself might rule alone.

Anti-Machiavel:

Severus intending to leave the government of the empire to his two sons together, flatterers about them disposed it otherwise… Those two young princes fell into so great and mortal enmity, that not only they hated all each other's friends and servants, but also those who would have reconciled them. As soon as their father Severus was dead, Laetus, one of the marmosets of Bassianus, persuaded him to slay his brother and feign that he was assailed by him. This counsel was found good by Bassianus, who was audacious enough and ready to give the blow with his own hand. One morning he entered into the chamber of empress Julia, Geta's mother, and finding him there he slew him between his mother's arms.

French Academy:

And it is greatly to be feared that such unskillful and ambitious men will in the end show themselves both in will and practice to be imitators of one Cleander, an outlandish slave, who being preferred by Commodus the emperor to goodly offices and great places of honor, as to be great master of his men of war and his chief chamberlain, conspired notwithstanding against his lord, seeking to attain to the imperial dignity by seditions which he stirred up in Rome between the people and the soldiers. But through good order taken, his enterprise took no effect, except the loss of his own head and destruction of his house.

Cleander was another marmoset who succeeded in his place; who at the beginning made some show that he would do better, but soon did worse. He practiced many cruelties, and sold the estates and governments of provinces to those who would offer most. There happened at Rome then a great famine and pestilence. The people, who always lay the cause of public calamity upon the governors, bruited abroad that Cleander was the cause of the plague and the famine, and therefore should die. Cleander, to stop this rumor and cause the people to hold their peace, had the emperor's horsemen rush through the town and suburbs, slaying and wounding innumerable. But the people began to take houses and fight from the windows so well that the horsemen were constrained to retire. Fadilla, the sister of Commodus, seeing this civil war commenced and raised by Cleander, went to find her brother, whom she found among his harlots. All bewept she fell on her knees before him, saying, "Sir, my brother, you are here taking your pleasures, and know not the things that pass, nor the danger wherein you are. For both yours and our blood is in peril, to be altogether exterminated by the war and civil stir Cleander has raised in the town. He has armed your forces, and has made them rush against the people, and has brought them unto a slaughter more than barbarous, filling the streets with Roman blood. If you do not soon put to death the author of this evil, the people will fall upon you and us, and tear us in pieces." Saying these words, she tore her garments and was very sad, as it were desperate. Many also who were present increased the fear of Commodus by their persuasions; fearing some great danger to himself, he sent in haste for Cleander, who knew nothing of his complaint. As soon as he arrived, Commodus had his head cut off and carried on a pike through the town, and the sight of the head appeased the people.

French Academy:

And lastly, for the upshot and perfection of all happiness and felicity in this world, he instructs him how he may lead a quiet and peaceable life in beholding the wonderful works of the divinity, which he is to adore and honor, and in the amendment and correction of his manners naturally corrupted, by squaring them after the pattern of virtue, that so he may be made worthy and fit to govern human affairs, for the profit of many; and at length attain to the perfection of a wise man, by joining together the active life with the contemplative in the certain hope and expectation of a second, immortal and most blessed life.

Anti-Machiavel:

Very true it is, that among Christians there must be some contemplatives, that is to say, studious people who give themselves to holy letters in order to teach others. But we do not find by the documents of that religion that there is allowed any idle contemplation of dreamers, who do nothing but imagine dreams and toys in their brains; but a contemplative life of laboring studious people is only approved, who give themselves to letters to teach others. For after they have accomplished their studies, they ought to put in use and action that which they know, bringing into an active life that which they have learned by their study in their contemplative life. And those who use this otherwise do not follow the precepts of the true Christian religion.